C000193891

Selling the Korean War

SELLING THE KOREAN WAR

*Propaganda, Politics, and Public Opinion
in the United States, 1950–1953*

Steven Casey

OXFORD
UNIVERSITY PRESS

OXFORD
UNIVERSITY PRESS

Oxford University Press, Inc., publishes works that further
Oxford University's objective of excellence
in research, scholarship, and education.

Oxford   New York
Auckland   Cape Town   Dar es Salaam   Hong Kong   Karachi
Kuala Lumpur   Madrid   Melbourne   Mexico City   Nairobi
New Delhi   Shanghai   Taipei   Toronto

With offices in
Argentina   Austria   Brazil   Chile   Czech Republic   France   Greece
Guatemala   Hungary   Italy   Japan   Poland   Portugal   Singapore
South Korea   Switzerland   Thailand   Turkey   Ukraine   Vietnam

Copyright © 2008 by Oxford University Press, Inc.

Published by Oxford University Press, Inc.
198 Madison Avenue, New York, New York 10016

www.oup.com

First issued as an Oxford University Press paperback, 2010

Oxford is a registered trademark of Oxford University Press

All rights reserved. No part of this publication may be reproduced, stored in a retrieval
system, or transmitted, in any form or by any means, electronic, mechanical, photocopying,
recording, or otherwise, without the prior permission of Oxford University Press.

Library of Congress Cataloging-in-Publication Data
Casey, Steven.
Selling the Korean War : propaganda, politics, and public opinion in the United States,
1950–1953 / Steven Casey.
    p. cm.
Includes bibliographical references and index.
ISBN 978-0-19-530692-7; 978-0-19-973899-1 (pbk.)
1. Korean War, 1950–1953—United States.   2. United States—Politics and
government—1945–1953.   3. United States—Foreign relations—1945–1953.
4. National security—United States.   I. Title.
DS919.C35 2008
951.904'21—dc22   2007028884

Printed in the United States of America

For Gemma and Lauren

ACKNOWLEDGMENTS

One of the great pleasures of finally completing a book that has taken six years to research and write is the chance it affords to thank the numerous individuals who have made it possible. I must begin with the tangible—that is, financial—debts. The Truman Library Institute has been particularly generous. In August 2001, it provided me with a travel grant that enabled me to work slowly through the tremendous resources it has to offer. In 2004–5, it gave me the Truman Scholar's Award, which I used to buyout my teaching, move temporarily to Washington, and complete the bulk of the writing. I would also like to thank the University of London Central Fund, which provided me with a research grant in 2003, and the George C. Marshall Foundation, which awarded me a Marshall/Baruch Fellowship in 2006.

Since 2001, the London School of Economics has been my intellectual home. The members of the International History Department, as well as providing a stimulating environment, have also given me that enormously precious commodity: time to undertake the research and writing. I would particularly like to thank MacGregor Knox, David Stevenson, Odd Arne Westad, Nigel Ashton, Antony Best, Piers Ludlow, Mick Cox, David Easter, and Kristina Spohr Readman. I also owe a special thanks to those students who have taken my two courses, HY422 and HY311.

A number of people have generously given their time to read through earlier versions of the manuscript. I am particularly grateful to William Stueck, whose unrivaled knowledge and perceptive comments greatly strengthened the finished manuscript; and Ralph Levering, who read an earlier draft with enormous care and whose numerous critical insights immeasurably improved the finished product. I would also like to thank Matthew Jones, Ken Osgood, and Colin Brazier, who all provided helpful comments on different aspects of the project; and Saki Dockrill, George Edwards, Jonathan Bell, and Kendrick Oliver, who each provided a forum in which I could present my evolving arguments. This book has also been greatly improved as a result of the careful evaluation by two anonymous reviewers. Needless to say, any errors of judgment or fact are mine.

Over the years, a number of other people have offered support, encouragement, and advice. I am especially indebted to Richard Crockatt and Roberto Franzosi. I would also like to thank Wolfram Latsch, Michael Fullilove, Priscilla Roberts, Marilyn Young, Rosemary Foot, Bob O'Neill, Louise Fawcett, Adam Roberts, and Raymond Cohen.

Some of the arguments in this book have been published in slightly different form in the following articles: "Selling NSC-68: The Truman Administration, Public Opinion, and the Politics of Mobilization, 1950–51," *Diplomatic History* 29 (2005): 655–90, © 2005, Society for Historians of American Foreign Relations; "White House Publicity Operations during the Korean War, June 1950–June 1951," *Presidential Studies Quarterly* 35 (December 2005): 691–717, © Center for the Study of the Presidency.

At Oxford University Press, my editor, Susan Ferber, has once again been extremely supportive, helpful, and efficient, ever since I first broached the idea for this book in October 2000. I would also like to thank Brian Desmond and Martha Ramsey for their help and expertise during the production stages.

In the course of my research, I have visited numerous libraries and archives. All the staff have been extremely helpful, but I would particularly like to thank Michael Devine, Dennis Bilger, Randy Sowell, Liz Safly, Pauline Testerman, and Lisa Sullivan at the Truman Library; Herb Pankratz and Dwight Strandberg at the Eisenhower Library; James W. Zobel at the MacArthur Memorial Archives; Bob Aquilina at the Marine Corps Historical Center; and Bob Reynolds at the Meany Memorial Archives.

Last, but definitely not least, there is my family. My parents, Margaret and Terry, and my sister, Louise, have—as always—been enormously supportive. Gemma and Lauren both enjoyed our tremendous year in the United States, but they have also had to endure my numerous research-driven absences. This book is dedicated to them.

CONTENTS

ABBREVIATIONS

AP   Associated Press
CIA   Central Intelligence Agency
CPD   Committee on the Present Danger
DNC   Democratic National Committee
HUAC   House Un-American Activities Committee
KMAG   Korean Military Advisory Group
NAACP   National Association for the Advancement of Colored People
NATO   North Atlantic Treaty Organization
ODM   Office of Defense Mobilization
OPI   Office of Public Information (Defense Department)
PA   Office of Public Affairs (State Department)
PAD   Press Advisory Division
PI   public information
PIO   Public Information Office
PR   public relations
PSD   Press Security Division
RCT   Regimental Combat Team
ULPC   United Labor Policy Committee
UMST   Universal Military Service and Training
UN   United Nations
UNC   UN Command
UP   United Press
WSB   Wage Stabilization Board

Selling the Korean War

INTRODUCTION

America's experience during the Korean War defies simple classification. Initially a conflict of wildly fluctuating fortunes, during its last two years it bogged down in a bloody stalemate contested over a narrow stretch of land. Although ultimately a war fought for limited objectives, U.S. officials were periodically tempted to push for the unification of the entire peninsula and on occasion even contemplated extending the war into Chinese territory. The first United Nations (UN) war, the American public initially basked in the aura of legitimacy accorded by the sponsorship of that body, before becoming increasingly exasperated by the lack of tangible support from allies. The first hot war during the Cold War era, senior U.S. officials were determined to keep Korea in perspective and not take their eyes off the vital European theater. They therefore moved to militarize America's whole containment strategy, seizing on the Korean crisis to implement NSC-68, the national security review completed in April 1950, which led ultimately to a 262 percent increase in defense appropriations.

How did the Truman administration sell such a complex war to the American public? Despite a vast and burgeoning literature on other dimensions of the conflict, in this area Korea remains very much the "forgotten" war. The reasons for this amnesia are various. During the 1950s and early 1960s, the first historians and political scientists who wrote about the war reached the conclusion that Korea, because of its very nature, had been basically impossible to sell. Americans, they insisted, only ever wholeheartedly embraced all-out crusades designed to compel the unconditional surrender of the enemy. As a result, they implied, any limited conflict that stopped short of complete victory was doomed to unpopularity, inexorably squeezed between "hawks" who wanted to use maximum force and "doves" who wanted to get out altogether. In such an environment, any publicity efforts the government might have made were likely to be ineffectual at best.[1]

3

After the searing Vietnam years, Korea then faded into the background. Whenever America's home-front experience received a fleeting mention, this tended to be in the form of an explicit comparison between Korea and Vietnam, with Korea appearing to be a far easier war to sell. After all, during the 1950s the Truman administration never had to worry about a large peace movement.[2] Nor, it has been widely assumed, were generals in the field burdened with an unmanageable media. To be sure, during and shortly after the Korean War, some leading participants and official historians did complain about biased reporting, condemning journalists for "inexact and exaggerated news dispatches," even labeling them "home-front distorters" who pedaled a "disaster school of journalism."[3] But such barbs were quickly forgotten amid the intense military-media conflict of the Vietnam years. In fact, from this new vantage point, the early 1950s now marked the apogee of "objective journalism," a time when reporters relied on "official facts" to develop their stories and had not yet become devoted to the "investigative" techniques that became common in the 1960s and 1970s. And in the Korean battlefield zone itself, the military also seemed free of all the problems that plagued the Vietnam experience—with the absence of television, the relative ease of controlling journalistic access to the fighting in a more conventional conflict, and a more rigid censorship code detailing what reporters could write.[4]

Subsequently, even broader analyses of the opinion-policy relationship have tended to ignore the government's efforts to drum up support for the Korean War. Thus political scientists often focus on the simple relationship between casualties and domestic support, positing that when casualties rise, the public tends to turn against a war, thereby implying that the government is effectively powerless to reverse such an inexorable process.[5] From a different perspective, analysts of how presidents use the "bully pulpit" to promote their agenda tend to view the Truman administration's experience during the Korean period as a distant event, of little import to contemporary affairs because the basic political environment was so different in the 1950s.[6]

In recent years, to be sure, an increasing number of historians have focused on the Truman administration's efforts to construct the Cold War consensus at home. But there have been few efforts to explore the specific impact the Korean War had on this campaign. Instead, historians have generally agreed that, from 1947 onward, the president and his advisers believed they could best drum up popular support for their Cold War policies by "scaring the hell out of America," by using overheated rhetoric that locked U.S. policy into an "ideological straitjacket," perhaps even by engendering a "war scare" to "deceive the nation."[7] When scholars briefly address the Korean War period, they suggest that the Truman administration simply persisted with this strategy, attempting to drum up domestic support for the NSC-68 mobilization plan by launching a "psychological scare campaign."[8] Yet, surprisingly, no one has explored the government's specific public actions in any great detail.

Nor do we have a clear sense of how its efforts to promote rearmament actually interacted with the problems thrown up by fighting the Korean War.

Simply put, then, the Truman's administration's effort to sell the Korean War still lacks its own comprehensive history. One reason to attempt to fill this important gap is the wealth of primary source material now available, much of it untapped, that documents the work the main government departments undertook, not to mention the reception of the war by correspondents in the field and politicians and the media back home. But such a history is not just important because it fills a gap and utilizes new sources. The Korean War is now widely recognized as a watershed moment in American history. As well as being the first limited war the United States fought in the contemporary period, it sparked the emergence of the national security state to oversee a militarized version of global containment. Moreover, although a large antiwar movement was lacking, this war was an increasingly unpopular conflict, one that largely wrecked the Truman administration during 1951 and 1952 and helped to secure the election of a Republican president for the first time in more than twenty years.

Government Propaganda

This book is first and foremost about the government's efforts to sell the war at home. Most of the recent literature on American propaganda in the early Cold War has focused on the international dimension: how Washington tried to disseminate its message to the world. As a number of historians have shown, the 1950s were a time when both the Truman and Eisenhower administrations undertook important efforts not only to penetrate the Iron Curtain but also to win the hearts and minds of people living in neutral and even allied states.[9] This is an important story, but it is largely beyond the scope of my work. In the following pages, I focus firmly on the government's propaganda initiatives *inside* the United States.

Although propaganda is a word loaded with negative connotations, it has a neutral, scholarly definition: "the *deliberate* attempt to persuade people to think and behave *in a desired way*."[10] In times of war, this often entails withholding information, perhaps through overt censorship, perhaps through more subtle methods of persuading the media not to publish certain stories, in order to protect both the troops at the front and the morale of the folks back home. Propaganda also requires convincing the public that the enemy is worth fighting. In the United States, the rallying of popular support has normally been achieved, first, by a presidential "war address"—"typically thoughtful rather than angry narratives that explain the origins of the immediate crisis and the necessity for war"—and then by a series of keynote speeches that attempt to articulate America's aims in visionary ideological terms, say, as a war to make the world safe for democracy or to defend basic freedoms.[11] During world wars, presidents have also created propaganda agencies in order to define the enemy and enunciate war aims, as well as to coordinate the activities of the sprawling bureaucracy. But particularly after Woodrow Wilson's Committee on Public Information grossly exaggerated the nature of the German menace during World War I, presidents, politicians, and the public have all been leery of propaganda in its most overt form. Selling war has thus tended to devolve into more informal channels, with national security officials forging behind-the-scenes alliances with key media outlets in order to disseminate the government line.[12]

During the Korean War, six venues bore the brunt of these propaganda activities. President Harry S. Truman's keynote speeches naturally formed the centerpiece of the government's message. Not only were they drafted after careful consultation with all the relevant departments and agencies but, once "frozen" in their final version, they were meant to be the basic reference point for all other official efforts. Increasingly, too, the president and his aides made a variety of efforts to improve the delivery of their message, from the creation of what one journalist dubbed a "speech factory" to the production of a regular television show in conjunction with NBC.[13]

In important respects, however, Harry Truman was never particularly comfortable practicing the arts of the rhetorical presidency. Often ill at ease when reading a prepared set piece speech, he had an instinctive distaste for publicity stunts and had little time for the polls, surveys, and focus groups that were beginning to be used at that time and that drive so much of the content of today's speeches.

Nor did Truman have the personnel support enjoyed by presidents today. In total, his White House staff numbered only about twenty-five. Charles S. Murphy acted as the president's chief speechwriter, responsible for overseeing a drafting process that was invariably conducted by committee. Charlie G. Ross was his press secretary, in charge of handling day-to-day relations with the fourth estate. Ross, a longtime friend of Truman, was highly respected by the Washington press corps. But, as one historian has pointed out, he was a "better newsman than news handler, he never established a policy of coordinating news releases throughout the executive branch, frequently fumbled details, never developed (probably never thought of developing) a strategy for marketing the president's image, and failed to establish a strong press office."[14] After the outbreak of the war, he was also increasingly overworked. Indeed, the press office soon became morbidly known as the "homicidal center" because of the killer levels of stress suffered by incumbents, with Ross succumbing to a fatal heart attack in December 1950 and his successor, Joseph Short, "a taut, tense, 'ulcer-type,'" dying of a heart condition in September 1952.[15]

Elsewhere in Washington, the State and Defense departments often took up much of the publicity burden, especially on the details of substantive policy questions. At the top, both Secretary of State Dean G. Acheson and Secretary of Defense Louis A. Johnson had been plagued by PR problems. Acheson, to be sure, had many of the qualities of a perfect advocate; his confident manner, articulate speech, and clear control over the subject matter often combined to impress even the most hostile audience. But these virtues could easily turn into vices, for Acheson could also be overweening, almost arrogant, his barbed tongue all too swiftly demolishing foolish or ill-informed questioners.[16]

Johnson's difficulties were also self-inflicted. Desperately ambitious, he had acquired a well-deserved reputation as a slippery customer. Instinctively hostile to Acheson and staunchly opposed to key aspects of State Department policy, he was perhaps Washington's most inveterate leaker. Since taking office in March 1949, he had forged close relationships with leading Republican critics of the administration—in Washington, for instance, it was an open secret that he was friendly with Owen Brewster (R-ME), the chair of the GOP congressional campaign committee; that both men lived in the Mayflower Hotel, where they had "ample opportunity for secret huddles"; and that Brewster's efforts to discredit Acheson were doubtless aided by inside information from the Pentagon. By 1950, however, such underhand actions had started to backfire, and a number of leading media figures now considered him a "practiced liar, without scruple."[17]

Under the sway of these two domineering, controversial personalities, the State and Defense departments had both recently established their own PR bureaus. In the Pentagon, however, the Office of Public Information (OPI) had not been a happy innovation. Although intended as an effort to mute the vicious interservice rivalries, which were habitually played out in the nation's media, the OPI lacked support at the top. Before Korea, it failed to become a central clearinghouse for military statements, the services guarded their information functions jealously, and Johnson preferred to handle his own press relations. With the outbreak of war, the OPI did establish a new "nerve center," to deal with the sixty or so visits and more than five hundred telephone inquiries the military now received each day.[18] But even now, the OPI was unable to become a major player. And with its harassed officers increasingly overburdened with work, the press soon condemned it for being "clumsily ineffective in the face of crisis."[19]

Inside the State Department, meanwhile, the Office of Public Affairs (PA) was a stronger organization. It was headed by Edward R. Barrett, an experienced public advocate, who had previously been both an executive editor at *Newsweek* and a domestic propaganda chief during World War II. Acheson, who valued both PA's purpose and its output, also gave it important backing. But PA still faced important difficulties. Just before the war, it had been forced to shed some of its staff, who had been reallocated to the regional bureaus. The aim of this reorganization was to place PR officers with experts in various fields, in the belief that their exposure to specialized knowledge would help them develop more refined and effective public statements. In practice, however, PA emerged from this reform in a weakened state, left only "with the task of defining and coordinating information policy which affects more than one region." It also continued to be widely distrusted by "old school" diplomats in the State Department, who viewed the whole public opinion function as "unnecessary," even "dangerous."[20]

Outside the capital, the United Nations debates in New York were another vitally important venue, for the administration worked hard to wrap its Korean intervention in the cloak of legitimacy provided by UN endorsement. In the UN, Warren Austin, the U.S. ambassador, was often at the forefront of the administration's efforts to define objectives and counter Soviet propaganda efforts, a task that was given a greater profile by the wall-to-wall coverage the fledgling medium of television gave to the UN, particularly in the early months of the war.

In terms of domestic propaganda, however, UN support was not to prove an unbridled asset. In part, this was because of the familiar complaints from politicians and the press that America's allies were demanding too much of an input in policy decisions without shouldering a sufficient burden of the fighting. But there was another important dimension to the problem. Inside the UN, Austin often had to undertake a delicate balancing act between responding to Soviet jibes on the one hand without alienating America's allies on the other. Back in Washington, officials also had to temper and tailor their rhetoric in significant ways so that it conformed to the whole ethos of an international collective security enterprise, rather than a unilateral U.S. Cold War intervention.[21]

In the battlefield theater itself, General Douglas MacArthur, the UN commander based in Tokyo, was the author of the most famous unauthorized public outbursts of the war, on a range of sensitive questions from the strategic importance of Formosa to the need to push for complete victory in Korea.[22] These eruptions would result in the most notorious political event of the conflict—MacArthur's dismissal in April 1951—and they naturally cast a long shadow over Washington's whole information campaign.[23] But MacArthur's command in Tokyo also played another extremely significant PR role. In the first six months of the war, it was often the central source of official information on the fighting. As well as its regular communiqués and press releases, which purported to provide the most comprehensive and up-to-date assessment of how the war was progressing, it established the ground rules for the hundreds of war correspondents who flooded into Korea. Initially, these guidelines were vague and nonbinding, for MacArthur was convinced that censorship was "abhorrent" to the American free press. But after endless clashes between the military and the media over what constituted a security breach, in December 1950 the Tokyo command ultimately bowed to the inevitable and instituted a formal code for the first time.[24]

The actual implementation of censorship took place in Korea, where public information (PI) officers attached to the Eighth Army—the UN's main fighting force during most of the war—were given the sensitive task of deleting copy that contained security breaches. Before the advent of censorship, the Eighth Army's PI activities in Korea had been distinctly subordinate to those in Tokyo. In the first six months of the war, the central tasks of PI officers in the field were largely confined to conducting regular briefings, maintaining telephone and cable connections back to Tokyo, and providing accommodation and transport, where possible.[25] The lack of censorship, however, made many briefing officers wary about giving out too much information and guidance, for fear that their comments would simply be printed in tomorrow's newspaper. And a basic lack of equipment often made it difficult for the Eighth Army's Public Information Office (PIO) to provide satisfactory logistical support.

The institution of censorship at the end of 1950 initially made relations between the military and media even worse. In Korea, the Eighth Army continued to lack experienced PI officers to oversee the new code. And the whole process was adopted in such haste that reporters received no prior warning about the extent of the clampdown or the severity of the sanctions. By March 1951, however, the Eighth Army had made a concerted effort to recover its position with war correspondents. And with the removal of MacArthur the following month, together with the emergence of trench warfare over the next two years, the military built on this achievement, adopting numerous innovations and improvements that helped to change the way the conflict was covered.

Propaganda, Politics, and the Press

If the first focus of this book is on all these individuals' and institutions' efforts to sell the Korean War, the second is on the interaction between the administration and the key mediating institutions in the American polity. This is vital because of the obvious fact that officials are not always in the vanguard of the debate, setting the agenda at will. As Bernard Cohen points out, frequently their efforts are reactive; in this mode, they have "to 'put out the fires,' to respond to 'errors,' charges, criticisms of policy, programs, or institutions as they appear."[26] An important part of my analysis must therefore focus on the complex relationship between officials on the one hand and the politicians and the media on the other. Such an exploration also sheds light on some of the significant questions of this period—the extent to which political debate was stifled and the political spectrum truncated, the difficulties inherent in sustaining support for a limited war, and the importance of Korea in shaping American attitudes toward the Cold War.[27]

Party politics was a dominant concern for two reasons: fighting the war required Congress to pass numerous pieces of legislation, and partisan battles often overshadowed the whole domestic discourse on the war. To be sure, as political scientists have suggested, when it came to securing congressional support for specific legislation, Truman was in some respects a premodern president, who generally favored private bargaining rather than the more confrontational policy of "going public." According to Samuel Kernell, bargaining was the strategy of choice for presidents who came before the advent of modern communications like television and air travel when politicians had fewer ways to reach the mass public. It was also the preferred mode of operation in a period when powerful committee chairs could still be relied on to shepherd bills through the complex procedures of both houses of Congress.[28] At the start of the Korean War, moreover, Truman should have been in a position to co-opt, rather than confront, leading Republicans, since the advent of a real international crisis often serves to foster an elite consensus. Certainly, in such situations opposition parties are placed in a difficult dilemma, wanting to highlight specific flaws in the way the government is conducting the conflict without being accused of undermining the entire war effort.[29]

Yet the extent to which the Korean War was marked by a cozy, consensual relationship, with political elites doing much of their business behind closed doors, must not be exaggerated. Even before Korea, the bipartisan cooperation that had characterized the 1947–49 period, when Democrats and Republicans had united behind vital measures like the Marshall Plan and the North Atlantic Treaty Organization (NATO), was starting to wane. It was the victim of a myriad developments, including Truman's unexpected election victory in 1948, which Republican nationalists blamed on the campaign strategy of their candidate, Thomas Dewey, with its "me too" embrace of the Democrats' foreign policies; the shift in power away from moderate Senate Republicans after Senator Arthur Vandenberg (R-MI) was struck down by illness; and the emergence of a real ideological cleavage, as the focus of waging the Cold War shifted from supplying economic aid to Europe to the vexatious questions of where to draw the line in Asia and how to mobilize U.S. military resources.[30]

To make matters worse, Truman also faced major problems inside his own party. True, Democrats in the Eighty-First Congress were generally more cohesive and more responsive to their leaders than were Republicans.[31] But many southerners felt betrayed by their president because he had placed civil rights at the top of the political agenda in 1948.[32] Truman, for his part, was increasingly "fed up with our leadership on the Hill," convinced it had not been aggressive and effective enough in pushing his policy goals.[33] And even the president's relationship with internationalist legislators was somewhat strained, as many of his core supporters called publicly for a more imaginative approach to international relations in the wake of the Soviet A-bomb test of September 1949, including ideas like UN reform or a disarmament conference.[34]

Because such a fractious Congress seemed less susceptible to behind-the-scenes pressure, the Truman administration often had little choice but to adopt the more confrontational strategy of "going public." By drumming up broad-based popular support for specific initiatives, this approach promised to provide a degree of leverage over legislators. By aggressively stating what the administration was trying to achieve, it would also help to counteract Republican efforts to reframe the whole nature of the crisis. This, at least, was the view of key presidential aides at vital moments of the war.[35] Although Truman did not always take their advice, his experience during the Korean War had much in common with later presidents who, when stymied in the capital, have taken their cause to the country. But the unruly nature of the Washington environment was not the only reason the administration increasingly eschewed behind-the-scenes bargaining. Also important was a basic lack of resources, which made it far more difficult for officials to bargain with legislators on foreign policy, as opposed to domestic, issues. "It must be remembered," the State Department's chief of congressional relations pointed out at one particularly low point in the war, that State "is practically unique among all government agencies in having practically nothing with which to trade, even in good 'horse trade' fashion, to secure the ends which it seeks.... We are a unique eunuch."[36]

Although perhaps a "eunuch" in its private interactions with Congress, the administration was far from powerless when it took its case into the public arena. As well as the traditional tools—speechmaking, press conferences, and private briefing sessions with reporters—the Truman administration had developed a close working relationship with the Democratic National Committee (DNC), which had been particularly useful in supporting Truman's surprisingly successful whistle-stop campaign in 1948.[37]

In the foreign policy sphere, the Truman administration had also established an enviable record in working with private actors to garner support for its policies. Such state-private networks were important, because they enabled the government to disseminate its message without the opprobrium that the public, traditionally chary of official propaganda, would have attached to a more direct government campaign. And in the years before Korea, these networks had been constructed in a variety of different forms. Perhaps the most notable occasion had been in 1947–48, when officials had worked closely with the Committee to Sell the Marshall Plan, a pressure group led by prominent private citizens, to drum up popular enthusiasm for European aid.[38] But the government had also established more routine relationships. Indeed, one historian has depicted Acheson "deftly" using James Reston's columns in the *New York Times* to disseminate his views to the wider public.[39] Others have explored the activities of the Advertising Council, which exploited its extensive media connections to circulate commercials aimed at fostering broader support for American internationalism, and have uncovered the efforts the White House made to work with the main networks in the budding new medium of television.[40]

After the Korean War began, the administration had—in theory, at least—even more potent tools to shape media coverage. As political scientists frequently argue, during periods of crisis, the press tends to be particularly keen to echo the government line. Editors and reporters invariably conclude that they are in a weak position to second-guess officials who have access to the latest top-secret information. They also recognize that an overly negative piece can easily be depicted as rocking the boat—perhaps even as disloyalty—at a time of dire peril.

At this particular moment, the accusation of disloyalty could be particularly disastrous. The 1950s were the high point of the great Red Scare, a time when right-wing politicians accused anyone left of center of being procommunist, when advertisers bailed out of shows featuring "controversial" personalities, and when even big news organizations like CBS introduced loyalty oaths for their employees. In such a torrid environment, it would not have been surprising if debate had been stifled, as reporters, columnists, and commentators played it safe by eschewing controversy and accepting the dominant assumptions of the day.[41]

During the 1950s, moreover, the basic work culture and operating routines of the media also provided the government with important potential leverage. For one thing, the structure of "pack" reporting, especially in Washington, ensured that journalists not only covered a familiar beat, attending the regular briefings at the White House, State Department, and Pentagon, but also carefully constructed relationships with officials in each institution that would be fatally compromised if they wrote a highly critical story. For another, "objective" journalists were supposed to base their accounts on attributable sources. Since most reporters considered the executive to be the central authority on foreign policy questions, in practice this meant that "official facts" from the White House or State Department were generally given priority.[42] Small wonder, then, that one recent account has concluded that "the very routines of objective journalism supposed to guarantee freedom of information fit the needs of the national security state and embraced the specific and virulent anticommunism of the early Cold War."[43]

In Korea, meanwhile, the military also had powerful tools it could employ to influence war correspondents' coverage. True, in any war there tends to be a fundamental difference of perspective between war correspondents and the military, summed up by the maxim "The essence of successful warfare is secrecy; the essence of successful journalism is publicity." War correspondents also tend to have a more egotistical and subversive self-image than their counterparts back home, viewing themselves as "exceptional individuals in exceptional circumstances," courting danger to bring back "news from hell" and being less hemmed in by the routines and structures binding others in their profession. Yet despite their heroic self-image, war correspondents are often subject to important constraints. Most obviously, the military can impose formal censorship and directly control what journalists tell the outside world. But even without such a brutal mechanism, war correspondents are not simply free agents. Back home, their editors and newsdesks can bury any story deemed too critical or controversial; they can also subtly determine which stories are covered and how they are framed. In the battlefield zone itself, skillful PI officers can develop close working relationships with particular reporters, swapping useful information, transport, and access to communications in return for a good press, while their superiors have more coercive means at their disposal, including even the banishment of reporters from the war zone altogether, in order to send a "chilling" message to the rest of the pack to toe the line.[44]

What all this means is that far from assuming an unregulated marketplace of ideas—what one work on the Korean period has termed a "laissez-faire" system[45]—we have to be aware of all the tools, both formal and informal, that civil and military officials could employ in an effort to dominate the debate. But we must also be careful not to take this too far. Indeed, the idea that officials had the power to mold, manipulate, or control media coverage would have come as a major surprise to many of the leading participants of the time, most notably the president, who were far more convinced of their own limitations in this sphere. As Truman explained in his memoirs, "it is a characteristic of any system where free expression of opinion prevails that the critics and the malcontents will be heard more often than those who support the established policy." This was partly because "our means of communicating and consolidating public opinion—the press and the radio—emphasize the differences of opinion rather than agreements." But it was also due to the actions of biased publishers, whose "campaign of vilification and lies and distortion of facts... was the greatest asset the Soviets had."[46]

This glaring conflict between historians, who stress a partnership between the government and media, and officials at the time, who were convinced that the media had it in for them, can partly be explained by their differing conceptions of what constituted criticism. To thin-skinned politicians, what often stood out were the press's barbed assaults on specific policies and events. To historians writing from a more distant vantage point, what seems most striking is the large degree of consensus over the basic thrust of how the United States should wage the Cold War. But what both perspectives obscure is the enormous complexity in the relationship between two institutions that were far from monoliths. On the one hand, there were obvious conflicts within the diffuse and disparate administration, which were often played out in the public eye, as competing sides used briefings and leaks to influence the policy debate and denounce rivals. On the other hand, even at the height of the Cold War consensus, when the "sphere of legitimate controversy" was fairly narrow, there were also important cleavages within the media.

One was the partisan coloration of particular newspapers. Of the big media organizations, the numerous Hearst newspapers, the Luce empire, which published *Time* and *Life*, and the Scripps-Howard chain, which encompassed both nineteen daily newspapers and the United Press wire service, were all vehement in their support for Chiang Kai-shek's nationalist regime on Formosa and hypercritical of the administration's soft stance toward communism in Asia.[47] Elsewhere, the president could always rely on newspapers like the *Chicago Tribune* and the *Los Angeles Times* to be strident opponents, at least in their editorial pages, while outlets such as the *New York Times, Washington Post*, and *News and Observer* (Raleigh) tended to be supportive of his foreign policy stance. But beyond this, there was great variation. Even on the most highly charged issue of the day—Senator Joseph McCarthy's (R-WI) claims that the State Department was infested with communists—the press, rather than being cowed into a stifling conformity, was divided along complex lines. Although a small minority of diehard administration opponents echoed McCarthy's allegations, a number of conservative critics of the State Department, including the Scripps-Howard chain, the *Philadelphia Inquirer*, and *Cincinnati Times-Star*, were equally critical of the Wisconsin senator.[48]

Nor was partisanship the only cleavage. Pack reporters working the capital beat were divided between those employed by the main wire services on the one hand and those writing for the dailies and weeklies on the other. Although the U.S. press was highly decentralized at this time, with thousands of regional and local newspapers, in practice all except a few leading players relied heavily on the wire services. Indeed, as one close observer wrote, the massive wire service companies were the "backbone of the industry and, to a certain extent, its central nervous system . . . with a labor force large enough to monitor every major news" development. Speed and intense competition characterized wire service reporters' entire professional existence. All day they were under constant pressure to get a new "lead," and a matter of seconds or minutes could determine whether a reporter scooped his or her rival.[49] In contrast, correspondents for the large Washington bureaus of the major newspapers, not to mention the journalists working for weeklies like *Time* or *Newsweek*, had more leisure to check their sources and develop their thoughts.

Of course, regardless of what news organization employed them, all journalists were meant to embrace the norms of "objectivity" and "straight" news reporting—norms that were widely viewed as "one of the great glories of American journalism." To be clear, "objectivity" did not mean the absence of bias; rather, it was a series of journalistic practices that entailed distancing the reporter from the story, normally by basing it around hard evidence, attributed where possible, and containing every effort to present the opposing viewpoint. Because "official facts" were given priority, the administration theoretically was in a powerful position to dominate the news agenda.[50] But "objectivity" could also work in more complex and subtle ways. For instance, since priority was given to facts rather than underlying causes, unscrupulous government critics could exploit "objectivity" to make all manner of accusations, safe in the knowledge that these would be reported before anyone had a chance to check their veracity—a technique used to great effect by Joe McCarthy, who managed to spark no less than 845 Associated Press (AP) stories in 129 newspapers during February 1950 alone.[51] Moreover, since any story based on "hard facts" conformed to the reporting norms of the day, editors were likely to stand by correspondents who produced such copy, even in the face of intense criticism from officials and generals. As a result, far from producing a press that always parroted the government line, objectivity sometimes provided the media with an important degree of protection from official condemnation or intimidation.

Even in this period, then, the relationship between the administration and the media was far from straightforward. In exploring how it operated during the Korean War, we need to go beyond a simple analysis of what the government hoped to achieve, its interactions only with those outlets it enjoyed close relationships with, and the basic contours of consensus inside media circles. We need to examine, more broadly, the specific areas of agreement and disagreement, even during periods of intense crisis. We need to assess the extent to which all the wire services and the daily newspapers relied on official sources, and thereby had their stories heavily framed by the administration. We also need to look at the extent to which other, more subtle forms of influence worked or failed to work, by using available sources that detail private media calculations and shed light on editorial calculations, such as self-censorship on the one hand or a determination not to be intimidated by the government on the other.

In the months before Korea, the Truman administration had faced a complex domestic environment. McCarthy's witch hunt against internal "subversives" had scarred the political landscape. Recent debates over the "loss" of China, the Soviet A-bomb test, and the president's decision to build the H-bomb had also generated enormous unease. For the first time since the end of World War II, many Americans had become apprehensive about the chances of another global conflagration; more than half were convinced that it would erupt within the next five years.

But during the spring and summer of 1950, it had not all been doom and gloom. At the start of June, in an effort to calm public fears, Truman publicly stated that the world was closer to peace than at any time since the end of World War II. And his message seemed to resonate. For the first time in months, press criticism had abated, and even critical columnists like the Alsop brothers (Joseph and Stewart), Drew Pearson, and Mark Sullivan were willing to say friendly things about the administration. McCarthyism also appeared to be on the wane. In New York, a grand jury assessing one prominent disloyalty charge tentatively supported the government's position. In New England, moderate Republicans issued a stinging rebuke to those in their party who sought to make partisan gain from reckless redbaiting. Meanwhile, on Capitol Hill, as tempers cooled over foreign policy issues, legislators even began to make progress with key parts of the administration's liberal reform package, passing extensions to rent controls and contemplating substantial increases to social security.[52]

Deeply gratified by all these developments, Truman was in a relatively carefree frame of mind when, on the last sultry weekend of June, he left the capital for his hometown in Missouri. Desperate for a rest, the president passed a lazy Saturday afternoon trying to escape the heat. Unbeknownst to him, it would be his last such peaceful moment for quite some time. For thousands of miles away, in a land fourteen time zones ahead, a conflict had just erupted. The war in Korea—a war that would dominate Truman's last thirty-one months in office—was about to intrude on America's peace.

Part One

The War against North Korea, June–November 1950

1

KEEPING THE HOME
FRONT COOL

The telephone rang at the president's home in Independence, Missouri, shortly after 9:15 on the evening of Saturday, June 24, 1950, rudely interrupting Harry Truman's attempt to snatch a brief "back-porch vacation." On the other end of the line was Dean Acheson, the secretary of state. "Mr. President," Acheson quickly reported, "I have very serious news. The North Koreans have invaded South Korea."

To both men this was a shocking development. South Korea was, in many respects, an American "creation," occupied by its forces in the immediate aftermath of World War II and supplied with economic and military aid after its troops had departed in 1949. Only a week before, John Foster Dulles, a special consultant to the secretary of state, had promised the Korean National Assembly in Seoul that "you are not alone. You will never be alone so long as you continue to play worthily your part in the great design of human freedom." Now this client state had been attacked by a North Korean regime that Washington believed was completely beholden to Moscow. North Korea was "a tightly controlled Soviet satellite," the Central Intelligence Agency (CIA) had concluded earlier the same week, "that exercises no independent initiative and depends entirely on the support of the USSR."

Seen in this light, the invasion could denote only one thing: the Soviet Union had decided to escalate the Cold War, boldly switching its target from Europe to Asia and changing its expansionist methods from internal subversion to armed invasion and war. Truman was keenly aware of these implications, and his first instinct was to return to Washington immediately, so that he could monitor developments more closely and consult with his key advisers. But Acheson demurred. A night flight was risky. It might also alarm the American people. It was better for the president to stay put until more information was available.

By the next morning it was clear that the situation in Korea was continuing to deteriorate. About eighty-nine thousand well-armed North Korean troops had plunged across the thirty-eighth parallel, and were already threatening Seoul. On receiving an update from Acheson, Truman now decided to hasten back to Washington. After a hurried Sunday lunch, he arrived at the airport in Independence, where reporters had already gathered, anxious to get a glimpse of the president and hopefully even a statement. Before boarding the plane, Truman was clearly "stern faced" and "grim." But he was also anxious to tell journalists how to cover this new story. Don't exaggerate the seriousness of the attack, he instructed. "Don't make it alarmist."[1]

In the coming weeks, Truman's unfolding reactions to the Korean crisis would continue very much in this vein. Behind closed doors, neither the president nor his advisers doubted that the attack was an alarming new Cold War challenge. And within a week, they would decide to send U.S. ground forces into action for the first time since the end of World War II. Yet, despite the bold and decisive nature of this response, the president's initial public posture remained decidedly low-key. "Don't make it alarmist" became something of a motif for his early information campaign. As one shrewd observer noted at the time, "the real idea was to fix in the public eye a picture of the government in a calm mood...to keep Korea in its place: a pint-sized incident, not a full-scale war....Official Washington was doing everything it could to keep a firm line against the communists, and keep the home front cool at the same time."[2]

A Low-Key Public Posture

Sunday, June 25, as Truman flew back to the capital and other decision-makers hastened to their Washington offices, was a time for taking stock. On hearing news of the North Korean attack, virtually everyone in the administration agreed that it would be desirable for the United States to take some sort of action, not because Korea was strategically valuable in its own right but because of South Korea's "symbolic significance" now that it had been so brazenly assaulted. Indeed, throughout the administration there was an almost instinctive recognition that something had to be done—that to do nothing would undermine U.S. credibility with Asian and European allies, while emboldening the communist bloc, just as the meek appeasement policies had emboldened the Axis powers back in the 1930s.

Yet with the situation on the ground in South Korea still extremely murky, it was not entirely clear what the United States could or should do. Some officials, having recently received a few rosy reports about South Korean military capabilities, briefly clung to the hope that Seoul could repel the invasion; they even fleetingly thought that perhaps Moscow might be prevailed on to restrain its North Korean proxy. Most, however, feared that this brazen act of communist aggression heralded the start of something far bigger—that it was the first shot in a world war and that the Soviet Union might be preparing to attack other places, from Tito's Yugoslavia, which had recently sought to distance itself from Stalin's Eastern bloc, to Iran and the Middle East.[3]

These were the imponderables that faced Johnson, Acheson, and James E. Webb, the undersecretary of state, as they met Truman's plane on Sunday evening and headed back to Blair House for dinner and a crisis meeting with the Joint Chiefs of Staff, the secretaries of the army, navy, and air force, and three other leading State Department officials.

While the president had been away in Missouri, the State Department had already taken the lead. That afternoon, it had convened a session of the UN Security Council in which a resolution had swiftly been adopted calling on the North Koreans to withdraw behind the thirty-eighth parallel. Now in Blair House, the president's temporary residence while the White House was undergoing extensive renovation, Acheson was firmly at the forefront. Dapper and domineering, he led the discussion as the conferees agreed to send all available military supplies to the South Koreans, to utilize U.S. air and naval power in the region to enable the safe evacuation of American dependents, and to rush a military survey party to South Korea to assess what else could be done.

After sanctioning these limited initiatives, Truman turned to public presentation. With the distinct likelihood that far more momentous decisions would be taken in the next day or two, he asked the State Department to start work on a speech that he could deliver in person to Congress on Tuesday. This would clearly be a vitally important statement, perhaps making the case for direct U.S. involvement in an Asian war, and the president asked "the department to put its best brains on it." Until it was ready, however, Truman wanted to keep a tight rein on official statements. He therefore ended the meeting with a clear instruction. He directed that (in the words of the official minutes of the meeting) "no statement whatever was to be made by anyone to the press until he speaks [sic] on Tuesday," stressing that "it was absolutely vital that there should be no leak in regard to this matter and he wished everyone to be careful. They should not even make any background comment to the press." Senior policymakers were then ushered out the back entrance of Blair House to avoid the assembled reporters, while the White House press office announced that a meeting had taken place but that at this stage "there was nothing to add."[4]

Earlier that Sunday, before this absolute presidential prohibition on speaking out, the State Department had been fairly active in the PR sphere. Certainly its decision to call an immediate emergency session of the Security Council had been taken with one eye on domestic opinion. Of course, inside the State Department there was a natural, almost knee-jerk, tendency to view the whole matter through the prism of the UN, since this had been the framework used to establish and sustain the South Korean regime since 1948. But for senior State Department officials, the timing of the decision had been very much driven by newspaper deadlines. It was "of utmost importance," Dean Rusk, the assistant secretary of state for Far Eastern affairs, explained, to get moving on this question before 2:30 on Sunday morning—even though the department was still awaiting final confirmation of the attack—so "that the decision to present the case to the Security Council should appear in the morning papers simultaneously with the news of the North Korean attack."[5]

Later in the day, Rusk's deputy met the available members of the Senate Foreign Relations Subcommittee on Far Eastern Affairs, filling them in as best he could on developments both in Korea and at the UN. By early evening, with the UN resolution having passed, members of the U.S. delegation in New York also talked freely with reporters, stressing that although this resolution failed to mention sanctions, the Security Council's swift action clearly carried the threat of stiff countermeasures if the North Koreans continued with their invasion.[6]

But would such countermeasures include U.S. troops? Now that the president had stopped everyone from speaking out, officials were suddenly tight-lipped on this pressing question. On Monday, the White House barred both Acheson and Johnson from mentioning Korea in their testimonies before congressional appropriations committees. Instead, all that emanated from the administration that day was a brief White House press release, which simply expressed "concern over the lawless action taken by the forces of North Korea" and "sympathy and support" for the people of South Korea.[7]

Keen to puncture this veil of secrecy, on Sunday night and Monday morning reporters bombarded the press offices in the White House, State Department, and Pentagon with numerous questions, from whether or not U.S. commanders had ordered alerts in Alaska to the veracity of the claim that General Douglas MacArthur had once declared that he "would defend Korea as he would the shores of California." The Defense Department alone received more than fifty requests for background briefings on Korea and interviews with the Joint Chiefs—neither of which were forthcoming. The Pentagon was also swamped by personal visits from reporters who hoped that a face-to-face meeting might enable them to inveigle an off-the-record comment from their administration sources.[8] But on Sunday and Monday, very little hard information leaked out. "Just what this government will do now," remarked NBC's David Brinkley in a typical comment, "aside from rushing in more arms, is not made public.... A kind of lid has been put on all the town's usual sources of information—maybe because no one is sure of what there is to say."[9]

Reporters did have more joy up on to Capitol Hill, where, true to form, legislators were anything but reticent. But at this early stage, even senators on the important Foreign Relations Committee appeared confused about the nature of the new crisis. On Sunday, the immediate reaction of Alexander Wiley (R-WI), the second-ranking Republican on the committee, was to ask whether the battle in Korea was "a fight between Koreans or a communist assault egged on by the Russians," while on the other side of the aisle, Elbert D. Thomas (D-UT) had no such doubts, inclining "to the view that legally this was a civil war and not an act of aggression." Although such apostasy was effectively drowned out by an emerging congressional consensus that the invasion was indeed Soviet sponsored, it was soon replaced by a growing pessimism about South Korea's chances of survival. Recently Tom Connally (D-TX), the chair of the Senate Foreign Relations Committee, had publicly conceded that the communists would be able to overrun South Korea whenever they chose to do so. On Monday, Connally's committee deepened the mounting gloom by releasing secret testimony given a month before by the U.S. ambassador to South Korea, John J. Muccio, which had grimly concluded "that if the North Koreans attacked there was little hope of stopping them."[10]

Such evidence seemed like a gift to Republicans, especially those on the conservative wing of the party who had become increasingly vocal in their claims that Truman and Acheson had pursued a disastrous "appeasement" policy in Asia. Of course, Republicans in the Eighty-First Congress were hardly a cohesive group. On most of the important roll call votes of the past eighteen months, the administration had ultimately got its own way, often with the help of East Coast Republican internationalists like Leverett Saltonstall (R-MA), Irving M. Ives (R-NY), Margaret Chase Smith (R-ME), Ralph E. Flanders (R-VT), and Charles W. Tobey (R-NH).[11]

In terms of raw numbers, then, the nationalist wing of the GOP was not terribly potent, with only between ten and twenty Republican senators habitually voting against the administration's foreign policy. But what diehard opponents like William E. Jenner (R-IN), James P. Kem (R-MO), and Kenneth S. Wherry (R-NE) lacked in strength, they had more than made up for in a high-profile effort to reframe the public debate on foreign policy. That spring, Joseph McCarthy had become by far the most reckless—and the most newsworthy—of their number, with his claims that the State Department was infested with communists, claims that reverberated across the country and sparked a high-profile investigation that was currently preoccupying the Senate.[12]

For conservative leaders in the Senate like Robert A. Taft (R-OH), the advent of Joe McCarthy's anticommunist crusade created both an opportunity and a threat. Convinced that the State Department was politically vulnerable and hoping that some of McCarthy's charges might stick, during the spring Taft had moved cautiously to endorse the Wisconsin senator. But he remained anxious. As he remarked in private, McCarthy "doesn't check his statements very carefully and is not disposed to take any advice so that it makes him a hard man for anybody to work with, or restrain." Nor was Taft hopeful that McCarthy would ever bring the different wings of the GOP closer together—not with seven internationalist Republican senators signing a public Declaration of Conscience in mid-June, charging that certain elements of their party hoped to ride to electoral victory "through selfish political exploitation of fear, bigotry, ignorance, and intolerance."[13]

Rather than identify too closely with the specifics of McCarthy's charges, which in any case fluctuated between 57 and 205 communists in government, depending on the audience, the Taft wing had increasingly focused its attention on the Far East. This had a number of potential advantages. By latching on to the government's apparent neglect of Asia, Taft was able to effect a closer working relationship with the China lobby. These were internationalist senators like Alexander Smith (R-NJ) and William F. Knowland (R-CA), who tended to support the government's policy in Europe but had become increasingly angered by Truman's reluctance to protect Chiang Kai-shek's regime on Formosa.[14] Moreover, by adopting the China lobby's combative stance, Taft hoped to turn the tables on Truman. He was driven partly by pure politics, convinced that the Republican defeat in the 1948 election had been the result of Thomas Dewey's disastrous "me too" consensus strategy. But Taft also wanted to challenge Truman's often-repeated charge that the Ohioan and his ilk were excessively negative, always opposing everything and never providing positive alternative courses of action.[15]

Throughout the first six months of 1950, however, the White House and State Department had refused to rise to the bait. While Truman steadfastly opposed a more vigorous policy toward Formosa, Acheson notoriously placed both Formosa and Korea outside America's "defensive perimeter." Now, as soon as word reached Washington that the apparently defenseless South Koreans had been attacked, diehards like Wherry and Owen Brewster instinctively reiterated all the old charges of administration "appeasement" in Asia. In the House, Congressman Walter H. Judd (R-MN) went even further by charging that the administration had effectively "invited the attack."[16]

But could the fractious GOP forge a united position? On Monday morning, twenty-eight of the party's forty-two senators assembled for a prearranged meeting of the Republican Conference to discuss the Military Assistance Program. In recent years, Taft had worked hard to bring an element of unity to GOP policy positions, creating the Minority Policy Committee as a forum to coordinate both policy ideas and assaults on the administration. But this particular caucus turned out to be something of a desultory affair, as many legislators rushed off halfway through to attend an appropriations hearing (in the vain hope that Acheson and Johnson would fill them in on what was happening in Korea), and those who remained only briefly discussed the breaking crisis.[17]

With no clear party line, the Republicans' responses to the unfolding situation veered off in different directions. Some Republicans continued to tell journalists that the North Korean invasion was simply further evidence of the administration's total neglect of Asia. Others were quick to depict the Democrats as the party that always seemed to lead America into wars. But the most coverage was given to Senator Eugene Millikin (R-CO), widely viewed as Taft's sidekick in the Republican leadership. Coming out of the Republican Conference Committee on Monday lunchtime, Millikin appeared to suggest that the GOP would be opposed to any vigorous action in Korea. "They [the Republicans] were unanimous," he told reporters, "that the incident should not be used as a provocation for war."[18]

It would soon become apparent that this statement did not really reflect the prevailing mood in the capital. Senior figures in the Republican Party were certainly quick to distance themselves from Millikin's comments, explaining that only a few Republican senators had been at the conference to the very end and adding in a somewhat convoluted and defensive fashion that Millikin's "account of their attitude was designed merely to inform those who were inquiring whether the U.S. is automatically committed to defend South Korea with its military forces."[19] Still, all this activity did serve to highlight one basic fact that would continue to plague the administration: in the absence of clear presidential leadership, speculation and confusion would abound, and journalists and political opponents would have the opportunity to put their own particular spin on events.

On this occasion, however, the absence of presidential leadership proved to be extremely short-lived, for on Monday evening, at a second Blair House meeting, Truman decided to adopt a more vigorous response to the unfolding crisis. With North Korean troops continuing to pour south, directly menacing Seoul, Acheson again kicked off, suggesting that U.S. air and naval power now be used against the North Koreans. Truman quickly agreed, albeit with the stipulation that for the time being, all American action should remain below the thirty-eighth parallel. The president then decided to deploy the Seventh Fleet to Formosa and accelerate U.S. aid to both Indochina and the Philippines. Contemplating the possible risks, Truman's mood was grave. The president reminded his senior advisers that "he had done everything he could for five years to prevent this kind of situation," adding, "Now the situation is here and we must do what we can to meet it." Perhaps it might be necessary to mobilize the National Guard, he continued, and the Joint Chiefs of Staff were instructed to consider this. But Truman clearly hoped the problem could be solved with only air and naval power. "I don't want to go to war," he stressed, as the meeting came to an end.[20]

Because of this keen determination to avoid war, Truman decided to scrap his earlier idea of delivering a set-piece address in person to Congress, in favor of a low-key private briefing for congressional leaders.[21] But this raised another, perhaps thornier, problem: exactly who should be invited to this briefing?

Back in January, the Republican Policy Committee had adopted a statement of principles that deplored the administration's failure either to cooperate with or give "adequate information to the Congress." In an attempt to defuse this charge, in April John Foster Dulles had been appointed as a special consultant to the State Department, while Truman and Acheson had also met with senior Republicans to try to restore a measure of trust. But neither initiative had silenced the criticisms of the Taftites. Back in the heyday of bipartisanship, Senator Vandenberg had not merely been the spokesman for the internationalist wing of the GOP; he had also muted much of the latent opposition from Taft and other nationalists, who despite their dislike of extensive and expensive overseas commitments, had nevertheless been willing to defer to his lead. Now that Vandenberg had been removed from the scene, however, struck down with a cancer that would kill him within a year, Taft was in the process of moving out of his shadow with a vengeance. Taft certainly did not want Republicans on the Senate Foreign Relations Committee speaking on his behalf, for the likes of Alexander Wiley, Alexander Smith, and Henry Cabot Lodge either lacked Vandenberg's clout or were too internationalist in orientation.[22]

Nor, for their part, did Truman and Acheson relish the prospect of dealing with Taft and his followers. As Acheson complained, recently Taft had appeared "to adopt the notion that almost *any* way to defeat or discredit the Truman plans was acceptable." And Acheson was equally scathing about Wherry, the Republican floor leader in the Senate, describing this fundamentalist midwesterner as "my old enemy . . . the Nebraska undertaker."[23]

In short, briefing such figures in the midst of a crisis might well be a recipe for disaster—an opportunity for bitter partisan wrangling rather than a consensus-building exercise as American air and naval forces went into action. Truman and his senior advisers therefore reached a fateful decision. They would exclude the diehards.[24]

The next morning, hundreds of reporters packed the large White House lobby, waiting expectantly for the fourteen legislators who had received an invitation. Arriving in a black limousine with Wiley, Thomas, and Alexander Smith, Tom Connally was clearly the star of the show. After first stopping to have his picture taken in the crowded lobby, Connally grabbed his straw hat, pushed the photographers aside, and strode into the Cabinet Room with the shout "Make way for liberty!"[25]

The meeting itself lasted slightly more than half an hour and was characterized by "a general air of approval" from the bipartisan delegation. Once everyone was seated, Acheson briefed them on the latest developments, Truman read out a short statement that would soon be released to the press, and the legislators were then given a few minutes in which to ask questions. With no hard-line administration critics present, it was not surprising that everyone seemed happy to endorse the president's decision to deploy air and naval power against the North Koreans. Sam Rayburn (D-TX), the Speaker of the House, even promised that he would avoid reporters after the meeting to ensure that the press would have only the president's statement on which to base its account.[26]

Released at midday, this press statement summarized the administration's overall public position now that U.S. air and naval power had been committed to Korea. Its first theme was straightforward enough: the United States was acting hand in hand with the UN to deal with the crisis.[27]

When it came to pointing the finger at the party responsible for defying the UN Charter, however, a studied caution characterized the official line. Indeed, back on Sunday, when Edward W. Barrett, the assistant secretary of state for public affairs, had told reporters that the North Koreans were utterly dependent on Moscow—that their relationship, in his colorful phrase, was like that between "Walt Disney and Donald Duck"—he had been swiftly reprimanded and told to "pipe down."[28]

As officials worked through the laborious process of drafting Truman's press release, their thoughts mirrored the trajectory of Barrett's unfortunate experience. Initially, many wanted to follow their gut instincts and place the blame squarely on "centrally directed Communist Imperialism." But by Tuesday, the White House and senior figures in the State Department thought this was too bold. After considerable debate, the statement they eventually released was watered down so that it simply referred only to the fact that "communism has passed beyond the use of subversion to conquer independent nations and will now use armed invasion and war." By implication, the Soviet Union was not held publicly responsible for the crisis.[29]

On June 28 and 29, official utterances continued in this subdued vein. On Wednesday evening, the president had the perfect opportunity to deliver a rousing radio address, making his case to the public for his latest Korean decision, when he made a preplanned appearance before the American Newspaper Guild. But Truman resolutely refused to make a major statement on Korea—much to the chagrin of the four radio networks, who broadcasted his rather lackluster speech live to an expectant public.[30]

The next night, Acheson addressed the same audience. Marshall Shulman, the secretary's main speechwriter, felt it would be disastrous if Acheson followed the president's example and failed to mention Korea. "There would be an adverse reaction," Shulman quite sensibly pointed out, "to a speech by the secretary of state which did not deal with the problem uppermost in everyone's mind."[31] Accepting this advice, Acheson decided to deliver a "calm and factual treatment of the Korean issue," which focused almost exclusively on the mechanics of how the decision had been made and only briefly blamed the invasion on ill-defined "communist forces."[32]

At his press conference that same day, Truman intended to be just as vague. At first, he refused to be drawn out on many issues, especially if they related to military strategy. But all of a sudden, one question brought a typically quick-fire response. "Mr. President, everybody is asking in this country, are we or are we not at war." "We are not at war," Truman emphatically declared, a statement he allowed reporters to quote directly. Anxious to get something more substantial, another journalist then prompted Truman with a trick that periodically worked at his press conferences: he put words into the president's mouth. Would it be correct "to call this a police action under the UN?" he inquired. "Yes," Truman replied, "that is exactly what it amounts to."[33]

In the months ahead, the term "police action" would become the sound-bite everyone would remember, and time and again Republicans would use it to attack the administration's methods of waging war. At this precise moment, however, the phrase made perfect sense. For one thing, it encapsulated the notion that the war was not the result of North Korea's drive for unification but rather the product of an illegal challenge to international peace and security. For another, the United States was not yet fully at war—it had only deployed air and naval power against the North Koreans.

Yet even as Truman spoke, the situation in Korea continued to deteriorate dramatically. On leaving his press conference, he returned straight to the West Wing to meet with his principal national security advisers. Although still determined not to "become so deeply committed in Korea that we could not take care of other situations as might develop," Truman nevertheless agreed to send a limited number of troops to protect the port-airfield in the Pusan area, on the southern tip of the Korean peninsula. This was only a limited measure—a move to protect supply lines and preserve order in an effort to facilitate the evacuation of Americans from Korea. But the next morning it was swiftly followed by a more momentous decision.

On Thursday, General Douglas MacArthur flew from Tokyo to witness the unfolding military situation firsthand. Landing on an air strip that had just been strafed by North Korean planes, his party drove in three "old, broken-down cars" to the edge of Seoul, where the general observed shell fire, burning buildings, and long lines of retreating troops and refugees. Told that only twenty-four thousand South Korean troops could be located out of an army that had totaled ninety-eight thousand at the weekend, MacArthur reached a firm conclusion. Two of the U.S. divisions based in Japan would have to be thrown "into this breach." Without these troops, the North Korean invasion would succeed.[34]

The Pentagon received MacArthur's recommendation at 3:40 Friday morning. Truman, informed an hour and twenty minutes later, decided to authorize the immediate use of one regimental combat unit from MacArthur's command in Japan. Then at 9:30, the president and his senior advisers took their most important decision of the week. Although still anxious "not to start a general Asiatic war," Truman nevertheless gave MacArthur "full authority to use the troops under his command." With this simple instruction, U.S. ground forces would soon be fighting in Korea.[35]

An hour and a half later, the president held another briefing session for congressional leaders. Fittingly, in light of America's deepening involvement in Korea, the group was now expanded to include one of the GOP diehards, Kenneth Wherry. The White House hoped his presence might take some of the edge off potential Republican criticisms. An imposing array of top brass, including cabinet secretaries, White House aides, and the Joint Chiefs of Staff, was also on hand to help Truman with this vital briefing and perhaps even to intimidate potential opponents into submissive quiescence. But Wherry, for one, refused to remain silent. At first, the consultation centered on areas where bipartisan agreement was possible, such as the need for other countries to supply troops and the desirability of making MacArthur the UN commander. Then Wherry rose and, in the words of the White House minutes, "addressed the president as though he were on the Senate floor, and wanted to know if the president was going to advise the Congress before he sent ground troops into Korea." Truman, trying to keep calm, responded that he had faced "an emergency. There had been no time for lots of talk," he explained. "There had been a weekend crisis and he had to act."[36]

Truman was clearly right to stress that the hectic and fluid nature of events during the past week had not allowed much time for extensive speechmaking or consultation. But now that the decisive action of sending ground troops had finally been taken, the president still did not think there was any real need to talk in public. In briefing legislators, he even misleadingly informed them only of the decision taken the day before, to send support troops to the Pusan area, and not the major decision, made a few hours earlier, to instruct MacArthur to send U.S. combat forces into battle.

After the legislators were ushered out of the West Wing, the White House press office released another presidential statement, but this merely announced, "General MacArthur has been authorized to use certain supporting ground units" in Korea. On Saturday, July 1, pointedly seeking to exude an air of calm, quiet confidence, Truman then headed off on a preplanned cruise on the yacht *Williamsburg*, accompanied only by eight members of the White House press pool, who had to tag along in an escorting destroyer. When the president returned on Sunday, reporters waiting expectantly on the shore were expressly forbidden to ask any questions.[37]

Motives

The contrast between Truman's public response to this Cold War challenge and his reaction during an earlier crisis was particularly striking. Back in

1947, having decided to send aid to Greece and Turkey, Truman had gone before Congress to deliver a ringing condemnation of the totalitarian danger. As historians have frequently pointed out, his goal then had been to drum up popular support for his foreign policy by "scaring the hell out of America" and placing events in Greece and Turkey squarely in the Cold War context. Now, during the first days of the Korean crisis, the president privately believed there was a very close parallel between these two events. "Korea is the Greece of the Far East," he remarked on June 26, peering at a globe in the Oval Office. "If we are tough enough now, if we stand up to them like we did in Greece three years ago, they won't take any next steps."[38] In the past week, Truman had certainly decided to stand up to the threat, this time with even tougher action than he had employed three years earlier. But his public utterances were nowhere near as tough—or as clear-cut—as they had been before. Indeed, although the president had now directly committed U.S. forces to battle for the first time during the Cold War, he had categorically refused to accompany this with a rousing, Truman Doctrine–style call to action.[39]

In part, this was because the bipolar, confrontational rhetoric that had characterized the Truman Doctrine was clearly at odds with the universal principles that lay at the heart of the UN. Back in 1947, most domestic criticism of the Truman Doctrine had revolved around the fact that the administration's Cold War posturing seemed to herald its abandonment of the fledgling UN.[40] Now that the United States was working so closely with the UN to beat back the North Korean attack, the State Department was particularly keen to avoid a repetition of such swipes. Officials therefore worked hard to ensure that official rhetoric conformed to the whole ethos of a UN-sponsored campaign. On June 27, U.S. delegates at the UN headquarters in Lake Success, New York, even explicitly rejected the possibility of using a UN resolution to extend the Truman Doctrine to Korea, on the revealing grounds that it was "not consistent with principle of keeping the Korean matter a *UN* rather than a *U.S.* affair."[41]

For the president, meanwhile, caution was vital because of a complex blend of fears and hopes about Moscow's next move. Initially, Truman and his senior advisers had worried that the Korean attack might be the harbinger of a new world war, with Stalin poised to unleash his satellites at other points on the Soviet periphery, from Europe to the Middle East. Moreover, if such a major conflict was in the offing, Korea was about the last place the Joint Chiefs wanted to make a stand. It was all well and good, senior officials agreed, to make a move to defend South Korea if this was an isolated incident, since such decisive action would serve to protect Japan, demonstrate U.S. resolve to the communist world, and build up American prestige among its European allies. But in a global conflagration, the Joint Chiefs believed that Korea held very little strategic significance. And they had long planned to abandon the peninsula to the enemy as part of an overall defensive posture in the Far East, while scarce American resources were concentrated in

Europe. Given these calculations, Truman was naturally anxious to obtain a detailed assessment of Moscow's short-term intentions before getting too embroiled in Korea. The conclusion he soon received was heartening. Neither the senior generals who attended the Blair House meetings nor the National Security Council consultants who assembled at a specially convened conference on June 29 believed that the Soviet Union was ready, willing, or able to launch a full-scale conflagration in the near future. The Kremlin "did not intend to bring about a general war or involve the USSR in a showdown with the U.S.," a National Security Council action paper concluded at the end of the first week. "Its aim was rather to acquire strategic control over South Korea," while also probing America's resolve.[42]

Still, it was clearly prudent to avoid overtly taunting Stalin—and, as many officials quickly grasped, a presidential statement publicly blaming the Soviets for the Korean invasion could easily prove to be a very serious provocation indeed. Not only might it serve to escalate the Korean crisis into a full-blown clash between the two superpowers—a clash the United States, with only ten army divisions, was patently unprepared to meet at the moment—but it might back Stalin into a corner, denying him the flexibility to end the North Korean attack and opt for a negotiated settlement if he so desired.[43] As Paul H. Nitze, the director of the State Department's Policy Planning Staff, reported to Acheson:

> Should the U.S. officially denounce the Soviet government as responsible for the aggression, it would be very difficult to avoid the logical consequences of such a position, i.e., branding the Soviet Union as the aggressor through UN action. Other steps, such as breaking diplomatic relations, etc., would be almost inescapable once the direct accusation was made.... In short, we definitely do not wish to see Soviet forces involved in this as it would complicate our military tasks and it could lead to a general conflict which we have no desire to see and for which we are distinctly not militarily prepared.[44]

As well as heading off such calamitous international consequences, officials had one eye firmly fixed on domestic public opinion. The president, to be sure, had an instinctive distrust of opinion polls, convinced that the major polling agencies were peddling a highly inexact science—a conviction only heightened by the fact that Gallup had erroneously predicted his defeat in the 1948 presidential election. Nor, as a matter of principle, did the president believe that popular opinion ought to play much of a role in the actual formulation of foreign policy. "It isn't polls or public opinion alone of the moment that counts," he once famously commented. "It is right and wrong, and leadership—men with fortitude, honesty, and a belief in the right that make epochs in the history of the world."[45]

Still, effective leadership obviously required some conception of the current mood. And the president, as one of his aides recalled, was always "very anxious to know, not only through his press office but through others on his staff, through the cabinet, and through people on the Hill, what the people out in the country were interested in and what they wanted." In fact, Truman the ex-senator was always highly sensitive to congressional opinion. Not only did he see the "Big Four" leaders each week but his daily diary was frequently filled with meetings with legislators, and the president was always willing to listen to those he considered "forward looking."[46]

In the State Department, meanwhile, PA's Public Studies Division had the main responsibility for monitoring popular attitudes toward foreign policy. Although PA was viewed with suspicion by some in the department, Acheson believed it had an important role to play, and, as Francis H. Russell, its director, recalled, Acheson was always "generous in giving it his time, in accepting speech requests, and creating an atmosphere in the department whereby all other officers knew they were expected to cooperate." Since the start of the year, Acheson had also paid particularly close attention to PA's opinion surveys, not least because in these turbulent months the popular mood had been especially volatile, oscillating rapidly between calls for disarmament and budding support for a preventive war.[47]

Two events had been particularly responsible for sparking this tense instability: the Soviet A-bomb test of September 1949, followed four months later by Truman's decision to build a "super" H-bomb. In February and March, a number of senior Democrats had reacted to these disturbing developments by calling for "disarmament all the way down the line."[48] Although their intention had been to counter Soviet propaganda, the State Department had fretted that a complacent public, which had "a false sense of security," might take such ideas seriously.[49] PA had therefore started to contemplate "a psychological scare campaign" to "whip up sentiment," while Acheson had made a series of speeches widely viewed in the media as the "toughest" of the Cold War and a firm riposte to all those who advocated a disarmament conference with the Soviet Union.[50]

Yet State Department officials had also been acutely aware that "scare" tactics had to be employed with extreme care, for complacency was only one aspect of the whole problem. From time to time, Americans had also seemed dangerously prone to panic. In one poll conducted during the spring, 40 percent of respondents had singled out war as their chief concern—"the highest...at any time since the end of World War II"—while 22 percent had expected war with the Soviets in one year and a further 57 percent had thought it would come within five years.[51] What had particularly alarmed officials was the prospect that a public convinced that war was inevitable might push for the United States to get its blow in first, with a preventive strike, rather than wait for the country to be destroyed by Soviet A-bombs.

In January, Acheson had listened angrily to a group of senators who claimed that their constituents were frequently writing in "with statements like 'why don't we get into this thing now and get it over with before the time is too late.'" This "attitude was growing by leaps and bounds in his state," one legislator stressed, "and...he was compelled to take note of it."[52] Thereafter, polls and media surveys had been scanty and inconclusive on the subject. But State Department officials had deemed it prudent to avoid saying anything that might generate a popular conviction that World War III was inevitable, lest they unintentionally create a demand for a preemptive strike now.[53]

The Korean crisis naturally enhanced the government's caution. Given the fear that the domestic mood might suddenly overheat, it seemed sensible to maintain the public conceit that the Soviet Union was not directly responsible for the North Korean attack, for this would help ward off public demands to take more vigorous action against the real perpetrator. "We must exercise a high degree of self-discipline under the present situation," one State Department official remarked to a friendly congressman on July 6, "and should carefully consider any measures likely to cause hysteria."[54]

Although there were thus good reasons to "avoid creating a feeling of panic among the American people," by the second weekend of the crisis, as the president tried to relax on his cruise along the Chesapeake Bay, a number of officials in the State Department began to worry that a clear tension had emerged between keeping the home front cool on the one hand and keeping Congress up to speed on the other. In part, this was simply a rerun of the hoary problem of consultation. As Acheson was only too aware, the two briefings for congressional leaders had hardly satisfied the rank and file's desire for information. In addition to Wherry's attack on Friday, over the weekend the State Department's congressional liaison officer, Jack McFall, found "a general desire" on the Hill for a full presidential report to a joint session of Congress.[55]

And there was also a deeper, more controversial, aspect to the whole problem: the absence, thus far, of congressional authorization for sending U.S. troops overseas. In a Senate speech on Wednesday, Taft had charged that the president had "no legal authority for what he has done."[56] Although the State Department's legal advisers soon disagreed, pointing to numerous precedents when U.S. forces had been sent abroad without expressed congressional approval, over the weekend others in the department felt it might be prudent to adopt a conciliatory stance toward the legislature. The administration had, after all, gone to great lengths to build up an international coalition to deal with the crisis; it seemed almost perverse to go it alone at home. If the conflict turned out to be a long-drawn-out and messy affair, a congressional resolution would also provide a measure of protection against partisan jibes that this was purely a "Democratic war." And, as a practical matter, soundings in

Congress suggested that such a resolution would enjoy widespread support, not only from Democrats and moderate Republicans but also from the likes of Taft, who had publicly stated that he would vote in favor.[57] On Saturday, Acheson met with senior Pentagon officials to discuss the whole question. In a second meeting on Sunday afternoon, State and Defense officials agreed on the text of a draft resolution that Acheson felt "would be helpful during the time ahead," especially if the conflict turned ugly.[58]

As soon as Truman returned from his cruise, Acheson prevailed on him to call yet another top-level meeting to discuss this subject, and so on Monday, July 3, senior policymakers returned to Blair House. Acheson again led off, stressing the growing demand on Capitol Hill for both a presidential speech and a congressional resolution, which the State Department felt ought to be met (although Acheson believed that the initiative for a resolution should come from the legislature rather than the president). On the subject of a resolution, however, the meeting soon bogged down in practical considerations. With Congress in recess, it would not be possible to get any action on a resolution before legislators returned the following Monday. The Joint Chiefs also feared a protracted congressional debate at a time when speed and unity were of the essence. Scott W. Lucas (D-IL), the Senate majority leader, agreed, advising that even after Congress returned a debate on a resolution might last a week. The president himself doubtless believed that, with midterm elections looming, any debate would simply be a chance for legislators to grandstand to their constituents.[59]

But what about a simple report to Congress, outlining the reasons for intervening in Korea? If practical considerations dominated the president's decision to reject calls for a resolution, then it was the familiar fear of sparking popular hysteria that dissuaded him from pursuing this more limited course. As Lucas pointed out, "to go up and give such a message to Congress might sound as if the president was asking for a declaration of war." "This was exactly the point," Truman agreed. Private consultations had been fine, he believed, but a high-profile speech at this stage, particularly since it would entail recalling Congress from its recess, risked engendering the very panic he and his advisers had studiously sought to avoid.[60] As one White House source stressed to reporters, "a joint session of Congress, addressed by the president, might contribute to a war hysteria."[61]

Indeed, at this stage little could deflect the president from his determination to adopt a low-key, laid-back public posture. The very next day, July 4, the first American troops were preparing to go into battle against North Korean forces at Osan, just 30 miles south of Seoul. Truman, however, continued to present a decidedly calm image, instructing his press office to tell journalists that he would be spending the July 4 holiday relaxing at Blair House with his daughter. As most news bulletins reported, Truman planned to hold no official engagements at all on Independence Day.

As a matter of fact, on Independence Day, the president did not stay in Washington and relax. In the afternoon, he secretly drove out to Leesburg, Virginia, to get the advice of two of the main military figures of the last war, generals George C. Marshall and Dwight D. Eisenhower. For a couple of hours, their conversation ranged widely over the issues and personalities of the past week—"China, Formosa, Japan, MacArthur, Chiang Kai-shek, and finally about the Defense Department." Anticipating a "terrific jam" as the holiday traffic headed back to Washington, Truman left early. But by the end of his visit, he had reached a significant conclusion: in the current crisis, the president had no doubt that General Marshall would make a far more effective head of the Defense Department than the incumbent, Louis Johnson.[62]

In recent weeks, Truman had been angered by Johnson's scheming with Republicans to undercut Acheson.[63] But he was not quite ready to oust his controversial defense secretary, not with the Pentagon just starting to establish what force levels would be required in Korea. On July 5, Johnson also temporarily staved off the threat to his own position when he decided it was time to lie low. All officials in the Pentagon, Johnson told reporters that day, would refrain from making public speeches for at least a month. Truman was visibly pleased; as he pointedly told journalists at his press conference the next day, he was "very happy that the Defense Department is going to devote all their time to their job over there, instead of making speeches."[64] Reporters were more flippant and cynical, however; as one privately remarked to his colleagues, "I've got my lead written already: 'Secretary of Defense Johnson today announced a plan for keeping his foot out of his mouth for the remainder of July.'"[65]

Consequences

Despite the president's obvious pleasure, it would soon became clear that Johnson's decision to keep the Pentagon quiet had left a gaping hole at the heart of the administration's already anemic information efforts. It was a hole made all the bigger because of Truman's own reluctance to do anything that might create a "war hysteria." And soon the resulting lack of hard information would not only create growing frustration among journalists; ominously, it would also provide Republicans with a relatively clear field to develop their own conception of why the conflict had erupted in the first place.

On the surface, to be sure, these worrying side effects were masked by the almost universal applause that greeted Truman's decision to intervene in Korea. By the end of the first week, Gallup reported that 81 percent of the mass public supported Truman's decision to aid South Korea, while the White House press office hastened to inform reporters that letters to the president were running ten to one in favor of sending U.S. support to Korea.[66] One survey by the AP found "no well-known paper opposing the president's policies" except the *Daily Worker* on the left and the *Chicago Tribune* on the right.[67] On Capitol Hill, congressmen burst into spontaneous applause on receiving word that the United States was committing air and naval forces. And apart from the most extreme diehards like Missouri's James P. Kem and Utah's Arthur V. Watkins, congressional Republicans, as one of their number put it, were "all elated by the news." As Eric Sevareid told his CBS listeners, "the remarkable bipartisan unity behind the president is at a pitch not seen since Mr. Truman's first weeks in office."[68]

Even privately, some of the administration's leading media critics were now willing to do their utmost to stand with their president in the midst of a real crisis. "We all want to help," Roy Howard of the Scripps-Howard press assured the White House. "No difference of opinion we may entertain about details or methods, and certainly no selfish interests of our own, will ever cause us, knowingly or intentionally, to become obstructionists or to give anything less than our all out support to the effort to win the war." As a practical step, the Scripps-Howard cartoonist was even instructed to tone down his caricatures of Truman. "No matter what anyone thinks of him," the chair of Scripps-Howard privately explained, "he will be president for the next two years and at a time like this I don't think it will add to the morale of our readers to picture the commander-in-chief as a grinning nincompoop. Many might wish for Eisenhower or MacArthur, but we have Harry."[69]

Truman was naturally gratified by these expressions of support, for they seemed to vindicate his response to the crisis. Yet it would soon become clear that this widespread endorsement only extended to the narrow decision to intervene. When it came to broader issues, such as why the North Koreans had invaded in the first place or how the U.S. intervention fitted into the broader pattern of the Cold War, the administration would quickly be plagued by a host of problems and criticisms emerging from two separate quarters.

One was the Washington press corps, which was becoming increasingly frustrated by the distinct lack of information emanating from official sources. Of course, in periods of crisis, presidents are usually able to dominate the news, by taking center stage and using their privileged access to sensitive information to explain their view of unfolding events. This was also the era of so-called objective journalism, when the dominant journalistic norm was to avoid editorializing in news pages and to rely instead on "official facts" when developing a story.[70] In practice, however, with the government now making very few "official facts" available, reporters soon started to look elsewhere for their stories. Many resorted to pure speculation. In the harassed press offices inside the West Wing and State Department, question-and-answer sessions now seemed utterly divorced from reality, as journalists speculated about the wildest of claims, from whether or not Molotov was in the Far East directing Korean operations personally to the rumor that Truman had called Stalin to discuss the whole crisis.[71]

Everything finally came to a head on Friday, July 7. At the end of the second week of the crisis, with U.S. forces now in contact with the North Korean enemy but with no presidential statement since June 30, journalists "swarmed" into the White House pressroom and lobby, apparently tipped off by sources in Congress that an important new policy announcement was in the offing. Yet, despite (or perhaps because of) the expectant and somewhat frenzied atmosphere, the White House was still keen to play down new developments. At a cabinet meeting that morning, the president had authorized the Pentagon to increase military forces by more than one hundred thousand in the next twenty-one months. But Truman and his military advisers hoped to get these men without extensive use of the draft. More to the point, the president was reluctant to release this information directly from the White House, fearing that it "might indicate we are on the verge of war." He therefore delegated the announcement to the Pentagon. All that came from the White House that afternoon was the relatively small decision to ask Congress for a supplemental appropriation for the H-bomb—a decision that had been anticipated for a long time, before the Korean conflict broke out, and was only for an additional $260 million to build a facility for a project that had already been agreed on back in January.[72]

For reporters and editors, however, denied a steady steam of hard information about Korea and believing that something serious was afoot, the time had come to abandon restraint. The next morning, even the normally measured *New York Times* led with only its second page-wide banner headline of the war so far, declaring: "TRUMAN ORDERS INCREASES IN ARMED SERVICES, DRAFT IF NEEDED." Underneath, in an article that focused on the H-bomb decision, the *Times* White House correspondent, Anthony Leveiro, explained why the press was making so much of these two issues:

> The [H-bomb] action was taken on a day that was notable for a marked rise in White House activity bearing on national security in general and the Korean conflict in particular. The request for funds, which was the first thus far made for the new weapon, was the only formally announced activity. The increased planning and actions to meet the problems arising from the Korean War were mostly shrouded in secrecy. The administration is making a studied effort to avoid sensationalism as part of a policy to avoid further complications in Korea and elsewhere. Reporters relied mainly on their observations of comings and goings of national leaders to uncover some idea of what was going on.[73]

It was a cautionary episode. The White House may have been seeking to avoid sensationalism, but on this occasion its strategy of providing little hard news had obviously backfired. By forcing journalists to rely on their own observations of what was going on, what was important, and how it should be presented, the administration had effectively lost control over the public debate. More worrying, far from keeping the home front cool, reporters were giving far too much prominence to the disturbing news that the draft was about to be enforced and an H-bomb built.

This type of journalistic speculation was alarming enough, but it was not the only unintended consequence of the president's PR strategy. By July 7, newspapers and commentators across the spectrum were also starting to conclude that the government's low-key posture was evidence of excessive complacency at the very top. Criticizing Truman's "optimistic" press conference remarks, the Scripps-Howard papers soon reverted to type, insisting that "this is no time for politics as usual—no time for Mr. Truman to be encouraging unfounded confidence." "We must do more than we are doing now," the *Washington Star* agreed, "and if we err it should be on the side of doing too much." Pointing out that the administration was trying to "shelter" the American public, the *San Francisco Chronicle* maintained that "there is a clear need for the entire country to face the facts." "There is a total war in Korea," Drew Pearson told his ABC listeners, "but there is only 50 percent war in Tokyo and about 10 percent war in Washington."[74]

As well as these press problems, State Department officials were worried that the government's muted information campaign had effectively left the field open to Republicans to present to the public their own version of the Korean crisis. The most extreme GOP interpretation came on June 28, when Taft charged that the administration had effectively "invited" the attack. In Taft's conception, the communists were only part of the problem. "The most dangerous threat to...peace," he declared, "is the kind of wavering foreign policy which this country has maintained."[75]

Given the strong desire to rally around the president, Taft's speech received "little sympathy" in the press. Initially, too, many of Taft's natural allies on Capitol Hill were unwilling to defend him. Unlike their intrepid leader, they were reluctant to go out on a limb while events in Korea were still in such a state of flux.[76]

Nonetheless, with the administration doing little to drive home its temporary advantage over Taft, the GOP's timidity soon started to evaporate. Launching a more subtle assault, leading Republicans like Styles Bridges (R-NH), Knowland, and Alexander Smith began to suggest that the administration's belatedly bold action had finally put an end to the "appeasement" of communism in Asia.[77] And in stark contrast to Taft's widely condemned speech, this subtler allegation quickly found a congenial audience. A number of mainstream newspapers and magazines—including the *Cleveland Plain Dealer*, the *New York Herald Tribune*, *U.S. News & World Report*, and the *Wall Street Journal*—hastened to repeat the claim that Truman's strong stand in Korea and Formosa "marks an almost complete reversal" in government policy.[78] "It almost amounts to 'vindication' of the attitude taken" by senior Republicans, the *New York Herald Tribune* editorialized. "The present action comes late," agreed the *New York Times*. But we have finally "learned the lesson that appeasement does not serve peace."[79]

Inside the State Department, this damning with faint praise seemed highly ominous, for if taken to its logical conclusion it could easily serve to place the pretext for war in a whole new light. Indeed, what should have been a straightforward matter of the United States and the UN uniting to halt a brazen act of communist aggression might instead be viewed as yet another byproduct of the administration's past neglect of Asia.

In the effort to counter "the allegation that the recent steps in Korea constitute a 'reversal' of American foreign policy," John Foster Dulles took the lead.[80] He had just returned from a two-week trip to Japan and Korea, and so had firsthand experience of conditions on the ground. He was also the administration's major symbol of bipartisanship, having been recruited in April to help glue back together the partisan perforations that threatened to become an irreparable tear. Appearing on CBS, Dulles now emphasized that the North Korean invasion had nothing to do with United States–induced weakness of Syngman Rhee's South Korean regime. Quite the opposite: it was a product of South Korea's growing health and strength. "The communists seem to have felt that they could not tolerate this hopeful, attractive Asiatic experiment in democracy," Dulles declared. "They had found they could not destroy it by indirect aggression, because the political, economic, and social life of the Republic was so sound that subversive efforts, which had been tried, had failed."[81]

Dulles's carefully chosen words were helpful in countering the "reversal" charge, but Acheson and his top advisers believed they were no real substitute for a keynote presidential address. Indeed, as one White House aide recorded, State Department officials were clearly worried "by the criticism of a few writers and they thought it essential for the president to go on air almost at once." Truman continued to disagree, however, remaining resolutely determined to avoid anything that might spark hysteria. Inside the White House, some officials even began to gloat, convinced that that Acheson had been unduly "panicked" while they had kept their cool and adopted the correct PR strategy. George Elsey, one of the president's aides, personally regarded Acheson's pressure for a presidential speech both premature and "highly offensive." Needless to say, he was extremely pleased that Truman continued to reject the State Department's advice.[82]

But Acheson persisted. Between July 10 and 15, he continued each day to make his case for a presidential pronouncement. Increasingly, events were on his side. By the middle of July, the situation in Korea was clearer. The crisis would obviously require more than just a short, sharp infusion of men and materiel. It was a full-scale war that might take many months to win. Congress would therefore have to provide additional funds, probably as much as $10 billion.[83]

Faced with this grim new situation, Truman finally relented to Acheson's pressure, allowing work to begin on a set-piece address to define what the war was about. The only question was whether it was too late. Already the president's decision to adopt a low-key public posture had created problems. As well as encouraging journalists to speculate, it had given Republicans the opportunity to put their own spin on why America was suddenly at war.

Now, as White House speechwriters set about their task, the attention of the press, the politicians, and the public started to shift away from Washington and toward the actual fighting in Korea. On July 5, the first U.S. troops were flung into the battle. Small in number, inadequately trained, and insufficiently supplied, they were soon forced into a headlong and demoralizing retreat. By the time the president finally took to the airwaves, there would thus be yet another dimension to the public debate: just why was the United States so unprepared to do battle with the communists?

2

"CENSORSHIP IS ABHORRENT TO GENERAL MACARTHUR"

In the first two weeks of the Korean War, Dean Acheson often fretted about the problem of how to dominate the domestic debate. As all the activity in Congress and the media amply demonstrated, even in the relatively limited environs of Washington in the midst of a real crisis, influencing what legislators said and reporters covered was far from easy. Now, as the focus shifted to the battlefield in Korea, maintaining any sort of control over the popular discourse would prove even more of a challenge.

This became clear at the very start of the crisis. On June 26, MacArthur's headquarters in Tokyo announced that it would coordinate the release of all relevant military information, making sure that "all news of non-strategic value or that will not aid and abet the aggressors will be released as early as possible."[1] But this initiative naturally had little effect on the few correspondents caught in the midst of the fighting in and around Seoul. Early on the first morning of the war, Jack James of UP grabbed a worldwide exclusive by breaking the story of the North Korean attack.[2] Later the same day, Walter Simmons of the *Chicago Tribune* wired back an eyewitness account of the fighting, describing "how the Korean civil war looks in the muddy fields and slippery mountains where it is being fought."[3]

To officials back in Washington, convinced that North Korea's invasion was part of the Cold War, rather than just a civil war between the two Koreas, Simmons's story was disturbing enough. But worse was to come a few days later, when MacArthur's headquarters released a communiqué announcing that the United States was "actively intervening in the Korean civil war."[4] In an effort to limit the damage, an exasperated State Department soon sent out clear instructions to every official stressing that "labels can be terrifically important." "Wherever practicable," PA advised, the terms "North Korean invaders" or "International Communist invaders" should be employed, rather than more neutral phrases like "North Korean forces" and the "Korean War."[5]

On June 27, the few reporters caught up in the war were joined by four more correspondents, who landed at Kimpo airfield outside Seoul just as the bulk of the U.S. Korean Military Advisory Group (KMAG) was preparing to evacuate the capital. The four correspondents—Keyes Beech of the *Chicago Daily News*, Burton Crane of the *New York Times*, Frank Gibney of *Time*, and Marguerite Higgins of the *New York Herald Tribune*—were greeted by the unmistakable signs of panic and defeat, by a pockmarked runway strewn with punctured beer cans, suitcases burst open, and discarded trucks. In the next three days, all four then witnessed a major military catastrophe firsthand.

The reporters' first destination was Seoul, which remained in friendly hands and had the facilities that would enable them to relay their stories back to Tokyo. But that first night they were forced hurriedly to flee the city, as rumors spread that North Korean troops were about to enter it. Heading south with thousands of refugees, they were in the process of trying to cross the Han River when panicky South Koreans suddenly blew up the major bridge across the river. Although now stranded on the north bank of the Han along with a large contingent of the South Korean army, all four managed to clamber across, where they joined the disorderly retreat to Suwon in time to meet the survey team sent by Truman to assess the military situation. Their problem now was how to get their story out. In Seoul, the four reporters had briefly telephoned Tokyo, relaying their initial impressions to an air force PI sergeant—who, as they later discovered, promptly buried each of their dispatches. With the fall of Seoul, even this tenuous line of communication was now gone. If they wanted to file their reports, the only realistic option was to fly back to Tokyo.[6]

Until now, the relationship between the handful of war correspondents and the thirty-three remaining members of the KMAG had been highly informal and unstructured. Amid the confusion of retreat, there had obviously been no time for orderly briefings or detailed interviews. The KMAG officers had been helpful in supplying transport and advice, but none had had much time to think about the causes of the conflict or its broader implications, let alone to grasp and disseminate the PR strategy that was currently being developed back in Washington. Nor were the members of the military survey team sent by Truman any better prepared to disseminate the official line. This became all too evident when certain officers, unaware of or unmoved by Washington's studied attempts to adopt a calm public posture, promptly told reporters that the Korean conflict was part and parcel of a Soviet plot. What would happen if the Soviet Union came in? Tom Lambert of the Associated Press (AP) asked Major General John H. Church, the head of the survey team, on June 30. "If the Russkies come down," Church bluntly replied, "we'll fight the Russkies." Hearing such comments and having seen the destruction wrought by the Soviet-supplied North Korean army, Keyes Beech was even more explicit. "I have a feeling," he wrote in a widely syndicated report, "that I have just witnessed the beginning of World War III."[7]

In the space of less than a week, then, signals emanating from the front had gone full circle, from reports about a purely Korean civil war to speculation of an impending superpower conflict. Moreover, as the crisis worsened, the prevailing view among journalists and many military personnel on the ground was that the United States had clearly tied itself to a South Korean regime that, as the fall of Seoul seemed to demonstrate, was deeply demoralized, if not utterly incompetent. As Lambert of the AP wired home, the South Koreans had basically quit fighting by June 30. Reliable sources in the new U.S. command post, Lambert reported, said that South Korean troops had "refused to mine roads and walked away from the fighting after having told the Americans they would keep battling." The UP was equally scathing, describing how the trigger-happy retreating South Koreans made it safer to be at the front than at the rear. "They blew up a bridge without warning," the UP correspondent explained, "when both Americans and South Koreans were on it. They laugh uproariously when a gun is discharged accidentally. Some South Korean guards have a habit of shooting first and challenging afterward, and several soldier hitch-hikers have fired on jeep drivers who would not give them rides." An American officer even told the UP that "South Koreans fight with 25 percent ferocity, when they actually fight, and there has been no report that they have taken prisoners on a mass scale. 'If World War III broke out,' the officer said, 'South Korea would be safer than New York state.' "[8]

Such reports clearly served to undermine the image Washington was trying to craft. Not only were senior administration officials anxious to avoid publicly connecting the Soviets to the conflict, they were also keen to assure the American public that U.S. troops would be coming to the aid of a vigorous, not discredited and lame-duck, South Korean regime. Desperately trying to counter these reports from the front, MacArthur's headquarters in Tokyo had already issued a communiqué declaring that reports of a South Korean collapse had been exaggerated, which was only "understandable due to war hysteria resulting from the unprovoked North Korean assault."[9]

But would this be sufficient to rebut all the eyewitness accounts? In Korea, the U.S. ambassador, John J. Muccio, believed that the presence of the reporters remaining in Korea after the fall of Seoul was a distinct "nuisance," and he tried to prevail on them simply to "go away."[10] But Muccio had little authority to enforce this wishful aspiration. In Washington, after hearing the eyewitness testimony of a diplomat who had recently been evacuated from Seoul, an interdepartmental information committee also felt that it was time to do something about "the way the newspapers have continually emphasized that the South Koreans are running away." But apart from issuing a few statements that were more optimistic, it was not entirely clear what they could do.[11] Perhaps MacArthur's command, now gearing up to send U.S. troops into battle, would have both a better idea and the necessary power.

MacArthur's System

In some administration circles, the prospect that MacArthur would assume command of all UN forces in Korea was viewed with a good deal of unease. Louis Johnson, who doubtless recognized another avid publicity seeker when he saw one, had already warned the president to keep a tight leash on the general. On returning from a two-week trip to Japan and Korea, John Foster Dulles was even more worried about what might be in store. Dulles had been in Tokyo when word first arrived of the North Korean attack, and he had been surprised by the general's temperamental moods—his blasé overconfidence one day that the invasion was just "a reconnaissance in force," followed by his black pessimism the next day that "all Korea is lost." Dulles had also been dismayed by MacArthur's haughty reluctance to attend an urgent teletype conference with the Pentagon. And on his return Dulles swiftly recommended to Truman that rather than being given command, MacArthur should be "hauled back to the United States immediately."[12]

In private, the president had long been critical of MacArthur's arrogance, and he agreed with Dulles that MacArthur could be dangerous. But Truman and the Joint Chiefs also felt that they had little option other than to place MacArthur in charge. Already, in the first week of the crisis, they had naturally turned to him as their man on the spot—the supreme commander of the Allied Powers, who, as well as being in charge of the occupation of Japan, controlled all U.S. forces in the Far East. Truman was also acutely aware of the domestic ramifications of bypassing or recalling MacArthur. As Truman explained to Dulles, "the general was involved politically in this country— where he has from time to time been mentioned as a possible Republican candidate—and... he could not recall MacArthur without causing a tremendous reaction in the country where he has been built up to heroic stature." In other words, if MacArthur were passed over, this would simply exacerbate partisan divisions; if he were given command, this would send out a strong signal to Republicans that the administration meant business in Korea. On July 7, when the UN passed a resolution recommending a unified command, Truman therefore had little hesitation. Within days he had placed MacArthur in charge of all UN forces in Korea.[13]

In Tokyo, MacArthur was deeply gratified by his appointment to yet another command, and in the next few weeks he moved swiftly to cobble together sufficient troops to try to halt the North Korean invasion. As well as three divisions from the Eighth Army, which were close at hand, having been engaged in occupation duties in Japan for the past five years, MacArthur soon received the Second Infantry Division, plus one marine regimental combat team (RCT), an airborne RCT, three tank battalions, and a variety of infantry RCTs. On August 10, the Joint Chiefs then decided to augment these forces with two additional divisions, the First Marine and the Third Infantry, which were scheduled to reach Korea toward the middle of September.[14]

As more and more U.S. troops headed toward Korea, American editors decided to beef up their own presence in the region. By July 8, there were fifteen reporters in and around the U.S. headquarters in Korea. A week later, this figure had risen to more than forty, and by the end of the month it was reaching two hundred. While the dailies quickly sent many of their experienced correspondents to compete with Beech, Crane, and Higgins, the two major wire services, the AP and UP, invested the most resources.[15] The AP even sent its big hitters, Hal Boyle and Don Whitehead, whose forty-nine-hour journey gave them an early exposure to the punishing conditions to come—a train trip from New York to Seattle that included drinking copious amounts of Scotch, followed by flights to Anchorage, the Aleutians, and Tokyo, where they spent five days in a steamy room while their inoculations and travel arrangements were finalized.[16]

This massive influx of journalists clearly necessitated a more structured relationship between press and military, and as early as July 2 MacArthur instructed his press officer, Colonel Marion P. Echols, to release a statement outlining his basic media policy. "The word censorship," Echols began, "is abhorrent to General MacArthur as it is to all believers in freedom of the news and a true democratic society." For this reason, there would be no compulsory system, such as that applied in World War II, when reporters traveling to a war zone had had to agree to submit all their copy to a military censor in order to get their accreditation. However, because "inaccurate and irresponsible reporting endangers our interests and the lives of our soldiers, sailors, and airmen," the media was asked to practice voluntary restraint. Journalists should not name "specific units, sizes, titles, places of landings, locations, and troop movements." Nor, more broadly, should they engage in the "vilification of our armed forces personnel," since this clearly undermined the security of the headquarters to which they were accredited.[17]

In effect, MacArthur's instructions gave war correspondents a wide degree of latitude. They were free to travel anywhere along the front. They would soon be provided with officers' uniforms, stripped of rank and insignia but with a large "C" patch sewn onto the left sleeve. Above all, they were permitted to report whatever they saw, taking care only to avoid detailed information that could help the enemy. If in doubt, particularly about the obvious gray area surrounding stories that might be construed as "vilifying"

American personnel, correspondents were encouraged to consult the army's Public Information Office (PIO). In Korea, the PIO was also available to edit and file copy on behalf of correspondents who did not have representatives in Tokyo. But there was to be no mandatory surveillance of reporters' copy. Unlike World War II, when censors in combat zones used their ubiquitous blue pencils to cross out anything deemed to be a threat to security, now the onus was to be very much on the individual journalist.[18]

That MacArthur should instigate such a loose and informal system was, in many respects, surprising. Back in World War II, he had acquired a fierce reputation for seeking to control media output. Often he had forced newspapers to rely almost solely on his communiqués for war news—missives notorious for being highly laudatory of his own military genius. In the past five years, the Japanese under MacArthur's occupation had been subjected to a good deal of high-minded talk about the freedom of the press. But this had invariably been accompanied with a very practical determination to censor any stories that were "even slightly critical of the supreme commander."

Nor in recent years had the American media escaped unscathed. In dealing with the Republican-leaning press, the supreme commander's aides had assiduously nurtured his image in order to float trial balloons for a presidential candidacy that never seemed to quite take off. In Tokyo, MacArthur himself had carefully cultivated a small "palace guard" that could usually be relied on to toe the official line. But the five-star general rarely had much time for mainstream newspapers like the *Christian Science Monitor*, *New York Herald Tribune*, *Chicago Sun*, and *San Francisco Chronicle*, whose articles and editorials on Japan, he complained, "have not only been slanted but have approached downright quackery and dishonesty." On at least one occasion, MacArthur had been perfectly willing to deny journalists from such papers access to Japan; at other times he had expelled recalcitrant reporters already covering the occupation.[19]

So why did MacArthur publicly embrace such an ostensibly noncoercive system now? His own public justification focused heavily on ideology—his conviction that democracies were different from the communist enemy principally because of their faith in freedom, particularly freedom of the press, and that publishers, editors, and reporters now had the perfect opportunity to demonstrate the efficacy of this democratic system in time of war.

At one level, MacArthur probably believed these platitudes. In the face of all the practical problems that were to mount in the coming months, he would certainly oppose the adoption of a formal code with a tenacity that suggested he was a true believer. Nor was the haughty general likely to be too bothered by the inconsistency of suddenly rejecting something he had so frequently utilized in the past. On a subject like the strategic importance of Korea, MacArthur had not only reversed course in recent months; he had also embraced his new position with the zeal of a convert. Moreover, energized by the war, he seemed to have a self-assured faith that he could control events in Korea and that everything would work according to his plans. His decision to gamble on a risky amphibious landing at Inchon and his breezy optimism that China would not intervene in the war would become the most (in)famous examples of this. But MacArthur's belief that a responsible press could be relied on to report his version of the war also fitted into the same general pattern of extravagant self-confidence.[20]

Yet, while MacArthur's talk about the responsibilities of a free press was to remain a constant throughout all the vicissitudes of the coming months, initially at least there were other, more hardheaded, reasons for his opposition to censorship. One was the obvious practical difficulty of directly supervising all the copy flooding out of Korea. Not only did it seem distinctly likely that a heavy-handed system of mandatory censorship, which strictly limited what reporters could say, would engender a real resentment among the press corps but, in any case, MacArthur's aides complained that they simply lacked the personnel to take on such a task.

In the first month of the war, the overworked staff in Echols's Tokyo PIO already had enough on their hands. Swamped with the job of responding to reporters' questions twenty-four hours a day—not to mention arranging their travel orders, airplane reservations, post exchange cards, and authorization to buy clothes suitable for the front—they were too busy even to provide daily briefings for the press.[21] In Korea, the Eighth Army initially lacked sufficient troops to stem the communist advance. And, as MacArthur reminded the Pentagon, in dealing with reporters, the Eighth Army's "facilities were very, very limited."[22]

During these grim early weeks, the Pentagon's own PI officers tried their best to help, scouring the reserve lists and training camps for suitable people to send to Korea. But the personnel problem was not easily resolved. Even when the air force was able to assemble a team of fifteen PI officers, it took twenty days to undertake briefings, gather equipment, and ship them out to Korea, so that they did not arrive before the end of July.[23] As for army reservists, meanwhile, the administration's studied attempt to keep the home front cool also discouraged many qualified PI specialists from volunteering their services. As Major General Floyd L. Parks, the army's chief information officer in the Pentagon, privately conceded, "right now in this limited emergency people who would not hesitate to serve in an all-out emergency are reluctant to leave their business and come into service, and I can't blame them."[24]

Such practical considerations were obviously important. But in Tokyo, MacArthur's PR aides were also confident they could exert a measure of control over the media by continuing to employ the system that had been very successful over the past five years. At the heart of this system had been the official communiqués. Although these purported to describe and explain recent developments, in reality they tended to be highly uninformative.

MacArthur's spokespersons justified this reticence on the grounds that the presence of press officers from TASS, the Soviet press agency, made it impossible to be more candid. The general's aides also provided a series of carrots and sticks for journalists who embraced or ignored the meager official offerings. Thus for reporters who spouted MacArthur's line, there was the reward of becoming one of the "palace guard," with the prospect of the occasional snippet of inside information, a route followed by wire service bureau chiefs like Russell Brines of AP and Earnest Hoberecht of UP. For reporters who ignored the communiqué and tried to delve deeper, however, there was distinct prospect of harassment by MacArthur's loyal lieutenants. Back in 1947 and 1948, MacArthur's press officers had frequently been downright abusive to recalcitrant members of the press. The current incumbent, Echols, had tried hard to construct a more positive relationship with the media, but even he was known to berate journalists. And as the Tokyo Foreign Correspondents Club complained in February 1948, MacArthur's other aides had plenty of ways to hassle perennial critics, from expulsion to raids on houses, from "derogatory letters to employers" to being branded a "security risk."[25]

That MacArthur now intended to continue with this style of media management was abundantly clear from his actions early on in the crisis. While a number of reporters headed straight to the Korean front, many flooded into Tokyo, where they augmented the sixty or so regulars who were already based in Japan. Luckily, the Tokyo Press Club had facilities to house this large new influx, for it was fitted out with sleeping quarters for two hundred, a bar, a dining room, and a barber shop. Situated in a narrow alley in Tokyo's business district, the Press Club was only a block from MacArthur's headquarters, and so journalists based here were conveniently on hand to receive the general's periodic communiqués and the command's daily news releases.[26]

MacArthur doubtless hoped that this proximity, plus the ease of simply reiterating the official line, would dominate stories coming out of Tokyo, drowning out any discordant notes that might emanate from the front. But to make doubly sure, the PIO quickly started to produce a wide variety of "feature articles, human interest stories, and analyses of operations" written in language tailored specifically to meet the demands of editors in the United States.[27]

Back in Washington, the Pentagon would also amplify MacArthur's message. Traditionally, the military top brass had deferred to the theater commander in matters of information and censorship. As Pentagon PR officers soon realized, they were simply too far from events to provide "spot news" on the actual fighting. After the first week, the Pentagon's twice-daily briefings therefore concentrated on providing only "the necessary background information to fill in and correlate the many communiqués and news reports originating in Korea and Japan."[28]

Meanwhile, for journalists back in Korea and Tokyo who ignored this official version of events, the threat of reprisal was still very much in the air. From the outset, Echols had made it perfectly clear that only certain types of reporting would prove acceptable to the supreme commander. The stories of the first week, he complained at a press conference on July 2, with their heavy emphasis on South Korea's swift collapse, had been "far from desirable." In particular, he warned the assembled correspondents, there had been a "lack of decency, honesty, observance of proper procedure."[29] To everyone who heard these words, the implication was only too clear: now that MacArthur had issued his voluntary code, future critical stories would be viewed in a distinctly unfavorable light, and might even be punished by some of the old harassment techniques.

The Military and Media at War in Korea

These sanctions might not have been necessary had there been a series of stunning victories for the correspondents to cover over the next few weeks. Unfortunately, however, throughout July the U.S. army did not prove any more successful in halting the communist advance than South Korean troops had been during the disastrous first week. The reasons for this failure were manifold. The American troops hurriedly sent over from Japan were more attuned to occupation duties than the rigors of combat. They had recently been given little training above the battalion level, were largely equipped with weapons of World War II vintage, and were thrown piecemeal into the fray. As they faced two of the best divisions of the North Korean army, equipped with large numbers of Soviet-made T34 tanks, a string of reverses rapidly ensued—at Osan on July 5, at Chonan on July 8, at the important Kum River defense line on July 16, and at Taejon on July 20. Within two weeks, the North Koreans had advanced 100 miles south of Seoul and were now 130 miles from Pusan, the key port on the southern tip of the Korean peninsula.[30]

From the vantage point of MacArthur's United Nation's Command (UNC) in Tokyo, this situation, though worrying, was far from catastrophic. Indeed for MacArthur and his senior advisers, these tactical reverses were simply an inevitable component of the overall strategic picture. At the moment, to be sure, American forces were being thrown back. But this was because the UNC only had a small number of troops at its disposal. It was vital that these limited forces do their best to slow down the North Korean advance before it reached the southernmost tip of the peninsula. A counteroffensive could then take place once all the reinforcements being sent over from the United States had finally arrived in Korea.[31]

This detached, measured perspective, refusing to be panicked by local reverses, infused all the official press releases and communiqués emanating from Tokyo during these weeks. But, significantly, there was far more to the official line than simply a cool, levelheaded confidence. In the past, it had also been very much part of MacArthur's makeup to accentuate the positive aspects of any military engagement. During World War II, his communiqués had frequently minimized the importance of reverses; some had even announced victories before they had actually occurred. Now, perceived military necessity reinforced this natural character trait. In MacArthur's opinion, it was essential to bolster morale, both among the troops waiting to go into action and among the public back in America. And the most obvious method of achieving this goal was to release a series of decidedly upbeat dispatches.

The official story emanating from Tokyo thus had an obvious slant. In reality, the North Korean advance was moving forward in a series of thrusts, interspersed with pauses while equipment and supplies were organized for the next offensive lurch. Time and again, however, MacArthur's communiqués insisted that whenever the communists stood still they must have been halted by American action. "North Korean offensive was curtailed, but probes continued," Tokyo announced on July 8, the day GIs had in fact been forced out of Chonan, completing a retreat of roughly 20 miles in four days. "Yank armor" was performing well in its first engagement with the enemy, an army spokesman insisted two days later, when actually it had performed "poorly," and U.S. forces had again been pushed back another 10 miles. When finally forced to admit that a retreat had taken place, PIO spokespersons were keen to emphasize that this had been undertaken in a planned, orderly fashion, with troops only withdrawing to "better lines of natural defense." On other occasions, Tokyo was careful to accompany casualty figures with announcements of enemy losses, in an effort to stress that these sacrifices had not been in vain.[32]

For a time, this bold attempt to influence the news agenda enjoyed a measure of success. Each day, many of the hundred or so journalists in Tokyo dutifully reiterated MacArthur's communiqués in their reports, and back home all the major newspapers from across the political and geographic spectrum consistently carried at least one story based on this official version of events. Yet the communiqué was clearly a weak tool to wield in the face of the growing influx of reporters to both Korea and Japan. From the very start, some in the Tokyo press corps complained to MacArthur that his news releases were "meager and inaccurate." More important, correspondents based in Korea soon relayed back a far more pessimistic picture of the war. In place of orderly withdrawals came news of "routs," ebbing morale, equipment failure, and a host of other "snafus."[33]

That correspondents in Korea should focus on a very different story was hardly surprising. Although MacArthur hoped to shape media coverage from the rear, a combination of professional self-image and journalistic competition impelled many reporters to the front. As a result, rather than parrot the UNC's broad strategic overview of the situation, correspondents tended to witness the war in microcosm. Indeed, theirs was a view of bitter fighting against superior enemy forces, often witnessed firsthand in hastily dug foxholes, or secondhand in interviews with harassed officers and disillusioned GIs.

Part of the attraction of the front was the traditional heroic model of the war correspondent as a breed apart in the journalistic profession. As a rule, war correspondents have always sought to differentiate themselves from their deskbound colleagues back home, by making "a fetish out of combat" and promoting a professional identity that "seems an endless dance with death...a life of close and constant contact with extreme violence."[34] Although this self-image often obscures the reality, since a lot of their time is necessarily spent at the rear trying to get a story back home, for correspondents in Korea, a determination to witness combat firsthand was a powerful motivating factor. They certainly took appalling risks, especially in the first stages of the war when the fighting was chaotic and fluid. By the end of July, in fact, no less than six had been killed, three wounded, and one captured. As the industry journal *Editor and Publisher* lamented, in just over a month more war correspondents had been killed than in the entire first year of World War II.[35]

At the front, journalists had plenty of sources to draw their stories from. The GIs themselves, though unschooled in the arts of PR and lacking much sense of how their distant superiors wanted the fighting to be portrayed, nonetheless made good copy. In the first days of the fighting, combat-shocked "sloggers" were quick to share their distress and disillusionment with reporters, bemoaning the fate of their green, dead colleagues, sacrificed in battles where the odds were no better than one hundred to one. And even when battle-hardened veterans arrived in Korea, they added to the sense that this was a grim and bitter conflict by making unfavorable comparisons to brutal battles in the last war. "This is worse than Tarawa or Iwo Jima," one veteran told Marguerite Higgins. "It's not the 'gooks' that are harassing the hell out of us. It's the terrible terrain and the sun." For reporters themselves, many of whom lost 15 to 20 pounds in weight following the troops around, the abysmal conditions naturally became a key part of how they framed the story. Indeed, many felt they had to write about their own experiences with a savage foe in the intense heat (sometimes rising to 110°F), not to mention the endless climbs up steep hills and mountains.[36]

Compounding this natural determination to report from the front was a familiar motive: rampant journalistic competition. Many correspondents were hardened old pros who had covered World War II, others were just starting out and anxious to make a name—and all were determined to obtain the latest scoop. Perhaps the best illustration of this was the breakdown in personal relations between Marguerite Higgins and Homer Bigart, who would not even speak to one another, despite the fact that both worked for the *New York Herald Tribune*. Though little more than a personality clash, the bad feeling between them nevertheless sparked a frenetic race to get the page 1 lead story. And, as one colleague later noted, "the delighted *Herald Tribune* sat back to enjoy some of the best coverage of the war while the more dignified *New York Times* dispatched a taskforce to compete with Maggie and Homer."[37]

Other reporters, meanwhile, were spurred on by more distant colleagues. As Wayne Thomis of the *Chicago Tribune* pointed out, most faced intense pressure from editors who shot off frequent "rockets" from the home office calling for more "I was there" stories, since these were what the reading public seemed to want. "This meant," Thomis complained, "that correspondents felt they had to take more chances and be with the men at the front in order to write the more personalized stories demanded."[38]

While competition among correspondents working for dailies was thus intense, the wire service reporters faced the most overtly cutthroat environment, since their whole professional existence depended on getting the story out first. In their world, a matter of minutes could easily mean the difference between selling a scoop to newspaper clients nationwide or being beaten to the punch by a rival.

By the middle of July, all the wire services had assembled large teams in Korea. These were loosely organized into the front-line correspondents, who fanned out with different units to the front; the collators, who were based further back at army headquarters and tried to craft a lead story from the various reports that flooded in all day; and the reporters based in Tokyo, who wired the stories from Korea back to the United States. In conditions that often seemed very primitive, the competing wire services invariably worked in close and uncomfortable proximity. At Pusan, for instance, one of them recalled that "all three news agencies—plus men from a couple of newspapers—were in one tent, sharing one telephone, which ran all night long. You screamed your stories into the phone. If you got your hands on an exclusive story, it was usually exclusive for exactly the length of time required to call it in."[39]

Still, despite the difficulty of protecting a scoop, competition remained the driving force for all wire service reporters. And it was greatly exacerbated by a basic resource imbalance that existed between the two major wire services, the AP and UP: the "unipressers" were habitually outgunned more than three to one by their AP rivals. Under constant pressure from their Tokyo boss, "Asia Earnie" Hoberecht, to "keep a tight hold over expenses, but don't come back without the story," UP correspondents often felt the need to push their reports just a little bit further in order to satisfy their demanding master, beat their high-powered rival, and sell their stories to the largest number of newspapers back home.[40]

The first clear sign that this group of hardened, competitive correspondents was gathering a very different perspective on the war emerged after the battle at Chonan between July 8 and 11. While Tokyo and the Pentagon heralded this as the first time that seasoned officers and well-equipped men had gone into battle, performing "very nicely" in their "first brush" with the enemy, the likes of Bigart and Higgins recorded a very different set of events. GIs were calling it a slaughter rather than a battle, Higgins reported in a widely syndicated article. "The young soldiers most of whom are green troops in action for the first time, told bitter tales of rough fighting against hopeless odds." Bigart, who had been in a foxhole that had briefly been surrounded by North Korean troops, was equally graphic. The troops were asking a very pertinent question, he wrote: "Since American front-line units now employed are outnumbered and outgunned, why commit them to positions quickly made untenable by North Korean flanking movements?" "Many times in World War II," he continued, "this correspondent observed American troops in conditions of adversity, but he never saw anything like the bitterness and bewilderment displayed at the front yesterday when the men received their orders to withdraw." The fall of Chonan, he concluded, was "a galling humiliation."[41]

In Tokyo, MacArthur soon bristled at such reports. On July 12, in a wire to the Pentagon, he complained privately that "voluntary press censorship has not been entirely satisfactory due to the insensate desire for sensationalism." MacArthur singled out UP, which had just released a story describing the "slaughter on a ghastly retreat," as the "principal service for defeatist head-lines." "Its stories," he insisted, "habitually omit or bury" UNC communiqués "and feature alarming generalities or alleged remarks by disillusioned retreating wounded US troops." Such dispatches, he concluded, "amount in fact to psychological warfare benefits to the enemy. They depress the morale of our troops and enhance the morale of the enemy. They are frequently so confined to a small incident as to be misrepresentative of what is really taking place."[42]

Yet even now, MacArthur remained surprisingly confident that voluntary censorship could be made to work. All that was really needed, he thought, was a conference in Washington between the Pentagon and "senior press people...to spur them to a more active realization of what voluntary cen-sorship entails."[43] For MacArthur, such optimism continued to rest on his professed faith in the responsibility of a free press. For the more discerning observer, however, there were grounds to suspect that beneath this rheto-ric, the military was starting to develop some other—more underhand—methods of controlling what was reported.

One tool the Eighth Army clearly had at its disposal was the daily press briefing. In the middle of July, when General Walton Walker, the overall commander of the Eighth Army, established his command post at Taegu, his PIO set up a correspondents' billet in an old schoolhouse. This was particularly vital for the wire services, which needed a base both to collate all the reports from their journalists in the field and to cable out their stories at the earliest possible moment. But conditions there were far from easy—"fleas, mosquitoes, and hole-in-the floor wooden toilets." And far more important, wire service reporters soon complained that the Eighth Army's briefings had introduced their own form of subtle manipulation.[44] Not only did the information handed out tend to lag behind actual conditions, but as one observer grumbled, after telling correspondents that there was "no censorship," the army spokesman invariably "warns them not to mention names of certain towns," or "forbids them to describe as 'cut off' a battalion that has lost contact with the main body because of intervening enemy troops," or "bans reference to a commanding general by name."[45]

Just as bad, even at Eighth Army headquarters it was still a nightmare transmitting stories to the outside world. Initially, the only channel of communication was a single radiotelephone circuit between Korea and Japan that the army and the correspondents had to share. With military personnel naturally having priority, reporters sometimes had only three minutes to dictate their stories to the Tokyo office. Matters were somewhat improved in the second half of July, when a second telegraph circuit was opened between Pusan and Tokyo. But even this was unable to deal with the growing demand, as correspondents attempted to relay out up to eighty thousand words in any given night. Some messages still took six or more hours to transmit, while the quickest for AP, the largest of the U.S. wire services, was an unimpressive three hours.[46] More to the point, correspondents were starting to suspect that since their stories had to be submitted to Tokyo via the army's teleprinter, yet another form of censorship was actually in effect. As the Pentagon informed Echols, many reporters had complained that the army "sees stories before they are transmitted and frequently calls attention to items objected to."[47]

While reporters found such developments highly irritating, they soon paled next to the very real threat of expulsion from the theater altogether. In the middle of July, at the height of the debacle along the Kum River defense line, Walker's headquarters informed Marguerite Higgins that she was being banished from Korea. The reason had little to do with her reporting and everything to do with the prevailing norms in the Eighth Army. As Walker explained, "there are no facilities for ladies at the front." By this, of course, Walker did not mean the lack of communication facilities that were currently driving the war correspondents wild, but the lack of latrines for women, not to mention the bad language that the troops were apt to use.[48] Higgins quickly appealed this decision, and with the help of her publisher in New York, together with MacArthur's hasty intervention, she was soon reinstated.[49]

But other expulsions soon followed. On July 15, Echols prevented Tom Lambert of AP from returning to Korea, accusing him of "giving aid and comfort to the enemy" in a dispatch that quoted a GI calling Korea "a damned useless war." The same day, Peter Kalischer of UP received exactly the same sanction, on the grounds that his stories "were sensational" and "made the army look bad." By singling out these two leading wire service correspondents, MacArthur's aides were clearly trying to mete out retribution for the stories of the past week, as well as firing a warning shot to other reporters who might still be tempted to stray from the official line.[50] But their high-handed action quickly backfired. In the United States, leading newspapers quickly pointed out that neither Lambert nor Kalischer had actually divulged anything of value to the enemy.[51] In Washington, the chiefs of the two wire services swiftly joined forces and descended on the Pentagon, asking if anything could be done "to smooth the situation." Meanwhile in Tokyo, recognizing the potential for disastrous publicity, MacArthur personally intervened, inviting the two men, plus their immediate bosses, to a meeting on July 16.[52]

MacArthur's office in the Dai Ichi building was an imposing affair. His uncluttered desk sat in front of large windows with impressive views of the Imperial Palace just a block away. Here on July 16, the general greeted his four visitors affably enough, and immediately announced that he was lifting the ban on Lambert and Kalischer. But as the group started to discuss the deeper causes of military–media friction, it soon became clear that there would be little meeting of minds. For their part, the wire chiefs felt their correspondents needed more guidance from the army, even if this came in the guise of censorship. They also favored regular briefings in Tokyo to amplify what was in the communiqués. Yet MacArthur refused to listen to such suggestions. In fact, in a curious reversal of roles, it was the general, not the media men, who extolled the virtues of a free press, arguing that sound coverage "rested on the almost intuitive judgment of the newspaper men." Censorship was "abhorrent," he reiterated, and as a practical matter, "the army was not trained to apply it." Nor would Tokyo be able to conduct regular briefings, because his staff was just too busy. In a revealing finale, MacArthur then became extremely defensive about his communiqués. They were "factually correct," he insisted, adding that his Pacific communiqués in the last war "also had been honest," even if "some people didn't seem to think so."[53]

Despite this parting outburst, the media men went away satisfied. At the very least, MacArthur had countermanded the expulsions of Lambert and Kalischer. Within days, he also reversed his stance on regular briefings. From the end of July, Echols and the PIO would undertake this task on a daily basis, replete with an up-to-date situation map "for the benefit of correspondents who wanted to check movements, locations, and the spelling" of place names in the unfamiliar Korean landscape.[54]

Even now, however, the old menacing threats did not suddenly go away. On July 26, the chief PI officer for the Eighth Army, Lieutenant Colonel R. L. Thompson, announced a new set of instructions, which declared, in stronger language than before, that "unwarranted criticism of command decisions or of the conduct of Allied soldiers on the battlefield will not be tolerated." There would be no ban on "fair and honest criticism," Thompson hastened to stress. But the army would nevertheless "be the sole judge and jury on whether criticism is unwarranted or not." In elaborating on this, Echols complained publicly about the "lousy stories" emanating from the front, and implored reporters to take more care. "Demoralizing accounts of the Korean fighting are frightening men who might otherwise fight on the democratic side," he concluded. "Please give these kids all the help you can."[55]

Back in the United States, the media's reaction to this flurry of activity was decidedly mixed. Some reporters and columnists, fearful for their careers, now deemed it prudent to hold fire on their criticisms of MacArthur and the military. One of the most prominent was Carl W. McCardle of the *Philadelphia Evening Bulletin*. McCardle had been with MacArthur at the very start of the crisis, and had returned home to write a series of widely read articles on the inside story. In private, he believed that the complacency in Tokyo during that first week had been appallingly reminiscent of Pearl Harbor. But, anxious to return to the theater and all too aware of MacArthur's low opinion of hostile journalists, in his published articles McCardle was "less critical of the proceedings of the U.S. headquarters than he would have otherwise been."[56]

Drew Pearson censored himself for similar reasons. Pearson was a highly influential and "flamboyant muckraker" who reached millions of Americans through his syndicated column and radio show. Widely famed as the scourge of politicians in general and of Louis Johnson in particular, in July he got his hands on a story that would have greatly added to the sense of mounting catastrophe in Korea, with its tales of outnumbered GIs, their useless anti-tank weapons, and the military's preparations for an orderly evacuation of Korea. But on this occasion Pearson remained uncharacteristically mute, fearful of being accused of defeatism and abetting the enemy at a moment of major setback in the Cold War.[57]

Higher up the chain of journalistic command, some editors and executives were also alarmed by the charge that certain reports were giving aid to the enemy, and a few moved to tighten up their procedures. Senior managers at the *Chicago Sun-Times*, for instance, publicly announced that they would only publish "official announcements which in our opinion will not endanger American lives"—and were promptly congratulated by MacArthur for a "commendable" demonstration of media responsibility.[58] CBS was equally restrictive. During August, its president, William S. Paley, who normally gave his public affairs broadcasters "a free hand," personally intervened to kill no less than five reports that he deemed were in contravention of MacArthur's new guidelines, including a dispatch by Edward Murrow that alluded to serious command mistakes and discussed the growing disenchantment of American troops.[59]

Yet such actions tended to be isolated incidents rather than evidence that the media as a whole had been cowed into submission. The wire services, in particular, saw little need to change their practices. Both the main companies, to be sure, would have preferred a formal censorship code to MacArthur's hodgepodge of vague guidelines and ominous threats. But both were totally preoccupied with getting their stories placed in the maximum number of newspapers. And as they soon discovered, despite all of Tokyo's threats, there was little indication that the U.S. press now suddenly preferred sterile, officially sanctioned summaries to good, old-fashioned scoops from the front. In August, the UP even complained that it had "lost the play several times because our opposition have over-reached and 'beaten' us by breaking security." This did not mean, UP vice-president Earl Johnson hastened to add, that the UP was now about to be reckless in its war coverage in order to regain the initiative. But it did mean that his "unipressers" were not going to be overawed by MacArthur's threats. "We have imposed no new rules on our war reporters," Earl Johnson told *Editor and Publisher* in the middle of August. "They are all old hands at covering wars and know enough not to send anything which would expose our troops to unnecessary danger." The AP adopted a similar stance. All AP staff were now instructed "to be guided by the appropriately stated and specified security embargoes." But they were also told "not to engage in self-censorship where no authoritative restrictions are imposed."[60]

For their part, editors at many dailies and weeklies concluded that MacArthur's guidelines were simply a cover for his desire to "sugarcoat" bad war news. At the heart of the problem was the obvious fact that the media still had not been told what constituted "unwarranted criticism." And many media men naturally feared that PI officers, acting as "sole judge and jury," would simply use this loose phrase to root out or silence correspondents who were even mildly critical of the army. In Washington press circles, there was even dark talk comparing MacArthur's system to "the method used by the Nazis who maintained they had no censorship, but a writer often found himself expelled from Germany on the slightest pretext." Nor, like the wire services, did many newspaper editors see any real need to suppress eye-witness accounts of battles based on interviews with soldiers on the spot, particularly if written by reliable professional correspondents. Indeed, the norms of objective journalism could work both ways. Often, it is true, the fact that reporters gave priority to official sources meant that their accounts were heavily influenced by the way the government framed an issue. But on occasion, "straight" reporting could also provide a degree of protective cover against official intimidation, since editors were apt to stand by stories that were based on hard facts, even if these facts came from interviews with battle-scarred GIs rather than official statements from army headquarters.[61]

Back home, moreover, reporters like Beech, Higgins, and Bigart who had based all of their reporting on such sources were quickly greeted as stars rather than pariahs. In the national press, their dispatches were given enormous circulation—in fact, the stories by these three controversial names not only appeared regularly in their own newspapers but were also frequently syndicated to a wide range of newspapers across the geographic and political spectrum. Seeking to exploit this new-found fame, leading magazines like the *Saturday Evening Post* were soon anxious to sign these journalists up for feature articles—although in a revealing insight into the prevailing values of the time, the *Post*'s editors felt that Bigart "could do a straight reporting job," while Higgins would be left to "do a kind of lady-in-battle piece," which would attract the "female clientele."[62]

Thus, MacArthur's attempts to place certain battlefield stories beyond the "sphere of legitimate controversy" had clearly failed. War correspondents were now bristling at his claims that their stories were based on dubious interviews with shell-shocked survivors. Reporters in Tokyo were becoming increasingly suspicious of the massaged version of events they were being fed in daily communiqués. And editors, driven by a competitive marketplace and determined to publish stories they deemed in the public interest, were refusing to be browbeaten by threats. Of course, at this stage no one in the mainstream media actually questioned whether or not the United States should be fighting this brutal war that seemed to be going so badly. But neither did anyone want to bury stories of American defeats, even when they were replete with tales of underequipped and disenchanted GIs being forced into a series of costly and humiliating withdrawals.

The View from the Pentagon

Back in the United States, the Pentagon viewed all this friction between MacArthur and the media with mounting concern. The Washington military establishment of midcentury was acutely concerned with the image it projected to the world. This was partly a product of the vicious interservice rivalries of recent years, when the army, navy, and air force had vied in public for a greater share of the ever-decreasing defense budget. Since World War II, the military had also made a conscious effort to make its PR more professional, setting up the Armed Forces Information School at the Carlisle Barracks in Pennsylvania. Since its inception, this school had churned out around five thousand graduates, some of whom were now either en route to Korea or employed in the Pentagon's OPI to deal with the huge demand for war news. All of these graduates had been taught a simple rule: namely, that openness was the best policy for dealing with the press—and that distorted statements or underhand initiatives would only alienate the Fourth Estate. As one of the school's former commandants put it,

> the newspaper profession has a high code of ethics and its members will respect your confidence. But they will instantly recognize bluffing, evasion, half truths, or attempts to slant the story and they will resent such tactics as insults to their intelligence. You must avoid these mistakes. So-called "bad" news stories are often the result of poor handling rather than of the facts themselves.... You can often forestall unfavorable repercussions by candid and honest release of information.[63]

Although such injunctions did not always sit easily in an organization that prided itself on secrecy in times of crisis and war, many senior figures in the Pentagon had nevertheless come to believe that it was simply common sense to treat reporters in as candid and as open a way as possible. In August, the army chief of staff, General J. Lawton Collins—himself a former head of the army's information section—remarked privately that while "some of our columnists seem to take delight in publicizing material that could well be a comfort to the enemy," most reporters "have honest and sincere purposes in mind." The present press problems were "our own fault," he frankly concluded, "for not providing them [with] better guidance."[64] Collins's PR deputy, Floyd Parks, fully agreed. Although Parks had "no schooling whatever" for his current information job, having previously served in a tank corps and as commander of an airborne army, he had struck up a close relationship with reporters, largely on the basis of a reputation for candor and honesty. "You cannot put a good face on an ugly fact," he firmly believed, "nor can you call back a bad story once it is in print. The correction or explanation never catches up with the original story. It is an axiom that you must have complete frankness and a reputation for honesty in dealing with the news media." Given the current problems brewing between the military and media, Parks now deemed it vital for journalists to be given far more direction about what they could not publish.[65]

Political pressures inside the United States underlined the wisdom of this course. In meetings with wire service chiefs, Parks quickly discovered that they favored a censorship code, particularly if it was accompanied with improved facilities so that correspondents could get their copy out more quickly.[66] On Capitol Hill, legislators from both sides of the aisle also jumped on the censorship bandwagon. For Democrats like Scott Lucas, reckless reporting inside the United States posed the biggest problem. "It seems to me

Major General Floyd Parks briefing the press, June 30, 1950. Courtesy of National Archives.

almost criminal," the majority leader declared on July 14, "for columnists and newspapermen to tell where our troops are going at this time. We are giving the enemy every opportunity for the destruction of our ships or to destroy our troops on the way." Republicans, meanwhile, tended to look to the Far East, where their hero was having a hard time. Convinced that war correspondents in Korea had been responsible for too many "alarmist" reports, they called on the Pentagon to give MacArthur the authority to impose censorship forthwith.[67]

Ironically, the Pentagon was more than happy to give MacArthur this authority—the problem was that he repeatedly refused to accept it. On July 14, the Pentagon sent its first cable to Tokyo on the subject, with Louis Johnson recommending that censorship be instituted in the combat zone immediately. When Tokyo failed to respond, Parks sent a second cable on July 22, only to receive the brusque reply that "it would be utterly foolish" to apply censorship in Korea without having it in Tokyo or the United States.[68] A week later, after a controversial article by Keyes Beech in the *Chicago Daily News* describing "how miserably unprepared—spiritually, physically, and materially—we were for the Korean War," the Pentagon decided to change tactics.[69] Along with Beech's dispatch, Parks was particularly struck by a *Washington Post* editorial that attacked MacArthur's media policies and pointed out that "censorship by obstruction and harassment of reporters can be more objectionable than more frank and openly practiced censorship of reporters' copy." The *Post* was especially savage in challenging MacArthur's contention that journalists could best decide what to publish. "The decisions of editors...must be made thousands of miles from the scene," the paper pointed out, "and in view of the handicaps of time, distances, and ignorance of the immediate issues, these decisions are preordained to be foolishly over-cautious or unintentionally risky." Agreeing with this editorial "one hundred percent," Parks decided to make a third effort to get MacArthur to accept such advice. Not only did Parks wire it directly to Echols but, to make doubly sure the message got through, he handed General Matthew B. Ridgway a copy to transmit to the UN commander when he accompanied Averell Harriman on a presidential mission to Tokyo.[70]

Until now, all the Pentagon's recommendations had come against the back-drop of the military retreats of July, as the meager U.S. forces were pushed back toward the Pusan perimeter, a precarious foothold in the southeastern corner of the Korean peninsula measuring about 100 miles north to south and only 50 miles east to west. By the start of August, however, Walker's Eighth Army was finally bolstered with sufficient reinforcements not only to stabilize the Pusan perimeter but also to contemplate a counterattack to relieve pressure on his hard-pressed troops. Gathering together four regiments into Task Force Kean, Walker intended to punch a hole in the North Korean lines in the south-ern part of the front and hopefully retake the town of Chinju. Although such an operation obviously demanded the highest security, Parks was soon dis-turbed by a series of wire service reports "giving the proported [sic] strength, composition, objective, and place of the attack of the 'Kean Task Force.'"[71]

On August 12, this task force failed to reach its objective. In blistering tem-peratures of 112° F, it ran straight into a North Korean offensive launched at exactly the same time. Fearing that the North Koreans had been tipped off by the U.S. press, senior officers in Washington decided that the time had come to make an even more vigorous effort to prevent such blatant—and costly—security violations. In yet another cable to MacArthur, Johnson stressed that "strong concern" was mounting "in executive, congressional, and civil circles," and again authorized MacArthur "to initiate censorship either on voluntary code operated with military assistance, or by outright military censorship on all stories concerning military operations in Korea." Crucially, however, the defense secretary still refused to issue a direct order to this effect, believing that he lacked the statutory authority to do so. MacArthur was thus given the discretion to ignore this recommendation and to continue with his loose, informal—and increasingly unpopular—system.[72]

By August, the Defense Department's anxieties about the media situation in Korea were being sharpened by its own growing problems with the press.

These stemmed partly from the familiar dilemma of what to withhold. In theory, PI officers were meant to avoid "evasions" and "half truths." But in the current politically charged environment, with officials and legislators talking ominously about the implication of security breaches, Pentagon press officers naturally started to err on the side of caution. By the middle of the month, reporters begun to note that increasing numbers of military documents were being given the mark of "administrative classification," which allowed officials to withhold relatively innocuous material from the public domain. And soon journalists were circulating joke cards designed for Pentagon press officers, with the barbed heading "If it's too much work for me it's a security violation."[73]

By this stage, too, the Pentagon had also been drawn into a highly damaging spat over the human cost of the war. As part of its upbeat assessment of the war, Tokyo consistently minimized the number of casualties U.S. forces were sustaining.[74] With military medical teams being one of the few success stories of the first weeks of the war, MacArthur's command also encouraged correspondents to follow these units around in Korea—and was delighted when reporters like Higgins duly reported that "the speed with which the wounded were tended and evacuated was one of the most remarkable performances this correspondent has seen in the Korean War."[75]

Yet stories of wounded GIs clearly had to be treated with care. When the first wounded soldiers started to return home in the second half of July, press interest was so intense that the Pentagon was obliged to formulate new guidelines with the purpose "of avoiding shock or anguish to the families of American casualties."[76] Visual images were particularly sensitive. Back in World War II, as historian George H. Roeder has shown, officials had "used images of pain and death to respond to what they perceived to be the PR needs of each phase of the war," banning ghastly pictures when morale was deemed fragile and releasing pictures of dead GIs when complacency seemed rife.[77] In this new emergency, the OPI adopted a similar policy. "Pictures and information concerning wounded which are likely to inspire patriotism or determination and otherwise contribute to the war effort" could be given to the media to publish, the OPI decreed in August. Not to be released, however, were "pictures showing wounded personnel in large numbers.... 'Horror' pictures such as those showing mangled bodies, obvious expressions of agony, severe shock, or conditions indicating doubt of patient's recovery." Pictures of "mental patients" were also restricted, as were pictures of the blind, the deaf and dumb, and amputees.[78] In other words, the visual images the American public was about to receive would offer a heavily doctored and sterilized view of the war, one far removed from that depicted in war correspondents' written reports from the front.

While the Pentagon went to great lengths to try to control the stories and images of the wounded, by August any official mention of casualties was apt

In the first weeks of the war, the military was keen to play up the role of its medical teams. Courtesy of National Archives.

to fuel growing claims that the military was actually massaging the figures. This suspicion came from various quarters. On Capitol Hill, senators on the Appropriations Committee were quick to spot a large discrepancy between the casualty figures the Pentagon had furnished them in a secret executive session and the official numbers found in newspapers across the country. According to the committee's ranking Republican, Styles Bridges, this difference indicated that the appalling cost of the war was "being concealed"—a fact that would shock and horrify the public when it learnt of "the whole truth."[79]

A number of prominent media voices echoed this point. Drew Pearson, no friend of Louis Johnson and not normally shy about exposing government distortions, claimed in his nationally syndicated column that "the army is holding back the true casualty lists in Korea," which he believed were in fact 75 percent higher than what had been announced. Meanwhile, Bert Andrews of the *New York Herald Tribune* latched on to a paragraph that had been "buried in a dispatch from Tokyo" by the war correspondent Keyes Beech. "The greatest source of anger and frustration here is Washington's apparent refusal to recognize the Korean War as a first-class war," Beech had written. "It may not be a first-class war in any conventional sense. But Americans are going to be in for a rude shock when they see the casualty figures." If this was a hint by Beech that the military had been glossing over the true state of affairs, then Andrews had absolutely no doubt whom he would believe. "Newspaper reporters who know Mr. Beach's [sic] reputation as an accurate reporter," Andrews declared, "are aware that he was saying between the lines that he knew what the casualties were, and that the shock when the true number was announced would be 'rude' indeed."[80]

On this occasion, however, as the Pentagon swiftly pointed out, this media frenzy was actually deeply unfair. Part of the problem was the fluid nature of the war, which meant that a company of soldiers who were encircled and listed as missing in action on one day might have fought their way back to U.S. lines the next—a fact of life that prompted the Pentagon to ask leading magazines like *Time* to postpone any publication of "box scores" of casualties until the front had been stabilized.[81]

The more fundamental aspect of the whole problem, though, was the time-consuming nature of confirming casualty figures. As early as July 4, the day before the first U.S. troops had gone into combat in Korea, MacArthur's headquarters had sent "qualified personnel" to the front "to assist local commands in improving [their] reporting technique" of casualties, while the Pentagon had insisted that World War II rules for casualty reporting be applied again in this conflict. Since then, the military had often been slow to compile complete lists. But this was only because it was at pains to ensure that it had got the facts straight and had notified the next of kin before releasing names to the press.[82]

Feeling "very strongly" about press allegations of a cover-up, the Pentagon quickly issued a public explanation. Although conceding that it had provided a Senate committee with classified casualty figures, it explained that these were only "unconfirmed flash figures"—and that the confirmed totals would "take considerable time to collect."[83]

On this occasion, then, the press had got it wrong. But in a sense, the Pentagon was now paying for all the overoptimistic communiqués that had emanated from Tokyo over the past month. After all, why should the press believe anyone in the army, when reporters had come to suspect that MacArthur's command had made a habit of sugarcoating the news on many other aspects of the war?

Stabilization

In August, as the battlefield situation started to stabilize, there was a corresponding improvement in military–media relations. Admittedly, the Eighth Army's defensive line along the Pusan perimeter was still weakly held in some areas, and a major North Korean breakthrough could easily spell disaster for the whole UN effort. On the ground, war correspondents also continued to focus on the dreadful conditions that still afflicted the average

GI, not to mention the fact that few of the men struggling against the savage enemy seemed to have a clear idea of what they were doing in Korea.[84] But most war correspondents were soon striking a more confident tone, their optimism bolstered by the arrival of the Second Infantry Division, a regiment of marines, and the three tank battalions.[85]

Perhaps the symbolic moment came on Friday, August 25, at the end of the ninth week of the war. That day, an eyewitness dispatch by Homer Bigart was published in numerous newspapers. A tough, hard-bitten professional, Bigart never hesitated to send home vivid and disturbing accounts of the defeat. But today he was far more upbeat, reporting that

> the enemy has been badly beaten and it is now very doubtful whether he could mount another serious onslaught against the bridgehead. One of the most cheering developments of recent days has been the remarkable rise in morale among American and South Korean troops. They felt today they had withstood the fiercest blows of the North Korean Reds and that the enemy was no longer capable of inflicting disaster.[86]

Still, two major problems persisted. One was the patent lack of security at the front. By the end of August, MacArthur had finalized his plans to launch a bold counterattack in the rear of the North Korean invader. His target was Inchon, a port just 25 miles west of Seoul. Its capture would deal a devastating psychological blow to the communists. As well as enabling the Eighth Army to break out of the Pusan perimeter, it would also, in MacArthur's grandiose estimate, save one hundred thousand lives. The Joint Chiefs were dubious, however, fearing that Inchon's brief high tides and large mud flats would make it difficult to land sufficient troops in the first wave. Even if this obstacle was overcome, UN forces would still be landing in the midst of a large city that would be easy to defend, while the Han River blocked the way to Seoul and might prove another formidable defensive barrier. On August 23, in a spellbinding briefing to senior officers, including two visiting members of the Joint Chiefs, MacArthur conceded that the Inchon attack was a five-thousand-to-one gamble. But, in no mood to brook dissent, he insisted that "we shall land at Inchon and I shall succeed."[87]

Despite their unease, the Joint Chiefs ultimately decided not to block MacArthur's plan. Nevertheless, such a risky operation obviously called for maximum security, so the Pentagon prepared yet another study on the question of censorship. Completed on September 7, this report effectively demolished all the practical obstacles that had been used to forestall censorship in the past. It stressed that the defense secretary had the legal authority under JCS 1968/3 to call for a formal code. And it concluded that "MacArthur has a sufficient nucleus of personnel within his command today, experienced in censorship, to immediately institute censorship in Korea if directed."[88]

True to form, however, MacArthur remained adamantly opposed to a formal code. His calculations remained partly practical: his command was still too overworked to oversee such a controversial measure. They were also professional: his belief that journalists were the best judges of what to print. But doubtless his stubbornness also derived from his original public characterization of censorship as "abhorrent," a statement so categorical that it would now be difficult to override. In a vigorous—and sometimes fanciful—defense, MacArthur even went as far as declaring that his system had "resulted in the most complete coverage for public information of any military campaign in history, without, as far as I know, a single security breach of a nature to provide effective assistance to the enemy. Correspondents assigned to war reporting are essentially responsible individuals," he reiterated, "and their ability to assume the responsibility of self-censorship has been amply and conclusively demonstrated" by the success of UN operations.[89]

Yet as officials in the Pentagon were all too aware, such a blithe assessment neatly ignored the political fallout this unfettered war reporting was generating back in the United States. Along with the flaps about security breaches and casualty figures, reporters, columnists, and politicians were also starting to delve deeper in their efforts to fathom why the U.S. army had performed so poorly against the North Koreans. They did not have far to look. As Homer Bigart recorded in one particularly influential account, U.S. soldiers were facing well-equipped communist troops with "old, rebuilt equipment." Leading with a photograph of a dead U.S. soldier "face down on a Korean roadside," *Life* was more emotive. The U.S. military had "not been kept in combat condition," it declared. Apparently, it had not even maintained the "inadequate equipment" it kept in stock, for "some of it has failed in combat."[90]

For many in the media, this lack of preparedness was baffling, because the Pentagon had reportedly spent huge sums since 1945—no less than $50 billion, more than twice the amount the country had actually spent to fight World War I.[91] But for others, there was no doubt where the blame for the current disaster should be directed. Over the past few months, the Alsop brothers (Joseph and Stewart) had already been relentlessly hounding the defense secretary in the pages of the *New York Herald Tribune* and *Saturday Evening Post*, insisting that his misguided notions of economy had left the U.S. military dangerously exposed at a time of heightened peril. Now, senior Republicans hastened to ask Louis Johnson for an accounting of all the funds that the Pentagon had actually spent, while even some Democrats started to press for his scalp.[92] "I cannot tell you how the feeling against Secretary Johnson is building up," Eleanor Roosevelt wrote to Truman, "because people feel that for political reasons he tried to go beyond what was asked for in the way of economy and is therefore responsible for our poor showing in the way of equipment."[93] Apart from getting rid of Johnson, the only remedy seemed to be a basic change in America's military posture for waging the Cold War.

3

MOBILIZING FOR A POLICE ACTION

Two and a half months before the outbreak of the Korean War, a special working party headed by Paul H. Nitze of the State Department's Policy Planning Staff had completed a top-secret national security review entitled NSC-68. In the wake of the Soviet A-bomb test, this document had depicted the Cold War struggle in stark, dark terms. The Soviet Union, it began, "animated by a new fanatic faith, directly antithetical to our own," was seeking "to impose absolute authority over the rest of the world," and the only way the United States could prevent this was by undertaking "a more rapid build-up of political, economic, and military strength" over the next four years. The danger was so great, NSC-68 concluded, that "budgetary considerations will have to be subordinated to the stark fact that our very independence as a nation may be at stake."

Before Korea, however, any attempt to disregard budgetary considerations had faced serious obstacles. One was Louis Johnson, whose determination to cut military spending and hostility toward the State Department threatened to derail the whole project. Ultimately, Acheson and Nitze had been able to isolate Johnson, partly by building up support inside the Pentagon among the Joint Chiefs and civilian service secretaries and partly by drafting the document in black-and-white language in the hope that this would "bludgeon" top officials into accepting its arguments. In April, Johnson had surprisingly succumbed to this pressure by endorsing NSC-68. But he remained a slippery customer, ever eager to brief his own partisans in the press against Acheson. More important, during the spring and early summer the president had been distinctly lukewarm to the whole program. Still publicly committed to a policy of cutting back on military spending, Truman's instinct had been to play for time, directing that absolutely "no publicity be given this report or its contents," while he consulted with more fiscally conservative officials about its conclusions.[1]

Until now, domestic pressures had also seemed to stand in the way of a large defense buildup. Before Korea, Congress had clearly been in a stingy mood, and it had escaped no one's notice back in January when Truman's state of the union address had been noisily interrupted from both sides of the aisle as soon as he proposed that "federal expenditures be held to the lowest levels."[2] Nor, more generally, did the mass of Americans seem willing to embrace the sacrifices necessary for a sustained mobilization. During the spring, even champions of NSC-68 had been pessimistic about the prospect of persuading a majority of the public to support their rearmament ideas, convinced that the popular mood was basically volatile, with many Americans all too willing to lapse periodically into a state of apathy and complacency. "I fear that the U.S. public would rapidly tire of such an effort," Edward Barrett of the State Department's PA had gloomily noted in April. "In the absence of real and continuing crises, a dictatorship can unquestionably outlast a democracy in a conventional armaments race." "The American people have a false sense of security," Acheson had agreed,

> and do not realize that the world situation, which is called a cold war, is in fact a real war and that the Soviet Union has one purpose in mind and this is world domination....The American people must be made to realize the gravity of our situation and must become reconciled to the fact that we must make certain sacrifices in order to meet the problem of Soviet aggression.[3]

As we have seen, one of the most important consequences of the initial Korean reverses had been to dispel this "false sense of security." Yet as the debate over mobilization unfolded, even NSC-68 advocates would realize that the relationship between the situation in Korea and the issue of mobilization was complex and tangled.

Crafting a Program and a Message

On July 9, MacArthur's request for eight divisions to fight the war shattered any lingering illusions that "the North Korean bandits" could be suppressed relatively cheaply. Even the compromise the Joint Chiefs cobbled together in the next few days, which sent an additional division to Korea, plus some RCTs dotted across the United States and Pacific, placed tremendous pressure on both the general reserve and America's global commitments. Within days, the Joint Chiefs therefore requested that the army be enlarged from 630,000 to 834,000 men. As well as calling up individuals serving in the army's reserve, they also mobilized ninety-two National Guard units.[4]

Under sustained political attack because of the early defeats in Korea, Johnson was in no position to stand in the way of these proposals. Indeed, at a crucial cabinet meeting on July 14, he was effectively marginalized. With Acheson making a forceful case for massive hike in defense spending, together with powers to control the allocation of scarce strategic resources, the president finally came down on the side of the State Department's hawkish position—a decision that clearly had a cathartic effect.[5] "It was the most satisfying cabinet meeting he [had] ever held," Truman told aides shortly after. "Everybody let his hair down. We discussed all phases of the Korean problem, including industrial controls, manpower controls, and price controls. It was no kidglove affair but there were no recriminations."[6] Just as important, now that a general agreement on how best to proceed had been reached, intensive work could finally begin on a keynote presidential speech to be made the following week.

Truman's eagerly anticipated message appeared in two installments on July 19. At noon on that hot and humid Wednesday, members of both houses of Congress assembled to hear a clerk read a long, detailed statement. This largely fulfilled the State Department's often-expressed desire for a "formal" document that "would bring the whole [Korean] story together in one official narrative," thereby countering GOP charges that Congress had not been consulted.[7]

That evening, Truman then took to the airwaves to deliver a fireside chat on the war. Before a vast audience estimated at around 130 million, the president began with a short history of the Korean incident, stressing exactly why GIs had been sent to this "small country, thousands of miles away." The reason was simple. The North Koreans had launched a brazen and premeditated act of aggression, Truman declared, against a small, independent country that was sponsored by the UN and supported by the United States. Speaking in a slow, measured manner, his anger barely concealed, the president insisted that this assault was a "direct challenge to the efforts of the free nations to build the kind of world in which men can live in freedom and peace." Placing the current crisis in its global perspective, Truman explained that Korea was likely to be only the first in a series of "sneak" attacks. America therefore had to be on its guard. It had to increase its strength and war preparedness to meet the new challenges that were bound to emerge. This meant making a "considerable adjustment" to the country's economy, both to ensure that defense industries had access to the raw materials they required and to "prevent inflation and to keep our government in a sound financial condition." It also meant raising taxes to pay for the $10 billion increase in defense spending.[8]

Truman's speech clearly marked an important step in the direction of NSC-68, ending the old retrenchment policy that had placed a $13.5 billion ceiling on that year's defense budget and calling for important changes to the economy in order to spark a broader rearmament program. Yet in significant ways, the president still held back from a wholehearted endorsement of the full NSC-68 program. His reasons were partly practical, since detailed estimates for a sustained buildup could not be compiled overnight.[9] In the meantime, his attention was still firmly fixed on "stopgap" measures to meet the current crisis. Indeed, although Truman finally decided to ask for a supplemental appropriation of $10 billion, which would almost double that year's defense budget in one fell swoop, around half of this would be earmarked either for essential personnel and supplies for Korea or to replace units sent from the now threadbare general reserve. What was left was intended for a more general expansion of the armed services. But this was still a far cry from the $50 billion estimates that NSC-68 advocates had prepared during the spring. And for the time being, Truman was not entirely willing to abandon his old fiscal conservatism. As he remarked on July 22, he wanted to avoid "putting any more money than necessary in the hands of the military."[10]

The president's call for limited economic controls was also far less radical than some officials seemed to want. In the first week of July, officials in the departments of State, Interior, Commerce, Agriculture, and Labor all believed that some form of price and wage control would soon be needed to contain the inflationary pressures unleashed by war. Inside the National Security Resources Board, the new head, Stuart Symington, a persuasive and dynamic administrator from Missouri, also urged the administration to "embark promptly on whatever program is necessary," perhaps even with an emergency powers act that would drive home the extent of the sacrifices that would be necessary. But Truman rejected all this advice. He doubtless recalled the deep hostility toward wage and price regulation during World War II, when the Office of Price Administration had become "a target for all the frustrations and disappointments of people unaccustomed to regimentation and control," not to mention the 1946 midterm elections, when Republicans had successfully campaigned on a platform to swiftly terminate wartime controls. Unwilling to return to such an unpopular path in the current limited emergency, Truman concurred with his political and economic advisers, like Averell Harriman and Leon Keyserling, who "were profoundly convinced that the country and Congress were not yet ready for an all-out mobilization bill." Consequently, all that appeared in the administration's defense production measure were powers to allow the president to allocate resources and facilities for the buildup, to control consumer credit and commodity speculation, and to provide loans to small businesses to help them participate in the production of military hardware.[11]

That the administration's mobilization plan was distinctly limited would naturally become a focal point for all the public explanations during the coming weeks. The president would not ask for sweeping powers "until he thinks they are essential and that Congress would grant them," Dr. John Steelman, assistant to the president, told one *Time* reporter in a background briefing. "That wouldn't be until we are in a real emergency and I wouldn't say that we are in such an emergency now."[12] "We are not, at this time, calling for an all-out mobilization," Symington explained to the Senate Banking and Currency Committee on July 24, at the start of the hearings on the administration's program.[13]

Yet officials also had another option: they could use the crisis mood to lay the groundwork for the longer term sustained mobilization that was clearly in the pipeline. After all, senior State Department officials were acutely aware that the public's attention span was short and that Americans might soon lapse back into a mood of complacency. During the spring, Acheson had also contemplated the possibility of exploiting the next Cold War flashpoint in order to drive home the need for sustained vigilance.[14] Why not use this particular incident to drum up domestic support for NSC-68, perhaps even employing the "clearer than truth" rhetoric historians have so frequently alluded to?

The reason officials decided to eschew this course was simple. As they realized, exploiting a small incident to generate domestic support for a defense build-up was one thing; it was quite another to magnify a major crisis like Korea. Indeed, the public was already edgy. If it now became convinced that a major war with the Soviets was in the offing, it might start to clamor for highly dangerous courses of action.

Even before the outbreak of the Korean War, officials contemplating how best to sell NSC-68 had been preoccupied with the dangers of such a popular hysteria. As Adrian Fisher, the State Department's legal adviser, had pointed out in a meeting on June 6, a fundamental problem facing any effort to go public with NSC-68 was that "by indicating the necessity of building up forces you automatically create a frame of mind which considers that war is immediate and this in turn makes it impossible to achieve our objective which is preventing war." Other State Department officials thought that it was particularly essential to reject proposals from the National Security Resources Board, which focused on civilian defense measures to be adopted *after* a war had started, because if the assumption took hold that "we are fighting a war tomorrow," then "the inevitable result will be to make this assumption come true."[15]

In the middle of July, as news of defeats from the censorship-free battlefield multiplied, a series of statements erupted with "volcanic force" on Capitol Hill, reinforcing the fear that the domestic mood might disastrously overheat. On July 13, Owen Brewster, chair of the Republican Campaign Committee, publicly urged that MacArthur be given the discretion to use the A-bomb, while Congressman Lloyd Bentsen (D-TX) proposed giving the North Koreans a week to withdraw behind the thirty-eighth parallel or face a nuclear attack.[16] Two days later, John M. Vorys (R-OH), the ranking Republican on the House Foreign Affairs Committee, was equally bellicose, privately telling State Department officials that "war with the Soviet Union is inevitable. Perhaps our thinking should now concentrate not on how to avoid it but how best to win it." Perhaps, he even suggested, the focus of such planning ought to be firmly fixed on our current superiority in the air and in atomic weapons.[17]

Faced with such bellicose pronouncements, senior administration officials deemed it prudent to maintain their subdued public posture, shunning anything that might fuel calls for an escalation of the Cold War.[18] Acheson even abandoned much of the NSC-68 imagery that had characterized his speeches during the spring, with its portrayal of the Cold War as a simple conflict between freedom and slavery, and its depiction of the communist world as a monolithic bloc in which the Kremlin called all the shots. Instead, Acheson and his aides remained firmly wedded to promulgating the fiction that the enemy in Korea was the vaguely defined international communist movement. The Soviets were still not held directly responsible and, when mentioned, were merely condemned for failing to force the North Koreans to halt their attacks and withdraw back behind the thirty-eighth parallel.[19]

Inside the White House, meanwhile, Truman remained anxious to avoid any action that might engender or exacerbate a "war psychosis" among the American public. On July 19, he even refused to go up to Capitol Hill and deliver his speech in person, lest this create the impression that he was asking for a declaration of war. The speech itself had also been carefully crafted to limit expectations—as Dulles found out when he proposed issuing a statement to ratchet up domestic support for a larger and more sustained preparedness program. Swiftly and firmly disabusing him of the whole idea, Barrett stressed that

> the mobilization for which he [the president] is asking is for the purpose of replacing the wastage in Korea and generally improving the defense of the United States. It does not constitute full war mobilization. He therefore feels that in the passage cited it would be desirable not to relate the measures now being taken to the expectation of general war.[20]

Such manifest caution also helped scupper an interesting suggestion that Truman reorganize his cabinet to include key Republicans in an attempt to foster a bipartisan spirit to meet the current crisis. By the middle of July, the war was already starting to have an impact on the policymaking machinery. The president was now regularly attending National Security Council meetings for the first time. In the State Department, various proposals were also under consideration for establishing some sort of coordination with the Pentagon, from weekly dinner meetings between Acheson, Johnson, and Harriman to the creation of joint Defense-State working groups to discuss key issues.[21] At a cabinet meeting on July 21, Truman then announced that everyone present, plus Harriman and Symington, would constitute a "war cabinet." Most of those around the table duly nodded their assent, no doubt pleased that this key decisionmaking body would not be kept small enough to exclude them. But Vice President Alben Barkley, who spent his days presiding over the Senate and had a keen sense of the mood on the Hill, quickly broke in to express his concern. The "only reservation," he averred, "is that there may be a clamor for Republican membership in the cabinet."[22]

There was certainly an obvious precedent for constructing a coalition government in a time of great peril. Just ten years earlier, in the midst of a similar international crisis, Franklin Roosevelt had appointed two prominent Republicans, Henry Stimson and Frank Knox, to important positions in his cabinet, and both had soon proved to be formidable spokesmen, publicly making the case for a string of controversial measures. As the World War II mobilization got under way, Roosevelt had also been keen to bring on board key figures from both business and labor, in the (often vain) hope that this might quell dissent from both ends of the economic spectrum. In stark contrast, Truman's current cabinet hardly represented all the diverse strands of American life, let alone all the politically potent blocs in Congress. Of the senior posts, Acheson was essentially a foreign policy expert with no constituency or clout in Congress; Johnson had attempted to hook up with leading Republicans but in such an underhand way as to seriously damage his own credibility; and Treasury Secretary John W. Snyder was not only widely viewed as one of Truman's Missouri cronies but also deeply distrusted by liberals.[23] Restructuring the cabinet could clearly help to make it more representative, perhaps if the appointment of a senior conservative was balanced with the elevation of a union representative to a key job in the defense setup—something that top labor leaders meeting with Symington at the Washington's Statler Hotel on July 11 intimated might be a condition for their support of any wide-ranging mobilization package.[24]

Writing his memoirs from the safety of retirement, Acheson also recognized the strengths senior Republicans might have brought to the administration at this point. In a significant passage, he recalled how moderate Republicans like Thomas Dewey and Earl Warren, his "friends of a good many years," had deflected and silenced criticism from the Taft wing of the GOP. At the start of June, Acheson had attended a governors' conference where he had been forced to endure a barrage of hostile questions for almost four hours. Only when Dewey and Warren had intervened on his side had the attacks started to ease. "They objected to loaded questions," he remembered later, "getting them rephrased; protested against sneers and insults stated as questions, insisting that the chair rule them out of order; and corrected misstatements of fact embedded in long-winded questions." Of course, it was one thing for Acheson to reminisce about the political strengths of Dewey and Warren in his retirement, and quite another for him to have advocated bringing such a figure into the Washington maelstrom in the summer of

1950, when his own position was widely perceived to be far from secure. But even at the time it was obvious that such a leading Republican could now bring important strengths to the administration, perhaps in the increasingly embattled Pentagon, where Johnson's position was highly fragile.[25]

Truman was adamant in his opposition, however. The intensely partisan president was never very comfortable with the thought of opposition politicians (even from the moderate wing of the GOP) holding prominent positions inside his government. Even Dulles's appointment back in the spring had been made reluctantly, "to preserve some semblance of bipartisanship," and Truman balked at the idea of promoting another Republican whose ego might be just as "monumental."[26] Nor did Truman think much of Roosevelt's experiments of balancing businessmen and union leaders in the same agencies, since the chaos that tended to ensue violated his instinctive preference for neat and orderly administrative arrangements. Yet these were not his only motives. In the middle of July, when Senator William Knowland also called on the president "to establish 'a government of national unity for as long as the crisis lasts' by inviting Republicans into his cabinet," Truman's instant rejection had come with a very revealing reason. As a White House spokesman told reporters, "for the president to appoint a 'coalition cabinet' . . . might imply that we are going into a global war, whereas the Korean conflict might not lead to one."[27]

It was a telling statement, demonstrating the White House's keen determination to ensure that key actions remained symbolically subdued. The only problem with such a posture was that it provided Republicans with the perfect opening to go on the offensive.

Republicans and Mobilization

During periods of war, opposition parties are normally faced with a perilous balancing act, wanting to highlight specific flaws in the way the government is conducting the conflict without being accused of undermining the entire war effort. This balancing act tends to be particularly precarious when governments offer forceful leadership, depicting the issues in black-and-white terms, as an all-out struggle between good and evil. In the early days of the Korean War, however, the administration had eschewed this course. By so doing, it had immediately provided the opposition with an opportunity to go on the offensive. After all, there had been no declaration of war, no full consultation, no attempts to share the responsibility by constructing a government of national unity. There was not even strident language coming from the White House, stressing the need for unity at a moment of dire peril.

That the administration's low-key stance had left it vulnerable to a Republican counterattack was underscored by a series of polls and surveys published during the summer. Indeed, when one of the first focus groups was assembled in New York City to watch Truman's July 19 speech, the pollsters' central conclusion was that "the president was not in advance of the national mood.... If anything, the public would evidently have gone along with somewhat stronger language regarding communism."[28] More traditional surveys also found that the government's partial mobilization program lagged well behind what most Americans wanted. As PA explained, "the main criticism of the administration's actions since June 25 is that the actions are inadequate and that mobilization should be faster and greater in magnitude."[29]

This criticism was spearheaded by a number of influential spokesmen, with the financier Bernard Baruch leading the way in his testimony before the Senate Banking and Currency Committee. An influential and respected figure, with vast experience in managing the home front dating back to World War I, Baruch did not pull any punches. "Events have left us with no choice," he stressed. "We have to mobilize. Already our young are being called. Casualty lists are coming in." Viewed in this light, there was one major weakness with the president's program: it did "not go far enough."[30]

Other prominent Americans agreed. Leading radio commentators like Walter Winchell and Gabriel Heatter called for "all-out" mobilization "now," to ensure that America had "enough power to frighten Stalin and make him back out." In a similar vein, William Green, president of the American Federation of Labor, released a statement stressing that the nation must have "all-out preparedness for any eventuality," including the mobilization of labor.[31]

Responding both to these cues and the unfolding debacle in Korea, mass opinion clearly favored more vigorous action. According to Gallup, 53 percent of respondents believed that plans should be worked out "NOW for the total mobilization of all U.S. citizens—that is, in case of another war, every able-bodied person would be told what war work he would have to do, where he would work, and what wages he would get." If support for such regimentation was surprising in itself, Gallup also found that 70 percent would endorse higher taxes to fund a larger military. "Rarely has the Institute in its fifteen years of measuring public opinion," Gallup concluded, "found such heavy majorities expressing a willingness to pay more taxes for any public purpose."[32]

While all this hard-line sentiment gave the GOP a perfect opening, the party's leaders were not entirely sure where best to strike. There was clearly little mileage to be gained from attacking the conduct of a war that, despite all the battlefield reverses, was only a few weeks old. And, in any case, Taft was well aware that Congress lacked the military intelligence to offer a pertinent critique.[33]

Nor, at first, did the Republican leadership in the Senate seem ideally placed to capitalize on the growing public demands for all-out mobilization. It had long been an article of faith among those on the Taft wing of the party that government spending should be kept as low as possible, that excessive state control over the economy stifled initiative, and that every effort should be made to stop the executive branch from wielding yet more influence over American life.[34] The day before Truman unveiled his mobilization plans, Taft and Joseph W. Martin (R-MA), the Republican leader in the House, had remained wedded to this credo, issuing a joint statement warning that they would carefully "scrutinize" every administration proposal "to make sure it was actually necessary." As the mobilization hearings got under way, Senate conservatives, rather than lambasting the administration for not going far enough, then tried to exploit its subdued rhetoric to bolster their own calls for minimal mobilization.[35] In one revealing exchange, the "bulldoggish" Homer Capehart (R-IN), who carried the bulk of the GOP attack, arriving early and well-briefed to all the committee meetings, asked Barcuh: "How are we going to sell the American people on 100-percent mobilization ... when the president himself has told the American people that the Korean incident is simply a police action?"[36]

Yet this conservative carping was clearly wide of the mark, and soon the central line of Republican attack, especially in the House, veered decisively away from the Taft-Capehart position. Indeed, within days of Baruch's testimony, observers soon noted "an upsurge of sentiment" for all-out mandatory price and wage controls. On July 27, one Democratic leader (who refused to be identified) told reporters that there was suddenly a fifty-fifty chance that the House would adopt a package far in advance of what the administration had asked for. Giving substance to this claim, the House Banking Committee failed by only one vote to ditch the administration's defense production bill on the grounds that it "was not drastic enough" and replace it with a GOP measure that would put a ceiling on prices across the economy. Tellingly, Republicans in the House, led by John Kunkel (PA), based their bill on a program Baruch had championed during the last war, with the transparent intent to maneuver the Democrats into an embarrassing position. As one journalist paraphrased their motives, "If Truman's piecemeal program goes haywire now, they can always say, 'We offered the Baruch plan, which would have worked, but the Democrats wouldn't take it.'" Equally tellingly, around forty Democrats in the House, doubtless recognizing the danger, seemed ready to break with their leadership and vote with the Republicans. "Sentiment for all-out mobilization [is] sweeping through both houses of Congress," one reporter concluded on July 31. "Administration forces virtually conceded that the president's limited program would be expanded."[37]

It was not difficult to discern why Congress was so susceptible to bolder measures—not with midterm elections just over three months away and polls demonstrating that the folks back home favored more vigorous action. But a stubborn Truman was determined not to bend to the prevailing political wind. As his economic advisers hastened to point out, extensive economic controls would be a nightmare to administer. They might also do more harm than good to the economy, perhaps even undermining the future prospects for a long-term, sustained defense buildup. The president himself was angered by the obvious politicking behind the GOP strategy in the House, complaining to one aide that the opposition was merely "seeking headlines." Rather than cave in to such opportunism, on August 1 Truman met with the congressional leadership to devise a response. With Rayburn and Majority Leader John W. McCormack (D-MA) deeply concerned that the House could easily spiral out of control, Truman agreed to a limited compromise. He would send a message up to the Hill agreeing to accept any measure that contained standby or permissive controls, which the president himself "could invoke when the need arose."[38]

Ultimately, this concession would provide a compromise position around which most congressmen could rally, but during most of August the mood on the Hill remained dangerously chaotic. Debate on the House floor began on August 1. During the next four days, legislators proffered such a bewildering array of amendments that on one occasion members were only allotted seven-eighths of a minute to outline their proposals. With the House being asked to vote so hastily on a range of complex issues, cries of "confusion" abounded. By August 4, the situation had become so tangled that Democratic leaders, after meeting with the House parliamentarian, decided to scrap all the previous work and start again. The floor debate was also postponed for five days, to give the leadership time to forge a measure acceptable to both Congress and the White House, while also providing a breathing space in which, it was hoped, tempers could cool. In the interim, Rayburn and McCormack went to work behind closed doors, pressuring potential Democratic defectors into line with personal appeals—"We need your help"; any problems will be ironed out in Conference; "but let's don't let the Republicans walk off with the ball on this one." By the time the measure came back on August 9 and 10, all this lobbying had clearly paid off, and the party leadership's measure was finally voted through by wide margins.[39]

In the Senate, the main effort to stiffen the legislation came on August 3, when J. William Fulbright (D-AR) introduced an amendment during the Banking Committee hearings that would roll back prices and wages to the level prevailing before the start of the war. After this initiative was voted down the next day, the Senate leadership still faced numerous challenges— no less than fifty-two amendments in total. But these were generally aimed at the Senate's traditional concern: protecting against an open-ended measure that would greatly enhance presidential authority.

On August 21, many of these amendments were successfully added to the bill during the last eight hours of debate.[40] Attention now shifted to the Conference Committee, which attempted to iron out the differences between the House and Senate versions. During more than a week of hard bargaining, the main sticking point proved to be an amendment that would have effectively backed the president into a corner by compelling him to invoke controls across the board whenever he moved into any area of the economy. A complex compromise was finally worked out that attempted to strike a balance between discretion and compulsion by only forcing him to control wages for any commodity subject to price controls. When the committee then got stuck on whether to terminate the measure in one or two years, Omar N. Bradley, chair of the Joint Chiefs, was called in to make the case for a termination date in 1952, which he stressed was vital because defense contracts normally took two years to fulfill. Again, a convoluted compromise was reached, extending the allocations and priorities provisions of the legislation until 1952 but prohibiting the making of new contracts after June 1951.[41]

Compared to some of the ideas that had swirled around Congress during July and August, this final compromise proved something of a victory for the administration, for it gave the president the ability to impose standby controls, while only eliminating the authority to regulate commodity exchanges from his original proposal. Yet in strictly political terms, this was a Pyrrhic victory. Many Republicans certainly believed they had now found a new line of attack to use in the upcoming midterm campaign. The president "has been negligent in leaving the American people in the dark about the gravity" of the international situation, Senator George D. Aiken (R-VT) charged in August. "Can we wait until after the November elections to tell the people the real truth?" he asked; complete mobilization was essential now.[42] In the House, fifteen Republicans from the internationalist wing of the party (including Richard M. Nixon [R-CA] and Gerald R. Ford [R-MI]) even issued a statement declaring that Korea "has exposed the fact that a tragic diplomatic and military inadequacy exists." Stressing that a "lack of leadership at this time will breed hysteria or complacency," they called for a "vigorous program of positive action of which the American public is aware."[43]

Truman's reaction to that summer's other major item of legislative business appeared to give greater force to Republican charges that his administration's response to the Korean crisis was dangerously complacent. Almost inevitably, the outbreak of the Korean War gave an enormous boost to the nationalist Republicans and conservative Democrats who had long believed that the United States faced a real threat from the "enemy within." "The present situation is an open sesame to the communists," Karl E. Mundt (R-SD), one of the most vocal and prominent of their number, declared on July 24. "It is a wide-open invitation for espionage, sabotage, and destruction.... Are men so gullible and naïve at this late date when we are fighting communism abroad as to assume that the communists in America will do nothing to help their associates in Korea?"[44]

What Mundt and his allies now wanted was stiffer legislation to protect against this threat, particularly passage of a bill that had been stuck in

Congress for over two years that would require "communist political organizations" to register the names of their officers and members with the Justice Department. In July, the Republican Policy Committee placed the Mundt bill on its "must list." The time was ripe, its sponsor stressed, to stop "coddling" communists at home while American boys were being killed in Korea.[45]

Truman was clearly unhappy with the Mundt bill, telling one aide that it "adopted police-state tactics and unduly encroached on individual rights." As pressure in Congress built up behind the measure, he decided to use the same device that was proving so successful in forging a compromise position on economic controls: he issued a public statement calling for a measure based not on hysteria but on a proportionate response to the danger. On August 8, exactly a week after he issued his public letter conceding the case for standby controls, Truman sent a new message to Congress in which he accepted that the threat of communist subversion, espionage, and sabotage required closer supervision of aliens, the registration of foreign agents, and enhanced security at national defense installations. But he also warned the nation about extremist conservatives "who urge us to adopt police state measures." "We must all act soberly and carefully," Truman concluded, in a now familiar refrain. "This is important not only to our own country, but to the success of the cause of freedom in the world."[46]

Yet in stark contrast to the debate over controls, Truman's attempt at compromise now fell on decidedly deaf ears. The reasons are instructive. Unlike the defense production debate, where Republicans remained divided between fiscal conservatives and those willing to go further than the administration, on this issue the party was united. Before Korea, to be sure, internationalist Republicans had been leery of the most controversial manifestation of the mounting internal anticommunist hysteria: Joe McCarthy's reckless charges that the State Department was infested with Reds. But moderates like Aiken, Tobey, and Wayne Morse (R-OR), who had all denounced McCarthy at the beginning of June, increasingly faced discontent among their own ranks—including, in Tobey's case, a stiff primary election fight from a conservative challenger, replete with allegations that he was a "Truman Republican."[47]

Outside the halls of Congress, in fact, the war in Korea had clearly changed the prevailing political weather, churning up storms that threatened to submerge any moderate daring enough to oppose Joe. Inside the Senate, meanwhile, it was Millard E. Tydings's (D-MD) mishandled investigation into McCarthy's charges that now created a new squall.

Tydings's investigation, which had started in the spring and was concluded just after the Korean War began, united Republicans of all stripes. All were convinced that the Maryland senator was guilty of a series of underhand procedural shenanigans. Some expressed anger at his effort to smuggle out a final report without a full meeting of his subcommittee. Others were convinced that he should have investigated McCarthy's charges and not McCarthy himself. And all were inflamed by Tydings's "bare-fisted" denunciation of McCarthy on the Senate floor, which, although a reaction to McCarthy's own antics since the spring, clearly contravened the norms of senatorial courtesy and etiquette. When Tydings's report finally came up for debate in the middle of July, the Senate divided on straight party lines to have it filed. On the back of this rare display of party unity, zealots like Jenner enlivened proceedings by shouting, "How can we get the Reds out of Korea if we cannot get them out of Washington?" From the packed galleries, many applauded.[48]

The fallout from the Tydings report was important, because it papered over the cracks in the GOP and prevented the exposure of McCarthy's dubious claims. It also worried leading Democrats, who now fretted about getting caught on the wrong side of such an explosive issue. When one group of Democratic senators met to discuss the bill, they were in no doubt that it was "a bad measure" that ordinarily ought to be rejected. But they also concluded that "those who faced the electorate THIS year would be taking too great a risk if they voted right because of the popular lack of understanding and hysteria over the issue." Even liberal Democrats felt the need to trim their sails. As the congressional debate intensified, a group that included senators Paul H. Douglas (IL), Harley Kilgore (WV), Herbert Lehman (NY), and Hubert Humphrey (MI) decided that they could only head off the bill's registration proposal with the even more radical expedient of interning suspected subversives whenever the president declared an emergency—a measure that would, at least, give the executive control over the whole issue, while switching the terms of the debate away from a general witch hunt and toward the rooting out of specific security threats.[49]

In the defense production debate, the administration had been able to quell some of the panic in Democratic ranks by leaning heavily on the Speaker, the majority whips, and powerful committee chairs. Now, however, the anticommunist measure was in the hands of Pat McCarran, chair of the Senate Judiciary Committee and no friend of the White House. An Irish Catholic from Nevada, McCarran was not only highly skilled in the arts of moving legislation through the complex procedures of the Senate but also determined to pass a stiff measure. For a brief moment, it seemed possible that the White House might be able to outmaneuver this experienced parliamentary bruiser, as eight influential administration supporters, including Scott Lucas, chief whip Francis J. Myers (D-PA), and three Democratic members of the Judiciary Committee prepared to introduce a mild bill along the lines of Truman's public statement. But then McCarran swiftly and unexpectedly engineered a version of the more radical Mundt proposal out of committee by a nine-to-three vote, although this was now widely—and tellingly—known as the McCarran bill. Once on the Senate floor, there was little doubt that the political wind was blowing lustily behind McCarran's cause.[50]

With the debate about to start in both chambers, the White House decided to undertake a sustained publicity campaign to warn of the dangers of the subversive bill. After spending a dismal weekend at Shangri-La (the Maryland presidential retreat later renamed Camp David), marred by unseasonably cold weather, Truman hoped to spend the week conducting what one reporter described as an "educational campaign" on the pitfalls of the McCarran measure, in yet another attempt to dampen down the popular mood and ward off the passage of hysteria-driven policy.[51] But such a campaign seemed all too reminiscent of the government's posture on other key issues. And it quickly ran into the obvious GOP riposte that the president was once again adopting a stance of too little, too late. "It is high time that the administration give immediate attention to proper ways to get at this menace to our people and our institutions," Homer S. Ferguson (R-MI) declared in a typical comment. "Recent history has always been one step ahead of this administration.... When does this administration propose to wake up and anticipate developments? Must we always be the victims of hostile actions before we prepare ourselves?"[52]

On the floor of both chambers, few legislators were willing to challenge such logic. Lucas, facing a close election in November, and Tydings, hoping to recoup some of the ground lost in the protracted controversy surrounding McCarthy, even engaged in a parliamentary sleight of hand that added the liberal detention measure to the McCarran bill, before rushing the whole unwieldy package to a voice vote, which it passed with just seven senators dissenting. In the House, the verdict was equally decisive, with only 20 votes against and a massive 354 in favor.[53]

Such margins made the prospect of sustaining a presidential veto dim indeed. Not wanting to hand the Republicans a powerful campaign issue, Democratic leaders urged Truman to sign the bill and thereby take the whole matter off the political agenda. But the White House demurred. In a series of private debates, presidential aides concluded that no political credit would accrue to the administration, since Republicans would claim that Truman "signed it only under enormous pressure from the Congress and the people." The president would also back himself into a position where he could be portrayed as both a hypocrite and appeaser—a hypocrite because he would now be signing a bill he had forcefully attacked in public and an appeaser because it would simply encourage Republicans "to cry for still more repressive legislation." Stressing that there "is at least a fighting chance of sustaining a veto in the Senate," White House aides prodded the president to issue a forceful veto message. Even if this failed to convince legislators, it might prove an effective piece of gesture politics, rallying liberal support and perhaps even putting down a marker for the 1952 election, by which time the flaws of the measure would have become evident.[54]

Fully persuaded, Truman moved to stiffen the language of his veto message. The main provisions of the McCarran bill, he declared, are not directed toward the real and present dangers that exist from communism. Instead of striking blows at communism, they would strike blows at our own liberties and at our position in the forefront of those working for freedom in the world. At a time when our young men are fighting for freedom in Korea, it would be tragic to advance the objectives of communism in this country, as this bill would do.[55]

Not content simply to rely on rhetoric, the White House also made sure the veto measure was mimeographed onto top-quality paper, with the text double-spaced for easier reading. In an unprecedented move, Truman even sent each member of Congress a personal note, signed with a careful facsimile of his signature, in the hope that such cosmetics would make the Congress "read and heed" his message. Clearly this was gesture politics with a vengeance.[56]

Yet it had little impact on the House, which was so desperate to override the president's veto that it barely listened to the veto message before voting 248 to 48 against it. In the Senate, a small band of liberals and mavericks did lead a thirty-hour filibuster in the hope that, as one of them told a reporter, this would give the country both time to digest the president's message and a chance to wire their colleagues supporting the veto. But when this wishful scenario failed to come to fruition, the filibuster came to an inglorious end, with William Langer (R-ND), its chief spokesman, collapsing on the Senate floor, before his colleagues promptly voted to override Truman's veto, fifty-seven to ten. Not to be outdone in terms of eye-catching publicity stunts, Taft even flew from a campaign speech in Ohio directly to Washington to cast his vote against the veto, before heading straight back to the stump. No one could doubt that Republicans believed they had now acquired a powerful tool for the upcoming election.[57]

Efforts to Regain Control over the Debate

That the election would now be fought on the administration's record of combating communism was confirmed when the Republican members of the Senate Foreign Relations Committee published a white paper on foreign policy in the middle of August. This was the brainchild of Alexander Smith, the senior senator from New Jersey, who since the start of July had been working on a foreign policy statement that every Senate Republican could subscribe to. Consulting widely with all groups, Smith's task was far from easy. On one side, Vandenberg and Lodge balked at anything that was too negative and neglected Truman's achievements in Europe. On the other, conservatives like Bourke B. Hickenlooper (R-IA) wanted a full-scale assault on "communists in government," echoing McCarthy's line that communist sympathizers associated with the State Department had prodded Acheson toward his malign neglect of Asia. Only through a protracted process of negotiation were these divisions narrowed. The ailing Vandenberg proved useful here, using his lingering influence over colleagues to moderate the tone of the document. Dulles, too, played a key role, one perhaps befitting his ambiguous status as a State Department counselor, for he helped to keep "the statement on a rather conservative plane" and excised "exaggerated adjectives," but—reflecting the fact that he was not a major administration player—he also viewed his role as editor rather than censor and saw no reason to step in and scupper the whole process.[58]

The end result was released on August 13. That day, Smith and his colleagues provided briefings for influential journalists like James Reston of the *New York Times*. At a Republican Conference Committee meeting, Taft called on senators to "amplify the statement in floor speeches," while the publicity arm of the Republican National Committee was put to work distributing the document to a wide audience. At a time when politicians still attempted to pay at least lip service to the idea of bipartisanship, this Republican white paper created quite a splash, and was soon on the front cover of most of the nation's press. It began mildly enough, with the standard call for everyone to unite behind the stand taken in Korea. But it then moved quickly to the offensive, charging that the administration had been blind to the "true aims and methods of the rulers of Soviet Russia," had constantly underestimated the dangers of Asian communism, and had failed "vigorously to build strong American armed forces." The implication was unmistakable: the administration's past neglect had contributed to the current crisis. "These are the facts which must be faced," the white paper concluded. "The American people will not now excuse those responsible for these blunders."[59]

This highly partisan assault deeply alarmed many in the administration. "It is not ordinarily within the province of this staff to recommend approaches to be taken in domestic political problems," a worried Nitze wrote Webb on August 14, "yet the grave implications of the [GOP] statement as it affects the future conduct of U.S. policy, particularly the far-reaching program envisaged in NSC-68, cannot be overlooked." After all, NSC-68 clearly assumed the maintenance of "national solidarity in support of the major undertakings in American foreign policy and security." The Republicans, however, seemed more bent on attacking the administration at each and every opportunity.[60]

But what could be done? Nitze himself recommended that the administration ignore the GOP attack, because a forceful rebuttal would merely do further "injury to the bipartisan principle in the critical months ahead." Others agreed. At a strategy lunch on August 15, officials from the White House, State Department, and Pentagon recommended that Truman adopt an air of studied aloofness. "It was decided that the president's statement should be very brief," one of them recorded. "He should attempt to minimize the statement by the Republican minority and should do nothing which would be viewed as an effort to break up the bipartisan policy."[61]

Yet such official reticence only served to reinforce the growing impression that the administration's whole Cold War strategy was distinctly lackluster. Indeed, from the perspective of the White House and State Department, there may have been good grounds for refusing to engage in public polemics, from concerns that a forceful rebuttal would further undermine bipartisanship to fears that a more vigorous and stark presentation of the danger would precipitate demands for more radical action. But by August, it was clear that this low-key posture had not worked. For one thing, it had provided Republicans with the perfect opening to outflank the administration by claiming that they were the party that espoused timely and vigorous—not laggardly and complacent—Cold War policies. For another, it had exacerbated the very ills officials were trying to avoid.

This became abundantly clear on the subject of preventive war against the Soviet Union. Far from dampening down demands for bold action, during the summer the government's subdued PR efforts were actually starting to fuel them. Thus, in the middle of August a delegation of leading internationalist legislators from both parties descended on the State Department. Believing that the administration's muted public statements had patently failed to bring "a new measure of hope to the American people," they warned of "a growing disposition on the part of the American people to support the concept of preventive war. This growing attitude is aired in fear," they stressed, "and will continue to grow in volume unless some bold alternative course of action is presented by the government."[62]

If this were not disturbing enough, Republicans from both wings of the party now latched onto the charge that the administration was not being sufficiently tough on the Soviet Union. On the floor of Congress between July 31 and August 2, a number of diehard administration opponents lined up to call for direct action against the Kremlin, perhaps even a preemptive nuclear strike. This might be "cruel and murderous, "conceded Clare E. Hoffman (R-MI). "But when was war anything but just that? How many times have we been told by those in authority that Stalin intends to bomb us when he has the ability? Why sit around, waiting for him to destroy us?"[63]

Ominously, even internationalist Republicans now inclined toward tough action. In the House, congressmen Robert Hale (R-ME), Christian A. Herter (R-MA), and Walter H. Judd (R-MN) filed a concurrent resolution that was clearly a slap at the State Department's failure to indict the Soviet Union directly. Their intention, the legislators declared, was "to make it absolutely clear that, insofar as the Congress is concerned, Soviet Russia can no longer inspire its satellites to aggressive action without being held accountable for such action through the appropriate agency—namely, the Security Council of the UN."[64] On the radio, Harold Stassen was more belligerent, declaring that another communist assault anywhere in the world ought to mean that "war will come to Moscow, to the Urals, to the Ukraine." Congress itself had to "take the leadership and issue this warning," added Stassen, a likely contender for the GOP's 1952 presidential nomination, "because the Truman administration had been almost unbelievably confused and inefficient."[65]

In this fervid atmosphere, about the last thing the State Department wanted was any official encouragement of the notion that war was inevitable or that the United States should seek to provoke a showdown in the near future. Unfortunately, however, officials in Foggy Bottom had very little control over the actions of the central policymaker in the Pentagon. Indeed, by the summer the State and Defense Departments were themselves like two warring powers. Relations between Acheson and Johnson had completely broken down. And despite a few forlorn attempts to build bridges, State Department officials were often forced to rely on scraps of information, sometimes even hearsay and gossip, to discern what the defense secretary was up to. Piecing this together, it soon became clear that Johnson was grasping every opportunity—in private, off-the-record comments to journalists and legislators—to shift the blame for America's poor showing in Korea, not just by badmouthing Acheson but also by depicting himself as the administration's leading hawk and a proponent of ideas that clearly bordered on preventive war. "He said there is a surprising amount of sentiment within the services and from intelligent persons outside for the U.S. to 'make' an incident in Europe and start soon with our atomic bombs," Arthur Krock, the *New York Times* columnist, noted privately after one meeting with the defense secretary. "He told us very plainly that we have plenty of bombs close at hand and there is no question that we can fly big bombers from U.S. bases and return."[66] "A lot of people now feel that war is inevitable," Johnson told an executive session of the Senate Foreign Relations Committee in the middle of August. If the country continued to move in the direction of high defense spending and a large military establishment, "there will be a lot of pressure to use our strength." In contemplating this, an aide reported back to Harriman, Johnson's inference "appeared to be that he personally believed both that war was inevitable and that, at the end of three years, we might have to engage in a preventive war."[67]

On August 25, Johnson's sentiments erupted into the open. That evening, before a massive audience at Boston Naval Yard, Francis P. Matthews, the secretary of the navy, publicly declared that America had to be prepared to pay "any price, even the price of instituting a war, to compel cooperation for peace." Although there was no direct evidence linking Johnson to this speech, word in press circles and the Washington cocktail circuit was that "Matthews' speech was, of course, inspired by Johnson."[68] This was a disturbing conclusion. Four years earlier, a very public dispute over foreign policy between two leading officials, Henry A. Wallace and James F. Byrnes, had foreshadowed a disastrous defeat for the Democrats in the 1946 midterm elections. Now, countless journalists hastened to emphasize the obvious parallel. And Taft, never one to let a good opportunity pass, charged that the administration "has so many conflicts within itself, it's like a man with no brains who is unable to develop a consistent course of action."[69]

Deeply worried by such criticisms, at the start of September Truman made a series of efforts to try to gain control over the public debate. The most prominent victim was Louis Johnson, who was not only clearly out of sympathy with the administration's whole mobilization strategy but also far too willing to share his doubts with reporters and opposition politicians.[70] Crucially, Johnson was losing friends fast on the Democratic side on Capitol Hill, especially as the media inquest into America's lack of preparedness to wage war in Korea gathered momentum. His most vocal critic was Anthony F. Tauriello, an obscure freshman congressman from Buffalo, who issued two public calls for his resignation in August.[71] But far more ominously, powerful southerners like Sam Rayburn and Lyndon B. Johnson (D-TX) were privately concerned that "public confidence" in the defense establishment "has been shaken deeply." Both now began to intimate that they would be far from upset if Johnson were to go—although they were also wary about going public with such sentiments, on the grounds that the more Johnson was attacked the more the ever-loyal president would stand by him.[72] They need not have worried, for Truman's patience had finally snapped.

The denouement to Johnson's turbulent political career came in two grueling Oval Office meetings, in which he tearfully pleaded with the president to reconsider his decision to replace him. Truman remained adamant, however, determined that he would now appoint General Marshall to this post. In practical political terms, this was probably a mistake, for it meant passing over the chance to appoint a leading Republican who could shield the cabinet against partisan attacks. Marshall had also been tarnished with the whole "loss of China" issue during his earlier stints as both mediator in the Chinese Civil War and secretary of state. And scathing Senate critics like Taft and Jenner did not miss the opportunity to paint his appointment as "a reaffirmation of the tragic policy of ... encouraging Chinese communism which brought on the Korean War."[73] Yet Truman was delighted that Marshall was back on board. He revered the saintly general. He also recognized that his new defense secretary, as well as having good relations with Acheson, had unparalleled experience in the problems of mobilization. As for the comments of Republican critics, a shocked Truman brushed them aside with the acidic observation that they had "set an all-time low for attacks in the Senate."[74]

In the first weeks of September, as Marshall prepared to take over the reins at the Pentagon, the president and his senior aides moved to clamp down hard on other officials who espoused the preventive war heresy. Matthews himself was spared after releasing a suitably contrite press statement, which stressed that his preventive war speech represented his "own personal thinking" and not that of the administration.[75] But Major-General Orvil A. Anderson, the commandant of the Air War College, was not so lucky. In a public speech, Anderson had declared that "waiting until your hit first is un-American," adding that the United States "could wipe out Russia's five A-bomb nests in a week." With Drew Pearson fueling the controversy by giving these comments a wide circulation in the media, on September 2 Anderson was immediately suspended from his post. General Hoyt S. Vandenberg, head of the air force, hastened to explain the reason. The military's primary purpose was to prevent war, Vandenberg told reporters. "The premise that war is inevitable is not only untrue but is most dangerous."[76]

Of course, firing recalcitrant officials was a decidedly heavy-handed sanction that could only be used sparingly. A far better solution was to try to prevent such insubordinate outbursts in the first place. One obvious method of achieving this would be to establish some sort of propaganda agency, which would act as a clearinghouse for administration speeches, as well as refining and developing the administration's overall PR campaign. Clear precedents existed for pursuing such a course. In World War I, Woodrow Wilson had created the Committee on Public Information, which had not only coordinated official utterances but also produced its own particular brand of rabid anti-German propaganda. In World II, Franklin Roosevelt's Office of War Information had been a less powerful and more restrained body. As such, it briefly seemed to offer a more appropriate model for the current crisis.[77]

Senior officials first started to contemplate the creation of a new Office of War Information at the start of August. They were responding partly to all the problems surrounding MacArthur's lack of formal censorship arrangements. As the mobilization debate got under way, they also recognized that even the release of relatively mundane economic figures could be problematic. Unsurprisingly, Louis Johnson was behind much of the trouble, particularly angering the National Security Resources Board with claims one day that manpower figures were top secret, only to leak them to the press the next. But even the Commerce and Labor departments were at each other's throats, publicizing their caustic spats about whether or not to urge workers to take jobs in essential war industries.[78]

On the back of such disturbing developments, key PR officials held a series of meetings to debate the desirability of creating a propaganda agency. They even consulted Elmer Davis, who had headed the Office of War Information during World War II, and his long and detailed history of his bureau was circulated inside the White House. Ultimately, however, Truman's press secretary, together with publicity chiefs of the State Department, Pentagon, and

Truman and his senior advisers after the sacking of Louis Johnson. *Left to right*: Special Assistant Averell Harriman, Defense Secretary George Marshall, President Harry Truman, Secretary of State Dean Acheson, Ambassador Philip Jessup (partly obscured), Treasury Secretary John Snyder, Army Secretary Frank Pace, and General Omar Bradley. National Park Service Photo, courtesy of Truman Library.

National Security Resources Board, all agreed that the time was not ripe for such an organization. Their reasons were manifold. Congress's traditional distrust of anything that smacked of propaganda was all too familiar, and naturally overshadowed discussions. The president was also known to favor neat and tidy chains of bureaucratic command, and normally shied away from creating new agencies to meet new problems. But there was one calculation that clearly clinched the argument. The Office of War Information (like the Committee on Public Information in World War I) had been a creature of total war. A limited conflict did not warrant its own separate propaganda agency.[79]

Instead, officials decided simply to tighten up existing procedures. An informal interagency committee, which had once operated under the auspices of the State Department, was reactivated. Meeting twice a month, it would distribute background materials, instructions, and guidance to other departments, informing them of the official line. If anyone was still in doubt as to what to say, they were instructed to approach the White House press office for clearance.[80] The president's speeches were also intended to provide a clear statement of U.S. policy, which subordinates could then try to amplify.

For this reason, the White House now took the unprecedented step of arranging two nationwide addresses in the space of just over a week.

On Friday, September 1, Truman took to the airwaves to enunciate America's eight goals in Asia. The United States, he insisted, was working hard to ensure that the fighting in Korea did not expand into a general war. His administration was also categorically opposed to any "aggressive or preventive war." Nine days later, having just signed the Defense Production Act, he then tried to clarify the administration's mobilization policy, explaining that the United States would now have to double its defense spending in future years. More sacrifices would thus be required, from working longer hours to using voluntary restraint to quell inflation without formal controls. "This defense program cannot be achieved on the basis of business as usual," he declared. "All of us—whether we are farmers, or wage earners, or businessmen—must give up some of the things we would ordinarily expect to have for ourselves and our families."[81]

Mobilizing the Wider World: The UN and Korea

One of the beneficiaries of the government's rearmament drive was Sperry Gyroscope, a manufacturer of top-secret equipment for the U.S. armed forces. In the summer of 1950, Sperry's major war plant in Lake Success, a suburb of New York City, suddenly hit the headlines twice. On the first occasion the media latched onto a three-year pact concluded between the management and unions, in which labor leaders agreed to a nonstrike pledge in return for an inflation-linked wage increase—the sort of pact that conformed perfectly with the administration's desire for voluntary sacrifice and restraint. But it was the second occasion that grabbed most attention. In recent years, Sperry had been sharing its Lake Success plant with the UN Security Council while the UN awaited completion of its new headquarters in Manhattan. Now, as America's military mobilization started to gather speed, Sperry decided that it would have to evict 750 members of the UN Secretariat, to free up space for the massive influx of new war orders. A development fraught with obvious symbolism, this eviction swiftly prompted reporters to emphasize the stark contrast between a Sperry plant "bustling with war orders" in one wing of the building, while "the UN is still striving for peace in the other quarter—659,000 square feet which it rents for $202,831 annually."[82]

From the administration's perspective, this symbolic clash was not terribly incongruous, because the UN had now become an integral part of its Cold War strategy. And officials were keen at every turn to stress that the immediate goal of their mobilization program was to fight the conflict at the behest of this international organization. For government critics, however, the fact that UN officials were being evicted from the Lake Success building so that American workers could move in to make a concrete contribution toward the containment of communism seemed all too emblematic of the more general division of labor in Korea, where Americans bore the brunt of the action and UN partners were increasingly notable by their absence.

In fact, this sense that America's UN allies were not pulling their weight had pervaded the debate in Washington since the very start of the war. By the middle of July, newspapers as diverse as the Scripps-Howard chain, the *Denver Post, New York Journal of Commerce, Kansas City Star,* and *Christian Science Monitor* had all reacted to the growing defeats by declaring that "this is a UN show and the others should be sending their soldiers and equipment to fight in the police action."[83]

Given that the cloak of legitimacy provided by the UN was at the very heart of the administration's case for war, such grumbling distinctly disturbed the State Department. In the middle of July, it therefore launched a concerted diplomatic campaign "to encourage the maximum direct participation by all members of the UN in support of the UN effort in Korea."[84] Trouble soon came from MacArthur, however, who told reporters that U.S. and South Korean forces were still bearing the sole burden of fighting the war.[85] Picking up on the general's barbed comments, Republicans in Congress also bemoaned "the fact that the American boys who are fighting and dying on the battlefields of Korea today, with their backs to the sea, do not have a single nation we have helped so much, outside of Korea, fighting alongside them."[86]

The arrival of the first contingents of British troops on August 29 helped still some of this criticism, although the PA's media surveys continued to note "disgruntlement that other nations have not cooperated more fully in the military effort in Korea."[87] By this stage, however, the public debate on the UN had shifted to the deeper problem of how the international community should be organized in this new, more dangerous phase of the Cold War.

Among many internationalists, it had long been an article of faith that the UN machinery established in 1945, with its Rooseveltian emphasis on a concert of great powers rather than a purer, Wilsonian vision of collective security, would have to be strengthened at some stage. Although numerous ideas had circulated for months, the outbreak of the Korean War gave a massive fillip to this campaign for UN reform.[88] One much-discussed notion—which garnered support from an improbable cross-section of individuals and institutions, from the *Christian Science Monitor* to the AMVETS, from Hubert Humphrey to Homer Capehart—was the creation of an international police force that would always be on hand to deal with crises like Korea. Far more popular, though, was the idea of an Atlantic Union.

On paper, it was not entirely clear how strengthening the political bonds between the United States and its NATO allies would dovetail with the UN's mandate—whether it would swiftly supersede the international organization or whether it would mark the first step toward a wider international federation. But by the summer, the concept of an ever closer Atlantic Union could, according to its champions, count on no less than half the members of the Senate and about one hundred members in the House. Ominously for the administration, many of these legislators were core supporters of its foreign policy. Equally ominously, Atlantic Union advocates were quick to tap into the general sense of unease at the subdued nature of official utterances. Indeed, as one congressional delegation informed Acheson in the middle of August, the Atlantic Union was just the sort of "bold plan...that will afford a new measure of hope to the American people."[89]

While internationalists pushed for some form of enhanced international machinery to keep the peace, old isolationists reemerged with a far simpler expedient: the eviction of the Soviet Union from the UN altogether. Back in May, former president Herbert Hoover had called for the international community to make the Soviet Union's abstention from the UN permanent. Hoover had stressed that this was the easiest way to turn the international organization into "a phalanx of free nations," but the public's reaction had been decidedly lukewarm.[90] Once again, however, Korea suddenly changed the political dynamic, especially when Jacob Malik, the Soviet ambassador to the UN, returned to Lake Success in August to take up the presidency of the Security Council.

Malik's return created such a sensation because of the way his propaganda tirades and endless obstructionist tactics were covered by a new medium. The month of August proved a boom time for television. On the August 13, in an effort to reach the 20 million or so Americans who now owned television sets, senior government officials began a series of weekly broadcasts, entitled *Battle Report, Washington.* Working closely with NBC, their goal was to use "the magic of television" to provide weekly briefings on the latest developments in Korea.[91] Yet the administration was soon playing second fiddle to Malik, whose UN speeches were given wall-to-wall coverage on television. PA even fretted that the networks were providing the UN with so much airtime that Malik was in danger of becoming a "byword" for TV itself. "Probably there has never been a single factor that has so influenced public thinking on a matter of international policy," PA recorded, "as has the television coverage of the Security Council."[92]

Of course, amid such hyperbole, it was easy to forget the Malik's activities were deeply counterproductive to the Soviet cause. Certainly, UN officials believed that the Soviet ambassador had become such a hated figure inside the United States that they deemed it prudent to increase his bodyguard contingent, lest irate New Yorkers were to vent their anger through violence. As James Reston of the *New York Times* pointed out, Malik also seemed likely to prove a boon to the administration in its efforts to generate congressional support for large defense appropriations. "If Mr. Acheson will hire two television sets," Reston quipped, "fix it with Leslie Biffle [the secretary of the Senate] to put them in the cloak rooms of the Senate and House on Capitol Hill, the U.S. rearmament will jump a billion dollars every hour the Soviet delegate is on the screen."[93]

Still, when it came to the specific matter of the future of the UN, the Soviet Union's high-profile return to the Security Council seemed only likely to redound to the credit of Herbert Hoover, for it threw into sharp relief the obvious fact that America had only been able to use the UN in Korea because Moscow had been temporarily boycotting the institution. Opinion polls certainly revealed a sharp increase in support for the Hoover plan, with 50 percent now in favor. And even on Capitol Hill, the mood seemed to be shifting. Although the Senate Foreign Relations Committee ended its hearings on UN reform in the middle of August without any specific recommendations—and certainly no endorsement for evicting the Soviets—by now Republican internationalists like Knowland and Lodge were clearly exasperated with events in the UN, comparing Malik's presidency to Al Capone heading the FBI or an arsonist being put in charge of the fire department.[94]

Inside the State Department, there was little sympathy for an Atlantic Union, which officials thought would simply scare vital allies like the British with the specter of a fundamental loss of political sovereignty. There was even less support for Hoover's plan, which officials felt would leave the UN in the same enervated condition the League of Nations had been reduced to after the Axis powers had withdrawn in the 1930s. But the State Department was worried by the direction the public debate was heading. And by late summer, it was convinced that something had to be done to counteract the growing appeal of such dangerous ideas.[95]

With so many Americans now glued to the current airing of differences between Malik and the West, in August the State Department decided to revisit the question of how to frame the Korean crisis. Although Acheson remained reluctant to unleash his subordinates in Washington, still fearful that overheated rhetoric might inflame congressional opinion and provoke Moscow, he was willing to countenance a limited change in the U.S. posture at the UN, so that the U.S. delegation could respond to Malik's tirades and fight fire with fire. In sanctioning this limited change, Acheson recognized that the U.S. ambassador at Lake Success, Warren Austin, would be a perfect advocate. Austin, after all, was a Republican, whose record as a staunch anti–New Dealer would appeal to the opposition party. In the public sessions at the UN, his steady and polite manner also marked a stark contrast to Malik's highly abrasive public persona.[96]

On August 8, Austin began his counterattack. Although stopping short of directly holding the Soviets responsible for the war, he responded to Malik's allegation that the United States was the offender in Korea by pointedly asking who had the power to call off the North Korean invasion. Two days later, Austin was even more explicit, describing North Korea as a "zombie regime" that not only was supplied by the Soviets but also had waited for a signal from Moscow before launching the invasion.[97] "The 'astuteness and skill' with which Mr. Austin has balked the Soviet maneuvers has been applauded," PA soon reported. "Many commentators greeted with relief the American delegate's speech 'pointing the finger of accusation' directly at Russia for its responsibility in the Korean aggression."[98]

In a further effort to shore up popular support for the UN, Acheson intended to use the opening of the General Assembly to deliver an address of "extraordinary importance."[99] Armed with a new initiative, arrestingly entitled "Uniting for Peace," Acheson mounted the General Assembly podium at 3:45 on September 20. In contrast to the studied caution of his June speeches, he began by ostentatiously naming names—indicting the Soviets for creating "a terrible peril for the rest of the world." But his main aim was to devise a way to stop this menace from paralyzing the UN in the years to come. To sidestep a future veto in the Security Council, Acheson proposed to give the General Assembly greater powers to meet swiftly and act when faced with a breach of the peace. In a future emergency, the General Assembly could be called on twenty-four-hour notice, and would have the

Warren Austin addressing the UN Security Council. Courtesy of National Archives.

authority both to send inspection teams to the scene and to establish a Collective Measures Committee to report on ways to maintain the peace.[100]

This initiative promised immediate benefits. In the international sphere, it would pave the way for the United States to continue to use the UN to wage its battle against communism, particularly in Korea, safe in the knowledge that it could currently garner a majority of General Assembly votes to bypass any Soviet veto in the Security Council. In the domestic sphere, the speech was designed to undermine the domestic momentum for the Hoover plan and other unsavory reform packages. It was certainly a hit. As PA recorded, editorial reaction "was widespread and impressively favorable."[101]

The only problem was that PA had itself muffed the perfect opportunity to ensure that Acheson replaced Malik as television's newest political star. Before the speech, hopes had been high after Acheson had made an impressive TV debut on September 10. As well as having the opportunity to make the administration's case directly to the public, without the distorting mediating influences of conservative commentators and Republican politicians, Acheson had clearly been at ease, oozing confidence and obviously in control of the subject matter. "The secretary emerges as the very real person that he is," PA reported, "in fuller color, before a larger number of people, than is possible in any other way."[102] It was therefore galling when the major networks only devoted five to ten minutes to the Uniting for Peace speech, especially in light of all the airtime they had devoted to Malik's endless offerings during August. "I think we should raise hell with the networks about this," one indignant PA official complained the day after the speech, "and bring home to them the fact that their cooperation on a thing of this importance is indispensable if we are going to lick Soviet propaganda."[103]

But any thought that this might be the occasion to wield threats against the new medium soon evaporated. As an internal State Department post-mortem discovered, a major part of the problem stemmed from the lack of notice PA had given the networks about the importance of the speech. At the same time, the broadcasters themselves remained unapologetic. In a revealing insight into their priorities at the new medium's inception, television executives swiftly informed the State Department that because their afternoon audience tended to be "small and unworldly," it would find such a speech hard to take.[104]

Such a remark about viewers' attitudes was hardly the most auspicious beginning for this significant new relationship. But for the moment this episode was swiftly lost amid the stunning news that U.S. forces were on the offensive in Korea, news that dispelled the gloom of recent weeks and held out the prospect that Uniting for Peace might soon have a tangible impact on Korea's future.

4

ON THE OFFENSIVE

In the first two and a half months of the war, the Truman administration had faced the unenviable task of selling a conflict that was going badly. In the middle of September, MacArthur's astonishingly successful counterattack at Inchon suddenly transformed the situation. The North Korean army, outflanked and outfought, crumbled away. The thirty-eighth parallel lay largely undefended, presenting Washington with the enticing prospect of uniting the whole peninsula. And with a stunning victory on the horizon, and a large share of the credit bound to reflect on the successful commander in chief, Democrats now looked to the upcoming midterm elections with an unfamiliar sense of optimism.

Yet Inchon soon generated its fair share of problems. In the Far East, PI officers continued to berate reporters for security violations. In Washington, Pentagon officials began to worry that their mobilization program would suffer, since if past experience was a guide, public opinion tended to lapse into complacency as soon as a crisis had passed. Even in October, Truman and the Democrats would find it surprisingly difficult to make political capital out of victory in Korea. The following month, the Democratic campaign would suffer greatly from the news that China had entered the war—a turn of events that was largely due to the most troublesome consequence of victory: what were America's objectives in this limited war?

"Operation Common Knowledge"

Inchon did surprisingly little to quell the tense atmosphere that persisted between MacArthur's command and most American war correspondents. On the contrary, security was now an even more acute irritant. In the weeks leading up to the assault, so many rumors about an impending offensive had circulated around the Tokyo Press Club that reporters had begun to dub it "Operation Common Knowledge." While this confirmed the Pentagon's worst fears about the dangerous consequences of MacArthur's lax censorship policies, journalists were hardly appeased by the fact that, despite knowing of an attack, they were not consulted in advance about coverage requirements. "The Inchon operation may go down as one of the worst handled in history from the viewpoint of the press," CBS's Robert Martin complained. "Correspondents were given no choice of the units they would accompany." "The result," as Marguerite Higgins lamented, "was that magazine writers and columnists rode on the first wave of assaults and many first-rate daily newsmen with urgent deadlines arrived about three days late."[1]

Nor were American journalists impressed by the way Inchon was first revealed to the world. At Pusan, Bill Shinn, a young Korean-born, American-educated AP reporter, spent the morning of the attack gathering information from his sources in the South Korean military. By lunchtime, he had hard evidence that the offensive had succeeded. Determined to have this major scoop confirmed by a high-ranking officer, Shinn approached the South Korean army chief of staff, Chung Il Kwon, asking if he could name the general as his main source. The minute Chung agreed, Shinn relayed his story to Tokyo. It hit the wires at 2:05, creating an immediate sensation.

Indeed, MacArthur's headquarters instantly tried to have the story killed, insisting it was premature. But the AP stubbornly refused to back away, pointing out that Tokyo had not denied the accuracy of the report. To the consternation of the other wire services, who had lost the biggest scoop of the war so far, the army's official announcement trailed in nine hours after Shinn's dispatch. To the dismay of the AP, the next day MacArthur's PIO denied Shinn the use of the military telephone from Korea to Tokyo, ruling that he was not an accredited reporter, even though he had enjoyed the same privileges as other correspondents until now. At their annual meeting, AP members in the United States shot back an immediate protest, which highlighted how deep feelings now ran. The military's treatment of Shinn, insisted William P. Stevens, executive editor of *Minneapolis Star and Tribune* and assistant director of the press division of the Office of Censorship back in World War II,

> appears to be an act of military caprice, not an act prompted by the needs of security....The present "write-what-you-want-and-we'll-shoot-you-if-we-don't-like it" Korean policy is an insidious, vicious, and unfair form of censorship, inconsistent with the rights of free men, the principles of the UN, and the requirements of the U.S. Constitution.[2]

The one saving grace was that at least the media now had a series of impressive victories to cover, from the breakout at Pusan to the recapture of Seoul, all of which created a mounting sense that the war would soon be won. Yet victory also created another set of home-front problems. As the State Department's PA soon recorded, the staggering change of fortunes naturally served "to widen and intensify the [media] demand that the UN must formulate a 'plan' for postwar Korea—that it must make decisions concerning the crossing of the thirty-eighth parallel, the occupation of North Korea, and the future government of the war-torn land."[3] In a CBS radio broadcast, Eric Sevareid pithily summed up the prevailing new mood when he told listeners that victory had now brought about "a happy kind of crisis": how to bring the "police action" to a successful conclusion.[4]

Crossing the Thirty-Eighth Parallel

Because Korea was a limited "police action," the answer to this question seemed self-evident: the United States and UN would stop at the thirty-eighth parallel. Such a prudent policy had obvious advantages. It would be perfectly in line with the UN mandate for intervention.[5] It would go down well with allies, who were both leery of the risks of rollback and recoiled at the thought of Rhee's brutal regime dominating the whole peninsula.[6] And, crucially, it would conform to Truman's basic strategy of doing nothing to provoke Stalin into a full-blown clash with the West. As Acheson explained to a secret session of the Senate Foreign Relations Committee in early September,

> North Korea and perhaps all of Korea is a matter of considerable importance to the Russians. They have fought two wars over it.... They surely would be extremely sensitive to Western troops fooling around in North Korea. It would be highly desirable not to have this happen.... The very great object of policy is not to do anything which will unnecessarily bring the Russians into it.... The same thing is true with the Chinese. You don't want to get them into it.[7]

Yet within weeks of making this statement, Acheson and his associates would give a green light that enabled UN forces to go "fooling around in North Korea." It was a fateful decision, for it not only dragged China into the war but greatly complicated the task of sustaining domestic support for the conflict in the years to come.

At the time, however, the administration's calculations were straightforward enough. Even in the early days of the war, when the military situation was bleak and the possibility of Soviet or Chinese intervention was a nagging concern, many officials were enticed by the prospect of unification. In crossing the thirty-eighth parallel, the United States would not only fulfill its UN obligations and eliminate the North Korean threat; it would also cement its relations with the South Korean ally and demonstrate to the world that aggression did not pay. At the same time, a major success in the Cold War would have the added benefit of halting the "dangerous strategic trend in the Far East" against the United States, which had been steadily gathering momentum since the communists' advent to power in China. Closer to home, more politically inclined officials also relished the promise of partisan advantage. At a time when Republicans were accusing the administration of softness on all manner of questions—from mobilization to internal subversion—a clear-cut outcome in Korea would undoubtedly give the Democratic Party a much-needed boost.[8]

With all these pressures pointing toward rollback, senior officials soon began to lay the political groundwork. During August and September, to be sure, Truman and Acheson refused to be drawn out in public on the specific matter of whether or not U.S. troops would be allowed to cross the thirty-eighth parallel. It was simply too early to tell, Truman told reporters whenever he was asked. "The business of the thirty-eighth parallel and what we do there," Acheson told four leading journalists in one background briefing, "probably depends on how we get there."[9] But even with UN forces still on the defensive, the administration began to put out a number of public signals that suggested its ultimate goal might be more than simply restoring the prewar status quo.

Austin led the way at the UN. "Shall only a part of the country [Korea] be assured freedom?" the ambassador asked both his fellow diplomats and a large television audience on August 17. "I think not. . . . Korea's prospects would be dark if any action of the UN were to condemn it to exist indefinitely as 'half slave and half free,' or even one-third slave and two-thirds free." As sources in the U.S. delegation hastened to tell reporters, Austin's speech did not represent a fundamental change in policy, for the simple reason that the United States still hoped to achieve this unity through negotiation and political means.[10] But this disclaimer only partly served to distract attention from the fact that officials were now talking about the paramount importance of Korean unity. As the president declared on September 1, in his major speech on Asian policy, "We believe the Koreans have a right to be free, independent, and united—as they want to be. Under the direction of the UN, we, with others, will do our part to help them enjoy that right."[11]

Of course, such pronouncements did not mean that the United States had definitely decided to fight for Korean unity. During August and early September, officials continued to stress to reporters the distinction between the long-term political aspiration of unity and the short-term aims of the current military campaign. Meanwhile, in private policy debates even the government's hawks recognized that a move into North Korea carried the risk of a direct confrontation with Soviet or Chinese forces. And with U.S. mobilization still in its infancy, everyone agreed that this dangerous prospect had to be avoided at all costs.[12]

But as the fighting unfolded in Korea without any overt action from Moscow or Beijing, officials increasingly concluded that the Soviets and Chinese had missed the boat. According to their private analysis, Stalin and Mao Zedong would be most likely to send their troops into Korea well *before* UN forces ever reached the thirty-eighth parallel, since this would give the communists the best chance to protect their North Korean ally without risking a more general conflagration with the United States. Nevertheless, the administration's growing confidence remained tempered by the fear that pushing into North Korea would be risky. Even NSC-81, the formal policy statement the president approved on September 11, which strongly supported the "complete independence and unity of Korea," only advocated this course in the "unlikely" event that Moscow and Beijing had decided to adopt a "hands-off policy" on the peninsula. Only then would UN forces be authorized to push into North Korea.[13]

Four days later, the stunning military success at Inchon clinched the argument. With North Korean forces in full retreat, crossing the thirty-eighth parallel now entailed little risk of costly battles. It also promised the chance both to mop up the remnants of continued North Korean resistance and to eradicate this menace once and for all. With the Soviets and the Chinese having failed to intervene, the odds even seemed good that going north would not trigger a wider war—although to make doubly sure, Washington was keen to instruct MacArthur to use only Korean forces on the borders of China and the Soviet Union. In a further effort to deter the Soviets and Chinese, the State Department also deemed it prudent to obtain a new resolution from the UN, which the British introduced on September 29. Passing the General Assembly on October 7 by forty-seven to five, this resolution authorized "all steps to be taken to ensure conditions of stability throughout Korea." In the debate, both U.S. and British spokespersons had stressed that UN troops would *not* carry the fight into Chinese or Soviet territory, as well as emphasizing that the UN occupation would be brief.[14]

Yet such efforts at deterrence would ultimately fail. In October, Mao Zedong, driven by a determination to protect his fledgling revolution from the aggressive Americans, as well as a desire to promote the Chinese communist cause throughout Asia, decided to intervene in the war. Although this decision was not finally ratified until the middle of the month, mainly because it took time for Mao to obtain sufficient support both from his bureaucracy and the Soviet ally, on October 2–3 Zhou Enlai, China's foreign minister, met with the Indian ambassador in Beijing, K. M. Panikkar, and issued a portentous warning. China, Zhou declared, would enter the war if U.S. troops crossed the thirty-eighth parallel.[15]

Fatefully, Washington chose to ignore this warning. This was partly because officials did not trust a message routed through Pannikar, whom they considered pro-Chinese and something of a loose cannon. Coming at the height of the UN debate over a new resolution, the administration also perceived Zhou's message as little more than a diplomatic gambit that aimed to drive a wedge in the Western bloc. But above all, the Americans simply failed to take the Chinese seriously as a potential adversary. It would be "sheer madness" for China to get involved, Acheson confidently believed, especially at a time when Mao needed to prioritize economic reconstruction and political consolidation in the aftermath of a grueling civil war.[16]

While all these considerations encouraged officials to ignore China's warning, other pressures prodded the Truman administration forward. Not least was the domestic environment. Indeed, if going north promised political gains at a time when Republicans were accusing Truman and the Democrats of excessive softness toward Asian communism, then a presidential order halting the advance into North Korea pointed toward political catastrophe. Official statements had, after all, created the impression that Korean unity was in the offing. Crucially, just days before Zhou's missive, Washington had also given MacArthur his marching orders to cross the thirty-eighth parallel.

Senior members of the Truman administration were perfectly aware of MacArthur's views on war aims. The victor of Inchon was determined to destroy North Korean forces as a precursor to "composing and uniting" the peninsula.[17] When thwarted, MacArthur's favorite mode of operation was also ominously familiar. Only recently, he had issued a public critique of the administration's Formosa policy, complete with jibes at those who advocated appeasement and defeatism in Asia. Although Truman had immediately ordered MacArthur to withdraw this statement, the Formosa episode offered a clear warning: MacArthur, if restrained now, would undoubtedly take his case to the public, buttressed by highly vocal support from the Republican right and the China lobby.[18]

And the public would certainly listen. On October 3, the day Washington received Zhou's message, a PA media survey recorded that "strong demands for a General Assembly decision to cross the thirty-eighth parallel persist from all parts of the country." Soon after, Gallup published the first poll on the subject, which further underlined the drift of popular sentiment. According to Gallup, only 27 percent wanted the fighting to stop at the thirty-eighth parallel, while 64 percent advocated pushing into North Korea.[19]

By the start of October, so much momentum had built up behind the decision to push into North Korea that it was all but impossible for officials to contemplate staying put at the thirty-eighth parallel. The political costs were just far too great. And with leading officials frankly dismissive of the prospect of Chinese involvement, the possible pitfalls were also discounted. "A greater risk would be incurred by showing hesitation and timidity," Acheson remarked privately on October 4; "the only proper course to take was a firm and courageous one and . . . we should not be unduly frightened at what was probably a Chinese communist bluff."[20]

Initially, this determination and confidence seemed to pay off. On September 30, units of the South Korean Third Division crossed the parallel, followed a week later by the first U.S. troops. Meeting relatively light resistance from the demoralized North Koreans, on October 19 UN forces captured Pyongyang—a city that would soon earn the distinction of being the only liberated communist capital to host a production of the *Bob Hope Show*. Five days later, MacArthur discarded the restrictions on U.S. forces marching to the Yalu River, pressing his officers "to drive forward with all speed and full utilization of their forces." And, in public at least, senior Washington officials were equally sanguine. In the final phase of the war, Truman declared on October 10, the UNC and the new UN Commission on Korea would work together to establish "a unified, independent, and democratic Korea." As well as a clear-cut victory, such an outcome would have far wider ramifications. "The successful accomplishment of this peaceful mission of reconstruction," the president triumphantly insisted, "can serve as a pattern for other efforts to improve the lot of people all over the world."[21] With a midterm election looming, it was heady stuff.

Preventing a Letdown

Yet for officials charged with implementing the NSC-68 mobilization program, this optimistic talk about victory contained a decidedly troubling aspect. The basic problem, they believed, stemmed from the inherent instability of the domestic mood, which was too prone to panic during the periods of crisis and defeat, but tended to become mired in complacency the minute victory had been achieved. This, at least, appeared to be the lesson taught by the American experience in both world wars, when the public had initially been reluctant to get involved in the fighting but, once roused, had been determined to crush the enemy, only to descend swiftly back into its old lethargy as soon as the fighting was over. It was also the common conclusion of a recent spate of highly influential social science literature, as academics like Thomas A. Bailey, Martin Kriesberg, and Gabriel A. Almond exploited the growing volume of polling data to try to ascertain the basic nature of American opinion. By 1950, PA officials had fully digested these studies' central conclusion, and it gave intellectual credence to the notion that the popular mood was highly unstable, often characterized by "sudden shifts of interest or preference." As Almond succinctly put it, "the superficiality and instability of public attitudes toward foreign affairs creates the danger of under- and overreaction to changes in the world political situation."[22]

Actually, in the aftermath of Inchon, there was little evidence to suggest that the American mood was about to enter a dangerous downswing. According to a Roper poll published in the middle of October, two out of three

Americans still supported helping other countries in the event of a communist attack, while Gallup found that there remained a "great public willingness to support higher taxes and domestic controls."[23] Yet the accumulated wisdom of past precedent and recent social science research completely overshadowed these current data. Inside the Policy Planning Staff, planners were certainly fretful that Inchon would "lead to a let down in public support [for] our preparedness and collective security programs." Inside PA, officials were thus instructed to keep a "close watch for any significant signs of relaxation."[24] But perhaps the biggest worrier along these lines was the new secretary of defense, whose World War II experience had convinced him of the dangers of "pendulum" thinking and the public's basic "emotional instability." As Marshall pithily put it, "Whenever you win a victory overseas, you get in trouble back here."[25]

For Marshall, like other officials who thought in this vein, public opinion was a somewhat abstract concept. Rather than the specific statements of reporters, editors, columnists, and politicians, or even the concrete surveys of mass opinion undertaken by the pollsters, it was the vague mood of the nation. Although this mood had little influence on the specifics of the policy agenda, it was vitally important in determining the overall fate of national security strategy, because when on a down cycle, it could lead to a widespread slackening off, a mounting opposition to higher taxes, and a general shying away from work in the armed forces or defense industries.[26]

How could the administration head this off? According to some later commentators, Marshall's response was straightforward enough: his fears about the likely ramifications of a "letdown" after Inchon simply "encouraged" him and others to engage in a series of risky policies, from crossing the thirty-eighth parallel to ignoring warnings about a possible Chinese intervention, in the hope that a prolonged war might save the rearmament program.[27] The main evidence for this contention comes from the recollections of Frank Pace, the army secretary, almost twenty-two years after the event. Recalling a discussion with Marshall over MacArthur's promise to have the troops home from Korea "by Christmas," Pace stated that Marshall had found this prospect "troublesome," for the simple reason that "too precipitate an end to the war would not permit us to have a full understanding of the problems that we face ahead of us." When Pace balked at this type of thinking, Marshall shot back: "but you didn't live through the end of World War II the way I did, and watch people rush back to their civilian jobs and leave the tanks to rot in the Pacific and the military strength that was built up fade away."[28]

Such a statement clearly confirms the importance of lessons from the past in explaining why Marshall believed that the public was prone to violent mood swings. But does it necessarily mean that Marshall, along with other senior officials, was reckless, even willful, in his misjudgment of Soviet and Chinese intentions, "continuing the march to the Yalu River in spite of clear indications that the Chinese were planning to intervene"?[29] The simple answer is no. In Marshall's opinion, domestic support for NSC-68 would have to be sustained over the long haul. Quite apart from the obvious fact that it is extremely doubtful that officials would contemplate dragging the Korean conflict out for a long period of time just for domestic mobilization purposes, Marshall's mind was clearly moving in a number of other directions.

The most obvious way to protect against a letdown was to scale down the size of the buildup, so that it was "predicated not on anxieties of the moment but on a long-term politically and economically feasible basis, one that Congress and the public would continue to support." Given the current fears of a "letdown," the Pentagon swiftly decided to reduce the total five-year estimate from $260 billion to $190.6 billion, while also cutting $9 billion off another supplemental appropriations package planned for the current fiscal year.[30]

At the same time, officials adopted a new public posture. Over the coming months, they would finally begin detailed planning for a sustained and intensive information campaign to sell NSC-68, with the timetable governed by the prospect not only that the Korean crisis would soon be over but also that the Eighty-Second Congress would assemble for the first time early in the new year. More immediately, they would move to abandon the soothing tones and low-key actions of July and August, which had been so essential to protect against hysteria, replacing them with a series of calls for vigilance, which would hopefully protect against any creeping signs of complacency and apathy now that the Korean conflict seemed to be won.

On September 24, Commerce Secretary Charles Sawyer delivered the opening blast, stressing that home-front mobilization must continue even after victory in Korea. It would be "extremely naïve, even stupid," he warned, "to assume that, if this episode is closed in our favor, we can forget the whole thing." With Marshall now at the helm, the military establishment was keen to amplify this message. "We face a grueling period of hard work, self-denial, and danger," the new secretary of defense declared on September 27. "I ask you to bear in mind that if the fighting in Korea should cease tomorrow, our increased responsibility would still be with us." "The greatest danger," Bradley stressed the same day, was that once the fighting was over, "this nation will let down its guard."[31] At the start of October, after Truman endorsed Bradley's comments in a press conference, at least one close observer believed that "these warnings are not independent, but are part of a consolidated White House plan." For the first time, officials were certainly determined to reveal more of the conclusions contained in NSC-68. As Marshall now told members of the Business Advisory Council, the country had to prepare for a massive production program that would last at least four years.[32]

That Marshall was now taking the government's case to organizations like the Business Advisory Council was symbolic of another of the government's

PR responses to the problem of letdown. Until now, the bulk of official publicity efforts had been traditional in scope—speechmaking, press conferences, private briefing sessions with reporters. But from September, the administration moved more aggressively to disseminate its message in other arenas. In the White House, aides sought to exploit existing connections with the Advertising Council, which—despite its opposition to much of Truman's domestic Fair Deal legislation—had long been an enthusiastic supporter of the administration's foreign policy. Before long, the council had agreed to set aside September and October for intensive drives to drum up enthusiasm for UN Day and the Crusade for Freedom. It also used a "generous part" of its $80 million annual budget to produce spot announcements calling for more volunteers for the armed services and bond saving by the public.[33]

Inside the Pentagon, meanwhile, officials now set up meetings with organizations like National Business Publications in order to explore ways in which business magazines could help to disseminate the official line on manpower needs.[34] Before Korea, the Pentagon had begun to work with ABC to produce a radio series, *Time for Defense*, which was designed "to let the people—high and low, who are making Defense news—speak for themselves." In the first months of the war, this show had been "devoted almost entirely to eye-witness recordings from the battle area by our defense reporters." But it now started to shift gears, with "a new series of interviews with our top officials and [ABC] commentators, plus leading newspapermen," all designed to keep "the public fully informed as we enter a new phase of the 'Cold War.'"[35] Complementing these broadcasts, the army undertook an informal effort to get the motion picture industry to produce films intended to "create an awareness in the American people of the present dangers facing this country." An officer from its psychological warfare division was even put to work developing brief outlines for between ten and twelve films, "which, if produced by [the] industry, would achieve a marked impact on the American public."[36]

Inside the Pentagon, the new team being assembled by Marshall was also well placed to reach out to those at the core of the nongovernmental national security establishment—university presidents like James B. Conant of Harvard, Harold Stassen of the University of Pennsylvania, and Dwight D. Eisenhower of Columbia University; or past office-holders like William Clayton, Robert P. Patterson, and Tracy S. Voorhees. While most of these individuals had been exasperated, even alienated, by the cost-cutting emphasis of Louis Johnson's tenure, they held Marshall in high esteem. Many had also developed a close relationship with Marshall's new deputy, Robert A. Lovett. Formerly Harriman's banking partner and an assistant secretary of war during World War II, Lovett has been aptly described as a "classic insider's man," the sort of person who was "regarded by those within the Wall Street and Washington Establishment as a touchstone of things safe and sound." In the last war, part of his job had been to function as "the reliable focal point for a group of bankers, lawyers, journalists, and public officials who viewed themselves as the backbone of a nonpartisan foreign policy elite."[37] He would now perform a similar function in the new conflict.

At the end of September, the current members of this elite started to meet, organize, and plot. Some attended a conference at the Waldorf-Astoria Hotel in New York City, where Conant and Eisenhower held sway, calling for an armed force of three million to be generated by the institution of "universal military service and training" (UMST) male adults. Soon afterward, another group led by Voorhees, and backed by Conant, Clayton, Patterson, and others, met with Lovett to discuss how they could best help the mobilization drive. Buoyed by Lovett's positive response, they began to talk openly about forming a new elite pressure group.[38] Dubbed the Committee on the Present Danger (CPD), it promised to be of immense help in 1951, when substantive items of legislation would have to be shepherded through Congress.[39]

In the meantime, on October 24, as their first initiative, the CPD sent a letter to Marshall. "We feel that bringing about in fact the 'all-out effort' of which the president speaks will become far more difficult with the ending of the Korean War," they stressed. "We believe that even yet the gravity of the civilized world's peril is not adequately understood, and that it will not be easy to obtain action to take and carry out the hard decisions necessary." This new group was therefore prepared to undertake a big effort to help sell key initiatives, such as sending more troops to Europe or introducing UMST. But they were also keen to emphasize that their goal was deterrence, not war. Indeed, in a thinly veiled attack of the approach adopted by the recently departed Louis Johnson, their letter ended by pointing out that new efforts to mobilize the military were "necessary not because of a fatalistic acceptance of the inevitability of war, but because they together constitute the best and perhaps the only means of keeping the peace."[40]

Exploiting the Policy Agenda

In one area of the administration, however, the ghost of Louis Johnson lingered. This was the Navy Department, where Francis Matthews clung to his job in spite of his preventive war speech, partly because of his prompt apology for uttering this heresy but mainly because he was highly active in Catholic circles and thus carried clout inside the Democratic Party.[41] Still, Matthews retained his unfortunate ability to say the wrong thing in public. On September 20, this trait again became clear when he attended a large lunch with his fraternity friends at Hogate's Waterfront Sea Food restaurant. Midway through a convivial afternoon, Matthews was suddenly called to the phone by the manager. On the other end of the line, an aide told him that an unconfirmed UP dispatch had just come over the ticker, quoting a U.S. army spokesman as saying that the North Koreans had asked for a twenty-four-hour cessation of hostilities to discuss an armistice. Throwing caution to the wind, Matthews immediately shared this news with his fellow diners, who duly responded with a large roar. Unfortunately, the press swiftly picked up on the fact that a leading official was declaring an end to the war. By 4:00, the story was all over the capital; by 6:00, the Pentagon press office was stressing that Matthews was mistaken, while the White House hastened to deny reports that he had been forced to resign.[42]

For Matthews, this brief episode was yet another personal embarrassment. But at a deeper level, by highlighting a pervasive confidence that the war would soon be over, it not only undercut the government's new emphasis on the need for vigilance but also underlined the need to sustain public interest in the broader Cold War struggle, lest the actual end to the Korean War result in an actual return to the Johnson-inspired economies in the military budget. Luckily for leading officials, they had more to rely on than just rhetoric, or even a growing network of support from leading nongovernmental individuals and institutions. They also had a very crowded policy agenda, which they now hoped to exploit in order to sustain public interest in Cold War mobilization.

One important new development was the emergence of a civil defense plan in case of an all-out war with the Soviets. In September, the National Security Resources Board published its 162-page Blue Book on civil defense, which its head, Stuart Symington, hoped "will hit the American people with tremendous impact."[43] In crafting a message for this book, officials had been determined, first and foremost, to counteract the possibility that a "nuclear terror" would grip the country. This was vital, because a public that was hysterical about nuclear weapons might soon become a public that would prefer to capitulate—or retreat into isolation—rather than face the prospect of a nuclear holocaust. Attempting to reassure the public, in order to stiffen its determination to sustain a policy of deterrence, was therefore at the very heart of the government's civil defense campaign.[44]

But there was another dimension to it. Officials were also intent "on hammering home the idea that an impending attack was imminent." As one authority has put it, the whole idea was "to produce a manageable level of fear that could then be channeled into civil defense operations and training, thus preempting panic." "The civil defense program for this country," the Blue Book stressed, "must be in constant readiness because for the first time in 136 years an enemy has the power to attack our cities in strong force, and ... that attack my come suddenly, with little or no warning."[45]

In driving home the twin themes of the possibilities of attack and the probability of survival, the administration was not always sure-footed. Most conspicuously, Truman was unable to get congressional support for a proposal to move key parts of government departments to a series of new towns outside Washington. The president had hoped that this dispersal plan would make the capital a "less attractive target" for Soviet A-bombs, while also ensuring that any attack would not be able to shut down the government. But on Capitol Hill, there was a good deal of muttering about wasting money to "save the hides of bureaucrats," while some opponents charged that the "whole thing seems to have been born in hysteria."[46]

A similar skepticism greeted another administration initiative. Between September 25 and 29, almost two thousand representatives from twenty states and 150 cities, towns, and counties assembled in Chicago for a massive civil defense exercise. Its ostensible aim was to demonstrate the great strides that had been made toward protecting the public. But many outside observers were highly dubious about its actual impact. According to one acerbic witness, officials "struggled against heavy odds to prevent the exercise becoming a Democratic Party convention," while "some of the local politicians viewed the civil defense jobs as a means of settling a large proportion of the demands for patronage." Still, the Chicago exercise was not entirely without value. At the very least, like the Blue Book, it served to dramatize the continuation of the broader Cold War threat, despite the optimistic news from Korea.[47]

For a time, senior officials were hopeful that progress toward a west European defense force would have a similar impact. The omens appeared particularly good during September. At the start of the month, Acheson and Johnson reached a rare meeting of minds when they agreed to recommend sending additional U.S. forces to Europe, together with the early creation of an integrated European army containing German troops. At the end of the month, after leading officials of the NATO countries met in New York, senior officials were optimistic that they would soon be able to publicize a major breakthrough in providing the NATO alliance with a coherent command structure and a large infusion of new troops.

True, the attitude of the French was likely to remain a major sticking point, particularly given that the administration remained wedded to a "package plan" that linked the sending of U.S. troops to the issue of German rearmament. For the Americans, a German contribution was vital if NATO was to become a viable defense organization. For the French, however, the whole question of German rearmament raised obvious and deep-seated security fears. It also threatened to undermine their claim to the leadership of western Europe, both by strengthening German ties to the United States and Britain and by weakening the regional structures they were hoping to construct to circumscribe German independence. Yet in the New York talks, the French had demonstrated signs of flexibility in their position. The French Foreign Office was certainly keen to compromise, fearing that outright opposition to German rearmament would result in diplomatic isolation, at best, and at worst a complete loss of influence over the whole process.[48]

After the September meetings, Acheson thought Robert Schuman, the French foreign minister, was "like an active trout which has been well hooked and which puts up a terrific battle."[49] Along with Marshall, he thought the reeling-in process would be tough, but he had high hopes that his prey would be landed during the upcoming meeting of defense ministers in Washington, which had been pushed back to October 28 to give the French more time to work out their position. Anticipating a big PR success, officials even began publicly mooting that a new supreme commander would be appointed at this meeting. When Eisenhower was then brought to Washington in a military plane on October 27, helpfully telling reporters that it was his "duty as a soldier" to accept whatever command was offered him, the press was clearly primed to expect a major achievement.

By engineering these expectations, officials intended to place added pressure on the French to concede ground on German rearmament. If such pressure ended in a constructive conference, they also hoped to silence growing opposition from the Republican right, which was skeptical of the extent and expense of the U.S. military presence in western Europe.[50] More generally, with officials convinced that the public was prone to a letdown, they thought a "dramatic" achievement was vital to sustain domestic support for a vigorous Cold War posture. As one Pentagon official put it, if Eisenhower took the job, this "would have a great psychological value everywhere, particularly in the United States, where Eisenhower back in Europe lends a real feeling of urgency to the international situation."[51]

As the conference approached, however, Marshall and Acheson began to realize that these preliminary public moves were likely to backfire. At the root of the problem was continued French intransigence on the question of German rearmament, which the September New York meetings had obscured rather than overcome. Nor did it help that the U.S. negotiating position was rigidly tied to a simple quid pro quo: America would only move forward with a command structure and additional troops if the French agreed to German participation. After four days of fruitless talks, the Washington conference was adjourned. In public, Marshall tried to put the best possible gloss on the situation, stressing to reporters that the whole German problem was being referred to NATO's Council of Deputies, where, it was hoped, it could be resolved "within a matter of weeks." But having raised press expectations, the administration could hardly avoid the widespread media verdict that the meetings were "a complete flop." Off the record, angry Pentagon officials were also keen to fan the flames, revealing that Marshall had closed the whole conference "abruptly."[52] With polling day looming, such stories were about the last thing the administration needed, especially given the Republican accusations that officials had excessively prioritized the European theater while neglecting Asia.

Korea and the 1950 Midterm
Elections

Although the temporary collapse of the NATO talks was a blow, at first glance most developments during September and October appeared likely to give the Democrats' unfolding campaign strategy a much-needed boost. Inchon and the crossing of the thirty-eighth parallel certainly seemed set to silence the GOP effort—unveiled by Guy Gabrielson, chair of the Republican National Committee, at the start of September—to make the "blundering" in Korea the focus of the election. In fact, along with the official calls for continued vigilance and preparedness, the Korean victories promised to give the Democrats a perfect opportunity to stress their Cold War achievements.

At a relaxed and jaunty cabinet meeting on September 29, top decision-makers discussed their strategy. Filled with good intentions, they agreed to eschew personal attacks on leading Republicans, and focus instead on the administration's successful record in fighting communism in Greece, Iran, Turkey, and western Europe. By polling day, it was hoped, Korea could emphatically be added to this list. As Acheson announced, a successful war followed by an intensive reconstruction effort could be "used as a stage to prove what western democracy can do to help the underprivileged countries of the world."[53]

It soon became clear, however, that the administration would find it difficult to capitalize on the Korean victory. Part of the problem was the aggressive nature of the Republican opposition. Although historians have naturally focused most attention on this aspect of the GOP campaign, which was to reach its shrill apogee in McCarthy's controversial efforts in Maryland, it is important to remember that not all Republicans up for election were firebrand critics of Truman's foreign policy. In the aftermath of the primary campaigns of the spring and summer, it even seemed possible that the GOP as a whole was shifting toward the bipartisan center. In California, New York, and New Jersey, internationalist Republican governors like Dewey, Warren, and Alfred E. Driscoll all won renomination handily. At the same time, leading nationalists, such as Taft in Ohio, Millikin in Colorado, and Forrest C. Donnell in Missouri, all faced tough campaigns for reelection. Small wonder that seasoned observers believed that the dominant trend appeared to be toward "moderate liberals rather than extreme left or right."[54]

Yet such portents hardly served to silence conservative Republicans. On the contrary, before Inchon, what had captured the most headlines were the vehement assaults that still emanated from this quarter—the allegation that Acheson had effectively given the communists the "green light" to invade South Korea, and the constant claim that South Korea had received only $200 of the $10 million Congress had appropriated to it before the war.[55]

In August, Wherry charged that Acheson was directly responsible for the war. "The blood of our boys in Korea," he shouted on the Senate floor, "is on his shoulders, and no one else"—a statement Truman immediately labeled "contemptible."[56] Even more reckless was Joe McCarthy, who campaigned vociferously in Maryland against Tydings, his nemesis of the summer, accusing Tydings of "protecting communists for political reasons."[57]

Conservative Republican leaders tolerated such antics out of a genuine conviction that Truman and Acheson had pursued a dangerously soft policy toward communism in Asia, not to mention their firmly held view that

Republican Party campaign poster, 1950. Courtesy of Eisenhower Library.

bipartisanship had been responsible for the electoral defeat of 1948. The administration's own low-key rhetoric of July and August also gave Republicans the opportunity to launch such vigorous assaults (see chapter 3). But these were not their only calculations. As the aftermath of Inchon made clear, sheer political opportunism also drove GOP behavior.

Before the UN offensive, Republican strategists had recognized that any improvement in the Korean battlefield situation "would take some of the steam out of the [Korean] issue." It would also effectively outflank their calls for bolder Cold War policies.[58] Having planned for this eventuality, in the weeks after Inchon, the GOP was fully prepared to switch gears. On the campaign trail, Republicans swiftly discarded the more militant Cold War language that had been at the heart of their rhetoric during the retreats and defeats of July and August. Instead, they focused more broadly on the government's "incompetence," which, they claimed, had been manifested in both its inability to "provide an adequate national defense"—of which the sacking of Louis Johnson had been an admission—and its failure to avoid twenty thousand casualties in Korea.[59] Republicans also placed the administration's recent efforts to prevent a "let down" in the firing line. The government's recent calls for vigilance, they claimed, were ample evidence that it was relying on "the bastard art of manipulating opinion by sloganeering and shock."[60]

This effort to shift the nature of the debate was given wide circulation because of big improvements the Republican Party had made to its basic machinery in recent years. Nationally, the Republican National Committee was able to raise more money in the first seven months of 1950 than it had done in the past two election years, although it still lacked the funds to give more than $1,000–$1,200 to each congressional district.[61] More important, the different branches of the party were much more tightly organized and now worked fairly harmoniously with one another. Under Gabrielson's energetic leadership, the committee also tried hard to adopt a middle position that would alienate neither of the party's flanks. Meanwhile, the congressional and senatorial committees headed by Leonard Hall and Owen Brewster, respectively, helped individual legislators who were up for election by furnishing radio slots, suggesting advertisements, and writing short speeches, often pursuing the more aggressive emphasis the conservative wing of the GOP favored. As the campaign went into high gear, the congressional committee even pioneered the new technique of "visual aid presentations," which enabled Republican speakers to accompany their attacks with a short film, *Korea—the Price of Appeasement.*[62]

In stark contrast, the Democratic Party, which had been so effective in helping Truman to his surprising win in 1948, had fallen into disrepair. The publicity arm of the DNC was still in operation but, as one critic pointed out, was now mostly ineffective and reactive, "repeating hackneyed Roosevelt-era portrayals of the Republicans as isolationist pawns of big business." Just as damaging, the DNC Research Division had been disbanded, despite having provided vital information to respond to Republican attacks in the 1948 campaign, and despite constant lobbying by senior White House figures for its revival.[63]

With the DNC at a disadvantage, more responsibility devolved on Kenneth W. Hechler, the White House aide who generally served as "a lightening fast researcher, fact-finder, and compiler of background information, particularly in the field of political research."[64] Throughout the summer, he worked hard to provide material on the administration's policy positions for about 80 percent of the Democratic candidates standing for election. In dispensing editorial advice, Hechler frequently called for "more hoop-la," particularly after the Inchon counterattack gave Democrats the perfect opportunity to take the offensive. But for the most part, all his prodigious activity never strayed beyond providing "simple language on the background on Korea, the reasons for setting the thirty-eighth parallel boundary, reasons for withdrawal of American troops, and answers to common charges and misconceptions about the Korean situation." In fact, most of it was dryly factual in tone, particularly the number-crunching responses that Democratic candidates were instructed to give whenever Republicans claimed that the administration had effectively abandoned South Korea to the communists.[65]

That much of this White House output had a distinctly defensive feel naturally worried senior officials. Convinced that the Republican opposition was successfully dominating the basic narrative of the campaign, they decided to take the fight to the GOP in a few key battleground states, such as Ohio, Indiana, and Missouri, where Taft, Capehart, and Donnell all appeared vulnerable. Here, the administration hoped to capitalize on a bout of intense activity by labor unions, especially in Ohio, where the American Federation of Labor and the Congress of Industrial Organizations had joined forces in an attempt to oust Taft, the author of highly controversial labor legislation.[66] Abandoning its earlier aspirations to a lofty campaign that would rise above personal assaults, the White House also sent out Harriman to respond to the aggressive GOP attacks in kind. "When you look at Mr. Taft's record," Harriman declared at an American Federation of Labor convention in Houston, taking aim at the administration's principal target, "you can't escape the conclusion that if the Congress had adopted his position communist objectives would thereby have been furthered."[67]

At a press conference the next day, Truman stood fully behind Harriman's comments.[68] In an ideal world, the intensely partisan president would have loved to deliver such an attack himself. But, apart from one blatantly partisan speech at the end of the campaign, he ultimately refrained from overt politicking.

Truman's abstention was the product of numerous calculations. Conscious of his presidential role, he deemed it unseemly for the head of state to be grubbing for votes while American boys were still fighting and dying in Korea. A keen student of history, Truman also believed that his direct involvement would be counterproductive to the Democratic cause. He was particularly troubled by Woodrow Wilson's disastrous experience in the 1918 midterm campaign, when Wilson had called on the electorate to endorse his peace plan, only to see the Democrats go down to defeat. Convinced that this episode vividly demonstrated that "people do not like to be told by the Chief Executive how to vote," especially in wartime, Truman remained determined not to board the campaign train, even when faced with increasingly desperate pleas from "shaky Democrats" like Brien McMahon in Connecticut, Myers in Pennsylvania, and Lucas in Illinois.[69]

With the president deciding to abstain from direct electioneering, other ways had to be found to place the Democrats' major election asset in the public eye. By far the most conspicuous was the plan hatched by White House aides during September to get Truman to fly to the Pacific to meet with MacArthur. For Truman's advisers, such a trip would "be good public relations." It would also underline his role as commander-in-chief now that U.S. forces were on the offensive. Although Truman, with his instinctive "distaste" for such publicity stunts, was initially hostile to the idea, in the first week of October, during yet another Potomac cruise, he finally succumbed. On October 10, Ross announced to reporters that the president would leave for Wake Island in the Pacific the next day.

Word of the trip swiftly "created something of a sensation" among reporters, and "there was an immediate rush of newsmen to go." Working feverishly to set up the press pool, the White House arranged for a separate plane to take reporters. This plane would leave slightly ahead of the presidential party, so that journalists would be on the ground and ready to cover Truman's arrival on each leg of the journey. Ross also promised the press that there would be adequate communications facilities, so that reporters would be able to wire their stories promptly back to the United States[70]

The president left a warm Washington on the afternoon of October 11, on a round trip of 14,425 miles that took him across seven time zones. Arriving at Wake Island early on the morning of October 15, Truman chatted privately with MacArthur for thirty minutes in a small Quonset hut by the ocean. The two men then moved to the freshly painted Civil Aeronautics Administration building, which barely had room to hold their retinue of seventeen aides and advisers.

In the mythology that would later surround these meetings, especially after MacArthur was recalled the following April, officials, reporters, and biographers would often play up the differences between the two central

Truman and MacArthur at Wake Island. Courtesy of National Archives.

protagonists—the fact that MacArthur "appeared irked, disgusted" at being called away from the war for a political stunt, or Truman's apparent exasperation with the general's disrespectful manner, especially his failure to salute his commander-in-chief, the informality of his "greasy ham-and-eggs cap," and his evident desire to leave Wake at the earliest possible moment. But although the two meetings were indeed brief, and although they resulted in no major changes in policy, at the time the president had much to be happy about. Not only did MacArthur reveal his conviction that North Korea's "formal resistance" would end "by Thanksgiving" but, when asked by Truman about the prospect of Soviet or Chinese involvement, he briskly replied: "We are no longer fearful of their intervention. . . . If the Chinese tried to get down to Pyongyang there would be the greatest slaughter." On departing the island, the general was just as cocky. "Come to Pyongyang," he invited reporters. "It won't be long now."[71]

Yet despite MacArthur's triumphant parting comment, as a PR stunt, Wake had important limitations. Before they left, Truman and his aides doubtless hoped that their trip would be something of a reprise of Roosevelt's famous media coup of 1944. That summer, facing a tough wartime election, Roosevelt had traveled to Pearl Harbor to meet with MacArthur, and the symbolism of the whole occasion had gone a long way to neutralize

Republican charges that he had focused too much attention on the European theater. Six years later, however, Wake was to prove a very different affair. The main problem was the obvious lack of substantive achievements. Whereas at Pearl Harbor, Roosevelt had established Pacific strategy for a decisive phase of the World War II, the Wake meetings were little more than an opportunity for MacArthur to brief Truman and for the two men to get acquainted. Even the official communiqué released at the end of the conference conceded as much, stating that the president's purpose had been little more than to get "firsthand information and ideas" from the general.[72]

During the grueling plane journey to and from the island, relations between the presidential party and reporters were also strained. Merriman Smith of UP was the main culprit. On the outward journey, Smith wired out a report that punctured the image of a dapper and ever-alert president, depicting a somewhat disoriented Truman alighting from his plane at Susian airfield in California. Truman was reportedly "madder than hell" with Smith, and in the coming days he would constantly pepper his remarks to reporters with allegations of press distortion and bias.[73]

Nor were other members of the press pool all that enamored with Smith, especially when he scooped everyone by grabbing an early copy of the communiqué and sending it out as a UP exclusive. As well as breaking the press pool agreement, Smith's action jammed Wake's limited transmitting facilities—highlighting in turn the fact that the extra communications facilities the White House had promised reporters before the trip had failed to materialize. Ross then compounded the error by allowing Anthony Leveiro of the *New York Times* to send out an additional story. As Robert Nixon of the International News Service recalled, "all hell-fire broke loose." On the way home, feelings ran so high that there was almost a fistfight between reporters. As one of them privately put it, "after that trip, with no sleep, no filing facilities, and not much news, it is a wonder that any of us are still friends."[74]

Meeting with reporters after his return, Truman tried to put the best gloss on the whole affair, declaring that it had been a "most successful conference." When pressed about past policy differences with MacArthur, however, the president was quick to reveal his irritation, and even accused certain sections of the media of disloyalty.[75] Such an outburst was hardly the best way to win over journalists, but many mainstream newspapers were nevertheless willing to applaud the Wake Island meeting as a "wise" and "timely" move. Particularly supportive were the mainstream organs like the *New York Times*, *Philadelphia Inquirer*, *Washington Post*, and *Washington Star*, who all congratulated the president for making the trip. Typical of this positive coverage was a widely repeated assessment by the columnist Arthur Krock, who concluded that Wake had been one of those rare instances when presidential duty and party politics were served at the same time.[76]

Still, the very fact that even favorable stories stressed the political nature of the trip worried senior officials. Although PR may have been the main motive, about the last thing the White House and Pentagon wanted were accusations of an expensive jaunt across the Pacific simply to boost the Democratic vote in November. To make matters worse, PA soon reported that "a sizable minority" of the media had greeted the whole episode "coolly," expressing "disappointment at the brevity of the meetings and the absence of any specific results—in terms of policy—from the conference. Many of these commentators have charged that the meeting was motivated by 'politics.'" As the *New York Herald Tribune* concluded, in a characteristic comment, "the notion that the elaborate and well-publicized affair was arranged simply to hitch a political bandwagon to the five stars of the general of the army would be extremely repugnant to the American people and derogatory to the dignity of this country."[77]

About the best that could be said was that Wake had at least placed the president back in the public eye. It also provided him with the opportunity for an ostensibly nonpartisan speech on October 17, when he reported to the nation on his meetings with MacArthur. A week later, he then delivered a long-planned address to the UN General Assembly. The White House had particularly high hopes for this occasion. Since the start of the war, the UN had been accorded a central position in the administration's foreign policy. Since Acheson's Uniting for Peace address, the State Department had also been lobbying hard to secure support from allies for his plan to give greater authority to the General Assembly. A presidential speech before this body would give both efforts an obvious boost. But White House aides also had their attention fixed on developments closer to home. As one of them revealingly pointed out, the UN speech would "permit the president, without the slightest taint of 'politicking,' to emphasize his (and the Democratic Party's) foreign-policy plank for the November elections."[78]

If pure "politicking" was the goal, then Democratic fortunes would best be served by jaunty and triumphant language. Yet as Truman's two October speeches went through their lengthy drafting process, a series of pressures intervened to prevent him from fully driving home the scale of the Korean success. One was the familiar concern about a "letdown." Rather than focus on the sparkling prospect of looming victory, Truman felt obliged to pursue the drabber "theme of not letting our guard down" in the ongoing Cold War struggle.[79] A second consideration was the whole ethos of a UN-led collective security enterprise. Again, instead of talking about the impending triumph, this required a magnanimous tone, even in the midst of a bitterly fought election campaign at home. As Acheson advised the White House after reading an early draft of the October 17 speech:

The whole idea of victory should be taken out. We should not be talking about victory. This is out of keeping with the UN. There are no victors or vanquished in this kind of situation, only an adjudication. The only victor is peace and perhaps this should be said in this way. To talk in terms of victory makes this too much of a U.S.-USSR conflict. This part of the speech should be done with great restraint, should be sober, with a sense of responsibility.[80]

Infusing these presidential speeches with a sense of restraint, it was hoped, would also have a third, vitally important consequence: dissuading Moscow or Beijing from intervening in the war. Despite MacArthur's brazen optimism at Wake, this prospect suddenly became all too real when on the day after Truman addressed the UN, the first Chinese volunteers clashed with South Korean troops near the Yalu River.

In retrospect, these battles marked the start of China's First Phase Offensive, a fortnight of attacks between October 25 and November 6 that smashed the South Korean II Corps in northern Korea and would soon create a flurry of panic in Tokyo and Washington. But at first, U.S. officials were privately sanguine about the news, convinced that the sudden appearance of Chinese troops was not a full-scale intervention. As the CIA concluded, they were merely an indication of China's desire "to establish a limited 'cordon sanitaire' south of the Yalu River." MacArthur reinforced this optimism, informing the Joint Chiefs on November 4 that while it was impossible to provide an authoritative appraisal, full-scale intervention by China "appeared unlikely."[81]

Still, not everyone in the military was so confident, and their concerns soon began to appear in print. As early as October 31, the media ran "unofficial reports" indicating Chinese involvement "at least in regimental strength." The next day, as editorial writers and commentators started "to evoke concern" about such a disturbing development, PA hurriedly prepared a possible response.[82] As well as gathering together in one document all the administration's past efforts to calm Chinese fears about U.S. intentions, PA thought the time was ripe for "a new and forceful reassurance." In its view, a comprehensive statement of U.S. intentions would signal "to the American people and others that every effort has been made to convince the Chinese communist regime of the groundlessness of any legitimate fears that might be the instigation of their action." If the worst did materialize, it would also "make it easier to demonstrate that the Chinese action was explainable only in terms of overall communist strategy stemming from Moscow."[83]

With a week to go before polling day, however, PA's suggestion was quietly shelved. This was partly because the situation on the ground in Korea remained murky. According to some observers, it was also because Truman "did not want to risk a charge from his bitter Republican critics that he was attempting to appease the communists."[84] But as a practical matter, any new initiative was quickly buried amid the hectic and troubling first seven days of November.

The grim month of November began with two Puerto Rican assassins trying to kill the president, walking up to his temporary residence at Blair House and exchanging gunfire with White House police officers. Although Truman was unharmed, one of his bodyguards was killed. Six days later, just before the country went to the polls, MacArthur suddenly—and very publicly— changed his tune about the situation in Korea. The communists, his daily communiqué now declared, had moved "alien" forces across the Yalu River, in "one of the most offensive acts of international lawlessness of historic record." Back home, an already uneasy press greatly amplified MacArthur's new-found pessimism. On election eve, PA recorded that a growing number of media observers now thought "that the U.S. must 'be prepared' for a continuation of the 'murderous' struggle." On election morning, many more concluded "that the UN is faced with the 'gravest crisis' in its history."[85]

Quite naturally, Republicans moved swiftly to exploit such headlines. Internationalist senators like Smith, Ives, and Flanders hurried to make the familiar claim that this new crisis was merely the result of the "administration's policy of appeasement in the Far East." For their part, leading Democrats privately recognized the obvious danger posed by China's intervention. As Captain Victor Harding, the manager of the Democratic Congressional Campaign Committee, conceded, news of China's intervention would suggest to many voters that Truman was "incapable of bringing off a clean-cut, effective, and not-too-bloody victory."[86]

But even this was not the only dimension of the problem. Well before MacArthur had publicly conceded the presence of Chinese troops in Korea, the administration had found it difficult to capitalize on the period of success after Inchon. Engineering events had not really worked, for the NATO talks had foundered on French intransigence, and the Wake conference had merely produced a new bout of press irritation and skepticism. Trying to counteract the shrill Republican assaults had given the Democratic campaign a defensive feel. And even when leading officials had tried to focus on the battlefield victories in Korea, they had been anxious not to strike too triumphant a tone, fretful that such a course would lull the public into a false sense of complacency, would be completely out of sync with the ethos of a collective security enterprise, and might further provoke Moscow and Beijing. Thus, when confirmation of China's intervention finally seeped into the public domain, it simply fed into a Democratic campaign that was already faltering in its efforts to exploit the Korean issue effectively.

Certainly, when Truman arrived in Independence, Missouri, to cast his vote, he could not have been optimistic about the outcome. The party that holds the presidency traditionally performs poorly in off-year elections. While newspapers filled their pages with stories about China's intervention,

White House officials were "showing increasing alarm at the turn of events in Korea." Ominously, the president even spent election morning conferring with Acheson by phone. It all seemed like a strange case of déjà vu, for Truman had been in Independence back in June when he had first got word of the North Korean attack. His initial reaction then had been to say and do nothing to alarm the American public. Now, with that public about to go to the polls, his instinct was exactly the same. The president, Ross announced to reporters, "is not yet ready to comment publicly on the Korean setbacks."[87]

After voting in Missouri, Truman flew straight back to an unseasonably mild and sunny Washington. By the time the first returns came in, he was trying to relax on the *Williamsburg* as it sailed along Chesapeake Bay. But even the early results were grim. As one of his aides recalled, that evening the president was so low that this was the only time the aide "recalled seeing him unmistakably showing the effects of too much drink." To Truman, bourbon seemed the best way to handle the news that the Republicans had picked up five seats in the Senate and twenty-eight in the House.[88]

Dealing with Limited Setbacks

In the weeks to come, a variety of officials, party strategists, and reporters all pored over these results. Despite the president's gloomy reaction, the State Department's PA was fairly upbeat. The Democrats, after all, had retained numerical control of both chambers—something they had conspicuously failed to do in the last midterm election. As PA pointed out, the victories of Dewey and Warren for governor, and James H. Duff (R-PA) and (perhaps) Richard Nixon for the Senate, were also a strong indication that the voters were still attracted to internationalist Republicans.[89] And even the high-profile Democratic losers had been undone as much by local issues as by their foreign policy stance—Lucas in Illinois by corruption charges leveled at the Democrat's candidate for sheriff in Cook County; Tydings in Maryland by growing opposition among core Democratic constituent groups toward his long antilabor, anti–civil rights voting record; and Myers in Pennsylvania by growing Republican strength in a state that had voted for Dewey in 1948.[90]

Yet few shared PA's breezy optimism. Republicans certainly interpreted their gains as a vote of no confidence in the nation's foreign policy–makers in general and Dean Acheson in particular. Having kept a low profile during the campaign, Acheson then let off steam—and inflamed his critics even more—with an ill-judged speech on November 17 in which he accused the Republican right of seeking to undermine the whole fabric of America's Cold War strategy with their partisan-driven calls for a policy reexamination. The antics of the GOP, he claimed, were similar to those of "the farmer who tears up the crops every morning" or "the man who doesn't know whether he really loves his wife." Even moderates took offense at this, objecting to Acheson's "name-calling." And among Republicans on the Hill, moves would soon be afoot to pass a party resolution calling on the secretary of state to resign.[91]

Elsewhere, few doubted that Tydings's defeat by John Marshall Butler—widely viewed as McCarthy's candidate—demonstrated the powerful popularity of Red Scare tactics against the State Department. Nor did anyone miss the fact that other leading cheerleaders of the right, such as Taft, Millikin, and Capehart, who had all been targeted by the administration and had all been deemed vulnerable back in September, now emerged with resounding victories.

On Capitol Hill, Democratic survivors were particularly perturbed by the extent of the Republican gains. Les Biffle, the influential secretary of the Senate, privately admitted "the shock to the party is almost if not quite as deep as when the Democrats lost the Congress in 1946. This time, for all practical purposes, the Republicans have taken over the Congress without having to take over the responsibility for its acts." In the House, where Democratic strength had fallen from 260 to 234, Rayburn and McCormack now guessed that a further twelve to twenty Democrats might defect on crucial votes, which would greatly reduce their freedom to push administration measures through. In the new Senate, the problem would be qualitative as much as quantitative. While Tydings's defeat might prove a blessing in disguise, as it would elevate the respected and influential Richard Russell (D-GA) to the chairmanship of the Armed Services Committee, the loss of majority leader Lucas and majority whip Myers had few redeeming aspects. Among the new GOP members, Duff and Nixon might follow the bipartisan line. But Wallace F. Bennett (R-UT), Frank Carlson (R-KS), Francis H. Case (R-SD), Everett M. Dirksen (R-IL), and Herman Welker (R-ID) were all clearly allied to the Taft wing of the party, which would undoubtedly use its new clout to scrutinize administration proposals more carefully.[92]

Republican opposition was also likely to become stiffer if the conflict in Korea persisted. In the first days after the election, news from the front continued to be alarming, as Chinese troops drove UN forces back at considerable cost. On November 8, one grim CIA estimate calculated that thirty thousand to forty thousand Chinese troops were now in Korea, with a further 350,000 lying in wait across the border.[93] More alarmingly, MacArthur now decided that the only way to prevent further Chinese infiltration into Korea would be to bomb the bridges across the Yalu River. MacArthur also wanted to allow his air force to engage in the "hot pursuit" of any communist plane that sought sanctuary over Chinese territory. In Washington, however, the State Department and Pentagon saw major problems with these ideas, and they immediately placed restrictions on both.[94] Deeply annoyed, MacArthur took solace from the fact that Chinese forces melted away almost as suddenly as they had appeared. By the middle of November, the Korean front was again relatively quiet. And MacArthur was so confident that he could push all communist troops out of Korea that he began to talk of a swift and total end to the conflict, to be achieved by one final UN attack before Christmas.[95]

Back in Washington, many senior officials were uneasy about MacArthur's "end-the-war" offensive. Marshall fretted about a yawning gap between UN forces pushing up the two sides of the peninsula, which a new Chinese intervention could easily exploit. Lovett was alarmed by MacArthur's fluctuating estimates of the situation on the ground. Inside the State Department, where officials had to deal with British calls for a halt well south of the Yalu River, there was even brief consideration of some sort of demilitarized zone along the Korea-China border.[96] At the very least, the State Department and White House recognized that the time was now ripe to implement the idea, first aired before the election, of presenting Beijing with yet another reassuring indication of Washington's limited objectives. With his senior advisers concerned that "the American public have little understanding of what really has been done diplomatically and psychologically" to dissuade China from entering the war, in the middle of November Truman used his weekly press conference to emphasize that the United States had no designs beyond the restoration of "a unified, independent, and democratic government established throughout Korea."[97]

In the weeks after the election, the mood in Washington was thus tense. Recalling this period in later years, Acheson would bemoan his reluctance to intervene decisively in the policy debate, condemning himself and others for sitting "around like paralyzed rabbits while MacArthur carried out his nightmare."[98]

Yet even at this time, the doubts and fears that so obviously gripped senior officials also coexisted uneasily with a lingering but still potent hope that MacArthur would indeed succeed. After all, the general's earlier gambles had often paid off handsomely. As a result, Marshall and the Joint Chiefs remained reluctant to second-guess the commander on the ground. Nor were they enthusiastic about the British proposal to halt well south of the Yalu River, equating this with appeasement and pointing out the practical difficulties of enforcing such a political situation in the midst of fighting hard battles. Reluctantly, Acheson held back from challenging this position. Ready to defer to Marshall's experience, and wounded by the mounting Republican assaults on him, he agreed that MacArthur should not be restrained. The victor of Inchon was thus free to launch a new attack, planned for November 24.[99]

With the prospect of victory still possible, it was time for Truman and his advisers to take stock. Over the past five months, the war against North Korea had not been easy to sell. This was partly because, with one notable exception, the fighting had not gone well. It was also due to the changing nature of U.S. objectives, which had been ambitiously widened to include Korean unity—a fact that would cast a long shadow over sustaining support for the war during the grim winter months to come.

But there was a deeper reason, too, one that underpinned and influenced many of the problems that had plagued the administration. This was the problem of selling a limited war. Because Truman and his advisers were so keen to stop the fighting spilling out of the Korean peninsula, they had faced obvious constraints on what they could say and do. Not wanting to provoke the Soviets or inflame domestic opinion, they had abdicated leadership at key moments and, when they had spoken out, had invariably shied away from ratcheting up the rhetoric. Viewing Korea as a short-term emergency, they had also been reluctant to make basic changes in the mechanics of opinion persuasion, like the creation of a new propaganda agency. Although such restraint had helped to calm a dangerous international situation, in domestic political terms it had had negative repercussions. It had helped to dissipate the "rally-'round-the-flag effect" that normally accompanies a dire international crisis. It had provided an opening for the Republican opposition to sharpen its attacks. And it had underpinned some of the antagonism that working reporters had directed toward the government's information providers.

Still, in recent weeks, with victory seemingly imminent, officials had recognized the need to change course. Their thinking had been driven by the need to sustain the broader Cold War mobilization drive, especially since a far more unruly Congress would soon be heading to town, while the mass public was always prone to complacency the minute a crisis appeared to be over. Animated by these concerns, officials now agreed to begin an intensive effort to publicize NSC-68 in the new year. The president's State of the Union address would provide the launching pad. It would be followed by a series of speeches and by committee testimony from senior officials, not to mention vigorous activities of the prominent public figures gathered together in the CPD. Inside PA, officials even thought the time would now be ripe to publicize actual portions of the NSC-68 document, especially those that pointed to the continued risks to American security and the importance of pursuing a "Strategy of Freedom."[100]

In conception, all these exertions promised a stark contrast to the rather subdued, sometimes anemic endeavors of the early months of the war: they would be vigorous, far-reaching, and hard-hitting. This was certainly the thrust of Acheson's advice when, on Monday, November 27, he went over to the Oval Office to finalize these ideas. He found Truman in an accommodating mood, his earlier reservations about a large defense budget seemingly a thing of the past. As Acheson recorded, Truman now "thought that the administration should take a vigorous fighting attitude in support of our foreign policy." On the specific subject of mobilization, Truman even agreed that all the State Department's PR ideas "were wise and suggested that we go ahead developing these as rapidly as possible."[101]

Yet what neither man knew was that two days earlier, MacArthur's "end-the-war" offensive had run headlong into the Chinese forces still lurking in northern Korea. And the Korean War, far from coming to an early end, was about to be transformed into a much more dangerous conflict.

Part Two

The War against China,
November 1950–July 1951

5

AN ENTIRELY NEW WAR

The weekend of November 25–26 was bitterly cold in Washington. A fierce storm ravaged the whole northeastern seaboard, with temperatures dropping to 15°F, as snow, ice, and strong winds blacked out 350,000 homes and caused more than two hundred deaths.[1] The short session of the outgoing Eighty-First Congress was scheduled to meet on Monday, November 27, but many members were left stranded in their homes, unable to take trains or planes back to the capital. With attendance so sparse, the House adjourned after just forty-one minutes. In the Senate, a planned meeting of the Republican Policy Committee had to be postponed to the next day, because Taft was unable to get to Washington in time. But on the Senate floor, the few members in attendance were quick to rehearse their familiar lines. "All this talk about 'bipartisanship' and 'you've got to consult the Republicans,'" Connally declared, still smarting from the Democratic reverses at the polls; "—to hell with that! If a man is an American he ought to stand for an American foreign policy in the interests of the people of the United States!" In response, Wherry launched into yet another attack on Acheson, contending that the secretary of state had been operating "a one-man foreign policy" that had proved "an absolute failure."[2]

At 6:15 the next morning, Tuesday, November 28, Truman received a call from General Bradley. The Pentagon had just received "a terrible message" from MacArthur, Bradley explained, that two hundred thousand Chinese troops had struck UN forces in Korea. MacArthur had suddenly abandoned all hope that the Korean conflict could be kept localized. "The Chinese military forces are committed in North Korea in great and ever increasing strength," MacArthur stressed. "No pretext of minor support under the guise of volunteerism or other subterfuge now has the slightest validity. We face an entirely new war."[3]

Truman, like the Pentagon, was shocked. One observer that morning recorded that "his mouth drew tight [and] his cheeks flushed" as he considered the news. "This is the worst situation we have had yet," he spluttered. But he was reluctant to lash out at MacArthur directly, even in his private moments, despite the general's promises that the troops would soon be home, his patent lack of intelligence detailing the existence of large numbers of Chinese troops, and his "end-the-war" offensive that had walked straight into a massive Chinese trap. Instead, Truman's first instinct was to single out his Republican critics—the likes of Wherry, who only yesterday had issued yet another denunciation of his secretary of state. Such "vilifiers," the president explained to his staff, wanted to tear the country apart. "We can blame the liars for the fix we are in this morning. . . . What has appeared in our press, along with the defeat of leaders in the Senate, has made the world believe that the American people are not behind our foreign policy."[4]

Yet the new crisis clearly demanded that the public—including the press and the opposition—finally pull together. How could this be achieved? Perhaps the extent of the danger, now that U.S. forces were in direct combat with Chinese armies, would engender a real and enduring "rally-'round-the-flag effect." Perhaps—but with the prospect of a massive defeat suddenly looming large, there was obviously scope for recriminations on a monumental scale.

The war's objectives were also far murkier than before. Over the summer, U.S. goals had expanded from pushing communist troops out of the south to uniting the whole peninsula. Now, however, the chances of completing this rollback mission were slim; for a time, it even seemed possible that UN forces might be evicted from the peninsula altogether. There were also some—especially among America's allies—who suspected that China's intervention had at least been partly provoked by MacArthur's march to the Yalu River. Nor was it clear exactly what measures the United States and the international community should take to respond to China's attack—whether they should escalate the war on the one hand or opt for a cease-fire and negotiation on the other. Crafting an information campaign in such a complex environment was going to prove no easy task.

Conflicting Public Signals

Within hours of receiving MacArthur's "terrible message," the president convened a special session of the National Security Council. Although details from the battlefield were still unclear, the Pentagon was convinced that UN forces were now in a "very gloomy" predicament, highly vulnerable to further attacks either from Chinese reinforcements or from Soviet MIGs. For this reason, the Joint Chiefs were desperate to avoid provoking Moscow and Beijing. And Acheson fully agreed. Looking at developments through a broader lens, he worried that a protracted war in Asia could deflect the American focus from Europe, the key Cold War battleground, creating dissension among the Western allies and undermining attempts to solidify the NATO alliance. As Acheson stressed, to get sucked into a broader war with the Chinese communists "would be to fall into a carefully laid trap."[5]

Apart from a general desire to avoid escalation, no clear decisions were taken at this meeting, not least because the battlefield situation was so fluid that no one could predict how severe a defeat the Chinese were likely to inflict on MacArthur's forces. In the next three days, there was even some optimism that, as Acheson put it, the military situation was "serious but not in any sense disastrous."[6] Perhaps, some senior State Department officials mused, a new battle line might soon be stabilized. Initially, they hoped, such a line could provide the basis for a cease-fire agreement. At a later date, it might even be given some form of "sanctity" by the international community.[7]

Because the situation in Korea was so unclear, officials were hamstrung in what they could say to the public. "The deepest secrecy" thus covered Tuesday's National Security Council meeting. When reporters cornered the vice president on his way out, his tight-lipped response—that he was "not the talking member of the firm"—was typical.[8]

During the course of that tense day, as anxious crowds gathered outside the White House, Truman also abandoned plans to make a prompt appearance before Congress, since "there were no major recommendations that could be made" at this time. Such a speech, he decided, would be more effective "when the situation clarified a bit, but no date was set."[9] Rather than dramatizing Korea with a big set-piece address, Truman would try to foster the impression that he was not being diverted from his regular routine. As one White House correspondent privately noted a few days later, "the president kept pretty much to his normal schedule this week despite the pressing developments. He did not put himself on a war-footing."[10]

At first glance, all this was eerily familiar. Back in June, Truman had been reluctant to speak out promptly, preferring to cultivate an image of business as usual. But this reticence had provided Republicans with an opportunity to reframe the crisis in their own terms, as part and parcel of the Democrats' abject neglect of Asia. The president's refusal to go before Congress in the first days of the war had also alienated many legislators, who even now continued to grumble about executive arrogance, the bypassing of proper constitutional mechanisms, and a general sense that "the White House was inaccessible to them, except for very brief and stilted meetings with the president."[11] To make matters worse, on the select occasions during the summer when officials had gone public, their subdued rhetoric—particularly their failure to indict the Soviets directly and their unwillingness to characterize the conflict as anything more than "police action"—had provided yet more ammunition to government critics, who constantly charged that Truman and his advisers were too slow in recognizing the danger, too complacent in proposing an effective response, and too lackluster in providing vigorous leadership.

Acutely aware that saying and doing little in public was a dangerous strategy, this time senior officials wanted to avoid their earlier mistakes. Thus, although the White House continued to keep a keen eye on the symbolism of presidential actions, eschewing anything that might appear to be a radical break with normal routine, Truman and his top advisers were determined not to create another massive information vacuum. Wednesday, Thursday, and Friday, therefore, saw a flurry of activity—a radio speech by Acheson, and by Truman a carefully worded policy statement delivered at his weekly press conference as well as a longer written message for Congress that explained the reasons for the crisis and offered a series of preliminary recommendations to meet the new situation. Moreover, in all of these efforts, both the White House and State Department pulled few punches. In his Wednesday radio speech, Acheson insisted that the Soviet Union was behind the events in Korea. Two days later, Truman endorsed this line. China, he insisted, had launched a premeditated act of aggression—"equally as naked, deliberate, and unprovoked as the earlier aggression of the North Korean communists." While "reckless" in the extreme, China's attack had a clear purpose: "to further the imperialist designs of the Soviet Union."[12]

Behind closed doors, senior officials were quick to concede that the new crisis could easily be viewed in a very different light. Back in October, China's leaders had warned Washington that China would intervene in the war if U.S. forces crossed the thirty-eighth parallel. The administration had blithely ignored this warning, however. Only a week ago, it had also sanctioned MacArthur's "end-the-war" offensive, which envisaged U.S. and UN forces pushing right up to the Yalu River, where they would be able to peer directly into Chinese and Soviet territory. Clearly, such a catalogue of events might easily be used to frame the new crisis as an act of self-defense on China's part—an effort to protect its territory from MacArthur's marauding forces.

One way this interpretation could be avoided was by refusing to go into specifics about the recent past. A few days into the new crisis, the White House mooted the possibility of releasing a revised white paper, replete with documents and a detailed commentary, "so that the American people can have the full and accurate facts about Chinese intervention in Korea." But the State Department swiftly rejected this idea, acutely aware that any effort to provide precise factual material raised numerous potential problems. As one official revealingly explained, a white paper, "if it were to carry conviction with the public, would necessarily have to answer the vital questions that have been raised concerning developments in our Korean policy," such as why the United States had effectively ignored China's warnings back in October, the reasons for Tokyo's disastrous intelligence failure, and whether

MacArthur had "disregarded instructions and political guidance." To answer such questions fully and candidly would be difficult, however, for it might "drive a wedge between us and our friends in the UN." At the very least, it would "emphasize differences within our own government"—a result that, given MacArthur's connections with the Republican right, could easily prove to be political dynamite.[13]

In short, a fully documented account of the reasons behind the current crisis would raise too many embarrassing questions. Rather than pursue this risky course, Acheson and other top officials preferred to go public with a much more vague rendering of recent events. In his major speech on Wednesday, November 29, Acheson merely said that UN forces had been "approaching the successful conclusion of their mission," which was to allow the Korean people to establish their own free and independent government, when the Chinese struck. When forced to delve a little deeper, Acheson and his subordinates scrupulously avoided discussing their own actions—how they had responded to China's warnings or how their intelligence had assessed the Chinese danger. Their focus, rather, was on what the Chinese had done. As Acheson declared in his Wednesday speech, China's attack was unprovoked, because U.S. officials had offered numerous reassurances that the UN had no aggressive designs on Chinese territories. Moreover, given the numbers of Chinese troops involved and the planning that had been required to place them in Manchuria and Korea, China's decision to assault UN forces had probably been taken in August, before the United States had even decided to cross the thirty-eighth parallel.[14]

That China's intervention, at the behest of the Soviets, was thus "a fresh and unprovoked aggressive act, even more immoral than the first," also meant that the international situation was truly perilous. In sharp contrast to the summer, neither Truman nor Acheson was willing to mask this fact from the public. The country faced "a situation of unparalleled danger," Acheson insisted. If the Chinese continued their attack, "they will vastly increase the danger to the whole fabric of the world." "The gravity of the world situation," Truman told Congress, meant that an extra $16.8 billion was needed immediately "to support our part in the United Nations military action in Korea, and to increase the size and readiness of our armed forces should action become necessary in other parts of the world."[15]

Yet even now, officials were clearly determined not to overdo the scare mongering. Both Truman and Acheson, in particular, were keen to balance their utterances with calls for calmness. We must demonstrate numerous qualities, Acheson declared in his speech on November 29—"steadiness, moderation, restraint, constancy of purpose, and flexibility in action, imagination, wisdom, maturity." The next day, Truman planned to reiterate this message of "firmness and confidence" when he met with the press for the first time since the start of the new crisis.[16]

Truman entered a packed Indian Treaty Room promptly at 10:30 on the morning of Thursday, November 30. Once the two hundred or so correspondents were seated, he began by reading a statement designed to be the authoritative declaration of government policy. "The forces of the UN have no intention of abandoning their mission in Korea," he insisted. If they cut and run, this would only encourage aggression elsewhere. Events in Korea, he continued, were "only part of a worldwide pattern of danger to all the free nations of the world." It was thus necessary for the United States and its allies to speed up their preparedness measures.

Then the questioning began. Reporters were eager to discover whether MacArthur would be allowed to expand the war, say, by bombing Manchuria. At first, the president stuck to the script, responding carefully that this would depend on UN authorization. But when pressed, he brusquely snapped, "We will take whatever steps necessary to meet the situation, just as we always have." "Will that include the atomic bomb?" someone asked. "That includes every weapon that we have," Truman replied. "Does that mean that there is active consideration of the use of the atomic bomb?" a reporter shot back. Yes, the president retorted. "There has always been active consideration of its use." When probed still further on whether the United States would only use the A-bomb with UN authorization, Truman compounded the damage potential of his outburst by explaining that "the military commander in the field will have charge of the use of weapons, as he always has."[17]

As reporters rushed to the doors to file their stories, the president's opening written statement was swiftly forgotten. In the hours to come, the only lead story would be the stunning news: "use of bomb under active consideration," with MacArthur having the authority to consider its deployment. "TRUMAN PONDERS A-BOMB USE" blared a typical headline the next morning.[18]

In the reaction that followed, some officials privately thought that this barbed threat might have a useful impact on Beijing and Moscow. As a general proposition, Admiral Forrest Sherman, the chief of naval operations, deemed it in America's interests to keep these two adversaries guessing. Rusk, in a meeting with the Belgian ambassador shortly after the press conference, was suitably ambiguous, telling him that he "could not say whether or not we were going to use the atom bomb."[19] In an off-the-record meeting with a reporter, Admiral Sidney W. Souers, the executive secretary of the National Security Council, was even willing to explain the thinking behind such statements. As Souers stressed, the A-bomb would not be of much use in Korea. But neither did he "think that would Truman said could hurt, and it might possibly help, in the councils of China and Russia," perhaps by calling to their attention the dire consequences that could ensue from this new bout of aggression.[20]

Yet what might be helpful in the councils of Moscow and Beijing could also have disastrous impact on allies and congressmen. America's main allies were certainly shocked by Truman's comments. Already convinced that MacArthur had been excessively reckless in Korea, Britain and France were hardly reassured by the notion that he might now have the authority to use the A-bomb—and that they might be cut out of the decisionmaking process altogether.[21]

In London, where the Labour government only held office by a slim parliamentary majority, the mood was particularly nervy. Just the day before Truman's press conference outburst, the British ambassador to the UN had expressed his concern to Austin that half a dozen Labour members of Parliament might abstain in any debate on the Chinese intervention, adding that if the government lost such a vote, it would probably fall. Now on Friday, with a hundred members of Parliament signing a hastily drafted letter protesting the possible use of the A-bomb, Prime Minister Clement Attlee decided to visit Truman immediately in order to discuss the matter directly. As news reports from London soon confirmed, the British prime minister planned to "urge Mr. Truman to avoid a formal war with China at all costs."[22]

Domestically, too, Truman's comments on the A-bomb generated feverish debate and speculation. A few hours later, the White House press office issued a clarification, confirming that "only the president can authorize the use of the bomb and no such authorization has been given."[23] In a private meeting with reporters, Harriman also denied "that Truman was using the news conference to make an informal threat to the Chinese and the Russians when he could not make a formal threat through diplomatic channels."[24] But the damage had already been done. As the *Washington Post* correctly noted, Truman's outburst "took the headlines away from the prepared statement that had carefully been read out at the start of the press conference." As Murrow pointed out to CBS radio listeners, "the explanations will never catch up with the original indiscretion."[25]

On Capitol Hill, Truman's gaffe certainly framed the debate throughout Thursday and Friday, shifting the agenda away from official efforts to strike a note of calmness and determination. On Thursday afternoon, just hours after the president's ill-fated press conference, senators lined up to give their verdict on the A-bomb. Not all were hawks. Moderate Republicans like Alexander Smith believed the ultimate weapon should only be unleashed as a last resort, while Eugene Millikin thought it should not "be used impetuously." But a powerful cross-section of opinion was far more strident and bellicose, with Owen Brewster, Margaret Chase Smith, Burnet R. Maybank (D-SC), and Richard Russell all in favor of considering atomic operations. The next day, Senator Ralph Flanders tried to stem the tide in a powerful speech that explored the disastrous consequences that would ensue if the A-bomb were dropped. But an angry Brewster was quick to respond that MacArthur should be given authority to use every weapon in the U.S. arsenal—a tough line that struck a chord with many of his colleagues on that panicky Friday afternoon.[26]

To make matters worse, over the weekend the administration's private estimates of the battlefield situation suddenly became even gloomier, ending the brief lingering hopes some officials had entertained during Tuesday, Wednesday, and Thursday. In western Korea, the Second Division had been chewed up on November 30 in a harrowing retreat from Kunu-ri, with the loss of about a third of its fighting strength. This grim rearguard action had at least helped to cover the retreat of the other divisions in the west. But it was still not clear if these forces could avoid encirclement, especially with Chinese forces apparently poised to scythe through South Korean troops on the right flank, presenting the enemy with a chance to sweep west to the sea.[27] The situation was equally fraught in the east, where the strung-out units of X Corps were surrounded by about sixty thousand Chinese troops and faced the prospect of having to fight their way back almost 80 miles to safety across icy terrain. And overshadowing all was the prospect that the Chinese and Soviet air forces might suddenly launch an attack "aimed to extract the greatest possible degree of attrition on UN personnel and equipment" as the forlorn retreat of MacArthur's battered and frozen army gathered pace.[28]

In a flurry of meetings over the weekend of December 2–3, Marshall conceded that "the situation looked very bad indeed," while Bradley "also took an extremely pessimistic view of the military situation and thought that not more than forty-eight to seventy-two hours would elapse before it reached a crash state."[29] From Tokyo, MacArthur informed the Joint Chiefs that he lacked sufficient troops to establish a defense line across the waist of Korea. Stressing that his command was extremely small in contrast to the massed ranks of the Chinese, MacArthur glumly concluded: "unless some positive and immediate action is taken, hope for success cannot be justified and steady attrition leading to final destruction can reasonably be contemplated."[30]

But what could the Pentagon send? Chinese nationalist troops were again ruled out, because this might provoke Beijing into an even greater escalation of the war, while also alienating allies unconvinced of Chiang's staying power. Nor could reinforcements be provided from the United States. In this bleak situation, the Pentagon began to contemplate the prospect of evacuation, for the sooner this was planned and undertaken, the greater was the likelihood that all the UN forces could be saved along with their vital equipment. Once these allied troops had escaped Korea, then perhaps the United States could retaliate against the Chinese communists with a naval blockade and air strikes.[31]

Ultimately, however, senior Pentagon officials were not ready to embrace the extremes of escalation and withdrawal. For one thing, with the battlefield situation still not so desperate that the complete destruction of UN forces was imminent, officials retained the (dubious) luxury of waiting on events before making a final decision. For another, since the Joint Chiefs no longer entirely trusted—in the wake of his failure to predict the massive Chinese intervention—MacArthur's desperate diagnosis of the situation, they decided to send General Collins, the army chief of staff, to Tokyo and Korea to make his own assessment. In the interim, officials agreed that there was little choice but to hang tough in Korea.[32]

When Attlee arrived in Washington on Monday afternoon, December 4, Truman and Acheson were equally determined to disabuse him of the notion that a negotiated settlement could be reached. Over the next five days, the president and prime minister held a series of formal meetings, usually in the 22- by 30-foot White House Cabinet Room, where more than twenty participants were squeezed in. Acheson felt that too many people had been invited to these meetings, and that the overcrowding made them overly formal and "rather rigid."[33] But Acheson's own policy stance hardly made the discussions any more flexible, for he was opposed to paying for a cease-fire with the offer of either a seat for the People's Republic of China in the UN or a communist takeover of Formosa. "This moment for negotiations with the communist movement is the worst since 1917," Acheson grimly concluded.[34]

If such unyielding talk dismayed Attlee, he also came away with reassurances that the Americans had no desire to escalate the war. As Acheson was quick to remind everyone at every opportunity, "the central enemy is not China but the Soviet Union. All inspiration for the present action comes from there." "Regarding the question of all-out war against China," Acheson continued, "if this meant land, sea, and air action, there were not many of the president's advisers who would urge him to follow that course." In reiterating this vital point, Truman also sought to reestablish the essential legitimacy of the conflict by emphasizing America's earlier pledges not to threaten Chinese territory. "We have made every possible move to keep out of war with the Chinese communists," Truman told Attlee. "We do not want such a war and have shown great forbearance so far in withstanding their attacks."[35]

Despite the deteriorating military situation, the administration's private position thus remained clear: a "dogged determination" to hang on to Korea without expanding the war. Unfortunately, however, the same sort of clarity did not extend to the government's public utterances on the crisis. For these soon jerked uneasily from Truman's hints on November 30 that the A-bomb might be used to a raft of suggestions made in the second week of the crisis that the United States might cut and run from Korea altogether.

Part of the problem was MacArthur. In Tokyo, the general was struggling hard to come to terms with the reality of defeat, putting in longer and longer hours at his Dai Ichi office, before spending most of the night awake, pacing restlessly around his room while mulling over what to do.[36] Desperate to salvage his reputation, he swiftly entered into an intensive bout of public correspondence with leading reporters. He defended his drive deep into North Korea by claiming: "Washington's restrictions prevented a short, successful end to the war."[37] Along with his closest aides, he also hastened to dramatize the perilous situation facing his troops. As senior officials in Washington soon complained, General Charles A. Willoughby, MacArthur's intelligence chief, seemed overly anxious to hold press conferences "in which he speculated about the possible courses of actions, and the dire consequences which would flow from alternate courses."[38] On December 4, MacArthur then issued a communiqué that soon became the basis for press accounts that the Chinese had a million-man army in and around Korea. His command, MacArthur estimated, now faced three separate echelons of Chinese troops: first, the 268,000 soldiers actually fighting in Korea; second, the 550,000 men poised on the Yalu River to support the forward combat forces; third, a reserve including all the Chinese men under arms, and especially the 200,000 troops presently moving north into Manchuria.[39]

That the UNC was so massively outnumbered carried the obvious implication that Korea might have to be abandoned. This grim prognosis was soon reinforced by news reports from the battlefield itself, where war correspondents continued to operate in a censorship-free environment. For journalists caught up with the imperiled American Second Division, which engaged in a bitter and murderous fight to cover the Eighth Army's retreat from Kunu-ri, the situation was especially grim. "The result," Homer Bigart recorded, "was slaughter. Many wounded had to be left behind. It was as ghastly a night as the veteran troops had ever spent."[40] Rounding up all the reports on December 2, the *New York Herald Tribune* summarized the situation in a short dispatch that appeared in numerous newspapers: "Masses of Chinese are still pouring southward down the center of the Korean peninsula and already are closer to Seoul than are most of the UN forces. It would take a major miracle now to effect a union of the Eighth Army force with the U.S. X Corps, which has been fighting an independent war in northeast Korea.... It appeared that the supreme crisis was near."[41]

With such reports creating the impression that UN forces might soon be forced out of Korea altogether, the initial instinct of many senior military officials in Washington was to try to counter this new wave of excessive public pessimism. "It always looks worse at first," General Collins privately told reporters on December 1. Tokyo's estimate of communist troops "is undoubtedly exaggerated," he stressed; when the situation clarified, "we'll find that there weren't nearly that many." "Morale," Admiral Sherman acidly agreed, "seems to be lower at Tokyo headquarters than anywhere else."[42]

But these attempts to reassure reporters had been made on Friday, before the private despondency of the weekend. By Monday, December 4, few military figures were willing to stick out their necks with such upbeat assessments. In theory, all were under firm instructions to keep quiet about the military situation, and officials thus went to great lengths to avoid reporters, from changing the venues of meetings to using side entrances and back doors. But with a sense of desperation growing in the Pentagon, senior Washington correspondents had little trouble piecing together the military's true view of the crisis. James Reston of the *New York Times* was perhaps the most successful. In a page 1 story on December 4, he pointed out:

> every official movement in the capital today, every official report from Tokyo, and every private estimate of the situation by well-informed men reflected a sense of emergency and even of alarm about the state of the UN army in Korea. Not even the fateful night twenty-three weeks ago when the Korean War started was the atmosphere more grim.... It was learned on responsible authority that [senior military officials] now regarded the immediate military situation with unrivalled anxiety.[43]

Even government efforts to consult Congress—and thereby avoid the charges of arrogance that had abounded during the summer—added to the deepening sense of doom. Late on Sunday night, Acheson called all the available Democratic and Republican leaders from both Houses to the State Department for an emergency briefing. On leaving, some like Connally and Wiley "were extremely close-mouthed about what they were told." But others—who remained unnamed—were not, telling reporters they had been informed of the "grave consequences" of the situation.[44]

Two days later, General Bradley, chair of the Joint Chiefs, then testified in executive session before the Senate Foreign Relations Committee. Within hours, one legislator had leaked the story that the army was planning a Dunkirk-style evacuation from Korea. Horrified, Bradley offered an immediate clarification, which denied that any such withdrawal was in the cards. He tried to explain: "Any reference I made to evacuation was in connection with the hard-pressed troops in the extreme northeast sector, which are now moving back to a concentration in a bridgehead. Any reports other than this are misleading and merely speculation."[45]

Coming just five days after the president's clarification about the A-bomb, Bradley's original statement hardly created the impression that the government was firm in its determination to hold its position in Korea without expanding the war. Coming in the midst of a welter of news stories implying that the outnumbered UNC might soon be forced to evacuate, his statement even raised real questions about the feasibility of hanging on in Korea. Bradley tried his best, to be sure, to demolish claims that he had uttered the fraught "Dunkirk" phrase.[46] But as a sense of disaster gripped Washington, his disclaimer was easily lost in a jumble of speculation. And it was only made worse by the president's own decidedly odd public actions.

As defeat gathered pace in Korea, Truman was clearly a man under intense pressure. In private, he started to lash out at editorial writers, labeling them "prostitutes of the public mind."[47] In public, he soon left no one in any doubt about how he felt. This first became clear at his ill-fated press conference on November 30. At the end, after most print reporters had rushed out to file their stories about the A-bomb being under "active consideration," Truman remained behind to film a retake for the newsreels. Spotting someone from the UP, he immediately lashed out at a recent UP editorial entitled "While Men Are Dying." It was, he told the UP man, "one of the rottenest things I have ever read in my life," adding a barbed swipe at the Scripps-Howard boss for good measure, labeling him "Roy Chiang Kai-shek Howard." Only a swift damage-limitation intervention by Ross, who told reporters that all comments made during the newsreel session were off the record, stopped an embarrassing story.[48] But the pressure on Ross soon proved too much. Never in the best of health, he had been under intense strain in the past week. As well as clarifying his boss's incautious remarks, he had been charged with satisfying the intense press demand for news about the Attlee talks. In the early evening of December 5, while waiting for NBC to set up its equipment for a brief television interview, he was joking with reporters when all of a sudden he collapsed. Although medical help was immediately rushed to the press room, within minutes Ross was dead of a coronary occlusion.[49]

Consequences

On December 8, the administration received its first piece of good news since the start of the new crisis: Collins, who had been sent on a fact-finding mission to Tokyo and Korea, returned home to reassure everyone that the battlefield situation was no longer critical. In the west, he informed Truman and Attlee, the "Eighth Army is not in danger." In the east, it even looked as if X Corps could hold a bridgehead for a considerable period of time before effecting an orderly withdrawal without serious loss.[50] Shortly after fortifying senior officials with this timely "ray of sunshine," Collins went out to brief reporters along similar lines. "Our forces will be able to take care of themselves without further serious losses," he insisted. A debacle would be avoided.[51]

After ten days of bad news, the sense of relief inside the administration was palpable. Collins's assessment changed the whole atmosphere of the Truman-Attlee talks, which now ended on an upbeat note. It also went some way toward stiffening the government's "dogged determination" to stay the course in Korea, especially in a Pentagon that was perhaps prone to panic.[52] Yet in terms of the domestic mood, it clearly came too late to stem yet another tide of rabid political attacks and competing policy prescriptions. This was hardly surprising. Before Collins's upbeat appraisal, official cues had been far from coherent or reassuring, and this jumbled information policy had in turn exerted an obvious effect on popular sentiment. "It is no exaggeration to say that public opinion is confused and uncertain," the ABC broadcaster Edwin Lanham stressed in a comment typical of those made at this time. "It needs calmness and it needs information."[53] In the absence of either, a wealth of evidence suggested that public opinion had now begun to cleave into two extremes.

On the one hand, partly fueled by Truman's press conference comments on the A-bomb, the ranks of the hawks started to swell. According to a Gallup poll published over the weekend of December 2–3, a plurality of 45 percent would be willing to drop the A-bomb on China if a full-scale war developed, while 7 percent favored its use as a last resort, and only 38 percent completely opposed its use. On Monday, perhaps reflecting this disturbing finding, the mood on the Senate floor remained distinctly bellicose. From the right, Harry P. Cain (R-WA) now joined those pressing for MacArthur to be empowered to use the A-bomb at his discretion. Meanwhile, William Knowland proposed launching a conventional air strike against Manchuria, and a number of senators from both wings of the GOP called for the use of Chinese nationalist troops in Korea.[54]

Yet such belligerence was far from the norm. "A much larger group of commentators," PA pointed out, "including some of the most influential opinion leaders, warn of the perils of becoming embroiled in a full-scale war with Red China." Although the views of this group had not completely congealed, a combination of the dismal stories emanating from Korea and the downbeat statements from the Pentagon had helped to spark a spate of worried calls for the United States to " 'get out' of Korea"—to "disentangle ourselves from the Asian struggle by the best means available, even if it means 'buying off' or 'appeasing' Red China."[55] On December 4, when Lovett appeared before the House Armed Services Committee, he certainly found that pessimism was rife, with most legislators now convinced "that our entire entry into Korea had been a mistake and that we ought to pull out as rapidly as possible."[56]

Elsewhere, a cross-section of influential newspapers, including the *Atlanta Constitution, Christian Science Monitor, New York Post, St. Louis Post-Dispatch,* and *Wall Street Journal,* all favored a negotiated settlement. And even Henry Luce's *Time* magazine was overcome with despondency. Calling the current situation the worst defeat in American history, *Time* outlined five alternatives before plumping for a withdrawal of U.S. troops to Japan in order both to wage an air and naval war against China and to strengthen America's allies in western Europe.[57]

All this congressional and media discussion about escalation and withdrawal underlined an obvious but disturbing point: few opinion-makers were willing to rally behind the administration, despite the dire nature of the new crisis. Initially, the administration had been hopeful of stitching back together a measure of cross-party cooperation, its confidence buoyed by a number of encouraging signs. On November 29, for instance, even a diehard like Wherry had publicly declared his intention to stop partisan mudslinging. Four days later, those attending a meeting with Acheson had agreed "to close ranks" and cease their attacks on the State Department.[58]

Now, though, with defeat possible and the administration's public efforts ever more confused, this fleeting moment of unity swiftly gave way to the more familiar sound of bickering. The usual suspects on the right were naturally in the vanguard. On the Senate floor, James Kem led those extreme nationalists who openly questioned the president's authority to make concrete arrangements with the British.[59] In talking to reporters, Taft continued to complain about the lack of adequate consultation on key policy decisions.[60] Yet what was truly ominous was the rumbling that now started to come from both internationalist Republicans and senior Democrats, suggesting that the political situation was far worse than anything to date. The prospect even loomed of the total collapse of a bipartisan coalition, and with it the end of the administration's authority and influence on the Hill.

In the first week of December, this nascent antiadministration mood threatened to coalesce around two issues. One was the fate of Dean Acheson. On the Hill, Republicans of all stripes were convinced that Acheson no longer enjoyed the public's confidence. In the opinion of some East Coast internationalists, such as Irving Ives of New York, it was even time for the GOP as a whole to unite around an unprecedented resolution calling for Acheson to be fired.[61] For their part, many senior Democrats were increasingly dubious about the president's continued loyalty to his wounded secretary of state. This was particularly true of Lucas, Myers, and Tydings, who were all spending their last days in office after November defeats that they blamed partly on Acheson and the State Department. But other shaky Democrats were also troubled by a mailbag that was dominated with letters calling for the secretary of state's head. And in this grim environment, Acheson had few friends in Congress, even on the Democratic side of the aisle—and hardly anyone was brave enough to buck the prevailing political wind and speak out openly on his behalf.[62]

To make matters worse, many informed observers were also angry about the lack of informed statements coming from senior officials. Acheson was particularly assailed on this score, despite his best efforts to try to provide stronger leadership. As Walter Lippmann charged, Acheson had "lost the confidence of the people" because he had failed to "face candidly, debate openly, or make Congress and the people judge decisively." Ominously, many Democrats agreed. "This nation is confused and upset," the influential Richard Russell declared. "This is due to the tragic lack of any real leadership here in Washington."[63]

Still, not all administration supporters despaired. Tom Connally, in typically pugnacious style, thought much could be salvaged if only the president would take to the airwaves to explain his position.[64] A significant proportion of the Democratic rank and file agreed. They were calling for "action" and "leadership," one of Truman's aides discovered. "They want boldness and positiveness from the White House," he reported, not to mention a better sense of where the government was heading so that Democrats could keep in step with the administration and respond more effectively to Republican assaults.[65] The more partisan Democrats, increasingly frustrated that the administration always seemed to be on the receiving end, also recommended launching a powerful assault to place the GOP on the defensive for once. Their obvious target was MacArthur, whose close connection to the Republican Party suddenly seemed more of a liability than an asset. In a series of private conclaves, senior Democrats therefore "discussed the feasibility of building up a counter-drumfire of criticism against the great idol of the GOP," perhaps by holding him directly accountable for the military fiasco in Korea.[66]

Although many high officials had also lost patience with MacArthur, they were reluctant to sanction an overt campaign to darken MacArthur's reputation by blaming him directly for the unfolding military debacle. Acheson thought that such a political attack would have a "disastrous" impact on the whole war effort, while Truman disliked heaping blame on anyone whose fortunes were at a low ebb.[67] As a result, all that emerged from this particularly flurry of activity was a "gagging order" that was intended to shut the general up, and this would soon cause its own problems (see chapter 8).

Moreover, clamping down on discordant voices was only a negative tool. With support on the Hill threatening to dissolve, a number of White House aides agreed with Connally and others that it was now vital for the president to take to the airwaves at once. They were "hot after" Truman "to get on the air and tell the country what was going on in Washington and what would be going on in the future," one reporter noted after an off-the-record meeting at the White House. Some of the president's advisers even felt that the "psychological moment for rousing the country had passed," he noted. They were convinced that he should have gone on the air on Monday or Tuesday night, December 4 or 5, "when the shock of the communist assault in Korea had gripped the nation."[68]

But all was not lost—not with Truman finally prepared to act. By the third week of the crisis, he now considered a keynote speech possible, because the battlefield situation was clearer. It also helped that his talks with the British were over, for he "thought he would be freer to speak if Attlee were not in town." On the basis of these considerations, Truman at long last gave his speechwriters the go-ahead to start work on an address. It was scheduled for Friday, December 15.[69]

As they sketched their first drafts, White House aides had good reason to ponder how easy it had been to fall into the same traps that had plagued their way during June and July. True, in the first week of this new crisis, officials had gone to great lengths to try to learn from past mistakes. They had spoken out more promptly, stiffened their rhetoric, and tried to foster a greater degree of bipartisan cooperation on the Hill. But all too soon they had been forced on to the back foot, facing a string of familiar gripes and criticisms over their laggardly leadership, confusing public signals, and failure to consult with all stripes of congressional opinion.

Part of the problem stemmed from the absence of hard information about events in Korea—for in the first few weeks, officials had simply lacked an accurate sense of the scale of the impending disaster, which made it difficult to craft a message that struck the right note. Another complicating factor was the recurring difficulty of coordinating what was said, something made worse by MacArthur's determination to salvage his public reputation by talking repeatedly to the press. But the president was again at the heart of the problem. Despite intense pressure from aides and allies on the Hill, Truman was reluctant to deliver a major address in the first few weeks of the crisis. His only offerings in this period were a written statement, a press conference that spiraled out of control, and some unfortunate ranting to individual reporters, most of which showed him in a poor light.

Yet, significantly, even these belligerent efforts had had some effect— which further underlined the fact that Truman had again missed an important opportunity to dominate and frame the public debate. Although some media observers were scathing about the president's public displays of anger, questioning his mental fitness for the job, others had drawn the conclusion that perhaps it might be prudent to tone down their attacks, lest these provoke him into something rash at such a dangerous time.[70] This was certainly the case with Roy Howard, head of the influential Scripps-Howard chain. In the first days of the crisis, Howard's papers had called for a tough response— far tougher than anything the administration had announced. The United States is "at war with world-wide communism," was their basic editorial line. And this global fight could not be won under America's current "pussyfooting leadership."[71] Very soon, however, Howard was having second thoughts. "I think that the country is in a very jittery state of mind at the moment and that it behooves us to be very critical of all our own editorials before putting them out on the wire," he instructed a senior executive in the middle of December. "What I have especially in mind is the danger that I think is inherent in any editorial course which would seem to involve nagging or picking on Truman." In a revealing insight into how the president's unintentional explosions exerted an important influence over some of his critics, Howard elaborated:

> I feel that Truman's recent outbursts of temper and pettiness have very definitely created a fear on the part of the general public that we may be

going to sea with a captain who either has no chart or does not know how to read it. I do not think that the public has suddenly developed a new liking or affection for the president even though I think they are apt to be very critical of those who are critical of him. The public's attitude seems to me to be a bit like that of a third person riding in a car with a man who is not a very good driver in the first place and who is being made additionally nervous by a backseat driving wife. I have a feeling that the public feels that at his best Truman is not going to do a very good job, but that if he is the victim of too much nagging he is very apt to put the car in the ditch. If this happens, I think that the public's reaction will be to get sore at the critics rather than at the man criticized. It is by no means my idea that we should adopt a pollyanna-ish attitude. I believe, however, that, when we have to deal in criticism or condemnation, the criticism should be leveled at the incident, the policy, or the administration as a whole rather than at Truman as an individual.[72]

Not all media bosses were as sensitive to Truman's moods as Roy Howard. But the willingness of just a few to mute their attacks and engage in a measure of informal self-censorship was an unexpected bonus. In fact, it was one of the few positive developments for the administration at a time when the Chinese intervention sparked a new bout of animosity between the military and media, which, if anything, was even more intense than what had gone before.

6

DEALING WITH THE "DISASTER SCHOOL OF JOURNALISM"

During the first phase of the war, many of the three hundred reporters based in the Far East had reached two firm conclusions, one relating to MacArthur's UNC, the other stemming from conditions in Korea. The military hierarchy, they were convinced, had little sympathy for their day-to-day working requirements. MacArthur and his advisers, rather than providing clear guidelines and basic logistical support, had invariably attempted to manipulate coverage of the fighting through a combination of veiled threats, misleading communiqués, and control of communications. To make matters far worse, life at the front had been hellish. Faced with numerous hardships, from appalling billets to enemy ambushes, even the most experienced correspondents had wilted. In September, when Homer Bigart flew to Japan for a short rest, he had complained of being "so exhausted I could hardly walk." After a night in the splendor of Tokyo's Ambassador Hotel, he had felt a little better. But he had still considered his first tour of duty in Korea "the roughest ten weeks I've ever lived."[1]

Two and a half months later, however, Korean veterans like Bigart were looking back on these early days as something of a halcyon period. In the summer, life may have been grim and working facilities rudimentary. But in the wake of the massive Chinese offensive, everything soon got far worse.

A major defeat and the atrocious weather were partly to blame. Forced to embark on a series of long, chaotic retreats through a frozen landscape, war correspondents naturally turned a more jaundiced eye toward the whole Korean enterprise. In Tokyo, where MacArthur's command was under intense pressure, officers retaliated with a vengeance, condemning reporters for embellishing the extent of the military debacle. As relations between the two spiraled downward, leading correspondents began to hit back, pointing to a growing credibility gap between Tokyo's optimistic communiqués on the one hand and the reality they had witnessed on the other. In January 1951, when censorship was belatedly introduced, this increasingly bitter clash abated somewhat. But by now a good deal of damage had been done, especially back home, where the public had been able to follow one of America's biggest defeats in graphic detail.

The Military and Media at War

When the Chinese assault began, some of the best known correspondents were stationed with the Eighth Army along the Chongchon River line, including Bigart, Harold Boyle, Don Huth, Tom Lambert, and Reginald Thompson. For five unnerving days and nights, they worked the congested roads between Sinanju, where I Corps headquarters had a PIO camp, and the threatened towns of Kunu-ri and Sonchhon, on the Eighth Army's sagging right and center flanks. By November 29, extensive Chinese penetrations had placed this whole front in an extremely precarious position, forcing a series of hasty retreats. The situation was so bad in I Corps sector that when the war correspondents returned to the PIO base that evening they found that without any notice, it had suddenly gone.

In the mounting melee, the reporters decided to mimic the actions of their military counterparts by heading swiftly south in their own effort to "regroup." "Like homing pigeons," Don Huth of AP observed, "correspondents from all points along the front have filtered back to Eighth Army headquarters" in Pyongyang. There they found a large PIO office with the luxury of "two stoves, coffee, typewriters, and two telephones." But the respite was brief. Most spent the next few days battling the retreating traffic as they headed north to try to locate the collapsing front. "In any sector the situation may change in minutes," observed one. "Jeep-loads of newsmen stop frequently along the way to ask about conditions ahead. The answer they usually get is, 'I don't know any more than you do.'" On one occasion, the AP correspondent Tom Lambert visited the Second Division command post to interview the men before leaving to get out his story. "When he returned the next morning he found that the Chinese had broken into the command perimeter, killing officers and men in their tents. The post had moved to the rear during the night."

After hours on the clogged road to and from Pyongyang and a day spent witnessing such distressing sights, each night correspondents returned to Eighth Army headquarters to file their stories and briefly get some rest. But even this routine was soon ended. On December 5, the Eighth Army planned to evacuate southward. All the correspondents still in the area were brusquely instructed to get out fast. No one, came the order, should attempt a "last aircraft out of Pyongyang story."[2]

In Washington and Tokyo, these war correspondents' travails soon reached the top of the agenda, if only because of mounting concerns about the impact of their stories. These concerns came in three different guises. The most specific was a small but growing litany of security violations. Inside the Pentagon, some aspects of the media's coverage exasperated even the experienced Marshall. He was particularly scornful of the wire services' determination to locate the six hundred men of the Seventeenth RCT. The wire services deemed this to be highly newsworthy because this RCT had been one of the few U.S. units to reach the Yalu River, and its men now faced a perilous retreat across more than 100 miles of enemy-dominated terrain. But according to an angry Marshall, this particular "newspaper flurry" did little more than "needlessly upset and worry the relatives of the men."[3]

In Korea itself, the officers who were struggling with the myriad problems of withdrawal, retreat, and evacuation took an equally dim view of security breaches. They even thought that irresponsible correspondents' careless reporting was about to imperil the evacuation of X Corps from the Hungman beachhead.

By December 11, the scattered units of the beleaguered X Corps had managed to fight their way back to a relatively secure beachhead around the port of Hungnam, where they could be evacuated by sea. In the past week, some had come as far as 78 miles through enemy-held territory, fighting off Chinese attacks on their precarious escape route through frigid mountain passes that rose to 2,500 feet and in temperatures that fell to −35°F.[4] Tokyo, seeking to maximize their chance of escape, had already engaged in a creeping set of press restrictions.

As early as December 4, the UNC PIO, which had hitherto provided daily hour-long briefings for the press, began scaling these down to fifteen or so minutes. On December 9, these briefings were then temporarily suspended, before Echols called in a cross-section of media representatives to discuss the need for voluntary restraint. MacArthur's command was thus shocked when, just a day later, AP sent out a wire that provided details of the whole operation.[5] Immediately, General Doyle Hickey, MacArthur's acting chief of staff, sent out a missive instructing that "all evacuation references be 'cut off clean,'" an order that an irate Echols interpreted expansively to "mean the elimination of all references to X Corps evacuation, including previously transmitted matter." On December 14, in a hurriedly arranged meeting, eleven leading newsmen protested Echols's action, pointing out that it was foolish to try to kill material that had already been released into the public domain. But Hickey was unapologetic. "The situation is much graver than it has been and particularly with regard to the X Corps," he explained. "You know there is an enemy air potential and that potential could be diverted against the X Corps. The X Corps is going to be in a critical position for some time. References to its movements cannot be made."[6]

On the specific subject of security lapses, the military therefore had good reasons for their anger. But when MacArthur attempted to turn this into a broader two-pronged attack against the overall thrust of the media's coverage of the war, his barbs were often wide of the mark. The first aspect of Tokyo's more general assault on the media was Tokyo's claim that the press was deliberately exaggerating the number of U.S. casualties. As one UNC press release charged, the "unofficial, persistent, and speculative casualty reports from the Korean Theater" not only contributed to "the artificial nuance of 'disaster' that has been given to UN military operations" but also had "a detrimental effect" on the whole UN effort, by encouraging the enemy to attack units they thought had been weakened.[7]

It was certainly true that the press was determined to establish the cost of the current debacle. But any tendency to speculate and exaggerate stemmed less from deliberate sensationalism and more from the very practical difficulties of getting accurate figures. As in the summer, the army faced enormous handicaps in trying to issue prompt and full lists. Part of the problem was the time-consuming business of identifying bodies and notifying the next of kin. Although some efforts had recently been made to expedite the whole process, including experimenting with the "photoelectric transmission" of information from Korea to Tokyo to Washington, in the early weeks of this new crisis the Pentagon was still not in a position to release official figures on dead, wounded, and missing since the end of November.[8]

With nothing concrete to go on, reporters probed their sources. On December 8, one Pentagon official told a *Time* reporter—off the record—that overall U.S. casualties would be in the region of fifty thousand. The marines, meanwhile, initially estimated to the press that around seven thousand of their men would be lost trying to escape to the Hungnam beachhead. Determined to get harder proof, some journalists were highly inventive, picking up on developments like a Defense Department estimate that it would need ninety thousand pints of blood for its military hospitals in next few weeks.[9]

By the second half of December, however, reports based on such sources looked like scare-mongering, after the military presented revised estimates that greatly diminished the sense of catastrophe: total losses that approximated figures for similar battles in World War II, and marine casualties that were half the amount of those first expected.[10] But while the media had indeed jumped the gun and erred on the side of exaggeration, most accounts had been scrupulously based on the available evidence, either in terms of conversations with officials or more innovative efforts at verifications. This defense was important, for it was based firmly on the ruling norms of "objectivity" and "straight" news reporting. It was also a defense that would become increasingly familiar as MacArthur and his advisers sought to expand their attack on the media into a more general and damning indictment that impugned correspondents' motives and, at its most extreme, even blamed certain sections of the press for the unfolding debacle in Korea.

In the post-Vietnam era, this earlier bout of military–media mudslinging has largely been forgotten, but at the time the deep-seated animosity was real. Indeed, while MacArthur may have bristled at security breaches and inflated casualty estimates, what really grabbed his attention was the press's more general use of "such extravagant superlatives as " 'decimated divisions,' 'military debacle,' and such nonsense" to describe the current campaign. "The sensational reporting of our withdrawal movements," he remarked privately on December 13, "have produced a fear psychology which is just what the Kremlin would most desire."[11] In the weeks and months to come, his loyal subordinates would often make even more damaging claims. Some charged that journalists were simply disloyal, pedaling "irresponsible" charges akin to those that had been widely carried in the Soviet press. Others thought that the highly competitive correspondents had a misguided sense of their market, erroneously convinced that readers primarily wanted "to learn of mistakes, defeat, tragedy, incompetence." But all agreed that war correspondents were a large part of the problem—that they were effectively undermining domestic support for the war at home, if not contributing to the current string of military reverses in Korea itself. Most were "careless chroniclers" who subscribed to "the disaster school of journalism," General Willoughby charged, in a typical comment. "The typewriter attack from the rear," he concluded, "can sometimes be worse than the enemy."[12]

There could be no doubt that some of the media's coverage during December was negative. While MacArthur's command made an intermittent effort to put a rosier gloss on events, issuing a string of press releases that insisted that UN forces were "trading space for time," many correspondents on the ground depicted a much gloomier reality.[13] Leading the way was the Knight-owned *Chicago Daily News*, which used its copious coverage of the war as a key selling point in a circulation drive that would soon see its readership soar to over half a million a day.[14]

In the early weeks of the Chinese offensive, the *Daily News* published a series of punchy, pungent stories by its two main war correspondents that not only pointed to the hopelessness of the situation but also hinted at the recriminations to come. Fred Sparks, who was with X Corps during its retreat, believed this gruesome frozen march would be "irrevocably etched in the mind—and the conscience—of the American people. The etching will show frostbitten boys slipping, falling, and dying—but fighting, though facing a vastly greater foe, dragging out their dead and wounded, by hand, by jeep, by oxcart." Keyes Beech, who interviewed some of the survivors, pointed out that the marines were bewildered by what had happened to them. "Retreat is a word that doesn't appear in the marine vocabulary," Beech wrote. "Yet they were made to retreat. More than one marine wants to know why they should have been put in a position where they had to go back on the famous marine slogan: 'Retreat, ****, well we just got here.' "[15] In another dispatch, sent when he made it back to Seoul, the irrepressible Beech went even further. "A fog of defeatism and despair hang over this shattered capital like an oppressive cloud," he wrote on December 13. "Among U.S. Army and South Korean government officials there is undisguised gloom as never-ending vehicles rumble through the streets headed in one direction. General MacArthur's communiqués say the morale of UN troops is high despite their smashing retreat by the Chinese communists. Evidently, the general and I haven't talked to the same people."[16]

Elsewhere, two of the other leading names of the war, the *New York Herald Tribune*'s ultracompetitive Homer Bigart and Marguerite Higgins, also wired back eyewitness reports and interviews with battle-scarred survivors, Higgins from her exploits with X Corps in the east and Bigart following the Eighth Army's long retreat in the west. "The men were ragged," Higgins revealed, "their faces swollen from the cold and bleeding from the raw bite of the icy wind, their ears blue." Like Keyes Beech, whom she frequently traveled with to the front, Higgins was unwilling to speculate on who was responsible for this predicament. But Bigart, his long tour of duty coming to an end, had no such scruples. "The full impact of defeat—the worst licking Americans had suffered since Bataan—has not yet been felt by the great bulk of American troops in Korea," Bigart wrote on December 6. At the moment, these retreating soldiers were "too weary and too preoccupied with immediate concerns to think of the consequences," but there was bound to be "bitterness." In fact, Bigart revealed, "already some of the thoughtful officers are beginning to question the sanity of recent military decisions, which may not have caused, but which certainly accelerated, this crisis." "The most questionable" of these was MacArthur's decision to push for the Yalu River rather than hold the far more defensible position on the neck of the peninsula. "To fan out a small force along the rugged vastness of a 700-mile frontline with Red China and the Soviet Union simply made no sense. It was an invitation to disaster."[17]

It was stories like these that naturally inflamed senior officers in Tokyo, who did not handle criticism well at the best of times. Deeply angered, MacArthur and his subordinates chose to interpret them as the product of biased, even traitorous reporting. Yet on close inspection, MacArthur's cutting allegations were deeply unfair, for they were based on a highly selective reading of media coverage. They also ignored the fact that most dispatches were based on solid sources, including those from the general's own command.

For a start, viewed in its totality, American reporting of the war was far from uniformly negative. To be sure, those journalists who were becoming the

Keyes Beech was one of the most controversial correspondents in Korea. Courtesy of National Archives.

biggest names—and enjoying the widest syndication—were also those who adopted a more engaged and critical approach. But not all outlets succumbed to reporting that could be deemed misleading or overwrought. A brief survey of the big news organizations bears this out. Although the Knight chain was a constant thorn in Tokyo's side, the Scripps-Howard newspapers and Luce magazines were largely content to toe MacArthur's line and act in a "careful and cooperative" manner.[18]

Significantly, too, a number of dailies noted for the quality of their foreign reporting, such as the *New York Times* or *Christian Science Monitor*, generally opted for a detached, factual approach to the war. On their front pages, they ran long pieces under the bylines of their leading Far East correspondents, which used a combination of official press releases and wire service accounts to piece together a broad overview of the strategic situation. Generally, these dispatches contained little attempt to analyze the causes or consequences of the debacle, and included only the occasional human interest story or interview with soldiers. Meanwhile, for newspapers that invested fewer resources in foreign affairs, the wire services necessarily provided the bedrock of their coverage. This was true for the *St. Louis Post-Dispatch* on the left of the political spectrum and the *Chicago Tribune* and *Los Angeles Times* on the right. Despite the very different politics of all three, their basic reliance on wire dispatches meant that they all tended to lead with similar stories, invariably broad overviews by the wire services that were based on MacArthur's communiqués or army press releases, when available.[19]

Moreover, when handling the critical dispatches filtering in from the Far East, editors at some of the big organs pulled their punches in revealing ways. The *New York Times* was a case in point. In the key period between November 28 and December 10, when U.S. forces were in headlong retreat and formal censorship had yet to be introduced, the *Times* ran only two items that could be termed censorious or disparaging. One, by Michael James, described the U.S. evacuation as more of a "rout" than a withdrawal, "with UN forces, the great majority of them Americans, begging for 'rides the hell out of here.'" The other, by Richard Johnston, detailed GIs' ebbing morale as they began to realize that "their superiority in weapons, transport, medical treatment, rations, and a myriad of modern war devices was no guarantee for victory." But, significantly, both stories were only allotted a small amount of space. And both were safely buried on the inside pages.[20]

Of course, not all outlets were so timid. Papers like the *Chicago Daily News* and *New York Herald Tribune* reveled in the controversial writings of their high-profile correspondents, but they were also careful to ensure that such stories could be defended. It was here that the culture of "objective" reporting proved a useful protective device. Rather than resulting in stale dispatches that mirrored the official line, in the hands of a Beech or a Bigart, "objective" journalism became a way of challenging MacArthur's communiqués, since their bosses could be confident that their reports were based on solid sources. "Beech's facts are essentially correct," his publisher, John S. Knight, stressed after Tokyo questioned the veracity of one account. "They were obtained from sources which are both reliable and anxious to have the story brought to the attention of the American public."[21]

Often, these reporters had also witnessed the battles, and this led to a second obvious point in their defense. War correspondents in Korea were not simply conjuring up or fabricating a sense of disaster; December 1950 *was* a time of major defeat—a fact many senior officials themselves recognized in their anguished debates about whether the UN would be able to hang on in Korea. In northwest Korea, correspondents like AP's Don Huth and the *Baltimore Sun*'s James S. Cannon had been caught in the harrowing collapse of the Eighth Army's front at the end of November, Cannon having the misfortune to be with the Second Division, which was savaged as it tried to cover the rest of the army's retreat south of Kunu-ri. It was hardly surprising that as soon as they reached the relative safety of the rear, they would wire home stories of their awful experiences in the most inhospitable of climates.[22]

In the northeast, the situation was different. Both Marguerite Higgins and Richard K. Tucker were only flown into to Hagaru-ri on December 5–6, after it had become the base for stranded X Corps units who now faced the perilous task of breaking out of the Chinese encirclement in order to reach the evacuation point at Hungnam. On arriving in Hagaru-ri, they were greeted by troops who had fought a series of horrific engagements in recent days, and their early dispatches naturally emphasized the gruesome nature of this "death snare" in a "frozen hell." But the marines, in particular, were not slow to turn all this media attention to their advantage. And a raft of stories soon appeared praising the marines' grit, determination, and innovation. Some focused on their ability to overcome massive odds to reach safety. Others stressed their reluctance to leave their dead on the battlefield. But the incident that caught the eye of most correspondents was the marines' successful effort to fly in a portable bridge, which allowed thousands to escape to safety across a vital pass.[23]

All such stories, by focusing on the micro-level exploits of individual units, necessarily emphasized the horrors of war on the ground rather than the broader strategic perspective held by MacArthur's command. But this determination to focus on the human angle, to base stories on interviews with shell-shocked or demoralized survivors rather than rely on the more measured overview of army press releases, was not new. It had been at the heart of the previous military–media clash during the summer. And, like then, it was still driven by familiar motives—an abiding belief that the central story was with the "sloggers" at the front, mixed with a frantic competition for scoops, and exacerbated by "rockets" from restless editors back home. What *was* new was MacArthur's decision to scale back and then suspend his daily briefings in the first weeks of December, leaving reporters with only a daily printed news release. It was this restriction, some journalists now felt, that was a key part of the problem, since bureau chiefs in Tokyo increasingly lacked the information to piece together the "big picture" so as to place the micro-level stories from the front in their proper context.[24]

In other ways, too, reporters, editors, and publishers now believed that MacArthur was at least partly responsible for the very ills he was attacking. It was not simply that they lacked proper guidance. At a deeper level, some journalists reached the conclusion that the absence of censorship was contributing to the rampant competition—and with it the appalling risks—that were the hallmark of Korean reporting. Indeed, without censorship, Eighth Army briefing officers tended to be cagey about upcoming engagements, fearing that whatever they divulged would simply appear in tomorrow's newspaper. This, in turn, created an environment of uncertainty and anxiety for correspondents, since they could not be sure where to position themselves. It also exacerbated the frantic rush to get a scoop, since uncertain journalists would twist their sources' arms in an effort to beat their rivals to the main story, while those who were left behind might tempted to "overwrite"—that is, exaggerate—their dispatches to compensate.[25]

As both the defeat and the recriminations gathered pace, many correspondents also reached another, even more disturbing, conclusion. The military might accuse them of exaggerating the situation on the ground. But a number of prominent media figures believed that it was MacArthur's command that bore the main responsibility for creating the growing sense of disaster. The military, after all, had provided the initial hints of high casualty figures. The chair of the Joint Chiefs had first suggested the possibility of a "Dunkirk"-style evacuation (although he had quickly qualified this). And MacArthur himself had provided the hardest evidence to suggest that the UN's position in Korea was desperate. Indeed Tokyo's communiqués, for all their periodic effort to put a more optimistic spin on the war, had more frequently stressed that UN forces faced staggeringly bad odds.[26]

Seen in this light, MacArthur's attempts to indict war correspondents for pedaling a "disaster school of journalism" seemed almost perverse. Certainly, some of those on the general's hit list were outraged at this suggestion and keen to hit back with vengeance. Morale in the Eighth Army remained "good," Bigart reported at the start of December, "in spite of the bitter and unexpected reversal of fortunes, and it is safer to say there is less gloom here tonight than in certain quarters at Tokyo and Washington." Citing MacArthur's alarming estimate of one million Chinese troops in and around Korea, Bigart's employer even ran a scathing editorial challenging the veracity of Tokyo's whole assessment of the war. "On the record of the last three weeks," the *New York Herald Tribune* pointedly declared on December 7, "it is impossible to put any confidence in such figures; and it is becoming increasingly difficult to put confidence in the military capacity of a headquarters which has so gravely compounded blunder by confusion of facts and intelligence."[27]

For some at least, the credibility gap that had first opened up in the summer had now become a gaping chasm.

Censorship Revisited

Whatever the merits of these various complaints, officials in both Washington and Tokyo now agreed that the basic structure of the military-media relationship had to be refashioned. The laxity of the current code, MacArthur pointed out on December 10, had been acceptable when the enemy was just North Korea. In this smaller war, it had been "desirable to give the world the fullest information of UN action at the possible expense of military security," especially since North Korea's lack of air power meant it "did not have the ability to strike quickly on the basis of information obtained from the press regarding UN dispositions." Now, however, China had the capacity to strike "our weak points with unerring accuracy as long as we continue to publicize detailed dispositions of our forces as well as their movements to new positions."[28]

The new war therefore necessitated a new system; but what form should this take? Already, MacArthur's PIO in Tokyo had tried scaling down and then halting press briefings. On two occasions, senior officers had even called in leading reporters to discuss the growing problems. At the second of these meetings, held in the Radio Tokyo Building on December 14, Echols and Hickey first expressed their indignation at the premature revelation of Hungnam evacuation details, before announcing a range of practical steps to avoid similar incidents in the future. Four days later, the UNC PIO in Tokyo established the Press Advisory Division (PAD), headed by Colonel E. C. Buck-hart and staffed around the clock by three enlisted men. Its task, as Echols explained, would be to "furnish the press information on the military situation in Korea not involving security and advise correspondents on security phases of reports received from the field." It could "suggest rewrites and deletions in press copy, but will not censor it. The press will remain on a voluntary censorship basis."[29]

Significantly, then, MacArthur still shied away from formal censorship. Neither the extent of the current crisis nor his burgeoning suspicions of the media were enough to convince him that such a drastic step was necessary.

MacArthur's refusal to go beyond the PAD probably stemmed partly from his unequivocal public statement back in July terming the whole concept of censorship "abhorrent." But he also remained convinced that the basic problem was not just with reporters in the field; it was also vital to persuade editors and publishers back in the United States to restrain their charges at the front and stop sending "rockets" that forced them to exaggerate conditions on the ground. For this reason, MacArthur revived an idea he had first mooted back in July: a meeting in the Pentagon between senior Defense officials and media executives "to enlist cooperation against furthering security breaches."[30]

Yet if MacArthur hoped such a meeting would help to resolve problems short of formal censorship, he would soon be rudely surprised. Even back in the summer, senior army officials in Washington had called for the adoption of a formal censorship code. As the new bout of military–media wrangling intensified, Floyd Parks, the army's chief of information, wasted no time resurrecting his case. Bolstered by tacit support from a number of bureaucratic allies, especially in the State Department, Parks moved to demolish once and for all the practical case against censorship, particularly the idea that MacArthur's UNC simply lacked the trained personnel. Not only was it possible to train officers in a short space of time, but as Parks remarked to one newspaper executive in a planned indiscretion, the Pentagon had offered MacArthur all the censorship personnel he needed, only to be rebuffed.[31]

Just as important, it was now clear that many key media figures also supported a major reform. True, some—like the AP's executive editor, Alan J. Gould—remained lukewarm to outright censorship, pointing out that it could easily be used to withhold bad news from the public. Perhaps hypersensitive after Tokyo's ire at the AP's Hungnam evacuation revelation, Gould was eager to stick up for his reporters, stressing that the failure of the present system stemmed from an honest disagreement "as to what constitutes essential security or at what point the maintenance of secrecy can no longer be justified." But the AP's skepticism and defensiveness were not widely shared. Indeed, most media executives believed that some sort of clear and predictable code would avoid the friction and misunderstanding that currently hampered Korean reporting. As Barry Faris, editor-in-chief of the International News Service, put it, "we think it is the right thing to do in view of the security violations that have occurred recently. We are fully in accord with it." Crucially, working reporters in Korea and Tokyo tended to agree with this assessment. Long convinced that they had been given scant guidance on what constituted a security breach, correspondents also felt they faced a series of threats and sanctions that were basically capricious and unfair.[32]

An implicit consensus had already emerged, therefore, before the MacArthur-inspired meeting between senior Pentagon officials and media executives even took place. The conference itself was held during and after lunch on December 18. Marshall and three senior officials represented the military, while eleven leading media men spoke for the wire services, the National Association of Broadcasters, and the American Newspaper Publishers Association. Clayton Fritchey, the new head of the OPI, began by summarizing the recent messages the Pentagon had received from MacArthur: one complaining of security breaches during the Hungnam evacuation, the other suggesting that editors back in the United States practice voluntary restraint. With the media representatives still digesting both this and their lunch, Marshall took over and made some general remarks. Speaking "forcefully, with emphatic gestures, and with decided emphasis," he focused on a familiar theme—the basic instability of the popular mood—and "pleaded for public understanding based on real facts, rather than emotionalism growing out of misinformation." After Marshall left, Fritchey, Parks, and the media representatives then got down to business. It soon became clear that they all agreed that the crux of the problem lay in the Far East rather than the United States. Deciding to send MacArthur a message to this effect, the media men were united in the view that "security of information from the combat zone is the responsibility of the military. That responsibility cannot be passed to any other agency or group within the combat zone, or without."[33]

On receiving this dispatch, MacArthur concluded that the press itself wanted censorship, and in the coming weeks he would express his bemusement at this turn of events. "It is indeed a screwy world," he commented on one occasion, "when a soldier fighting to preserve the freedom of the press finds himself opposed by the press itself."[34] Yet even now, the general still hoped to get away with something short of outright censorship. On December 20, to be sure, Echols announced to reporters that any stories originating in Japan would have to be submitted "to the PAD for clearance before transmission." But in his press conference, Echols avoided using the word "censorship." And MacArthur himself refused to place more stringent controls on the reporters operating in the battlefield theater. No censorship would be imposed in Korea, the Eighth Army's chief PI officer stressed on December 21, after receiving new guidelines from Tokyo. "There would be no change in treatment of news copy in Korea," he added, except that some dispatches would be delayed or withheld if the military situation warranted it.[35]

It would soon become clear, however, that these actions represented the last gasp of opposition to formal censorship. The reason for this was simple: MacArthur, for all his continued determination to control media coverage through lesser means, was no longer in charge of events. He was already under mounting pressure from the Pentagon for tighter restrictions. As the end of the year approached, intelligence reports also indicated that the Chinese were poised to launch the third phase of their great offensive within days. And every tool at the military's disposal would now have to be marshaled to prevent a disaster of enormous proportions.

Hitting Rock Bottom

By the last week of 1950, as UN troops braced themselves for the new Chinese attack, their military situation was not entirely bleak. In the west, the Eighth Army, having broken off contact with the enemy at the start of December, had retreated 100 miles south of Pyongyang, where it had established new defensive positions along the Han and Imjin rivers. In the east, the last elements of X Corps were safely evacuated from the Hungnam beachhead on Christmas Eve. Taken by sea to Pusan, they would soon be redeployed in southern Korea, under the overall command of Eighth Army, to bolster its defensive positions.[36]

The Hungnam evacuation was the cause of much rejoicing back home. While newsreels heralded it as "one of the military miracles of the century," war correspondents lauded "one of the finest retreats in military history."[37] MacArthur himself used the occasion to issue yet another wide-ranging public defense of his recent actions. Brazenly ignoring the president's recent injunction to avoid controversial statements, he rehearsed all the familiar arguments about how his November 24 offensive had revealed China's secret aggressive intentions and had thereby saved his troops from an even bigger disaster.[38] Yet none of this could hide the fact that the Chinese offensive had only paused for breath. And as intelligence multiplied that a renewed assault was in the offing, many officers in both Korea and Tokyo were convinced that it was only a matter of time before the overwhelming number of Chinese troops rolled forward and pushed UN forces off the Korean peninsula altogether.[39]

In this perilous situation, the tightest security was essential. Bowing to the inevitable, on December 22 the UNC at long last ended any pretense that censorship could now be avoided. Four days hence, it instructed the Eighth Army PIO, the official censors would check all stories emanating from Korea for security violations. These censors would work in one of the new alphabet agencies that suddenly sprang up. In Tokyo, Echols had already established the PAD to monitor copy originating in Japan. In Korea, the Eighth Army would now have its own Press Security Division (PSD), which would be responsible for instituting censorship in two locations: the main headquarters at Taegu, where Major Melvin B. Vorhees, assisted by two officers, would delete any offending material, and an advance post nearer the front, manned by Major Jack G. Westbrooke and one subordinate.[40]

These censors were taken from the pool of PI officers already in Korea. Although most had at least some background in journalism, this was generally not very extensive—in fact, one had dropped out because he thought the profession "boring," and another had been drafted into the army before he could use his journalism degree. Three of the four had, however, been combat officers during World War II, and this experience shaped their conception of the job at hand far more than any expertise in reporting. As one of them commented, their primary task was "to protect the guy at the front."[41] Soon, they were provided with marching orders that reinforced their personal proclivities. These included instructions to be particularly vigilant about references to any unit other than Eighth Army, in order to withhold from the Chinese information that would enable them to establish the UN order of battle. Armed with their newly delivered stamps—"approved," "approved as revised," "delayed," and "disapproved"—they quickly set to work, scrutinizing 181 stories during the last six days of December and no less than 2,689 dispatches during the first month of the new year.[42]

Back in the United States, the first media responses to this belated introduction of formal censorship were highly favorable. This, at any rate, was the impression Floyd Parks sought to create in a series of gloating messages he wired to Echols. "Reception by press in this country is that censorship is proper and will be helpful to news media," one insisted. MacArthur ought to see clippings of the various editorials on censorship, another stressed, "because I think it would be very reassuring to him to know that in practically all cases it was favorable."[43] Yet what Parks failed to communicate was the fact that the media's support for censorship was conditional. The media executives had made this clear in their wire to MacArthur on December 18. In the next few days, even newspapers that praised the new code stressed that they wanted "to see restrictions kept down to a minimum and confined as much as possible to straightforward military operations."[44]

This underlying caveat was thrown into sharp relief during the first two weeks of January. On New Year's Day, the Chinese finally launched their new attack. Punching through South Korean lines along the Imjin River, an estimated 170,000 Chinese and North Korean troops forced the evacuation of Seoul on January 3–4. By that time, UN forces were again in headlong retreat. They had soon fallen back more than 50 miles below the thirty-eighth parallel, where they only gained a brief respite when the overextended Chinese logistical lines started to buckle under the twin pressures of antiquated equipment and UN air attacks. Nonetheless, China's advance took its toll on the U.S. military. Forced to retreat in extreme weather conditions, between January 7 and 17 the Eighth Army's morale hit rock bottom. On January 10, MacArthur then wired Washington, warning officials that his command faced the grim prospect of either evacuation or annihilation unless vigorous action was taken against China.[45]

As demoralization gripped many in both the Eighth Army and the Tokyo headquarters, war correspondents added to the mounting gloom. The usual suspects among the wire services and the daily press were quick to relay stories of yet another disaster. According to military officials, this time their exaggerations ranged from details about the collapse of an allied division to reports that the entire front had threatened to "split wide open."[46] Twisting the knife, Homer Bigart launched a scathing attack, arguing in a widely reported article that MacArthur had made such a "momentous blunder" back in November that the United States could no longer afford to "string along" with him.[47] If this was not bad enough, Keyes Beech had also got wind of MacArthur's January 10 wire to Washington, and he now chipped in with a story reporting that the general had recommended a prompt withdrawal from Korea.[48]

The reaction in Tokyo was typically apoplectic. Echols immediately denied Beech's story. Along with MacArthur's other close advisers, he also attempted to depict Bigart as little more than a subversive troublemaker, whose "article is obviously part of a campaign of propaganda and smear long underway to undermine public confidence."[49]

In Korea, meanwhile, as the defeat gathered pace, the harassed censors were deeply angered by a series of blatant security breaches by the UP. According to an Eighth Army investigation, these fell into two categories. The first was the premature release of unauthorized information, such as UP's announcement of the fall of Seoul on January 5, which infuriated both the military and the other wire services. The UP's competitors were angry, for they had held their own reports at the expressed instruction of the army and were piqued at being scooped. But the military was even more enraged, convinced that the UP had acted with outrageous stealth and dishonesty. In order to get the story out, a UP reporter in Korea had used a division telephone to bypass the censor and relate his dispatch directly to Japan. In Tokyo, another UP correspondent had then had the gall to lie to MacArthur's PIO, telling officers that the story had been cleared by Eighth Army.

And this was not the end of the deceit. Innovative wire service correspondents also developed the practice of "administrative interviews" to get around censorship restrictions. In telephone conversations, Tokyo bureaus would ask Korean-based reporters questions about material the censors had struck from dispatches. The Tokyo bureau would then rewrite the story, incorporating material that had previously been deleted, in the hope that they could slip the new dispatch past Echols's unwitting PAD. Again, UP was at the forefront of such shenanigans; as the Eighth Army PIO complained, it had "continually used this trick to breach security."[50]

When lumped together, this new bout of "disaster" reporting and security lapses appeared doubly alarming. Not only were correspondents still writing stories that seemed likely to deepen the Eighth Army's plight but censorship in its current guise appeared powerless to improve the situation. In Washington, harassed officials in the Pentagon decided to counterattack through conventional channels. Behind the scenes, Fritchey approached the wire services and asked them not to publish anything from unauthorized sources, "such as letters from the front, returning veterans, or private reports to home offices," particularly on the whereabouts of specific units, that might be of use to the enemy.[51] Seeking to put a lid on further exaggerations, the Pentagon also made a concerted effort to laud media restraint and condemn press excess. According to the OPI, *Life* magazine was a model of the former, particularly now that it had formulated "a good, workable code" that detailed for its reporters and photographers when, how, and why they should operate cautiously when covering the war.[52] On the other hand, the wire services, with the UP clearly in the vanguard, were even more irresponsible than before. Thus, on January 2, one officer called in wire service representatives in order to chide them for "overwriting" the story.[53]

In Tokyo, meanwhile, MacArthur's command decided to institute a total clampdown. In the second week of January, PI officers announced two new initiatives. Since the Eighth Army was in day-to-day control of the tactical situation, Echols now gave it the power to issue daily press releases. Tokyo's own activity in this sphere, hitherto so central to its efforts to influence media coverage, would be confined largely to "decorations, human interest stories, and other information not pertaining to current military operations."[54] At the same time, under the cover of unifying all the rules and regulations into one document, the Eighth Army released a new set of censorship guidelines to reporters. From now on, no mention was to be made of units, officers, troop movements, or towns and cities near the front. Other material would naturally be censored if it was deemed to be of advantage to the enemy; far more controversially, it would also be suppressed if it injured the morale of UN forces or caused embarrassment to the United States and its allies.[55]

Seeking to remedy earlier wire service attempts to get around censorship in Korea by amending the story elsewhere, the military also told war correspondents that they would have their privileges suspended if their dispatches were subsequently distorted by their home office. They would even be the target of sanctions if they used "words or expressions conveying a hidden meaning which would tend to mislead or deceive the censor and cause the approval by him of otherwise objectionable dispatches." The sanctions themselves were just as tough. Added to the earlier threats of losing accreditation and banishment from the theater, reporters were now faced with the prospect of court-martial should they ignore the new rules.[56]

These tough new guidelines clearly contravened the caveat that had been at the heart of the media's initial acceptance of censorship. While the media had been willing to endorse an agreed set of regulations that permitted the maximum dissemination of information, this new "penal code" was hastily implemented, with no consultation and no trial period, and it appeared to sanction sweeping restrictions enforced by severe sanctions. "What correspondents had hoped would be censorship for military security," lamented Keyes Beech, "has broadened into something that amounts to political and psychological censorship." According to UP's veteran reporters, the current regulations "were the most inclusive they had ever received from any army headquarters." These new rules must be explained further, UP's general news manager, Earl Johnson, stressed, "to eliminate implications that press conduct under voluntary code was so irresponsible that we must now be schoolmarmed into proper behavior."[57]

Ominously, such complaints were not restricted to those at the top of the military's hit list. From Florida, Nelson Poynter, the editor of the *St. Petersburg Times* and longtime Truman supporter, wired the White House claiming that the "sweeping" new censorship code was a "threat to the free press and the successful prosecution of the war."[58] In Washington, Senator Wayne Morse, a maverick Republican who often sided with the administration, used his position on the Armed Services Committee to demand a full text of the regulations, adding that he did "not think there can be any justification for denying to the American people, through a free press, information of the war in Korea which could not be classified as truly top secret."[59] But perhaps the most widely circulated criticism came from the trade journal *Editor & Publisher*. "The censorship clamped over correspondents in Korea," it declared, in an editorial that was syndicated across the country, "is not only unnecessarily stringent but is ridiculous in some extremes and implies a distrust of the correspondents which is unjustified."[60]

In the next few weeks, the military's implementation of censorship did nothing to deaden this media distress. Admittedly, with the battlefield situation still highly precarious, much of what the Eighth Army's PSD sought to restrict was clearly related to the security of UN troops. The censors, for instance, ordered a complete blackout on news from the battles around Wonju, where the Second Infantry Division was desperately trying to contain a concerted offensive by the North Koreans in the center of the allied front. But correspondents also suspected that a number of restrictions were based on more sinister calculations. Why, for instance, were they stopped from using the word "retreat" and forced to use the more neutral phrase "withdrawal"? Was it really the case that UN forces were only withdrawing for "tactical reasons, such as to shorten lines or to find a better battlefield," and were not being forced to retreat by enemy attack? Other suppressed stories seemed to reveal an even clearer pattern: the case of a Reuters correspondent who was refused billeting facilities after he complained of being denied the use of a telephone to relay a piece about GI "gripes"; the quashing of dispatches that detailed the burning of three Korean villages by U.S. troops; and the cuts made in wire service stories that told of the slaughter of GIs or that contained "derogatory" and "uncomplimentary" remarks about the South Koreans. Some veteran correspondents certainly thought the military had a clear agenda. As the *New York Times* recorded, they believed that "censorship, which was introduced here for 'security' purposes . . . was being used to cover up military errors and defeats."[61]

As these complaints multiplied, MacArthur could scarcely believe the virulence of the media response. Quite apart from his own belief that the war correspondents' reckless reporting had gone way beyond the bounds of acceptability, MacArthur was convinced that it was the media that had called for censorship, while he had long been its leading opponent. Neither did he accept the accusation that the Eighth Army's new guidelines were any more onerous than those imposed in previous wars. In fact, as Tokyo soon pointed out, the censors, in their hurried effort to produce more workable guidelines in the midst of a raging battle, had simply "lifted almost bodily" the regulations that had been applied to the correspondents who had accompanied U.S. army forces during World War II.[62]

This last defense was a telling one, for it effectively demolished the media's claim that the new guidelines were unprecedented in their harshness. But MacArthur was on more fragile ground when he sought to adopt the pose of a wronged man, attacked for something he had opposed all along by those who had talked him into it in the first place. Of course, no one could doubt that MacArthur had steadfastly opposed censorship until the very last minute. But it was not true, as he now maintained, that the media itself had called for a total clampdown back on December 18 and he had only reluctantly acquiesced. What the media had actually called for were guidelines that protected security while providing for the maximum dissemination of information. What they now had, many believed, was a series of rules that gave the military carte blanche to hush up all manner of events, with the threat of a court-martial hanging over anyone who dared speak up.[63]

In the coming days, some of MacArthur's traditional press defenders, such as the Scripps-Howard chain and the *Chicago Tribune*, were quick to accept the general's explanations.[64] But most reporters, editors, and publishers remained unhappy about the tenor of his remarks and unrepentant at their own actions. With relations between MacArthur and the media at rock bottom, the Pentagon decided to launch a charm offensive to soothe the angry press corps. In public, Floyd Parks now admitted that "some mistakes" had been made. Stressing that the censors themselves lacked experience and were overloaded with work, he pledged to try "to get experienced people to go over there and help." He also predicted that it would not be long before the PSD would be in the position to do "the job with facility and without friction."[65]

Over the next few weeks, Parks's efforts were supported by a number of other leading figures. On January 14, the Pentagon ordered Echols back to Washington, so he could brief senior officers on the new regulations. Almost at once, Echols began to make his own public appearances in an effort to clear the air.[66] Soon after, Collins, the army chief of staff, addressed the National Press Club in Washington. As well as paying tribute to the thirteen correspondents who had been killed at the front, Collins declared that the work of the press in Korea had been "excellent—marvelous." Speaking at the opening of the *Washington Post*'s new newsroom on January 28, General Marshall adopted a similar line. An independent newspaper, he averred, was "one of the most delicate instruments in America's arsenal for freedom." Those in uniform, he added, felt a "deep appreciation" for the "devoted services" of the correspondents in Korea. True, relations between the military and media had been "strained," but this was only a natural product of their differing viewpoints, and recently "the traditional gap between the censor and the correspondent has greatly narrowed."[67]

As attempts to take the heat out of the situation, all these efforts were well intended. But on their own they were unlikely to bring about a sudden thawing of relations in the military's cold war with the media. What was required was a substantive overhaul. Neither the Pentagon nor Tokyo was well placed to undertake such an effort, however. The Defense Department had long played a detached role, especially when it came to treating with war correspondents, convinced that this task was the responsibility of the commander in the field. More recently, Tokyo had abdicated the bulk of its responsibilities, giving the PIO in Korea the job of issuing daily news releases and censoring journalists' copy. As a result, the only organization that actually had much power to transform the situation was the Eighth Army—a fortunate turn of events, because the Eighth Army was itself in the process of undergoing a fundamental transformation, precipitated by the arrival of a new commander, General Matthew B. Ridgway.

Ridgway Comes to Korea

General Ridgway took command of the Eighth Army under the most inauspicious circumstances. On December 23, just a week before the start of China's Third Phase Offensive, General Walker had been killed in a jeep accident. In earlier discussions about command changes, MacArthur had personally asked for Ridgway to be placed at the head of the Eighth Army, if anything should happen to Walker; now this appointment was swiftly made. After a hurried departure, Ridgway arrived in Tokyo on December 26 and went straight to the Dai Ichi building. "The Eighth Army is yours, Matt," MacArthur informed him. "Do what you think is best."[68]

In the next few days, Ridgway's assessment of what was "best" included the evacuation of Seoul and pulling the Eighth Army back in a series of retreats to avoid encirclement. But he remained confident that things could be turned around. His goal, he told one division on January 9, was to "bleed China white. I have the fullest confidence," he added, "that we can stay indefinitely when delay merges into defense." It was necessary first, however, to instill a similar sense of confidence into the rest of his command, for too many officers had come to accept that the Eighth Army's days in Korea were numbered. It was also vital to get U.S. soldiers off the roads and into the hills and mountains, where they could attack Chinese troops who were exposed at the end of a long and tenuous communications network. And it was essential, too, to ensure that the army fought in a cohesive fashion, with units maintaining close contact with one another, so that they were neither isolated when attacked nor vulnerable when probing Chinese positions.

Toward the end of January, after China's Third Phase Offensive had run out of steam, Ridgway put these ideas into action. On January 23, he launched Operation Thunderbolt—a strong reconnaissance force in the Suwon area. The U.S. Second Division then fought a key defensive battle around Chipyong-ni during February 13–16, standing fast in a tight perimeter defense in order to turn back a much larger Chinese force. As the confidence of UN forces started to grow, Ridgway launched two limited offensives in the next fortnight—Operations Killer and Ripper—which, in a major reversal of fortune, led to the recapture of Seoul on March 16.[69]

Of all the factors that helped to defuse military–media tensions during February and March, these victories were the most important. There had, after all, always been a clear correlation between battlefield fortunes and military-media relations, with the earlier bouts of bitter bickering coming against the troubling backdrop of defeat and retreat. But this time, the relief was even greater. By February, senior officers were no longer bristling at stories of disaster or blaming reporters for exaggerating the extent of reverses. It was also evident, as the Eighth Army's PSD concluded, "that the censors'

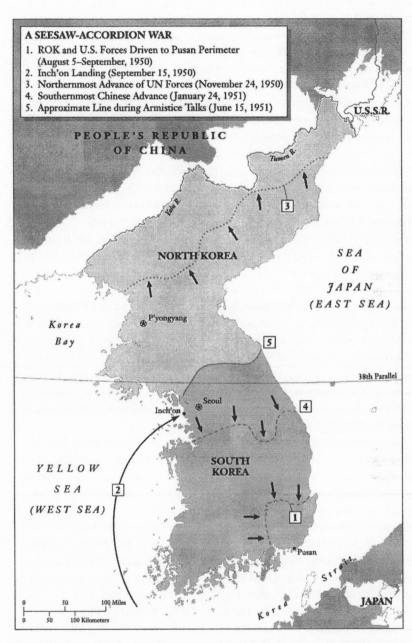

A SEESAW-ACCORDION WAR

1. ROK and U.S. Forces Driven to Pusan Perimeter
   (August 5–September, 1950)
2. Inch'on Landing (September 15, 1950)
3. Northernmost Advance of UN Forces (November 24, 1950)
4. Southernmost Chinese Advance (January 24, 1951)
5. Approximate Line during Armistice Talks (June 15, 1951)

From Robert L. Beisner, *Dean Acheson: A Life in the Cold War* (New York: Oxford University Press, 2006), 397.

problems are less pressing and the work less prejudicial when our troops are moving forward than when we are withdrawing." The reason for this was simple. With the UN holding the initiative, its clerks had more time to consider what to release and when.[70]

Still, victory was not the only dynamic at work. Also significant was the personality of the new Eighth Army commander, for Ridgway was never one to leave matters simply in the hands of fate. As in the military sphere, he was also determined to institute a series of changes that would place Korean PR activities on a firmer footing and make them able, he hoped, to sustain future reverses should the war continue to drag on.

In seeking to improve relations with the media, it helped Ridgway that he personally got on much better with reporters than Walker. Whereas Walker had been "an undemonstrative man in public," whose dour exterior had not endeared him to the press. Ridgway made for more colorful copy.[71] Initially, to be sure, much of what he had to say was hardly uplifting, not with the Eighth Army in such a precarious position. Ridgway also came down firmly in favor of the tough censorship code his PIO was in the process of instituting. And during his first turbulent weeks in charge, his own comments were often suppressed or could be quoted only after clearance from the censor.[72]

Nonetheless, even as the mudslinging between the military and media reached its zenith, Ridgway sidestepped its more vicious aspects. In contrast to MacArthur and his loyal lieutenants, with their inflammatory comments and idiosyncratic media guidelines, Ridgway seemed like a breath of fresh air. Ooozing charisma, he was immediately recognizable in his airborne trooper's uniform, visiting troops at the front with a grenade and first-aid kit fastened to his shoulder straps.[73]

On these endless inspection trips, Ridgway took care to make himself accessible to the reporters. Crucially, he also refused to hide the fact that war is hell. Unlike Tokyo, which seemed determined to bend reality to fit its own purposes, overemphasizing success one minute and exaggerating the size of Chinese forces the next, Ridgway sought to be more candid. In February, for instance, when the Pentagon objected to the use of the term "Operation Killer" on the basis that it "struck an unpleasant note as far as public relations was concerned," Ridgway refused to change the name. "I am by nature opposed to any effort to 'sell' war to people," he explained, "as an only mildly unpleasant business that requires very little in the way of blood."[74]

Ridgway was also determined to make the Eighth Army's PIO more professional. At the end of January, he appointed his own personal PR adviser, James T. Quirk. Currently a PR executive at the *Philadelphia Inquirer*, Quirk had come highly recommended on the basis of his previous stints as PR head for the First and Third armies in World War II, where he had been the press liaison for both Omar Bradley and George S. Patton.[75]

When he landed in Korea on January 31, Quirk's tasks were so vaguely defined that his immediate retort to any journalist who asked him to specify his job description was a friendly "I'm damned if I know." But Ridgway soon asked him to focus on two key problems: how to prevent another "letdown" like 1945–46, when calls to "bring the boys home" and "demobilize" had placed U.S. defenses in a parlous condition, and how to assemble and transmit information "so that our government can deflate the falsely acquired military reputation of communist China's armies." At a more practical level, Quirk also discovered that the Eighth Army's PIO section had prosaic problems his expertise could help to straighten out. Already the Pentagon was working to rectify the PIO's severe personnel problem, screening anyone in uniform with PR skills in an effort that would soon increase manpower by an impressive 60 percent. On arriving in Korea, Quirk was immediately struck by the lack of experience of the PI officers who were actually in day-to-day contact with working reporters—not to mention their "high state of timidity" toward an interloper suddenly parachuted in over their heads. But he worked hard to forge a team spirit, using his experience to improve both the PIO's daily briefings and its efforts to respond to damaging news reports.[76]

Perhaps the biggest improvement in these heady first weeks was the recognition of the link between censorship and briefings. One of the consequences of MacArthur's earlier informal code had been a reluctance on the part of many briefing officers to be candid about the extent and location of upcoming engagements, since they fretted that whatever they said might end up in the next day's newspapers. Now, the institution of censorship enabled Ridgway and Quirk to enhance the Eighth Army's briefing capabilities, using the cover of formal censorship to provide more useful information.

Inside the main pressroom at Taegu, correspondents soon noticed the difference. Although the censors continued to restrict what names and areas could be mentioned in dispatches, Quirk and his team worked hard to put each engagement in its proper context. From now on, they hoped, reporters would no longer mistake a small advance as the start of a new drive to unify Korea or a tactical withdrawal as the beginning of a rout. On February 1, for example, PI officers urged "correspondents to treat the drive toward the Han River as a 'limited offensive,' not to over stress the city of Seoul as the goal and not to treat the drive as a major effort." When this attack started to gather pace, they issued a further warning that, while the offensive might be "a sizable victory, in terms of enemy losses . . . no further implications should be attached to the present situation." In the opinion of the Eighth Army's chief PI officer, these careful efforts provided a perfect example of how censorship could be used not merely to restrict information but "as a means of establishing perspective."[77]

And crucially, reporters seemed to agree. From their perspective, part of the obvious appeal of these new reforms was that it placed them on the inside. Not only were they treated more like partners and less like spies but also they could plan more effectively. Armed with detailed briefings, they now had a clearer sense of where the main fighting would unfold—a simple improvement to their daily routine that swiftly ended the haunting old fear of setting off for the wrong part of the front and thereby missing a major scoop. Reporters also appreciated the military's new efforts to place the upcoming fighting in its proper context for them before they left for the front. Quirk's presence in Korea, one AP correspondent remarked, "has been a real shot in the arm to all of us"—especially his "interest in seeing that correspondents at Eighth Army headquarters were carefully briefed before" engagements so that they did not exaggerate their importance.[78]

Happy with these improvements, correspondents were even willing to give the censors a bigger break. In fact, most reporters now recognized that the tough new censorship rules had one clear virtue: because the military deleted any offending material before it hit the newsstands, there was far less chance that correspondents would be accused of putting the whole war effort in jeopardy. Furthermore, as the censorship operation settled down, reporters' other fears also ebbed. Some, like Richard Johnston of the *New York Times*, although still highly critical at the "stupid and precipitous" way censorship had been introduced, now conceded that its bark was worse than its bite. Others were more positive. Having witnessed the operation of censorship firsthand, Barry Faris, the editor-in-chief of the International News Service, was quick to pronounce that it was "working smoothly; a clear-cut operation." On the ground, many journalists were just as content, particularly with the army's efforts to clamp down on naming places and units, since this also eased their hectic work routine. As the PSD noted, the "correspondents' attitude, especially wire service representatives, indicated that this restriction, far from being oppressive, was desired since it eliminated the need for continually filing stories which described inch-by-inch advance on Seoul."[79]

By March, in fact, the new year furor seemed like an increasingly distant memory, little more than the birth pangs associated with a major reform. At the end of the month, the PSD even reported that it had just "experienced the quietest period of censorship to date. It was almost as though a truce had been declared across the front. Correspondents appeared ready to sit back and await developments. The only stories submitted were small actions and stories based on information received at morning briefings."[80] It was the type of situation Tokyo had wished for, but never attained, during the traumatic first six months of the war.

Tokyo versus the Eighth Army

On February 20, as the Eighth Army prepared to launch its first major offensive under Ridgway's command, MacArthur made his eleventh wartime trip to Korea. By now, a MacArthur trip had its own carefully choreographed routine. The day before, he would personally call members of his "palace guard," would apologize for interrupting their busy schedules, outline his own plans, and ask them if they wanted to go along. On the plane, MacArthur would often talk at length about the war, his aides stressing that it was all off the record. On arriving in Korea, he would then tour the front in a jeep, the press contingent following behind. After seeing various battlefields and talking with his commanders, MacArthur would brief reporters. Since the Chinese intervention, he had been far more careful in these sessions, reading slowly from a prepared statement, "so there would be no mistake."[81]

On February 20, MacArthur's press briefing took place in a tent at Wonju. Flanked by Quirk and Hickey, the general read a statement to ten correspondents that was nothing less than a bombshell. To the surprise and consternation of all present, MacArthur used the occasion to announce that he had personally ordered the Eighth Army to launch a new attack. In one fell swoop, he thereby undermined all the careful preparation PI officers had undertaken in the past few days.

As part of the planning process for Operation Killer—which was indeed scheduled for February 21—Ridgway, Quirk, and the PSD had devised a thorough set of instructions for the media. After briefing reporters ahead of time, they intended to place an embargo on all stories in order to protect the troops about to go into action. This plan, based on the improvements and innovations of recent weeks, seemed foolproof. But no one had factored in a publicity-grabbing performance by MacArthur just hours before the attack. Shocked and outraged, the censors initially wanted to include MacArthur's remarks in the overall news blackout, but this course was hardly practical. MacArthur clearly intended his statement to be relayed to the outside world. And with the wire services begging for its release, the censors relented. The very next day, however, as Operation Killer got underway, yet another outburst from Tokyo threw the Eighth Army's plans into further disarray. Without consulting anyone in Korea, MacArthur's command issued a new set of communiqués—the first it had produced since China's New Year's offensive—that again announced details of the impending operation. Appalled, the PSD had little choice but to lift its own blackout, even though troops had not yet made major contact with the enemy and were thus being denied the crucial element of surprise.[82]

Both Ridgway and Quirk were aghast. Ridgway was normally deferential toward his commanding general, but now he had been offered a vivid firsthand example of MacArthur's need "to keep his public image always glowing." Quirk, for his part, already had little time for a man he considered "fascinating but detestable." And now his anger grew. "MacArthur has no more to do with the victories in Korea than I do," Quirk complained in private, "but he always gets into the act when things go well and then wraps himself in a mantle of silence when the going is rough." What was particularly galling to both men was not so much the brazen headline-grabbing as the obvious security breach. Having repeatedly lectured correspondents about the need to omit anything that might aid the enemy, the Eighth Army now discovered it was unable to control MacArthur. "Our security people now had a heart attack on that one," Quirk sourly noted, "but no one could stop the supreme commander and the story ran everywhere.... At that point, Chinese intelligence could cut down their staff since all their work was done for them.... It's shocking."[83]

In a desperate attempt to prevent a repeat performance, Quirk immediately conferred with MacArthur's staff in order to establish yet another system for communiqué releases. It was soon agreed that the Eighth Army would "write the ground forces portion of the communiqué and send it to Tokyo for inclusion in their overall sea-air-ground communiqué." With reporters starting to pick up on signs of friction between MacArthur and Ridgway, Quirk also set about formulating ways of papering over the cracks, including a joint press conference the next time MacArthur landed in Korea.[84]

This visit came on March 7, but despite Quirk's best efforts, it was no more successful than the last. In planning the event, Quirk had envisaged the two men standing together before reporters, so that they would "appear to be absolute pals." But the reality proved to be very different. MacArthur studiously refused to play up his friendship with Ridgway. Even worse, he chose to read another statement. This time, he noted the Eighth Army's "satisfactory" military progress. But he also reprised familiar gripes about Washington-imposed limitations on "our freedom of counter-offensive action"—limitations, MacArthur declared, that would mean the war was bound to end in "military stalemate."[85]

To Ridgway and Quirk, MacArthur's gloomy utterances seemed likely to undermine the Eighth Army's recently rekindled fighting spirit. Seeking to undo the damage, a few days later Ridgway offered a public riposte, which praised the work of the fighting soldiers and emphasized their "tremendous victory" in defeating the Chinese. Obviously a thinly a veiled swipe at MacArthur, Ridgway's statement did little to dispel press rumors of a split between the two men.[86]

In the next few weeks, the rumor mill then went into overdrive in the wake of yet another round of bickering over the perennial problem of censorship. With relations between Eighth Army and Tokyo increasingly tense, eagle-eyed censors in Korea spotted a gray area between military and political matters. While the Eighth Army's PSD could suppress copy that threatened combat security, it was not clear who had authority over a string of nonmilitary subjects, such as "horror stories that affect the morale of the people at home," "stories that tend to discredit the ROK [Republic of Korea] forces or the South Korean people," and dispatches about "dance halls, beer joints, liquor sales, and the like."[87]

MacArthur's controversial press conference at Suwon, March 7, 1951. To his left are Quirk and Hickey. Courtesy of National Archives.

In order to clarify jurisdiction, the Eighth Army and Tokyo reached a verbal working agreement on March 8, which marked the first time in the new year that MacArthur's command assumed some responsibility over censorship. But this accord soon turned out to be just the thin end of the wedge. On March 16, Tokyo issued a new set of guidelines to correspondents. These stressed that no mention was to be made of the size of patrols, the results of ongoing operations, or the whereabouts of correspondents. Most of this was familiar enough, but there was a sting at the end. Henceforth, Tokyo announced, all stories emanating from Korea would have to be cleared not only by the Eighth Army's PSD "but also by the PAD Tokyo prior to being filed for release by the press."[88]

Coming at a time when military-media relations had finally settled down, Tokyo's sudden decision to introduce "double censorship" received a frosty reception. The press depicted it as an unnecessary duplication of effort. For their part, Eighth Army PI officers hardly appreciated Tokyo handing out guidelines on what ought to be suppressed, especially in light of MacArthur's outbursts during Operation Killer. Nor did they like the loss of authority. MacArthur, many PI officers were convinced, had been willing to concede Eighth Army control over PR operations during January, in the midst of impending disaster. Now that the situation had improved, Tokyo was "muscling" back in on the act.[89]

On March 25, the Eighth Army's chief censor therefore protested the new reform. When MacArthur merely brushed this complaint aside, Korean-based PI officers were distinctly put out. In their view, MacArthur's sudden introduction of double censorship, coupled with his apparent lack of concern for security at the front, would undo all the patient improvements of recent weeks. Significantly, many journalists agreed. While appreciating Ridgway's reforms, most working reporters no longer trusted Tokyo to fulfill their daily needs.

In truth, there was only one development that would defuse these simmering tensions: MacArthur's recall. But before Truman got around to this messy task, all the graphic and disturbing media reports that had emanated from the battlefield during the winter would exert a profound impact on two closely related debates that raged back in the United States: whether or not the United States should continue this grim struggle in Korea and how to wage the broader Cold War with the Soviets.

7

MOBILIZING WITH THE UTMOST SPEED

In 1950, Washington was a city littered with the artifacts of earlier wars. The Pentagon was the most notable of these, having been built on a Virginia swamp during 1941 and 1942 to house the more than twenty-seven thousand military personnel needed to plan and oversee the defeat of the Axis. But along the Mall were also thirty-eight squat, rectangular structures that had been hastily put up during both world wars, to serve as offices for the massive influx of new workers into all spheres of the federal government. In conception, these buildings reflected what had been the basic assumption about mobilization during earlier conflicts: they were designed to be temporary. This was certainly the case with the offices that scarred the vistas on either side of the reflecting pool between the Lincoln and Washington monuments, for these were drab and somewhat shabby, totally lacking in aesthetic appeal, not to mention amenities like air conditioning to ward off the humid Washington summers. It was even true of the Pentagon, which had only been sanctioned by a suspicious Congress on the grounds that it would be turned into a veteran's hospital after "peace is restored and the army no longer needs the room."[1]

In the years since 1945, as the Cold War had gathered momentum, hardly any of these "temporary" buildings had been demolished, while the military remained firmly and permanently ensconced in the Pentagon. In the months after June 1950, as pressure on office space again mounted, sheer necessity dictated that many of Truman's new mobilization agencies be moved into the ugly temporary structures that still lined the Mall. Yet this time, there would be a fundamental difference. Unlike the two world wars, this mobilization was not conceived as a temporary measure to meet a short-term crisis; it was a long-haul strategy, which would stretch into the indefinite future. And the capital's architecture would soon begin to reflect this assumption. As the temporary offices were finally torn down, shiny new permanent structures would be constructed in their place, so that Washington, as one historian has noted, would soon become "at heart, a military headquarters."[2]

In crucial respects, then, the emergence of the contemporary capital can be dated to this period, as numerous buildings were gradually erected to house the burgeoning national security state. But this was not an inevitable, linear process. There would be peaks and troughs, times of uncertainty and confusion—none, perhaps, greater than the period immediately after the Chinese intervention, when the thinking contained in NSC-68 came under close scrutiny, both by an administration that wanted to expedite the whole process and by a political opposition that questioned many of its basic components.

The Impact of Emergency

Just before 10:00 Wednesday morning, December 13, congressional leaders started to arrive at the White House in their black limousines. Back during the June crisis, the president had relied heavily on private briefing sessions with senior legislators, but this meeting would be different. As one of the limousines pulled up and opened its doors, out came not just Bridges, Wherry, and Wiley, who had all been present in the summer sessions, but also Millikin and Taft. As the waiting reporters instantly recognized, Taft's appearance signified that the current crisis was very serious, since this was only the second time that "Mr. Republican" had been allowed inside the building during Truman's tenure.[3]

As soon as the large bipartisan delegation had assembled in the Cabinet Room, the president started the meeting by stressing that it was "essential to speed up our military preparedness at the fastest possible rate." Marshall then explained that until the Chinese intervention, "the Pentagon had been working on the assumption that we would engage in a four-year buildup period"; now, the same goals would have to be achieved by 1952.[4]

But what precisely did this mean? In recent weeks, the Defense Department had privately drafted a "shoot-the-moon" plan, which called for NSC-68 objectives to be reached as soon as possible and envisaged, among other things, fivefold increases in aircraft production and ship modifications by the end of 1951.[5] Marshall, meanwhile, although recognizing the importance of expanding current output, was even more focused on constructing the basic framework of the nation's industrial capacity so that even bigger increases of defense materiel could be swiftly produced should another world war ever break out. All of this would naturally require massive new injections of money, together with wide-ranging controls. Already, the administration had submitted requests to Congress for an additional $16.8 billion. Now, as the bipartisan delegation listened intently, the president elaborated on the importance of another key initiative: a proclamation of national emergency. As well as enhancing his legal powers, he told the legislators, this "would have very great psychological effects on the American people." "It would help create a united front to enable us to 'meet the situation with which we are faced.'"[6]

With congressional leaders duly briefed, the administration engaged in a bout of furious activity to awaken the wider public to the need for faster mobilization. On Friday evening, Truman delivered a major address, carried not

A grim Truman signing the proclamation of national emergency, December 16, 1950. Courtesy of National Archives.

just by all the radio and television networks but also by nine movie theaters in the East and Midwest, which experimented with big-screen video feeds, hoping to attract the many Americans who still lacked a television set.[7]

The speech itself was straightforward and uncompromising. Despite some objections from military planners who continued to worry that an overt indictment of the Soviets might provoke a dangerous escalation of the Cold War, the president began his speech in unambiguous fashion.[8] "Our homes, our nation, all the things we believe in, are in great danger," Truman declared. "This danger has been created by the rulers of the Soviet Union." He then outlined a fourfold program to meet this heightened threat: continued efforts to work with the UN to uphold the principles of freedom and justice, including a rejection of "appeasement" in Korea; enhanced new efforts to strengthen the defense of western Europe, which was also acutely menaced by Soviet designs; massive increases in America's own military capabilities, including expanding personnel in the armed services from 2.5 to 3.5 million; and sustained measures to ensure that the U.S. economy remained "on an even keel," including cuts in nondefense spending, pay-as-you-go taxes, and wide-ranging controls to contain the perils of inflation.[9]

In the next few days, the White House undertook a series of "drastic actions" to begin the implementation of this heightened mobilization program. On Saturday December 16, while the Economic Stabilization Agency canceled the price increases for 1951 car models, a grim-faced president signed the declaration of limited national emergency.[10] On Sunday, the nine-member Wage Stabilization Board (WSB), consisting of representatives from business, labor, and the public, announced that the car freeze was only the first step and that a far broader attack on inflationary pressures would be needed soon.[11] This board was one of the many that had been created following the passage of the Defense Production Act in September, but now the president decided that even more machinery was required. On Thursday, December 21, he therefore moved to establish a new agency, the Office of Defense Mobilization (ODM), which would be headed by Charles E. Wilson, president of General Electric. A strong, uncompromising personality—described by one reporter as a "big bull-necked Irishman from New York's Hell's Kitchen"— Wilson only took the job after the White House agreed to give him sweeping powers to plan and coordinate mobilization.[12]

These bold new actions were markedly different from the administration's low-key rhetoric and studiously subdued mobilization actions of the summer. Officials now concluded that the intensity of the current crisis demanded sweeping new initiatives. They were also determined to learn from past mistakes, to ensure that in this crisis their flank would be protected from political attacks.

Here, Wilson's appointment was especially instructive. While he had extensive experience in the mobilization field, having been the number two man in the equivalent bureau during World War II, it was no coincidence that he was a moderate Republican and thus able to give the government a more bipartisan appearance. Bringing such a man on board, as the White House told reporters, was also "Mr. Truman's answer to those critics at home who have complained that the mobilization effort is too feeble."[13] But would it work? Could Republicans, emboldened by the success of their campaign during the summer and fall, be effectively silenced now?

The first signs were not encouraging. As already discussed (see chapter 5), the administration's halting and oscillating public actions during the first two weeks of the crisis had created a degree of confusion in the public mind, while also providing Republicans with a chance to continue their sniping. On December 13, as the congressional visitors to the White House mulled over the president's proposed national emergency proclamation, many from both sides of the aisle were lukewarm. Some, like Kenneth D. McKellar (D-TN), thought it would be misconstrued as a declaration of war. Others, like Connally, were not sure that "the people would know what it meant." But the most ardent opposition naturally came from Taft, Wherry, and Millikin, who all professed to believe that a proclamation would do little good. It might create a headline for a day or two, they contended, but then it would either be swiftly forgotten or would "needlessly alarm and confuse the people."[14]

Beneath these protestations, what truly troubled nationalist Republicans was the prospect that Truman's new gambit might actually succeed and that a declaration of national emergency might drastically reduce their future maneuvering room. This, at least, was the thrust of a briefing memorandum that staff members on the GOP Policy Committee drafted for Taft, Millikin, Wherry, Bridges, and Wiley. Truman, they concluded, was now trying to escape from all the problems that had plagued him—and benefited the Republicans—both during the summer and in recent weeks. In their view, a state of emergency would serve to "silence congressional and other criticism relating to the national predicament in foreign policy and domestic and domestic activities of the administration." It would also "put behind the present administration in the eyes of the public, the strength of something approaching a 'coalition' government in which the minority *shares responsibility* for operations and events along with the majority." Rather than seeing this as a boon, they worried that it would "compromise the Republican position." If the current crisis continued to escalate, "there might arise the question of the untrustworthiness of the executive branch itself. In such a crisis Congress might be the scene of a last ditch struggle for the preservation of the nation. Such a contingency should be borne in mind in considering any association with a declaration of national emergency, drawn to the president's prescription."[15]

The hostility of nationalist Republicans to a state of national emergency thus stemmed from more than a sense that it would confuse the American public; it was also based on a fear that Truman might be onto something. For if he finally began to exert strong presidential leadership, his likely success might undermine their continued efforts to present a distinctly Republican foreign policy agenda. Hurriedly leaving the White House meeting for an engagement in New York, Taft stopped to reveal his doubts to reporters, although he naturally put a different gloss on his motives. "As to the proposed declaration of a national emergency," he read from a cautiously worded statement, "we did not feel we were sufficiently advised as to the legal effect of such a declaration, or the program that should accompany it, to take a final position on that question."[16]

In the last two weeks of December, this GOP fear that Truman might at last be in a position to dominate the debate seemed well founded. Inside the capital, the short session of the outgoing Eighty-First Congress moved swiftly to grant the administration all it had asked. At noon on December 15, just hours before the president made his speech to the nation, the House began discussing the supplemental appropriations bill, which had now edged up from $16.8 to almost $20 billion. Opening the debate, the chair of the Appropriations Committee, Clarence Cannon (D-MO), "reluctantly" presented the measure, saying he believed there was "no alternative." "We must arm as rapidly as we can," he insisted. "We must be as strong as we can—as soon as we can." Equally reluctantly, even a noted economizer like John Taber (R-NY), the committee's ranking Republican, voiced his agreement, stating that the present crisis left no other choice. When it came to raising new taxes to pay for all this, however, conservative Republicans were not so quiescent, challenging the Democrats' plan, which had been under consideration since the fall, for an excess-profits tax that would bring in $3.3 billion in additional revenue. But the Democratic majority was solid for such a tax, and the president's crisis-focused rhetoric gave their cause obvious momentum. The House even held an unprecedented New Year's Day session in order to pass the two measures before the Eighty-First Congress expired the next day.[17]

Outside the capital, all the momentum seemed to be with the administration in the last two weeks of December. Even before Wilson could settle into his new job, it was clear that the president's declaration of national emergency was having an effect on key interest groups. On one side of the business-labor divide, the automobile executives swiftly agreed to "conform promptly" to the price freeze on new models, something they had hitherto rejected; on the other, ten thousand railroad workers ended a wildcat strike that had recently brought much of the rail system to its knees.[18] On the radio, the mainstream networks were "eager to keep the American public fully informed on the problems and dangers confronting us," especially now that advertising revenue was beginning to pour into news-based programs. On December 18, CBS even proposed a new weekly television show that would "explain the

specific steps which the government is taking in every field—military, for-
policy, industrial, labor, and agricultural—to make the nation's defenses
:ong that no enemy will dare strike," a proposal the Pentagon accepted
alacrity.[19]

'hile Congress and the media largely rallied to the administration's side,
:tate Department worked with overseas allies to improve U.S. defenses
trope. Here, along with the crisis mood, it helped that officials had laid
1 of the groundwork during the fall. Indeed, although the disappoint-
IATO talks of late October had been something of a PR disaster for the
nistration on the eve of the midterm elections, they had at least spawned
wed efforts to bridge the gap between the U.S. and French positions. In
it weeks, Charles Spofford, the U.S. representative to the North Atlan-
)uncil, had broached a compromise idea that soon proved acceptable to
sides. Spofford proposed the creation of German "combat teams." These
smaller than the infantry divisions the Pentagon had hitherto called for,
vould be placed into a NATO force under a supreme commander before
olitical institutions that France proposed had been constructed.[20]

1 December 17, after the French had reluctantly accepted this compro-
. Acheson set off for Brussels for a new round of talks that soon bore fruit.
were "briefer than had been expected," leading newspapers reported,
certainly more harmonious than some participants had foreseen." The
'ord compromise was ratified, which paved the way for Truman to make
key announcements. One declared that the United States would now
additional ground troops to the Continent as soon as possible. The other
led that Eisenhower would become the NATO supreme commander—
rucial appointment the president had hoped to make in October, con-
:d that it would have "great psychological value." Hoping to squeeze as
1 advantage as possible out of Eisenhower's new role, on December 18
Vhite House made the announcement at 6:30 in the morning so that
uld make both that day's European broadcasts and the morning radio
's in the United States.[21]

ell as these achievements, officials could be pleased that in the new crisis
onment, the Republican Party's renewed attacks were not always effec-
During December, Republican efforts to draw blood came in three guises.
first was a resolution Senator James P. Kem of Missouri introduced on
mber 6. Essentially a product of the nationalist wing of the GOP, which
ined suspicious of entangling alliances in general and Britain as an ally
rticular, this resolution stated that any agreements reached during the
nan-Attlee conference "should, under the Constitution, be embodied in
aty which should be submitted to the Senate for ratification." In defend-
uch a procedure, Kem was bland rather than strident, pointing merely
e constitutional proprieties of keeping the legislature fully informed. But

Democrats swiftly accused him of committing grave offenses. In addition to trying to circumvent the Foreign Relations Committee's normal prerogatives, they insisted that he was fostering disunity in the midst of crisis. With Connally and Lucas strongly urging its defeat, on December 19 the Kem resolution was voted down forty-five to thirty, with a solid front of Democrats picking up support from Margaret Chase Smith, Leverett Saltonstall, and Chan Gurney (R-SD).[22]

By this time, however, leading Republicans had pushed forward a far more ominous idea: a party resolution that would condemn Acheson and call for his resignation. Although Taft was particularly enthusiastic about such a resolution, he encouraged moderates to take the lead. As a result, its sponsor was Irving M. Ives of New York, an internationalist senator who normally supported the administration's foreign policy but who now favored a more aggressive stance in Asia. As Ives explained to reporters, "we can't have a situation in a desperately crucial time when the person with the highest authority in foreign affairs doesn't enjoy the confidence of the American people."[23]

Inside the White House, this Republican resolution was greeted with scorn. Truman was always quick to stand by subordinates when the going got tough; he was also convinced that the Republicans were simply playing politics in the midst of an emergency. Seething, he began his press conference on December 19 with a written statement. "How our position in the world would be improved by the retirement of Dean Acheson from public life is beyond me," he told reporters, since Acheson was the architect of most of the key elements of containment. "At this moment, he is in Brussels representing the United States in setting up a mutual defense against aggression." "If those groups attacking our foreign policy and Mr. Acheson have any alternative policies to offer," Truman concluded, "they should disclose them. . . . It is not a time for vague charges and pious generalities."[24]

Significantly, numerous internationalist Republicans agreed, and were soon seeking to distance themselves from the Ives resolution. At the root of their unease was the fact that Taft had acted so precipitously. At the key meeting on December 15, Owen Brewster, who was not normally known for either his restraint in attacking the government or his solicitude for Dean Acheson, had argued that it would be prudent to wait a day or two, during which time Republicans and Democrats could meet and perhaps confer with the president. But Taft had immediately intervened and, according to one account, "very earnestly and excitedly said, 'I am against consultation and I am against bipartisan action.'"[25] Quite apart from the brazenness of this statement, Taft's timing seemed all wrong. Some moderates like Alexander Smith favored a change at the top of the State Department but were opposed to playing politics with such a vital matter in the midst of an acute crisis.[26] Others were more specific. "It was a cowardly thing to do on the eve of [Acheson] going to Europe to represent the nation in this great contest,"

New Hampshire's Charles Tobey thought. "We took power from him by that attack. It was poorly timed and eminent men here, on a non-partisan basis, feel the same way."[27]

But even this act of overreach paled next to the third phase of the nationalist Republican assault. On December 20, the day after Truman wondered publicly whether his critics had anything more to offer than "vague charges and pious generalities," former president Herbert Hoover delivered a national radio address. Arguing that the West could never hope to compete in a ground war with the vast manpower resources available to the communists, Hoover rejected Truman's policy of sending more ground troops to Europe. Instead, Hoover envisaged a national security strategy based on the use of air and naval power to protect key overseas interests, essentially islands like Britain, Japan, Formosa, and the Philippines.[28]

While Hoover's speech was "instigated" by the MBS radio network, it proved such a newsworthy event that the other networks soon canceled their planned shows and carried it on a "delayed basis."[29] With its implied corollary that the United States would no longer seek to defend Continental positions in either Europe or Asia, it presented a major challenge to the administration's whole Cold War strategy. But officials soon counterattacked. Hoover, they stressed, "has been wrong in every great crisis of this generation." And his latest speech, they insisted, was little more than the last gasp of the discredited dogma of isolationism.[30]

State Department officials also hoped to use this occasion to expose the deep fissures inside the GOP. In this task, they had an obvious ally in John Foster Dulles, who was scheduled to make a major speech on the evening of December 29. That day, the State Department press office went to great lengths to give this speech advance billing.[31] Although this transparent effort to drive a wedge between him and the former president angered Dulles, his actual speech was a clear rebuff to the Hoover position. "The whole world can be confident," Dulles declared, "that the U.S. will not, at a moment of supreme danger, shed allies who are endangered and to whom we are bound by solemn treaty, by common heritage, and by past fellowship in war and peace."[32]

As the public digested these speeches, the available evidence suggested that the administration was getting the better of the argument. To be sure, the State Department's PA recognized that "the rude shock of the military retreats in Korea, coupled with a widely shared impression of apathy among our European allies, have awakened some doubts that American power should be irrevocably committed in Europe and Asia." But, it concluded, "the preponderance of American opinion still appears to reject any suggestion for pulling out of Europe. Editorial writers, commentators, and members of Congress continue to argue that US national security is inextricably dependent on the security of Western Europe.... All evidence continues to indicate powerful support for large-scale rearmament and mobilization measures." Hard data soon backed up these sketchy assessments. In January, one National Opinion Research Center poll found 78 percent in favor of the NATO alliance. Other surveys revealed a sharp increase in support for sending arms to Europe, up from 55 percent a year before to 71 percent now.[33]

In private, even Hoover and Taft recognized that they were swimming against the current tide. Although Hoover's associates told reporters that his speech had received a "tremendous, favorable response," Hoover himself remembered that a similar speech in a similar situation ten years before had been most unwelcome.[34] Taft, for his part, thought that "the internationalist press in the East and the New Deal columnists are determined to involve us in the project of a large American army in Europe, and they are doing everything possible to smear statements like that of President Hoover or my own." But though on the defensive, "Mr. Republican" had not abandoned hope. Indeed, recognizing that Hoover's language had been too "uncompromising," Taft worked hard in the first days of the new year to refine the nationalist challenge to government policy.[35]

Gearing Up for the Great Debate

On January 3, the Eighty-Second Congress met for the first time. Two days later, Taft delivered his own attack on the administration's foreign policy. Although more measured than Hoover's recent radio broadcast, Taft's address stressed that, fundamentally, his thinking was "in accord with Mr. Hoover's theory." True, there were differences. Taft added Indonesia, Australia, and New Zealand to Hoover's short list of countries that needed to be protected. He was also careful to stress that U.S. policy had to be global in scope and that there could be no simple withdrawal to the Western Hemisphere. But, like Hoover, he favored air and sea power. He also worried that the massive mobilization the administration envisaged threatened to result in economic collapse. Finally, he stressed that it was vital for a free society to air its differences, even in the midst of crisis. It was a wrong "theory" to maintain "that there shall be no criticism of the foreign policy of the administration, that any such criticism is an attack on the unity of the nation, that it gives aid and comfort to the enemy, and that it sabotages any idea of a bipartisan foreign policy for the national benefit."[36]

Of course, just by highlighting the existence of such a "theory," Taft was implicitly conceding that the president's recent actions had narrowed the maneuvering room on the home front. Historians have also tended to be dismissive of his effort to spark a "great debate," writing it off as little more than "a last-ditch" effort that "led a token force."[37] It was certainly true that events in recent weeks had been going against Taft, closing the window of opportunity that had seemed to open up during the first stage of this new crisis. More ominously, he now had to face the prospect that this challenge to the administration would have an enervating rather than energizing effect on the Republican Party itself. Only recently the fragile Republican coalition had barely held together on the vote over Acheson's censure. Now, there were ample signs that many East Coast Republicans would support key aspects of the government's mobilization program. Perhaps the most notable was Dewey, the party's 1948 presidential nominee, who had recently made a series of bold statements calling both for unity and for an all-out preparedness program even larger and swifter than the administration proposed.[38]

What, then, was Taft hoping to achieve? Although he faced clear risks in challenging the administration, Taft was not simply an ideological martyr, relentlessly pursuing convictions in the direction of likely political oblivion. His position, to be sure, represented deep-seated beliefs. In particular, he worried that extensive and expensive overseas commitments would corrupt the whole nature of the American polity, turning it into a "garrison state" in which the executive wielded executive power, the state interfered too drastically in the economy, and the people swiftly lost basic liberties.[39] But Taft was also a practical politician. And at a tactical level, he had a variety of reasons to hope this new campaign might prove successful, both by placing legislative constraints on the president and by reframing the whole public debate. Indeed, unlike many politicians, Taft did not just consult current surveys and then give up in despair if they opposed his point of view. Rather, he understood that the goal of any public campaign was to try to change the attitudes of the public, press, and fellow legislators. As both Taft and his opponents in the administration recognized, the political mood at the start of 1951 was confused and confusing. But from Taft's perspective, there were a number of grounds to hope for at least a measure of success.

One was the zeal of the nationalist Republicans in Congress, who generally were convinced that events were moving in their direction. The recent election campaign seemed clear proof that vigorous opposition to the administration reaped electoral dividends.[40] Before the new Congress convened, estimates of its basic orientation abounded and were notoriously unreliable. But it was clear that important new allies would bolster Taft. On the floor as a whole, even internationalist Republicans calculated that there were only twelve Republican senators "who regard the defense of Western Europe as a matter of urgent priority." The others could be divided into three schools: "the first is bent on economy"; the second would prefer to "throw our might in the Far Eastern area because it believes that area to be more important than the European area"; and the third "is for defending the Western Hemisphere and giving up on the policy of arming our allies who can't be trusted anyway." In the House, too, the constellation of forces seemed promising for the nationalist cause. Although the Democrats retained a nominal majority of thirty-four, early surveys of new members estimated that 125 would be strong adherents to the nationalist line and another 130 might be won over on certain issues.[41]

What united these legislators was a mixture of beliefs about both policy and process. On the one hand, many shared Taft's suspicion of growing overseas commitments, particularly in terms of sending large land armies to distant parts of the globe. This was the substantive side of the debate, which would revolve around two issues: whether to support Truman's decision to send additional American troops to Europe and whether to endorse the administration's proposal to extend the draft, including a provision for UMST. On the other hand, nationalist Republicans also shared a common belief that constitutional niceties were being ignored and bypassed by an overweening executive, one who barely informed congressmen of his foreign policy moves, let alone consulted them in advance. This was the thrust of the two resolutions that formed the "crux" of the "great debate": a resolution Wherry introduced in the Senate stating "that no ground forces of the United States should be assigned to duty in the European area for the purposes of the North Atlantic Treaty pending the formulation of a policy with respect thereto by Congress," and a resolution Frederic R. Coudert (R-NY) introduced in the House requiring "congressional authorization for sending military forces abroad."[42]

Because their challenge revolved around a complex mixture of different matters, nationalist Republicans had a number of opportunities for tactical maneuvering, any one of which might produce a victory. Their best chance was clearly on the procedural question of consultation, for this tapped into a long-running Republican gripe about the absence of proper bipartisan cooperation, as well as the obvious fact that Truman had failed to ask Congress for a declaration of war at the start of the Korean crisis and now seemed bent on sending more troops to Europe on his own authority. Here, sentiment in the Senate was particularly fluid, and a number of Democrats might be easily attracted to the cause, including Dennis Chavez of New Mexico, Allen Frear of Delaware, Thomas Hennings of Missouri, Spessard Holland of Florida, and John McClellan of Arkansas.[43]

In the House, GOP ranks were fairly solid for the nationalist cause; shortly, 118 of the 199 Republicans in the House would issue a ringing declaration that stated that the nation's foreign policy should "be determined with the full participation and approval" of Congress.[44] Although House Democrats, for their part, might be equally disciplined, as the debate broadened out to other aspects of mobilization, Republicans had a number of cards up their sleeves. They could try to link the issues together, say, by seeking passage of an amendment to the draft bill that would prohibit sending drafted troops to Europe. Because the administration thought time was of the essence, they could also use a variety of procedures to hold up key aspects of the mobilization program in return for concessions. One obvious delaying tactic was a concurrent resolution on troops to Europe, which both the House and Senate would have to vote on. If an impatient administration then tried to expedite matters by cutting off debate or by pushing for a resolution only in the Senate, this would simply confirm GOP charges of an arrogant executive. It might even bring further recruits to the cause, including habitual administration supporters like Mike Mansfield (D-MT) and Abraham Ribicoff (D-CT), who thought the House "should have a say."[45]

Outside the halls of Congress, too, Taft and his associates had reason to believe their campaign might enjoy some success. Despite the administration's recent attempt to seize on the crisis to foster unity, Taft was convinced it still had a glass jaw. The public, he believed, would not simply forget the mistakes of last summer: the bungling and incompetence, the public clashes between leading officials, the lack of adequate presidential leadership at the start of crises, the rhetoric that ebbed and flowed with events on the battlefield. For this reason, Taft continued to accompany his broader attacks with carefully aimed reminders of these leadership flaws. At the end of December, he even told reporters he had "no great confidence" in the judgment of America's military leadership. In a barbed assault that cut to the very heart of the administration's entire PR strategy, Taft charged that there is "a kind of wavering between panic and reassurance that goes right on up to the Pentagon."[46]

While Taft hoped to exploit past failures, his trump card was the current state of the war in Korea, particularly as casualty figures—often distorted and exaggerated—mounted and the fate of American forces in this frozen, faraway country continued to worsen. For Taft, an obvious starting point was to highlight the consequences of presidential adventurism, since Truman had gone to war in Korea without a formal declaration and this policy now seemed such "a costly failure." But he also hoped to exploit the public's growing impatience with allies, which reached its apogee during January, when the UN proved reluctant to pass a resolution condemning China's aggression (discussed in Chapter 8). If allies were so lackluster here, then surely they would be no better inside NATO, which would become another forum where Americans made all the sacrifices while supposed partners continued to wield an excessive influence over policy. Moreover, the whole subtext of GOP utterances was bound up with recent developments on the battlefield. Certainly, nationalist Republicans hoped to tap into a sense of unease about devoting more resources to Europe at a time when the conflict in Korea was going so badly. In particular, Taft's claim that the million men to be sent to Europe might easily be destroyed by "Russian hordes" was intended to feed in to the current concern about the fate of 110,000 GIs who were currently engaged in a long and painful retreat inflicted by the Chinese "hordes."[47]

During January and February, such rhetorical claims seemed likely to resonate. Already, widespread public fears about the course of the war in

Korea had affected army recruitment. As the UN position in Korea worsened, the army desperately needed replacements. With the Pentagon announcing that it would draft eighty thousand men per month for the first three months of 1951, two developments hit the headlines. One was the growing number of "draft delinquents" who failed to respond to their Selective Service call-ups, which in some areas was up substantially when compared to a similar period of World War II.[48] The other was a wave of panic enlistments at the start of the New Year. Rather than waiting to be drafted, thousands of college students were dropping out and volunteering for the military in order to pick which service to enter. This worried not only universities, which were soon lobbying the Pentagon for some help, but also the army, since the volunteers invariably picked the navy and air force—services that were traditionally more popular with recruits, but now had an added luster with so many GI casualties being reported in Korea. To try to halt such panic, on January 19 the Pentagon changed the draft criteria so that students could finish their studies and then pick what service to apply for.[49]

But this initiative did not end the manpower problem. In January and February, senior military officials also noted "considerable restlessness for rotation of troops on the battlefront."[50] If some forces were brought home, however, this would mean sending two National Guard units overseas immediately. Across the country, as the army's chief information officer conceded, there had been "a great deal of concern on the part of individual [National] Guardsmen as to their particular status." This concern was hardly alleviated by the army's own clumsy announcements, which baldly stated that thousands of reservists might soon be sent into the combat zone because casualties had been so high and army training centers had not been able to produce sufficient men.[51] In this panicky environment, it seemed distinctly possible that a Republican campaign that challenged both the underlying concept of a large land army and the immediate issue of sending more troops to Europe might well transform the contours of the debate, both substantively, through a congressional resolution, and more broadly, by changing the minds of a majority of Americans.

For its part, the administration certainly feared the possible consequences of this "great debate," and while nationalist Republicans marshaled their arguments and calculated their prospects, officials thought long and hard about their own posture.

For many, going public looked like the best bet. Truman, angered by the Republican challenge, initially told reporters that if Congress tried to prevent him from fulfilling America's treaty obligations, he would take the issue directly to the American public.[52] The State Department, having borne the brunt of vicious partisan attacks for so long, was also convinced that the time had come to take off the gloves.[53] Hoover's careless language had already provided an opening for government assaults at the end of December. Now, the administration began preparations to use the charge of "isolationism" against Taft, replete with a history of his past record at voting against vital foreign policy measures, from Lend-Lease in 1941 to more recent Cold War initiatives.[54]

And then there was all the planning that was already in the pipeline to launch an intensive publicity campaign to sell NSC-68, using the president's upcoming State of the Union address to begin a wide-ranging effort to convince the public of the need for sustained mobilization. Although this planning was a product of events that now seemed distant—events tied up with the post-Inchon euphoria and consequent fears of a public "letdown"—there remained much to be said for putting these earlier ideas into practice. For one thing, mobilization was more than "a one shot affair like a particular bill to be put through Congress"; it was a whole package of plans that needed the sustained support of both Congress and the public.[55] For another, a wide-ranging PR campaign to take the government's case beyond the confines of the capital would also build on the emergency declaration and the president's recent stark rhetoric, which—in its use of crisis imagery and its stark condemnation of the Soviet Union—had already complicated the calculations of the Republican right.[56]

Back in November, senior officials had envisaged using a "citizens committee" to amplify their mobilization message, and they now had an obvious vehicle at their disposal to do just this: the CPD. This committee had started to coalesce and organize in the late fall, but its early efforts had not gone much beyond private meetings in the Pentagon, placing advertisements in newspapers, and holding a press conference at Washington's Willard Hotel to support Eisenhower's mission in Europe.[57] Now, numerous officials envisaged turning the CPD into something much grander. Their thinking was heavily influenced by the Committee to Sell the Marshall Plan, a pressure group that had been organized in 1947–48 and had worked closely with the administration to reach out to the mass of Americans, sponsoring radio shows, disseminating pamphlets, and organizing speakers. In January, Francis Russell in the State Department's PA met with CPD leaders to prod them toward branching out into a series of local, grass-roots operations that would "both mold public opinion and also give expression to public opinion which already exists but which has no adequate medium through which to make itself heard."[58]

What all this seemed to suggest was that more would be needed than simply private bargaining with key legislators. It was now time to "go public" in earnest, using both the current crisis and the need for specific legislative measures to drum up widespread and enduring support for mobilization. Perhaps it might even be the time to launch the "psychological scare campaign" that some in PA had considered almost a year before, in order to end once and for all the nationalist Republican challenge and ensure the ascendancy of the administration's vision of mobilization.

When Truman went to Capitol Hill on January 8 to deliver his State of the Union message, he pulled few punches. On the podium of the newly decorated House chamber, resplendent in blue and white, the president exuded grim determination. Speaking in a slow steady voice, and ignoring the pointed lack of applause from the GOP side of the aisle, he told legislators that they faced "as grave a task as any Congress in the history of our Republic." Debate was essential, he stressed, but there was "a sharp difference between harmful criticism and constructive criticism." Turning to the source of the country's ills, Truman depicted the Soviet Union as an imperialist regime that was even more ambitious, crafty, and menacing than its czarist predecessor. "If Western Europe were to fall to Soviet Russia," he insisted,

> it would double the Soviet supply of coal and triple the Soviet supply of steel. If the free countries of Asia and Africa should fall to Soviet Russia, we would lose the sources of many of our most vital raw materials, including uranium, which is the basis of our atomic power. And Soviet command of the manpower of the free nations of Europe and Asia would confront us with military forces which we could never hope to equal.

The United States therefore had no choice. It had to work together with its allies to deter future Soviet aggression, providing them not just with military aid but also American troops. At home, moreover, the country had to move ahead with a ten-point mobilization plan, including yet more military appropriations, a revision and extension of the draft, price and wage controls, the housing and training of defense workers, and a major increase in taxes to meet these new costs.[59]

At first glance, this ringing call for unity and action appeared to be the opening salvo in the government's campaign to influence the "great debate." Just before he went up to Capitol Hill to deliver his speech, Truman met with the new Democratic leadership. Fully briefed by the State Department, he used the occasion to press senior Democrats to gear up for the fight ahead, by arranging for the party's most effective advocates "to make speeches on the floor in an organized program which the leaders personally keep on schedule." He also issued clear instructions to the State Department to make sure its officials were available to the Democratic leadership "on a day-and-night basis to help them and any members who are joining in this effort to clarify public understanding of the issues through furnishing materials, drafting speeches, and whatever else may be required."[60]

Planning was also under way for senior officials to make frequent appearances before key committees. Marshall alone was due to make five separate appearances before Congress between the middle of January and the middle of February. Even more prolific was Anna Rosenberg, the new assistant secretary of defense, who would testify on twelve of the fifteen working days between January 10 and 30.[61] Back in the fall, Rosenberg's appointment had been highly contentious, raising a series of protests (typically ill-founded or irrelevant) from Joe McCarthy. But now that she had settled in to office, Rosenberg brought particular PR strengths to her new job. As a renowned New Dealer, she could help mollify labor's growing unease at being kept out of the main government councils (discussed below). As the first woman in such a high-profile Pentagon post, she might also be able to assuage the fears of mothers who were generally reluctant to see their boys drafted. As Rosenberg pointedly noted whenever the opportunity arose, she was from "that sex which used to stay up at night waiting until every door was closed and every light was out to make sure that every member of the family, even though they may have reached the age of eighteen, was safely in."[62]

In terms of lobbying Congress, all these actions were significant and intensive. Yet in the final analysis, this furious bout of activity would be largely confined to the capital. When it came to reaching out beyond Washington, the government's efforts would remain curiously anemic. Even the CPD remained very much an elite pressure group. Although it engaged in a fund-raising drive, expanded its membership to one hundred, and opened a full-time office in the capital, it generally shied away from organizing grass-roots operations and only engaged in a limited bout of publicizing through a series of NBC broadcasts, newspaper ads, and private lobbying of key congressmen.[63]

Direct efforts by administration officials would be even more limited. Indeed, despite all the planning, and despite the widespread fears that the Republican campaign might unduly influence the mass of Americans, ultimately there would be no pamphlets or major speeches by key officials to ram home the message of the president's State of the Union address. Outside committee rooms of Congress, officials would remain largely mute.

Why was this? Why did the administration still shy away from a major effort to sell mobilization to the public? One of the major obstacles was the president himself. This was no longer because of his old suspicions of big defense budgets. By now Truman was committed to mobilization and reconciled to abandoning the domestic reform initiatives of his Fair Deal program.[64] Instead, what concerned him was the need to control the dissemination of sensitive material in the midst of a crisis. MacArthur's outbursts in December had already forced the White House to issue its so-called gagging order that prevented officials from discussing controversial subjects without authorization (see chapter 8). Now, the military was also in the midst of instituting censorship in the field, in a desperate effort to get control of the publication of troop movements, casualty figures, and the state of the army's morale.

On January 4, as the renewed Chinese offensive forced UN forces out of Seoul, an angry Truman met with the National Security Council. "Public disclosure of classified information regarding this government's national security policies and plans in these critical times," he complained, "has become so flagrant in recent weeks that I feel compelled to bring this matter to your attention at this meeting." He was particularly concerned about "recent disclosures in the press and radio of highly classified atomic energy information and top-secret data contained in the NSC-68 series," especially in stories written by the Alsop brothers. In the current crisis, he now deemed the divulgence of such material completely unacceptable. When officials talked to reporters, they would have to be far more careful about revealing details in the document—a presidential command that went a long way toward ending plans to publish extracts from NSC-68 in pamphlet form.[65]

Truman could be an impulsive president. This had its positive side: the renowned decisiveness of a leader who refused to agonize over issues but rather decided in an instant, once the "buck" had finally reached the Oval Office, and then never looked back. Yet during the Korean War, this mode of decisionmaking was not always an advantage. Often, Truman failed to play an important part in the early stages of planning on a particular issue, unwilling to step in and give guidance as his subordinates battled or agonized over their course. If a decision reached him, he rarely hesitated. But his choice was not always informed; sometimes it clashed with the basic recommendations of his senior advisers or even ran counter to months of hard work by his subordinates. Small wonder, then, that some historians depict him "playing a generally aloof but also a spasmodically disruptive role in the policy process."[66] In terms of public leadership, too, Truman's interventions could have a disruptive effect. As his January 4 command to the National Security Council indicates, just one statement by him could undo months of hard planning.

Still, Truman's personal whims were not the only reason for the administration's reluctance to go public in an aggressive fashion. Also important were a set of fears about the current state of public opinion, fears that were not simply confined to battling nationalist Republicans on the right. In fact, had the only public opinion problem been the Hoover-Taft-Wherry challenge, the government might well have engaged in a vigorous attempt to silence these critics by dramatizing the extent of the danger, for this had clearly worked its magic during December. But as the situation in Korea deteriorated, officials were also gripped by another familiar fear: the prospect that the home front might overheat in the midst of a crisis, resulting in burgeoning calls for a dangerous escalation of the Cold War.

For the most part, this fear was not based on hard evidence. There were no polls that suggested a public demand for anything that smacked of a preventive war. There was not even any concrete reason to believe that key opinionmakers were starting to incline in this direction. But as one senior State Department official pointed out, this line of argument was "no less dangerous because its authors have been unwilling to be perfectly frank."[67] More to the point, in the realm of rumor, officials received a number of indications that support for a preventive war was indeed growing, and that it might even encompass those on all sides of the political spectrum.

In the depths of the winter crisis, these rumors centered on the emergence of a new pressure group advocating preventive war, to be headed by the ex-communist Frieda Utley and supported by figures like Father Edmund A. Walsh, who had just provided the moral justification for such a belligerent course in a *Washington Sunday Star* article. Although the details were sketchy, a lieutenant colonel named Herschel Williams was thought to be at the heart of this embryonic organization, using his Washington home as a "political salon" to recruit opinion-makers in the media and military who were part of a growing "hate-Stalin-and-do-something-about-it-at-once school." In the frenzied environment at the start of January, some officials even worried that Williams and his ilk might attract support from an unlikely alliance of Republican nationalists, air power proponents, and senior members of the internationalist establishment.[68]

One figure who was known to be "a close personal friend" of Colonel Williams and had made frequent appearances to his political salon was Stuart Symington, the head of the National Security Resources Board. In early January, Symington sent an explosive memorandum to the president that described containment as "a dangerous and extravagant policy" and concluded that the administration's current stance was "not strong enough to match the organized and aggressive growth of communism." Truman immediately rejected this as pure "bunk," but it was clear that Symington was not an isolated voice.[69] Ominously, leading Republicans were again hinting that radical measures might be necessary. Although Taft always rejected a preventive strike, others to the right of the GOP were firm proponents of air power and were close allies of those, like General Carl Spaatz, the former air chief, who believed it was better to risk war with the Soviets "now than a few years hence, by which time Russia can be expected to have an A-bomb stockpile." Within weeks, Wherry would even call on Spaatz to testify in the "great debate."[70] And Wherry doubtless knew that some active officers in the air force were eager to tell reporters (off the record, of course) that by July the United States would have enough atomic bombs to "flatten" the Soviet Union in thirty days.[71]

Nor was this all. As the rumor mill went into overdrive, the State Department even heard that the CPD inclined in the same disturbing direction. As one journalist told a Policy Planning Staff official, in public, CPD leaders like James Conant and Vannevar Bush might be staunch opponents of preventive war. But behind the scenes, they were part of a group that "was convinced that time was *not* on our side and that this country should in 1951 force the issue with the Soviet Union. The conclusion was that the United States should use its atomic superiority against the Soviet Union this year."[72]

Top officials in the White House, State Department, and Pentagon remained adamantly opposed to a preventive war. Convinced that the United States was still too weak to prevail in a direct face-off with the Soviet Union, they decided to make another effort to confront a familiar problem: how to stop the home front from overheating, given the likelihood that this would create irresistible pressures for a dangerous escalation of the whole Cold War.[73]

The most obvious method was to scale back the crisis-focused rhetoric of December by issuing a string of reassuring utterances. As Marshall now explained, the country had to move ahead with its mobilization program "with determination, but also with patience and calm deliberation." Acheson, meanwhile, used a series of background briefings to quash forecasts of an impending superpower confrontation. He even denied that officials had a "date toward which we were aiming our military buildup." "He did not believe war was inevitable," Acheson told three reporters on January 18, adding that "he did not feel that any secretary of state should ever base his policy on the assumption that all our energies should be directed toward preparing ourselves for war at a given date."[74]

In earlier crises, Truman had also attempted to keep the home front cool by paying careful attention to symbolism—to the setting, timing, and frequency of speeches and other official actions. Now, the White House and State Department acted in an equally cautious fashion. On January 12, Acheson and Harriman stepped in to veto a Pentagon decision to send General Curtis LeMay on a high-profile fact-finding mission to Korea, on the basis that the superhawk air force commander "had become something of a 'Mr. Atom Bomb'" in the public mind, and his presence "would excite people unduly." Meanwhile, the president had become convinced that certain officials could not be trusted to talk to reporters at such a sensitive moment. Rather than launch an intensive campaign to reach out to the public beyond Washington, the White House moved to ensure that the government's efforts would be confined to lobbying Congress on specific items of legislative business, where it could hopefully exercise greater control over what was said and done. As a result, when it came to the scope of official actions, this debate would be "great" only inside the capital itself.[75]

The Great Debate

Congressional deliberations began in earnest in the days immediately following the president's State of the Union address. On January 8, Wherry introduced his resolution on the Senate floor. Two days later, as legislators digested this challenge to the president, a subcommittee of the Senate Armed Services Committee, under the chairmanship of Lyndon Johnson, began hearings into another key aspect of the government's program: a new draft bill that contained UMST. Over the succeeding weeks, as the debates on these two measures unfolded, there was one final reason the administration failed to launch a vigorous information campaign outside the capital: ultimately, behind-the-scenes maneuvering in the halls of Congress would prove sufficient to head off the Republican challenge, because on key mobilization issues the administration and its allies in Congress had clear advantages that helped them ward off a substantial defeat.

The first of these strengths was the support of powerful committee chairs, who generally sympathized with the government's agenda and were willing to work with it to set the basic rules of the game—rules that placed nationalist Republicans at a distinct disadvantage. Of course, this was an obvious consequence of the slim but significant majority the Democrats had been able to retain in the midterm elections. But two other developments also magnified the importance of committee leadership.

One was the lack of leading nationalist Republicans on either the Senate Foreign Relations or Armed Services committees. This was an obvious error by Taft and his associates, but it stemmed from a conscious calculation. Until now, nationalist Republicans had not believed there was much to gain by sitting on these key committees. In fact, by their absence they had been able to have it both ways. They could constantly complain about the administration's lack of consultation, knowing full well that it was difficult for officials to include them in a regular system of formal briefings without undermining the whole committee structure and antagonizing the ranking members on these committees. They could also continually criticize the content of the government's policy, safe in the knowledge that because they had not been consulted, they bore no responsibility for its formulation and implementation. Yet as the "great debate" would clearly reveal, there was an obvious downside to this outsider status: a lack of control over substantive items as they moved through the various legislative stages.

The other development that magnified the importance of the committee structure was a decision by Tom Connally to refer the matter of troops to Europe to a joint body, containing members of both the Foreign Relations and Armed Services committees. This was vital for a variety of reasons. The combined clout of both committees would make it extremely difficult for their findings to be reversed on the floor. In the joint body, the administration was also likely to prevail. Although the administration had lost powerful Democratic allies in the recent election, in the middle of December the White House and State Department had worked closely with the Senate Democratic Policy Committee to find suitable internationalist replacements.[76] More important, the merging of the two committees ensured that the whole subject was managed by two very different characters, Tom Connally and Richard B. Russell, who together would prove to be a complementary and effective mix that would greatly help the administration's cause.

Although they were both southerners, Connally and Russell could not have been more dissimilar in temperament, style, and to a lesser extent, policy orientation. Connally was something of a political showman, a pugnacious orator and debater whose outgoing political style was exemplified by his very first race for Congress, when he had gained visibility and notoriety through a variety of advertising gimmicks, including riding around Texas in a "shiny black" Buick with "the brightest red wheels you ever saw." Connally could also boast a long history as an ardent internationalist, dating back to the 1930s, when he had been an early opponent of attempts to keep the United States neutral as the Germans, Italians, and Japanese expanded. In recent years, this up-front senator had become one of the government's key spokesmen on foreign policy issues, using his debating skills to challenge dissenters on both the Senate floor and the radio airwaves.[77]

Russell, in contrast, shunned the spotlight. He distrusted reporters, for he was convinced that they "often twisted, garbled, or misstated the facts." He hated the showy, social side of Washington life, and would rather spend quiet nights in his lodgings in the Mayflower Hotel reading the *Congressional Record* and boning up on legislative business. And when it came to pushing this business through the Senate, he was also reluctant to be out front on any issue, preferring to work behind the scenes, where he could use his detailed knowledge and reputation for integrity to construct winning coalitions. On substantive matters, Russell had a somewhat ambiguous past. Ultimately a loyal Democrat, he had supported key administration policies on farming and education and had cast his vote for Truman in 1948, despite the temptation of the anti–civil rights candidate Strom Thurmond. But Russell remained a passionate opponent of the president's civil rights initiatives, and from time to time he had been known to join forces with Taft and the conservatives. Increasingly a staunch Cold Warrior who had always been a leading champion of strong defenses, Russell had also taken his time to become fully reconciled to the need for extensive overseas commitments. Indeed, he described himself as "by instinct, an isolationist," though one "who supports the flag when it is committed to any danger or trouble." At root, he thought that the United States should focus first and foremost on protecting its vital interests, rather than searching to solve the world's problems, especially with expensive foreign aid programs.[78]

That Russell was now working alongside Connally was important because it gave the whole debate a less partisan flavor. It was no longer just Connally, the administration's central spokesman, versus the Republican right. Although a Democrat, Russell was a less polarizing figure, someone southern Democrats and moderate Republicans trusted, someone whose knowledge, record, and demeanor could serve to dampen the passions that threatened to get out of control. Russell already effectively controlled UMST, which he ardently believed in, convinced it would achieve the unlikely combination of strengthening the nation's defenses while saving money.[79] Now, he could bring his impressive skills to bear on the other, more important, dimension of the "great debate."[80]

With Connally and Russell in charge, the rules of the game were swiftly established in the administration's favor. Just days after Wherry introduced his resolution, the State Department began working closely with Connally to ensure that only the Senate voted on any resolution. As well as speeding up proceedings when time was of the essence, this would ensure that whatever emerged at the end would only be advisory, not legally binding. At the same time, Connally also moved to transform the whole emphasis of the resolution. Rather than Wherry's negative attempt to block the sending of troops to Europe, Connally's substitute would become a positive affirmation of congressional support for the policy, thereby demonstrating unity and strengthening the whole policy at a stroke.[81]

Once the Joint Committee hearings began, Connally and Russell worked hard to structure their course, determining the order in which witnesses appeared, leading off with the first questions, and setting the length of the entire proceedings. Here, their trump card was Eisenhower, who, after accepting the commission to head NATO forces, had set off on a European tour on January 6. Ike's return would clearly be the single most important factor in the congressional debate, so the Democratic leadership postponed the committee hearings until he could present his detailed findings. In the interim, the administration also benefited from the marked improvement in the Korean situation in the wake of Ridgway's limited offensive, which obviously helped to undermine the GOP's effort to capitalize on battlefield defeat.

On February 1, Eisenhower briefed members of both houses on his European trip. In typically confident fashion, speaking only from a few notes, he insisted that the European allies were determined to play their full part in NATO, that their greatest need at the moment was arms and equipment, and that more U.S. troops should only be sent to the Continent in a ratio to those provided by the European countries. On February 2, Eisenhower then reiterated these arguments to a large radio audience, before opening up the Joint Committee hearings, speaking for two hours in executive session and repeating his conclusions.[82] "It was interesting and Ike was inspiring," one sympathetic Republican senator noted. Most members had confidence in him, another agreed, "and will be guided by what he has to say."[83]

Two weeks later, when Marshall and Acheson took the stand, the hearings were opened to the public. The administration's goal now was, first, to scotch rumors that the U.S. commitment to Europe would be huge. At the start of his testimony, Marshall "reluctantly and after much consideration" decided to divulge the precise nature of the American commitment. The U.S. plan, he told legislators, was to send only four additional divisions; the focus of America's effort would remain on air and naval forces. Marshall's revelation was a key moment, for it went a long way toward demolishing the Republican right's claims that the administration planned—once again—to shoulder the principal burden while so-called allies complained but failed to do their bit. In the following days, other senior officials buttressed the government's case. Acheson, keenly aware that he was a polarizing figure, adopted a mollifying stance, trying to narrow the differences between the administration and its critics by contending that the whole debate was only over means, not ends. The Joint Chiefs testified separately, all agreeing that the need for American troops was vital. Then came Dewey and Stassen, two leading Republican internationalists, who both strongly endorsed the administration's stance.[84]

The contrast between a united administration and a Republican Party now airing its divisions in public was striking. It also marked something of a departure from the situation of the summer, when the GOP had been able to forge a fairly united stance on issues like internal subversion and the government's lackluster response to the Cold War in Asia, while different branches of the administration had clearly been at loggerheads. On those earlier issues, moreover, the Republican challenge had generally been in the direction of doing more to meet the danger. Now, however, nationalist Republicans were being pushed onto the defensive, accused of adopting a negative and obstructionist posture toward a key Cold War initiative. This was not just a matter of where and how to combat communism, or even the fact that the GOP position was easily caricatured as isolationist, although both these developments were important. It was also a product of the underlying logic of the nationalist Republican argument, which was clearly a hard sell when stripped to its bare bones.

The basic problem stemmed from the mixture of optimism and pessimism that underpinned the Republican case. Taft, in particular, was upbeat about the international situation, in the sense that he thought Soviet military power was "overestimated," that the Kremlin was not ready to start a war, and that it was therefore unnecessary to send lots of U.S. troops to Europe. But he was also pessimistic about what the United States could afford, convinced that the country was economically, politically, and socially unprepared to send sufficient troops to the Continent. The taxes required were "beyond our economic capacity." The repercussions on the entire nation would also be grave: the loss of basic freedoms and the emergence of a "garrison state." "Nothing can destroy this country," Taft believed, except the type of "overextension" the administration envisaged.[85]

In response, the administration could deploy powerful arguments. In the midst of a desperate battle in Korea, which officials clearly blamed on the Soviet Union, it seemed prudent to prepare for the worst. Only extensive new efforts, such as training huge numbers of troops and sending some to Europe, could deter future acts of Soviet aggression. Moreover, it was in America's interest to offer protection to allies; for, as Eisenhower and Acheson both stressed, these countries contained two hundred million free people whose skills and resources contributed to the defense of the free world, and who, if lost, would greatly enhance the power of the Soviet bloc.[86]

Crucially, too, officials were in the healthy position of fulfilling what one historian has dubbed "the first commandment of American politics: thou shalt always be optimistic when addressing the electorate."[87] Administration spokespersons were certainly quick to emphasize that the country was in better shape to meet the current crisis than it had been ten years earlier, on the eve of Pearl Harbor. They also stressed the affordability and efficiency of current mobilization plans. As Marshall constantly reiterated, these were far more cost-effective than the nation's "destructive" tendency to "make short-term plans for immediate emergencies to be followed by abrupt demobilization" the moment the crisis abated.[88]

As the debate developed, nationalist Republicans soon recognized that they had been forced into an increasingly embattled and defensive position. Wherry, who had been one of the most aggressive and combative GOP spokesmen in the summer, now complained that he was the victim of a "vicious smear campaign" that had erroneously painted him as a "defeatist." Taft, meanwhile, was quick to lash out at the media. Still convinced that the American public widely supported his own position, he concluded that the problem must be "the wide influence of the administration with editors, columnists, commentators, and others on questions of foreign policy" who "seem to accept blindly whatever the administration is doing or proposing to do." Acknowledging that the "great debate" was going badly, he even started to fret that "the Republican Party cannot win an election until there is at least some independence on their part in the development of foreign policy."[89]

Overall, Taft's gloom was well justified. By March, it was clear that in broad terms, the administration was likely to get its way. Although much tough bargaining and debating was required both in committee and on the Senate floor, by the start of April, Senate Resolution 99 passed by sixty-nine to twenty-one votes. Based on an earlier Connally-Russell draft, this resolution approved not only Eisenhower's appointment as NATO commander but also the president's decision to send four additional divisions to Europe. Meanwhile, the administration's draft bill appeared to be in good shape, too. The Senate had passed a measure that lowered the draft age from nineteen to eighteen, increased the length of service to twenty-four months, and included the possibility of UMST after the current crisis had subsided. The House had moved more slowly and more reluctantly, but on April 13 it passed its own draft bill by 372 to 44, with just 37 Republicans and 7 Democrats voting against it. The bill was now scheduled to go to conference, where the differences between the House and Senate versions could be ironed out.[90]

Still, even with all its advantages, the administration's victory in the "great debate" was only conditional. In part, this was because the nationalist

Republican calculations of early January were not entirely unfounded. Inside Congress, a good deal of resentment remained toward America's allies in the wake of recent Korean War experiences. Legislators were also uneasy about what appeared to be a growth of presidential power that might leave little room for congressional input in foreign policy. Both sentiments resulted in the passage of nonbinding amendments to the Senate resolution that greatly annoyed senior officials. One called on NATO partners to provide "the major contribution" to western European defense; the other opposed sending additional American troops to Europe "without further congressional approval." The administration vigorously opposed this second amendment, since it placed a severe restraint on future action. But eleven Democrats abandoned their president, joining thirty-eight Republicans, mostly of a nationalist bent, in pushing it through. Some of these were habitual rebels, such as McCarran and Edwin C. Johnson (D-CO), who rarely voted for any of the government's policies. But others—like Frear, Holland, and Chavez, all of whom the State Department had viewed as persuadable back in January—had now defected. This was perhaps a good indication of how volatile the situation was in Congress, how small the margins were between success and failure, and how important the shrewd marshaling of forces had been to maintaining a key aspect of the administration's whole Cold War strategy.[91]

The Problem with Labor

In one of the least noticed initiatives of the period, the Commerce Department designated the first week of March "National Smile Week." Despite the continuing struggle in Congress, it seemed a fitting time for mirth and relaxation. The news from Korea was now better. Not only had UN forces contained the massive Chinese offensive, but under Ridgway's command, they were inching back up the peninsula and would soon be in a position to recapture Seoul. At home, other officials, departments, and bureaus were also sending out an upbeat message. The State Department picked this moment to release detailed figures to prove that the communists were losing ground all over Europe; Charles Wilson issued a report stressing that the country was rapidly reaching the point where it would be so strong that no enemy would be foolish enough to attack it; and, as if to underline the fact that the danger was passing, Truman and Acheson both left town, flying off to vacations in Key West and Bermuda, respectively.

Although these developments were hardly earth-shattering, when lumped together the overall message seemed clear: it was time to slacken off. As James Reston of the *New York Times* pointed out, this was a perverse message for officials to be sending out, because there were very real indications that the public had already reached the same conclusion, and the government's main focus ought to be on ending rather than encouraging such a dangerous notion. "The basic problem in Washington today," Reston noted colorfully on March 11, "is how to turn Uncle Sam, a good sprinter, into a marathon runner. For a guy with long shanks and knobby knees, old Mr. Whiskers can spurt faster than any bear this side of Vladivostok, but can he stay the course? That's what is worrying official Washington."[92]

Inside the Pentagon, Marshall was especially worried, for he was always inclined to believe that Americans were too prone to lapse into lethargy the minute a crisis seemed to have passed. On March 27, in an effort to change this new mood, he held a press conference. Pointing to the sense of crisis that had gripped the nation in December and January, Marshall recollected his prediction back then that the mood would soon change and that by 1952, if a new world war had not erupted, "we'd have a hard time with appropriations. I thought possibly we might even get it in September," he told the press, "but I never dreamed that we'd get it in February."[93] Marshall's concern was with the draft bill, which he hoped would include UMST but which he feared a new bout of congressional complacency might still derail. But as fears of a "letdown" intensified, perhaps the most threatened aspect of the government policy was its plan for economic stabilization.

The problem here came from labor. With the battlefield situation suddenly more stable, many unions no longer seemed ready to make the necessary sacrifices for the defense effort. The first flashpoint came on the railways. In December, at the height of the crisis in Korea, the White House had helped to broker a draft agreement between the railroad companies and the railroad brotherhoods to end a twenty-three-month pay dispute. By February, however, with union restraint weakening, this agreement had broken down, resulting in a series of wildcat strikes that brought the nation's rail network to a standstill and threatened both civilian and military production.[94]

Inside the administration, officials felt they had little choice but to clamp down hard on the rail strikers. Truman himself had always had a somewhat ambiguous relationship with labor. He had been happy to accept its endorsement during political campaigns, and had even considered its active support vital to his surprise reelection in 1948. But he was also convinced that unions should act responsibly and always bear in mind the needs of the community as a whole. Whenever they contravened such standards, as in the national rail strike of 1946, he was prepared to get tough, even to the extent of drafting strikers into the army.[95] In this case, the White House was also under pressure to end a dispute that was wreaking havoc both with defense production and civilian transportation. In Congress, Republicans and southern Democrats were calling for legislation to induct railroad workers with occupational deferments into the army, and even the new senate majority leader, Ernest W. McFarland (D-AZ), told reporters that the strikers were "ruining their public relations, not only with Congress but with the people, by hurting the war effort." Small wonder that the president decided to act decisively, calling out the army to break the strike, as "badly shocked" union leaders directed their members back to work.[96]

But even this was not the only flashpoint. While many officials fretted that the overall public mood was excessively cool and calm, the economy began to overheat. With more and more resources being sucked into the mobilization drive, the Consumer Price Index soon reached record highs, topping even the "great inflation" of 1948.[97] By January 26, the situation was so bad that officials believed they had no choice but to institute price controls. The decision, when it was announced, came "in an atmosphere of hasty improvisation," after the White House sent out orders demanding immediate action. In a frenzied press conference attended by more than a hundred reporters, photographers, and newsreel camerapersons, the head of the Economic Stabilization Agency, Eric Johnston, announced the immediate institution of sweeping wage and price controls, adding that this was only a "stopgap" measure, pending a more detailed policy with "a little more flexibility."[98]

Johnston's caveat was important, because none of these developments were likely to sit well with the American Federation of Labor and Congress of Industrial Organizations. Until now, the unions had enjoyed a fairly close relationship with the administration. Although militant action by the rank and file had periodically upset the president, the bosses of the big national unions were generally a conciliatory bunch. They also wanted to position themselves in the mainstream of the debate over foreign policy. As well as expelling communist members, they had been staunch supporters of all the major containment policies. "This mobilization," one senior leader declared in December, "may last a generation. . . . It is imperative that we keep our productive machinery going at full speed ahead."[99] Seeking to line up their membership behind the government, in the middle of December most of the main union leaders had even grouped together to form the powerful United Labor Policy Committee (ULPC), which immediately announced that it would tacitly support a wage freeze, as long as it included enough flexibility to permit upward adjustments to counteract the effect of inflation.[100]

By February, however, much of labor's earlier goodwill toward the administration had dissipated, and the ULPC was in open revolt against it. Significantly, senior union leaders were not so much troubled by the president's heavy-handed action in the rail strike, which was not the first time he had intervened in such a direct fashion. Nor were they overly disturbed by the introduction of price controls, which were widely seen as inevitable by January. What really riled them was the basic attitude of Charles E. Wilson, the man the president had chosen to head the mobilization effort.

As president of General Electric, Wilson had been known for his tough, nononsense bargaining with unions. As head of the ODM, he was fierce in his efforts to expand his bureaucratic domain, and had few qualms about taking over tasks that had previously been in the hands of key labor allies such as Maurice J. Tobin at the Labor Department or Symington at the National Security Resources Board. Nor was Wilson much of a diplomat. Although he went through the motions of consulting labor leaders, he often gave them the impression that his mind was already made up and there was little they could say or do to alter things.[101]

By February, the unions placed Wilson's specific sins into two closely related categories. The first revolved around the thorny matter of participation in the inner councils of government. At the start of 1951, labor could boast twenty-four representatives in official posts.[102] But what it really wanted was someone in the ODM of the same rank as Lucius D. Clay and Stanley Weinberg, Wilson's two principal assistants. Union leaders were particularly keen to balance the influence of Clay, who they deeply distrusted because of his past support for compulsory labor mobilization.[103] And when Wilson repeatedly vetoed their suggestions for a position of such stature, they became deeply annoyed.[104]

With mutual hostility mounting, union leaders soon began to think the worst about a more important bone of contention: the specific details of the new wage and price controls. Of course, any hasty wage freeze is bound to result in inequities, with workers who have just received a pay increase faring better than those who have not. But the hurried institution of controls on January 26 had been made with no input from labor. In the next few days, the WSB met to hammer out revisions that would inject greater degree of flexibility into the wage and price freeze. But labor members on the board, constantly outvoted by their business and public counterparts, felt their voice was again being ignored.[105]

Unable to make any headway in these private meetings, on February 16 the ULPC issued a stinging press release. Vigorously protesting "the unworkable and unfair wage formula adopted by the WSB," the ULPC announced that its members would withdraw from this body.[106] In the next few days, Truman and his aides worked feverishly behind the scenes to try to forge concessions that would mollify labor, including "escalator" clauses tied to inflation and productivity that would enable wages to rise above the imposed ceiling. By now, however, labor's resentment ran so deep that even such pocketbook concessions were not enough. This became clear on February 28, when a three-hour meeting between the ULPC and Wilson ended with the union representatives walking out of all the positions they occupied throughout government.[107]

Truman was now in an extremely awkward spot. His appointment of Wilson had been an attempt to broaden the administration, to try to give it more of a national complexion. In a sense, it had been a victory won by the Republicans and their constant criticisms since the summer, for the president had decided that his main vulnerability was on the right and that a successful mobilization strategy would have to include moderates from this flank. In a certain sense, too, it had worked, for many business leaders were content with the way things were going.[108]

Yet by tacking so close to the business end of the economic spectrum, the mobilization program had alienated labor. Inside the White House, aides worried that the ULPC walkout might herald a new bout of strikes, which would severely damage the overall preparedness program. The president's advisers were concerned, too, about the ramifications of alienating such a powerful member of the Democratic coalition. And in private discussions, they had few doubts that it was Wilson, not labor, who was largely to blame.[109]

But what could be done? Until now, private bargaining had failed. The White House was constrained in what it could propose, since a major concession to labor would be widely viewed as a direct repudiation of Wilson. Business leaders also made it clear that there were distinct limits to what they would accept. Behind the scenes, White House aides continued to think long and hard about ways to conciliate labor, but the basic clash would remain throughout March and April, with few signs that labor was about to return to government.[110]

The administration's frustration and anxiety was in full evidence on March 14, at a meeting attended by senior officials involved with mobilization. Eric Johnston led off, forlornly recounting all his labor problems, from the ULPC walkout to a series of strikes, ongoing and threatened, in the woolen and packinghouse industries. "Is the American public prepared to receive, or does it want to have stabilization?" he asked the meeting, adding that he feared many groups were now reluctant to make the necessary sacrifices. Marshall then stepped in with his own analysis. This disturbing situation, he insisted, had been "created to a considerable extent by the absence of an effective PR program to acquaint the general public with the underlying causes of a need for stabilization." Around the table, everyone nodded their assent. "The stabilization program must be continued," it was agreed, "or the result can only react to the detriment of national security. Accordingly, a carefully planned PR program to acquaint the American public with the need for stabilization must be undertaken."[111]

Yet implementing such a strategy was not easy. It was not just a matter of "National Smile Week" or the awkward timing of Truman's and Acheson's vacations. Wilson also proved to be a loose cannon. As well as antagonizing labor, he picked April 1 to issue his first public report on the nation's defenses on. Blithely ignoring the suggestions of other senior officials, his report was essentially a self-serving document that focused first and foremost on all the ODM's achievements under his command.[112] Indeed, the end result was so upbeat that rival bureaucrats and senior journalists were frankly puzzled over what he was trying to achieve. As one official on the National Security Resources Board complained, his claim that "everything is on the right track and going well" seemed to give everyone who wanted to leave a defense job the freedom to do so. "It is appropriate that the report is issued on *April First*," the official concluded acerbically. "I just hope it doesn't fool everybody!"[113] Others shared this sense of dismay. "The hard news on the front page of this morning's newspapers," Reston agreed, "illustrates why the ordinary American has trouble figuring out who's ahead." While in one building Marshall had told reporters that "he was astonished at the relaxation of public and congressional support for a long-term defense effort," in another building, "Mr. Wilson, in his first press conference since taking over the mobilization job three months ago, acted astonished about how well we were doing."[114]

Reston himself put the problem down to coordination, and even thought Washington could learn a lot from military-media relations in Korea itself, where Truman's gagging order had "worked fairly well."[115] Given the military's recent struggle to find a workable system to control war correspondents, this suggestion demonstrated just how bad things had gotten on the mobilization front. On returning from his vacation, Truman therefore decided to act. He was certainly troubled about the mounting public confusion over mobilization. But he was also worried by the fact that since the Chinese intervention, the administration had found it extremely difficult to provide a plausible public answer to another vexed question that was increasingly dominating the discourse: why were so many American boys still dying in faraway Korea?

8

WHY KOREA?

While many in Washington were preoccupied with the problems of mobilization, news of the unfolding tragedy in
Korea started to reverberate across America. "The hour is approaching,"
Raymond Gramm Swing told his large radio audience in the middle of January, "for the painful but necessary decision to pull out of Korea"—a point
that newspapers like the *Richmond Post-Dispatch* and *Seattle Times* endorsed.
Surveying the different arguments for and against withdrawal, in the middle
of January the *Washington Post* adjudged that those who advocated getting
out now had the "more impressive" case. For some, like Lippmann, a comprehensive Far Eastern settlement could only be achieved once the United
States had abandoned Korea.[1] But most, especially on the Republican end of
the spectrum, believed that a withdrawal ought to precede vigorous retaliation against the Chinese mainland. This was certainly the view of Taft, who,
when asked by one reporter what he would have done if he had been president in June 1950, replied, "I would have stayed out." "What would you do
now?" asked another. "I think I would get out and fall back to a defensible
position in Japan and Formosa. I certainly would if I thought there was danger by staying of losing any considerable number of men." But at the same
time, Taft hastened to add, the United States should also take the "shackles"
off Chiang Kai-shek and allow him to make a "full-scale diversion" in Korea
or South China.[2]

By the middle of January, such statements appeared to be both affecting
and reflecting the contours of public opinion beyond the confines of the capital. According to one Gallup poll, 66 percent of Americans now wanted the
United States to "pull out" of Korea altogether.[3] "There seems little question
that American opinion has moved a long way toward concluding that the
Korean action has been a mistake," the State Department's PA reported on

January 19. "For the American public the issue 'Why Do We Stay in Korea?' has become of primary importance." Since August, for instance, polls had demonstrated a sharp rise from 20 to 49 percent of the population thinking that the war was misguided. "It seems clear," PA concluded, "that the public sees the issue of continued U.S. support to the UN in Korea primarily in terms of military reverses, and it minimizes the moral obligation so generally supported at the outset."[4]

But what could be done? Toward the end of January, PA officials concluded that "a major high-level attempt to clarify" the importance of staying in Korea was "imperative." Fleshing out the details, the State Department's Working Group on Public Relations recommended that "the White House should take the lead in alleviating popular anxiety about 'getting the boys out of Korea' by having the president issue a strong statement." Acheson, Marshall, and Bradley could reinforce this message in a radio "Report to the People," in which "primary emphasis should be given to the broad military reason" for staying the course.[5]

Senior presidential aides agreed that something different had to be tried. According to Roger Tubby, the new assistant press secretary, it was essential for the administration to establish a rapid-response capability in order to counter the "glaring cases of distortion" the Luce and Scripps-Howard chains were frequently peddling, not to mention the increasingly furious partisan jibes coming from "Taft, Wherry et al."[6] According to White House aide George Elsey, it was vital for the president to launch a sustained campaign to revive domestic support for the war. "One or two statements or speeches will not be enough," he insisted in one memorandum to Truman; "what is needed is a hard-hitting, carefully-thought-out program whereby a number of speeches on the Hill are required in addition to more activity on the part of State and Defense." "A great many people are gravely troubled and worried at the present," he reiterated shortly afterward, "and there seems to be almost widespread confusion and uncertainty. It will be comforting and encouraging to the public to find the president identifying himself with the gravest problems that families face today."[7]

On February 2, as the cabinet members filed into the White House for their weekly meeting, the need to revive domestic support was at the top of their agenda. " 'Why are we in Korea?' " Truman began, "is a pertinent question," and it was vital to get a convincing answer to the American people. No one around the cabinet table dissented. But neither did anyone come up with any innovative solutions. "The exposé must be handled in a dramatic way," was about the best Vice President Barkley could suggest, "maybe in a speech by the president. We must maintain the morale of our own people." "If cabinet officers could have an outline of the facts," the attorney general chipped in, then "they could put the attack forcefully against the critics of our foreign policy."[8]

This was hardly stirring or novel stuff. It also begged the question of why the Truman administration had reached such a position. Why had the president and his advisers not acted before now, in the previous weeks, when the popular mood had already become so tense and disenchanted?

One reason was strikingly familiar: it was obviously difficult to launch a public information campaign when the government lacked an agreed-on policy to sell. This was certainly the case in the early weeks of the new year, when the battlefield reverses that had sparked such a dangerous shift in public opinion also engendered another spasm of uncertainty and despondency in official circles.

The Reticence of the Uncertain

On December 26, Truman abruptly ended his Christmas vacation, flying back to Washington from Independence twenty hours ahead of schedule for a meeting with his senior advisers. With intelligence reports indicating that a massive new Chinese offensive was in the offing, the restless president was particularly concerned about the fate of the Eighth Army in Korea. Nor was this only potential crisis point. In the past week, Marshall and the Pentagon had become increasingly worried by the prospect that the Soviets might suddenly strike at Japan, exploiting its "extreme vulnerability" now that U.S. occupation forces had been sucked into the defense of Korea. In Pentagon circles, there was even another round of talk about whether Korea should be abandoned altogether, so that U.S. troops could be regrouped to protect Japan—a far more valuable strategic asset.[9]

When the renewed Chinese offensive began on December 31, the Eighth Army appeared to be in a forlorn state, outnumbered by a foe who had a decisive manpower edge, weakened by the defeats and retreats in the bitter cold of the past month, and in the process of adjusting to a new commander after Walker's death just days before. In two alarming cables to the Joint Chiefs, one on December 30 and the other on January 10, MacArthur deepened the mounting sense of despondency. His command, the general began, had "insufficient strength to hold a position in Korea and simultaneously protect Japan against external assault." War correspondents, he added, were only making his task more difficult, since U.S. troops were increasingly "embittered by the shameful propaganda which has falsely condemned their courage and fighting qualities." The troops' "morale will become a serious threat to their battle efficiency," MacArthur warned, "unless the political basis upon which they are being asked to trade life for time is clearly delineated." In fact, the situation was so bad that the United States was now left with only two choices. It could persist with the present policy, but this was likely to end only in evacuation or destruction. Or it could retaliate directly against China, both by using naval and air power to destroy its "industrial capacity to wage war" and by unleashing nationalist Chinese troops "for diversionary action" against the mainland.[10]

The president was "deeply disturbed" by MacArthur's two messages. "We were at our lowest point," Marshall agreed.[11] If Tokyo was correct, then the choices were grim indeed. On January 12, in a mood of enveloping gloom, the Joint Chiefs met and "tentatively" approved a memorandum that echoed MacArthur's calls for retaliation. Among the Joint Chiefs, Admiral Sherman was particularly hawkish. On January 3, convinced that the United States was effectively at war with China, he had already recommended that the navy institute a blockade of the mainland, that Chiang's nationalist troops be allowed to launch guerrilla assaults, and that the U.S. air force begin a series of reconnaissance missions over Chinese coastal areas and Manchuria. Now, contemplating what ought to be done if UN forces were forced out of Korea, the Joint Chiefs listed sixteen possible courses of action, including the three Sherman had championed.[12]

With the battlefield situation so precarious, and America's whole Korean strategy being reconsidered, officials were clearly hamstrung in what they could make public. Certainly no one wanted to provide a hostage to fortune, announcing a specific policy that might soon be overtaken by events. When Truman suddenly flew back to Washington in the middle of his Christmas vacation, the White House press office thus released a studiously terse and low-key statement.[13] On January 12, when Keyes Beech of the *Chicago Daily News* provoked yet another bout of headlines, this time with a story suggesting that MacArthur had recommended withdrawing from Korea, the administration's denials were swift and vigorous, for officials were keen to repudiate any story that might fuel the growing public mood of defeatism and despondency. But the State Department's press office still chose its words carefully and then refused to elaborate. There would be no "voluntary withdrawal" from Korea, it starkly insisted.[14]

Three days later, Lawton Collins, the army chief of staff, and Hoyt Vandenberg, the air chief, arrived in Tokyo. In past crises, the Joint Chiefs had always sent representatives to the Far East to witness events firsthand, and they had invariably been rewarded with upbeat assessments that had dispelled the prevailing gloom. This time, with the situation so desperate, the need for hard facts was even more pressing. In a whirlwind five-day tour, Collins and Vandenberg visited all the corps headquarters in Korea and spoke to most of the division commanders. Their timing was impeccable, for Ridgway had just launched the first of his limited counterattacks. Reporting back to his superiors, Collins was suitably impressed. "Eighth Army in good shape and improving daily under Ridgway's leadership," Collins cabled on January 17. "Morale very satisfactory. . . . Ridgway confident he can obtain two or three months' delay before having to initiate evacuation. . . . On the whole Eighth Army now in position and prepared to punish severely any mass attack."[15]

Bolstered once again with this timely ray of sunshine, the same day the National Security Council met to discuss Korean policy. Less than a week earlier, with defeat possible, the Joint Chiefs had considered ways to escalate the war. Now, however, Acheson was able to wage a successful counterattack against such dangerous suggestions, declaring the Joint Chiefs' January 12 memorandum "quite inadequate" and pushing for a period of further study. Soon afterward, these contingency plans to escalate in the face of evacuation were quietly shelved. "Action with respect to most of them," Marshall concluded, "was considered inadvisable in view of the radical change in the situation which had originally given rise to them."[16]

In fairness, Truman had always remained determined to hold on in Korea. On January 8, in his State of the Union address, he called Korea a "symbol" of the global struggle "against oppression and slavery" and compared the UN's firm action now with the democracies' failure to act during the 1930s. On January 13, as morale among senior officials sank to its lowest point, the president then sent MacArthur a long telegram explaining his purposes. "A successful resistance in Korea," he insisted, would "demonstrate that aggression will not be accepted by us or by the UN" and provide "a rallying point" to unite the West against the Soviet threat; would deflate the military prestige of China and help the United States organize noncommunist resistance throughout Asia; would fulfill America's commitment to its South Korean ally and provide time to complete a satisfactory peace settlement for Japan; would lend "urgency to the rapid build-up of the defenses of the western world" and "alert the peoples behind the Iron Curtain that their masters are bent upon wars of aggression."[17]

All in all, Truman's telegram was an impressive document. On one level, it was an obvious attempt to respond with diplomacy and tact—with what Acheson later described as "infinite patience"—to MacArthur's repeated challenge to the administration's limited war strategy. At another level, the telegram was an elaborate effort to answer "Why Korea?" It was an "epistle" that, in the words of one historian, was one of "the most eloquent expressions for the reasons for American participation in the Korean War."[18]

Nonetheless, despite its eloquence, it proved largely ineffective. In Tokyo, MacArthur's resistance to Truman's points and patience was of course total, and would soon produce the major political crisis of the war.[19] But even among many Americans at home, these arguments would prove unpersuasive. Significantly, this was not because the president's basic case for war had suddenly changed in any major fashion. Essentially, his stated reasons for fighting in Korea were similar to what they had been during the summer: standing up to aggression, signaling America's credibility and resolve, and intensifying the workability of the UN and the cohesiveness of the West.

What had changed was the context within which the war was being fought. During January and February, developments at both the international and domestic levels combined to restrict the administration's opportunities to go public on the specific subject of Korea, thereby ensuring that Truman's eloquent "epistle" never received the public attention so many officials thought was essential for rallying domestic support.

The UN and the Aggressor
Resolution

At the beginning of January, the four hundred members of the international press corps who covered the UN beat moved from their temporary home at Lake Success to the new UN building alongside the East River in Manhattan. Here, they had much more space: more than 20,000 square feet on three separate floors. According to UN officials, they also had facilities that were "the most modern, efficient, and comfortable in the entire world."[20] In the next few weeks, however, the first major story these reporters would cover from their new offices threatened to undermine the very existence of the organization that now enjoyed such plush surroundings.

The basic problem centered around two proposed resolutions: one pushing for a cease-fire in Korea, the other seeking to condemn Chinese aggression. The United States was the driving force behind the latter. As far back as November 28, the day Washington had first received word of the massive Chinese attack, Acheson had insisted privately that the United States needed to "go forward in the UN to uncloak the Chinese communist aggression."[21] Throughout December, as members of an Arab-Asian bloc in the UN tried to foster some sort of peaceful resolution to the crisis, this idea got sidetracked. But at the start of the new year, as Chinese forces poured south across the thirty-eighth parallel, the United States was keen to push ahead. An aggressor resolution, the administration believed, would be in line with the UN's reaction to the original North Korean attack in June. It would confirm the UN's vitality as a collective security organization, demonstrating that it could stand up to both big and small powers. And, closer to home, it would also be good politics, silencing the growing body of opinion holding that the Truman administration had been too soft in its dealings with the Chinese.[22]

At the UN, however, many of America's key allies opposed such a move. The British, for instance, feared it might expand the whole war by giving legitimacy to the escalatory measures MacArthur was pressing for. Elsewhere, a number of Latin American and Asian delegations were adamant that any such "conflict with China would not find the support of the public opinion in their countries."[23]

But all was not lost. According to U.S. diplomats in New York, many delegations might be persuaded to vote for an aggressor resolution if another attempt was first made to engineer a cease-fire. So in the second week of January, instead of moving straight ahead with an indictment of Beijing, the General Assembly decided to make one last effort at peaceful reconciliation. After much wrangling over details, on January 11 a new cease-fire resolution was placed before the General Assembly. It was voted on two days later and approved by fifty to seven, with one abstention. Inevitably, this pushed initiatives aimed at condemning the Chinese on to the back burner. In fact, it was not until January 20 that the actual debate began on America's aggressor resolution. And even then, it was soon delayed because of yet more allied opposition, mainly regarding the wisdom of using an aggressor resolution as a vehicle to push for sanctions against China.[24]

Inside the United States, none of this played well. Even during December, many opinion-makers had equated a cease-fire resolution with craven appeasement. In the first days of the new year, as the new Chinese offensive gathered pace, public calls for an aggressor resolution swiftly grew in size and intensity, encompassing newspapers from the *Washington Post* to the *Los Angeles Times*, the *Philadelphia Inquirer* to the *New York Herald Tribune*. Throughout the grim month of January, when delay followed delay, media denunciations of the UN reached a pitch of anger. "The UN dillies, marks time, stalls," declared Albert Warner on NBC in a typical comment, "feebly twitching at the bare thought" of having to "rise up in dignity and honest wrath to call communist China what it is, an aggressor, and outright foe of the UN." By the middle of the month, opposition to the UN's reluctance to brand China an aggressor had united a powerful cross-section of opinion, including the Scripps-Howard and Knight chains and the *Baltimore Sun*, *Chicago News*, *Cincinnati Times-Star*, and *New York Times*. "Observers increasingly warn," PA glumly concluded, "that the UN's very existence may depend on its taking at least a strong moral stand on this issue."[25]

On January 19, the House of Representatives gave legislative substance to this impatience when it passed a resolution calling on the UN to brand China an aggressor without delay. Ironically, in the floor debate there was a good deal of grumbling about how hastily this resolution had been introduced, for it was thrust on the House on a Friday at noon, when only a quarter of members were present, and the House Foreign Affairs Committee had not been formally consulted. But the popularity of the measure soon drowned out these gripes about process. In fact, unlike most of the issues tied up with the "great debate," where the Democratic leadership had generally supported the administration, the House resolution cut completely across party lines. Initially, leading Republicans like Vorys and Martin had formulated the idea. But, fearing that the Democratic leadership would kill a purely Republican measure, they had worked swiftly and smoothly with McCormack, the floor leader. Once the debate began, the idea soon proved so "noncontroversial" that it was not even necessary to hold a roll call; the measure was simply nodded through by voice vote.[26]

Typically, the Senate moved at a more leisurely pace, but here, too, feelings were running high, with many denouncing the U.S. vote for a cease-fire as "a silly diplomatic minuet" and calling on the State Department to get tough. On January 23, when John McClellan introduced a resolution calling on the UN to label China an aggressor, it swiftly passed, this time by a roll call vote without any recorded dissent.[27]

Faced with a widening split between the UN and domestic opinion, the administration had to decide whether to vote for a cease-fire resolution that many Americans equated with gutless surrender. The choice, Acheson recalled later, "was a murderous one, threatening on one side the loss of the Koreans and the fury of Congress and the press and, on the other, the loss of our majority and support in the UN." Ultimately, Acheson opted to brave the domestic fallout and instructed Warren Austin to support the cease-fire resolution, but only "in the fervent hope and belief that the Chinese would reject it."[28]

When Beijing duly obliged on January 17, Acheson tried to limit the damage at home. He immediately issued a public rejection of China's counter-proposal, hoping thereby "to avoid any confused thinking, about our being a bunch of appeasers." With rumors swirling that an unhappy Austin was about to resign in disgust, the State Department made it clear that Austin had only cast his vote in favor of a cease-fire on the expressed instructions of his superiors.[29]

In the last two weeks of January, the State Department then tried to regain lost ground on the home front by pressing ahead with a resolution branding China the aggressor. Diplomatically, this remained a difficult task. Although key allies like the British were now willing to vote for a simple resolution, they still balked at any hint that this would be followed by actual sanctions against China. Along with India and Canada, the British also wanted to make another approach to Beijing, asking for clarification of its January 17 statement on a cease-fire. At first glance, this resistance on the part of allies threatened doom for the Truman administration. As Acheson explained on January 18, in supporting the cease-fire resolution, "we brought ourselves to the verge of destruction domestically," and he "could not take any further chances unless it made a great deal of sense to do so." If other countries failed to support the U.S. stance, Acheson warned a few days later, this would "seriously damage UN prestige and influence and jeopardize U.S. public and congressional support for UN."[30]

Ultimately, however, to narrow the gap, Acheson was willing to make one final concession to allies, agreeing that sanctions could be deferred if yet another attempt to find a peaceful resolution to the war made "satisfactory progress." Acutely aware that many informed Americans, especially in Congress, wanted to be more "rambunctious" than this, Acheson moved to head off yet another potential domestic firestorm. On January 25, he consulted with the relevant committees in both the Senate and House. The next day, he then cleared the new compromise with the president and cabinet. For their part, America's allies were somewhat reassured by all these efforts to tone down the aggressor resolution; most were also reluctant to alienate the Americans. And so on February 1, when the U.S. resolution finally came before the General Assembly, it passed by a large margin, with India and Burma the only noncommunist countries to vote against it. At long last, the UN had condemned China for its aggression in Korea.[31]

Historians have accorded a good deal of attention to this episode, viewing it as a classic case of allied and domestic pressures pulling officials in competing directions. But most have tended to minimize the domestic consequences of this episode, refusing to go beyond Acheson's rosy recollection that "fortunately the storm soon blew over."[32] On closer inspection, however, the ramifications of the whole UN debate went far deeper than this.

A large part of the problem, as Acheson recognized, was that all the maneuvering in the UN "completely confused the American people."[33] Certainly, throughout January, as the possibility of defeat loomed large, the UN was an easy target for resentment and recriminations. More important, the protracted UN debates also detracted from the simple reasons for waging the war. Back in the summer, the motivation for intervention had been relatively straightforward: the United States was acting hand in hand with the UN in response to a clear-cut case of aggression. In December, in a series of year-end speeches, some State Department officials now tried to recapture this old simplicity. "There is little danger," Ernest Gross claimed, "that the members of the free world will forget the importance of the action boldly taken and loudly cheered on June 25. The military setback which has ensued from the massive Chinese intervention," he insisted, "does not in any way detract from the morality and fundamental wisdom of the action taken by the UN on June 25."[34]

Unfortunately, however, these earlier developments had been, if not entirely forgotten, increasingly obscured by more recent events. Already, the State Department had shelved plans for a new white paper, because it did not want public and allied attention to focus too closely on awkward questions surrounding the Chinese intervention.[35] During January, the UN's reluctance to brand China an aggressor only served to muddy the waters still further. Indeed, in stark contrast to the summer, when the UN's swift denunciation of the North Korean invasion had provided the administration with a vital ingredient in its efforts to establish the legality and morality of the whole U.S. enterprise in Korea, now the UN's reluctance to promptly indict the Chinese created real questions in the public mind, not just about the UN's usefulness as a vehicle for U.S. policy but also about the basic correctness of America's participation in the war. Throughout January, PA pointed out, "there was much public pressure for withdrawal from Korea," partly "because of our military reverses" and partly "because the UN debate on the aggressor resolution tended to detract from the unequivocal moral position of the UN." "The pace at which the UN moves toward declaring the Chinese communists as aggressors," PA concluded, "reinforces the public notion about the 'futility' of the policy as a whole."[36]

But this was not the only consequence. As well as confusing the moral case for war, the machinations in the UN prevented the administration from going public with any great force and frequency. This was because Acheson and the State Department were reluctant to speak out about their policy goals, lest this complicate the delicate negotiations on the aggressor resolution currently underway in New York—negotiations that if they failed might very well undermine America's whole Korean War policy. As Acheson told reporters in a private interview on January 18, it was impossible at this stage to say anything specific about Korea or the effort to brand China an aggressor. Five days later, Acheson held a meeting with Lester Markel, the influential editor of the *New York Times* Sunday edition. When the discussion inevitably drifted onto the public confusion and disillusion that had emerged during the long wrangles in the UN, Markel insisted that "the domestic scene was more important than the foreign" and "concluded by saying that although he realized the amount of energy involved, it was absolutely necessary for the secretary to explain in simple terms our foreign policy to millions of Americans." Acheson agreed in principle, "but pointed out that there were so many things that were absolutely necessary to do that it was hard to do them all."[37] Put another way, he thought it vital to prioritize. And throughout most of January, he preferred to focus on the delicate task of alliance bargaining, even if this meant forgoing the opportunity to explain the government's Korean policy at a moment when public support was eroding fast.

Constraints and Diversions

In the days after the UN passed the aggressor resolution, midranking officials were more active and vocal in explaining the administration's views. In response to complaints from internationalist legislators on the Hill, who complained that they were finding it difficult to answer the mounting numbers of letters that asked "'Why should we stay in Korea,'" Barrett and PA now drafted a generic reply that congressmen could send to their constituents.[38] Dean Rusk also went public, delivering two "down-to-earth expositions" that repeated the central arguments of the president's State of the

Union address. "The issue in Korea," Rusk told an NBC television audience, "is aggression." If the United States and its allies ran away from the challenge, as the free world had done in the 1930s, the result would be world war. But if "we can show that we have both the will and the ability to defend ourselves, the main attack may be averted."[39]

Yet at the highest level, officials were still reluctant to speak out in a similar fashion. Indeed, despite the cabinet debate on February 2 and intense prodding from aides, Truman refused to issue a major statement on Korea in his next press conference. He then barely mentioned Korea in a string of routine speeches and statements during February and the first half of March, before heading off to Key West for his annual vacation. And Acheson was equally mute, failing to attend a string of speaking engagements that had been set up for him in during the cold, bleak days at the end of this long winter.

Why were senior officials so tight-lipped during February and March? One possible reason might have been the sudden shift in the popular mood that polls started to detect by the middle of February. Officials were always prone to believe that domestic opinion oscillated sharply between undue alarm and excessive optimism. As Ridgway's Eighth Army started to inch back up the Korean peninsula, retaking Seoul by the middle of March, polls seemed to confirm this basic assumption, recording a swift about-turn in those who advocated a complete evacuation from the peninsula. According to a National Opinion Research Center survey, 67 percent now wanted to stay in Korea as long as necessary, while only 20 percent supported pulling out—a finding that was seconded by a *Denver Post* poll that put the figure in favor of staying slightly higher.[40]

Still, not all polls were so optimistic. In February and March, a majority of Americans continued to think that the decision to intervene in Korea had been a mistake. Truman's own personal approval ratings also dipped dramatically, down to a dismal 26 percent—an all-time low.[41] Small wonder, then, that a number of PR specialists inside the administration still deemed it vital for senior officials to speak out. As one PA official noted on February 15, "the American people are still demanding 'leadership' from the administration by which they mean very clear, forceful enunciation of our policies."[42]

Rather than being a natural response to a sudden change in the popular mood, the administration's reticence was actually related to other domestic pressures—all connected to the familiar problem of fighting a limited war. One of the most important was the attention the administration, Congress, and the media were currently lavishing on the "great debate" (see chapter 7).

Fighting a limited war had always meant keeping Korea in proper perspective—as "a pint-sized incident, not a full-scale war." But on numerous occasions during the first three months of 1951, the reasons for fighting in Korea were largely eclipsed by the discourse surrounding mobilization. At the start of February, for instance, the cabinet debate on finding a plausible public answer to "Why Korea?" effectively came to naught, partly because in his next press conference Truman had to focus on a railroad strike, which necessitated calling out the army to force the strikers back to work. The next days were also dominated by Eisenhower's report on his fact-finding mission to Europe. And in the middle of the month, when Acheson and Marshall both made high-profile appearances, they did so only in framework set by the Connally-Russell committee on troops to Europe. The "protracted [great] debate with its emphasis on Europe," one White House aide complained soon afterward, "tends to make us forget other parts of the world that are important to world security. Western Europe is not the only place and we must not let our concern with that area detract us from efforts which we must make elsewhere."[43]

Acheson's appearance before the Connally-Russell committee was actually something of an anomaly. A year before, he had been the central spokesman for the government's foreign policy, an authoritative, knowledgeable voice, clearly in command of his brief. By the start of 1951, however, he was a man besieged, the most prominent target in the vicious partisan campaign swirling around Washington.

Because of the intense Republican assault on Acheson, by February the State Department considered itself impaled on the prongs of a painful dilemma. If it failed to speak out, Republicans would dominate the agenda and influence the public mind. "The whole administration as well as the State Department is fighting a battle with hands tied behind its back," Barrett complained on February 8. "In these critical days, the president and his cabinet must maintain a position of dignity, poise, and considerable non-partisanship. The opposition, on the other hand, has considered itself free to engage in unlimited mudslinging."[44] Yet Acheson was clearly such a deeply polarizing figure that if he entered the fray with a vigorous defense, Republicans would simply use it as an opportunity to launch another round of viciousassaults against the administration. "The secretary should avoid public speeches as much as possible in the next few weeks," the State Department's Working Group on Public Relations therefore reluctantly concluded, "since the criticism against him appears to be dying down, and... it seemed unwise to him to take the chance of stirring it up again."[45]

Preoccupied with the tricky problems surrounding European defense, Acheson accepted this advice. Thus tethered, about his only recourse was to engage in an intensive series of background briefings with reporters, in the hope that these would shape press coverage without provoking the diehard critics into a damaging retaliation. Yet such a low-key approach hardly met the growing need to explain "Why Korea?" As PA soon concluded, Acheson's background briefings were no substitute for frequent speeches—even if such speeches obviously riled the diehard critics. In March, when PA conducted a survey of the output of selected reporters with whom the secretary had met in recent months, it discovered that only one radio broadcaster out of all those wooed had actually changed his position on air and adopted a clear proadministration stance. This convert was CBS's Eric Sevareid, who "may be somewhat quicker to explain the department's position than he was a few months ago." But Sevareid's was a conspicuously lone voice.[46]

As they contemplated a way out of this dilemma, officials confronted yet another problem. In theory, an obvious solution would be to encourage more second-rank officials to follow Rusk's example and fill the void created by their superiors' unwillingness to speak out. Although no substitute for vigorous action by Truman and Acheson, a lower level campaign might exert some influence over media coverage of the war. But when it came to implementing such an idea, the State Department ran up against another familiar obstacle: the lack of a propaganda agency to encourage, coordinate, and amplify official efforts.

This lack was not from any want of internal discussions. Throughout December and January, officials again debated the desirability of establishing something along the lines of the old Office of War Information. No one could doubt that the need was acute, given the intensity of the current crisis and the growing demands for censorship. The president's hostility to a burgeoning bureaucracy had also dimmed, for he was currently constructing new mobilization bureaus with abandon. Nevertheless, even as rumors swirled around Washington that the government's emergency planning included a "revived OWI," senior officials ultimately rejected this course a second time. As in the summer, everyone recognized just how controversial the Office of War Information had been during the last war. In the final analysis, the White House also continued to believe that a propaganda agency was a creature of total war. To Truman, a new Office of War Information would have to await the eruption of a new global conflagration.[47]

But this decision left unresolved the central problem: how to get subordinates to toe the same public line. As the new crisis gathered steam, many in the White House and State Department fretted that discordant voices might well prove fatal to the war effort. "The worst thing that could happen at this point," Philip Jessup, Acheson's ambassador at large, explained to Barrett and Webb at a time when the Chinese communists appeared to have the whip hand in Korea, "was loose statements by government officials." Jessup wanted the White House "to issue an order stopping all speechmaking, press conferences, and interviews by individuals." He was even willing to sacrifice the State Department's ongoing program "of having correspondents see selected officials for background."[48] With MacArthur continuing to speak out of turn, Jessup's advice soon found a receptive audience. On December 5, Truman issued a "gagging order" that prohibited officials from speaking out on controversial foreign policy issues and ordered that all prospective speeches be cleared in advance.[49] A month later, he moved to clamp down on unauthorized disclosures concerning the implementation of the NSC-68 mobilization plan.[50]

Coming in the midst of a deep crisis, these gagging orders were a desperate attempt to stave off home-front disaster. But as the situation in Korea began to settle down, it soon became evident that they were operating in a perverse manner.

At first glance, gagging orders were simply blunt instruments that seemed to add to the information vacuum on the Korean War. Indeed, while a propaganda agency could act as a clearinghouse for official statements, as well as undertake its own efforts to amplify the agreed line, the very existence of a gagging order tended to deter everyone in the administration from speaking out.[51]

On closer inspection, moreover, these orders had an even more pernicious effect: they tended to silence loyal subordinates, those who were scrupulous in obeying White House commands and were reluctant to say anything that might be construed as controversial. Yet what these orders patently failed to achieve was to silence those who were out of sympathy with the central thrust of government policy, or those brought on board to give the administration a more bipartisan complexion. They certainly had little effect on Charles Wilson, who had few scruples about going public with a decidedly upbeat mobilization message at a time when most senior officials thought the administration ought to be protecting against a "letdown." Nor, most ominously of all, would they stop Douglas MacArthur from sharing his explosive opinions with the media about how the United States ought now to seek an end to the war.

In the absence of a formal propaganda agency, and with senior officials diverted and constrained by the complexities of waging a limited war, the State Department tried its best to muddle through. During February and March, PA began to produce materials for mass consumption. It also compiled a new information memorandum to be circulated throughout government, entitled "Why We are Staying in Korea." These new guidelines were intended to encourage loyal subordinates, perhaps intimidated by the "gagging orders," to speak out.[52]

But none of these activities seemed very effective. In March, when PA completed one detailed pamphlet that elaborated on the need to stay the course in Korea, some State Department officials were unimpressed, believing that the whole production was "forbidding to the ordinary reader." In other buildings, many thought PA's output was too often stuffy and elitist. "I think it is high time that the State Department be goosed into some soul-searching on its domestic information program," one White House aide complained. It must be hammered home that "you do not need to be dull to be dignified; that lower income groups have to be reached as well as the literati; and that it pays to be human.... For my money the State Department is not doing its job on the domestic side."[53]

Back in World War II, the government had successfully reached this wider audience by forging connections with Hollywood. Both the military and Office of War Information had worked with studios, providing them with technical support and script suggestions in order to ensure the production of movies that helped to sustain support for the war. As popular approval for the Korean enterprise continued to sag, while the administration struggled to find an effective way to get its message out, it was hardly surprising that some officials now turned their thoughts toward using the powerful medium of film.

Movies and Letters

Midcentury Hollywood felt itself besieged. This was partly due to the danger posed by television, still in its infancy but with a potential power to reach Americans in their living rooms that was readily apparent. In addition, increasing taxes, rising production costs, and growing restrictions in foreign markets had pushed all the major studios into implementing concerted cost-cutting drives. "Hollywood," one leading producer bemoaned in 1949, "is an island of depression in a sea of prosperity."[54]

What made this depression even worse was the meddling of politicians, as the close cooperation that had developed between Washington and Hollywood during World War II had dissolved under the pressure of the Red Scare. In 1947, the House Un-American Activities Committee (HUAC) had launched a high-profile investigation of communists in the movie industry that had ended with the indictment of ten unfriendly witnesses for contempt. Although the major studios had subsequently gone out of their way to demonstrate the political purity of their product—most notoriously, by instituting a blacklist that precluded the employment of any communist or subversive—this had not entirely ended the committee's harassment. And at the start of 1951, rumors abounded that the Republicans, emboldened by their gains in the recent election, would start new hearings before the HUAC, on the ostensible grounds that many of the individuals subpoenaed back in 1947 had never testified.[55]

On the subject of Korea, such a supercharged environment could have easily resulted in a spate of prowar films. It would, after all, clearly be good politics for the studios to embark on patriotic projects that lauded the fighting qualities of the average GI and espoused a hawkish Cold War line. It would also be good business. During 1950, World War II movies had been extremely popular at the box office. Of that year's top fifty earners, eight focused on the war, including *Battleground*, which had come in second and grossed $4.5 million, and *The Sands of Iwo Jima*, which had brought in $3.9 million.

Buoyed by these profits, many senior executives saw the new conflict as an obvious opportunity to improve their threatened position. The movie industry "thrives in a wartime economy," Ellis Arnall, president of the Independent Motion Pictures Industry, noted at the start of 1951. "The more difficult it is to obtain houses, automobiles, television sets, washing machines, the more money the public will have to spend on entertainment."[56] It was hardly surprising, then, that when the industry as a whole decided to come together under the umbrella of the Council of Motion Picture Organizations, its first statement pledged complete cooperation with Washington. The council "is prepared to handle any job given by the government," one of its spokespersons declared in the middle of December. Its "machinery is virtually all set to roll, and now all that is awaited is a specific assignment."[57]

Yet, in practice, nothing much materialized from this promise of cooperation, at least in the short term. Indeed, with one notable exception, Hollywood proved unable to do much to directly bolster support for the Korean War in early 1951, and even this exception ended in controversy. The reasons for Hollywood's failure to help sell Korea are not difficult to fathom. In large part, they all stemmed from the nature of the war itself, especially during the summer of 1950, when the decisions that influenced the output of the winter had been made.

At this early stage of the war, Hollywood, taking its cues from the government, had viewed the conflict as little more than a temporary crisis. Institutionally, this had meant there had initially been little impetus to change the industry's relationship with the administration, setting up new structures along the lines of the old War Activities Committee. Indeed, although the formation of the Council of Motion Picture Organizations had been under discussion for months, the numerous internal conflicts among big and large studios, producers, and theater owners were not ironed out until the crisis months of December and January. "It is regrettable," lamented the president of the new council, when it finally came into being in January, that "we weren't in Washington long ago—at the White House, before the Eighty-Second Congress, with other governmental agencies, offering the heart and hand of this most potent medium of communications, motion pictures. But it is too late."[58]

By the time of the Chinese intervention, it was also too late for most studios to rush feature films into production. Again, this stemmed back to calculations made during the summer months. At this stage, most movie executives viewed Korea as little more than a regrettable irritant that promised to disrupt their working relationships with the military, relationships which were essential to give authenticity to the spate of World War II movies then in production. True, the marketing people quickly realized that these films about the "good war" could be sold with the current police action in mind. And features such as Twentieth Century–Fox's *American Guerrilla in the Philippines* wasted no time playing up the similarities, showing many scenes "of marauding Oriental troops; of bearded, unkempt American fighters inhabiting alien hovels in alien lands and dauntlessly improvising devices and designs as they go."[59]

Nonetheless, most major studios did not deem Korea a big enough subject to warrant its own major features. One of the few exceptions to this thinking was at RKO, where Howard Hughes, after a telephone discussion with air force officials, decided to commission a picture that would dramatize the cooperation between air and ground forces. He immediately sent producer Sam Bischoff to Washington to meet with military officials, and it was soon rumored that Cary Grant was interested in playing the lead role—and was even ready to brave conditions in Korea, if it was necessary to do some filming on location.[60]

Almost as soon as this project was mooted, however, it was abandoned because of the Chinese intervention. With American forces falling back fast and disaster looming, RKO, like many other studios, now decided that the public would crave films of a "lighter genre": musicals, comedies, swashbucklers, westerns, mysteries, sci-fi, and horror. As *Variety* noted, "escapism" was the dominant trend of the sixty-eight pictures that went into production in the first six weeks of 1951, accounting for no less than three-quarters of the movies currently being shot.[61]

Hollywood's attempt to avoid the biggest issue of the day would not last long. By December 1951, as the fighting dragged on, some of the major studios would revisit Korea, most notably with Samuel Goldwyn's *I Want You* and Twentieth Century–Fox's *Fixed Bayonets*; the following year, six more Korean War films would appear.[62] During the crucial winter months of 1950–51, however, when public support for the war threatened to collapse, most movie executives decided that grim battlefield scenes were about the last thing their audiences wanted to watch.

With the major studios largely neglecting the war, the few exceptions soon stood out. In the second week of January, the first two films to focus on Korea hit theaters, both produced by smaller companies.[63] *Korea Patrol*, released by Eagle Lion Classics, was shot quickly on a small budget, and was a standard account of six GIs charged with demolishing a bridge during the early days of the war. *Steel Helmet*, released by Lippert, was made equally quickly, in twelve days, at the cost of just $104,000, and even used cardboard tanks. Although it started life as a standard World War II B-movie and was hurriedly changed to exploit the new conflict, it was an altogether more impressive and successful film, not to mention far more controversial.[64]

After pulling in respectable audiences in Los Angeles, *Steel Helmet* quickly became the subject of a political tussle on the East Coast, and demonstrated yet another potential pitfall of dealing with Korea. The controversy this time surrounded a scene in which a U.S. sergeant kills a North Korean prisoner of war. The producers claimed the Pentagon had sanctioned this scene. But with the communist *Daily Worker* shouting allegations of American brutality, the film soon found few friends. Across the country, the Hearst press began to talk ominously about a new HUAC investigation. In New York, rumors soon spread that that Loews theaters had canceled their bookings of the film. In Washington, the Pentagon moved quickly to remove itself completely from the controversy. "Army Pictorial Section officers were amazed when they saw the script," one radio commentator reported. "But it wasn't for the army to say whether the film could or couldn't be produced."[65]

Back in World War II, officials had been able to wield such editorial power over scripts. One of the most vigorous wielders of the censor's blue pencil in Hollywood had been Ulric Bell, a staunch internationalist and the head of the Office of War Information's Overseas Branch. Based in Los Angeles, Bell had used his powers aggressively, making numerous suggestions to studios to cut anything that might prove harmful to the war effort. If they refused to accept his suggestions, Bell would refer the film to the Office of Censorship, with an accompanying recommendation that it be denied an export license.[66]

By the beginning of 1951, with even the limited Hollywood output on Korea drawing fire, some officials doubtless pined for similar authority. In the Pentagon, the services did vet scripts of any films that required tangible military support. But only one movie of this kind was in the pipeline during this critical period, and it would not appear for more than a year.[67] More important, the administration as a whole lacked a new Office of War Information to oversee all of Hollywood's output. Instead, all it had was a small, informal network of support inside one particular part of Hollywood.

Significantly, this network included Ulric Bell. Reappearing in a new role as cowriter of a Twentieth Century–Fox short documentary, Bell now used all his old powers of advocacy to support Hollywood's main effort to give meaning to the Korean War. His film was shot under the close supervision of legendary producer Darryl F. Zanuck. Released at the start of 1951, its title was pithy and to the point: *Why Korea?* attempted to tackle head-on the question at the heart of many of the propaganda problems currently plaguing the administration.[68]

The answer Bell and his associates gave to this question closely echoed the line the government had developed back in the summer and fall. In fact, apart from the narrator, with his carefully chosen words, the only other voices in the film were those of Warren Austin, who was shown indicting the Soviets at the UN, and the president, whose October address calling for increased preparedness was liberally used. In the rest of the film, the central argument was simple: if the democracies had stood up to the aggressors back in the 1930s, then World War II could have been avoided altogether. American boys were now fighting and dying in this faraway place to prevent a repeat of this disastrous mistake. Korea, then, was the modern equivalent of Manchuria in

1931, Ethiopia in 1935, or Austria in 1938: the first round in a new wave of aggression that could be halted at a far lower cost if thwarted early.

In its presentation and style, *Why Korea?* had obvious weaknesses and strengths. Conceived and written before the Chinese intervention, it only briefly alluded to recent events and was unable to deal directly with the mounting sense that the whole moral case for war had in some way been undermined by the UN's failure to promptly pass the aggressor resolution. Nonetheless, the movie's writers and producers clearly recognized one thing that had thus far eluded the administration: the need to hammer the argument home through repetition. Time and again, the narrator asked why Americans were dying in such a faraway land. Time and again, he came back to the parallels between now and the 1930s.[69]

Whatever the movie's objective merits, the White House was delighted that at least one filmmaker was willing to step in and provide answers to this troubling question. At the start of the new year, Dr. John Steelman, often the White House point man on such matters, hastened to tell reporters that "the picture has been seen by the president and other high officials, and all have expressed the hope that the greatest possible number of people see it." As the movie's promotion went into high gear, Fox was keen to advertise the fact that it had produced the movie "as a public service" and had "no desire to make any profit from it." From the White House, Steelman even sent a note to movie theater owners, urging them to show it. "It is important," he stressed, "that the public sees this picture as quickly as possible. You can render a great public service to our country by cooperating in this activity."[70]

If film was an obvious way to reach a mass audience, then letters had been a traditional way for administrations to gauge the popularity of a war, not just with the home-front audience but with the citizen soldiers who actually did the fighting.[71]

By 1951, letters from the Korean front had become a staple of the political discourse. In the Far East, MacArthur's command had made no attempt to censor the GIs' mail, on the practical grounds that it took so long for letters to reach the United States that it was doubtful that soldiers could reveal any information of use to the enemy.[72] But as the war became more unpopular in the ranks, this policy created problems for the administration. Increasingly, soldiers' letters were full of complaints about appalling conditions, lack of equipment, and the absence of a rotation policy. Disturbed family members often forwarded such missives on to their local legislators. And congressmen were never slow to use them in speeches or to insert them in the *Congressional Record*.[73]

By the end of February, PA thought it was time for a rebuttal. Some PA officials even hoped to turn a necessity into a virtue, convinced that a sensitive and heartfelt letter of response by Acheson or Truman might prove an effective vehicle for reaching a wider audience.[74] Acheson wholeheartedly agreed. On January 19, he received a letter from John Moullette, a young corporal in the Marine Corps. Moullette summed up the disenchantment now felt by many, denouncing the outrageous expenditure of government money, the needless waste of human life, and the waning morale among the troops "because the American people are not behind them." "These men aren't afraid to fight," Moullette concluded, "it's just that they have no cause to fight." In a thoughtful four-page response, Acheson made an impassioned case for the war. He began by trying to explain that "Korea had already proved a great deal"—that the UN could act as a unified body, that the United States was determined to stand up to aggression, and that these sacrifices would help to create a better world. It was this generation's responsibility, Acheson insisted, "to take up the defense of freedom against the challenge of tyranny." Had America responded to aggression earlier in the 1930s, he concluded, in an obvious echo of Bell's Hollywood script, World War II could have been averted. Korea served the same purpose now.[75]

Moullette was delighted with Acheson's letter—indeed, he could not quite believe that someone so senior in the government "would take time out from his duties to write to an ordinary soldier like me."[76] Armed with this positive response, at the start of March, PA officials decided to release the entire Moullette-Acheson correspondence to the press. In a stark reminder of the obvious fact that senior officials have the clout to generate page 1 news, numerous newspapers led with the story. In one simple initiative, Acheson had thus finally made his case for "Why Korea." As the press hastened to report, he had also found at least one convert to the cause. Acheson's letter "has convinced me," the young corporal told journalists. "I've read the letter over a few times and talked it over with one of my friends. He has me thinking that maybe we could have avoided World War II if we had gone into Ethiopia. And I definitely think we ought to be in Korea."[77]

Unfortunately, however, not everyone was as impressionable as young Moullette. Although the Voice of America used Acheson's response to make its case to the wider world about Korea, at home the State Department received a flood of letters that lambasted Acheson's "rather sissified" statement, complaining that it failed to state "what we are going to do in Korea, how long we are going to fight there, are we going to continue to furnish about 90 percent of the troops, etc." Of those letters received, PA calculated, only a tiny minority endorsed Acheson's stance. Most either approved of Moullette's questioning attitude and endorsed his right to "rebel" or criticized Acheson's response "in bitter tones" and said the United States had no right to be in Korea.[78]

Such a negative general reaction might have been written off as yet further evidence that Acheson was now such a controversial figure that any public statement he made was bound to act as a lightening rod for vehement attacks. But the Moullette letter was not the only object of abuse. *Why*

Korea?—the other component of the administration's effort to reach a mass audience—received an equally dismal reaction. True, it was a clear hit with the critics, and would soon win the Oscar for best documentary. But commercially the response was lukewarm. Some theaters were reluctant to show it on practical grounds, arguing that, at thirty minutes, it was too long to run alongside *Halls of Montezuma*, the feature it was scheduled to accompany. Others had more straightforward political objections. At a time when regional movie theaters were quick to restrict circulation of movies they did not like, *Why Korea?* faced a hostile barrier, especially in the Midwest.[79] In an ominous indication of how high feelings were starting to run, in Ohio, P. J. Wood, the secretary of the Independent Theater Owners, publicly refused to circulate it unless the administration expressed its intention to make another film—"Why We Should Get Out of Korea." "There are millions of people in disagreement with the administration's policy in Korea," Wood explained, "and many of them will be *forced* to sit through the showing of the subject, and in such instances the exhibitor will thus lose the good will of many of his patrons."[80]

All in all, these different responses were troubling, for they suggested that even the administration's limited efforts to get its message across were at best failing to have much effect and at worst were actually proving counterproductive. But during February and March, even this was not the most pressing problem. For as the battlefield situation stabilized and the administration began to contemplate the prospect of a cease-fire, the matter of coordinating the government line suddenly became acute. In addition to the discordant voices on mobilization, General Douglas MacArthur picked this moment to reenter the public debate with a vengeance.

The Thirty-Eighth Parallel Revisited

Just days after the aggressor resolution passed the General Assembly, the State Department set about the task of working out an exit strategy. Inside the senior reaches of the administration, as Ridgway's forces crept back up the Korean peninsula, the confidence of September and the gloom of January were swiftly swept aside. Whereas both moods had prodded officials to think expansively, in terms of uniting Korea or taking the war to China, now there was a growing consensus that the battlefield situation ought to be stabilized somewhere in the middle of the country, as a precursor to a general settlement. This made sense for a variety of reasons: militarily, the size of Chinese forces made another march to the Yalu River unthinkable; diplomatically, America's allies would welcome a negotiated settlement; and strategically, it would also allow the United States to concentrate on other, more vital interests. In terms of a PR campaign, however, developments surrounding a possible end to the war created obvious difficulties. According to many historians, "the very concept of limited war, with no lure of outright victory, was alien to the American experience." As a result, these historians insist, the public was prone to reject any policy that was based on something short of outright victory.[81]

Yet during February and March, it was not so much the public's hostility to compromise that caused headaches. The problem was more prosaic: the difficulty of saying anything at all about objectives, which only added to the overall dearth of information coming from official sources on the whole subject of Korea.

There were numerous reasons the administration found it so difficult to speak out about war aims. The most fundamental was the abandonment of rollback. Back in October, with victory seemingly imminent, officials had insisted that the UN was fighting to unite the Korean peninsula. Any new statement would clearly be a retreat from this objective—as Warren Austin discovered in February when he proposed writing an article for the *New York Times Magazine* on the future of collective security. Austin wanted to make a forceful case for the much-lambasted UN. But when his first draft contained a spirited defense of the administration's earlier decision to push UN forces into North Korea, the State Department issued so many objections that he decided to abandon the idea. For officials in Foggy Bottom, it made far more sense to forget the earlier flirtation with rollback, especially since current aims were no longer so grandiose.[82]

If calculated amnesia underpinned the administration's determination to avoid talking about past objectives, then other considerations prevented it from speaking out on its evolving new exit strategy. One was the prospect of alienating the ally South Korea. As John J. Muccio, the U.S. ambassador, repeatedly warned Washington, "the more rabid" officials in President Rhee's government, including Rhee himself, "would never publicly acquiesce to drawing a line anywhere except on the old border at the Yalu River. They would undoubtedly scream and joust against any limiting arrangement, even though it was clearly evident that the situation had been forced by the international situation." With Rhee even talking "in rambling fashion" about the need to bomb Manchuria, while his South Korea press ominously used the word "betrayal" whenever the thirty-eighth parallel was mentioned, time was clearly needed to lay the diplomatic groundwork for any new announcement—time that could be used if not to persuade Rhee and his cohorts, then at least to dampen their opposition to the division of their country.[83]

Back in Washington, meanwhile, senior officials were unable to agree on the details of how and where to stop the fighting. Although Acheson thought the time was ripe to alter MacArthur's instructions, so that he no longer had authority to cross the parallel in overwhelming force, the Joint

UN forces crossing the thirty-eighth parallel once again. Courtesy of National Archives.

Chiefs thought this proposal was premature. For one thing, Ridgway's forces had to retain the freedom to strike into North Korea in order to implement a successful defense against a numerically superior enemy. For another, any move to discuss such matters with allies at the UN "would inevitably be disclosed to the Chinese and North Koreans who then could base their own courses of action upon known intentions of friendly forces." And for a third, the administration had still not worked out clear political objectives in the war. Although the Joint Chiefs agreed that there were "grave military risks" in trying to unite the peninsula by force, they opposed any straightforward division of Korea that would allow the communists to build up strength in the north as a precursor to a future military attack. On March 1, Marshall informed Acheson that he agreed with the Joint Chiefs' opposition to any new initiative. With the president about to depart on vacation, a decision on the whole tangled subject would have to be deferred for a few more weeks.[84]

With bureaucratic consensus impossible to achieve, both the military matter of whether to allow UN forces to push above the parallel and the political issue of a desirable place to end the war remained in limbo. More to the point, with any statement likely to spark political controversy, the administration decided to adopt a public position of studied silence. The president set the tone in his press conference on February 15, refusing to be drawn into specifics and merely stressing that MacArthur had all the instructions he needed to carry out his job.[85]

In Korea, officials instituted an even more vigorous clampdown. Determined to provide Ridgway's command with the flexibility it needed to gain the upper hand against the Chinese, the Pentagon wanted to avoid all press speculation on the subject. But reporters were incorrigible. As Eighth Army PI officers noted at the start of March, "as UN forces approached the thirty-eighth parallel, the press insisted on using the parallel as a reference point." Seeking to dampen comment on this explosive issue, on March 8 MacArthur's headquarters issued verbal instructions that briefing officers ought not to mention the parallel. Two weeks later, Tokyo then instituted an even more rigorous set of restrictions, ordering the Eighth Army censor not to pass "any mention whatsoever of thirty-eighth parallel." Symbolizing the extent of the new clampdown, reporters were even told: "no synonym in any form for 38th parallel will be cleared."[86]

The response to this creeping censorship was predictable enough. In recent weeks, the Eighth Army had been able to forge a constructive but fragile working relationship with journalists, using censorship as a shield to provide more informative briefings rather than as a tool to suppress embarrassing stories. Now, however, acrimony once again took center stage. By the middle of March, war correspondents had already started to rebel against Tokyo's efforts to institute "double censorship." When new orders preventing any reference to the thirty-eighth parallel were announced, they seemed to confirm the patent inability of MacArthur's headquarters to understand the working needs of the press. "All correspondents annoyed," the Eighth Army reported. Not only did they object strenuously to the censors' deletions of any mention of the parallel but they were busy "preparing angry 'gripe' stories on censorship being used for 'political purposes.'" Swiftly backtracking, Tokyo agreed to amend these rules so that correspondents could refer to the thirty-eighth parallel in their dispatches. But briefing officers were still instructed not to mention it. And the whole episode became yet another in a long list of friction points between the military and the media, one that partly undid the recent efforts to harmonize this fraught relationship.[87]

Nor was informed opinion any happier back in the United States. In one visit around New England, a planning adviser in the State Department's Bureau of Far Eastern Affairs "gained a strong impression that the frustration with regard to the Far East is more intense than ever." Worryingly, such angst was not confined to diehard Acheson-haters and Asia-firsters. Even "those who approved our resistance in Korea now find the present situation completely confusing and baffling." In one discussion in the offices of the *Providence Journal*, "which is probably one of the best newspapers on the East Coast and which has supported the department," the editor-in-chief asked the question that was at the root of much of the unease: "Why hasn't the president or secretary made a statement on how we end the war in Korea?"[88]

Inside the White House, officials who had long clamored for a more aggressive information policy were convinced that this type of thinking extended across the country. "At present," Elsey insisted, "most of the sag in the administration's fortunes is due to a widespread loss of confidence. There is confusion in the foreign area because of Korea, there is disappointment in the domestic area because of the prospect of higher taxes and the presence of higher costs. There seems to be no assurance of strong leadership." To rectify this, Elsey argued, there must be "more speeches, appointments, public appearances, and so on.... Above all, there has to be a most vigorous information program to make clear what is going on home and abroad.'[89]

It all seemed doubly frustrating because opinion polls and media surveys suggested that any effort to sell an armistice based on the thirty-eighth parallel would now garner widespread support. The dominant trend during March, PA recorded, "has been the growing desire among the public and commentators alike for a settlement of the conflict." According to Gallup, 73 percent of Americans now thought the United States should stop at the thirty-eighth parallel, if the Chinese also stopped fighting; in any settlement, 43 percent would approve of division of Korea, while only 36 percent would be opposed.[90]

That the public might be led on this question seemed to be confirmed when a senior figure finally spoke out. At a press conference on March 12, Ridgway told a group of assembled war correspondents that it would be "a tremendous victory" if the war ended with UN forces at the thirty-eighth parallel, for this would underline his command's success in defeating China's effort to drive it into the sea.[91] Shortly afterward, PA reported a "growing 'realism' about the nature of a settlement that might be obtainable in Korea." After Ridgway's remark, PA found that an increasing number of media commentators appeared willing to accept a return to the status quo of June 1950.[92]

Yet Ridgway's comment, rather than spur new efforts to define U.S. objectives, actually underlined the growing problems that buffeted the administration's PR efforts. For a start, the State Department was quick to distance itself from Ridgway, acutely aware that a bureaucratic consensus was still lacking on this explosive question. More important, Ridgway's statement was less a move to intervene in the political sphere and define what his command was now fighting to achieve than it was a simple effort to protect against ordinary GIs' sagging morale, which he thought was further threatened by MacArthur's recent public claims that a military stalemate was inevitable under existing policy.[93]

By this stage, MacArthur was an isolated figure. Although still surrounded by a loyal court of advisers in Tokyo, he privately seethed at the course of the war, not to mention Washington's continued rejection of his ideas for victory in Korea. Ever since the start of the war, he had been out of sympathy with some key elements of the administration's policy. Since the Chinese intervention, he had been subjected to a good deal of press criticism for his "end-the-war" offensive, while his efforts to establish a viable structure of military-media relations had largely backfired. Among allies, MacArthur was now widely depicted as a dangerous warmonger, too eager to push notions that might easily result in a new world war. With Ridgway on the scene, Washington officials had increasingly ignored MacArthur, often distrusting his assessments of the battlefield situation and invariably turning down his requests for bolder action, including one recent call to have A-bombs stationed in the region for use if the Soviets ever invaded Japan. Small wonder that one U.S. diplomat now found MacArthur "tired and depressed." Or as the official historians of the Joint Chiefs have put it, "the imposing figure in Tokyo no longer towered quite so impressively."[94]

MacArthur's response to this altered situation was to speak his mind in public. Authorities on his mood at this time portray him as a man determined to push his own agenda at any cost. This agenda might remain a vague set of prescriptions, ranging from the unification of Korea to expansive visions of dealing communism such a devastating global defeat that it could never recover. But MacArthur was now such a passionate believer in the need for "victory" that he was even willing to sacrifice his own career to ensure that the war was not ended in a shameful compromise.[95]

The form MacArthur's professional suicide took is well known: a series of on-the-record interviews with leading journalists during the first weeks of March that revealed his resentments and hinted at grander designs. At first, Washington was willing to greet such outbursts with a degree of toleration, telling worried ambassadors that it was only natural that MacArthur should chafe under the restraints of fighting a limited war and even suggesting that it would be "impossible" to censor him "in a democracy such as ours."[96]

Still, events were moving fast, and toleration was wearing thin. By the middle of March, UN forces had recaptured Seoul and were only a few miles from the thirty-eighth parallel. On March 19, the State Department and Joint Chiefs finally reached "a statement of understanding" on the basic objectives of the war. Although this was not formally ratified, senior officials nevertheless agreed that while the UN commander would be permitted to operate across the parallel for limited military objectives, he would not be given authority to attempt the forcible unification of the peninsula. The next day, with Truman about to return from his Florida vacation, the State Department and Joint Chiefs then formulated a presidential peace appeal. To keep Tokyo in the loop, MacArthur was informed that the UN was "now prepared to discuss conditions of settlement in Korea."[97]

Angry and dismayed, MacArthur viewed this message as the final straw. To scupper what he saw as "one of the most disgraceful plots in U.S. history," on March 24 (Tokyo time) MacArthur released another statement to the press. This stated that he would be prepared to consult with the enemy commander to discuss a cease-fire, but only under circumstances that would be tantamount to a Chinese surrender.[98]

Washington received word of MacArthur's mischievous message late on the evening of Friday, March 23. In an impromptu meeting that lasted into the early hours of the morning, Acheson, Lovett, and three senior State officials considered how to respond. An angry Lovett thought MacArthur ought to be fired. Acheson deemed his actions "insubordination of the grossest sort." The next day, in a further round of meetings, Truman and Collins joined the inquest. Although Lovett had simmered down and was no longer talking about dismissal, the president "appeared to be in a state of mind that combined disbelief with controlled fury." As an immediate matter, senior officials agreed on a State Department press release that described MacArthur's statement as "unexpected" and stressed that it had not been cleared with Washington. The Joint Chiefs would also send a private message to MacArthur, calling his attention to the president's "gagging order" of December and repeating that any further statements had to be coordinated through this mechanism.[99]

By demonstrating that MacArthur could not be trusted, this episode cast a long shadow over policy debates during the next two weeks. By the start of April, intelligence reports indicated that a renewed Chinese offensive was in the offing. With a substantial buildup of communist air power in Manchuria posing a major threat to the UN position, the Joint Chiefs drafted a new directive for the UN commander. These instructions would give him the authority to order the "hot pursuit" of communist planes into Chinese air space. But the Joint Chiefs were clearly uneasy about MacArthur wielding such power, fearing that he might use it to needlessly expand the war.

On the back of three more public outbursts from Tokyo, each one offering more criticism of the administration's way of waging war, senior officials began to contemplate MacArthur's dismissal. Marshall and the Joint Chiefs, convinced that he could not be trusted with the necessary authority and flexibility to meet the looming danger from China, advised "from a military point of view" that he be recalled. The president, exasperated with the continued evidence of MacArthur's public insubordination, steeled himself to act.[100]

As Truman's recognized, MacArthur's determination to wage his own unauthorized publicity campaign was particularly damaging because it came at a time when the administration had consistently failed to provide a lead. Recently, the president had invited his senior PR advisers to the Oval Office to discuss how the administration could do more in the public sphere. Eyeing the domestic environment with mounting concern, they had all agreed that the time was ripe to launch "a nation-wide speaking campaign in which cabinet officers and sub-cabinet officers would carry the message of the administration's policies and objectives to the forty-eight states." The problem, everyone recognized, was that "the administration's 'story' was not reaching the American public." To rectify this, the new speaking campaign would have to hammer away at just a few key issues, such as "the reasons for our fighting in Korea," which "cannot be told too often." To move things forward, Truman agreed to thrash the matter out in the cabinet, requesting each member to designate an assistant to work out detailed plans. He was even receptive to the idea of appointing a new administrative assistant "to supervise and carry out a coordinated program of speeches and similar PR activities."[101]

By the beginning of April, with senior officials increasingly convinced that MacArthur would have to be recalled, such a campaign was doubly vital. For the sacking of MacArthur was bound to cause a huge political explosion on the home front.

9

THE MACARTHUR
CONTROVERSY

Just before 1:00 in the morning on Wednesday, April 11, bleary-
eyed reporters were summoned to the West Wing of the White
House for a hastily arranged press conference. Once seated, they were
handed a sheaf of newly classified documents and bluntly informed that the
president had decided to fire MacArthur from all his commands because of
his insubordination, replacing him immediately with Ridgway. This sudden
nocturnal announcement had been sparked by a fear that the *Chicago Tribune* was about to break the news that MacArthur intended to resign. Determined to control the agenda, White House officials thought it vital to launch
a preemptive strike. But anger also drove their haste. "Why should we spare
the general's feelings," one asked, "when he behaved so outrageously toward
the president? In [an] unethical, insubordinate, insolent way?"[1]

Truman's decision to sack MacArthur would soon spark one of the most
intense public debates of the entire Cold War era, and this clumsy handling
was an inauspicious start. But not all the early signs were bad. To begin with,
the president had taken care to move only after consulting with senior officials, as well as leading Democrats in Congress, who would all be prepared to
support him in public if the going got tough.[2]

Moreover, to mute the likely domestic backlash, Truman was now determined, at long last, to undertake a vigorous public information campaign.
It began straightaway. All day that Wednesday, as he proceeded through his
routine meetings, the president let it be known that a central reason for sacking the general was to ensure civilian control over policy. As he told the ex-
congressman from Texas, Maury Maverick, knowing full well that Maverick
would share it with the large expectant crowd jammed into the press room,
"I had to choose between General MacArthur and the Constitution, Maury,
and I decided to save the Constitution."[3]

In between his scheduled meetings, Truman also set aside time to work on a nationwide speech to be delivered in the evening. Instinctively, he favored a tough, uncompromising approach, launching straight into a direct attack on both MacArthur and his right-wing Republican allies. As various drafts of the speech passed through different hands, however, it was gradually toned down. Officials in the State Department's Policy Planning Staff were particularly concerned to eliminate anything that was too personal or political. Reluctantly agreeing, Truman shied away from direct attacks and focused instead on the core issues: civilian control over the military, unanimity within the government, and above all the need to ensure that Korea did not escalate into a world war.[4]

"I have thought long and hard about this question of extending the war in Asia," Truman stressed that night to a massive radio and television audience. "I have discussed it many times with the ablest military advisers in the country. I believe with all my heart that the course we are following is the best course. I believe that we must try to limit the war to Korea for these vital reasons: to make sure that the precious lives of our fighting men are not wasted; to see that the security of our country and the free world is not needlessly jeopardized; and to prevent a third world war."[5]

During the remainder of the week, the White House then worked with a number of allies to amplify its case. On Wednesday evening, while Truman prepared to go on air, Oklahoma's Robert S. Kerr made a spirited defense of the president's actions. On the Senate floor, the mood was tense and angry; repeatedly, diehards like Capehart, Case, and Hickenlooper interrupted Kerr, determined to break his flow and challenge his assertions.[6] But Kerr, though a freshman senator, was an experienced speaker—his "stem-winding oratory" had entertained many a Democratic National Convention in the past—and he responded aggressively to all the Republican taunts. He even went as far as to blame "Magnificent MacArthur" for the fact that thousands of "American GIs are sleeping in unmarked graves in North Korea from which they will never return."[7]

Three days later, the president made sure that Kerr was not alone in launching a biting political attack, for he was scheduled to make his second major speech in a week, this time at the annual Jefferson-Jackson Day dinner. Traditionally, this speech was a chance for Democratic presidents to descend from their lofty perch as head of state and engage in partisan politicking. And Truman, in a combative mood after months of relative silence, was determined not to let such an opportunity pass by. As he told his speechwriting team, he wanted to seize the occasion to make MacArthur and his supporters look "ridiculous." While careful to remove specific references to Taft, "he wanted to make this speech hard-hitting and 'political,'" without getting "down in the gutter." This he would do by going after the "confusers"—the Republicans who had no policy of their own but wanted to confuse the public at a moment of extreme danger merely in order to win the next election.[8] "The long and short of it," Truman told his friendly audience, "is that they want defenses without spending the money, they want us to wage war without an army, they want us to have victory without taking any risks, and they want us to try to run the whole world and to run it without any friends."[9]

By the start of the second week of the controversy, all these actions appeared to be paying some dividends. To be sure, the White House was deluged by more than eighty thousand telegrams, most of them protesting MacArthur's recall. In Congress, diehard Republicans launched a "drumfire of speeches to keep the pot boiling" until MacArthur returned home. Inevitably, Joe McCarthy came up with the most notably outrageous comment, accusing the president of acting under the influence of "bourbon and Benedictine." But other senators were equally vehement. Jenner and Capehart accused Truman of "treasonable actions." Convinced that Acheson and his weak-willed diplomats were behind Truman's heinous act, Francis Case even introduced a bill that would abolish the State Department and replace it with a new department of foreign affairs.[10]

Outside the capital, all the usual suspects in the media were also savage in their condemnation. Organs like the *Cleveland Plain Dealer*, *Chicago Tribune*, and *Los Angeles Times* were appalled at "the hasty and vindictive" manner in which MacArthur was removed, blamed British socialists in Attlee's Labour Party for pushing Truman into this action, and assailed the limitations placed on Tokyo that had forced the general to speak out. For such critics, the president's speeches were "childish piffle," little more than "thin gruel to feed a worried and confused people." His words certainly failed to answer the central question: "How and when can conclusive decision be reached in the Korean War?"[11]

Yet such condemnation was far from universal, especially in the media, and within days there were mounting signs that the president was enjoying a significant measure of success in framing the key issues of the debate. Among a range of mainstream newspapers, including the *Baltimore Sun*, *Boston Herald*, *Boston Globe*, *Denver Post*, *New York Herald Tribune*, and *New York Times*, there was a tendency to take the president's cue and look beyond the abrupt end of an illustrious career. In their opinion, it was the "larger issues" that were crucial, especially the importance of civilian control over the military. As all these newspapers pointed out, the president had the unquestionable authority to fire an officer. Nor did they doubt that, because of MacArthur's repeated public outbursts, it was time for him to go. "Unless the basic policies of the U.S. and the UN were to be overturned," the *Christian Science Monitor* declared in a typical comment, "it became necessary for General MacArthur to conform, to resign, or to be removed."[12]

Perhaps the administration's biggest success was to fix the idea that MacArthur and his Republican allies favored an all-out war with China. As a State Department survey recorded, "the preponderance of press, radio, and other articulate opinion...shied away from the general's recommendations for dealing with the Korean conflict out of fear of the 'risk' of general war and the loss of America's allies."[13]

For senior officials, all this was an encouraging start. Clearly, though, it was only the first round in what promised to be a long-drawn-out battle. Truman himself thought that there would be about six weeks of rough going up on Capitol Hill before the mood started to settle down. He also recognized that after his own hectic week of activity, the administration would soon have to take a back seat to MacArthur, who was scheduled to return to the United States on April 17 and would address Congress two days later. This homecoming was bound to be a huge event. MacArthur had not set foot inside the country for almost fifteen years. Quite apart from the intense controversy surrounding his Korean War statements, the general was due a belated hero's welcome for his exploits during World War II.[14] As a result, there was little for the president to do but step aside gracefully. The White House even announced that Truman was "happy" to learn that MacArthur would be addressing a joint session of Congress, adding that the president would cancel a prearranged speech before the American Society of Newspapers on April 19 because this was MacArthur's day and he did not want to do anything to detract from it. Overall, as one reporter noted, Truman and his advisers decided to adopt "an attitude of relaxed, amiable waiting."[15]

Still, there was a limit to Truman's graciousness and amiability. To greet the general, the president sent Harry Vaughan as his personal emissary, which, because of Vaughan's reputation as a corrupt crony, was widely viewed as a snub. When MacArthur addressed Congress, the White House was keen to tell reporters that everyone in the building had been far too busy to watch his televised speech.[16]

The General Returns

MacArthur's triumphant return to the United States has been well documented. There were the parades in San Francisco, New York, and Chicago attended by millions of Americans who poured down tons of ticker tape in volumes that surpassed even those thrown on Charles Lindbergh in the 1920s and Howard Hughes in the 1930s. There was the general's keynote speech before a joint session of Congress, watched by an estimated twenty million, some of whom had acquired their new TV sets for this very purpose.[17] There was the speech itself, in which MacArthur challenged the claim that he wanted to send ground troops into China, contended that all his proposals for victory were fully supported by the Joint Chiefs, and argued that his own strategy in Korea—which included a blockade of China, aerial reconnaissance of

the Chinese mainland, and the use of Chiang's troops—would promise victory, whereas the administration's weak-willed policy would "mean a long,
indecisive war and the needless sacrifice of many American boys." There was
his rapturous reception by Republicans, including the (in)famous comment
by Dewey Short from Missouri: "we saw a great hunk of God in the flesh,
and we heard the voice of God." And there were the countless episodes of
emotion across the nation, from citizens in California stringing up effigies of
Truman from traffic light towers to longshoremen in New York walking out
of their jobs in protest of Truman's action.[18]

On Capitol Hill, some Republicans watched this amazing outpouring of
support with unmitigated glee. Out of power for almost twenty years, the
GOP had long lacked a charismatic, unifying leader. Coming at the very
time that Senator Vandenberg, their central voice on foreign policy matters
in recent years, had finally succumbed to cancer, MacArthur's triumphant
return home seemed providential. "This is the first 'voice' Republicans have
found in our time," one Washington commentator observed. "Enviously they
used to complain bitterly about the 'dulcet' and 'mellifluous' tones of Franklin D. Roosevelt. Now, in General MacArthur they have found an equal, with
that effective change of pace, that occasional drop at the proper moment
almost to a whisper—and a dash of corn that appeals."[19]

MacArthur wooing the masses on his return to the United States, April 1951.
Courtesy of National Archives.

Across the country, the depth and breadth of popular support for the general also seemed to suggest that the Republicans could use him to inflict mortal damage on the administration. On hearing word of MacArthur's recall, Republican leaders immediately called for both a formal congressional investigation of "the conduct of foreign and military policy" and a direct appearance by the general before Congress. Some even mooted the possibility of "impeachments"—the plural suggesting that they had both Truman and Acheson in mind. Their initial jauntiness was expressed by Styles Bridges, who bustled around the Senate cloakroom, telling everyone: "this is the biggest windfall that has ever come to the Republican Party."[20]

Admittedly, impeachment would be an extremely difficult task in a legislature the Democrats still controlled. But in the last weeks of April, as the domestic outpouring for MacArthur gathered force, impeachment did not seem impossible—not with GOP legislators reporting that they had received more than five thousand telegrams calling for such action in just one day. Nor did Democratic opposition appear an insurmountable obstacle. As one conservative columnist put it, nationalist Republicans hoped to take the issue to the country in an effort to "line up enough public sentiment to compel many of the Democrats in Congress to break with the president or run the risk of themselves being beaten at the polls on an emotional issue."[21]

Yet not everyone in the GOP was convinced that MacArthur was a political savior. Internationalist Republicans like Duff, Ives, Lodge, and Saltonstall were leery of tying the party too closely to a general who seemed out of sympathy with a Europe-first strategy; they also recognized that the president had the authority to remove any general, and were quick to go public with this point.[22] According to a widely syndicated article by Drew Pearson, even some nationalist Republicans had their doubts. Controversially, Pearson placed Taft firmly in this category, since it was an open secret that the Ohioan had intense presidential ambitions that would be swiftly dashed if MacArthur was built up into an irresistible force.[23] To counter this impression, Taft delivered a series of stinging speeches in which he tore into the administration for favoring a "soft war" in Korea and placed himself firmly in MacArthur's camp.[24]

Nonetheless, MacArthur's return clearly posed problems for Taft, quite apart from creating an obvious rival for the presidency. He was certainly poorly placed to support a general against the civilian authority of the U.S. government, for a central component of his current public philosophy revolved around fears of a "garrison state" and excessive militaristic influences on American life. Like most generals, MacArthur was also a strong supporter of preparedness, and his testimony might ultimately serve to detract from Taft's own campaign, reiterated amid a great fanfare on April 30, to cut current defense spending by a half, on the basis that the administration's proposals for a 3.5-million-man army would wreck the economy. Small wonder, then, that Taft was lukewarm to the idea of any congressional investigation being opened to television cameras or radio microphones. There was just no knowing what might happen if such media gave MacArthur extended exposure to the public.[25]

Nor was Taft the only MacArthur supporter who entertained private doubts. A complex blend of hope mingled with fear was in full evidence when Senator Alexander Smith traveled to New York City on April 26 to meet Herbert Hoover in his Waldorf Towers apartment. The two men had been close for more than thirty years, since Smith had worked under Hoover in the post–World War I economic relief effort. Instinctively, both were supportive of MacArthur—Hoover because he opposed the notion of getting too heavily involved in land wars in Asia and Europe but was perfectly willing to sanction U.S. air and naval power against China, and Smith because he agreed with MacArthur's assessment of the need to employ air strikes, a blockade, and Chiang's forces to win the war in Korea. Thinking through the GOP strategy for the upcoming hearings, both men agreed that if MacArthur was given a free rein, he could well be the perfect spokesman. But both were worried about what might happen in the heated partisan atmosphere of a committee room. Hoover privately thought that the general had a Napoleonic streak and "tended to couch his ideas in a manner resembling the King James version of the Bible." He also feared that "if MacArthur was cross-examined by hostile Democrats he might lose his temper and that this would be bad for the cause. Above all things," Smith noted, "Hoover feels that MacArthur should be kept on an even poise and not lose the enormous advantage" that had accrued from his recent appearances in San Francisco, New York, and Chicago.[26]

Because even MacArthur's supporters were worried about what the unpredictable general might do, most GOP strategists decided that the best approach would be to focus less on the personal issue between him and the president and more on the larger issues of U.S. policy in Asia since 1945. This promised various benefits. It would not make the party too beholden to just one person. It would unite the nationalist wing of the party with the Chiang Kai-shek boosters, like Smith and Knowland, who would be playing a leading part in the hearings. It would turn these hearings into a more general inquest into the Democratic policies that had ended first in the world's most populous country going communist and then the disastrous war in Korea. And it promised, by so doing, to inflict far more damage on the administration. Some Republicans even hoped that such a broader line of questioning would make the possibility of impeachment more likely, on the grounds that the president had "violated his oath of office by disregarding the Constitution of the United States in carrying on a war in Korea against China without the consent of Congress."[27]

On April 16, at a meeting of the Republican Conference Committee, the thirty-two senators in attendance all agreed on this strategy. As Millikin told reporters on his way out, GOP legislators were unanimous in their view that any congressional inquiry ought to be "virtually limitless" in scope. After such an extensive fishing expedition, Millikin intimated, impeachment might also result, perhaps on the basis that the president had waged war in Korea without asking for a formal declaration.[28]

Going Public

With MacArthur's triumphant return generating grandiose ideas of impeachment among some Republicans, the administration recognized the need to plan its next move with extreme care. In public, the president continued to adopt a jaunty, relaxed pose, confident that the furor would blow over as soon as "the facts are all known."[29] In private, however, the same developments that fueled optimism in Republican ranks looked deeply alarming from the point of view of the White House—and suggested that something more than simply getting out the facts would be in order.

Indeed, in the wake of MacArthur's homecoming, officials clearly faced a broader battle to win over the hearts and minds of the mass of Americans. As opinion polls demonstrated in the days after the general's return, the government had considerable ground to make up. According to one early survey, a mere 28 percent of Americans approved of Truman's decision to recall MacArthur. When asked about the general's specific prescriptions for ending the war in Korea, 56 percent favored bombing supply bases in China, and 58 percent approved the idea of giving aid to Chiang Kai-shek to attack the Chinese mainland, while only a quarter endorsed the administration's current strategy.[30]

Although many mainstream newspapers were supportive of the administration, there were numerous worrying trends here, too. In New York, for instance, elite-oriented organs like the *New York Times* and *New York Herald Tribune* stoutly defended Truman, but this was something of a mixed blessing. "I don't see that we have any cause for joy because conservative newspapers like the *Herald Tribune* side with the president on this issue," one White House aide observed. For one thing, such Republican organs could not really be trusted.[31] For another, the *Herald Tribune* and *New York Times* only had circulation figures of 345,400 and 505,400, respectively. In stark contrast, big populist papers like the *New York Daily News*—America's largest daily, with a circulation of 2.2 million—attacked the president savagely.[32]

Elsewhere, even some sympathetic newspapers found it difficult to hang tough behind the government. On the East Coast, leading figures at the *Christian Science Monitor* were instinctively opposed to MacArthur, convinced that his policy prescriptions ran counter to their basic editorial line. Yet the *Monitor's* editors were soon "getting heavy criticism in heavy volume from readers" who complained that the paper's reporting was biased against the general. Fearing a sudden dip in sales, at the start of May the *Monitor's* editorial board decided it had no choice but to instruct its journalists to be as balanced, "temperate, and objective as possible"—which, in effect, meant toning down any criticism of the widely venerated general.[33] On the other side of the country, meanwhile, the problem was somewhat different. As the publisher of the *San Francisco Chronicle* explained when Acheson thanked him for the paper's support, "he was not sure how long he would be able to 'keep off the wolves.'" It all depended on whether or not he could keep the newspaper's restive stockholders as far away from editorial comment as possible, for the money men were decidedly worried about being so obviously on the wrong side of the popular debate.[34]

Even more troubling was the prospect that certain core elements of the Democratic coalition now seemed poised to defect to the opposition. "There was a close kinship between MacArthurism and McCarthyism," one meeting of administration officials and supporters fretted, "both of which had gripped the urban masses in a way which was undermining one of the major supports of the administration."[35] Urban Catholics, in particular, seemed to be susceptible to MacArthur's position—a fact that prodded one young Democratic congressman from Boston to "regret" that the general had been removed. This was John F. Kennedy, who defended MacArthur by pointing out that he "suffered from a lack of direction from the U.S. in his assignment as commander of the UN troops."[36]

Among administration friends, another common complaint was that the White House invariably failed to provide effective leadership. This had clearly been the case during February and March, and had helped to magnify the importance of MacArthur's outbursts. Although the president had been more active in the first days after the recall, a number of sympathetic newspapers now urged him to do more to explain his policies and actions. "The sudden dismissal of MacArthur," the *New York Herald Tribune* insisted, "brings into dramatic focus the lack of direction and the confusion of policy which have characterized the administration throughout the conduct of the Korean hostilities. Neither President Truman nor his aides made clear to the country the objectives of our fighting or the outlines of a settlement." "What is needed, in our opinion," the *Washington Post* agreed, "is new leadership to occupy the political vacuum that General MacArthur is exploiting. MacArthurism is making a widespread appeal because the administration itself has offered the people so little light and leading."[37]

What all this meant was that far from simply trusting in the basic power of its case, the administration would have to engage in a range of strenuous efforts to try to win back the public mind. The hearings in Congress were vitally important, and intensive work was already under way to ensure that those who had to testify would be as well prepared as possible. But before they began on May 3, officials also had two weeks to try to launch a broader campaign, one that would undermine MacArthur's obvious appeal, neutralize the impact of Republican efforts, and help rekindle popular support for their policies in Asia.

To get the ball rolling, on April 17 the president's press secretary, Joseph Short, summoned a group of midranking officials from various departments to a meeting in the White House Fish Room. He began by calling for "a greatly stepped-up speaking program by cabinet members and little cabinet members," stressing that the president's December 5 "gagging order" had now been lifted. To facilitate a more intensive public effort, State and Defense would begin assembling material on relevant policies, which the White House would collate and circulate to officials throughout the executive branch. On receiving this information, officials were encouraged to get out of Washington and take their case to audiences all over the country.[38]

In providing support for these speeches, as well as to help out with preparations for the congressional hearings, the president appointed John A. Carroll to a temporary new post at the White House. Carroll, an aggressive liberal with impressive connections in Congress, had a well-earned reputation for being able to clarify and simplify the complex pressures at work in this fractious body. As well as liaison duties on the Hill, he was also to become one of the administration's point men in the vital effort to reach out to key groups beyond the confines of Washington.[39]

On his first day at work, Carroll was asked to formulate plans to liaise with "various segments of the population—labor, farmers, veterans, groups like the CPD."[40] A week later, a second group of Democratic workers and White House aides, led by John Barriere, met to consider the same problem on a more informal basis. Currently a staff member on the House Banking and Currency Committee, Barriere had previously worked on the DNC's Research Division, a body whose demise had been much lamented in the White House, since it had not only produced a wealth of ammunition to use against Republicans but also helped to reach out to core groups in the Democratic coalition.[41] Now, Barriere and his associates discussed how they might perform these tasks in the current controversy. It was particularly vital, they thought, to win back American Catholics, perhaps by enlisting liberal clergy like Archbishop Bernard J. Sheil in Chicago "to try and organize [an] effective opposition" to MacArthur, or by starting a quiet campaign "to get more friendly speakers at Communion breakfasts." It was even hoped that the accident-prone navy secretary, Francis Matthews, might atone for his gaffes the previous summer, for he was extremely well connected in influential Catholic circles and would be an ideal liaison man for the government.[42]

Beyond this, however, both Carroll and the Barriere group were at a bit of a loss. What the administration really needed was something along the lines of the interventionist groups of 1940–41, which had been grass-roots organizations consisting of "local committees, with eager beavers working, planning, and speaking all over the country." But such groups would take time to get off the ground. True, the CPD was already up and running, having played a role in helping to drum up support for mobilization. But after a good deal of internal discussion, and even a few consultations with CPD members, officials were left disappointed. "It was generally agreed that the CPD—consisting of people who are only interested in a high-level approach—was totally inadequate," Hechler noted. And in any case, "the CPD refuses to touch the MacArthur controversy, claiming it is 'all politics.' "[43]

Nor was this the only initiative that remained stillborn. Inside the White House, many officials now thought long and hard about the prospect of negative campaigning. One idea was to turn MacArthur's past triumphs against him. To dent his heroic image, they could publicize photographs of MacArthur wading ashore at Leyte in 1944 surrounded by a barrage not of Japanese artillery but of newsreel cameras.[44] They could try to tarnish his record in reconstructing Japan by investigating allegations that his command there had "fostered bribery, corruption, and a class social system."[45]

Another obvious target was the China lobby. Even before MacArthur was relieved, senior White House aides had considered pushing for an investigation that would uncover the extent to which senators like Bridges, Knowland, and McCarthy were financially beholden to a string of shady interests connected to the corrupt Chinese nationalists. Now, with MacArthur and his Republican allies talking about the need to unleash Chiang's troops in order to carry the conflict into mainland China, Carroll was asked to talk with his friends in Congress about how such an investigation might be started.[46]

Yet even as such ideas were mooted, White House aides recognized the need to move with care. Some of the more obvious slurs, such as claims of corruption in Japan, were hard to verify; others would be risky to use, and might easily backfire if traced back to official sources. On the proposed China lobby investigation, the State Department was particularly reluctant to act swiftly and only produced "a watery five-page memo" on the lobby's various activities, for Acheson remained firmly opposed to rushing "pell-mell into it until he has some idea of what the results of such an investigation might be."[47]

Still, the administration was not afraid to use some records from the recent past. On April 21, Anthony Leveiro of the *New York Times* revealed that he had been given access to the official record of the Wake Island meeting between Truman and MacArthur. Among other things, this demonstrated that MacArthur had been confident that the war would be over by Thanksgiving and that the Eighth Army would be withdrawn from Korea by Christmas. This dramatic leak created an immediate sensation. With rumors swirling around the Washington cocktail circuit that "it was Truman personally who gave the *Times* the Wake Island story," even internationalist congressmen wondered why friendly journalists had access to sensitive material while they had been kept in the dark. Ominously, less friendly Republicans began to mutter about official efforts to smear the general, while some even talked darkly about invoking the Espionage Act to find the person responsible for leaking such a top-secret document.[48]

Undeterred, the administration moved to bolster its case by exploiting the tremendous friction that had built up between war correspondents and MacArthur over censorship and security violations. Inside the administration, there was even some discussion about getting leading media critics to testify before the congressional committee, where their firsthand knowledge of MacArthur's methods would doubtless generate enormous interest among their colleagues. Although this idea was ultimately discarded, on the grounds that these hearings should be confined only to those in an official capacity, some officials still worked to make sure that the long-running controversies between MacArthur and the war correspondents now enjoyed a full airing. And in mid-April, the *Washington Post* ran two pieces exposing the growing rift between Ridgway and MacArthur, especially over the MacArthur's double censorship regime, "which reportedly was more political than military."[49]

As well as bashing MacArthur, the administration now moved to recalibrate its positive case for waging both the conflict in Korea and the wider Cold War. Key White House advisers were convinced that the president's rhetoric had to be far more direct, aggressive, and ideological.[50] Until this moment, Truman's Korean War speeches had often been low-key affairs, invariably restrained, and with an eye toward "gradually arousing the people to the peril they faced" rather than "scaring the hell" out of them in one overheated message. Now, however, Truman's speechwriters believed the time had come to offer a bolder vision, if not for the Korean conflict then for the whole Cold War, in order to counter MacArthur's popular calls for victory. "They feel that our present foreign policy has not been effectively enough 'packaged,'" Marshall Shulman, Acheson's main speechwriter, reported to his boss,

> and is therefore not well enough understood by our people, and cannot compete emotionally with such solutions as are offered by General MacArthur, and may be offered by others in the future. They feel that a more precise expression of our objectives in relation to the Soviet Union would give our policy more emotional appeal. In several recent speeches, they have sought to express our policy as being intended to achieve the overthrow of the Soviet regime, and the liberation of the satellite states.[51]

Senior State Department officials were leery of this kind of thinking, however. Although Acheson was happy to play up the idealistic elements behind American strategy, such as the use of the UN or the notion that free peoples would ultimately triumph over despots, he was reluctant to be too precise about how the Cold War might be brought to an end, especially if this meant talking explicitly about rollback. In his view, anything too radical would undoubtedly fuel domestic expectations, worry important allies, and undermine moves toward an armistice in Korea. On one occasion, he even rushed into the White House on a Sunday afternoon in order to excise a passage in a proposed presidential speech that he thought was "too optimistic about the internal collapse of the Soviet Union."[52]

Still, White House speechwriters were not easily dissuaded. According to Shulman, they continued to lobby for a keynote presidential speech along the lines of grandiose World War II declarations like the Atlantic Charter or Four Freedoms, which would declare America's ultimate goal in the Cold War to be "universal liberty." "Their feeling," Shulman concluded, "is that 'people need to see the light at the end of the tunnel,' to be willing to go along with the sacrifices being asked of them."[53]

In the first week of May, this White House effort to change the basic tenor of its message was centered on two messages—one on the budget, the other on civil defense. With the president poised to ask Congress for another $60 billion in defense spending, the budget message provided an opportunity to emphasize the government's ongoing efforts to deter future communist aggression by bolstering the defenses of the free world. Yet when the White House received the Pentagon's first draft, Truman's speechwriters were unimpressed, believing that the language paid no attention to the recent shift in the popular mood. "If I were favorable to the administration," one speechwriter remarked after reading the Pentagon draft, "I would hope for some indication at least of how to bring the Korean War to a close on the basis of its being a limited war in Korea." As it stood, the entire emphasis of the message was "proceed slowly and wisely, don't overbuy, don't put too much strain on the civilian economy, etc. In the present political temper of the country, I think this is just the wrong approach." Working hard to make it more punchy, the White House speechwriters replaced the Pentagon's staid prose with discussions "of the Kremlin, the central importance of being able to strike back at Russia, [and] the Korean fighting"—and were pleasantly surprised when neither State nor Defense protested their additions.[54]

Truman's civil defense speech, planned for May 7, was another ideal occasion to respond to MacArthur. Civil defense had always been a good way for the government to drive home the ominous nature of the Soviet menace on the one hand while stressing the horrible consequences that would accompany a world war on the other. Speaking at the Statler Hotel, with a large national radio audience listening in, Truman exploited this new opportunity to the fullest. He began by expressing his faith that "this country would survive and would win an atomic war," but hastened to add: "even if we win, an atomic war would be a disaster," with whole cities as casualties and civilian losses that would be "terrible." The corollary of this was clear. In an obvious swipe at MacArthur, Truman insisted that the central goal of the nation's foreign policy had to be to avoid a new world war. "I am confident," he concluded, "that the American people will not yield either to impatience or defeatism."[55]

Preparing for the Hearings

While the White House moved to sharpen the language of the president's speeches, attention moved inexorably toward Capitol Hill, where the hearings into the events surrounding MacArthur's recall were scheduled to begin on May 3. The administration now faced the prospect that for all its agonizing over how to get its message out to the average American, it might suddenly lose control over the debate. This was partly because MacArthur, as the first witness, would again have a major national platform on which to make his case. But Congress itself was hardly likely to be a pliant tool, loyally doing the government's bidding. Any high-profile congressional investigation tends to bring out the showman in even the most loyal legislator. As the leading scholar of a later investigation points out, in this type of inquiry the "individual and institutional interests of members of Congress inevitably blend with higher motives, thus creating a strange mixture of circus, morality play, exposé, and education."[56]

Many prominent Democrats in the Eighty-Second Congress were no strangers to such antics. Only recently, a number of them had used their committees as forums to make names for themselves, often at the expense of the administration—Lyndon Johnson in his probes of the preparedness program, William Fulbright in his examination of the Reconstruction Finance Corporation, and Estes C. Kefauver (D-TN) in his crime investigations.[57] The last had been particularly popular; when Kefauver had toured the country between January and March, his hearings had been televised by no less than twenty-five stations in twenty-one cities, and had reached audiences of around twenty to thirty million. Rarely off the front page, the Kefauver hearings had amply demonstrated the large rewards that hard-hitting, media-savvy questioning could reap.[58] And few legislators were likely to forgo the chance to make a name for themselves now—not with Johnson, Fulbright, and Kefauver all members of the MacArthur inquiry.

Nor did the administration have a series of reliable, close, and regular contacts with the fourteen Democrats who would sit on the committee. As a general rule, the Truman White House had "no form of organized, sophisticated type of congressional liaison" like those that subsequent presidents developed; as one congressional staffer recalled, "everything was done on an *ad hoc* basis."[59] In this instance, the White House could probably rely on about nine of the fourteen Democrats on the committee to stand up for the president, but some of these were mavericks like Fulbright and Kefauver.[60] When it came to the loyalists—senators like Lester C. Hunt (D-WY), Brien McMahon, and John J. Sparkman (D-AL)—the newly appointed Carroll had been asked to find ways to get them to ask the right questions, but thus far only McMahon had actively sought such support. The administration thus contemplated the start of the hearings with trepidation. Mostly reliant on the goodwill and skill of their sympathizers, it could only hope that these senators would prove effective.[61]

If some of the preparatory maneuvering was anything to go by, this trepidation was well placed. On April 13, Richard Russell, chair of the Senate Armed Services Committee, had announced his intention to open an investigation into the circumstances surrounding MacArthur's dismissal. Like other leading Democrats, Russell hoped that by championing an investigation early he could control both the participants and ground rules of any hearing.[62] But in the next few weeks, Russell was forced to make a series of important concessions to the GOP.

The first of these was related to the documentary record. Under intense pressure from Republicans, who responded to the leaking of the record of the Wake Island conference with accusations that the administration's declassification standard rested solely on the PR value of a document, Democrats broke ranks and agreed to push for the release of all material that had a bearing on the investigation.[63] This move was particularly ominous, because Russell had also agreed to widen the scope of the hearings. Initially, he had envisaged merely calling MacArthur before the Armed Services Committee to discuss the military matters surrounding his recall. But again Republican pressure was brought to bear. With the GOP Conference Committee unanimously calling for a "virtually limitless" inquiry into eight separate areas, including whether or not Acheson "should be removed in the public interest," Russell deemed it prudent to compromise. His hearings would not be the all-inclusive fishing expedition Republicans hoped to initiate. But to prevent allegations that he was heading a cover-up or "whitewash," Russell agreed that its scope would be "wide," covering both MacArthur's recall and the overall military situation in the Far East.[64]

Still, not all the portents were bad. While Russell had been forced into a few tactical retreats, on key issues he remained steadfast. This was heartening to the White House, because it was far from clear that Russell would be in the government's corner. As a Dixiecrat, he had staunchly opposed many of Truman's policies, especially on civil rights. As a senator jealous of his institution's prerogatives, he had been careful to avoid any formal contact with the administration since the start of the controversy. Now, however, on two important procedural issues Russell stood firm for positions that greatly strengthened the administration's position.

One was the question of open hearings. Despite concerns in some GOP quarters that MacArthur might self-destruct under hostile questioning, most Republicans were still eager to parade him under the full glare of television klieg lights, convinced that their popular hero would be an enormous hit with the public. From the outset, however, Russell was determined to keep radio and television away.[65] In committee, fellow Democrats gave him staunch support, voting down by twelve to nine a motion to open up the hearings. On May 2, Russell suffered a brief scare on the Senate floor, when a combination of Democratic absenteeism and the defection of the habitually awkward McCarran threatened to overturn the committee vote, but this danger was soon headed off by a timely filibuster from Matthew N. Neely (D-WV). When the subject came back the next day, sufficient Democrats were rounded up to block the renewed Republican effort. Russell then helped to rally the ranks by accusing the GOP of being prepared to risk the lives of American boys fighting in Korea in order to hold "a hippodrome and a circus" on the Hill. To counter persistent Republican charges that he was drawing an "iron curtain" around the proceedings, Russell then made sure that an edited version of all the testimony would be prepared immediately for reporters. A Pentagon censor would be on hand to see that vital secrets were not divulged. And Senators Knowland and McMahon would be appointed to ensure that these excisions were made for valid reasons and not simply to cover up embarrassing material.[66]

As well as denying MacArthur another public stage, Russell and other Democrats rallied together to ensure that a majority of the committee would be administration sympathizers. Republicans, recognizing that they effectively had been outflanked by the absence of their leading members from key committees during the "great debate," had mooted a number of plans to ensure a different outcome this time, such as the inclusion of members from the Senate Appropriations Committee, since this would allow at least two nationalist leaders—Wherry and Ferguson—to play a key role.[67] But Democrats again remained solid in their opposition. Rather than create a new committee, the Democratic leadership merely handed the matter over to the same body that had controlled the "great debate"— a joint panel consisting of both the Armed Services and Foreign Relations committees. As in February and March, many of administration's most potent critics would thus be spectators rather than participants. In fact, of the twelve Republican members, only seven were staunch MacArthur supporters.[68]

All these maneuverings on the Hill were important, because they ensured that once again the Democrats effectively controlled the rules of the game. But for the administration, perhaps the most encouraging development in the days leading up to the hearings came not from the partisan sniping in Washington but from the real fighting in Korea.

On April 22, China launched the "first impulse" of its great Easter offensive. According to Ridgway, this "was the strongest enemy attack we had yet sustained," with no less than fifteen communist armies seeking to punch through the UN defensive lines and recapture Seoul. If this massive enemy force achieved its goal, domestic support for MacArthur could well prove unstoppable. Officials were therefore enormously relieved when the new team led by Ridgway was able to report success. Although the fighting was again bitter, the Chinese failed to make a decisive breakthrough. By April 29, military spokespersons were able to tell reporters that the communist advance had been decisively disrupted, at a cost to the Chinese of about seventy thousand casualties. Four days later, they were even more upbeat. With the congressional inquiry scheduled to begin that day, the UNC euphorically announced it had won "a grand victory."[69]

The MacArthur Hearings

At 10:30 on the morning of Thursday, May 3, Senator Richard Russell gaveled his investigating committee to order. At that moment, the scene inside and outside the stately Senate Caucus Room was far from orderly. With MacArthur scheduled as the first witness, more than two hundred reporters had assembled to get a glimpse or a photo of him, while half a dozen picketers waved banners that read "We Don't Want a Truman-Rigged Hearing" and "Don't Cover Up Blunders With Secrecy." Having flown down from New York that morning, MacArthur seemed unperturbed. Determined to finish his testimony as quickly as possible so he could get back to wooing the masses, he agreed to testify for three straight days with scarcely a break even for lunch and refreshments.[70]

It was a grueling schedule for a seventy-one-year-old, but MacArthur initially seemed to be an effective advocate for his cause. Although he made no opening statement, convinced that his keynote speech of two weeks before had amply made his case, he dominated the sessions throughout Thursday, Friday, and Saturday. Even Democratic critics considered his performance "very dignified and impressive." Most were highly deferential to the man who had received such enormous popular support. And even hostile questioners felt obliged to preface barbed comments with reassurances that they were not being argumentative but merely trying to develop a "crystal clear" record of events.[71]

Submitted to a bewildering assortment of questions, as each legislator used his allotted time to ask about different aspects of the Korean War or to focus on his own pet project, MacArthur proved adept at handling questions from most directions. Despite some leading Republicans' concerns that the Democrats would goad him into anger and unfortunate remarks, MacArthur deftly refused to be drawn out on any matter outside the scope of his basic argument, especially if it meant undercutting the public position of Republican nationalists like Taft or Wherry.[72]

MacArthur also had a gift for distilling complex issues into simple and memorable phrases. He was particularly adept at contrasting his approach to winning the war, which was the "normal way," with the clueless and weak-willed strategy of the administration. But integral to his performance was his use of key words and phrases, deployed with an obvious eye to framing the unfolding political discourse. One of these was "appeasement," which he used in a broad fashion to characterize the government's limited-war strategy, implying that it was little better than the ill-fated response to the Axis powers during the 1930s.[73] Another was his constant talk about casualties—which marked a stark contrast to his earlier spasms of anger whenever journalists had even mentioned the losses his command was sustaining.

Focusing on casualties was particularly important to MacArthur, because it enabled him to draw out the bloody consequences of the administration's limited-war strategy, especially in light of his claim that the Korean campaign had cost more men than Eisenhower's decisive battle for Europe in 1944–45. It also allowed the general to take aim at broader aspects of administration policy. He especially wanted to raise and then demolish the idea that the Korean War was buying time for the Cold War mobilization strategy to take effect. All it was doing, he stressed, was "buying time at the expense of American blood."[74]

After three days of this kind of rhetoric, MacArthur's partisans on the committee were convinced he had made an "excellent showing."[75] Yet even at this early stage of proceedings, it was clear that MacArthur's strengths might easily turn into serious liabilities.

For a start, while the elaborate deference shown to the general created a comfortable environment for him to make his case, it also helped to take some of the sting out of the whole event. Certainly no Republican could claim, as many had during the Tydings investigation of Joe McCarthy, that the whole event was fatally flawed—not with MacArthur himself declaring that there wasn't "any man could criticize in the slightest degree either the conduct of the hearings, the scope, the methods."[76]

Even more important, MacArthur's studied vagueness on some issues, together with his tendency to sidestep thorny matters by insisting that they were outside his area of expertise, swiftly backfired. Put simply, he began to emerge as someone who was dangerously ignorant on some key questions of the day. On one occasion, he seemed to have no clear grasp of the basic organization of the communist enemy.[77] At other times, he confessed to having "very little" intelligence about U.S. or Soviet atomic weapons capabilities. Such issues, he hastened to add, were outside his area of responsibility. But this disclaimer hardly served to satisfy McMahon and Fulbright, who emerged as the Democrats' most effective interrogators. As McMahon pointed out, MacArthur should surely have thought more about such vital matters before advocating "a course of action that may involve us in a global conflict."[78]

In his defense, MacArthur was quick to stress that the Joint Chiefs, with their global perspective, had been willing to endorse his strategy in a memorandum they had written on January 12. This riposte satisfied most senators during the first three days of the hearings. But after MacArthur relinquished the stand on Saturday evening, Marshall, Bradley, and the three service chiefs would be next to appear. And between May 7 and 31, they would have eighteen days on the stand to challenge this crucial claim.

That the Pentagon would be quick to demolish MacArthur's allegations was clear to any informed observer.[79] Since his recall three weeks before, the Joint Chiefs had already given ample notice that they would stand by the president. On April 17, Bradley had even delivered his own keynote speech in Chicago, which had stressed the achievements that had followed from the decision to fight in Korea. Referring to those who despaired of the current stalemate in Korea and were in favor of an immediate showdown, Bradley had ended with a stinging rebuke: "Any such direct, unilateral solution to the military problem would be militarily infeasible."[80]

Three weeks later, when he took the stand at the hearings, Marshall engaged in a more specific counterattack. In his opening statement, he stressed that the now-famous Joint Chiefs memorandum of January 12 contained only tentative courses of action if evacuation from Korea ever became a real prospect, but that the rapidly improving battlefield situation in the days after it was drafted ensured that nothing came of these study proposals. Bradley, testifying next, went even further, declaring that the Joint Chiefs were convinced that MacArthur's proposals would "increase the risk of global war and that such a risk should not be taken unnecessarily." Bradley then employed a soundbite that eclipsed anything MacArthur had been able to muster. Any extension of the current conflict, Bradley famously declared, "would involve us in the wrong war, at the wrong place, at the wrong time, with the wrong enemy."[81]

While these statements were important in driving a public wedge between Truman's top military advisers and MacArthur, the two crucial witnesses in this phase of the hearings were the lesser known members of the Joint Chiefs. As an air power expert, Vandenberg was able to give short shrift to MacArthur's plan for ending the Korean War by bombing Chinese territory. As he explained, the likely result of such a campaign would be disastrous losses, which would thereby reduce, if not end, the air forces' ability to deter a future act of communist aggression, without having a decisive impact in Korea itself.[82]

As the leading proponent of escalatory measures in Korea, Sherman, the navy chief, threatened to be the weak link in the Joint Chiefs chain. Back in January, he had been the driving force behind the January 12 recommendations. Recently, he had privately hinted that the Joint Chiefs had not always been unanimous in their approach to strategy and their opposition to MacArthur.[83] But Sherman's testimony came in the midst of the successful UN defense against the Chinese Easter Offensive. In such circumstances, even he was ready to state that the present limited-war strategy, if it did not win the war, would at least inflict sufficient casualties on the Chinese army that "the war in Korea can be ended under conditions which will, in the long run, be advantageous to us." Crucially, too, Sherman was reluctant to endorse MacArthur's idea to blockade the Chinese coast, explaining that this plan would need allied support to work and such support would be impossible to obtain.[84]

This united front was vital in demolishing MacArthur's key charge, but it was not the administration's only strength. As the hearings unfolded, it became clear that the there was a massive resource imbalance between the two sides. At the start of the hearings, MacArthur tried to turn this to his advantage by drawing attention to the fact that he was now the humble private citizen, traveling light to Congress every day to answer questions, without the aid of copious files or a coterie of advisers.[85] As the hearings developed, however, this man-against-the-world status placed him in a weak position to respond to the administration's arguments.

MacArthur certainly lacked heavyweight support. In his new base on the thirty-seventh floor of the Waldorf-Astoria, General Courtney Whitney, MacArthur's closest friend, did hold a series of press conferences. But these tended to be little better than the uninformative sessions that had so infuriated war correspondents in Tokyo during the winter. And soon New York reporters were talking of their "frustration" at the lack of good copy.[86] Meanwhile, at the actual hearings, MacArthur's supporters did try to locate weak spots in the Pentagon's case. But the solidity of the senior officials was so impressive that by the end of the second week of the hearings, leading Republicans were desperately trying to cut short the testimony of the military men.[87]

In stark contrast to MacArthur's lack of resources, the administration had Carroll's office in the White House, not to mention numerous PR officials in the Pentagon and State Department, who all followed the nuances of the debate and worked hard to devise an effective message. This capability was particularly important when it came to MacArthur's claims about pointless casualties. Privately, officials fretted that MacArthur's repeated claims about the country being "bled white" for no tangible gain would undermine domestic support for the war. Their concern was only heightened when his partisans on the committee claimed that the administration was hiding the true human cost of the Korean debacle. Such accusations had first been raised the previous summer, but they now became entangled with a GOP effort to include nonbattlefield casualties in the overall casualty figures. On the surface, nationalist Republicans repeatedly professed their concern for the thousands who had suffered from frostbite throughout the winter. But they knew full well that juggling the figures this way would inflate the overall casualty total to around 140,000, and thereby fuel the sense that this was an excessively costly war fought for no clear-cut object.[88]

Inside the Pentagon, the number crunchers went to work to refute these Republican claims. Since MacArthur had explicitly contrasted the casualties sustained in the current conflict with all those inflicted on Eisenhower's command during its successful sweep across Europe in 1944–45, an obvious starting point was to provide the committee with hard data that completely demolished this assertion. Since Cain and Hickenlooper were making so much noise about nonbattlefield casualties, the army also produced impressive statistics that showed that such casualties were actually much smaller at the front in Korea than they had been at the rear in Japan. Moreover, as Collins hastened to tell the committee, "of all the non-battle casualties, so-called, in the Far East Command, including both Japan and Korea, 90.4 percent have been returned to duty in the Far East."[89]

The "so-called" in Collins statement was another vitally important dimension of the administration's efforts. Rather than accept the buzzwords that MacArthur and his allies were trying to force on the debate, senior officials sought to reframe the discourse in their own language. Collins was particularly anxious to avoid the term "nonbattle casualties." If only everyone "could get away from our military lingo and talk plain English a bit more," he implored at one stage, "we would name these so-called non-battle casualties what they really are—that is sick and injured." It was "sheer doggerel" to think of them as anything else.[90]

After four weeks of testimony by the military men, events seemed to be moving in the administration's direction. As the White House hastened to point out, its mailbag was now declining sharply in volume but rising steadily in support for the recall. One survey of 350 reporters working in Washington, Tokyo, and Korea found that 85 percent endorsed the president. Another rough tabulation of press reaction estimated that 60–70 percent of journalists were "now favorable to the administration on both foreign policy and the broader issues involved."[91] More tellingly, the reporters actually covering the hearings had no doubt who was winning the battle. Off the record, some were even convinced that the Pentagon had made "MacArthur out to be a liar."[92]

As such encouraging indications multiplied, Truman's optimism that the whole episode would soon blow over seemed well founded.[93] But not all officials were so jaunty. Some pointed out that while the administration had steadily gained some ground among elite opinion, polling data still made for upsetting reading. Indeed, a clear majority of Americans continued to disapprove of the decision to fire the general. Ominously, among those following the hearings, 39 percent were inclined to agree with MacArthur's arguments and only 19 percent with Bradley or Marshall, largely because of MacArthur's "long experience in war and his familiarity with Asia and its problems."[94]

As some White House aides pored over such findings, their sense of alarm started to grow. "I don't like to be a kill-joy," Elsey commented, "but I wonder if we aren't a little too optimistic about the way things are going on the MacArthur row," especially "the extent to which the public understands the president's position and sympathizes with the administration in the firing of MacArthur." Elsey was particularly concerned that the government's message did not appear to be getting beyond the halls of Congress, or at least beyond elite opinion. "It seems to me," he stressed to the president's senior advisers, "that we cannot afford to slack off in our constant emphasis and reiteration that MacArthur stood for war and the president's stands for peace. This and this alone," he believed, "will sink in with the general public, while technical arguments about 'civilian control' won't mean a thing to the people at large."[95] Other leading Democrats were equally pessimistic. As Fulbright pointed out, the administration's policy of restraint was difficult to translate "into language that is appealing to the press and the people." It "don't look good in headlines," he observed, particularly when contrasted to the MacArthur's approach, which "has a great deal more sex appeal in a political sense."[96]

That the military had enjoyed, at best, only limited success was deeply disturbing, because the hearings were about to enter a new phase. No longer would the focus be on MacArthur's dubious claims about the Joint Chiefs' support or his dangerous proposals for ending the war. Instead, from the start of June, the inquiry was about to enter the territory Republicans were convinced would inflict the most damage: Acheson, the State Department, and China. The secretary of state, in particular, seemed to be highly vulnerable. A week before he was scheduled to appear at the hearings, James Reston—whom some considered Acheson's mouthpiece in the media—had spoken openly about his inability to foster congressional and public support for America's foreign policy, before concluding that it was time for him to go.[97] And just the day before Acheson's appearance, even his closest advisers had worried "that the public attitude toward the secretary is now perhaps as unfavorable as it has ever been." Given the depths it had plunged to the previous winter, this was quite a statement.[98]

In this perilous environment, the State Department worked hard to counteract its main vulnerabilities. Although Acheson refused to sanction any public statement that was too optimistic about the internal problems inside the communist bloc, he was more than willing to toughen the administration's language on China. At the UN, Acheson directed U.S. officials to push for economic sanctions against Beijing. At the same time, the Pentagon also announced enhanced military aid to Formosa, suggesting that Chiang's nationalists now ranked with western Europe as a priority in terms of arms and munitions shipments.[99]

Then, on the evening of May 18, Dean Rusk made a few unrehearsed remarks to a China Institute dinner in Manhattan. Before an audience of eight hundred staunch Chiang supporters, including Henry Luce, who was presiding, Rusk affirmed America's commitment to the nationalist regime on Formosa. He then launched into a stinging attack on Red China, describing it as little more than a brutal and alien puppet regime—"a Slavic Manchu-kuo," in his immortal phrase.[100]

Inside the large dining room, Rusk's remarks immediately received loud applause. The next morning, however, the response was more ambiguous. Although a number of newspapers immediately hailed his speech as a significant change of course, Acheson and Truman liked neither Rusk's language nor the stories that he had announced a major review of policy. Seeking to undo the damage, Acheson issued a public clarification. While conceding that Rusk's speech was perfectly in line with long-established government policy, Acheson suggested that some of his language had not been "well-chosen."[101]

To many close observers, it looked like yet another instance of confusion at the top reaches of government. Arthur Krock, who undertook a detailed investigation for the *New York Times*, was especially brutal, concluding that Rusk's speech was the product of "neglected liaisons" with other departments, as well as "a heavy working schedule which prevented Mr Rusk from giving thought" to the potential "dynamite" of his statement.[102] Yet this gloss neglected the administration's deeper publicity calculations. True, Acheson was surprised and angry by some of what Rusk had said. But Rusk was not speaking entirely out of turn. Just the day before, the State Department, White House, and Pentagon had agreed on a new policy statement for Asia, NSC-48/5. This document formalized the stiffer stance toward China that had been emerging in recent months, confirming that U.S. policy would continue to recognize the nationalist government on Formosa while seeking to undermine the communist regime on the mainland.[103] Coming at a time when many officials were convinced that the government's case needed more "sex appeal," publicizing this new policy had obvious merit. Coming at a moment when many in the White House felt the State Department had dragged its feet in ratcheting up the rhetoric, Rusk's speech hardly seemed like the careless words of an overworked and isolated official. It looked more like an effort to toughen and clarify government thinking in the lead-up to Acheson's vital appearance before the joint committee.[104]

Acheson began his testimony on Friday, June 1. In the past few weeks, he had prepared intensively. On four separate occasions, his senior advisers had gathered in his huge office, surrounded by maps, clocks, and imposing paintings borrowed from the Smithsonian, in order to hone his response.[105] As well as going through all possible questions, his aides hammered home the fact that Acheson had to avoid any appearance of arrogance or ill temper. "The secretary should be urged to take it easily and calmly," they had advised. In the past, he had sometimes "allowed himself to appear irked by one or two questions." This time, it was vital that he "show sincerity, good humor and good will, and a complete absence of condescension, irritation, or resentment."[106]

Primed with all this preparation, Acheson proved experienced and skillful enough to fend off everything that the Republicans threw at him. During eight days on the stand, he faced constant efforts to focus the hearings on the catalogue of events that so obsessed the China lobby, such as Yalta; Marshall's efforts to negotiate an end to the Chinese civil war in 1946; and the lack of U.S. aid to the nationalists. But, with support from sympathetic Democrats, he consistently deflected such questions and focused on his own agenda.

It helped that Acheson was given the chance to present his own uninterrupted version of the nation's China policy, which took up a good deal of one morning session. In this presentation, he also took care to toughen his language, endorsing Rusk's claim that the Beijing regime was little more than a "Slavic Manchukuo."[107] Halfway through, even a critic like Alexander Smith was forced to admit (in the privacy of his diary) that Acheson "is very suave and makes a good witness—but doesn't say very much."[108]

As a comment on Acheson's success in neutralizing GOP efforts to draw blood on China, Smith's last point was well taken. But Acheson also saw the hearings as much more than a damage-limitation exercise. Although still wary about using language that explicitly referred to the prospect of freedom triumphing soon in the communist world, he nevertheless sought to inject a greater sense of ideological purpose into his testimony. His opening statement contained warm references to the Four Freedoms and the Atlantic Charter, which, he hastened to add, had not just been "cynical slogans" in World War II but had stood for an idea that "our people felt in their hearts was worth fighting for." Now, too, Americans had a cause: their nation's whole effort in Korea was intended to give concrete expression to the collective security principles embodied in the UN Charter.[109]

At the heart of much of Acheson's testimony was his faith in America's ultimate ability to win the Cold War. Time was clearly on the U.S. side, Acheson insisted in his opening statement. "We and our allies have the capacity to outproduce the Soviet bloc by a staggering margin." This was not merely a matter of a superior infrastructure or even the capitalist system of production. It was also, crucially, due to the "will" of free peoples. "The future belongs to freedom if free men have the will to make time work on their side," Acheson insisted. "I believe the American people and their allies do have the will, the will to work together when their freedom is threatened. This is the ultimate source of our faith and our confidence. A free society can call upon profound resources among its people in behalf of a righteous cause."[110]

After more than a week of this kind of talk, Acheson was in the clear. While his testimony had been eloquent and upbeat, its most decisive impact was to help kill the lynch-mob mood that had prevailed in some quarters in the wake of MacArthur's recall. In fact, by the end of Acheson's testimony, interest in the controversy was clearly starting to wane. The hearings themselves were moved from the impressive Senate Caucus Room to a smaller room on the second floor of the Senate Office Building. Many editors also began to relegate stories about the controversy to their inside pages, a decision made easier by polls that recorded the public's indifference to the whole affair. "The Senate hearings on what we should do about Korea may have created a big stir in Washington and other capitals of the world," Gallup noted on June 9, "but, in the language of Broadway, the performance has 'laid an egg' as far as many Americans are concerned." After the drama of MacArthur's return home, the Senate sessions were a distinct "anti-climax." Amazingly, Gallup found, "a total of 30 percent of those interviewed quite frankly admit they have not read anything about the hearings."[111]

The final few witnesses were hardly likely to breathe new life into the proceedings. Given the public's patent lack of interest, the committee agreed to cut the list of potential remaining witnesses from more than thirty to just six.[112] Of these, Republicans had the highest hopes for Louis Johnson, for he had an obvious axe to grind against the president and had never been shy, even in office, about voicing his jaundiced opinion of Acheson and the State Department. Yet Johnson was also remarkably loyal. In 1940, he had refused to speak ill about Roosevelt, even after he eased Johnson out of the War Department to make way for a Republican—a move Johnson believed had broken a solemn promise. Since September 1950, he had been similarly taciturn about Truman, despite the ugly nature of his "resignation."[113] It was perhaps not surprising, then, that Johnson refused to seize the moment for revenge. Although Republicans constantly goaded him, he was unwilling to criticize the president's decision to recall MacArthur. All in all, Johnson's testimony proved to be an important, if surprising, boon to the administration.[114]

The Balance Sheet

In the large literature on the MacArthur hearings, historians have reached a variety of different conclusions about its consequences. A few contend that the whole controversy faded quickly.[115] Far more common, however, is the claim that it greatly undermined the administration's ability to govern. As Truman's biographers have stressed, after the summer of 1951 his approval ratings never recovered; he no longer had much clout with Congress; and he was unable to do much more than preside as a caretaker president.[116]

Analysts of the Korean War tend to agree, insisting that the MacArthur controversy greatly reduced the administration's room to maneuver on the home front. The argument here is that nationalist Republicans were now quick to step up their attacks on the administration, in the firm belief that they could exploit MacArthur's arguments for political gain during the 1952 election cycle. In this conception, the GOP diehards now clearly held the initiative. In general terms, they sought to encourage the public's traditional dislike of wars that end in anything less than "outright victory and the surrender of enemy forces." More specifically, they constantly reiterated MacArthur's warnings against an "appeasement peace," which would be a total waste of the "140,000 casualties and billions of dollars" it had thus far cost America.[117]

On close inspection, however, the balance sheet was far less gloomy than these arguments suggest. In fact, in a number of important respects the controversy actually gave the administration an important boost.

For a start, things could have been a lot worse. Although most Americans continued broadly to support MacArthur's basic policy prescriptions, the popular mood lacked the frenzied intensity of mid-April. Only 36 percent of the public, for instance, now believed the general would make a good president, while 55 percent thought he would not.[118] Across the country, such findings were also borne out by the ever smaller crowds that now greeted him as he continued his tour to woo the masses.[119]

The administration could be thankful that inside Washington, too, the controversy had not spiraled out of control. By the summer, impeachment was no longer seriously entertained even on the Republican right. Mobilization also remained on track. Although the Senate-House conference on UMST had been pushed back a couple of weeks because the members of the Senate Armed Services Committee could not give it their full attention while also preparing for the MacArthur hearings, the overall mobilization program faced few other setbacks. Quite the contrary—the hearings had actually given the Pentagon the chance to drive home its case for more money, since the whole thrust of the Joint Chiefs' testimony was that the United States currently lacked the capabilities to confront the Soviet Union directly.[120] And opinion polls suggested that the public had taken this message on board. At the start of June, PA conducted an opinion survey of popular attitudes toward "the national objectives set forth in NSC-68" and found that the public "appears by all reliable objective criteria to be favorably disposed." Indeed, 83 percent wanted to continue the current levels of high spending on rearmament, 52 percent supported economic assistance to allies, and 57 percent favored sending U.S. troops to Europe.[121]

At a more practical level, one of the most disturbing episodes of February and March—labor's walkout from the mobilization process—was also brought to an end at the very height of the MacArthur controversy. At first glance, the two events seemed to have very little linkage, since the administration simply ended the union boycott by granting labor leaders the official positions they craved. But on closer inspection, the MacArthur controversy did help to bring the White House and organized labor to a renewed meeting of minds. For one thing, many union bosses stood squarely behind Truman's decision to fire MacArthur. And in May, with the administration desperately requiring logistical support to take its case to the masses, the White House worked with the Congress of Industrial Organizations to disseminate pamphlets supporting the case for a limited war in Korea.[122]

At the same time, Truman was now in a far stronger position to resolve the dispute that had precipitated labor's walkout in the first place. Back in February and March, the White House had blamed much of the conflict on Charles Wilson's intransigence. But at this stage, the president had been poorly placed to enforce an agreement based on these instincts. He had, after all, only just appointed Wilson, granting him wide-ranging powers to expedite the mobilization process. Had he now tried to broker an agreement that satisfied labor while effectively censuring Wilson, he would have risked, at best, alienating a vital official already known for his independence and, at worst, provoking a damaging resignation that would have thrown the whole mobilization effort into chaos. As it was, Wilson continued to speak his mind in public, even when he enjoyed the president's clear backing. Most damaging, at the end of March, at the very time that MacArthur issued his insubordinate outbursts from Tokyo, Wilson delivered a series of upbeat statements that seemed to belie the Pentagon's warnings of another "letdown."[123]

Officials and reporters alike were quick to link the actions and fates of Wilson and MacArthur. Both, it was widely observed, had closer ties to the Republican opposition than to the president. Both also seemed to have carte blanche to say whatever they wanted in public. Seen in this light, Truman's firm and decisive action against MacArthur sent an obvious signal to Wilson. Certainly, it did nothing to strengthen his position inside the administration. Far from it: rumors soon swirled around Washington that "Wilson is being undercut." "He still holds all the powers delegated to him," Business Week observed at the end of April; "but he no longer has complete freedom to use them."[124] With Wilson thus chastened, Truman felt in a stronger position to insist on a series of concessions to labor, safe in the knowledge that his ODM director was no longer well placed to offer damaging opposition.

And it was not just Wilson on the defensive. Republican nationalists also found themselves in a weaker position. This point is rarely made in the literature, and it is worth exploring in some detail. Most historians insist that the MacArthur hearings emboldened the Republican right and further weakened the embattled administration. They reach this conclusion by focusing on the high-profile statements made by Taft, McCarthy, and a few others. This gives a sense of a political environment that was more overheated than ever, especially at a time when McCarthy launched a two-hour tirade on the Senate floor against George Marshall, accusing the venerable general of being part of a "conspiracy of infamy," or when Taft told an NBC television audience that the Korean War was a "useless and expensive waste."[125] Yet beneath such strident language, many nationalist Republicans were deeply anxious about the drift of events during the spring and summer.

Republicans certainly recognized that the MacArthur hearings had, at long last, given the government the chance to make its case in a concerted and vigorous manner. Admittedly, officials had been forced to operate under the least auspicious of circumstances—they had been thrown on the defensive, forced into battle with a returning war hero who had intimate inside knowledge of the issues. But even under such trying conditions, the administration had still retained vital strengths. Throughout the hearings, officials utilized bureaucratic support mechanisms to the fullest to demolish false claims, release key documents, and develop their own narrative about key issues, from casualties to appeasement. In contrast, MacArthur was effectively a lone voice, dependent on just a few aides for advice, lacking access to materials that would support his claim, and reliant on Republicans on the committee who were not generally of the first rank. Crucially, too, the administration coupled its efforts inside the committee room with a vigorous campaign in the country at large. An important dimension of this attempt to reach the American people had depicted MacArthur and his allies on the Republican right as dangerous figures whose views, if ever implemented, would plunge the United States into a global conflagration with the Soviets and Chinese.

These dynamic efforts were very different from earlier periods of the war when the administration had often abdicated the task of leadership. Back then, the paucity of official information had provided Republicans with a chance to shape the debate. Now, the weeks of forceful and united utterances by senior officials had placed GOP diehards firmly on the back foot. Taft was particularly annoyed that the administration had mischaracterized his position—and even more irate when the media seemed to follow the government's lead. Indeed, when the AP claimed that he was a firm supporter of escalation, an angry Taft accused the press bureau of "deliberately attempting to overstate the Republican position in order to support Mr. Truman's arguments."[126] It was a telling moment. Although Taft felt he had little choice but to issue such a vigorous denial, by so doing he was giving wider currency to the initial accusation, however false. He was, in effect, being forced to fight on ground of the administration's choosing.

That the Taft wing was now on the defensive was illustrated by another important development. On April 17, at the height of the public excitement over MacArthur, Senator Harry Cain of Washington introduced a resolution calling on Congress to recognize that a state of war existed between the United States and China. Cain saw this initiative as little more than a move to formalize the state of relations between the two nations. But as all close observers soon recognized, he had clearly gone too far. Privately, the administration saw Cain's resolution as a golden opportunity to confirm their contention that those on the Republican right were basically a bunch of reckless warmongers. And with polls demonstrating that 61 percent of the public opposed starting a war with China, even Cain's Republican allies realized he had made a massive tactical mistake. According to one account, when Cain's resolution came before the GOP Policy Committee, "his colleagues agreed it was politically ill-advised, and ripped into him unmercifully."[127]

This mounting perception that the Republican right had overreached was to prove important inside the corridors and cloakrooms on Capitol Hill, for it helped to prod prominent GOP internationalists back toward the bipartisan center. Again, this was an important contrast with what had happened at earlier stages of the war. Back in December, in the immediate aftermath of the Chinese intervention, it had seemed briefly possible that all forms of bipartisan cooperation might soon collapse. The Republican resolution calling for Acheson's resignation had marked the low point, for it had not simply been the work of the GOP diehards but had also garnered strong support from Republican internationalists like Irving Ives of New York, Robert C. Hendrickson of New Jersey, and Leverett Saltonstall of Massachusetts. Since then, however, these moderates had started to gravitate away from their diehard colleagues.

Many were nudged in this direction by the excessive assaults coming from the right. During the "great debate," most internationalists considered the language of Hoover, Taft, and Wherry too loose and too close to unreconstructed isolationism. During the recent MacArthur controversy, they had also recoiled from the Taftites' extravagant talk about impeachment and the need to escalate the war in Asia, not to mention the overblown rhetoric of McCarthy and his ilk.[128]

Democrats, on the other hand, had gone out of their way to make it easy for the internationalists to adopt a more cooperative attitude. Particularly important here was the role of southern Democrats who, by remaining steadfast in their support of the administration, had helped to take much of the sting out of foreign policy debates during the first six months of 1951. In fact, on Capitol Hill the crucial dynamic at work was not so much the eye-catching antics of the Republican right on which historians have lavished so much attention. Rather, it was moderates' quieter efforts to reconstruct a bipartisan internationalist coalition. Put another way, the key figures were not so much Taft and McCarthy as Richard Russell and Leverett Saltonstall.

Russell, in particular, was crucial both in the "great debate" and the MacArthur hearings. In key committee hearings, his leadership style had a dulling, deadening effect, which was vital at a time when passions were running so high, for it successfully reduced the political temperature on the Hill.[129] Moreover, his reputation as a highly knowledgeable legislator who had no particular love of Truman also provided a degree of political cover for those Republicans who now drifted away from the Taft wing of the party.

One of the most important of these was Saltonstall, the GOP whip in the Senate. In December, this "genteel patrician" Yankee from Massachusetts had been willing to risk the ire of his internationalist constituents by voting for the party resolution that called for Acheson's head.[130] But since then, he had gradually returned to the bipartisan fold, first by agreeing with Eisenhower's position on troops for Europe and now by refusing to sign the majority GOP report on the MacArthur hearings.

This majority Republican report on the hearings rehearsed all the old criticisms—the need for victory in Korea, the weak-willed appeasement policy of Truman and Acheson, and even the basic areas of agreement between MacArthur and the Joint Chiefs. Wayne Morse was the first internationalist Republican to dissent from this critique, when he publicly declared that Truman would have been "derelict in his duty" had he not fired MacArthur. On August 20, Saltonstall made even bigger headlines. Although he disparaged the clumsy way the president had gone about sacking the general, he stressed that he had had every right to do so. Saltonstall also applauded the administration for using the hearings to clarify its Far East policy, singling out the State Department's stiffer language toward communist China for particular praise.[131]

Coming from the lone internationalist among the GOP leadership in the Senate, Saltonstall's dissent was another telling moment. Indeed, it symbolized a drift in the thinking of a significant group of Republican internationalists who would play a major role in the upcoming presidential campaign. In the opinion of these moderates, although Truman and his advisers had made their share of tactical mistakes, the administration's fundamental strategy, both in Korea and in Europe, remained sound.

By August, the administration had thus emerged from the hearings not in a mortally wounded condition but with an important degree of flexibility on the home front. Its chief opponents had been placed on the defensive. Its natural allies among southern Democrats and Republican internationalists had ultimately proved to be more supportive than at other moments in the recent past. And underpinning everything, administration officials had at last made a forceful case for their own policy.

Nowhere was this process more crucial than in paving the way for a negotiated end to the fighting in Korea. Back in March, when officials had first mooted the possibility of an armistice, three obstacles had stood in their way: MacArthur, whose insubordination had torpedoed the first initiative; the

Chinese, who had been furiously preparing for a major new offensive; and the American public, whose attitude toward negotiations had remained unclear. Now, however, all these obstacles had been removed. With Ridgway in charge in Tokyo, the administration had a commander it could rely on to carry out any talks in a sensible and compliant fashion. With both phases of the Chinese spring offensive ending with important defensive victories for the UN and the battlefield having stabilized just north of the thirty-eighth parallel, the enemy was more likely to be ready to come to terms. And with the MacArthur hearings now over, administration officials were also confident that they had substantial public support for a negotiated settlement.

Throughout the grinding weeks of testifying on the Hill, the government had finally made it clear that it would accept a cease-fire that would keep Korea divided.[132] Crucially, opinion surveys suggested that the public would endorse such a settlement. According to one poll, support for a truce that would leave Korea divided at the thirty-eighth parallel had increased from 43 to 51 percent between March and July. According to the State Department's Working Group on Public Relations, "the overwhelming majority" of press and radio commentators would also approve a cease-fire that would end in partition.[133] Even a figure like David Lawrence, the conservative columnist who had talked enthusiastically about the possibility of a presidential impeachment in April, now recognized that such an end to the war would further consolidate Truman's position. "Politically speaking," he wrote on June 25, "the administration will have gained a victory."[134]

All that was needed now was an indication that the communists were willing to start negotiations.

Part Three

The Stalemate War,
July 1951–July 1953

10

INTERMINABLE TRUCE TALKS

The first firm suggestion that the enemy might be willing to negotiate an armistice came on June 23. In a radio address delivered
from the Soviet delegation offices at the UN, Jacob Malik announced that the
Soviet Union believed a peace settlement possible in Korea, perhaps based on
the thirty-eighth parallel.[1]

In Washington, the official response was muted. The State Department
wanted more details before it would commit. The president, due to travel to
Tullahoma, Tennessee, to give a speech on the first anniversary of the start
of the war, kept to his prearranged script, which once again emphasized the
reasons for fighting in Korea and only at the end briefly alluded to Malik's
new peace proposal.

For senior officials, this caution was an obvious byproduct of their deep-
seated skepticism about the communists' ability to negotiate in good faith.
Only when the enemy offered the necessary reassurances that the negotiation process would be strictly limited to military matters, and would not
involve thorny political subjects like the status of Formosa or China's seat
at the UN, did Washington signify its willingness to begin talks. After some
haggling over the location and date, the UNC agreed with the Chinese and
North Korean commanders that their liaison officers would meet on July 8
at Kaesong, the old capital of Korea, which was located 35 miles northwest
of Seoul.[2]

With the start of the negotiations, the Korean War entered a new phase.
On the battlefield, the fighting settled down into a bloody stalemate, as both
sides dug in along defensible lines mainly north of the thirty-eighth parallel. Each day, border patrols were sent out as part of a constant jabbing to
wear out the opponent. In the late summer of 1951, the UNC also ordered a
series of limited ground offensives against targets that soon became known

by names like "Bloody Ridge" or "Heartbreak Ridge." And throughout this period, the U.S. air force launched savage raids, first against the North Korean road and railway systems, and later against hydroelectric plants, mines, and irrigation networks. From now on, though, there would be no more major offensives by either side—no renewed efforts to throw the enemy off the Korean peninsula altogether. At the truce talks, held first in Kaesong and then at Panmunjom, a similar stalemate soon emerged. Here, the negotiating teams haggled for more than two years over the demarcation line, over ways of enforcing an armistice, and ultimately over the fate of the prisoners of war.

As both the war and the truce talks dragged on, officials naturally worried about the fragility of public support, especially with an election year looming. In Korea, the military also had to recalibrate its PR facilities. As well as setting up new billets and channels of communications to deal with the massive influx of war correspondents, this entailed making calculations about exactly what to divulge to reporters each day. More fundamentally, as the negotiations continued, Washington had to connect the progress of the talks to the basic objectives of the war, and this task was to prove far from easy.

In most wars, American aims have evolved over time. But the normal trajectory has been from minimum to maximum goals, from initial presidential war addresses that "are typically thoughtful rather than angry narratives that explain the origins of the immediate crisis" to far-reaching statements that are efforts to articulate America's aims in visionary ideological language.[3] In this war, however, the evolution threatened to be very different. What had been, for a brief time during the fall of 1950, a conflict to unite Korea and turn the whole peninsula into a shining beacon of freedom and democracy had increasingly become a war to defend just South Korea. Moreover, as the negotiators haggled endlessly over the details, the differences between the two sides gradually narrowed. In terms of PR, this was far from desirable, especially since the remaining differences proved impossible to reconcile. As well as sparking a measure of popular impatience, this raised the prospect that the reason for the continued fighting—and the burgeoning casualties—would be just one of the small sticking points on the negotiating agenda. In short, what had once been a war to unite Korea might effectively become a fight over whether or not to allow the communists to construct and rehabilitate airfields or, more ominously, a fight over prisoners of war—and not even American prisoners but, as Edward Barrett, the assistant secretary of state for public affairs, pointed out, "some Chinese and North Koreans who are not political defectors but POWs who were once shooting at us and who surrendered to save their own skins."[4] Clearly this would be a hard sell.

First Phase of the Talks

At the beginning of July, with the truce talks scheduled to begin at Kaesong, the UN established its base in Munsan-ni, a small town just to the south of the negotiating site. Because of lack of accommodations and "severely limited road approaches," the military decided that the media would have to operate from Seoul. Working fast, the PIO expanded the Eighth Army press camp so that it could house up to two hundred correspondents, but it was scarcely able to keep pace with the enormous demand. In Seoul, accommodations for reporters were invariably cramped and overcrowded, while teletype facilities were so overworked that transmission times to the outside world were again measured in hours and not minutes.[5]

Still, even these inconveniences paled next to the reception that greeted reporters when they traveled the 25 miles from Seoul to Munsan-ni. On July 6, the UNC announced: "press coverage will be by official communiqué and daily briefing."[6] When the talks began, reporters would be denied access to the negotiating site at Kaesong. Worse, when the five officers of the UN negotiating team returned to Munsan-ni, they would be placed in a form of quarantine, walled off from prying press eyes in a specially erected tent compound that was heavily guarded by two rings of barbed wire and military police. The only chance correspondents would have to question these delegates was when they briefly emerged from their compound to make the short trip to the helicopter pad for the flight to Kaesong. But even this was far from satisfactory. While print correspondents had to try their best to shout questions before the negotiators got away, photographers immediately complained that another barbed-wire fence, this one around the helicopter landing area, made it impossible for them to take pictures.[7]

Nor were reporters enamored with the obvious difference between their own limited billeting facilities and those lavished on the UN negotiators. As correspondents were quick to write, with ill-concealed envy, the negotiators' compound at Munsan-ni was located in an apple orchard, which provided a degree of welcome shade from the heat and humidity of the Korean summer. Inside, one reporter wrote, this compound "is as well appointed as field accommodations and circumstances permit, and at first sight looks something like a millionaire's safari camp. The food is reported first-class with thick steaks, fresh vegetables, and desserts."[8]

Within days, these resentments bubbled to the surface. On July 8, UN liaison officers flew to Kaesong for a preliminary meeting with their communist counterparts. Back at Munsan-ni, as one AP correspondent noted, "it was a long, hot, nerve-tingling afternoon."[9] Reporters waited anxiously for more than seven hours for the UN delegation, headed by Colonel Andrew J. Kinney, to return. When his helicopter finally landed, Kinney looked "tired and grim." Determined to avoid questions, he ordered the waiting jeeps to speed his delegation away to the restricted area, "shaking off correspondents and all but running down photographers who tried to get 'one more shot.'"[10]

That first evening, Kinney staged a formal press conference, flanked by Lieutenant Colonel Walter J. Preston, the official censor. Kinney's aim was to provide a "straight chronological account," avoiding specific details on substantive discussions, but the restive reporters soon peppered him with angry questions. One problem came when Kinney revealed that armed guards had accompanied the communist delegation. Fred Sparks of the *Chicago Daily News* immediately pointed out that Kaesong was meant to be an "open" city. If it was in communist hands, Sparks shouted, he was going to say so in his dispatch. "If you do," Preston replied, "military censorship will not pass it." "I will not accept your decision," Sparks angrily retaliated—and was instantly supported by his colleagues. Already riled, the rest of the press corps "went on the warpath" when they discovered that while they had been denied access, communist photographers and newsreel cameramen had been at Kaesong. "We rather strongly protested," Sparks wrote the next day, "further heating the humid, blacked-out room."[11]

Yet if this shouting match was ominously reminiscent of the military–media friction of a year earlier, the follow-up was very different. On July 9,

Colonel Andrew Kinney returning from Kaesong, July 1951. Courtesy of National Archives.

Ridgway, who was in the area to monitor the start of the talks firsthand, began the task of trying to smooth things over. Meeting with reporters, he pledged to do everything possible to grant them access to Kaesong. Within hours, his PIO then announced that a limited number of journalists—perhaps sixteen—would accompany the senior delegation to the substantive talks soon after they began on July 10.[12] The next morning, when the enemy objected to the presence of allied reporters, Ridgway refused to let his negotiators return until this matter was resolved; and it was, four days later, when the communists conceded the matter. From then onward, the press pool that traveled to Kaesong would consist of twenty members, all chosen by their colleagues.[13]

When it came to logistics and communications, the military also made significant improvements. As soon as the talks got under way, dispatches from the press pool were relayed straight to the censors, who in turn mimeographed them for the other correspondents using a new portable machine brought in especially by PI officers. At the press billet in Seoul, the Signal Corps installed telephone and teletype facilities that would allow about one hundred thousand words a day to be sent out, while the air force laid on a courier service to take additional material back to Tokyo. And then, in the most eye-catching stunt of all, the PIO unveiled its press train. Located in a siding a mile to the west of Munsan-ni, the eleven carriages turned out to be "slightly seedy." But 80 of the 106 correspondents covering the talks immediately clambered on board, scrambling to claim lower or upper berths. Inside, they found greatly improved working and communications facilities. The press train, the Eighth Army PIO believed, "has proved ideal." "Releases were usually in the hands of the press and the news radioed or cabled to all parts of the free world within a mater of minutes from the time the information was telephoned from advance headquarters."[14]

That the PIO was able to rectify many of the media's complaints so quickly was due in large part to personnel changes. On taking over the UNC from MacArthur, Ridgway immediately recruited his own PR personnel. Not all liked or trusted reporters. Brigadier-General Frank A. Allen, who became Ridgway's special adviser on PR matters, firmly believed that "no one will ever be able to convince the press that their problems are understood."[15] Colonel George P. Welch, who replaced Echols as the head of the UNC PIO, sometimes complained about certain correspondents' slack standards.[16] But unlike MacArthur and his close court of advisers, Ridgway and his new team were generally sensitive to reporters' needs. Welch, for instance, was a steady old pro who had been responsible for PR in various commands during World War II. In early July, he made a point of flying to Munsan-ni, with six officers and one enlisted man, in order to supervise all PIO activities associated with the talks. He was thus on hand to deal with problems as they arose, giving a speed and suppleness to the military's response that had been altogether lacking a year before.[17]

Correspondents crowded into the press train at Munsan-ni. Courtesy of National Archives.

Still, the changes Welch and his team made were largely limited to access and logistics. The problem of exactly what to divulge to reporters remained acute. The talks themselves got off to an excruciatingly slow start. After they reconvened on July 15, it took more than ten days for both sides to reach agreement on the agenda; the main sticking point revolved around the UN's determination to avoid discussing the withdrawal of all foreign troops. By the last weekend in July, with the agenda finally fixed, substantive negotiations got under way. But they immediately bogged down on the complex matter of exactly where to fix the truce line. The communists favored the thirty-eighth parallel, while the allies held out for a zone based roughly on the present battle line, which in most places was to the north of the thirty-eighth parallel. When the communists recessed the talks on August, ostensibly in retaliation for a number of alleged UN violations of the neutral truce site, this item was still a long way from resolution. When the negotiations resumed at Panmunjom on October 25, this disagreement soon narrowed, but specific terms were not hammered out until the end of November.[18]

As the negotiations followed this tortuous path, the PIO faced a real test. It could not divulge too much information on the details of the talks without inflating public expectations and undermining its bargaining position. With the press pool chafing at the lack of information, some correspondents became critical of the military's PR, while others looked to the communists for updates. On at least one occasion, the PIO retaliated by accusing certain journalists of fraternizing with the enemy under the influence of alcohol—charges that deeply angered the press pool.[19] But just how bad was the overall situation at Munsan-ni? The scanty but impassioned literature on this subject has focused exclusively on the negatives. Was it really the case, as one influential account has it, that the U.S. military pedaled "a mixture of lies, half-truths, and serious distortions"? And when reporters rebelled at this treatment and refused to toe the line, was it true that "censorship at the peace talks became total"?[20]

There is little doubt that correspondents were frequently frustrated by a lack of information from official sources. During the last two weeks of July, in particular, as the two delegations battled over the precise details of the agenda, the military's information policy remained highly restrictive. At Kaesong, the members of the press pool who had finally gained admission to the talks complained of long, "dreary hours" sitting on the porch of an outhouse "waiting either for the rain to cease or the session to adjourn." With little to occupy their time, some adjourned to a small summerhouse, where the communists laid on "flattish but strong" beer and cigarettes that were "large, fat, fully packed, a trifle tight on the draw but good enough." Thus fortified, reporters waited expectantly for the delegates to emerge from their daily sessions, only to be disappointed when they generally refused to say much of note.[21]

Certainly Admiral C. Turner Joy, the leader of the UN delegation, was far from charismatic—to many reporters he appeared to be little more than a "soft-spoken, publicity-shy sailor."[22] But there was more to Joy's reticence than personal demeanor; he was under firm instructions not to talk to reporters. During July, everything that could be divulged was to be handled either by formal press conferences at Munsan-ni or by official communiqués disseminated by Ridgway's headquarters in Tokyo. Yet this output was rarely informative. In one session on July 17, for example, PI officers were unable to answer even the most basic questions, such as how many items were likely to be on the agenda, let alone what these were or what had proved to be the main sticking points. Reporters, an exasperated *New York Times* representative wrote that day, "have little in the way to judge progress of the talks except by examining the facial expressions of the conferees and guessing what information they can therefrom."[23]

After the talks moved on to the substantive agenda, some correspondents still complained about "vague" briefings and the absence of hard data on the UN position. But for the most part the military now made important efforts to improve the flow of information. Indeed, in this phase of the negotiations, it was simply not true, as some accounts claim, that correspondents were forbidden to speak with officers who had attended the negotiating sessions.[24]

On the contrary, from July 27 General William P. Nuckols, who traveled to Kaesong each day, was given the task of filling the information void, thereby rectifying the central problem that had so antagonized reporters during the first three weeks of the talks.

Described by reporters as "the man in the middle," Nuckols was yet another of the highly knowledgeable officers Ridgway had placed in an important position.[25] Before Korea, he had accumulated enormous experience working for a PR company in New York City during the 1930s, before rising to become the chief information officer for the Allied Expeditionary Force during World War II. Since 1950, he had been based in Korea as the chief PIO for the Far East Air Forces, so he knew all about the potential pitfalls that awaited him at Kaesong. His new job was a task "no one wanted." Not only did it entail sixteen-hour days in the heat of a Korean summer but also it meant arbitrating endlessly between negotiators who wanted absolute silence and reporters who were hungry for more information. In some subsequent accounts, Nuckols emerges as a rather sinister figure who consistently sided with the military's desire to dissemble and suppress information. At the time, however, American correspondents saw him in a very different light. As the *New York Times* put it in a friendly profile, "virtually the only reliable source of information about the cease-fire conference these days is a tall air force officer with a casual manner and a slight stammer...[who] has managed quite skillfully as a mediator between the press and the delegates."[26]

For sure, as soon as he settled in to his job, Nuckols could be maddeningly elusive in his daily briefings, especially on the central issue of the demarcation line. Yet he was never as mendacious as some accounts make out. For one thing, he did not, as some suggest, distort the communist position by insisting that it was the enemy, and not the Americans, who refused to accept the thirty-eighth parallel.[27] On the contrary, officials at all levels of the administration were keen to explain that the United States no longer considered the parallel a viable border, even for a temporary truce. What they would accept, Nuckols implied, was a demilitarized zone based on the current battle line.[28]

But what exactly did Nuckols mean by a truce based on the battle line? In the talks, Joy and his team had opened with a bold position, claiming a demarcation line well to the north of the current fighting, which would mean a substantial territorial retreat by the communists. To support this position, Joy had introduced the "basic concept" of three battle zones: ground, air, and naval. Because the UN enjoyed superiority in the air and naval spheres, he explained to the communists, it should be rewarded by additional territory on the ground.[29]

When it came to elaborating on this position for reporters, Nuckols was initially far from forthcoming.[30] But his reticence was not driven by an instinctive mendacity or a mounting distrust of reporters. Rather, it stemmed from a genuine fear of what might happen if the UN negotiators conducted their bargaining strategy in the open.

In private, the initial UN position was a classic textbook ploy. By opening high, Joy hoped to initiate a process whereby both sides would gradually whittle down their demands so that the final compromise outcome would be something close to what Washington really wanted, which was a truce line based on the battlefront and not the thirty-eighth parallel.[31] But in terms of PR, this strategy presented problems. A candid revelation of Joy's "basic concept" might easily backfire, especially if American popular opinion became so attached to this opening position that it would view any retreat as craven appeasement. Largely for this reason, the Pentagon instructed Ridgway and his negotiators to refrain from giving too much information to reporters on a daily basis. "Arranging for an armistice during the progress of actual fighting is one of the most delicate negotiations in human affairs," Parks cabled on July 8, "and must necessarily be conducted in strictest secrecy." "Ultimate success," he emphasized, "must depend in some measure upon the willingness of the public to await concrete results and especially to refrain from violent reaction to incomplete or unfounded reports and rumors."[32]

Still, any attempt to obscure the UN's private stance carried obvious risks. As experience had amply demonstrated, whenever the administration cut reporters out of the equation, they were apt to speculate. On the opening day of the conference alone, correspondents filed 300,000 words of copy, while the daily average thereafter was around 180,000—which, according to some estimates, tied up around 60 percent of the army's telephone and teletype facilities between Korea and Tokyo.[33] In the absence of much hard information, the reporters responsible for this vast flow of wordage groped for ways to frame the issues. As Ridgway's chief PI officer saw it, most tended to "sit around feeling sorry for themselves and write stories that in many instances are pure 'think pieces' and have no bearing on the conference."[34] More ominously, some mainstream correspondents even started to turn to broadcasts from the communist radio station in Pyongyang or comments by communist journalists at Kaesong, on the revealing grounds that they had frequently "given many more details on the conferences than pass through allied censorship."[35]

This is certainly what happened on the crucial subject of the truce line. On August 1, Radio Pyongyang broadcast the communist claim that Joy was insisting on an armistice line well above the current battlefield, somewhere in the vicinity of Kosong in the east and the Ongjin peninsula in the west. In both Munsan-ni and Tokyo, the military's first instinct was to dismiss this as pure communist propaganda—or, in the colorful words of one high UN source, "a lot of malarkey." In normal circumstances, this spirited rebuttal might well have satisfied journalists, but within days it was undermined by another problem that periodically afflicted official public information efforts:

lack of coordination. While briefing officers at Munsan-ni vigorously denied reports that the UN "had demanded a demarcation line well north of the present combat area, as the communist radio has been reporting," Ridgway's Civil Information and Education Section in Tokyo revealed a very different reality. "The military demarcation line upon which we must reach agreement," it declared in a background briefing for Japanese reporters, "lies somewhere between the air and sea front on the Yalu and the ground front in the area of Kaesong, Pyonggang, and the Yangjin River."[36]

The obvious contradiction between these two positions could have been a real embarrassment for negotiators and PI officers alike, fatally undermining their credibility. But in fact the whole episode soon blew over. This was partly because Nuckols's briefings had been opaque rather than false, always containing the caveat that the UN claim was for a truce line that "should maintain the approximate military balance of power existing at the time it was signed." This carefully worded statement had just enough elements of Joy's "basic concept" to be defensible when the communists tried to expose the UN position on the radio. And the military was quick to offer a vigorous justification of its actions. What the negotiating team really wanted, a series of communiqués declared, was not Korean real estate but "a defensible line." As Joy explained to reporters, as soon as an armistice was concluded, the UN would lack the massive aerial and naval superiority that currently allowed it to contain the massive communist land forces. He was therefore pushing for a truce line further to the north, but the UN stance was not rigid. "We have repeatedly stated that we were willing to discuss the proposal jointly on a map," Joy told reporters in the middle of August, "with a view to making such adjustments as would be acceptable to both sides."[37]

In the face of this barrage of statements, most in the media were willing to give Ridgway and his negotiators the benefit of the doubt. Although some like Henry S. Hayward, the chief Far East correspondent of the *Christian Science Monitor*, considered the demand revealed by the Civil Information and Education Section "surprisingly stiff," back in the United States, the military's hardball position was hardly viewed as a bad thing.[38] Mainstream newspapers like the *Baltimore Sun, New York Herald Tribune*, and *San Francisco Chronicle* staunchly opposed any withdrawal from ground currently occupied by American troops and warmly applauded the "toughness" UN negotiators were demonstrating at the talks. On Capitol Hill, a bipartisan group of House veterans issued a manifesto that began: "No retreat from areas won ... and no further recognition of the thirty-eighth parallel as the division line in Korea."[39]

Meanwhile, most correspondents in daily contact with Nuckols seemed content with the service they were receiving. Nuckols's briefings, according to one journalist, "are full and factual." When faced with the obvious discrepancy between his statements and Radio Pyongyang's broadcasts, the majority of reporters ultimately dismissed the communist stance as little more than rabid propaganda. With a regulated press pool up and running, many newspapers were also content to run accounts by unnamed wire service reporters, who lacked the clout to take on the top brass and were invariably content to reiterate what they had been told by U.S. officers. In August, moreover, this controversy was treated by much of the media as a sideshow. For press attention had shifted from the minutiae of the negotiations to the series of communist allegations that the UN was deliberately violating the neutrality of the Kaesong area, allegations that led to the breakdown of the talks at the end of the month.[40]

Panmunjom

Formal negotiations remained stalled until October 25, as both sides haggled over responsibility for their collapse and discussed a new location that would be less vulnerable to military attack. When they finally resumed in a specially constructed tent camp in the tiny village of Panmunjom, the Korean winter was already starting to loom. The cars in the press train, which had been "like ovens" during the July and August, soon became so cold that "reporters have been known to try to write with mittens on their ice-numb hands." In these worsening conditions, the size of the press pool started to dwindle; sometimes only eight reporters now made the 20-mile trip each day from Munsan-ni to Panmunjom.[41]

Still, if anything, this smaller contingent of reporters proved to be a far greater headache for the military. In fact, it was in October that the UNC PIO issued its first written warning to a reporter; two months later it issued its first "discreditation." Yet these episodes should not be exaggerated. The warning and discreditation were both for relatively minor infractions unrelated to the talks. And the military also made great efforts to improve its public information efforts. In October, senior officers toured the press train and recommended changes to make it more comfortable. Censors were also placed on the train so that they could check radio copy on the spot—an innovation that enabled radio reporters "to make their broadcasts closer to the source of the armistice talks." More important, briefing officers now provided correspondents with detailed information on the UN's demarcation line position. Contrary to the claims some writers have made, Nuckols even offered reporters a candid explanation of the thorniest issue that currently divided the two sides—the status of Kaesong.[42]

As soon as the talks resumed, the communist negotiators offered a major concession on the truce line, accepting the UN claim that it should be based on the current battlefield. In response, Joy and his team pushed for a further concession: they now wanted to keep Kaesong out of communist hands, largely because of its symbolic value as the old Korean capital. In a series of angry exchanges, however, the communists balked.[43] To put pressure on the enemy and generate support for the U.S. stance, Ridgway decided to launch a propaganda offensive, issuing a string of press releases that played up "the characteristics of the proposed zone and the fairness of our solution."[44] This deluge of detail solved one problem. From the very start of the armistice negotiations, PI officers had recognized that "the critical tone of the news stories largely disappeared after official information was made available to the correspondents." Now they were happy to note that the "allied press was grateful for the release of information on a timely basis."[45]

Nevertheless, by providing specific facts, Nuckols and his team immediately created an even greater difficulty for the negotiators. The basic predicament was one that would recur time and again over the coming months. Because the differences between the two sides had narrowed, officials back in Washington worried that the press, politicians, and public might all reach the conclusion that the administration was effectively waging war for the flimsiest of reasons. As the Joint Chiefs cabled to Ridgway on November 6, "judging from press reaction here it would be hard to make people understand why negotiations broke down, if such should happen, over Kaesong." In Washington's opinion, it was far safer to compromise on this question, so that the talks could move on to the next agenda items.[46]

In Tokyo and Korea, Ridgway and Joy disagreed. Both favored a tough stance on the armistice line. Both were afraid that an early agreement here would result in a de facto cease-fire, since neither side would sacrifice men for ground that might soon be given back. For Ridgway and Joy, this prospect was so troubling because it would deprive them of their main tool in dealing with the communists: military pressure. Washington adamantly called for a compromise, however, convinced that the endless wrangling over Kaesong was "too subtle for general understanding." But the Pentagon did offer one sop to its belligerent commanders in the Far East: the current battle line would be used as the final truce line, but only if the remaining items on the agenda were resolved within thirty days.[47]

As Joy and Ridgway feared, even this compromise position was problematic. On November 27, after an agreement was finally reached on the truce line, UN generals instructed all units to reduce "operations to the minimum essential to maintain present positions."[48] By a remarkable coincidence, the next day happened to be exactly a year since Washington had first learned of the massive Chinese intervention. As reporters searched for a suitable way to mark the occasion, they noticed the sudden decline in battlefield activity. At the front, one AP correspondent was told by "an extremely reliable source" that U.S. troops had been instructed to "avoid all casualties" and to "demonstrate [a] willingness to honor a ceasefire." In Washington, the UP went one better. "Orders from the highest source, possibly from the White

House itself," it declared, "yesterday brought the Korean ground fighting to a complete if temporary halt. The communist infantry came out in the open, played ball games, and after dark lit glaring camp fires in full view of UN troops who held their fire."[49]

As soon as these stories hit the wires, senior officials declared them a "serious breach of security." In Tokyo, Ridgway's command launched an immediate investigation into their origin and how they had made it past the censor. In Key West, Truman interrupted his vacation to issue a strong denial. His action was not taken lightly, since many of his PR advisers were convinced that a rebuttal from the top would only fuel interest in the whole matter. But Truman felt he had to refute the UP claim that a cease-fire order had come directly from the White House.[50]

And there were also deeper considerations. Although the negotiators at Panmunjom had agreed that the current battle line would only become the truce line if the remaining issues were resolved within four weeks, senior officials were not terribly optimistic that this timetable could be kept. Both sides still had to agree on ways to enforce the armistice, a matter that was bound up with tricky issues like when foreign troops would be withdrawn, the extent to which either side would be able to inspect the military facilities of the other, and whether the communists would be permitted to construct and rehabilitate airfields. Debate on these issues was bound to be long and fractious. In private, officials fretted that the public would soon become impatient with the delay; Truman even "feared that the increasing 'home for Christmas' idea" might force the United States to make excessive concessions, especially if Americans became convinced that a de facto cease-fire was already in place.[51]

What made this prospect was even more disturbing was the fact that the negotiators had not even started to address the thorniest of all issues—the fate of prisoners of war—a subject that had obvious emotional overtones for many sectors of American society.

Prisoners of War

By the fall of 1951, the military listed 10,624 American soldiers as missing in action (MIA) in Korea. Although the Pentagon had little concrete evidence as to whether these had been taken prisoner, killed in battle, or murdered in cold blood, unofficial estimates calculated that perhaps as many as 4,500 had survived and were in a string of prisoner-of-war (POW) camps dotted across North Korea and Manchuria.[52]

Inside the top reaches of the administration, most officials initially thought that the truce talks ought to focus on getting these men back as soon as possible. True, this would mean swapping them for more than 130,000 communist

POWs in UN custody, which in turn raised both a military problem—effectively giving the enemy the equivalent of twelve divisions for just 4,500 U.S. men—and a humanitarian question: what to do if those who feared retribution in China or North Korea refused to return.[53] But an "all-for-all" exchange would be perfectly in tune with the Geneva Convention. It was also what the American public expected. In July, before the truce talks had begun in earnest, Republicans in the Senate had demanded that the immediate release of American prisoners "be made a primary condition." While the inclusion of POWs on the truce agenda had mollified this sentiment, many legislators remained "greatly concerned by the constant reports of the dire circumstances in which American prisoners find themselves."[54]

And small wonder. Since the start of the war, communist brutality against POWs had been a common refrain of administration propaganda. No less than a third of all reports issued by the UNC between July 1950 and October 1951 had contained some mention of savage communist acts.[55] Since the summer of 1950, officials had also supplied the media with searing photographic images to bolster these verbal descriptions. To be sure, the Pentagon was careful "to prevent release of 'horror' photographs of American recognizable wounded and dead" that "would distress relatives and friends." But senior PI officers were convinced that the publication of carefully chosen atrocity pictures "may serve a useful purpose in drawing international attention to the crimes of the enemy." They were therefore quick to clear pictures and stories that showed the basic brutality of the enemy without revealing the specific identity of the victim.[56] And the media avidly published this material. Some magazines had shown awful pictures of dead GIs lying face down in a ditch, executed in cold blood after capture. Many newspapers had also detailed the beatings, death marches, and lack of food for the bedraggled survivors who had made their way into communist POW camps.[57]

As the horror mounted, influential voices on the Hill searched for ways to help these survivors. Throughout the fall of 1951, Lyndon Johnson used his position on the Senate Armed Services Committee to pressure the military into finding a way of getting winter clothes to U.S. POWs, because reports from Korea suggested "that the Chinese are in no position to supply these prisoners with warm clothing, even should they want to do so." In private, the Pentagon was skeptical that anything practical could be done before an armistice was concluded, but it also recognized the obvious political risks of ignoring this request. Facing mounting pressure, Robert Lovett, Marshall's recent replacement as secretary of defense, therefore instructed his subordinates to exhaust every possible avenue to help American captives.[58]

Although Lovett's instruction simply focused yet more attention on U.S. prisoners, within weeks it was completely overshadowed by what one military PI officer considered the "biggest flap on a news release" since the start of the Korean War. On November 14, Colonel James N. Hanley, chief of the Eighth Army's War Crimes Section, released a report to a small group of South Korean newsmen that claimed the communists had murdered 5,790 U.S. soldiers. In Tokyo, Ridgway's command was appalled by this unauthorized action. As Welch hastened to point out, Hanley's figures were unsubstantiated. Moreover, by releasing them to just one group of reporters and not the whole press corps, Hanley precipitated a furious bout of media indignation, as scooped correspondents charged the army with discrimination. Back in the United States, the Pentagon was even more worried by the likely impact Hanley's action would have on those families with next of kin listed as MIA or captured. It was clear that something would have to be done to sort out the mess.[59]

After flying straight to Korea on a fact-finding mission, Welch immediately prepared a "clarifying" press release for Ridgway's signature. This verified that atrocities had indeed occurred, but rather than sanctioning Hanley's figure it only confirmed 365 deaths.[60] Yet within days, even this number was the subject of intense dispute. As an intrepid reporter in New York discovered, Ridgway's clarification was itself misleading, because his own command had earlier reported "approximately 8,000 U.S. military personnel... as war crimes victims." The media immediately latched on to the discrepancy. As *Time* pointed out, this "clarifying" press release made Ridgway "a greater exaggerator and hastier reporter than Hanley." It also meant yet more "cruel anxiety to the wives and parents of U.S. men captured or MIA"—an anxiety that prompted a wave of letters and telegrams to the Pentagon and White House protesting against the confusing government statements and calling for clarification.[61]

Whatever the exact figures, opinion from across the political spectrum viewed the Hanley flap as a timely reminder of the vital need to get American POWs back home as soon as possible. "It is scarcely relevant that these disclosures may have been made at the wrong time or that the figures may have been exaggerated," opined the *New York Times* in a typical comment. "The fact is that communist troops have butchered prisoners in cold blood. No truce would be tolerable which would leave them in the position of holding other prisoners as hostages."[62] In the House of Representatives, the reaction to Hanley's release was so intense and angry that the chair of the Armed Services Committee immediately proposed the appointment of a special subcommittee to investigate the whole matter, and was only deterred when Lovett personally intervened and warned him that such an investigation could torpedo the Panmunjom talks.[63] But other legislators were not silenced so easily. One bipartisan group even called on the administration to retaliate by breaking off the talks and dropping the A-bomb on communist troops. "No moral question was involved," Frank Wilson (D-TX) insisted, since "we are dealing with a brutish people who have no morals and are just bloodthirsty."[64]

Mulling over the intense furor, State Department officials privately concluded that Hanley's original statement "was not motivated by any desire to, or expectation that it would have any effect on the armistice negotiations." In fact, they considered it "entirely probable" that Hanley thought he was merely "recapitulating information which had already been released."[65] Yet, regardless of his intention, the resulting controversy had served to dramatize the political explosiveness of the fate of American POWs just at the time that the truce talks were starting to focus on this issue. And media attention would become even greater a few weeks later, when the talks themselves resulted in another important development: an agreement by both sides to issue lists detailing exactly whom they held in their camps.

Given the almost total lack of detailed information about American POWs, the media was "intensely interested" in obtaining the communist list as quickly as possible. Trying to help out, Ridgway's PIO laid on a special jet to collect what the communists had released. That evening, however, the Korean winter intervened, delaying the jet's departure. In Ridgway's teeming media center, tension swiftly mounted. With families back home desperate for information on their loved ones, editors applied tremendous "pressure on their correspondents in Tokyo for the utmost speed in obtaining and transmitting the names," and the correspondents in turn shifted "the pressure to the PIO." But the weather did not abate sufficiently for the jet to make its way to Tokyo until early the next morning. When the list was finally handed to the group of weary and anxious reporters, it contained details of just 3,198 Americans, including General William F. Dean, who had been reported MIA in the early days of the war. Other POWs, however, were only identified by serial numbers, so the Pentagon had to rush to establish the names and addresses. But even this effort was not enough for many impatient newspapers, who attempted their own identifications by trawling through reference libraries.

After going to such trouble, the media naturally lavished enormous attention on the POW list. Across the United States, metropolitan newspapers ran special editions, while radio networks broadcast each and every name. In the runup to Christmas, it seemed there was no end to the public's demand for information about the Americans who had survived all the barbarities that the savage communists could throw at them.[66]

In stark contrast, most Americans paid little attention to what was going on in the UN camps that housed communist prisoners. As a matter of fact, this was a sorry tale. During the North Korean collapse of October 1950 and the failed Chinese offensives in 1951, the UN had captured more than 130,000 prisoners, including 95,000 North Koreans, almost 21,000 Chinese, and 16,000 South Koreans.[67] Many had been placed in thirty-two compounds on the island of Koje-do, off the southern coast of Korea. Because of the vast numbers and a shortage of space, these compounds were cramped and over-loaded. A lack of heating, poor food, and parlous sanitary conditions resulted in waves of dysentery, malaria, pneumonia, and tuberculosis, which had killed as many as six thousand inmates by the end of 1951. And manpower shortages at the front meant that the U.S. and South Korean troops who policed the compounds were invariably poorly trained and sometimes prone to mistreat their charges.

These UN guards also tended to confine their patrols to the entrances of the compounds, which effectively allowed discipline and control inside to pass into the hands of different factions. On one side were the national-ist compounds. Here troops from Chiang's Kuomintang army, though pro-hibited from fighting on the peninsula, were drafted into service as prison guards and interrogators. Their presence obviously intimidated a number of POWs, but these guards also found a receptive audience. Indeed, some Chinese prisoners had initially fought for the nationalists during the Chinese Civil War. Once inside the camps, they tended to abandon their tenuous loyalty to the communist cause and began to establish anticommunist orga-nizations, setting up their own administrations and removing rivals, often with force and brutality.

But not all POWs were coerced or persuaded by these organizations; many remained loyal communists. Angered by UN efforts to introduce indoctrina-tion classes to teach them the virtues of democracy (which were in violation of the Geneva Convention), communist prisoners began to dominate a string of compounds, using violence and propaganda to consolidate their position and make life difficult for their captors.[68]

By 1952, the UN camps were thus an incendiary mix of grim living condi-tions and ideological enmity. But little of this was reported to the American public. During the winter of 1951–52, as Welch explained, "Koje-do was not a matter of great interest to newsmen in Japan and Korea, preoccupied as they were with the conduct of hostilities and progress of the so-called armi-stice negotiations." Nor was the military overly keen to shed light on this subject. Apart from a riot in February that resulted in the death of an Amer-ican and was thus difficult to keep quiet, the censors were eager to steer reporters away from the seedier side of prison life. On one occasion, they prevailed on Keyes Beech to withhold a dispatch that focused on the alleged mistreatment of POWs, insisting that this would play straight into the hands of communist propagandists. At other times, the military exploited its con-trol over access to the compounds to ensure that correspondents' visits were carefully orchestrated.[69]

As a result, on those few occasions when journalists did cover the story, their conclusions tended to be highly favorable. Indeed, the basic thrust of the intermittent reports that appeared during December and January was that the allies' kindhearted treatment of prisoners could not be more different from the awful conditions their American counterparts suffered. As William L. Worden vividly concluded in a *Saturday Evening Post* feature,

> War in general has become more brutal with the years, until nothing is left of the sportsmanship, mutual respect of fighting men, protection of civilians, or any other virtues it may once have had. The lone exception to this trend is the treatment of prisoners by Occidental nations. At Koje-do, this humanity is being tried out on Orientals, most of whom have never known humane treatment even in the best days of their lives. Some of the results are immediate and encouraging. No healthy prisoner has lost weight in this sprawling camp. Most records show weight increases of five to ten pounds. The camp health record may be the best for any 150,000 Orientals in a single group in Asia. There have been no epidemics. Fatal diseases are far below nationality averages.[70]

Of course, if such American munificence was the norm, then it might easily translate into a desire among many communist prisoners to stay in the West. Yet the military had done little to raise public expectations on this issue. True, it had given a few reporters access to its efforts to educate POWs that "democracy offers a better deal than communism." But, as Collins explained to Lovett on November 15, UN psychological warfare programs had "scrupulously avoided" the subject of "asylum to Chinese communist forces or North Korean military personnel."[71] Just as important, the scanty media coverage had generally discounted the prospect that prisoners would want to defect. Even Worden conceded that it was difficult to ascertain the effect of the UN education campaign on communist prisoners. Less sanguine observers judged that most of those prisoners in UN compounds were "servile and steadfast followers of their communist masters."[72]

Inside America, then, the balance of interest could not have been clearer: while desperately worried about the fate of U.S. prisoners, most observers evinced little concern for those captured communists who seemed to be enjoying the fruits of American generosity. Yet at Panmunjom, the UN negotiators were about to unveil a bold proposal. Rather than base their position on the fate of American POWs, Joy and his team would insist on applying the principle of voluntary repatriation to communist prisoners.

The decision to plump for voluntary repatriation had little to do with domestic politics and everything to do with the firm views of a few key policymakers, especially the president. On October 29, in a meeting with James Webb, the undersecretary of state, Truman first revealed his views on the subject. "He does not wish to send back those prisoners who have surrendered and have cooperated with us," Webb recorded, "because he believes they will be immediately done away with."[73] Bowing to the president's wishes, the State and

Defense departments began to consider ways to amend their position so as to avoid forcing any prisoner to return who believed his life "would be endangered thereby."[74]

The culmination of this rethinking came on December 7, when senior officials presented Truman with a new directive to Ridgway that the president duly endorsed. This instructed the UN negotiators to push for an agreement whereby, prior to their release, "all POWs held by either side would be screened by teams composed of members of each side; individual POWs expressing a desire not to be exchanged would be permitted to remain under jurisdiction of their captors." On January 2, Joy revealed this position to the stunned communists, who immediately rejected it, well aware that if large numbers of their prisoners refused to return to North Korea and China, this would deal a massive blow to the legitimacy of their revolutions.[75]

The communists' strident opposition engendered a spasm of dejection inside the administration. The president was particularly downcast. On January 27, he penned the most notorious of his private "unsent" memoranda. Tired and anxious, he was in no mood to contemplate a compromise over POWs. Instead, he mulled over the prospect of giving the communists a ten-day ultimatum, along with a warning that if it was ignored, the UN would blockade the Chinese coast, destroy military bases in Manchuria, and eliminate a swathe of cities from Moscow to Vladivostok, in order "to accomplish our peaceful purposes."[76]

A few days earlier, at a senior Pentagon meeting, the mood was scarcely lighter. Officials not only fretted that the United States had "completely lost the initiative in the peace talks"; they also "doubted that the American people would continue much longer to support us in this apparently abortive effort."[77] Opinion surveys certainly bore out this last point. "Gloom over the prospects for an agreement at Panmunjom deepens further," PA concluded on January 23, "and some commentators caution that public opinion may not 'tolerate' continuance of the present situation much longer."[78]

With such pessimism and frustration rife, the voluntary repatriation policy inevitably came under the spotlight. The problem was simply put: was it wise for the administration to continue to wage war on the basis of the fate of communist POWs? Officials with an acute sense of the popular mood thought not. True, a number of influential voices, including the *New York Times*, Walter Lippmann, and the Alsop brothers, had recently emphasized their staunch support for the principle of voluntary repatriation. But opinion was far from unanimous, especially when attention shifted to the Americans who were languishing in communist camps. "Isn't our first business rather to return to their homes the American and other Allied prisoners the Reds have reported to be alive?" John Vandercook asked, on his radio program on January 24.[79] Tellingly, PA agreed. If the negotiations were broken off because of this one issue, Barrett stressed, "we could be accused of sacrificing the moral obligations of any government to rescue its own prisoners.... We could also be accused of causing countless thousands of additional casualties."[80]

Despite such warnings, on February 27 Truman and Acheson reached a firm understanding that there would be no forcible return of unwilling communist prisoners. Their decision was based partly on a combination of humanitarian and ideological considerations. "To use force to turn over the communist prisoners who believe they would face death if they returned," explained Acheson in a pivotal memorandum to the president, "would be repugnant to our most fundamental moral and humanitarian principles on the importance of the individual, and would seriously jeopardize the psychological warfare position of the U.S. in its opposition to communist tyranny." Truman was receptive to this argument, but he was also driven by a stubborn determination not to cave into an enemy that lacked "honor." And he probably lacked information about the true conditions in the UN camps—both the practical problem of how to discover which prisoners wanted to return home and the deeper unrest that was starting to percolate, especially inside the communist compounds.[81]

Having decided to hang tough on voluntary repatriation, the White House and State Department faced the problem of selling this policy to the public. Convinced that there was little popular support for their position, officials decided that they would have to stimulate it. Recognizing that the public would prefer a swift end to the war and the immediate return of American prisoners, they concluded that potential opposition would have to be neutralized.[82]

One way to drum up public support would be to use voluntary repatriation to turn the war into a moral crusade for human rights. Ever since the administration had backed away from the clear goal of unifying Korea, UN aims, as PA privately conceded, had become "more and more beclouded and misunderstood."[83] Now, however, the administration had a chance to turn the war it into something more than just killing the enemy. "This issue," claimed Charles Marshall of the Policy Planning Staff, "gets to the heart of the contention between communism and the tradition we live by. It bears on the rights of men to make choices and to claim protection."[84]

During February and March, the State Department periodically contemplated sponsoring a congressional resolution to ram this point home. Such a move would also serve other functions. It would ensure that the legislature shared responsibility for any continuation of the conflict on this one issue. It would give officials a degree of bipartisan cover with elections looming. And, crucially, it would also provide the legal backing that had been so conspicuously absent from the original decision to intervene in Korea.[85]

Yet pursuing this course presented one practical problem: the senators and congressmen who were willing to introduce such a resolution were the hawks who could scarcely be trusted to do the administration's bidding. In the Senate, the leading proponent of a resolution was William Jenner, the firebrand Indianan whose outlandish outbursts placed him close to McCarthy. In the House, the main mover was Orland Kay Armstrong (R-MO), a freshman Missouri Republican who fancied himself as something of an expert on Far Eastern affairs, having visited Japan, Korea, and Formosa in 1951. He was also part of a band of veterans in the House who were always on the lookout for ways to "strengthen the hands of our negotiators and protect our interests in Korea." But like so many other congressional "experts," he was a champion of ideas that were dangerously close to those proposed by MacArthur. Using such legislators could therefore be hazardous. Armstrong was hardly the most dependable man for the administration to lean on, and the resolution he finally prepared patently ignored the POW issue altogether.[86] Neither was Jenner—and his intimation that most senators supported his position was difficult to verify and soon appeared to be something of a chimera.[87]

With the prospect of congressional action far from appealing, officials switched their attention to the media and mass opinion. Already Joy and his team had unveiled the new policy with great fanfare, taking care to ensure that the press was fully and swiftly briefed.[88] In Washington, the administration now planned ways to drum up grass-roots support. Senior Asia specialists in the State Department met with religious leaders to brief them on the importance of the administration's POW stand, aware that leading Catholic and Protestant newspapers were united in their opposition to forcibly repatriating prisoners back to godless communism. In addition, PA contemplated trying "to put the administration's viewpoint on POWs before some fifty outside organizations," in the hope that they would then amplify the message to the wider public.[89]

Still, even if this activity reaped rewards, one crucial problem remained. "We all felt there would be a great uproar," one senior State Department official privately noted, "if this was the only issue preventing the conclusion of an armistice and the return of our own prisoners." To head off the domestic unrest that would probably ensue, the White House, State Department, and Pentagon all agreed that their information campaign would have to contain another essential ingredient: "In the event that negotiations are to be broken off, every effort should be made to drive home the impression that *this was not the only issue* on which agreement could not be reached."[90] In practice, this translated into the "package proposal." By lumping together the main points of dispute at Panmunjom—which included Soviet membership of any inspection regime, the communists' right to rehabilitate airfields, and the fate of POWs—the administration hoped to avoid the appearance that the talks had collapsed over its obdurate prisoner stance.[91]

Then, in the second half of March, a breakthrough at Panmunjom suddenly seemed possible. Not only had the differences between both sides narrowed on inspection and airfield construction but, crucially, the communists seemed ready to compromise on POWs. On March 19, they indicated a willingness to discuss new prisoner lists "from which some of those not desiring repatriation could be eliminated." Communist reporters at the talks also hinted that further concessions might be possible if the daily sessions were held in secret, for this would permit both sides "to express themselves freely, informally, and frankly."[92]

Hopeful that executive sessions would help the talks progress, Ridgway and his negotiators readily agreed to this initiative. But secrecy had obvious drawbacks. Many media commentators condemned "the executive sessions on POWs as a sign that the US was planning to compromise with principle." The American Federation of Labor was particularly outspoken, issuing a ringing statement "against any possibility of appeasement or fake compromise scheme affecting the Chinese and North Korean POWs." Secrecy, it feared, might simply mask "some tricky formula" designed to fudge the moral stance the United States had now adopted. In Congress, members of the China lobby were quick to reiterate these warnings. As Judd declared, any compromise on the prisoner issue would mean turning over thousands of men to an "atheistic" system in which "human beings are no more important or sacred than mosquitoes."[93]

All these worries were unfounded: secrecy was merely used to cast a veil over the screening of communist POWs in the UN camps. Since January, officials had convinced themselves that this exercise would produce a breakthrough, for if the UN could state precisely how many prisoners it would return, then the enemy might be ready to do a deal. Before the screening had begun, the UN negotiators had duly told the communists to expect the return of around 116,000 prisoners, basing this figure on a staff study estimate. But officials had given little thought to how the screening process would actually work.

In theory—and in administration rhetoric—all inmates would have a free choice between staying in the West and returning to their communist homeland. No one would be forced to return against their will; nor would anyone be coerced into remaining. In practice, however, conditions in the UN camps made such a free screening process impossible. Simply put, many inmates were in compounds dominated by violent anticommunist guards. With a large number of these prisoners too intimidated to state their true preferences, the final screening revealed that only 70,000 wished to be repatriated.

When the UN negotiators revealed this figure at Panmunjom, the communists reacted in savagely negative terms. By the end of April, with the talks about to collapse on the POW issue, both sides agreed to lift the veil of secrecy.[94]

Nuckols paved the way for the UN, briefing reporters on all that had happened during the weeks of executive sessions. In basic factual terms, he pulled no punches, revealing that the communists would have probably accepted the return of 116,000 prisoners but had balked at the far lower figure of 70,000. When it came to the underlying reason for this, however, officials were naturally keen to play down the actual condition in the camps. Instead, they implemented their plan to turn the whole issue into an ideological success story, giving chief billing to the fact that large numbers of prisoners had chosen the freedom of the West over the so-called godless, collectivist, and brutal system of the East. As Acheson stressed on April 24, the "UN believed in the worth of the individual," a fact fully recognized by thousands of prisoners who refused to return to their communist homelands.[95]

This focus on the ideological appeal of democracy was at the heart of the administration's effort to use the POW issue to instill a new moral purpose into the war effort. But it had to be handled with care, for officials were determined to avoid an appearance of the talks breaking down on this one issue. Earlier, the UN negotiators had unveiled their package proposal to the communists. When it was rejected, officials moved into high gear. On May 7, Ridgway issued a press statement explaining that the three remaining issues on the truce agenda "could not be solved separately," that the UN negotiators had presented "a just and integral solution," and that this was a position "from which we cannot and shall not retreat." In Washington, Truman, Acheson, and William C. Foster, the acting defense secretary, all sanctioned Ridgway's stance. As the president declared, America's refusal to force prisoners back to China and North Korea, where many would doubtless face torture and even execution, was not the only issue between the two sides. The UN's package proposal, he insisted, offered the only fair and final way to resolve all outstanding issues and thereby end the war.[96]

Koje-do

May 7 proved an eventful day. While senior officials released their carefully choreographed statements on the package plan, Ridgway was in the process of handing over the UNC to General Mark C. Clark. As the two men prepared to fly from Tokyo to Korea for briefings on the tactical situation, news came over the wires of unrest at Koje-do. Communist prisoners had overpowered Brigadier General Francis T. Dodd, the camp's commanding officer, and were holding him hostage.

Although Dodd was released after more than seventy-eight hours in captivity, his freedom was bought at a stiff price. Brigadier General Charles F. Colson, who was sent to Koje-do to sort out the situation, negotiated an agreement with the communist POWs. This saved Dodd's life, but Colson was forced to make some highly embarrassing admissions, conceding that "many

POWs have been killed and wounded by UN forces" and suggesting that the screening process had failed to offer inmates a free choice, especially in those compounds controlled by the anticommunists. .[97]

In Tokyo and Washington, senior officials were appalled. Clark immediately repudiated this agreement, declaring that it had been signed under duress. He also instituted disciplinary proceedings against Dodd and Colson that would soon lead to their reduction in rank.[98] In press briefings, Defense Department spokespersons were equally critical. To clarify what had happened in the camps, the OPI chief told reporters that the military had not engaged in forcible screening, nor had it been responsible for bloodshed, except to put down communist-inspired riots. "The U.S. Army," one official declared, when asked about the outcome of Colson's negotiated settlement, "was put in about the same position as a man who has never beaten his wife in his life, but agrees not to do it in the future."[99]

Yet these statements did little to quell the mounting sense of outrage. In Congress, as rumors circulated that Dodd had been "ordered to 'coddle and appease'" enemy POWs, legislators demanded explanations and threatened investigations.[100] Across the political spectrum, editorial writers united to denounce the "unholy mess." Many recognized that the Koje-do incident had been a massive propaganda victory for the communists and had greatly complicated the U.S. position at the truce talks. "The propaganda weapon the communists have been handed," the *Washington Post* opined, "will go a long way toward making a mockery of all the months of haggling at Panmunjom." This incident, the columnist Edgar Mowrer agreed, had "virtually destroyed the magnificent moral and political victory we achieved by our recent refusal to return unwilling captives to their communist master."[101]

In private, State Department officials ruefully agreed that the incident threatened the whole package proposal. Indeed, by raising questions about the screening process, it called into question the government's claim that prisoners had made a free decision to stay in the West. Because America's allies would be reluctant to intensify the war on the basis of this shaky POW policy, the State Department also concluded that it would be impossible "to present a clear package proposal and then suspend negotiations on a take-it-or-leave-it basis." Instead, what was needed was "a clear cut move on our part" in order to "restore domestic and international confidence in our position."[102]

Within days, the State Department decided it would have to rescreen the prisoners. Senior officials also deemed it vital for the United States to launch a propaganda campaign of its own.[103] For many months, the communists had been pushing the idea that the United States had been using germ warfare in Korea. In the early spring, as the Soviet and Chinese campaigns had become even more intense, the State Department had fretted that the

enemy had made "some headway" in the Far East.[104] But these germ warfare allegations had not been widely reported in the United States.[105] Nor
had they worried America's allies, some of whom had worked to cut off
debate on the subject in the UN.[106] Now, however, the administration was
suddenly concerned that the communists had achieved a big success by
linking "their claims of atrocities [at Koje-do] and our use of germ warfare." The administration's response was decisive. In indictments "of exceptional sharpness," Acheson and other officials accused the Soviet Union
of committing an "international crime" by repeatedly mouthing the false
germ warfare allegations.[107]

In Korea, meanwhile, the military moved to salvage something from the
Koje-do crisis. In the wake of Dodd's kidnapping, its main task was to establish control over those compounds dominated by communist inmates. Clark
immediately gave this thankless task to Brigadier General Haydon L. Boatner,
well aware that Boatner was a media-savvy figure who would prove a hit
with correspondents.[108] Throughout the next few weeks, Boatner then maintained tight control over the flow of information, which he used to blame the
enemy for all the carnage and killing. Indeed, his press releases detailed disturbing hauls of spears, gasoline grenades, knives, clubs, hatchets, and ham-
mers, not to mention anticommunist prisoners, emaciated and beaten, who
had been subjected to "kangaroo justice." And journalists avidly followed his
cues, reporting on the "full story of communist terrorism, torture, and mur-
der of anti-Red prisoners," paying special attention to the victims who had
been "garroted, stabbed, burned, tied, and hanged."[109]

When the time came to send in UN units to break up the communist-
dominated compounds, Colonel Roswell P. Rosengren, the Eighth Army's
chief PI officer, made sure that a group of friendly reporters would be able
to cover the new Koje-do story easily and efficiently. On the day before
the operation, he flew thirty-seven journalists to the island, put them up
in Quonset huts, plied them with bacon, eggs, and toast, and even made
sure they had time for a drink before the bar was subjected to the normal
curfew. The next morning, after Boatner briefed them, they were driven to
seats just 50 yards from the start of the action, which saw UN infantrymen
supported by tanks kill 31 prisoners before the communist resistance was
finally broken. "Except for some delay occasioned by the heavy communication load," Rosengren recorded afterward, "the press was very pleased
with the operation."[110]

In fact, everything went so well from the perspective of media relations
that Rosengren was convinced he had discovered a deeper lesson. All this
army assistance, he concluded, "illustrated a sound general rule for army
treatment of newsmen during a major news event: tell them what is going to
happen, then let them watch it happen."[111]

Public Opinion and the War

May and June 1952 were a terrible time for the Truman administration. The Koje-do incident forced it into a series of defensive moves, including an obvious retreat from its publicly stated "final position." Just as bad, on May 25 Rhee declared martial law in Pusan, his temporary capital, and began arresting members of the legislature—actions that inevitably called into question America's stated goal of defending democracy in Korea (see chapter 12).[112] Meanwhile, at home the administration's mobilization plans also took a high-profile knock when Truman, anxious to avert a steel strike that threatened supplies to the Korean front, seized the steel industry, only for the Supreme Court to strike down his action as unconstitutional.[113]

Yet for all these travails, support for the war held up surprisingly well. In fact, by June, there had actually been something of a turnaround in the domestic mood, compared to a year earlier.

Indeed, for much of 1951 polling data had made grim reading for officials. After the Chinese intervention, Truman's personal approval ratings had dropped markedly. The low point had come in December 1951, when only 23 percent of voters thought he was doing a good job, a paltry number that pollsters put down to a mixture of dissatisfaction about corruption allegations, rising inflation, and the lack of progress in the Korean truce talks.[114] Just as bad, support for the war had been fragile. At the start of 1951, with Seoul evacuated for a second time and war correspondents sending home stories of a major disaster, Gallup had found that two-thirds of Americans wanted to pull out of Korea altogether. Although this particular figure had proved to be a blip, other surveys had been almost as gloomy. Some had revealed that the proportion of those thinking the United States had a "made a mistake going into Korea in the first place" had shot up from a fifth to half the population. In one October poll, Gallup had even found voters divided roughly five to three in favor of the proposition that Korea was "an utterly useless war."[115]

In the first six months of 1952, however, the mood brightened. Although casualties continued to mount steadily, the president's approval ratings bounced back a little, edging up to 28 percent in May and 32 percent in June.[116] These figures were hardly earth-shattering, but support for the war was far stronger—and this was an even bigger change from a year before. In January, 56 percent thought the United States had been right to intervene in the war, while only 16 percent were in favor of "pulling our troops out of Korea."[117] Although these numbers slipped slightly in the next few weeks, by June 54 percent thought an armistice based on the division of Korea would be a success for the United States, up from 30 percent a year earlier.[118]

In the late spring, public opinion also rallied firmly behind the administration's POW position. Just before officials began their vigorous effort to sell the package plan, one poll found the public skeptical of the policy, with no less than 81 percent willing to "accept *in*voluntary repatriation either to hasten an armistice (38 percent) or if necessary in order to secure the return of captured Americans (43 percent)."[119] Within weeks, however, the public mood had changed completely. Even with the chaos on Koje-do, Americans now seemed convinced by the government's POW position. Despite a big petition drive calling on the government to focus its attention of getting U.S. prisoners back, by July a significant majority of 58 percent now supported the administration's stance on voluntary repatriation, whatever the cost—up 8 percent from a few weeks before.[120]

With the war continuing to drag on, casualties mounting, and the truce talks at an impasse, this was a surprising picture. And it naturally begs the question: why was popular support for the war so robust? The administration's effort to inject a new moral dimension into the war certainly helped. But it was only part of the answer. Also important was how the media covered the fighting, for this in turn shaped the way the public perceived the distant war.

11

STEADY IMPROVEMENTS

B y the second half of 1951, after more than a year's experience with war, it had become an article of faith among many officials that process rather than policy was at the heart of most of their propaganda problems. If you only ended the petty irritations that so often sprung up—if you made the flow of information from the government more efficient, took pains to ensure that reporters lives were more comfortable, and generally began viewing Congress and the press less as meddling irritants and more as helpful partners—then you would swiftly acquire better coverage, if not close allies or compliant tools. Put another way, officials throughout the different layers of the administration believed that many in the press, and even in Congress, were not opposed to the basic thrust of what the government was trying to achieve. But these mediating voices frequently gave the administration such a hard time because they felt slighted by a lack of adequate consultation, faulty logistics, and unnecessary security restrictions.

During the long stalemated months of 1951 and 1952, this assumption would be amply put to the test. In one sense, UN military fortunes were vastly improved from the low point of December and January 1950–51. The fighting front had, in most places, been stabilized north of the thirty-eighth parallel, there was little chance of UN forces being pushed off the peninsula, and U.S. commanders were able to confidently pronounce: "in the process of destroying huge segments of the enemy, Eighth Army has developed into a powerful military machine, stoked with confidence, combat knowledge, and a will to fight."[1]

Yet this new stalemate war was still a very tricky sell. The border patrols and limited offensives that characterized the final two years of fighting were certainly a big departure from the great eye-catching battles that had grabbed the nation's attention during 1950. The objectives in this new war were also far from "sexy"—simply to maintain the rough battle line, kill the enemy, and wait for the endless armistice negotiations to come to fruition. And all the while, American boys continued to die on this faraway peninsula—indeed, the United States sustained 45 percent of its overall battlefield casualties during this two-year period when the battle line hardly moved.[2]

Nonetheless, despite the claims made in some accounts, the basic relationship between officials and the media in this period was far from "disastrous."[3] The reason for this was simple. Although in many respects the war itself was a more difficult sell, this was counterbalanced by a variety of improvements in the underlying structure of relations between the government and the media, improvements that were the product of new personalities, changing bureaucratic interactions, and a learning process that enabled officials to avoid many of the mistakes of the early days of the war.

Changes in the Far East

In April 1951, after MacArthur was fired, Truman had to reshuffle the UNC. While Ridgway was promoted to take over in Tokyo, Lieutenant General James A. Van Fleet assumed control of the Eighth Army in Korea. To many in Washington, Van Fleet was "the natural selection" to assume this command, not just because of his stellar record as a divisional and corps commander in World War II but also because he had headed the American military mission in Greece in 1948–50, and Truman, for one, thought his performance here had been crucial to containing the communist guerrillas. Still, the sudden timing surprised Van Fleet, who was enjoying a short Florida vacation when Collins called with the curt instruction "Get a plane from the air force, get back here, and get ready to go at once to Korea to take Eighth Army."[4]

During Van Fleet's first hours as Eighth Army commander, senior officials in the Pentagon did their utmost to ensure that he did not blurt out any statement that reporters could seize on. Acutely aware that in the midst of the MacArthur controversy the press was playing up each and every comment, Van Fleet was a willing accomplice. On his way to Korea, he refused to be baited by the journalists who swarmed the Washington airport lounge. When he arrived in the Far East, it soon became clear that he had a keen sense of the importance of PR. Like MacArthur, this could sometimes take the form of self-glorification. Indeed, Van Fleet had no qualms about approving press releases that painted him in glowing terms—as "a crystal hard military man with a soft-shelled heart," a sixty-year-old who looked and acted much younger, a commanding officer who "prefers to live and fight in the field with his beloved infantry."[5]

Yet, as in the case of Ridgway, Van Fleet's concern for PR also had a more positive dimension. As mentioned earlier (see chapter 6), Ridgway understood the need to continue improving the day-to-day relationship between the military and the media in the Korean theater. Van Fleet, too, recognized the importance of cultivating all the press, not just a small "palace guard." From time to time, he accepted invitations to the correspondents' billet, provided personal background briefings, and agreed to be interviewed by the major magazines. His general approach was to be blunt and to the point—he was, his biographer reports, "guileless, friendly, positive, optimistic." Although sometimes angry when reporters read "hidden meanings into his words," overall his personal demeanor and media-friendly actions, like those of Ridgway, marked a welcome change from the MacArthur era.[6]

Van Fleet meeting correspondents on the press train at Munsan-ni. Courtesy of National Archives.

That the two men at the top were acutely concerned with publicity had another important consequence: both were determined to bring more PI officers into the theater. In the early phases of the war, the lack of experienced personnel on the ground had often had a debilitating effect on the military's relations with the press. Now, however, both Ridgway and Van Fleet worked to rectify this problem with a dual recruitment policy. On the one hand, they enlisted their own personal PR advisers. In his early days in Korea, Ridgway had relied heavily on James Quirk, an experienced newsman, who soon received numerous plaudits for his informative briefings and his overall media savvy. Later, Ridgway brought in Burrows Matthews, an editor at the *Buffalo Courier-Express*, who used his wide experience in all aspects of smaller newspaper publishing to improve the general's relationship with correspondents.[7] Not to be outdone, Van Fleet recruited his own expert: James C. McNamara, an award-winning veteran radio reporter from California, most known for his vivid on-the-spot coverage of Howard Hughes's famous one-minute flight in the Spruce Goose, the gigantic airplane, back in 1947.[8]

Along with these changes at the top, Ridgway and Van Fleet worked hard to boost the overall size of their PIOs. This was important because the activities of even the most experienced and skillful men at headquarters could easily be undone if PI officers working at the divisional level, and lower, were overburdened, for many reporters still made daily forays to the front to collect useful information. So to improve operations lower down the chain of command, senior officers undertook a big recruitment drive. Back in December 1950, at the time of the Chinese intervention, the Eighth Army's PIO consisted of just ten officers and ten enlisted men. A year later, after a concerted effort to bring in more men, the whole UNC had a total of 21 officers and 10 enlisted men working on censorship alone, and another 97 officers and 127 enlisted men engaged in the other dimensions of PI work.[9]

Still, this infusion of new recruits, though important, was no panacea. In fact, these burgeoning PR bureaucracies had the potential to exacerbate another problem that had plagued the military since the early days of the war: individual and interservice rivalries. It certainly did not help that the likes of Quirk, Matthews, or MacNamara were effectively outsiders who were immediately promoted over the heads of regular officers. Moreover, while these personal PR advisers had all worked in media and advertising, the regular PI officers generally hailed from a combat background and had little PR expertise beyond what they had learned on military training courses. Because of their decidedly different backgrounds, Quirk, Matthews, and McNamara were far more attuned to the needs of the working correspondents, while regular PI officers tended to think first about the need for strict security to protect the GI at the front.[10]

Nor was this the only potential friction point. A broader dimension of tension already existed between the UNC in Tokyo and the Eighth Army in

Korea. In MacArthur's last months, senior Eighth Army officers had come to resent first his attempts to gain credit for battlefield victories and then Tokyo's efforts to reestablish a role in the censorship sphere. Although MacArthur's recall removed a major cause of tension, Van Fleet's appointment clearly had the potential to make any improvement in relations between the two commands extremely short lived.

Ridgway and Van Fleet were certainly not close. It was an open secret that the two men did not always see eye to eye on the handling of the war. Ridgway, who had played such a pivotal role in reviving the Eighth Army in January, was naturally keen to keep a tight rein on his former command—so much so that Van Fleet sometimes felt smothered and complained that Ridgway was "all over the place" in Korea. On strategic matters, Ridgway thought that Van Fleet could be too "aggressive," that he wanted to expand the war in ways that were not militarily or politically feasible.[11] With the two men also acutely concerned about the image they presented to the world, it did not take too much to imagine that the PR gripes between the two commands would continue unabated.

Yet what was most striking about the military's information efforts during 1951 and 1952 was the fact that these underlying tensions, although ever present, were never truly damaging. In large part, this was because a basic division of labor had emerged by the summer of 1951. From July, Ridgway's PI officers concentrated much of their time and effort on handling reporters attending the armistice negotiations. Meanwhile, the Eighth Army PIO focused its energies on the tactical situation at the battlefront, conducting briefings, arranging billets, and facilitating communications for those correspondents still covering the fighting.[12]

When it came to censorship, the lines of authority were also clarified during the summer of 1951. Having witnessed at first hand the ill-feeling and resentment that had built up over MacArthur's "double censorship" policy during the early spring, Ridgway immediately recognized the need to centralize censorship functions. His problem was where to place ultimate authority. Both commands had exercised this function at different times, and any change seemed bound to ruffle some feathers.

Even before he took over in Tokyo, Ridgway had been sympathetic to the idea that ultimate censorship authority ought to be vested in the UNC, since only this higher command had all the relevant information on the overall strategic picture.[13] After his promotion in April, however, such a decision could easily be interpreted as a personal power grab, and so Ridgway decided to move with extreme care. To effect this centralization in the smoothest possible fashion, at the end of May he sent Welch to Korea on a five-day mission, charging him with "setting in motion a system of censorship aimed at expediting copy and photographs filed in Korea." The upshot of this trip was a formal commitment to end double censorship by the middle of June.

From then on, the UNC would take over all censorship functions, but its PAD clerks would be based at Eighth Army's headquarters, not Tokyo. By placing all censors closer to the action, it was hoped they would have a keener sense of the issues. By getting them to work alongside Eighth Army, it was expected that this would avoid some of the friction that had built between the two commands. And by centralizing the whole job under censors who had the authority to make judgments on all issues, it was anticipated that many of the problems that had plagued relations with the media over the winter would now be avoided.[14]

In many respects, this smoother relationship did materialize. In the first months of 1951, correspondents in Korea had been permitted to telephone their dispatches back to their Tokyo offices after the censors had cleared them. But this had allowed some unscrupulous journalists in Tokyo to reinsert information or to engage in "question and answer sessions" over the phone to probe for information censors had struck out. Now, however, PAD clerks would be in charge of transmitting all copy out of Korea. As well as ending the old question-and-answer loophole, this reform made moot the unpopular sanction whereby war theater correspondents could be suspended if their home office distorted their dispatches after they came in. The centralization of all these functions, along with the military's decision to take over transmittal, also promised to speed up the whole process, a fact that wire service correspondents duly noted and appreciated.[15]

Overall, these developments marked a big change from the first year of the war, when bureaucratic friction had often sapped the effectiveness of military PR activities. True, there was one important exception: the age-old enmity between the army and the Marine Corps. But even this feud was to have its upside. For here, it was the continued existence of friction that was instrumental in sparking a spate of significant improvements.

The Army versus the Marines

A year into the war, the Marine Corps had a fearsome reputation for aggressive selling. In the early days of the fighting, bureaucratic rivals had frequently complained that the marines were teaming up with pronavy reporters in order to attack the other services, and thereby drum up political pressure for more money and resources. In one notorious public outburst, the president had even suggested that the Marine Corps had "a propaganda machine that is almost equal to Stalin's"—a statement he soon had to retract amid a firestorm of protest from the marines and their domestic allies.[16]

Despite Truman's diplomatic retraction, the marines' reputation had considerable grounding in fact. During World War II, Brigadier General Robert L. Denig had "fathered" the idea of combat correspondents. At his suggestion, young reporters had been enlisted into the Marine Corps and given full training. They had then been sent into battle charged with writing copy for use by the national newspapers and with helping "civilian correspondents in any way they could."[17]

As soon as the marines appeared in Korea, this successful innovation was swiftly revived. At First Marine headquarters, Major Carl E. Stahey worked hard to maximize output. Using the extensive experience he had gleaned from years working in a range of Ohio newspapers, Stahey organized the PIO headquarters along the lines of a metropolitan newsroom. By November 1950, thirteen men had been allocated to his PI section—a figure that was soon raised to twenty-five. At any one time, Stahey could therefore send three or four combat correspondents to each marine regiment, placing them in a front-row spot to cover key events, such as the first liberation of Seoul or the harrowing retreat to Hungnam. From this vantage point, they produced a steady stream of copy, all of it extolling the exploits and virtues of the corps. Back at headquarters, Stahey and the other officers then acted as rewrite men and editors, refashioning this material "into proper news style."[18]

Back in the United States, many editors were drawn to the output of marine combat correspondents, with its punchy focus on the individual deeds of real fighting men, their successes against overwhelming odds, their humorous and irreverent comments at the height of battle, their toughness, and their never-say-die attitude. Some pithy comments by marines were already legendary, especially the declaration that the marines did not retreat, they simply attacked to the rear. But even on a routine basis, marine combat correspondents were adept at churning out human interest stories of heroism. Typical were the exploits of Joseph Vittori of Beverly, Massachusetts, who "virtually single-handedly, while bleeding from two wounds, . . . met one of the most ferocious mass charges of the Korean War and killed at least forty of the enemy before a grenade took his own life," or the comments of an enemy soldier now "sulking in a POW camp" who, when captured, was said to have exclaimed: "Me no more communist. Me no like to fight marines— they fight too hard!"[19] Receiving a constant stream of such stories, it was hardly surprising that editors would often sanction eye-catching headlines such as "MARINES SAVED UN IN KOREA."[20]

Of course, even for the well-organized marines, covering this distant, bloody, and grueling war presented innumerable problems. Like the army, marine PI officers often bemoaned the lack of trained personnel and new equipment, not to mention the complete absence of media sensitivity among the rank and file of the corps, who could easily spark a bad press with an offhand comment.[21]

What rivals saw, however, were not these practical problems but the steady flow of marine-friendly copy, which, they complained, seemed to dominate media coverage of the war. Floyd Parks, the army's chief of information, was particularly obsessive on the subject, for he was convinced that the marines were using their massive publicity advantages to belittle the army's contribution in Korea. It was becoming "fixed in the minds of the American people," Parks repeatedly complained, "that the army is being run over by the Chinese and the marines are going around picking up after them."[22]

Parks's biggest concern was that the army's patent PR inferiority might have a deep impact on morale. Part of the problem stemmed from the marines' unilateral announcement in February 1951 that they were instituting a rotation policy, which would enable those troops with extended battlefield experience to return home. Because the army had yet to act in a similar fashion, Parks naturally fretted that "every army man's relatives back in the States who reads this Marine Corps' publicity [will] wonder why the army can't take care of its soldiers in the same way."[23] More generally, with the military's mobilization plans predicated on drawing more than half a million men a year from civilian life into the army, Parks and his subordinates worried that the marines' PR preeminence allowed them to recruit the best of the bunch. Once in action, marine publicity also helped to build their troops' morale, perhaps to the detriment of army units. As Parks explained to Van Fleet,

> I certainly would like to see individual army units get credit similar to the marines. I don't want you to infer by this that I am opposed to the marines. I am not. I merely am interested in seeing that the army gets as much credit for its valor as the marines. As a matter of fact, I envy them their esprit de corps and the way in which every individual in the Marine Corps from private to commandant plugs for the marines on all occasions. I hope that at some future day this will be true about the army.[24]

As the last comment suggests, Parks, though often bitter about particular PR stunts by the marines, was determined to learn from them. In fact, whereas earlier clashes between the two had tended to have a debilitating effect on military public information, during 1951 and 1952 the continued friction now sparked something akin to competitive creativeness, as the army went to great lengths to emulate the achievements of its great rival.

For a start, Parks was keen to demolish the mounting impression that the marines were winning the war almost on their own. In large part, the absence of stories about specific army exploits stemmed from the fact that censorship rules decreed that individual units could not be identified in communiqués— a constraint that did not apply to the marines, who had only one division in Korea and who, in any case, bypassed the censors by sending much of their material directly to Washington. To rectify this problem, Parks began a prolonged lobbying effort to get the Eighth Army to relax its censorship regime in this sphere. He was especially concerned to boost the profile of the Second Division, which had fared disastrously over the winter of 1950–51. Along with Collins, he therefore pushed Van Fleet to specify in his communiqués the achievements of this and other army units, albeit without revealing the order of battle to the enemy.[25]

During 1951, the army also turned its attention to emulating the success of the marines' combat correspondents. As well as opening the Home Town News Center in Kansas City, Missouri, whose task was to try to place the army's own articles with local newspapers, the Eighth Army's PIO worked hard to make its output more appealing to editors. Combat correspondents were instructed to produce fewer but better stories, marking exceptional items so that headquarters could circulate them to civilian correspondents. Calls went out, too, for "some hard-hitting, well-written facts" about various platoons, regiments, and divisions, while researchers compiled a biographical release on each unit so that the PIO could issue it on request.[26]

Competition with the marines also prompted important army campaigns in the United States. In April 1951, the army finally announced its plans to rotate troops back home. By the summer, the army hoped to trump anything the marines could do by rotating twenty thousand men a month, based purely on length of combat experience.[27] In October, with GIs already complaining publicly about the intense cold, the Pentagon then made a bolder promise. In testimony before the Senate Armed Services Committee, Anna Rosenberg pledged that no combat soldier would have to spend more than one winter in Korea. Although many in the media were skeptical that this "risky promise" could be met, Rosenberg was quick to issue progress reports. And in January she triumphantly told legislators that of the quarter of a million American combat troops currently in Korea, only 80 enlisted men and 201 officers had been in the theater for more than fourteen months, and all of these were specialists for whom replacements were not readily available.[28]

When these men finally returned home, the army made sure they were met with appropriate fanfare. Out west, PI officials worked with numerous organizations to ensure that, as one revealingly put it, the "welcome was spontaneous and sincere." The local press in ports like Seattle and San Francisco were also keen to cover each episode. And to protect against a rapid ebbing of media interest, the Pentagon initiated a project to keep the activities of those who had done their bit in Korea before the public eye. Indeed, starting in September 1951, all PIOs working in the United States were "urged to publicize the return of reservists to their home communities. The 'hometown' phase of the program is now in operation."[29]

Learning

For the army, then, learning was at the heart of many of its PI initiatives during 1951 and 1952. But the army did not just learn from the marines.

After more than a year of war, many officers now had more experience and a better idea of what worked well. Senior figures also analyzed the major mistakes made in the first months of the fighting and then launched a concerted effort to ensure that these were not repeated.

One obvious lesson was the need to provide regular and informative briefings. Although secrecy was often vital, especially when it came to identifying tactical plans, excessive secrecy also created resentful reporters, who then tended to speculate or base stories on their own experiences and not the military's preferred line. As the UNC PIO concluded in July 1951, it was "significant that the critical tone of the news stories largely disappeared after official information was made available to the correspondents. The object lesson in this respect is that professional reporters at or near the scene of a major news event do not cease reporting simply because the flow of official information is turned off."[30]

In trying to avoid information vacuums, it helped that senior PI officers were more adept at providing the press with usable information. At the Eighth Army's headquarters, PI briefing officers strengthened their links to the intelligence section in order to acquire a clearer idea of the tactical situation. With the advent of censorship, PI officers could then pass this information on to reporters as background without worrying that it might end up in tomorrow's headlines. And, as the Eighth Army PIO noted, these changes in turn diminished "the possibility of half-informed correspondents" prematurely or unwittingly releasing "information that might be detrimental to tactical operations." For a similar reason, by the end of 1951, the Eighth Army instituted a program of supplemental briefings, normally held at the correspondents' billets in Seoul. These covered subjects often ignored in the daily tactical sessions—such as the role of army light aviation, the work of medical teams, and efforts to eradicate the guerrilla threat in southwest Korea.[31]

In the field, perhaps the most obvious problem of the first months of the war had been the lack of trained PI officers who were fully briefed on the military's preferred PR line and able to steer war correspondents in a particular direction. In fact, many of the so-called negative stories during 1950 had been the product of reporters bypassing the PI network altogether and interviewing disillusioned, battle-scarred GIs who had just survived harrowing battles.

A year later, with the influx of new PI personnel, enormous efforts were made to coordinate the military's message at the front as well as the rear. Before PI officers left for Korea, they attended a revamped fourteen-week course, with more time set aside for the practical work of dealing with the media.[32] Once they arrived in Korea, officers and enlisted men were invited to a series of conferences hosted by the Eighth Army PIO. These served a variety of purposes. Some were designed to acquaint all PI officers with "new problems, policies, and methods of coordination"; others were aimed at improving cooperation between the different layers of the military machine. In February 1952, the Eighth Army PIO also instituted a regular two-day staff orientation program. On the first day, new recruits were given the chance to meet reporters based in Seoul, and received briefings on how the correspondents' billets, censorship, and communications all operated. On the second day, they attended seminars with titles such as "Where the Information Section Fits In" and "What We [PIO headquarters] Can Do (and What We Can Do for You?) Administratively."[33]

All of this was a far cry from the haphazard and ad hoc nature of earlier media-military relations. As the war progressed, military public information became more structured, more bureaucratized. PI officers with hands-on experience had a better sense of what worked and what merely riled reporters. On the basis of this knowledge, they drafted guidelines and procedures at the center, and these were disseminated to the increasing numbers of officers working in the field. Although this occurred in all areas of PI work, nowhere was it more obvious than in the formulation of new censorship guidelines. Whereas the early Korean debates on censorship had been conducted in a crisis-driven atmosphere, with the military lurching into a series of actions that were not widely understood by reporters, now senior officers used their experience in Korea to devise a new set of rules.[34]

The "preparation of detailed plans, procedures, and directives, with respect to the establishment and conduct of field press censorship in combat areas" took up most of 1952. Inside the Pentagon, a joint working committee was established to hammer out an agreement between the services. Much of the legwork was done by Colonel Richard H. Merrick, an efficient, intense officer in Parks's Plans and Policy Office. As well as establishing clear rules, Merrick oversaw the drafting of a new curriculum at the Armed Forces Information School. Using both officers with recent experience in Korea and a set of practical primers as key texts, this revamped program aimed to educate a new generation of military men so that in the next crisis a lack of trained personnel would not be an excuse for avoiding censorship or establishing it in a clumsy fashion.[35]

When the plans to revamp censorship were first mooted, senior officials had presumed that the Korean War would be over and that the implementation of these new field guidelines would have to await the next Cold War crisis. By December 1952, however, with the truce talks bogged down and the stalemate war showing no signs of abating, Korea became the testing ground. Merrick, who had provided much of the drive for the project, was sent to the Far East for sixty days to put his theories into practice. Merrick's aim, based on his intensive study, was to liberalize procedures. He thought it particularly vital to reduce the role the intelligence and operation staffs played, convinced that such officers "cannot simply impose 'stops' but must demonstrate to the censor's satisfaction why important and newsworthy information should not be released." Underpinning Merrick's thinking was a positive view of the press. "The field press censor," his new guidelines stressed, "never forget that correspondents as a whole are reasonable human beings, above average in intelligence and public spirit. They are impressed with good reasoning and violently impatient with bad reasoning."[36]

And, crucially, reporters were indeed impressed. During 1951, the military continued to receive sporadic complaints about the inexperience of those working in PAD. From time to time, stories also appeared in national newspapers griping about the "erratic" implementation of restrictions, with rules and regulations being "formulated as the censors went along."[37] By 1952, however, these stories had ceased. And some correspondents even had kind words for the military's new operation. The army, stressed Walter Simmons of the *Chicago Tribune*, has not imposed "an arrogant censorship." "The censors," agreed Howard Handleman of the International News Service, "do not to my knowledge hold back anything except military security information."[38]

The Changing Nature of the War and Its Coverage

While the learning process the war generated was thus vital in sparking certain key improvements, it was not the only development at work. The nature of the fighting also changed dramatically after the summer of 1951, as both sides established elaborate defensive positions. And this in turn had a number of practical side effects, all of which ensured that the basic relationship between the military and media would now be far smoother.

For reporters, the war was now a less intense experience. Although this caused some problems, especially since attention back in the United States was starting to ebb and there were no longer opportunities to make a big splash, it also brought an obvious upside, for reporters now faced far fewer "rockets" from editors demanding that they be at the front. As Robert Schakne, a staff correspondent with the International News Service, explained:

> The daily tactical story, once the front page banner story across the country, is of less importance today. From day to day it changes little. The effort once concentrated on obtaining latest tactical developments, today goes into the search for feature stories and atmosphere pieces. It is a far cry from the days when competitors raced to file stories on the capture of a city or a major hill mass; today only outposts change hands, so competition centers around the feature.[39]

The more leisurely pace also made covering the war a lot less dangerous. During 1952, there were still a few casualties—in August newsreel cameramen were injured in a guerrilla attack on a train, and in October a CBS radio correspondent was wounded by shrapnel at the front—but nothing like the large numbers of dead and missing that had been a feature of the early days of the war.[40]

For the military, meanwhile, the lack of intensity also promised numerous payoffs. For one thing, major newspapers no longer sent their big hitters to the front. By mid-1951, of the correspondents who had won the Pulitzer Prize for their aggressive coverage in Korea, only Keyes Beech remained (Higgins was now a columnist, Bigart was in Europe, and Sparks was covering the U.S. election). In their place, newspapers across the geographical and political spectrum increasingly relied on the output of the big wire services, and this had two further benefits. Both AP and UP now tended to produce broad overviews culled from various sources. Because these contained no byline, AP and UP reporters were no longer so tempted to follow the path of, say, Kalischer and Lambert, who in the early days of the war had made a name for themselves through hard-hitting and controversial reporting.[41]

On a practical level, this growing wire service monopoly also meant that censors simply had fewer stories to process. Back in 1951, the PAD had often been forced to wade through more than ten thousand "takes" a month (a "take" being a portion of a story, normally 200–250 words long). This massive workload had made mistakes and misunderstandings almost inevitable, but it was now a thing of the past. During 1952, the pressure eased significantly. Not only did the PAD receive an influx of new personnel but its overall workload was effectively cut in half.

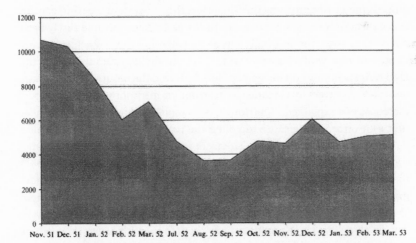

Volume of Censored Stories, 1951–53. Source: Far East Command, PIO, Staff Section Reports, November 1951–March 1952, RG 407, National Archives.

For reporters who remained in the Far East, basic living conditions also improved. In Korea, with the war settling down along a stable front, the Eighth Army could establish a more permanent headquarters to cater to correspondents' needs. In Seoul, the press billet was renovated during 1952, with hot water and electricity often available. As one journalist commented, "the food is [now] better, the billets cleaner and more livable, the rats, fleas, and lice under better control, the communication problem considerably eased, and the guerrilla and infiltrator problem eliminated in most areas."[42]

Equally important, correspondents now found it far simpler to get their stories out. By the middle of 1951, the military had established two relay stations, one at Eighth Army's main base in Seoul, the other close to the front. At both, the wire services placed a manager, who gathered all the incoming dispatches, passed them straight on to the censor, and after they were cleared sent them to Japan.[43] Meanwhile in Tokyo, the PIO had been organized along the lines of a newsroom of a large metropolitan newspaper. Equipped with two teletype machines, it was a massive improvement on the primitive organization of 1950. Indeed, whereas communications had been so poor at the start of the war that it often took journalists six hours to get their copy out, now the army had the facilities to handle more than three hundred thousand words a day. And even when there were occasional problems—such as faulty equipment or the mangling of copy in transmission, which, as the PIO ruefully noted at the start of 1952, "had become the source of considerable bad will on the part of the press toward the armed forces"—the military now had sufficient expertise to swiftly restore the service.[44]

From the military's perspective, the less intense, more stable nature of the fighting therefore had a number of important benefits. But perhaps the crucial change in Korea was the simple fact that it was now easier to control exactly where correspondents went. In the early days, this had rarely been the case. In 1950, the war had moved so swiftly that there was just no way to prevent reporters from witnessing firsthand the disasters that befell the Eighth Army in July and December. Now, however, the nature of trench warfare made reporters less inclined to head out for the front without an expert escort. As one explained, "it no longer is a simple problem to reach a combat unit as it once was, because too often the roads leading to the line of fire during daylight are impassable. There are many newsmen, of unquestioned courage, who think twice today of a front-line visit that two years ago would have presented no problem."[45] Moreover, with the battle line hardly moving, the military could also shepherd and monitor correspondents far more closely. Even with a high-profile event like the Koje-do riots, reporters were completely reliant on the military to fly them to the island, give them a tour of the facility, and brief them on what had occurred. When it came to the two major bouts of fighting during this period—the battles of September 1951 and October 1952—correspondents were similarly dependent.

The improved working conditions for correspondents at the press billet in Seoul. Courtesy of National Archives.

From late August 1951, Van Fleet launched a series of attacks in an effort to keep the enemy off balance. By capturing high ground around the "Punch-bowl" on the eastern side of the front, his specific goal was to prevent a communist attack in a vulnerable boundary between U.S. and South Korean troops. But the going was tough. Torrential rain hampered the movement of men and materiel. The North Koreans, firmly entrenched in a sophisti-cated defense line, fought tenaciously. And after weeks of intense combat, casualties were so high—an estimated sixty thousand UN losses between August and October, of which twenty-two thousand were American—that the target terrain of these attacks was soon being dubbed "Bloody Ridge" and "Heartbreak Ridge."[46]

For the troops caught up in the carnage, conditions were just as appall-ing as anything they had encountered at earlier stages of the war.[47] But, crucially, little of this reality was relayed home. At a time when the truce talks, although in recess, were still at a fairly early stage, Van Fleet was acutely sen-sitive to possible domestic criticism. In the first seventeen days of the fighting, he therefore instituted a total clampdown on news. It was not until the first partial victory had been achieved that the Eighth Army finally allowed cor-respondents to report that the UN had launched a series of "limited objective attacks" whose aim was to wrest key areas from the enemy "with a minimum of casualties to UN troops." Even then, this news was carefully orchestrated. In Tokyo, Ridgway released intelligence suggesting that the communists were preparing another major offensive and implying that the UN effort had been undertaken to forestall this. In Korea, Van Fleet told reporters that action was vital to the morale of his troops. "A sitdown army," he explained, "is subject to collapse at the first sign of an enemy effort." And he was determined to prevent his men from becoming "soft and dormant."[48]

All of these efforts cast a long shadow over how the battles were reported. Indeed, in the face of the army's determination to wield its censorship powers aggressively, media coverage was belated, vague, and largely favorable. In a number of accounts, for instance, the label "Bloody Ridge" was used *not* to describe the awful conditions faced by UN forces but to depict the terrible suffering of enemy troops, whose "positions had been shattered by a tremendous torrent of artillery—390,000 rounds." Moreover, because the censors only released the first stories on this battle after the target had been captured, the sacrifices could be depicted as worthwhile. As the UP put it in a typical and widely syndicated account, while the battle had only been won after more than two weeks of "savage fighting," the last stage had been nothing less than a rout, as "demoralized communist troops broke and fled, abandoning many starved and wounded North Koreans who were later taken prisoner. The final phase of an important allied victory was won without the firing of a shot."[49]

A year later, when the next offensive came, the military's problem was quite different, for it was the communists who now initiated the attack. But the Eighth Army's PR response was just as effective. Now, along with withholding certain information, Van Fleet's PIO exploited its growing new cohort of combat correspondents for the first time.

In October 1952, the first major flashpoint of this renewed fighting was White Horse Mountain, where South Korean troops were pitted against the Chinese. Because of the suddenness of the communist assault, few civilian reporters were in the area. And because South Korean troops were carrying the defensive burden, American correspondents would also have faced a language barrier that, as the Eighth Army's PIO explained, would have "prevented personal interviews." For these two reasons, the Van Fleet's command justified excluding the press. Instead, the military's own combat correspondents, working alongside the South Koreans, wrote stories on the spot and wired them to the Eighth Army's headquarters in Seoul, where the news agencies had little choice but to incorporate them into their own dispatches. In fact, as a triumphant officer calculated, PIO personnel were responsible for as much as 90 percent of all the agency-filed material on this story.[50]

By monopolizing the coverage, army combat correspondents ensured that coverage was, in their words, "authentic" and "reliable." It was certainly more disengaged. True, there were numerous comments about the "bitter" fighting, not to mention the destruction and casualties both sides were inflicted on each other. But unlike many stories that appeared in the first months of the war, these included no shocking eyewitness details. Perhaps the best indication of this was an AP report that appeared in the *Chicago Daily News*. Two years earlier, this newspaper had led the way with firsthand accounts by its star reporters Keyes Beech and Fred Sparks. Now it simply offered a wire service story of the most anodyne kind. "The crest of White Horse Mountain was a shell-shattered no-man's land," AP recounted. "It had changed twelve times in forty-two hours of almost continuous fighting."[51]

Lingering Problems

Thus, as the war settled down into a stalemate, a number of factors combined that made it easier for the military to sell: more personnel were recruited, guidelines and bureaucratic structures were streamlined, communications were enhanced, and censorship was made more effective.

True, not everything went entirely smoothly. Recruitment, for example, was a growing headache, especially by the end of 1952, for the UNC PIO found it difficult to retain staff, largely because lower ranking officers recognized they "could earn much more in civilian life."[52] Inevitably, censorship also engendered sporadic resentments, even if the overall day-to-day operation had now become much smoother. Perhaps the biggest clash occurred in December 1951, when one correspondent published a story that Ridgway had suffered a heart attack—an erroneous dispatch that immediately sparked an intensive investigation into how the censors had let it reach the public domain.[53]

Overall, however, the basic relationship between U.S. officers and American print reporters was far smoother. The central problem now occurred in the interactions between the U.S. PIO and the non-American journalists who were covering the war. The reasons for this were various. With the U.S. military dominating briefings, communications, and access to the fighting, foreign correspondents periodically claimed bias or rebelled at restrictive practices. In one flashpoint in November 1951, a correspondent from the London *Daily Telegraph* complained about discrimination, especially the censors' refusals to identify Commonwealth units. In another that erupted a year later, members of British and Canadian media joined forces to protest the U.S. navy's decision not to allow non-Americans to cover an action by a UN amphibious task force.[54]

Beneath these surface clashes, deeper problems existed. Often, PI officers were not terribly sympathetic to foreign reporters' different problems, approaches, and work routines. Hardly any American officers had experience outside their own country. In the final analysis, they also faced few political costs in ignoring the demands of the non-American press. Indeed, whereas the trials and tribulations of U.S. correspondents always made good copy for American editors, which in turn created political pressure for change, the complaints of foreign journalists were invariably met with deafening silence in the United States.

In some respects, this parochialism is surprising. As a number of historians have pointed out, new technologies were now making territorial borders more permeable. As a result, the American media could easily pick up on stories in the foreign press, turning foreign resentments into domestic political storms.[55] This, at any rate, was now possible. But for most of the Korean War, it was not how the U.S. media operated. As already mentioned (chapter 10), American newspapers gave little space to the enemy's efforts to make propaganda advantage out of the truce line. When it came to the foreign correspondents' gripes about how the U.S. PI officers treated them, most editors calculated that these had little news value in America. And those who did not ignore the story altogether buried it deep in their inside pages.

By 1951, newspapers and magazines were not the only media the military had to deal with. Television also presented a problem. With about a third of American households now owning TV receivers, the major networks were keen to enhance their coverage of the war.[56] As well as government-produced shows like NBC's *Battle Report, Washington* or DuPont's *Pentagon-Washington*, each network had fifteen-minute news slots each night, as well as longer debate programs on "egghead Sunday."[57]

In many respects, the U.S. military was in a strong position to influence this infant TV coverage. Cameras were cumbersome. It required three men to carry gear that weighed as much as 50 pounds, with cables, batteries, and sound equipment adding to their load.[58] Because it was so difficult and expensive to get such apparatus anywhere near the front, many television companies were happy to rely on the army's Signal Corps output—and in 1951 alone, the Pentagon's PIO provided the networks with some 55,000 feet of footage.[59] But even for more intrepid companies like CBS, who used their own crews, combat images were hard to come by. When Murrow presented his famous special *Christmas in Korea* in 1952, "the best picture he could get," he explained to his colleagues, was "a single GI hacking away at a single foxhole in the ice of the Korean winter or a guy on an icy road trying to change a flat tire in zero temperature."[60]

These were hardly the type of pictures guaranteed to generate outrage across the land, but television coverage did have its troubling side. Teething problems were partly to blame. Although the Signal Corps provided a good deal of the material the networks used, it was not always calculating when presenting images of the fighting. The worst instance came in October

1952. At a time when combat correspondents went to enormous lengths to influence print coverage of a new Chinese offensive, the Signal Corps released footage that, as the Eighth Army's PIO complained, focused on "the damage and destruction suffered by our positions and equipment but has shown little of what we have done to the enemy."[61]

The networks naturally seized on such windfalls with alacrity, but their own coverage could also contain a sting. Murrow's *See It Now* broadcasts were a case in point. In many respects, Murrow and CBS were keen to do the military's bidding. By sending camera crews to Korea to follow GIs around as they went about their daily routine of patrols, recreation, and rest, their aim was to construct an emotional bond between the troops and the home front at a time when the public's attention was clearly sagging. The troops were thus asked to introduce themselves, giving their names and hometowns. In an early incarnation of reality television, CBS wanted the viewer to connect and empathize with them as individuals. But there was an obvious snag. At the end of his broadcast, Murrow made a solemn announcement. Since filming, he intoned, half the men the audience had watched and come to identify with had become casualties in this ongoing stalemate war.[62]

Even in its infancy, then, television had considerable power to drive home the tragic costs of war. But this power should not be overstated. Only a minority of Americans had television sets. And even those who tuned in regularly were more likely to watch sports or entertainment. In short, TV was a medium for the future. Newspapers remained the major source of news in the 1950s. And it was in dealing with print correspondents that the U.S. military had been at its most effective.

"The Mess in Washington"

So even when these lingering problems are taken into account, the central process at work in the Far East during 1951 and 1952 was one of steady improvement, as the military tried hard to put an end to the majority of irritants that had plagued its working relationship with the press. Yet all of this could easily be overshadowed by what was happening in Washington. What, then, did officials in the increasingly embattled Truman administration do in its last months in office?

There were certainly problems. By mid-1951, the government was suffering from the normal tiredness and attrition that always seeps in after almost eight years in office. But while an infusion of new blood was vital, few men of caliber were willing to accept the call for a post unlikely to last past January 1953. This was particularly true in the State Department. Here, John Foster Dulles had performed a vital task since 1950, serving as the "bipartisan accommodator" and helping to dampen some of the worst Republican excesses.[63]

In October 1951, however, Dulles turned down Truman's offer of the ambassadorship in Tokyo with the biting remark that "there was no point being at the end of a transmission line if the power house was not functioning"—a decision and a comment that underlined the obvious fact that he was leaving the administration to become the Republican Party's leading spokesman on foreign policy.[64]

Nor was it easy to fill vacancies in PA. During the fall of 1951, the bureau received a vicious mauling at the hands of nationalist congressmen who questioned its domestic propaganda functions and proposed budget cuts of 25 percent or more in an effort to "seriously cripple" its activities. Although PA ultimately emerged largely intact, saved by a combination of intense lobbying by the White House and staunch backing by both loyal Democrats and congressional mavericks, it was clearly the new "whipping boy" for the Republican right.[65] Consequently, when Barrett resigned as assistant secretary of state for public affairs in January 1952, few leading lights were keen to replace him. As C. D. Jackson quipped when approached, "I would not touch Ed Barrett's job with a twenty-foot barge pole."[66]

Unable to appoint an outside specialist, Acheson turned to Barrett's deputy, Howland Sargeant. In many respects, Sargeant was an ideal choice, since he knew both how the department worked and how to get the secretary's ear. He also had a keen sense of the need to devise PR programs that would on the one hand "soften the punch" of the many attacks that were still directed at the State Department and on the other develop a positive approach on a small number of key issues where there were obvious target groups that could be swayed. But Sargeant would be operating in a highly constrained environment. For in an effort to dampen the Republican right's rising anger with PA, Barrett's old job had been split in two and the international component hived off to a businessman, Wilson Compton. Even then, Sargeant's new domestic duties were considerably narrowed. In February, he became merely "staff officer to the secretary on information matters."[67]

With the election campaign looming, Sargeant and his subordinates in PA recognized that they would have to be highly circumspect about what they said, shying away from anything that could be construed as helping Truman, Acheson, and the Democrats. Inside the Pentagon, too, caution was the new buzzword. In September 1951, Lovett had taken over as secretary of defense, after Marshall retired due to ill health. With Lovett on board, the president had someone in the Pentagon who was extremely well connected within the East Coast establishment; but Lovett was no public advocate. "I have only two claims to remembrance in Washington," he joked in early 1951. "One is that I'm the most photogenic man in government service, and the other is that [I] had only one press conference in five years during the [last] war. Now," he insisted, "I would hate to break either of those two records."[68] Indeed, Lovett was of the firm opinion that "the military is supposed to be and, in fact, is, I think, non-partisan." With the campaign starting to hot up, he was especially reluctant to go on the record, where his words could be "picked up by one side or the other and used as a battering ram." When his PR advisers approached him with a plan for public appearances, Lovett therefore readily agreed to make no more than one or two speeches every three months and restrict his engagements to those that had a "direct intimate bearing on Defense Department activities."[69]

Still, even now it was not all doom and gloom. Perhaps the most surprising success story of this period was Dean Acheson. Having weathered everything that the GOP had thrown at him in recent years, in mid-1951 Acheson started to receive public plaudits from some extremely unlikely quarters.

An important backdrop to Acheson's recovery was the conclusion of the Japanese Peace Treaty in September, an obvious success for the U.S. delegation. With Acheson leading the way, the Americans pushed through a generous settlement for Japan without totally alienating other Asian states, all while freezing the Soviets out of the process. It was a performance that, for the first time was seen by a national television audience, as the State Department "pushed hard" to ensure that transcontinental coaxial cable was installed before the conference convened—and an estimated 20 percent of the population duly tuned in to some of the conference.[70] More to the point, it was a performance that won widespread praise for Acheson, including "accolades" from none other than senators Bourke Hickenlooper, Alexander Smith, and Robert Taft. Acheson, observed *Time*, another unlikely convert, deserved thanks for his "urbane even-handedness and parliamentary precision."[71]

Soon afterward, Acheson's aides sought to capitalize on their boss's newfound popularity. In January, Lincoln White, the department's press officer, held a series of informal chats with leading members of the press corps. As he discovered, reporters had long viewed Acheson as "one of the most effective extemporaneous speakers in Washington," but they all felt that his strengths were rarely reflected in his press conference performances. "They fear that with the other burdens upon you," White reported, "you have unconsciously come to regard the weekly press conference as something of a bore, that you want to get through with it in the briefest possible time, with the least said the better." Armed with this critique, White, Sargeant, and other PR officials met to discuss possible reforms. What was needed, they agreed, was an end to the old "shotgun" approach, where reporters were free to fire questions "from all directions on all subjects." Instead, the secretary of state ought to focus each session more firmly on one issue per week. With Acheson sympathetic, his PR advisers devised a series of proposals for getting his public statements disseminated more widely, including an idea to ensure that every statement by a senior official in the department would "receive at least some attention on radio and television throughout the country, possibly by developing techniques of pulling out short and punchy excerpts for special use."[72]

Although some of these ideas proved difficult to implement, the fact that they were being mooted marked a far cry from a few months earlier. At the start of 1951, Acheson had been such a polarizing figure that his PR advisers had implored him to stay out of the public eye. By the summer of 1951, however, he filled part of the gap that the caution of PA and Lovett opened up. As well as playing a prominent role in the effort to explain the U.S. stance during the truce talks, he bore a large part of the burden when it came to a tediously familiar problem that suddenly reemerged with a vengeance.

This was the prospect of a letdown on the home front. As soon as the truce talks got under way in July, senior officials deemed it vital to launch a vigorous and innovative program to prevent any possible reversion to complacency, apathy, and withdrawal.[73] On Capitol Hill, the portents looked particularly ominous. With the Defense Production Act due to expire at the end of June, Congress was reluctant to renew it. In contrast to a year before, when legislators had been under enormous popular pressure to act aggressively, now right-wing Republicans returned to their normal posture of opposing excessive state interference in the economy, while many southern Democrats were reluctant to sanction further price rollbacks on agricultural products in general and beef in particular. This familiar alliance had begun to jell during May and early June, as both houses of Congress conducted hearings on renewing the measure. It was then given further impetus by the testimony of powerful interest groups, as industry, labor, and farm groups lined up to protest against controls that impinged on their own interests.[74]

For the administration, defeat on the Defense Production Act was unthinkable. As one informed observer pointed out, the vote on controls "will be taken as an index of the congressional mood on taxes, military spending, and foreign aid."[75] Desperate to prevail on this test-case issue, during the summer of 1951 the administration launched one of the most intensive publicity campaigns of the war. Its goal was to drum up the same sort of public demand for controls that had been evident a year before, not just by relying on the congressional hearings and keynote speeches but also by joining forces with the DNC and labor to reach out to the grass roots.

Although much of the administration's activity focused on familiar arguments, the issue's importance prodded many officials to develop a bolder message. Here Acheson played a vital role. As well as speaking out frequently, he recognized the need to persist with the radical rhetoric he had unveiled during the MacArthur controversy, with its faith that the Cold War would end not in stalemate but in an amazing American triumph. "We confidently believe that time is on the side of freedom so long as we make good use of it," Acheson declared in one speech. "We can meet the test of time better than they can. We have faith that free societies can out-last, out-produce, and out-build a police state, and can better stand the tensions of mobilization. We of the free world have geography, resources, manpower, and moral values on our side."[76]

In the first weeks of July, with the House debate coinciding with the start of the truce talks, administration efforts crescendoed. To put direct pressure on legislators, the chair of the DNC called on party members to "shower Congress with letters and telegrams," while the labor bosses at the ULPC, now firmly back in the administration fold, urged the 150,000 wage earners it represented to follow suit. With senior mobilization officials "barnstorming the country," the culminating event came on July 9, when Wilson made a nationwide radio appeal. "I am shocked to learn," the mobilization chief began, "that, even before a truce has been arranged, there is a movement in some quarters to wreck this country's defense program." It would be impossible to carry out the required mobilization drive, he insisted, without adequate economic controls.[77]

Like the boy who cried wolf, however, the administration's campaign now suffered from the law of diminishing returns. This was the third occasion that officials had warned against a letdown, and many Americans now tuned out. As the *New York Times* pointed out, "the administration's campaign was a fizzle." A Missouri Democrat who sent out twenty-six thousand questionnaires asking his constituents for their views on the issue got only

Acheson addressing the UN in 1952. Courtesy of National Archives.

one thousand back. As an official at the Capitol Hill Post Office concluded, "the people aren't writing any more than usual." An administration senator, when reporters asked him about the chances of a tough new controls bill, shrugged his shoulders. "There's no public pressure to keep or improve the present control on prices," he sadly concluded.[78]

Without such pressure, politics on Capitol Hill threatened to return to prewar normalcy, as a GOP-Dixiecrat coalition formed with the intent to stymie the government's efforts to pass significant domestic legislation. By the middle of July, the outlook seemed so gloomy that the administration's floor manager in the House conceded that Republicans and southern Democrats had "enough votes to put any kind of amendment into the bill it [the coalition] wants to"—a power they used to insert seven major amendments, all of which loosened controls the administration deemed vital.[79]

Yet ultimately the government's campaign was not without effect. According to one Gallup poll, 65 percent now favored controls, while 45 percent wanted them strengthened and only 16 percent were for termination. On Capitol Hill, the administration's attempts to translate such sentiments into usable pressure might have proved disappointing, but legislators were not entirely deaf to the official case. True, Truman suffered a clear rebuff on two issues: authority to control agricultural prices and a plan to give the president the power to build defense plants. But it could have been a lot worse. Toward the end of July, the Republican-Dixiecrat coalition finally started to crack, and in tense late-night sessions the House ultimately scrapped the wage and price provisions that officials regarded as an "inequity."[80]

When the bill finally reached his desk on July 31, Truman was angry and upset. The controls it sanctioned, he complained, were "gravely deficient" and threatened to spark rather than dampen inflation.[81] But the lame-duck president, faced with a major letdown on the home front in the wake of the truce talks, had at least been able to salvage something from a highly recalcitrant Congress. And the bill was not so bad that he felt compelled to hand down a veto.

Pentagon Propaganda

Meanwhile, across the Potomac, Pentagon officials were also busy. Just as Acheson and the president's economic advisers tried to salvage the Defense Production Act, the Defense Department launched three campaigns, all of which touched on Korea in some shape or form.

Recruitment was at the root of two of these. During the Korean War, the debate over who should be called up never reached the intensity of the Vietnam era. In these years, there were no protests about the way the draft operated, let alone efforts to dodge military service or burn draft cards. In fact, selective service was widely popular, both in Congress, where its extension was approved with wide bipartisan support in June 1951, and among mass opinion, with polls consistently finding that about 60 percent favored the current system. It was also remarkably successful, delivering 5.5 percent more men than requested during the first year of the war.[82]

Still, even with the success of the draft, each branch preferred to rely on volunteers, who were not only cheaper but also served a longer term of duty. For the army, however, this preference raised real problems. To begin with, the public widely viewed slogging GIs as far less glamorous than flyboys or sailors. For potential army recruits, the probability of being sent straight to the Korean front was hardly a major draw. But under the current censorship regime, this grim prospect was not even compensated by a chance to make a name, for the folks back home were only belatedly told what units had been thrown into in action. Inside the Pentagon, deeper fears also existed. As nationalist Republicans continued to talk about an emerging "garrison state," officers wanted to emphasize that the burgeoning size of the army would not result in the excessive militarization of American life. More practically, they had to reassure incoming recruits that time spent in the army was not time wasted—that GIs learned just as many transferable skills as those who went into the marines, the navy, or the air force.

For all these reasons, in late 1951 the army instituted an intensive effort "to contribute to the prestige of the infantryman." The military already had a contract worth almost a million dollars with the major advertising companies to drum up recruits for the services.[83] Now Parks drew up "a long-range plan to push the importance of the ground soldier into the public mind." As part of this campaign, the army worked with CBS to produce a thirteen-week television program that traced the progress of inductees through a training period, in an effort to show the public the discipline, team-building, and practical proficiencies instilled into new recruits. As well as dispelling myths about what went on in the army, all this activity was intended to demonstrate that recruits would fit neatly back into American society as soon as their enlistments were over. As a senior Pentagon official explained in July 1952,

> it is especially important that we convey a true picture of the *kind* of young men we are returning to civilian life: the benefits which they have derived from military service, their physical condition on their release (as compared with their condition on induction), their educational advancement under the army school system; a measure of their new technical and mechanical skills; an appraisal of the character and self-confidence which they have developed in training and combat.[84]

As more young Americans were called to arms, the military also faced an even thornier problem: race relations. Although the Pentagon had been at

Signal Corps Photo, November 6, 1950. Courtesy of National Archives.

the very center of this particular storm since 1948, when Truman had issued
an executive order calling for integration, during 1949 and 1950 implementation had been slow. Not only were many senior officers opposed to the idea
but integration seemed likely to alienate powerful southern Democrats on
Capitol Hill, many of whom controlled key committees. By 1951, however,
pressure was building for change. As personnel officers recognized, segregation was simply impossible to maintain, for the simple reason that black
Americans were now being drafted and volunteering in such large numbers.
Indeed, on the basis that the army in Korea would need twenty-five thousand

replacements a month, in the spring of 1951 the Pentagon calculated that the proportion of black recruits would be 15 percent for May, 21 percent for June, and 22 percent for July—and there was just no way all these men could all be placed in black-only units.[85]

Leading black spokespersons were also increasingly savage in their denunciation of the military's reluctant and laggardly implementation of a presidential order. At the very start of the war, the black press and leading civil rights groups had generally been supportive of the administration's Korean policy. Organizations like the National Association for the Advancement of Colored People (NAACP) had firmly supported Truman's decision to intervene. Like the government, they had framed the conflict in classic Cold War terms and had few qualms about calling for a decisive "victory over disruptive and sinister communist forces." On numerous occasions, African American newspapers had also expressed pride in the fighting achievements of individual black soldiers and airmen. But all these voices were also quick to condemn the continued existence of segregation in the armed services, which the fighting in Korea often threw into sharp relief.[86]

Black spokespersons were particularly irate about constant press reports that all-black regiments, such as the Twenty-Fourth Infantry, had a patchier fighting record than integrated units. The NAACP considered such claims to be politically motivated—"an attempt to discredit the combat ability of black soldiers and return them to labor duties." They were equally angered by the military's handling of disciplinary matters, particularly the courts-martial of thirty-six men in an all-black regiment. The NAACP even sent Thurgood Marshall to Korea and Japan to review these cases. And Marshall reached a damning conclusion. "The men were charged in an atmosphere making justice impossible," he declared. As long as segregation persisted, the military injustice dispensed in these cases was inevitable.[87]

During 1951, leading liberals in the Senate took up the cry of integration now. Hubert Humphrey and Herbert Lehman were firmly in the vanguard, both men deeming it unconscionable that the army had moved so slowly on such a vital issue. Crucially, too, key southern Democrats no longer stood in their way. Richard Russell, chair of the Armed Services Committee, told one Pentagon official in confidence that he could tell the secretary of the army "that I won't help him integrate, but I won't hinder him either—and neither will anyone else."[88]

Under mounting political and practical pressure—and with powerful legislative obstacles melting away—the army finally got its act together in the second half of 1951. Not only did it integrate those units fighting in Korea but also, in a marked change of direction, it unveiled its policy with great fanfare. During the first months of the war, with segregation still the norm, the military's instinct had been to avoid the whole issue. As one OPI official had pointed out in August 1950, its publicity policy was to issue "information to the press without special emphasis on the race of the individuals concerned. This, we feel, is in keeping with the spirit of considering our men in the service as Americans only."[89]

A year later, however, as integration finally began in earnest, the Pentagon suddenly viewed race relations as an achievement to be accentuated rather than a matter to be avoided. Pace, the army secretary, called it "a notable advance in the field of human relations." Senior officers in Korea chipped in with evidence that integrated units were extremely efficient in combat. And even the Pentagon's flagship radio show, *Time for Defense*, which ABC carried every Monday evening, now lauded the exploits of black troops, such as a "daring rescue" by the navy's "first Negro aviator," who was awarded a Medal of Honor and a trip to the White House.[90]

These recruitment and integration campaigns were important in generating more positive coverage for the military as a whole, but they only tangentially touched on the actual conflict in Korea. As the war dragged on, what was also needed was an intensive effort along the lines of the old World War II bond drives, which had played such an important role in focusing attention, generating support, and sustaining morale. In the late summer of 1951, the Pentagon began preparations for such a campaign. Its focus would be the somewhat unpromising subject of blood.

By the fall of 1951, reserves of dried human blood plasma were severely depleted. Although medics needed 300,000 pints per month to ensure sufficient reserves to treat Korean casualties, the figures for June and July were only 50,000 and 36,000 pints, respectively. To make up this enormous shortfall, the Pentagon decided to join forces with the Red Cross. In September, senior figures like Marshall, Bradley, and Ridgway began issuing statements and making speeches, imploring citizens to visit Red Cross centers to give blood. The Magazine and Book Branch of the OPI worked with a range of organs, including *Business Week*, *Collier's*, *Harper's*, and *Life*, getting them to publish posters, articles, and editorials to ram home the message. The Defense Department appointed a PR specialist, Paul Gaynor, to liaise with the Advertising Council, coordinating the enormous amount of material the council could disseminate through the radio and print media. And at numerous manufacturing plants, management and labor joined hands to encourage employees to boost the output in blood donor programs.[91]

Across the country, these efforts proved an immense success. To meet its goal, the Pentagon needed 75,000 pints per week. In the seven days before the campaign was launched, this figure was only a pitiful 9,537. By October 1951, however, supplies were up to 60,000, and by November the 75,000 target was regularly being exceeded. As Christmas approached, officials fretted that there would be some slippage, since the armistice negotiations seemed to be going well and the public was preoccupied with its annual shopping binge. But the Advertising Council specifically revamped its output so that it now had a "factual, emotional, and even *seasonal*" feel, with emphasis on "the idea of Christmas giving" and the need to make blood donation a New Year's resolution. As predicted, over the holiday period there was a dip in supplies for two weeks, but this proved temporary, and targets were regularly met well into 1952. As the Advertising Council was quick to conclude, this was undoubtedly "one of its most important as well as one of its most successful campaigns."[92]

It also helped to sell the war. To be sure, an important dimension of the message was hardly uplifting. "Korea," the OPI repeatedly stressed in its literature, "is one of America's costliest wars in numbers of casualties compared to forces engaged in fighting"—a fact that made the blood drive essential. But this campaign did allow the military to focus public attention on something that really worked: its medical teams in Korea. In the aftermath of the MacArthur hearings, the Pentagon was exceedingly anxious to undermine the GOP claim that American casualties were huge. It was especially keen to demolish the Republican effort to add battle and "nonbattle" casualties together. Now it had an ideal opportunity to shift the terms of the debate altogether. Although this was a costly war, military advertisements stressed time and again, overall death rates were far lower than in previous conflicts. "Out of every 100 wounded American servicemen who reach the most forward hospitals in Korea," asserted one poster, "ninety-seven are being saved." And the reason for this was clear: "Medical authorities credit this splendid record almost entirely to the prompt use of plasma and whole blood."[93]

By demonstrating what those on the home front could do in a practical sense to save lives, the blood campaign was also consciously aimed at forging a greater bond between civilians and fighting men. "I believe with all my heart that you will not permit the loss of [American] lives," Ridgway told his compatriots in November, in a typical comment. "I believe you will, each of you, within the next few days give of your blood to our men. To our men who daily and gallantly stand ready to shed their blood for you, having given your blood, I know you will feel a newer, deeper kinship for those who represent you in combat."[94]

Like all the other improvements introduced during the later stages of the war, the blood campaign was important because it shaped the way Americans perceived the distant conflict in Korea. The changes in the Far East helped to ensure that the old graphic micro-level stories of death, destruction, and defeat were no longer the central output of war correspondents in the field. To a lesser extent, the reforms and campaigns carried out by the administration in Washington served to focus attention on some of the more positive aspects of military policy at a time when war weariness and exasperation with the interminable truce talks were starting to mount.

These innovations, it is true, did not suddenly make the war massively popular. But when combined with the Truman administration's efforts to rededicate the war, they did help to create a relatively stable floor below which popular disapproval did not plunge. And with a presidential campaign about to begin, this was important, because the election and the conflict would inevitably interact in unpredictable, even dangerous, ways.

12

THE ADVENT OF EISENHOWER

O n June 4, 1952, Eisenhower returned to Abilene, Kansas. Although his main task was to lay the cornerstone for the new Eisenhower Foundation, his real purpose was politics. Two months before, he had asked to be relieved of his duties as NATO supreme commander. With a highly professional campaign team already in existence and with primary victories to his name in New Hampshire, Minnesota, and Oregon, Eisenhower was coming home to begin his formal bid for the presidency.

Naturally, Ike's campaign managers had gone to enormous lengths to guarantee the success of this opening event, arranging television coverage and taking "special pains to make sure that the newspapermen had a place to sleep, eat, and write."[1] But they could not legislate for the weather. By the afternoon, a torrential storm had turned the park surrounding the dedication site into a swamp. Although the planners had predicted a crowd of around fifty thousand, the horrendous conditions kept many away. The empty seats surrounding Ike's podium made a poor impression on the millions who had tuned in to watch the event on their televisions, but worse was to come. Eisenhower, no longer resplendent in his military uniform, wore a raincoat and gray suit, and as one account put it, "with a bald pate that was glistening with raindrops," he looked older than his years. Before delivering his speech, he even had to suffer the indignity of rolling up his trouser legs in order to wade through deep puddles. "Probably," Eisenhower recalled later, "no televised speech up to that moment was ever delivered under greater difficulties and more uncomfortable circumstances."[2]

It was not until his press conference the next day that Ike excelled, wooing reporters with a series of artfully constructed responses on the main issues of the day. On Korea, he was particularly cautious. The United States, he insisted, had initially intervened for legitimate and justifiable reasons. In the midst of a dangerous Cold War with an implacable enemy, it was neither possible to "retreat from the area we occupy" nor obvious that additional military steps would end the war swiftly. "In other words," he concluded, "I do not believe that in the present situation there is any clean-cut answer to bringing the Korean War to a successful conclusion."[3]

This opening statement was symbolic of the role Korea would play in the 1952 campaign. Although the conflict continued to drag on, and although there was an inevitable ratcheting up of the rhetoric as polling day neared, in a number of crucial respects both major candidates would help to take the sting out of it as a campaign issue.

Korea and the 1952 Election

That Korea would play a relatively muted part in the election was not inevitable. Had there been different candidates, the war would undoubtedly have been the subject of far more venom and bile, an unrestrained partisan brawl with both sides exaggerating its necessity and what it had achieved—something akin, in fact, to the midterm campaign of two years before.

And before July 1952 it did indeed appear likely that there would be different candidates. On the Democratic side, Truman's chances were bleak. Privately, he had long intimated to confidants that he would not run for reelection. With his approval ratings so low, it seemed merely a matter of time before the Democratic torch passed to someone else—someone like Estes Kefauver, the early front-runner who was making increasingly hawkish noises on Korea.[4] But Truman was a fighter. With no obvious heir, he refused to rule himself out of the running in the first months of 1952. And even if he failed to obtain the nomination, he still hoped to play a leading role in the campaign, influencing the choice of his successor, maintaining influence over the party machine, and launching a vigorous defense of his record.

In the past, Truman as a candidate had always been keen to strike savagely at his partisan rivals. And this year promised to be no different. In private strategy sessions, the White House planned to play hardball, hitting straight back at any effort to exploit Korea for electoral gain. "Republican leaders," one presidential aide suggested, ought to be assailed whenever they threatened to fiddle "with our frustrations on Korea by using fake labels and giving us phony prescriptions." They ought to be lambasted whenever they suggested an easy way out of the war.[5]

While the White House plotted strategy, Taft emerged as a real contender for the Republican nomination. In the primaries, he repeatedly labeled Korea "Truman's War." He attacked the excessive secrecy that had mired the United States in this "useless" and unnecessary conflict. He constantly reminded voters of MacArthur's recall, claiming that the war would already have been won "if we had followed the advice of our greatest soldier." And he ostenta-tiously pled guilty to not playing the bipartisan game. "It is the right and the duty of the Republican Party," Taft declared, "to point out the mistakes and the unbelievably bad judgment of those who have conducted our foreign policy."[6]

A Truman-Taft face-off would thus have presented the nation with a fundamental clash of opinions on Korea. And significantly, both men were intrigued and attracted by the prospect. In October 1951, the president told reporters that he hoped Taft would be the Republican nominee. A few days later, when Taft returned the compliment, the Ohioan's reasoning was revealing. "I don't want this to be a mutual admiration society," he explained in a press conference, "but I would like to see President Truman as candidate on the Democratic ticket. We then could go to the country on the real issues between the Republican Party and the Democratic Party."[7]

Yet this clash was not to be, in large part because both men were to become high-profile victims of Korea. By the spring, Truman's slim hopes were dashed. The steady flow of corruption stories about his administration had eroded away his popularity, but so had the persistent conflict in Korea. Despite a brief burst of optimism during the spring that an armistice might soon be concluded, at the end of March Truman formally announced his decision not to run.[8] After a long and painful courtship, he finally threw his weight behind Adlai Stevenson, the governor of Illinois, at the Democratic Convention in July. Truman's backing was extremely important in swinging the nomination to Stevenson, but he was slow to show his gratitude. Fearing that too close an association with the president would be political suicide, in the summer Stevenson adopted a posture of symbolic aloofness. Rather than base his cam-paign headquarters in Washington or New York, as was the custom, he set up shop in Springfield, Illinois. He then angered Truman by replacing the DNC chair with his own man, by his reluctance to ask the president to campaign, and by his tepid endorsement of the administration's record.[9]

Stevenson's style of campaigning was also very different from Truman's. Whereas the president reveled in what one Stevenson aide described as "tart or acidulous comments," Stevenson was an elegant, cerebral figure who spent more time crafting language to sell a positive liberal program than he did getting into partisan scuffles with the opposition. In recent years, he had "embraced a nonpartisan approach to state and local government."[10] Now he was convinced that candidates "for the presidency of the United States in this age and day, should not treat...[the electorate] as fourteen-year olds but as adults." More specifically, he wanted to shift the campaign away from the fraught subjects of Korea, corruption, and communism.

Stevenson naturally feared that all three were GOP issues that held out little prospect of success for the Democrats. But he was also convinced that they "were not really controversial issues at all," since no one wanted more graft, more treachery, and more casualties in a faraway war. "These were all questions of men and methods," Stevenson believed, "not of objectives or good intentions." Once he took to the stump, he wanted to turn the campaign into something more than a slinging match on tactics. He saw "a great opportunity to educate and elevate," to debate the fundamental issues of the day "sensibly and soberly," and to give the voters a real choice between two different philosophies of government.[11] In short, Stevenson had little time for the slashing partisan jibes that had been at the heart of Truman's furious whistle-stop tour four years before.

On the Republican side, meanwhile, it was a similar story of a more moderate candidate displacing a braying partisan. And again, Korea played a crucial role in the outcome, albeit for different reasons. Eighteen months before, in the immediate aftermath of the Chinese intervention, Taft had been convinced that his best chance for victory in 1952 lay in a series of furious assaults against the administration. But this campaign had soon created a backlash. With the primary season looming, moderates like Duff, Ives, Lodge, and Saltonstall were convinced that Taft was "backward-looking at home and utterly ignorant of the facts of life abroad." Worried that the Ohioan was the clear favorite with party bosses and could boast support from an estimated four hundred Convention delegates, they desperately began to search for an alternative. Among party regulars, there was no obvious candidate. Leading internationalist in the Senate were all too young or too lacking in charisma, while Stassen was widely believed to be overly opportunistic. Only Eisenhower seemed to have a chance of stopping Taft. But would Eisenhower leave his job in Europe? Would he be willing to campaign? Was he even a Republican?[12]

In trying to persuade Ike to run, GOP moderates had a number of advantages. They could rely on Eisenhower's intense ambition and desire for the top job. They could also garner support from a powerful network of political operatives and media luminaries, like Henry Luce, Paul Hoffman, and Lucius Clay, who had the knowhow and wherewithal to generate grass-roots support in the primary campaigns. And above all, they could play on the fact that Ike shared their deep distrust of Taft and the right.[13]

In early 1951, Eisenhower had arranged a private meeting with Taft to hear firsthand the senator's foreign policy vision. Before the meeting, Eisenhower had told his advisers that he would "kill off any further speculation about me as a candidate for the presidency" if Taft agreed to support America's broad involvement in European security arrangements. But the talk did not go well. According to Ike, Taft seemed to be "playing politics" with foreign policy, and was obsessed with "cutting the president, or the presidency, down to size." Disturbed by these sentiments, Eisenhower decided he would have to run for the top job, if this was the only way to avoid the GOP turning to such an unreconstructed isolationist.[14]

By early 1952, Eisenhower's premonition had come to pass: he was convinced that he was the only person who stood in Taft's path. From the very start, then, Ike's candidacy was not only based on the normal hostility toward an opposition incumbent. Crucially, it also revolved around his distrust of the Republican right and its sharp attacks on current Cold War strategy.

Indicative of Eisenhower's basic position was his instinctive sympathy with John Foster Dulles, the GOP's main bipartisan accommodator. In April, Dulles sent Ike an advance text of an article he was about to publish in *Life*. With its attack on the excessive passivity of the Democrats' containment policy and its call for the liberation of peoples languishing under communist rule, Dulles's article would shape an important component of Republican rhetoric in the upcoming campaign. But, befitting of someone who had been in government for the past two years, Dulles's critique was measured and limited. "The administration's policies are not without good elements," he insisted.

> They have evoked a show of national vitality which, even if somewhat ill-directed, has in many ways heartened our friends and caused the Soviet leaders some concern. In Korea—for all our failure to deter attack—we did respond nobly when the attack came. President Truman's decision that the U.S. should go to the defense of the Korean Republic was courageous, righteous, and in the national interest.[15]

This determination by both sides to take the most explosive foreign policy issue out of the campaign was nothing new. In 1944, Roosevelt and Dewey had reached an informal agreement not to mention prospective U.S. membership of the UN; four years later, Dewey had again devised a message that had scarcely found fault with the Democrats' handling of foreign affairs. Now, some internationalist Republicans wanted to formalize bipartisan consultation during the current election period. In a widely discussed plan, Alexander Wiley even proposed a series of meetings on "basic and continuing international problems" between the administration on one side and leading Republican experts on the other.[16]

In the early stages of the campaign, such procedures hardly seemed necessary. Eisenhower emerged from the GOP convention as the party's nominee, winning on the second ballot largely on the basis that he was the only Republican with sufficient standing and charisma to reverse the party's parlous record in recent presidential polls. Ike also had a platform that, despite rhetorical flourishes on "liberation," was widely depicted in the media as moderate, internationalist, and a firm rebuff to the Taft-Hoover-MacArthur wing of the GOP.[17]

Moreover, Eisenhower's Democratic opponent was a man who had so much respect for Ike's record that six months earlier he had wondered privately about his availability for the Democratic ticket. Once the campaign got under way, Stevenson also played up Eisenhower's moderation on the war. "My distinguished opponent," Stevenson declared in September,

> has already had occasion to disagree with conspicuous Republicans on foreign-policy issues. He has differed sharply with members of his party who have assailed the American action in Korea to stop and turn back aggression. He has gone further to set himself against the views of important members of his party who have called for enlarging the Korean War. I think he has done us all a service by saying these things.[18]

Yet as the fall campaign got under way, it became impossible to maintain this basic consensus on the war. Part of the problem was the Republican Party's desperation to win. Ingrained in the minds of all Republicans was the haunting memory of Dewey's shock defeat four years before, which was widely perceived to be a product of complacency and an aversion to hitting the Democrats where it hurt. Determined not to repeat this mistake, the Eisenhower team would ultimately stiffen its message. But in the weeks after the convention, its initial focus was on repairing the fissures inside the GOP.

On returning from a brief vacation, Eisenhower's first order of business was to make overtures to Taft, since the Ohioan's support would be vital in the crucial Midwest. On September 12, in Ike's home in Morningside Heights, New York, the two recent rivals reached an understanding. Taft agreed to campaign strongly for the Republican ticket; in return, Eisenhower pledged that if he won, he would consider nationalist Republicans for official positions and would work hard to reduce taxes. The Democrats immediately dubbed these concessions the "surrender" at Morningside Heights, but it would not be Ike's last effort to woo the right. He had already chosen Richard M. Nixon as his running mate—a shrewd decision, since Nixon was both an internationalist in foreign policy and a notorious diehard when it came to hunting internal subversives. At the end of September, in a campaign trip to Wisconsin, Eisenhower not only appeared with McCarthy but also agreed to delete a passage from his speech praising Marshall—a move that, given McCarthy's vicious attacks on Marshall, was widely seen as Eisenhower betraying his old mentor in a bid to buy support from the most extreme wing of the GOP.[19]

Ike's visit to Wisconsin came during one of his grueling whistle-stop tours. As he traveled through thirty-seven states, delivering brief remarks from the back of the train or making bigger set-piece addresses in city centers, his message slowly evolved. Recognizing that theirs was the minority party, GOP publicists drafted a plan aimed both at the party's twenty million or so core voters and at an estimated forty-five million "stay-at-homes" who only bothered to go to the ballot box "when discontent stirs them to vote against current conditions." Both groups, party bosses thought, could be won for Eisenhower if he savagely indicted Truman's record in three areas: corruption, communism, and Korea.[20]

Increasingly, Ike and his staff agreed with these conclusions. They thought it necessary to attack the administration on the corruption issue, so as to capitalize on the growing consensus that the Democrats had become stale and dishonest after twenty years in office. Ike and his staff were also determined to indict "Acheson's disastrous foreign policy." Indeed, although Eisenhower was leery of making too much of the controversial notion of "liberation," he was keen to batter the administration on its broader mobilization program. In speech after speech, he insisted that the country needed a national security strategy that did not doom it to excessive taxation, cumbersome controls, and eventual economic collapse. Reprising the party's vigorous campaign rhetoric of 1950, he even lambasted the information strategy the administration had used to sell its mobilization plan. The United States, he told an audience in Baltimore, had to end the current "stop-and-start planning," which emanated from the government's "swing[s] from optimism to panic." National security, he insisted, required "plan[ning] for the future on something more solid than yesterday's headlines."[21]

When it came to Korea, however, Eisenhower and his advisers remained far more moderate, at least in the first phase of the campaign. True, during September Ike often spoke about the United States "stumbling" or "fumbling" its way into war. He also linked the conflict's causes to the famous litany of events: the "loss" of China and Acheson's reckless announcement that Korea was outside America's "defensive perimeter" in Asia. And he referred repeatedly to the 117,000 casualties the country had suffered, before coming to the inevitable conclusion that it was time for a leadership change at the top.[22]

But Ike's rhetoric had another dimension, too. Apart from recommending that South Korea carry more of the burden, he offered no panaceas for ending the war and was adamantly opposed to echoing MacArthur's calls for escalation. Despite suggestions from his speechwriters, he was reluctant to repeat the staple charge that the Democrats were the "war party" who had presided during America's past four conflicts. Above all, he was determined to stress the basic legitimacy of the conflict. "I proudly salute the gallant American fight in Korea," he declared in his major foreign-policy address in September. "Moreover, I believe that the decision to fight to hold Korea ... was an inescapable decision."[23]

The problem Eisenhower faced was that such statements hardly set the campaign on fire. They also intersected with other troubling questions. Had Ike's attempts to appease the Republican right alienated moderate voters? What about Nixon's place on the ticket, which was called into question in the middle of September by press allegations that he had benefited from a "secret fund"? Although Nixon effectively countered this accusation in his famous

"Checkers" speech, Eisenhower's headquarters continued to be racked with growing pangs of doubt and alarm.

By the end of September, polls revealed that Ike still had a commanding nine-point lead over Stevenson. But senior Republicans, obsessed by Dewey's 1948 defeat, reacted to every subtle shift in the popular mood with exaggerated alarm. "There is a great amount of ferment and unrest," the campaign's pollsters recorded at the start of October, and "the trend is generally down. It must be stopped."[24] Agreeing with this gloomy assessment, Eisenhower and his advisers thought the time was ripe to place the campaign "on another level."[25]

But what exactly did this mean? How could Korea best be exploited? In the weeks before polling day, a combination of factors would merge to provide Eisenhower with the perfect answer.

One development was the ebb and flow of partisan politicking, the normal action-reaction cycle that characterizes any campaign. Thus far, the Democratic campaign had lagged in vital areas. Organizationally, Stevenson's Springfield-based team had been slow to construct close relations with the party's highly influential local bosses, whose support was vital in getting out the vote in the big urban areas. In the South, many key figures remained deeply resentful of Truman's civil rights record and highly suspicious of a Democratic nominee who was ready to embrace it.[26]

When it came to dealing with the media, moreover, Stevenson made elementary mistakes. Throughout the campaign, he used only the standard thirty-minute television slots, not the short, snappy commercials developed by the Republicans. Even then, he was so loquacious that the television networks sometimes had to cut him off in midsentence when his speeches dragged on beyond the allotted time. The central problem was his perfectionism. Supported by an enormously impressive speechwriting staff, which included Arthur Schlesinger, Jr., Kenneth Galbraith, and David Bell, Stevenson spent hours polishing his public utterances, and rarely left his aides sufficient time to gauge whether a speech would be too long. As one friendly commentator conceded, he also "gave reporters constant trouble—they could never count on getting his copy in time to meet their deadlines."[27]

Unable to keep pace with Eisenhower either on organization or fostering party cohesion, Stevenson had to rely on his lofty rhetoric, as he traveled some 30,000 miles across the country and delivered more than 250 speeches. In his early statements, Stevenson was determined to fulfill his own high standards. "He has been analyzing, not asserting," Eric Sevareid recorded on October 2; "he has been projecting, not an image of the big, competent father or brother, but of the moral and intellectual proctor, the gadfly called conscience." On Korea, Stevenson's approach not only meant backhanded compliments for Eisenhower for defying the GOP diehards. It also translated into at least one high-minded speech at the start of the campaign in which he depicted stopping communism in Korea as the essential prerequisite for undertaking America's main task in Asia: a developmental aid package that would help aspiring nations to govern themselves and develop their resources. On another occasion, Stevenson also did something almost unheard-of in modern politics: he admitted that his side had made mistakes—that demobilization had proceeded too swiftly in 1945, that the Soviets had been allowed to develop undue military superiority in the next couple of years, that a security guarantee ought to have been extended to South Korea before the war, and that "it might have been wiser if American forces had not crossed the thirty-eighth parallel in the fall of 1950."[28]

Of course, such candor and contrition hardly went down well with Truman, who had been in charge when all these "mistakes" had been made. As the campaign entered its final weeks, the president was determined to hit the road to defend his own record against the explicit attacks from the Republicans and the implicit censure of his own candidate. By now, the relationship between the two leading Democrats was extremely strained, but within days Stevenson recognized the splash made by the president's spirited efforts. Behind in the polls and smarting at Eisenhower's willingness to embrace GOP extremists, Stevenson decided to sharpen his own attacks. The GOP, he began to stress, was "hopelessly divided over foreign policy." An Eisenhower administration, he continued, would be in thrall to the right wing in Congress. And to cap it all, Ike's notions of liberation were "dangerous" and "reckless" in the extreme.[29]

On Korea, Stevenson increasingly assailed Ike for his selective use of history, for participating in decisions that he now attacked, and for deliberately distorting the content of Acheson's "defensive perimeter speech." As the campaign reached its culmination, he also made his most impassioned statement on the reasons for intervening in the first place. "Every one of us knows in his heart why we have to stand up and fight in Korea," he told a television and radio audience. "We all know that when the communists attacked across the thirty-eighth parallel that was the testing point for freedom throughout the world."[30]

Yet these barbs and justifications were a difficult sell in the last weeks of the campaign. In the early summer, public support for the war had remained surprisingly robust, even after the POW issue reached an impasse and the Koje-do camps erupted in violence. But this would not last. At the start of October, the moribund truce talks at Panmunjom went into indefinite recess, after senior officials agreed that the enemy would only listen to renewed military pressure. Later in the month, a series of high-profile propaganda tirades from the Soviet delegation at the UN General Assembly session confirmed that diplomacy was at an impasse.[31] Across the country, editors began to ask: "How long must we go on without a plan?" For many, the only alternative was massive escalation. On the West Coast, the *San Francisco Chronicle* and *Los Angeles Times* endorsed the bombing of Manchurian air bases. On the radio, ABC commentators advocated a blockade of the China coast. And on Capitol Hill, a subcommittee of the Armed Services Committee toured the Pacific and returned home to call for the use of Chinese nationalist troops.[32]

Although senior officials continued to oppose these familiar panaceas, the Pentagon did endorse a new bombing campaign to "ginger up" the peace talks.[33] But rather than still domestic dissent, these raids merely whetted the hawks' appetite for more. This became clear at the end of June, when the air force launched a series of massive strikes on hydroelectric installations in North Korea. As well as bipartisan anger at the British government, which was outspoken in its criticism of the American bombing, this episode provided the backdrop to a series of belligerent comments from U.S. legislators up for reelection. "We should go all-out in Korea or get out entirely," Representative Harold A. Patten (D-AZ) insisted. "The time has come to quit pussyfooting in Korea," Representative Lawrence H. Smith (R-WI) agreed.[34]

To make matters even worse for Stevenson, during October the ground war suddenly flared up. On the October 6, the Chinese communists launched an assault on White Horse Mountain, in the center of the allied line. For ten days, the enemy sent wave after wave against UN positions, failing to dislodge South Korean troops but inflicting substantial losses. In response, Van Fleet initiated a series of counterattacks that "resulted in bitter and costly fighting for several inconsequential hills"—so costly in fact that they resulted in nine thousand casualties during the month.[35]

This bloody battle, as Albert Warner pointed out to his NBC listeners, "did not sound like an armistice negotiation, it did not look like a police action; it was war." On the right, the Hearst and McCormick newspapers took the communist assaults as irrefutable evidence that fifteen months of truce talks had "accomplished nothing except the buildup of the enemy's strength and the waste of American lives." And even moderate opinion reached ominous conclusions. According to commentators like Walter Lippmann and Walter Millis, for instance, this new fighting pointed in one obvious direction: a large number of GIs would have to remain in Korea indefinitely. As Millis glumly asserted in the *New York Herald Tribune*, "it will be a long time before the South Koreans, brave as they are, or any other non-industrialized Asian peoples, can wage independently and on their own the kind of war" being fought in Korea.[36]

As the election campaign entered its final phase, many Americans responded to these stories with frustration, dissatisfaction, and even disgust. Whereas in January only 33 percent had viewed Korea as one of the gravest issues facing the country, by October this figure had shot up to 52 percent. More significantly, as Election Day neared, one poll found that 56 percent of the population had reached the conclusion that "the war in Korea was *not* worth fighting"—a level of disillusionment not recorded since the depths of defeat in January 1951. And another survey recorded that a plurality of 40 percent felt that our government had not done "all it should have done" to keep the communists from invading South Korea in the first place.[37]

With the electorate clearly pained by events in Korea, Eisenhower had an obvious opportunity to energize his candidacy. On October 24, in a nationally broadcast speech delivered in Detroit, he placed Korea squarely at the center of the campaign. "In this anxious autumn for America," Eisenhower began, "one fact looms above all others in our people's minds....One word shouts denial to those who foolishly pretend that ours is not a nation at war. This fact, this tragedy, this word is: Korea." The country, he continued, could not rely on the Truman administration "to repair what it failed to prevent." This task required new leadership. It also needed a "personal trip" by someone with impeccable credentials in war and peace. "I shall make that trip," Eisenhower concluded. "Only in that way...[can] I learn how best to serve the American people in the cause of peace. I shall go to Korea."[38]

By common media consent, this simple statement changed the whole dynamic of the campaign. "That does it—Ike is in," reporters immediately told Eisenhower's campaign chief. According to moderate newspapers like the *New York Herald Tribune*, in one sentence Eisenhower had "raised the spirits of men and cast a sudden ray of hope over a scene that has been obscured by uncertainty and doubt." He had tapped into the growing unpopularity of the war, coming up with a formula that, combined with his own enormous prestige, suggested to many voters that he was the one man who could end the bloodletting.[39]

Moreover, seen from a slightly different perspective, Eisenhower, like numerous other candidates running for office, had also fueled the public's disillusionment with Korea. Indeed, by October there was a symbiotic and circular relationship between the campaign and the war: as the conflict dragged on it became increasingly unpopular; this naturally encouraged candidates to attack it; and this in turn helped to fuel the domestic discontent. Eisenhower's pledge to visit Korea was the most high-profile, if vague, manifestation of this process. But even Stevenson was caught up in the logic. In his closing speech on election eve, he dubbed the war a "miserable stalemate."[40]

All the same, it is important not to exaggerate this dynamic. Although the campaign helped to undermine support for the war, it could have been a lot worse. As already mentioned (see chapter 11), the battles that erupted in the weeks before polling day were covered *not* by aggressive civilian reporters but by the army's own combat correspondents who presented a highly sanitized version of the fighting. Back in America, meanwhile, Eisenhower never challenged the basic legitimacy of the conflict.[41] And even his pledge to go to Korea was essentially a moderate statement. "The origin of the speech was simple and inexorable in political logic," its author explained later. "It rose from the need to say something affirmative on the sharpest issue of the day—*without* engaging in frivolous assurances and *without* binding the future administration to policies or actions fashioned in mid-campaign by any distorting temptations of domestic politics." In other words, its goal was place Korea at the center stage of the campaign, but without embracing the simple panaceas of escalation so beloved of the Republican right, and in such a way that a future Eisenhower administration would retain freedom of maneuver.[42]

On Election Day, Ike's restraint was to prove successful as well as statesmanlike. Across the nation, he garnered an impressive 55.1 percent of the vote, compared to Stevenson's 44.4 percent, which translated into an Electoral College victory of 442 to 89. Vital in this big win was the support of moderates, both independents and registered Democrats. This became clear in the elections for the Eighty-Third Congress, where Ike ran well ahead of the rest of the Republican ticket. Although his coattails were big enough to drag in a twelve-seat majority for the GOP in the House and a single-vote majority in the Senate, some of the most vocal critics of the war did not fare particularly well. Extremists like McCarthy and Jenner ran far behind him. And, significantly, Harry Cain of Washington state, who had been the most vocal critic of Korea on the floor of the Senate during 1951 and 1952, was easily defeated by a Truman Democrat, Henry "Scoop" Jackson.[43]

Of course, Korea had not been a vote-winner for the Democrats. On the contrary, this increasingly unpopular war had helped end their twenty-year hold over the White House. Most close analysts of the result also concluded that the voters had expressed a clear desire for a swift exit from Korea. Nonetheless, Eisenhower's campaign statements had not committed him to a specific course of action; they had merely provided him with a degree of flexibility he could use to find a way out of the Korean morass in the less frenzied postcampaign environment.

Transition

At 5:30 in the morning on Saturday, November 29, Eisenhower and his party left New York City for Mitchel Field, where two large Constellation airplanes were waiting to take them on the first leg of the long journey to Korea. After brief stops in California, Hawaii, Midway, and Iwo Jima, the president-elect landed at Kimpo Airport on Tuesday evening (Korean time). Security was intense, for the Korean police believed that 138 communists remained at large in the vicinity. But this was not the only inconvenience. After balmy weather across the Pacific, Ike and his advisers were immediately struck by the intense cold of Korea. As they were driven in an armed convoy through the streets of Seoul, they were also shocked by the scars of war—block after block of rubble, hundreds of thousands of Koreans using the remnants of buildings as primitive shelters, thousands more refugees outside the city gathered around fires, and black market hawkers "selling everything from a hairpin to a jeep."

Still, amid the chaos and destruction, Rhee's government had made an obvious effort to provide a fitting welcome. Everywhere there were large posters of Ike that bore an uncanny resemblance to Rhee, while banners and illuminated signs had been strung across telephone poles proclaiming "Welcome President-elect Eisenhower," "Destroy Communism," and "Unification Under a Free Korea."[44]

During the next three days, despite intense activity, Ike's much-touted trip was to prove little more than a series of troop inspections and meetings with senior officials. In a sense, it resembled Truman's PR-driven visit to Wake more than two years before. Indeed, although Eisenhower now had an opportunity to ascertain the strength of the enemy, the morale of GIs, and the fighting qualities of the South Korean forces, this trip, like the earlier Wake conference, was largely devoid of concrete results.

In stark contrast to Wake, however, it did prove a real hit with the media. This was largely due to mechanics. Whereas Truman's journey across the Pacific had proven little short of disastrous in terms of his dealings with the press, especially since correspondents had found it difficult to

Eisenhower's trip to Korea, December 1952. Clark is behind Ike. Courtesy of National Archives.

access and file the story, Ike's trip would reveal the operation of a smooth, professional PR outfit. And partly as a result, Eisenhower would escape the condemnation that had earlier been thrown at Truman.

Yet this success was not inevitable. Before Ike left, his press secretary, James C. Hagerty, headed off a potential storm of protest by finding extra spaces on the plane for wire correspondents.[45] Once the president-elect hit the ground in Korea, similar problems threatened to intrude. In anticipation of this trip, the population of the press billet in Seoul had recently risen from 40 to more than 110. With security paramount and transportation scarce, the military, after consulting reporters, arranged to set up two pools, both composed of twelve representatives, who would travel with Eisenhower each day.[46] But this immediately raised the question of whether to exclude members from the United States or the international wire services. Hagerty again provided the solution. Recognizing that Eisenhower was determined to give this trip an overwhelmingly American flavor and focus—if only to placate members of his own party who had been convinced that Truman had conceded too much to America's allies—Hagerty decided to extend this policy into press relations. "I said we'd cut the three [American] wire-services into each pool," he explained; "after all, Ike was president-elect of the U.S. and the American wires were entitled to complete coverage."[47]

With media representation settled, Hagerty worked closely with the Eighth Army's PIO to ensure that correspondents had plenty to report. A few hours after Eisenhower's arrival, Hagerty visited the press billets to apologize for the fact that correspondents had been prevented from witnessing the touchdown, explaining that it was all down to security. He then tried to compensate by providing them with "a blow by blow description of our 'escape' from New York City and our trip to Korea," detailing how journalists back home still thought that Ike was in his Morningside residence, hoodwinked by press releases of dummy meetings. More substantively, Hagerty also promised them daily briefing sessions at 8:30 each evening, where he would provide details of that day's events.[48]

The trips themselves were logistical nightmares—flights near the front, landings on dirt strips or, when these were vulnerable to enemy artillery, long jeep drives in the bitter cold. Yet despite all the hardship, officials went to great lengths to make life easy for reporters. Along with Hagerty's constant attentiveness, the army's top PI brass was on hand to make "the spot decisions, which solved problems as they arose and contributed to the smoothness of the operation," from chasing up transport to ensuring that equipment caught up with the two press pools. Although a news blackout was in force until Eisenhower was safely on his way home, the Eighth Army's PIO also worked hard to ensure that copy on each day's events flowed out of Korea in a timely and efficient manner, providing two special daily couriers to relay material to Tokyo and another jet plane to fly out any "last-minute material."[49]

And by all accounts the press was highly pleased with this service. Hagerty was certainly a hit with reporters, who appreciated his flexibility, diplomacy, and tact, not to mention his extraordinary efforts to meet their needs in a timely and efficient fashion. In Korea, the military also came in for enormous praise. The AP bureau chief in Tokyo commended "its fine performance and outstanding cooperation," and considered the whole event "the finest PIO job we've ever seen in this theater." The Far East correspondent of the *Christian Science Monitor* echoed this sentiment, reporting that the number of "slip-ups appears to have been microscopic," before congratulating all concerned for providing material in good time for the first edition after the blackout. "As on no other occasion within memory," the UNC PIO happily recorded, "the press corps went out of its way to show appreciation."[50]

Significantly, this smooth media operation also rubbed off on the coverage. Commentators in the press and on the radio, as PA pointed out, were quick to list a string of definite "gains" from the trip, including the fact that Eisenhower "has come away with a firmer grasp of the situation"; that "the potentialities of the South Koreans as soldiers have been seen and studied[;] and that the 'complications' in our relations with the South Korean government have been assayed." When Ike released a statement about the trip, while sailing aboard the *USS Helena* on his leisurely journey home, media comment was even more favorable. Although he warned the country that there were no "panaceas" for ending the war and offered no clear policy prescriptions beyond the need for "deeds," not "words," his ambiguous comments received almost universal praise. "The president-elect has satisfied virtually all schools of thought," PA recorded.

> In fact, many of those who opposed the general in the presidential campaign have happily concluded that the visit to Korea brought Eisenhower amazingly close to President Truman's and Governor Stevenson's concepts of the Korean problem. Among the president-elect's supporters, both those who demand a more vigorous military policy in the Far East and those who stress the risks involved were encouraged by Eisenhower's statements.[51]

This first venture was a big boost for the incoming Eisenhower team, but in one respect it owed as much to the past as to the future. The highly professional PIO operation in Korea was, after all, merely the culmination of all the steady improvements the military had made over the past eighteen months, as PI officers used their acquired knowledge to avoid the friction that had been common during the first six months of the war.

In Washington, the outgoing Truman administration believed it had lots of additional lessons to teach Ike and his advisers, and in November and December it invited them to a series of briefing sessions.[52] Like most incoming administrations, however, Eisenhower's was largely deaf to this well-meaning advice.

It had just won the election by repudiating, not endorsing, the incumbent. During the campaign, Ike had savagely attacked Truman's "mismanagement," which, he argued, had involved an inability "to develop a comprehensive, integrated, national strategy." Once in office, the new president would move to implement a variety of structural changes. In place of Truman's system, which Eisenhower deemed too sloppy and too reflective of each department's parochial concerns, he wanted a far tighter operation. The focal point would be the regular weekly meetings of the National Security Council. These would be attended by fully briefed senior advisers, supported by a planning board whose task would be to look beyond messy compromises forged by warring departments, and chaired by a president who would take firm control over the decisionmaking apparatus.[53]

On assuming office, Eisenhower was also determined to pay close attention to selling his policies. He hoped that his tightly coordinated national security system would be less prone to the debilitating public clashes that had scarred Truman's tenure, but this was only a start. In Ike's opinion, it was also essential to make a major effort to win over Congress, partly to avoid Truman's obvious failures on the Hill but also because the nature of his congressional party. Along with having only razor-thin majorities in both houses, the GOP remained deeply divided.[54] It also had little experience of supporting the incumbent in the White House. As Eisenhower explained to his cabinet nominees just days before taking office, congressional Republicans had been so used to a Democratic president that their instinct was to automatically oppose anything that came from the executive branch. "Now that we have a Republican Congress their job is to hold up the hands of the executive departments, but they have not learned that yet. It hasn't become part of their automatic thinking. Their automatic thinking is to tear them down."[55]

To protect himself against these destructive tendencies, Eisenhower planned to meet with Republican leaders at least once a week. He also appointed Major General Wilton B. Persons to head his congressional liaison office. A warm and cordial man, Persons had enormous experience, having performed this delicate task for the army. As well as keeping the fractious Republican right on board, Persons put feelers out to many key Democrats, for Ike was determined to try to obtain as broad a consensus as possible, especially on foreign policy issues.[56]

The first obvious flashpoint between the new administration and the new Congress would be the ratification of new appointees. Although Eisenhower selected a number of well-known businessmen for key positions—such as Charles E. Wilson of General Motors, who became secretary of defense, and George M. Humphrey of the Mark A. Hanna Company, who became secretary of the treasury—his failure to consult with Taft beforehand created early resentments.[57] And the Taft wing was even less enamored with Eisenhower's proposed foreign policy team, which was generally drawn from East Coast internationalists. The main controversy in the early months of 1953 centered on the nomination of Charles Bohlen as ambassador to the Soviet Union, a choice the Republican right hated because of the prominent positions Bohlen had occupied in the Roosevelt and Truman administrations. But even less contentious appointments, like Dulles as secretary of state or Lodge as ambassador to the UN, did not sit particularly well with nationalists. To compensate, Dulles picked his subordinates with care, bringing on board Scott McLeod, a former agent of the Federal Bureau of Investigation and a current ally of Styles Bridges, whose appointment to oversee internal security was widely seen as a nod to the McCarthyites, and Walter Robertson, whom the China-obsessed Walter Judd recommended for the position of assistant secretary of state.[58]

Eisenhower and the End of the Korean War

Eisenhower finally took the oath of office just after 12:30 on January 20, 1953. Delivering his inaugural address minutes later, the new president spoke in lofty terms, enunciating broad principles rather than specific policies. But he still managed to convey the central priorities of the incoming administration. He affirmed the importance of collective security, thereby repudiating the Taft wing's go-it-alone approach. His references to the vital importance of economic health implied that a cost-cutting reassessment of national security policy would soon be under way. And his firm rejection of appeasement suggested that any Korean truce would not be bought with major U.S. concessions.[59]

This was a deceptively simple agenda. If it came off, it also promised to pay enormous domestic dividends. It would garner support from China lobby senators who thought an armistice could be achieved through tougher policies. It would cement relations with the Taft wing of the party by balancing the budget. And above all, it would appeal to the mass of Americans tired of the stalemate in Korea. During his first four months in office, however, Eisenhower would have endless problems turning these basic preferences into a popular package.

A large part of the problem stemmed from the new president's decision-making structure. While his reforms of the National Security Council system promised a new era of thoroughly debated and well-informed policy choices, they also came with an obvious downside: it took time for these decisions to be reached. "I feel it a mistake for a new administration to be talking so soon after [the] inauguration," the new president recorded in his diary on February 2; "basic principles, expounded in an inaugural talk are one thing, but to begin talking concretely about a great array of specific problems is quite another. Time for study, exploration, and analysis is essential."[60]

In its first few months, the new administration therefore launched a lengthy policy review. On the budget, Humphrey and Wilson undertook an intensive effort to make major savings over the next few years, but this predictably ran into opposition from the Joint Chiefs, who insisted that big cuts would "pose a grave threat to the survival of our allies and the security of the nation."[61] On Korea, Eisenhower and his top advisers were even slower. In December, Eisenhower had been exposed to suggestions for escalating the conflict, both from Mark Clark in Tokyo and MacArthur in New York, but he was reluctant to listen to their advice, let alone embrace it. In his first weeks in office, he then faced such a crowded agenda that the National Security Council did not address Korea until February 11, and then the discussion was confined to the wisdom of launching an attack around Kaesong. Six weeks later, Eisenhower asked Wilson to assess the cost of a "massive blow" aimed at pushing communist forces back to the Korean waist. He also instructed his Planning Board to reassess all military options. But these directives merely sparked nearly two months of debate, during which time Korean strategy remained in abeyance.[62]

With senior officials groping their way forward, the administration obviously had little to announce to the public. True, it emitted a number of hints that it would be tougher than Truman. In his first State of the Union address, Eisenhower included a special section on Korea that focused on the need to get more South Korean troops to shoulder the burden, as well as the eye-catching decision to "unleash" Chiang's nationalist forces by removing the Seventh Fleet from the Formosa Straits.[63] Lower down the chain of command, officials engaged in some further bellicose talk during February and March. At the UN, Lodge used his new position to issue a stinging indictment of covert Soviet aid to the North Koreans and Chinese. On the Hill, Wilson publicly intimated that expanded military operations were impending. But beyond these threats and hints, senior officials made few firm statements about how the war would be waged or whether the United States was still fighting for the same objectives.[64]

This reticence was bound to cause problems. As Truman had discovered on countless occasions, saying little only tended to fuel speculation and encourage the airing of competing policy prescriptions. Now, numerous voices quickly filled the new information vacuum. As early as January 22, just two days into the new regime, Luce's *Time* magazine called on Eisenhower to define a new Far East agenda, recommending that he include the restoration of a united noncommunist Korea and the destruction of the Chinese army fighting the UN. According to numerous newspaper reports, Republican leaders in Congress had recently held a series of secret sessions to find some way of bringing the fighting to a hasty conclusion, their anxiety "heightened by the fact that they are receiving an increasing amount of mail reminding them of their campaign promises to end the war quickly." A blockade of the Chinese coast was particularly popular with many GOP legislators, especially those like Knowland and Smith who were leaders of the China lobby.[65]

In the next few weeks, with a dearth of information coming from administration sources, more voices entered the debate. Lewis Gough, the national commander of the American Legion, declared that the United States ought to announce a deadline for the conclusion of negotiations, adding that if the Chinese balked they should be greeted with bombing and a blockade. General Edward M. Almond, who had commanded X Corps during the vicious winter fighting in 1950–51, told *U.S. News & World Report* that the United States ought to impose a blockade on China and institute other "diversionary" efforts to cut the communist supply lines in Korea. And Marguerite Higgins, whose reporting from Korea back in the early days of the war had created such a splash, urged an immediate all-out offensive, including the use of atomic bombs.[66]

But by far the most conspicuous comments came from Van Fleet. On handing over the Eighth Army to General Maxwell Taylor in January, Van Fleet was in such demand that he was soon fielding lucrative offers from *Life* to write a series of articles.[67] Never one to dodge the main issue, he immediately generated an enormous amount of comment by claiming that his command had faced an acute ammunition shortage. Fanning the flames, he also told the House Armed Services Committee that the conflict could still be won. The present situation, he declared, was not "a stalemate" but "a sitdown of our own choice."[68]

Eisenhower was inevitably drawn into the Van Fleet controversy. At a symbolic level, the president appeared to endorse the general's ideas, first by awarding him the Distinguished Service Medal and then by giving him the opportunity to brief senior officials on how the war could be ended. But ultimately, Eisenhower's public stance remained cautious. In his press conferences, he would not be drawn on Van Fleet's hawkish recommendations, stating that he would only decide on a new course of action after all the proper authorities had thoroughly discussed it. "I don't believe in doing these things haphazardly," he brusquely informed reporters, "and on an individual and arbitrary basis."[69]

This cursory response hardly satisfied the media, however, and speculation soon began to mount. Many reporters tried to read hidden meanings into the president's sparse statements; they were especially convinced that Ike's decision to remove the Seventh Fleet from Formosa was a starting rather than an end point, with measures like a blockade of China bound to follow soon. Other journalists circulated "a welter" of rumors, including "supposedly secret testimony" by Dulles and comments by a senator "that we might use Formosa as an air base to bomb the mainland of China."[70]

By the middle of February, this frenzied conjecture had become so rampant that the capital's leading commentators felt the need to rebuke their less restrained colleagues. A "great deal of bad feeling is being generated" and much "mischief wrought" abroad and at home, Walter Lippmann stressed, "by men who are discussing not the president's policies but what somebody has said they might or ought to be." "Evidently," the Alsop brothers agreed, "President Eisenhower and the State Department policy makers did not foresee the consequences of their psychologically justifiable but militarily meaningless gesture of 'unleashing' Chiang. Plainly, they did not expect the ensuing orgy of wishful thinking and irresponsible talk about painless, miraculous ways to humble the Chinese communists and end the Korean War."[71]

This confused public debate confirmed a simple truth: what had worked before the inauguration was not necessarily effective now that the candidate had assumed power. Indeed, whereas during the campaign the media and GOP legislators had granted Eisenhower a wide degree of latitude, now the same voices looked to their president for more concrete guidance. Without it, their fevered ruminations started to reach such a pitch that they threatened to reduce Eisenhower's freedom for maneuver. As one senior presidential adviser mused privately at the end of February: "how does a discreet, responsible White House assert its leadership—beside a Congress clamoring for public attention?"[72]

Yet just as the domestic debate started to spiral out of control, the international context dramatically changed. On March 5, Stalin died. Ten days later, Georgiy Malenkov, the new chair of the Soviet Council of Ministers, publicly signaled his desire for détente. At the end of the month, the communist negotiators at Panmunjom then accepted an earlier American proposal to exchange sick and wounded POWs. From Beijing, Zhou Enlai even intimated that China would reconsider its stance on all prisoners held by the communists.[73]

These major changes in the communist posture promised to break the impasse that had halted meaningful truce talks for almost a year. At Munsan-ni, PI officers immediately prepared to deal with the massive influx of journalists who were bound to want to cover the handing over of sick prisoners. Relying heavily on the lessons learnt during Eisenhower's visit, the PIO refined its public position and honed its transmission facilities.[74] But, as senior officers soon recognized, this new operation, dubbed Little Switch, would prove far more of a headache than Ike's brief inspection trip a few months earlier.

One major difficulty stemmed from Washington's determination to prevent reporters from interviewing "certain types of POWs." The Pentagon was convinced that journalists could be fobbed off with the explanation that some sick and wounded prisoners were simply too frail to face the media spotlight. But this was not its real concern. In Washington, many officials feared that a number of prisoners had been so inculcated with communist ideas that on release they would immediately start to spread the enemy's message. As Clark pointed out, however, it was hardly practical to spirit away a proportion of the 150 non-Korean prisoners slated for release. Not only would it attract publicity, all bad, but it was unworkable, since the press corps would doubtless uncover the names of those kept in isolation. Still, the Pentagon was adamant, and Clark had no choice but to comply. When he announced this policy to the media on April 19, he did his best to soften the blow. Apart from this one restriction, he reassured reporters that their "efforts to cover the story would be facilitated to the greatest possible degrees."[75]

Operation Little Switch began the next day, and within two weeks the UNC had sent 6,224 sick and wounded prisoners back to the communist side in return for 684 of their own. As Clark had predicted, however, the effort to hide those suspected of being indoctrinated soon fell apart. San Francisco newspapers were particularly determined to locate and interview a local soldier who had made a number of propaganda broadcasts for the communists. Although UNC did its bit by keeping this GI in quarantine, as soon as he returned to the West Coast, the situation changed. In San Francisco, reporters pieced together a comprehensive portrait of this man from "candid statements" by staff at the military hospital and even from the soldier's own comments. Clark was incensed. The resulting stories, he complained, "completely negated the care with which the theater had followed instructions to separate these men, and reversed the original policy. In addition to being embarrassed, the theater commander unjustly was made to appear responsible for the completely unrealistic procedures which have been forced upon him, over his protests."[76]

To make matters worse, in "controlled interviews" with other released prisoners, most correspondents soon latched on to another fraught issue: the atrocities and war crimes the communists had apparently committed. Picking up on rumors and intelligence that had circulated since 1950, they sought to establish once and for all that U.S. prisoners had been exposed to forced marches, beatings, lack of food, and summary executions. At UNC headquarters, senior officers dismissed this "atrocity storm" as "largely synthetic," more the product of the media's preconceptions than a reflection of what had gone on in communist camps.[77] But in the United States, the dominant reaction was very different. "Many of us are shocked by the reports," Senator Bridges told journalists on April 21, before calling on his Appropriations Committee to hold hearings to find out "precisely what steps this government will take." The *New York Times* and *Philadelphia Inquirer* both welcomed Bridges's "swift action." Ominously, many newspapers also attacked the military's apparent lack of concern. The *Boston Herald* demanded that these atrocity reports "not be 'hushed up'"—a view that Earl Godwin and Ray Henle echoed on NBC. The *U.S News & World Report* even claimed that the military had intentionally "played down and sometimes suppressed" such stories in an effort to discourage demands for "a more vigorous prosecution of the war."[78]

In the next few days, the White House and the State Department moved to dampen the furor. While the president cautioned reporters that hasty denunciations might seal the fate of those still in captivity, Dulles's deputy convinced Bridges to hold off an investigation by assuring him that everything would be done to collect evidence for a later war crimes trial. Yet these efforts only partially quelled the discontent. On Capitol Hill, some legislators complained loudly that the enemy had only returned a small proportion of sick and wounded U.S. prisoners. At a time when the administration was also trumpeting the communist threat to Indochina, others reached the troubling conclusion that the tricky communists had engaged in yet another ruse to distract the West while preparing offensives elsewhere in Asia. As Judd succinctly put it, "We are getting back a few boys in exchange for a continent."[79]

Nationalist Republicans were often paranoid about the designs of the enemy and the alleged perfidy of their own government. But on this occasion, a report in the *New York Times* appeared to confirm their fears of a larger sellout. At the start of April, at an off-the-record dinner Dulles hosted for a group of leading reporters, the secretary of state casually remarked to Walter Waggoner of the *Times* "that a trusteeship for Formosa had been considered in the UN and might be considered again." The next day, Waggoner passed this comment on to Anthony Leveiro, the paper's White House correspondent, who promptly wrote a story that senior officials were contemplating a settlement based on a division in Korea and a trusteeship for Formosa. Predictably, Chiang boosters like Knowland and Smith exploded in outrage at such a "Far Eastern Munich." Placed uncomfortably on the defensive, an angry Dulles privately threatened to cut the *New York Times* off from future interviews. Publicly, the White House also issued a firm denial about a trusteeship for Formosa, while adding that "the administration has never reached any conclusion that a permanent division of Korea is desirable, or feasible, or consistent with the decisions of the UN."[80] In two keynote speeches on April 16 and 18, delivered both to probe Soviet intentions in the wake of Stalin's death and to solidify support for the long Cold War struggle that still lay ahead, Eisenhower and Dulles emphasized this point. America's goal, they insisted, was an armistice that would lead to "a free and united Korea."[81]

As the media digested this episode, its response was ominous. The *New York Times*, although it accepted that its story had been misleading, lashed out vigorously at the administration's heavy-handed threats. Elsewhere, Dulles's alleged trusteeship statement was the biggest item on the news agenda for a few days, eclipsing even the progress being made over POWs. And most accounts were distinctly negative. "The 'confusion' over the administration's post-armistice policy on Korea and Formosa," PA recorded, "all but crowds out discussion of developments at Panmunjom and the UN." Across the political spectrum, journalists, commentators, and editorial writers also used these events to revisit their views on an acceptable peace. On one side, the *Christian Science Monitor*, *Newsweek*, *Washington Post*, and *Washington Star* were all broadly supportive of an armistice based on division. On the other, a number of staunch Republican voices, including *Time*, *Life*, the *Washington Times-Herald*, and David Lawrence, all vigorously opposed such a settlement, adding for good measure barbed jibes at Dulles for "fumbling the ball badly."[82]

In the wake of all this domestic unrest, Eisenhower and his national security advisers continued to discuss how best to end the war. During April, their deliberations proceeded on two levels. First, there was a basic debate over the most desirable ends and means. Despite the administration's recent press statement affirming America's goal as the ultimate unification of Korea, no one in the National Security Council believed that this could be imposed by military force. About the most that could be hoped for was a renewed push north to the narrower strip across the peninsula known as the waist. On a number of occasions, Eisenhower mused about the possibility of expanding the war, perhaps even employing tactical nuclear weapons to achieve such a truce line. But Dulles was the most outspoken hawk. Convinced that the United States needed a big victory to regain the initiative in the Cold War, anxious to restore his position with the Republican right, and certain that South Korea needed more territory to be economically and politically viable, Dulles constantly advocated a military drive to the waist.[83]

Yet such an ambitious operation presented obvious problems. As the Joint Chiefs repeatedly pointed out, a conventional offensive deep into North Korea would be extremely costly, while a nuclear attack would not remove the Chinese from their deeply entrenched Korean positions. Allies would also balk at the use of A-bombs. And public opinion presented yet another potential obstacle. Although many voices on the Republican right were baying for a vigorous new offensive, preferring to escalate the war into China rather than accept a truce near the thirty-eighth parallel, others were far less belligerent. During April and May, Taft was focused on the budget. Upset that the administration had found only $8.4 billion in savings, he wanted deeper cuts in defense spending. Ending the war quickly would obviously help.[84] Escalation, however, would inevitably prove expensive. As private government estimates suggested, something in the range of an extra $4 billion would have to be found for any expansion of the fighting.[85]

Any attempt to escalate the war would thus have to address the deeper question of whether this would undermine the administration's attempt to make economies in the overall national security budget. In the aftermath of Operation Little Switch, it would also have to be related to a second set of considerations: the UNC's specific negotiating position at Panmunjom. Although the exchange of sick and wounded had not gone terribly smoothly, Little Switch had provided enough momentum to restart the truce talks. As senior officials debated what stance to take, they recognized that their hands had been tied by the earlier agreements reached at Panmunjom. As Eisenhower was quick to point out, any U.S. demand for a truce at the waist would mean reopening the entire negotiation process. Dulles agreed, but saw no problem. Personally, he told the rest of the National Security Council, he favored approaching the communists with an ultimatum: accept a new truce line at the waist or face a renewed UN offensive. As Eisenhower was quick to point out, however, "the American people would never stand for calling off the armistice and going to war in Korea again." Nor would America's allies be happy with such an outcome. Indeed, Britain, France, and Canada were already convinced that the U.S. negotiating stance had been far too rigid and that the time was now ripe for the West to make sufficient concessions to end the bloodshed.[86]

On April 26, when the armistice talks finally resumed at Panmunjom, both sets of negotiators immediately returned to the hoary problem of the POWs. The communists opened with a proposal based on Zhou Enlai's earlier public statement. On May 7, after the UNC's negotiating team rejected this out of hand, the communists returned with a series of concessions. These were very close to an Indian-sponsored UN resolution that the United States had endorsed in December, but Eisenhower and his advisers still balked. On May 13, the UNC's negotiators responded with yet another proposal. This stipulated that all Korean nonrepatriates would be released to civilian status as soon as an armistice was agreed. Non-Koreans would be held by a neutral commission for sixty days. This five-member commission would decide their fate by unanimous vote; those whose disposition had not been agreed on by the end of the time period would be released to civilian status.[87]

America's May 13 proposal was an obvious upping of the ante, for it was clearly biased in favor of ensuring that as many prisoners as possible remained nonrepatriates. And the next day, the communists predictably dubbed it "absolutely unacceptable," before threatening to break off negotiations altogether. Eisenhower was now in a dangerous position. While America's European allies were appalled by his administration's unwillingness to embrace what they saw as a good chance for peace, Republicans on the Hill viewed the latest position as too soft and only endorsed it on the grudging grounds that "there was no practical alternative."[88]

To extricate himself from this hole, Eisenhower decided on a three-pronged policy. For a start, he recognized that America's partners would not tolerate the continuation of the war, let alone its escalation, on the basis of the May 13 package. A week later, he therefore agreed to refine the U.S. bargaining position, toning down various elements to bring it closer to the communist proposal. Thus the neutral commission would work on the basis of a majority vote (not unanimity), Korean repatriates would be treated the same as the Chinese (not released immediately), and the time frame for persuasion would be ninety days (not sixty).[89]

Still, these concessions threatened dangerous consequences. On the one hand, the communists might turn down this latest package, thereby dooming the war to continuing indefinitely. On the other hand, the right wing of the GOP might refuse to endorse this compromise, thereby rupturing the party. To protect against the first danger, the administration decided to intensify the war in a limited fashion, launching a series of intensive bombing strikes against irrigation dams in North Korea. Using back channels, officials also threatened the enemy with dire consequences if they refused to agree to America's final proposal.[90]

Meanwhile, to shore up support on the home front, Eisenhower and his senior advisers made a concerted effort to brief and consult the congressional leadership. Privately, they even revealed the threats they had recently transmitted to the enemy, thereby implying that the administration, far from caving in to pressure, was in effect coercing the communists to come to terms.[91] The president also quashed rumors that a deal in Korea would merely be a precursor to a broader settlement that would recognize Red China. "As long as recognition meant approval in the case of communist China," Eisenhower pledged to GOP leaders on May 19, "he was against it."[92]

This last assurance was particularly important for China-lobby senators who obsessively hated Mao's regime. But these legislators also decided to stand by Eisenhower out of party loyalty. Knowland was an obvious case in point. A staunch supporter of the Chinese nationalists, who believed that a blockade of the Chinese coast would bring far more favorable terms, Knowland was not anxious to see the party implode so early in the congressional session.[93] At the start of June, he therefore acquiesced in the administration's new position. Although far from happy, he was even prepared to release a public statement supporting an armistice based on division and voluntary repatriation.[94]

Knowland's action was vital in shoring up support on the Hill. But it also had another purpose: to encourage Syngman Rhee to sign up to the settlement. For after June 4, when the communists accepted the new U.S. position on POWs, Rhee became the last remaining obstacle to the conclusion of an elusive armistice.

South Korea

Rhee's South Korean regime was no bastion of freedom and democracy. Even before the war, he had been an embattled figure, challenged by the legislature and losing ground in popular elections. Once the war started, his henchmen extracted brutal revenge on opponents. Alleged guerrillas were massacred during the first retreat in the summer of 1950; those accused of collaborating with the communists were slaughtered as soon as UN forces recaptured lost ground in the fall.[95]

In the United States, these actions were only intermittently reported. The brutality of Rhee's police force hit the headlines twice in 1950, when a few leading organs published grisly eyewitness accounts of mass executions.[96] In an effort to counteract the bad publicity, Rhee pledged to review all death sentences and promised that future executions would not be carried out en masse.[97] This prompt action calmed his most vociferous critics, but many Americans in South Korea continued to gripe about his numerous other failings.

In private, U.S. diplomats often found Rhee an infuriating ally: a skillful nationalist leader, yes, but also a stubborn, volatile, and untrusting man. For the most part, these diplomats kept their negative thoughts either to themselves or for their private memoranda. But the U.S. military was far less restrained. In public, officers frequently wondered why "our Koreans" fought less tenaciously than those on the other side. In talking to reporters, enlisted men sometimes complained that the Korean people lacked gratitude for all the American sacrifices.[98]

Then in June 1952, Rhee sparked a political crisis by declaring martial law, jailing his opponents, and brazenly seeking an additional term in office. Leading U.S. officials, unable to hide their disgust, told reporters that Rhee had "developed a dictatorship complex" and wanted "to do away with the legislature in favor of a personal rule of his own." Responding to these cues, and shocked that Rhee's new censorship rules even applied to the Voice of America, many in the media were quick to point out that Rhee's "autocratic actions" threatened South Korea's "democratic form of government."[99]

All the same, the most striking thing about the American debate was not these periodic outbursts against Rhee. Rather, it was the media's basic lack of interest in a country America was ostensibly fighting to defend. The Rhee regime clearly had its dark side. But in the U.S. discourse, this tended to remain shrouded from public view, only briefly and sporadically paraded in the open whenever it proved impossible to ignore.

The reasons South Korea only made rare and invariably rosy intrusions into the U.S. debate are not difficult to fathom. The administration, for its part, did a remarkable selling job. Its constant focus on the global dimension of the war naturally helped to direct the attention of the politicians, press, and public away from the internal civil conflict. Increasingly, too, the military's enhanced PR capabilities played an important role in shaping perceptions, especially after the Pentagon decided in the summer of 1952 to increase the size of the South Korean army. In the space of a few weeks, Eighth Army PI officers went to great lengths to emphasize the improved fighting qualities of these troops, keeping correspondents well briefed, supplying them with "color side-lights," and facilitating special assignments for reporters from the UP and *New York Herald-Tribune*.[100]

Throughout the war, officials also engaged in skillful damage-limitation exercises. On the few occasions when correspondents published gruesome stories of mass executions, senior officials were quick to respond. They released a barrage of information detailing the positive aspects of Rhee's regime, such as its handling of the serious refugee problem, the fact that its troops were sustaining enormous casualties, and how, despite the turbulent environment, it was "gradually becoming stabilized, encouraging public education, [and was] responsive [to the] popular will." Ominously, senior officials also muttered darker hints about Rhee's press critics "falling unconsciously for [the] commie line"—suggestions that could easily prove career-threatening in 1950s America.[101]

As Bruce Cumings points out, a number of reporters were indeed "afraid to print what they witnessed in Korea, given the Cold War atmosphere of the time."[102] But the media were not merely cowed into submission. In many cases, they became willing accomplices. Their coverage of the guerrilla war in the South was a case in point. The fighting in Korea had not begun in June 1950. In the months and years before the North Korean invasion, Rhee had launched vicious counterinsurgency sweeps to eradicate a well-organized and extensive guerrilla movement. Although these had enjoyed a good deal of success, the guerrilla problem had not gone away. Replenished by soldiers from defeated units during the great battles of the first year of the war, by the end of 1951, according to the estimate of the UNC as many as eight thousand guerrillas remained in the southwest of the peninsula.[103]

In an effort to eradicate this guerrilla threat, in December 1951 South Korean military forces launched Operation Ratkiller. Despite its distasteful name, the Eighth Army was keen to facilitate media coverage of a major South Korean operation. It not only transported nine reporters to the scene but also provided a series of background briefings for those correspondents who chose to remain at the press billets.[104] Yet to no avail. Back in the United States, the rare stories on the subject were given just a few lines and buried on the inside pages. Editors made the simple commercial calculation that their readers were simply not interested in the South Korean scene, especially at a time when so much attention was being lavished on the fate of American POWs. But they reached a deeper conclusion, too: the guerrilla operation did not fit into the simple frames most newspapers used to convey the war. It was, after all, a South Korean operation and not an American-led affair. It involved counterinsurgency and not conventional warfare. And rather than emphasize externally directed communist aggression, it suggested that Rhee faced a significant internal threat to his rule.[105]

On the other occasions when America's basic narrative of the war was open to challenge, journalists and editors used additional means to obscure the import or deaden the impact. Reports of South Korean executions, for instance, were greatly eclipsed by accounts of North Korean atrocities. From time to time, senior reporters also engaged in self-censorship, such as excising "nasty references to the Korean people" from their interview accounts with GIs, well aware that these were no help to the UN cause.[106] Meanwhile, their editors rarely saw much mileage in covering the impact of the war on life in Korea. And even on those rare occasions when major newspapers and magazines looked beyond American actions, they were keen to find a good-news angle. *Time* was typical. In the summer of 1951, one of its correspondents, after interviewing Red Cross workers, wrote a story that focused on the devastation wrought by the bullets, shells, and napalm unleashed by both sides. But in *Time*'s account, there was still a positive dimension. "Amid death, destruction, and homelessness," it concluded, "millions of Koreans held on to a simple fact: they would rather live where the Americans are than where the communists are."[107]

For many media voices, even Rhee's unsavory power grab in 1952 had its upside. True, he had been highhanded. But this needed to be viewed against the backdrop of war, inflation, and the basic fragility of a new state. For some, it could also be justified by the fact that Rhee was apparently popular throughout his country, not to mention the fact that he was attempting to establish the direct election of the presidency—which would make the Korean system more like that of the U.S. Constitution.[108] As Greg MacGregor of the *New York Times* argued, for all its faults, Rhee's South Korea had one saving grace: a close affinity between us and them. "So far there has been virtually no outward inclination of hard feelings between the Koreans and the Americans," he insisted after spending months in the country. "Since the war began the Koreans have looked up to the Americans and tried to pattern their actions, their dress, and in some cases their government on United States lines."[109]

By 1953, in fact, South Korea could count on an enormous amount of sympathy inside the United States. It was especially popular on the right, where Rhee was seen as another Chiang, and any hint that the United States was seeking to distance itself from him was immediately interpreted as an effort to "lose" another ally to communism.[110] But even moderate opinion was far from critical. This became clear at the start of June, when the communists accepted America's latest proposal at Panmunjom. "All commentators," PA reported, " 'sympathize' with South Korea's 'anguished protests' at the prospect of a compromise truce which would leave the country divided." Although only a few supported Rhee's demand to continue fighting until the communists were pushed to the Yalu River, the majority thought Eisenhower was correct to extend "assurances" to Rhee that his country would not be abandoned. And many were quick to point out that an armistice agreement was not a final settlement, and that the United States would still be working for unification through political means after the fighting had stopped.[111]

On June 18, however, Rhee pushed America's sympathy to the limit when he unilaterally tried to scupper prospects of an armistice by allowing twenty-five thousand Korean nonrepatriate prisoners to escape. Eisenhower was furious. Convinced that it was time to get tough, he initially considered withdrawing U.S. troops and saying "goodbye" to Korea altogether. At the very least, he agreed to let Clark place pressure on Rhee by slowing down aid shipments and generating the impression that the United States was now preparing to leave.[112]

Inevitably, some of these actions leaked into the public sphere. On NBC, Morgan Beatty claimed that the administration was ready to warn Rhee that unless he complied with a truce, the UN would send in more troops to "enforce the decision." Picking up on plans that had been drafted in May, *Newsweek* even reported that officials were discussing the possibility of "displacing" Rhee.[113]

Yet any effort to coerce South Korea carried clear political risks.[114] In the media, to be sure, a range of newspapers, including the *Christian Science Monitor*, *New York Times*, *New Orleans Times-Picayune*, *St. Louis Post-Dispatch*, and *Washington Post*, were "stunned, dismayed, and angered" by Rhee's action. Some, like the *Chicago Sun-Times* and *Kansas City Star*, even depicted him as "an international traitor to the cause of peace."[115]

But on Capitol Hill, the situation was far trickier. The right was already uneasy with the administration's foreign policy record—the lack of big budget cuts, the reluctance to take the war to China, and the prospect of a truce that left Korea divided. Thus far, as one expert put it, nationalist Republicans had swallowed all of this "with painful grimaces." But their patience was wearing thin, and Rhee's staunch opposition to the current truce package gave them a perfect opening to air their dissatisfaction.[116] Ominously, even moderates were restive on this subject. In consultations with congressional leaders, officials found absolutely no support for ousting the South Korean leader. Nor would Congress take kindly to a unilateral U.S. withdrawal.[117] An avid Ike partisan like James Duff summed up the prevailing mood when he contrasted the Chinese communists with the South Korean ally, before stressing the enormous dangers of making "a compact with a perfidious enemy over the head of a very wonderfully patriotic people."[118]

In the wake of the prisoner release, the president thus faced a conundrum. Any compromise with Rhee seemed likely to anger the communists and torpedo the Panmunjom talks. If the United States stood firmly against Rhee, however, the administration risked alienating its own base on the central issue of the day. With his options few and far between, Eisenhower decided to send Walter Robertson to Korea to see if he could reach some sort of agreement with Rhee. Ike was not optimistic about the outcome, but he thought the mission would "at least help out with our own Congress."[119]

When Robertson arrived at Pusan, he found Rhee in a typically stubborn mood, determined to oppose any truce that would divide his country. After twelve long meetings, however, the two men reached a basic, if vague, understanding. The very fact that the United States had sent someone so senior had given Rhee the political cover to retreat from some of his more strident claims. It also helped that Robertson, an ardent Chiang booster, was instinctively sympathetic to Rhee's position. Rhee, for his part, was under intense pressure to compromise. He had already received implicit threats from Tokyo, underscoring just how reliant his army was on U.S. supplies. In the middle of July, the Chinese unleashed a series of limited offensives, which pushed his forces back some 6 miles and further exposed the vulnerability of South Korea's military position.[120]

Back in Washington, moreover, the administration worked hard to rally Congress behind its position, and this also exerted pressure on Rhee. At first, senior officials feared this latest crisis might finally rip the fractious Republican coalition apart. Along with its disagreements over the budget and the truce, the Senate party was in some disarray after Taft had been diagnosed with cancer at the start of June and had relinquished the leadership to Knowland. In his first days in the job, the Californian had not covered himself in glory. Not only had he pandered to the right by bringing up a vote on the Bricker amendment (reducing the executive's ability to conclude agreements with other countries) but he had angered Democrats by employing overly sharp tactics. Eisenhower moved swiftly to heal this partisan breach, calling in Democratic leaders for a series of briefings.[121] He also worked hard to turn Knowland's elevation into an opportunity, recognizing that whatever his weaknesses as a tactician, Knowland could at least use his reputation as a senior member of the China lobby to bring on board some of the most suspicious legislators. Perhaps the decisive moment came at the end of June, when Alexander Smith agreed to make a public appeal to Rhee. Declaring "a stalemated truce is to be preferred to a stalemated war," Smith urged the South Koreans to remain partners with the United States, insisting that this was the only way "this idealistic war for the freedom and independence of Korea" could ultimately be won. Coming from a firm friend of the South Korean regime, it was a powerful demonstration of the drift of opinion in Washington.[122]

Robertson finally left Korea on July 11. After a grueling three-week mission, his final deal with Rhee was by no means straightforward. Rhee merely agreed not to obstruct an armistice, and for a few nervy days Robertson was unsettled by news reports that Rhee was about to repudiate even this minimal commitment.[123]

Still, Robertson's efforts were widely viewed back home as a success. It certainly helped that he had been canny enough to set the media agenda before he returned to Washington, briefing reporters about how he had prevailed on Rhee to yield on point after point. Congress promised to be a trickier audience, but in separate appearances before the foreign relations committees in the House and Senate, Robertson was able to satisfy legislators that Rhee had pledged "in black and white" not to undermine final U.S. efforts to conclude a truce.[124] He also unintentionally benefited from the expectations game. Before Robertson had gone to South Korea, senior officials had been gloomy about the prospect of reaching any sort of understanding with Rhee, and their doubts had inevitably been transmitted to reporters. When Robertson then returned home with some sort of compromise, commentators across the political spectrum praised him for making "headway" in Seoul.[125]

With the South Korean obstacle overcome, the way was finally clear for an armistice to be signed. This would be a major success for the Eisenhower administration, but it had not been achieved without cost. The new officials, to be sure, had learned some lessons from the Truman years. They had tried to streamline the national security bureaucracy, partly to make it less susceptible to great public clashes. They had spent more time consulting Congress, largely to avoid the major scuffles Truman had endured with the right. And they had engaged in some tougher rhetoric, thereby protecting themselves against charges of softness and appeasement. At the same time, they had also inherited the major improvements made at the lower levels of the military during 1951 and 1952. These had been particularly important during Eisenhower's first postelection jaunt—his trip to Korea—when he had been fortunate to benefit from all the recent changes made to logistics, censorship, and briefings, not to mention the less tense atmosphere that now prevailed between the military and media on the ground.

Yet Eisenhower and his new team had also made their fair share of mistakes, many of them alarmingly similar to the pitfalls that had tripped up their predecessors. They had created an information vacuum in their first weeks in office, which in turn led to a frenzy of speculation and competing policy prescriptions. They had missed a big opportunity for a PR coup in Little Switch, largely because they ignored UNC's advice not to place excessive restrictions on whom reporters could interview. And as the diplomatic bargaining at Panmunjom and Pusan reached the end of its tortuous path, they had frequently found themselves on the defensive, having to engineer a strategy that reconciled the apparently irreconcilable, with the allied and domestic audiences invariably pushing in different directions.

Even the prospect of a settlement sparked little enthusiasm. True, recent polls demonstrated that a plurality of 48 percent would consider a truce along the present battle line to be a success, while 69 percent now approved of an armistice that left Korea divided. A majority of media opinion also thought the last round of negotiations had been a victory for the United States

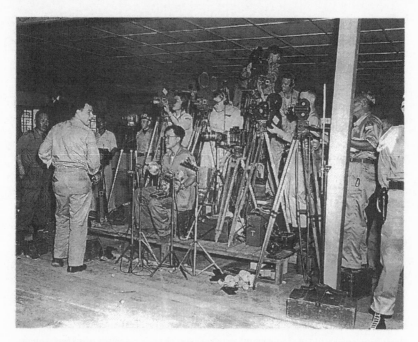

News cameramen wait to cover the armistice ceremony in the peace pagoda at Panmunjom, July 27, 1953.

because "just about all the concessions" had been made by the enemy.[126] But there was little rejoicing. The armistice, after all, would only halt the fighting in Korea; it was not a peace treaty that would end the wider struggle against communism. And it would be marked in a suitably restrained way: with relief, yes, that the fighting was coming to an end after more than three years and 140,000 American casualties, but with little exultation—as this was the first time the United States had been involved in a conflict with no clear-cut decision.[127]

CONCLUSION

After two years of protracted and thorny negotiations, the Korean armistice ceremony was a brief and suitably ill-tempered affair. Outside the new "peace" pagoda at Panmunjom, which had been built specially for the occasion, more than fifty correspondents assembled, waiting to be shepherded into the building where they would be placed opposite the UN delegation as it signed the historic document. Inside, the two delegations, kept apart by a table, entered from different doors and declined even to make eye contact. General Clark, who refused to attend, affixed his signature to the armistice document at Munsan-ni, before telling reporters that it was vital for both U.S. and UN forces to remain in South Korea for the foreseeable future. Back home, the president was no more exultant. In a brief and somber speech, he reminded his compatriots that this was merely "an armistice on a single battleground—not peace in the world." Convinced like Truman and Acheson before him that a letdown was on the cards, he also exhorted the public not to relax its guard.[1]

Nonetheless, despite these obvious efforts to play down the importance of the day, the administration's publicity efforts were extremely professional and effective. In the tense weeks leading up to this moment, UNC's PI officers had faced many familiar problems. The wire services had been in uproar over what they considered limited teletype and telephone facilities. Some old faces had also returned to haunt the Eighth Army, including Marguerite Higgins, who had inflamed the censors by refusing to submit a piece that one of them depicted as "a typical piece of inflammatory Rhee propaganda." But ultimately all these difficulties had been overcome with some aplomb. Higgins's indiscretion had been diplomatically ignored. The wire services' complaints had been resolved by laying on extra courier flights and stopping reporters from filing the same story more than once. And a number of smaller

357

efforts had been made to ensure that the day went smoothly, from providing journalists with a kit that summarized all the details of the truce provisions to laying on extra censors in tents outside the pagoda so that copy could be released immediately.[2]

This last act of the war was thus a testament to the major PR improvements made at different levels of the government over the past three years. But it had not always been this way. For long periods, the government had faced enormous problems in trying to spark and sustain support for this distant and messy war.

Selling a Limited War

The most obvious of these difficulties was the sheer complexity of the task. This was partly a matter of coordinating the government's message, as individuals and institutions in the sprawling national security bureaucracy competed in the public sphere. But there was also another dimension. Korea was a multifaceted war. At one level, the government had to worry about how the fighting was being relayed back home—whether stories of death and destruction were too much for a squeamish public to bear. At another level, it had to convince Americans that these casualties were worth sustaining—that the reason for war was clear-cut and the outcome would be some sort of victory. And at a final level, it had to demonstrate how this limited war intersected with the bigger picture of the Cold War.

Historians have often seen a neat fit between these different levels. It is often argued, for instance, that the outbreak of war, together with the big defeats in 1950 and 1951, were the pivotal catalysts for the massive mobilization the Truman administration undertook during 1950 and 1951.[3] In a sense, this line of argument is correct, since the Korean conflict undermined the position of those officials who wanted to suppress defense spending, while also generating congressional and popular pressure for greater preparedness. But historians have missed the deeper complications and tensions that emerged between the Korean War and mobilization: the fact that mobilization often distracted domestic attention away from efforts to define what Korea was all about, or that the war initially sparked a new wave of partisanship that threatened to undermine the task of constructing domestic support for a long-term preparedness program.

A second problem in the early phase of the war was the cautious nature of the propaganda message that generally emerged from official channels. In their interactions with elite opinion, Truman and his major advisers saw themselves traversing a tricky path. On the one hand, they were plagued by congressional pressure to wage a more aggressive Cold War, perhaps even including a preventive strike against the Soviets. On the other, they faced the lingering appeal of isolationism, voiced by a number of leading politicians who called for a retreat from expensive and expansive overseas commitments. Such sentiments, they believed, could not simply be dismissed as the ranting of discredited opinion-makers on either extreme of the political spectrum, for the simple reason that the broader mass of popular opinion was far too unstable. Whenever the international situation was quiet, most Americans tended to be too complacent about the danger and too inclined to focus inward. But the minute an international crisis erupted, they suddenly seemed to be gripped by hysteria. In such a volatile situation, leading figures in the Truman administration believed that the task of leadership was far subtler than simply launching a scare campaign. Leadership had, instead, to be acutely attuned to the needs of the moment—to be soothing during periods of crisis and more strident whenever the immediate danger appeared to have passed.

That the Truman administration was determined to stop the domestic mood from overheating was inextricably intertwined with a third problem: the difficulty of selling a limited as opposed to a total war. In the extant literature on limited war, the focus is almost exclusively on what the public will accept rather than what the government can do. Limited conflicts are inherently unpopular, so the argument goes, because the American people are repelled by limitations being placed on how the war is fought, and nothing the government can say or do will change this basic logic.[4] What this perspective neglects, however, are the constraints that fighting a limited war puts on leadership. During the first months of the Korean conflict, Truman and his advisers were cautious, in the sense that they were determined to avoid a wider superpower conflagration, especially one that involved the Soviet Union. They were also convinced that the public was prone to overreact during periods of intense danger. For these reasons, the exigency of waging a limited war exerted a profound influence over their rhetoric. In periods of crisis, senior officials studiously avoided inflammatory remarks and, on occasion, even refused to speak out at all, lest this antagonize the Soviets or engender a "war psychosis" at home. When it came to selling mobilization, they also fretted that overdrawn, "clearer-than-truth" rhetoric might fuel popular pressures that would be difficult to control.

As well as having a dampening effect on rhetoric, limited war placed other constraints on the government. As the Pentagon realized, many qualified PI specialists were reluctant to leave their careers and families to serve in a small police action. And the resulting lack of PI volunteers initially meant that the overworked offices in the Pentagon, Tokyo, and Korea did not have the personnel to provide better guidance to the press. At the same time, senior officials also believed that certain courses of action were more suitable to a total war, and wanted to keep them in reserve in case Korea, or another Cold War crisis, escalated out of control. This explains their reluctance to tinker with the machinery of government, either by creating an administration of national unity or a propaganda agency. As a White House aide tellingly remarked, "for the president to appoint a 'coalition cabinet'...might imply that we are going into a global war, whereas the Korean conflict might not lead to one."[5]

In the first year of the war, these actions had vitally important consequences. In Korea itself, the lack of censorship and proper guidance fueled a series of deep-seated resentments on both sides of the military-media divide. The ambitious war correspondents who thronged to the theater in the summer of 1950 were certainly mystified by the combustible mixture of laxity and arbitrariness in MacArthur's system of media relations. They were also irritated by the basic lack of facilities, which made covering this war enormously grueling and dangerous. Meanwhile, MacArthur and his advisers were increasingly angered by what they saw as a group of biased reporters who seemed bent on undermining the whole war effort. And when these senior officers vocalized these views at the depths of the winter crisis in 1950–51, they not only came close to precipitating a complete breakdown in media-military relations but also exacerbated the command's bad press at the height of a massive military defeat.

Back in the United States, other problems resulted from the way the administration sold the war. In periods of crisis, the government's low-key public posture tended to create an information vacuum. With reporters being denied their normal diet of "official facts," some resorted to speculation, while others turned to Republicans, who were quick to exploit the opportunity by charging that the crisis stemmed largely from the Democratic administration's bungled Asia policies. On the subject of mobilization, the administration's determination to dampen rather than raise the public temperature also permitted Republicans to depict officials as dangerously soft on a range of issues, from the speed of rearmament to the extent of economic controls. At the same time, the administration's failure to create new bureaucratic structures to cope with the information demands of war provided part of the backdrop for the growing media stories of chaos and confusion in official circles, while its reluctance to bring Republicans into senior positions in the government did nothing to dampen the increasingly shrill tenor of GOP attacks.

That the government's own publicity efforts had a series of damaging consequences is particularly pertinent when it comes to explaining the breakdown of bipartisanship. What the extant literature has tended to miss, with all its emphasis on the ideology and opportunism of the Republican right, is the symbiotic relationship between the administration's propaganda campaign and the GOP's response.[6] What the literature neglects, in particular, is the fact that the administration's subdued public posture often afforded the Republican opposition the perfect *opportunity* to take the offensive. This can best be illustrated by a simple counterfactual. Had the government, from the start of war, engaged in a forceful leadership drive, depicting the issues in black-and-white terms, as an all-out struggle between good and evil—had it done, in fact, what historians have often claimed it did—then this would have greatly reduced the Republican Party's freedom to maneuver. In this situation, the public pressure would have been much greater for everyone to forget past differences and focus on the global struggle ahead. The parameters of political debate would have thus been narrowed, the possibilities of dissent curtailed. As it was, even in this "police action," GOP leaders moved somewhat cautiously, with staunch government critics going out of their way to stress that "Republicans should give every possible support to the conduct of the war."[7] Yet at the same time, senior Republicans also glimpsed an obvious opening to go on the offensive. Simply put, a limited conflict had clearly given them the scope to offer the government only limited support.

Steady Improvements

In the last two years of the war, the government's domestic problems threatened to became even more intense. For one thing, the reasons for fighting in a faraway land were even murkier, especially with the UN failing to swiftly condemn the Chinese intervention, the administration retreating from its earlier goal of driving all the way to the Yalu River, and the truce talks bogging down over increasingly smaller issues. For another, historians have also argued that the Truman administration was now poorly placed to sell the war. The president himself was clearly a "lame duck," his capacity to govern effectively at an end after his controversial decision to recall MacArthur. The political environment had also become more heated, with a presidential election year looming and the Republican right keen to step into the vacuum left by the wounded president.[8] And all the while, casualties continued to mount. Indeed, even though the fighting was now waged over a narrow area with little territorial gain for either side, America sustained 45 percent of its casualties in this period of stalemate war.[9]

Yet on close inspection, it is apparent that some of these problems have been overstated. At the same time, in both Washington and Korea a set of countervailing processes were now at work that ensured that the constraints associated with fighting a limited conflict no longer cast such a long shadow over the government's publicity efforts.

Learning was one of these processes. After more than a year's experience with war, officials had a profound sense of what worked and what merely angered reporters. Misleading communiqués and heavy-handed restrictions fell firmly into the latter category, and major efforts were made to eradicate both, especially after MacArthur's recall made reform possible.

Closely related to this learning process was the bureaucratization of the government's publicity operations. Although Truman and his senior advisers still rejected the creation of a propaganda agency, convinced that such a controversial institution would have to await the outbreak of a world war, the administration's PR efforts were no longer as haphazard and as ad hoc as they had been in the initial phase of the fighting. Indeed, as the war progressed, experienced PI officers drafted procedures at the center, which were disseminated to officials working throughout the large bureaucracy. In the Far East, for example, the military established training courses for new censors, ran seminars for new PI officers, and repeatedly issued commands and suggestions to guide the large influx of enlisted men.

In Korea, the evolving nature of the war also eased the military's task. As the fighting bogged down in trench warfare, the conflict became less newsworthy. With editors looking to other flashpoints like Indochina and Iran to fill their pages, PI officers operated in a less pressured environment. Indeed, with the war increasingly covered by second-string reporters whose output had no byline, the military no longer faced big-name correspondents with both the clout and incentive to make a splash by writing controversial stories. At a more practical level, because far less copy now emanated from the theater of war, the censors found it far easier to sift through these stories in a timely, efficient, and tactful manner. Furthermore, as the battle line stabilized, the military established a permanent headquarters to cater to correspondents' needs. This immediately alleviated two of the practical problems that had soured military-media relations in 1950: appalling billets and antiquated communications. But these were not the only positive repercussions. In the later stages of the war, the military also found it easier to control exactly where correspondents went, putting an end to the old situation in which reporters could base their copy on eyewitness accounts of a major defeat or firsthand interviews with tired and demoralized GIs.

In Washington, meanwhile, another important development was at work: the government's attempt to stiffen its message, which would end in a successful effort to rededicate the war. This rhetorical change was initially driven by desperation. After saying and doing little to sustain support for the war in the first months of 1951, senior officials found themselves fighting for their political life in the wake of MacArthur's recall. In the spring and summer, they therefore implemented major changes in an effort to get their case across to the mass public. Some were organizational, such as creation of a temporary new White House position to coordinate the government's message. Others were undertaken at a departmental level or in conjunction with key pressure groups, such as the big campaign in 1951–52 to boost blood supplies. Far more crucial, though, was the tougher new message propagated by the men at the top. To be sure, even now, Truman and Acheson shied away from labeling Korea a "war."[10] They were also leery of anything that was "too optimistic about the internal collapse of the Soviet Union," fearing this would antagonize enemies, worry allies, and raise excessive expectations on the home front.[11] But in the spring and summer of 1951, both men did make efforts to stiffen their public posture, especially toward Red China, while also stressing their faith in America's ultimate ability to win the Cold War.

A year later, the Truman administration then made an even more significant change. With the truce talks bogged down, officials worried that the war might in effect drag on indefinitely over one small sticking point on the Panmunjom agenda. By this stage, Korea already lacked a moral dimension. This, after all, was no longer a war to turn the whole peninsula into a shining beacon of freedom and democracy. Nor was the administration able to capitalize on the international legitimacy provided by UN endorsement, not with the tardiness of the UN's condemnation of Chinese aggression, as well as the absence of tangible support from many UN allies.

In looking for a way to rededicate the war, the Truman administration ultimately latched on to the POW issue. Although strict adherence to a policy of voluntary repatriation promised to prolong the fighting, it also provided an opening to portray the war in more appealing ideological terms—as a moral crusade fought on behalf of America's traditional respect for human rights, as well as a symbol of the West's appeal to people who were subject to communist tyranny.

Still, these alterations to structure and message were only starting points. As the political scientist George Edwards points out, even the most rigorous White House–led PR campaigns often have disappointing results. The reason for this is straightforward: presidents have to compete with Congress and the media in order to get their message to the mass public. Only when there is an elite consensus, with Congress and the media both falling in line behind the official version of events, is it relatively easy for the White House to set the agenda and get its arguments across.[12] In the first year of the Korean War, of course, an elite consensus was virtually impossible to achieve. During 1951 and 1952, however, the situation was not quite so gloomy.

Historians often insist that the political environment became more problematic for Truman the longer the war persisted. It is certainly true that McCarthy continued to launch his savage attacks on communists in government, while Taft stepped up his claims that the Korean War had been a "useless and expensive waste."[13] But these eye-catching antics were not the only—or even the most important—development in the later stages of the war. Far more significant was the fact that a number of internationalist Republicans shifted decisively away from their right-wing colleagues and began to gravitate slowly back toward the bipartisan center. This development was momentous for two reasons: it helped to mute the overall potency of the Republican Party's attacks, and it enabled the government's own enhanced efforts to gain greater visibility.

What was behind this process? The role leading committee chairs played was vital. Whereas Tydings's clumsy handling of McCarthy in 1950 had helped unite the GOP, the shrewd and tactful actions of Russell and Connally in 1951 not only avoided Tydings's earlier errors but also provided a degree of cover that smoothed the way for Republican internationalists to adopt a more cooperative attitude with the Democrats. The administration's new public posture had a similar impact. Indeed, its tougher rhetoric not only made it less vulnerable to partisan attacks but also ensured that nationalist efforts to gain political advantage from foreign policy issues appeared increasingly shrill. Caught in the middle, GOP internationalists soon lost patience with the hard-line rhetoric the Taftites employed, much of which verged dangerously close to isolationism on the one hand or reckless warmongering on the other.

As these cracks in the façade of Republican unity demonstrate, the nature of political debate underwent a fundamental shift after the Chinese intervention. Before, GOP dissent had been tactical, positive, and optimistic. Indeed, most Republicans had not challenged the basic premise of the administration's Cold War policy. They had simply attacked it for being too slow and weak in responding to communist moves—a position that the restrained language coming from official sources made all the more plausible. After China entered the war, however, the Republican assault threatened to become more fundamental. In Korea itself, nationalists called either for escalation or withdrawal. More broadly, they disputed the president's ability to send troops to Europe, attacked the administration's willingness to listen to allies and the UN, and questioned the whole basis of a Cold War posture that threatened to turn America into a "garrison state." By expanding the boundaries of political debate, however, Republican nationalists created a backlash. Although some moderates flirted with Taft in the immediate wake of the big Korean defeats in December and January, by the summer of 1951 the weak glue holding the GOP together had lost its adhesiveness, not least because many East Coast legislators could not countenance the radical assaults the Taft wing of their party was unleashing.

Two events symbolized the Republican moderates' move toward the administration as they became increasingly at odds with the nationalists in their own party. One was the outcome of the MacArthur controversy, which saw important internationalists refusing to sign the GOP report. The other was the advent of Eisenhower, who was largely motivated to run for the presidency by concerns about what Taft and his allies stood for. Indeed, Eisenhower's candidacy meant that election year rhetoric would not be based on fundamental foreign policy differences. On Korea, although Ike concentrated on the broader "mistakes" the administration had committed before the war, he never embraced the ideas that had guided MacArthur and the nationalist Republicans. And he never questioned the basic need to send U.S. troops to defend Korea.

All these developments were significant: the emphasis on voluntary repatriation helped infuse the war with a new moral dimension; the improvements the military made shaped the way the public perceived the fighting; and the relatively muted political debate ensured that there was no fundamental partisan divide on the war. But the impact of these developments was basically defensive. They certainly did not help Truman's approval ratings, which collapsed in 1951 and scarcely recovered thereafter. Nor did they generate widespread enthusiasm for the bloody stalemate war. What they did create, though, was a relatively stable floor during much of 1952, below which popular disapproval never descended. Without these changes, things could have been a lot worse: indeed, support for the war could easily have plummeted a lot further, especially if war correspondents had continued to write micro-level stories that emphasized defeat, destruction, and death, not to mention if Taft had won the GOP nomination and then used his candidacy to denounce Korea as a "useless" conflict. As it was, although Eisenhower helped to fuel disenchantment with the conflict toward the end of the 1952 presidential campaign, his rhetoric was sufficiently vague to provide him with freedom to maneuver once he made it to the White House.

When Eisenhower finally concluded a truce six months into his presidency, the terms were little different from those Truman had sought. Across the country, the armistice was greeted with relief rather than rejoicing. And on Capitol Hill, most legislators were so keen to avoid this politically toxic issue that, as one close observer noted, Congress's inclination was "to keep hands off and to let the White House have all the credit and all the possible blame alike." Nonetheless, as the truce settled down and no major flare-ups were reported, the bulk of Americans increasingly considered the resolution of this strange war—the first in the nation's history without a clear-cut decision—to be Eisenhower's greatest achievement during his first year in office.[14]

In the ensuing years, Korea came to occupy an ambivalent place in the nation's consciousness. On the one hand, a "Korean syndrome" of sorts did develop. Less than a year after the armistice, few Americans were keen to get involved in another war in Asia, this time to help the ailing French effort to regain full control over its colonies in Indochina. After the French finally left, the United States provided South Vietnam with substantial aid in an effort to prevent this part of Indochina from falling to the communists. But for the next decade, many politicians, recalling the political damage the limited war in Korea had done to Truman's presidency, were reluctant to use U.S. troops to achieve their goals in Vietnam.[15]

Yet this "Korean syndrome" was never an all-powerful constraint, stopping decisionmakers from waging another "brushfire" land war in Asia. On the contrary, by 1965 the dominant image from this earlier experience pointed in the direction of waging a new limited conflict on the same continent.

Korea, after all, could be considered a success as a containment operation. By acting decisively in June 1950, Truman had stopped the south of the country from falling to communism. Although the more grandiose goal of unifying the peninsula had not been achieved, South Korea remained an American ally—a state of affairs Washington was desperate to achieve in Vietnam. By 1965, both Lyndon Johnson and Dean Rusk, who had been at or near the forefront of the Korean policy debates, thought these "lessons" could be applied again. Rusk, in particular, was "convinced that what we had done in Korea was a good thing to do." As a State Department colleague recalled, he believed "we had finally won in Korea and therefore by applying enough effort and enough time we should be able to prevail in Vietnam as we had in Korea."[16]

Once the United States escalated its presence in Vietnam, the Korean analogy created other grounds for hope. By scrupulously avoiding a rerun of October–November 1950, when pushing north had triggered the Chinese intervention, officials thought they could contain communism without dangerously intensifying wider Cold War tensions. Because the media had done so little to report the awful horrors of the Korean conflict, from the saturation bombing to the repressions of the Rhee regime, officials were also confident they could wage another war without too much scrutiny into its unsavory implementation. Thus, with Korea as a guide, a limited war in Vietnam not only seemed possible but also promised to be relatively painless at home.

In reality, of course, it was no such thing. Vietnam proved to be such a disaster that it holds the spotlight whenever Americans now think about war. The Korean experience, in contrast, is invariably consigned to the dim shadows. Beyond the commonplace statements that Korea came at a time of McCarthyite mayhem and stifling consensus, or the mechanical assertion that in this, as in other wars, approval ebbed as casualties grew, few have made the effort to analyze the complex dimensions of America's domestic debate. This is a shame because while Korea provides no simple parallels for other generations, a close assessment of this episode certainly illuminates some of the central dilemmas associated with waging a small, limited conflict in the midst of a broader struggle with an implacable enemy.

As we have seen, part of the story that unfolds from such an assessment is surprising. In Korea, the government did have some power to salvage a degree of popular support even when the fighting dragged on, in part because officials at all levels of the government had the astuteness to learn from their mistakes. Put another way, in this war there was no linear relationship between public opinion and casualties. It was not simply the case that support collapsed as the costs mounted, for the government found ways to redefine its objectives, while also improving its relationships with key mediating voices in the polity.

But this conclusion should not be taken to mean that selling a war is easy. In Korea, Truman had important strengths. The United States was involved in a conventional conflict, which by the middle of 1951 had reached a stalemate. The reasons for America's initial intervention were clear-cut: the United States was responding to naked aggression. Because the North Korean attack also shocked many in the international community, Washington acted at the behest of the UN. And despite all the political attacks directed at this body, its support gave the Korean War the veneer of legality and legitimacy.

As a result of all these advantages, Truman was in a far stronger position to spark and sustain support for a war than have been his successors who have tried to fight costly guerrilla conflicts in which the pretext is unclear, widespread international support is lacking, and the chances of any sort of meaningful victory are slim. But even in Korea, selling war was a complex job. The government had to devise multifaceted messages to sell to a multilayered audience. Its efforts to keep the conflict limited also placed considerable constraints on what officials believed they could say and do. On the one major occasion that the administration abandoned this caution and embraced rollback, it generated even bigger problems. Indeed, by expanding their war aims to embrace Korean unity, officials not only precipitated China's intervention but also created a good deal of public confusion over what would constitute a successful outcome. When the war dragged on for two more years while negotiators haggled over details at the truce talks, it was not surprising that public exasperation and impatience grew. What is striking, however, is the fact that public support never collapsed. Here was where the Truman administration enjoyed its biggest success, but it was essentially a negative achievement—it prevented popular resentment of Korea from totally overwhelming Truman's whole Cold War policy.

Overall, then, we ought to see the record in Korea as a cautionary tale. Even in the relatively favorable environment of the early 1950s, when officials at all levels made impressive efforts to refine and improve their propaganda efforts, both the Truman and Eisenhower administrations often floundered and foundered when faced with the fraught task of selling a costly, protracted, messy war. Eisenhower escaped relatively unscathed. But for Truman, Korea was the catalyst that first brought about the downward spiral in his approval ratings and then ensured that the Republicans recaptured the White House for the first time in more than twenty years. In a war that took millions of lives, including more than thirty-five thousand Americans killed in action, this result was scarcely the most important. But it ought to act as a stark and brutal reminder of the severe political costs associated with taking the nation into a "limited" war.

NOTES

Abbreviations Used in Notes

AFL	American Federation of Labor
AP	Associated Press
AWF	Ann Whitman File, Eisenhower Papers, Eisenhower Library
Chief of I&E	Chief of Information and Education
CoS	Chief of Staff
CPD	Committee on Present Danger
CQ	*Congressional Quarterly Almanac*
CR	Congressional Relations
DA MC	Dean Acheson, Memorandum of Conversation, Acheson Papers, HSTL
DDEL	Dwight D. Eisenhower Library
DNC	Democratic National Committee
DOPS	Daily Opinion Summary, State Department, Foster Files, boxes 5–6, RG 59, National Archives
FEC	Far East Command
FO	Foreign Office
FRUS	*Foreign Relations of the United States*
HSTL	Harry S. Truman Library
HU	Harvard University, Houghton Library
LC	Library of Congress
MCHC	Marine Corps Historical Center
MemCon	Memorandum of Conversation
MHS	Massachusetts Historical Society
MSAO	Monthly Survey of American Opinion on International Affairs, State Department, Foster Files, box 12, RG 59
NA/CLA	National Archives/Center for Legislative Archives

NA-UK	National Archives-UK
NSC	National Security Council
OF	Official File
OH	Oral History
OHC	Ohio Historical Center
OPI	Office of Public Information, Defense Department
PA	Office of Public Affairs, State Department
PC	Press Conference
PIO	Public Information Office
PIO Command Report	Eighth Army, Public Information Office, Command Report, RG 407, National Archives
PIO, SSR	Far East Command, Public Information Office, Staff Section Report, RG 407, National Archives
PRWG	Public Relations Working Group
PSF	President's Secretary's File
PU	Princeton University
RG	Record Group, National Archives (unless otherwise stated)
RNC	Republican National Committee
SCAP	Supreme Commander for the Allied Powers
SMOF	Staff Member and Office Files
TelCon	Memorandum of Telephone Conversation
TP	Truman Papers, Truman Library
UP	United Press
WHS	Wisconsin Historical Society

Introduction

1. Osgood, *Limited War*, 13; Spanier, *The Truman-MacArthur Controversy*, 2–7; Higgins, *Korea and the Fall of MacArthur*, viii; Rees, *Korea*, x–xvi. For an incisive discussion of the limited-war literature see Herring, *LBJ and Vietnam*, chs. 1 and 5. For a recent discussion of some of these issues, see Stueck, *Rethinking*, ch. 8.

2. Hamby, "Comments," 170

3. Willoughby, "Truth about Korea," 37; Vorhees, *Korean Tales*, 80–96. The army's official historian of the war often peppered his accounts with criticisms of press coverage. See Appleman, *South to the Naktong*, 264–65; *Disaster in Korea*, 61; *Escaping the Trap*, 339.

4. As one account puts it, during World War II both the military and media decided "that cooperation held more benefits than confrontation. The mood continued throughout the Korean conflict. Although tensions increased, relative harmony still prevailed." Not until Vietnam did a sense of "corrosive animosity" start to evolve. Hammond, *Reporting Vietnam*, ix. See also Hallin, *"Uncensored War,"* 38; Prochnau, *Once upon a Distant War*, 33. For a review of the Vietnam literature, see Carruthers, *Media at War*,

110–120. Brief assessments of the military-media relationship during the Korean War can be found in Knightley, *First Casualty*, ch. 14; Braestrup, *Battle Lines*, ch. 3. But neither were based on extensive use of primary source materials; as Braestrup pointed out in his study, since "much relevant archival material remains to be explored," his judgments on Korea were "tentative."

5. Mueller, *War, Presidents, and Public Opinion*.

6. Kernell, *Going Public*; Edwards, *Public Presidency*; Hart, *Sound of Leadership*.

7. See, for example, Gaddis, *United States and the Origins of the Cold War*, 351–52; Freeland, *Truman Doctrine*; Paterson, "Presidential Foreign Policy, Public Opinion, and Congress," 3–4; Kofsky, *Truman and the War Scare of 1948*.

8. See, for example, Gaddis, *Strategies*, 108; Christensen, *Useful Adversaries*, 125–27, 180–81; Hogan, *Cross of Iron*, 300–301; Bernhard, "Clearer Than Truth," 561–63; Fordham, *Building the Cold War Consensus*, 68–69, 115–16.

9. See, for instance, Hixson, *Parting the Curtain*; Krugler, *Voice of America*; and Osgood, *Total Cold War*.

10. Taylor, *Munitions of the Mind*, 6.

11. Campbell and Jamieson, *Deeds Done in Words*; Smith and Smith, *White House Speaks*, 23.

12. For a good survey of U.S. propaganda before Korea, see Osgood, *Total Cold War*, 15–39.

13. "Truman Sets Up a Speech Factory," *U.S. News & World Report*, November 10, 1950; Carlin, "Harry S. Truman," 40–67.

14. Hamby, *Man of the People*, 300–301.

15. For background on Ross's career, see Farrar, *Reluctant Servant*. On stress in the press office, see Heller, ed., *Truman White House*, 109, 145.

16. Barrett, OH; Beisner, *Acheson*, 96.

17. McNaughton, "Johnson-Acheson," September 1, 1950, folder 601, *Time* Dispatches, HU; McFarland and Roll, *Johnson and the Arming of America*, 225, 262–64; Beisner, *Acheson*, 123.

18. Erwin, "Voluntary Censorship Asked in Korean War"; "60 Now Cover Pentagon for News, Briefings"; both in *Editor & Publisher*, July 8 and August 5, 1950.

19. Rearden, *History of the Office of the Secretary of Defense*, 1:80–83; Condit, *History of the Office of the Secretary of Defense*, 2:26–27.

20. Reston, "Acheson Acts to Increase Foreign Policy Information," *New York Times*, November 3, 1949; FO, Research Department, "Reorganization of the State Department, 1949–50," February 16, 1950, FO 371/81614, NA-UK. Russell, OH. Bernhard, *U.S. Television News*, 70–71.

21. See, for instance, Gross to Austin, June 27, 1950, UN: Korea, Secret Reports, box 5, Austin Papers, University of Vermont; Shulman to Jessup, October 12, 1950, SMOF: Murphy, box 8, TP.

22. Throughout the text, I have used "Formosa" rather than "Taiwan," because that was the common usage in the United States at the time.

23. These eruptions have been the subject of much scholarly interest. See, for instance, Rovere and Schlesinger, *MacArthur Controversy*; Spanier, *Truman-MacArthur Controversy*; James, *Years of MacArthur*; Weintraub, *MacArthur's War*.

24. As well as being UN commander, MacArthur was commander in chief of U.S. forces in the Far East. In many documents of the time, his command was thus referred to as FEC or FECOM. However, to avoid confusion, and because the Joint Chiefs of Staff instructed MacArthur to emphasize the UN label, I refer to his command as the UNC throughout the text. I also use *Tokyo* as shorthand for MacArthur's headquarters.

25. Steward, "Monthly Historical Report—PI Section," September 2, 1950, Unit Records: 1st Cavalry Division, box 5, RG 338.

26. Cohen, *Public's Impact on Foreign Policy*, 172–73.

27. For an excellent discussion of these issues, see Stueck, *Rethinking*, ch. 8.

28. Kernell, *Going Public*.

29. Edwards, *On Deaf Ears*, 241; Zaller, "Elite Leadership of Mass Opinion," 187–88. Periods of crisis are the one exception to Edwards's main argument, which is that presidential leadership of public opinion is often surprisingly "ineffective not only for achieving majority support [for a president's program] but also for increasing support from a smaller base," largely because presidents have to compete with other mediating voices in order to get their message to a mass public that, in any case, is often apathetic and inattentive.

30. Westerfield, *Foreign Policy and Party Politics*; Caridi, *Korean War and American Politics*; Kepley, *Collapse of the Middle Way*.

31. Truman, *Congressional Party*, esp. 280–92.

32. Leuchtenberg, *White House Looks South*, 178–210.

33. Notes on Cabinet Meeting, July 8, 1950, box 1, Connelly Papers, HSTL.

34. DA MC, August 14, 1950; Wooley, *Alternatives to Anarchy*, 85–120.

35. Darby, "Prex Week II," December 8, 1950, folder 621, *Time* Dispatches, HU. Elsey to Truman, February 2 and 9, 1951, PSF (General): Elsey, box 119, TP.

36. McFall, Memo, March 1951, CR Asst. SecState, subject file, box 3, RG 59.The State Department's PA also had to promote policies without violating the Smith-Mundt Act of 1947, which prohibited spending money to influence Congress. Beisner, *Acheson*, 116.

37. Savage, *Truman and the Democratic Party*, 74–80.

38. Wala, "Selling the Marshall Plan at Home," 247–65.

39. Cumings, *Origins*, 2:44, 416–17. See also Beisner, *Acheson*, 316.

40. Griffith, "Selling of America," 388–412. Bernhard, *U.S. Television News*.

41. Caution was particularly evident in the new medium of television. See Barnouw, *Tube of Plenty*, 112; Whitfield, *Culture of the Cold War*, 154–5, 166–67; Bernhard, *U.S. Television News*, 56–59; Doherty, *Cold War, Cool Medium*, 19–36. For a strong argument that the media fully shared the Cold

War ideology the government propagated, see Fousek, *To Lead the Free World*, 186–88.

42. Cater, *Fourth Branch of Government*, 4–6; Cohen, *Press and Foreign Policy*, 21–22, 55, 81–89; Sigal, *Reporters and Officials*, 42–49, 104–15, 119–33.

43. Bernhard, *U.S. Television News*, 2–3.

44. Pedelty, *War Stories*, 6–8, 29, 72–76; Carruthers, *Media at War*, 5, 15; Ginneken, *Understanding Global News*, 65–75.

45. Braestrup, *Battle Lines*, 47.

46. Truman, *Years of Trial and Hope*, 433–36, 441, 470; Acheson, *Present at the Creation*, 415, 526–27.

47. Tucker, *Patterns in the Dust*, 145–53. Baughman, *Luce and the Rise of the American News Media*, 154–55; Trimble, *Scripps-Howard Handbook*, 3–8, 171–215.

48. PA, "Press and Radio Opinion on the Senate Investigation of State Department Personnel," March 17, 1950, Foster files, box 20, RG 59.

49. Cater, *Fourth Branch of Government*, 3. For background on the wire services, see Morris, *Deadline Every Minute*; Ritchie, *Reporting from Washington*, 111–18.

50. Miraldi, *Muckraking and Objectivity*, 14–17; Tuchman, "Objectivity as Strategic Ritual," 660–79.

51. Bayley, *McCarthy and the Press*, esp. 66–78.

52. Truman, *Public Papers*, June 1, 1950; Paige, *Korean Decision*, 47–48; Rose, *Cold War Comes to Main Street*, 164.

Chapter 1. Keeping the Home Front Cool

1. Ayers Diary, June 25, 1950, box 20, Ayers Papers, HSTL; "Truman Flies to DC for Conferences," *Washington Post*, June 26, 1950. On the first hours of the crisis, see Paige, *Korean Decision*, 93–94, 113–15; Foot, *Wrong War*, 56; Appleman, *South to the Naktong*, 18–19.

2. "March of the News," *US News & World Report*, July 14, 1950. Ellipses in original.

3. *FRUS, 1950*, 7:50; Paige, *Korean Decision*, 96–100; Donovan, *Tumultuous Years*, 197.

4. *FRUS, 1950*, 7:157–161; Ayers Diary, June 25, 1950.

5. *FRUS, 1950*, 7:128; Beishline to Collins, June 25, 1950, Central Decimal File 091 (Korea), box 557, RG 319.

6. Merchant to Rusk, June 25, 1950, CR Asst. SecState, subject file, box 1, RG 59. "Radio Broadcast for ABC," June 25, 1950, UN: Korea, Secret Reports, box 5, Austin Papers, University of Vermont; Paige, *Korean Decision*, 120–21.

7. DA MC, June 26, 1950.

8. OPI, Activity Reports, June 26 and June 27, 1950, box 151, RG 330. Ayers Diary, June 26, 1950.

9. DOPS, June 27, 1950.

10. Connally, "World Policy and Bipartisanship," *U.S. News & World Report*, May 5, 1950; Murrow, "With the News," June 26, 1950, Murrow

Papers, LC. "North Korea's Attack Catches 'Hill' Committees by Surprise," *Washington Post*, June 26, 1950. At the same time, some in official Washington were confident that the South Koreans could survive on their own. See Connally, *My Name Is Tom Connally*, 344–6.

11. "Voting Statistics," Voting Records file, ML 3, box 63, Tobey Papers, Dartmouth College. On the "fluidity" of the Republican Party in the Eighty-First Congress, see Truman, *Congressional Party*, 280–81. See also Westerfield, *Foreign Policy and Party Politics*; Caridi, *Korean War and American Politics*; and Kepley, *Collapse of the Middle Way*.

12. The term "diehard" is taken from Lubell, *Revolt of the Moderates*, 88.

13. Reeves, *McCarthy*, 297, 308–11; Patterson, *Mr. Republican*, 446–51.

14. Leary, "Smith of New Jersey," 132–54. Montgomery and Johnson, *One Step from the White House*, 81–93.

15. Kepley, *Collapse of the Middle Way*, 64–68.

16. DOPS, June 26, 1950.

17. Meeting, June 26, 1950, Republican Minority Policy Committee Minutes, box 3, RG 46; Smith Diary, June 27, 1950, Smith Papers, PU. For background, see Ritchie, *A History of the U.S. Senate Republican Policy Committee*.

18. Murrow, "With the News," June 26 and 30, 1950, Murrow Papers, LC; Albright, "Congress Eyes Chance of War; Keep Calm, Its Leaders Urge," *Washington Post*, June 27, 1950.

19. Krock, "In the Nation," *New York Times*, June 27, 1950; "Republicans: Critical, but in Line," *Newsweek*, July 10, 1950, 24–25; McNaughton, "Congress Week," June 26, 1950, folder 588, *Time* Dispatches, HU.

20. *FRUS, 1950*, 7:178–83.

21. *FRUS, 1950*, 7:182. "Preparation of President's Message to Congress on Korea, July 19, 1950," subject file, Korea, box 71, Elsey Papers, HSTL.

22. Meeting, January 23, 1950, Republican Conference Minority Policy Committee Minutes, box 3, RG 46; Kepley, *Collapse of the Middle Way*, 80–82; Patterson, *Mr. Republican*, 444–49; Berger, "Bipartisanship," 233–36.

23. DA MC, April 27, 1950, *FRUS*, microfiche supp.; Acheson, *Present at the Creation*, 364.

24. *FRUS, 1950*, 7:182; Murphy to Connelly, June 27, 1950, SMOF: Murphy, Korea, box 22, TP.

25. Bookman and McNaughton, "Add Korea Running," June 27, 1950, *Time* Dispatches, HU.

26. *FRUS, 1950*, 7:200–202.

27. Truman, *Public Papers*, June 27, 1950; *DSB* 23:43–46.

28. Barrett, *Truth Is Our Weapon*, 157.

29. *FRUS, 1950*, 7:169. Truman, *Public Papers*, June 27, 1950.

30. Truman, *Public Papers*, June 28, 1950; Paige, *Korean Decision*, 202, 212. .

31. Shulman to Barrett, June 28, 1950, subject file, Korea, box 71, Elsey Papers.

32. *DSB* 23:43–46.

33. Truman, *Public Papers*, June 29, 1950.

34. James, *Years of MacArthur*, 3:425–26.

35. Truman, *Years of Trial and Hope*, 388; Paige, *Korean Decision*, 245–46; Schnabel, *Policy and Direction*, 47.

36. Minutes of Meeting with Congressional Leaders, June 30, 1950, subject file, Korea, box 71, Elsey Papers.

37. Truman, *Public Papers*, June 30, 1950; Ross, PC, June 29, 1950, box 17, Ayers Papers.

38. "Truman's Conversation with Elsey," June 26, 1950, subject file, Korea, box 71, Elsey Papers.

39. The prospect of another Truman Doctrine speech was widely discussed. In August, MacArthur would tell Harriman that the Truman Doctrine was "great" and should be expanded to Asia. See Harriman, Mem-Con, Korean Trip folder, box 306, Harriman Papers, LC. At the Wake Island meeting in October, MacArthur would also pressure the president to deliver a Truman Doctrine for Asia; the president would decline. See *FRUS, 1950*, 7: 956–57.

40. Hamby, *Beyond the New Deal*, 176–77.

41. Gross to Austin, June 27, 1950, UN: Korea, Secret Reports, box 5, Austin Papers. Emphasis in original.

42. *FRUS, 1950*, 7:158 and 1:325–26, 330, 337–38. Minutes of NSC Meeting, June 28, 1950, box 2, RG 273. Gaddis, "Korea in American Politics," 281–83; Foot, *Wrong War*, 57.

43. The U.S. ambassador in Moscow and the British ally both advised against publicly connecting the Soviet Union with the attack. See *FRUS, 1950*, 7:158, 169–70, 186–87; Farrar-Hockley, *British Part in the Korean War*, 31–32.

44. Nitze to Acheson, July 23, 1950, PPS files, Congressional folder, box 8, RG 59.

45. Hamby, *Man of the People*, 558; Eisinger, *Evolution of Presidential Polling*, 45–46.

46. Heller, ed., *Truman White House*, 146; Donovan, *Tumultuous Years*, 81

47. Russell, OH. See also Elder, *Policy Machine*, 137–50.

48. DOPS, February 2, 1950. McMahon, "The Hydrogen Bomb," February 2, 1950; "Peace and Problems of Atomic Energy," March 1, 1950; both in Address and Press Releases file, box 7, McMahon Papers, LC.

49. Elsey, Memo, November 10, 1950, Speech file, box 47, Elsey Papers.

50. *FRUS, 1950*, 1:185–87, 225–26; *DSB* 22: 272–74, 427–30. For observations on Acheson's speeches, see British Embassy, "Weekly Political Summary," March 18, 1950, FO 371/81611, NA-UK.

51. Paige, *Korean Decision*, 47.

52. *FRUS, 1950*, 1:140–41.

53. Russell to Rusk and Nitze, February 6, 1950, CR Asst. SecState, subject file, box 3, RG 59.

54. Johnson, interview with Kruse, July 6, 1950, CR Asst. SecState, subject file, box 1, RG 59.

55. *FRUS, 1950*, 7:287.

56. Taft, "Korean Crisis Caused by Wavering Foreign Policies of Administration," June 28, 1950, Senate (Foreign Policy): MacArthur Hearings, box 628, Taft Papers, LC.

57. Smith Diary, June 29, 1950, July 1 and 5, 1950; "Proposed Joint Resolution," undated, box 100, Smith Papers.

58. DA MC, July 3, 1950.

59. *FRUS, 1950*, 7:287–91; Notes on Cabinet Meetings, July 8, 1950, box 2, Connelly Papers, HSTL.

60. *FRUS, 1950*, 7:288.

61. Albright, "Truman Calls Senate Leaders to 4th 2-Party Meeting Today," *Washington Post*, July 11, 1950.

62. Marshall to Truman, July 10, 1950; Truman to Marshall, July 15, 1950; both in American Red Cross Papers, General Correspondence, folder 164/5, Marshall Papers, Marshall Library. Ferrell, *Off the Record*, 192.

63. Ayers Diary, June 29 and July 3, 1950; Acheson, *Present at the Creation*, 373–74. For evidence of Johnson's publicity campaign against Acheson, see typescript of staff meetings, February 8, 1950, box 147, Johnson Papers, University of Virginia.

64. "Press Briefings and Interviews," July 7, 1950, Chief of I & E files, Unclassified Central Decimal File 000.71, box 5, RG 319. Truman, *Public Papers*, July 6, 1950.

65. Beal to Bermingham, July 7, 1950, folder 590, *Time* Dispatches, HU.

66. MSAO, June 1950; Gallup, "Survey Finds 8 of 10 Voters Approve U.S. Help to Korea," *Washington Post*, July 2, 1950; Hassett to Ross, June 29, 1950, OF 471B, box 1305, TP.

67. DOPS, June 29, 1950.

68. Albright, "Truman Gets Full Backing from Congress," *Washington Post*, June 28, 1950; Hinton, "Legislators Hail Action by Truman," *New York Times*, June 28, 1950; Smith Diary, June 28, 1950; Sevareid, "News Analysis," June 28, 1950, box I:D5, Sevareid Papers, LC.

69. Howard to Truman, July 21, 1950, City file (Washington): General, box 251; Hawkins to Howard, July 24, 1950, City file (NY): Hawkins, box 249; both in Howard Papers, LC.

70. Kern, Levering, and Levering, *Kennedy Crises*, 7–9. For the argument that the press simply echoed the administration's line during the early stages of the Korean crisis, see Aronson, *Press and the Cold War*, 107.

71. Ross, PC, box 17, Ayers Papers, July 3, 1950.

72. Ayers Diary, July 7, 1950; Notes on Cabinet Meetings, July 21, 1950, box 2, Connelly Papers.

73. Leveiro, "President Asks 260 Millions to Expedite Hydrogen Bomb," *New York Times*, July 8, 1950.

74. DOPS, July 7, 10, and 12, 1950.

75. Taft, "The Korean Crisis Caused by Wavering Foreign Policies of Administration," June 28, 1950, Senate (Foreign Policy): MacArthur Hearings, box 628, Taft Papers, LC.

76. DOPS, June 30, 1950; Special for Guylay, June 28 and 29, 1950, Radio Reports, 1950 Campaign folder, box 276, Taft Papers; McNaughton, "Congress Week," July 1, 1950, folder 590, *Time* Dispatches, HU.

77. Smith Diary, June 29, 1950. Smith, "The Korean Crisis and American Policy in the Far East," July 5, 1950, copy in Legislative: Korea, 1950, box 670, Taft Papers. For similar charges, see *Congressional Record, 1950*, 9994, 10560, 10558–59.

78. "Story of America's Policy Shift," *Wall Street Journal*, June 28, 1950; "Political Hay in Korea," editorial, *Cleveland Plain Dealer*, July 3, 1950. See also DOPS, June 28, 1950.

79. Andrews, "U.S. Far East Policy Reversed by Truman's Order for Action, *NYHT*; "Truman Act Given Support by U.S. Press," *Washington Post*; both June 28, 1950.

80. Russell to Shulman, June 29, 1950, box 10; Russell to Howe, June 30, 1950, box 4; both in PA Asst. SecState, subject file, RG 59.

81. *DSB* 23:49–50.

82. "Preparation of President's Message." DA MC, July 10, 1950.

83. DA MC, July 10 and 14, 1950.

Chapter 2. *"Censorship Is Abhorrent to General MacArthur"*

1. SCAP, press release, June 26, 1950, PIO, subject file, box 27, RG 331.

2. Erwin, "Newsmen Deployed for Fast Coverage of Korean War," *Editor & Publisher*, July 1, 1950, 11; Detzer, *Thunder of the Captains*, 60–64.

3. Simmons, "*Tribune* Writer Tells How War Looks at Front," *Chicago Tribune*, June 26, 1950.

4. Parrott, "U.S. Force Fighting," *New York Times*, June 28, 1950.

5. PA, "Aggression in Korea," July 17, 1950, Info Memos, box 2, RG 59.

6. Beech, *Tokyo and Points East*, 107–22; Higgins, *War in Korea*, 16–34.

7. Murrow, "With the News," June 30, 1950, Murrow Papers, LC; AP, "South's Soldiers Walk Away after Enemy Armor Breaks Defense Line on Han River," *Washington Post*, July 1, 1950.

8. AP, "South's Soldiers Walk Away after Enemy Armor Breaks Defense Line on Han River"; UP, "Trigger Happy Koreans Make Front Safer Than Behind Lines"; both in *Washington Post*, July 1 and 5, 1950.

9. SCAP, press release, June 27, 1950, PIO, subject file, box 27, RG 331.

10. Higgins, *War in Korea*, 30.

11. Minutes of Meeting of Interdepartmental Info Committee, July 6, 1950, PA Asst. SecState, subject file, box 4, RG 59.

12. Ayers Diary, July 1, 1950, box 20, Ayers Papers, HSTL; Allison, *Ambassador from the Prairie*, 132–38. A teletype conference consisted of MacArthur in Tokyo and the Joint Chiefs in Washington sending each other messages by a coded teleprinter. They could read what the other had written on screens, allowing prompt if primitive communication. See Weintraub, *MacArthur's War*, 38.

13. Ayers Diary, July 1, 1950, box 20, Ayers Papers, HSTL; Allison, *Ambassador from the Prairie*, 132–38; Schaller, "MacArthur's Japan," 5–7.

14. AMG, G-3, July 9, 1950, Geographic file: Central Decimal File, CCS 383.21 (Korea), S.23, box 38, RG 218. Schnabel and Watson, *Joint Chiefs of Staff and National Policy*, vol. 3, 1:74–84; Blair, *Forgotten War*, 121–22.

15. SCAP, Correspondents Location Register, July 17, 1950, PIO, subject file, box 24, RG 331.

16. Boyle to Boyle, August 7, 1950, correspondence folder, box 1, Boyle Papers, WHS.

17. Echols to Correspondents, July 2, 1950, General Correspondence, box 4, RG 6, MacArthur Papers, MacArthur Memorial Library; Erwin, "Voluntary Censorship Asked in Korean War," *Editor & Publisher*, July 8, 1950.

18. Erwin, "2 American Correspondents Lose Lives in Korean War," *Editor & Publisher*, July 15, 1950; Echols, "Information in the Combat Zone," 61–64. On World War II censorship see Sweeney, *Secrets of Victory*, 3, 51.

19. Martin, "MacArthur Censorship," 3–4. Coughlin, *Conquered Press*, 1–2, 46–58, 111–40. James, *Years of MacArthur*, 2:89, 164–65, 277–78, 708–9; and 3:304–6.

20. On MacArthur the "visionary" during this period, see Cumings, "Introduction," 53; James, *Years of MacArthur*, 3:467.

21. FEC, PIO, "Narrative Historical Report," January–October 1950, box 362, RG 407; Echols, "Information in the Combat Zone," 61–64.

22. MacArthur to Department of Army, July 7, 1950, WARCXDA folder, box 26; MacArthur to Department of Army, September 12, 1950, DACX folder, box 24; both in RG 9, MacArthur Papers. On the lack of trained PI personnel, see also Almond to Harrison, July 30, 1950, Chief of I & E files, Central Decimal File 000.74, box 194, RG 319.

23. Oldfield, "USAF Press Relations in the Far East," 40–45.

24. Parks to Lockhart, September 21, 1950, Chief of I & E files, Unclassified Central Decimal File 000.73, box 5, RG 319.

25. FEC, PIO, "Narrative Historical Report," January–October 1950, box 362, RG 407; James, *Years of MacArthur*, 3:304–5.

26. Hoberecht, "190 Reporters Augment Corps at Tokyo Club," *Editor & Publisher*, August 5, 1950; Pomeroy, *Foreign Correspondents in Japan*, 13–14.

27. FEC, PIO, "Narrative Historical Report," January–October 1950, box 362, RG 407; Almond to Harrison, July 30, 1950, Chief of I & E files, Central Decimal File 000.74, box 194, RG 319.

28. Dorn, "Briefing the Press," 36–41.

29. "News Cooperation Asked by MacArthur," *New York Times*, July 3, 1950.

30. Appleman, *South to the Naktong*, 179–81.

31. Collins to Truman, July 16, 1950, OF 471B, TP.

32. SCAP, press releases, July 8, July 11, July 12, July 13, July 20, 1950, PIO, subject file, box 27, RG 331; "Yank Armor Said to Fight 'Very Nicely,'" *Washington Post*, July 10, 1950. For the actual record of what was developing in Korea, see Appleman, *South to the Naktong*, 82–86, 94.

33. Erwin, "Voluntary Censorship Asked in Korean War," *Editor & Publisher*, July 8, 1950.

34. Pedelty, *War Stories*, 29–30, 130; Carruthers, *Media at War*, 5, 15.

35. Erwin, "Korean War Claims Dozen Casualties among Reporters," *Editor & Publisher*, August 5, 1950.

36. Higgins, "Marines Find Action Worse Than Tarawa," *Washington Post*, August 9, 1950; Lambert, "Wounded GIs Fight to Their Last Cartridge," *St. Louis Post-Dispatch*, July 9, 1950. For a good sample of such micro-level stories, see Boyle's dispatches for the AP, Speeches and Writings folder, box 6, Boyle Papers.

37. Beech, *Tokyo and Points East*, 171.

38. "Thomis Has No Beef with Korean Censorship," *Editor & Publisher*, October 14, 1950. For an example of UP sending a correspondent to the front with instructions to write "human homespun stuff" in the mold of Ernie Pyle, see Baillie to Howard, August 1, 1950, City file (NY): UP, Baillie, box 250, Howard Papers, LC.

39. UP Ad, "Front Line to By-Line," *Editor & Publisher*, September 16, 1950; Baillie, *High Tension*, 261; Morris, *Deadline Every Minute*, 321.

40. Pomeroy, *Foreign Correspondents in Japan*, 35; Prochnau, *Once upon a Distant War*, 65–66.

41. Higgins, "Not a Battle, but Slaughter, Dazed GIs Say"; Bigart, "Outnumbered, Outgunned GIs Bitter at Untenable Positions"; both in *Washington Post*, July 9, 1950. For the battle, see Appleman, *South to the Naktong*, 82–88.

42. MacArthur to Department of Army, July 12, 1950, WARZXDA folder, box 149, RG 9, MacArthur Papers; SCAP, communiqué no. 72, July 13, 1950, PIO, subject file, box 27, RG 331.

43. MacArthur to Department of Army, July 12, 1950, WARZXDA folder, box 149; Department of Army to MacArthur, July 14, 1950, WARWX folder, box 113; both in RG 9, MacArthur Papers.

44. Morris, *Deadline Every Minute*, 321; Boyle to Boyle, August 7, 1950, correspondence folder, box 1, Boyle Papers.

45. AP, "M'Arthur Cancels Ban on Reporters," *New York Times*, July 16, 1950.

46. "Teletype to Speed Korea War Reports"; "News from Korea Cut Off for Hours"; both in *New York Times*, July 19 and August 20, 1950. "Correspondents Wait in Line for 1 Korean Phone," *Editor & Publisher*, July 15, 1950.

47. Parks to Echols, July 22, 1950, Chief of I & E files, Unclassified Central Decimal File 000.73, box 5, RG 319.

48. Higgins, *War in Korea*, 97; Erwin, "Censorship, Communications Worry 200 K-War Writers," *Editor & Publisher*, July 22, 1950.

49. Reid to MacArthur, July 17, 1950, I: D96; Higgins to Reid, undated, I: D95; both in Reid Family Papers, LC.

50. Erwin, "Censorship, Communications." "Korea War Censorship Looms," *Washington Post*, July 16, 1950.

51. "Varieties of Censorship," editorial, *New York Times*, July 17, 1950.

52. Early to Parks, July 15, 1950, Chief of I & E files, Unclassified Central Decimal File 000.73, box 5, RG 319.

53. "M'Arthur Cancels Ban on Reporters," *New York Times*, July 16, 1950.

54. FEC, PIO, "Narrative Historical Report," January–October 1950, box 362, RG 407; Almond to Harrison, July 30, 1950 Chief of I & E files, Central Decimal File 000.74, box 194, RG 319.

55. Erwin, "Korean War Claims Dozen Casualties," *Editor & Publisher*, August 5, 1950.

56. Gore-Booth to Graves, July 10, 1950, FO 115/4486, NA-UK.

57. Gore-Booth to Haydon, July 14, 1950, FO 115/4486, NA-UK. On Pearson, see Bayley, *McCarthy and the Press*, 57, 165

58. MacArthur, telegram, July 15, 1950; MacArthur to Akers, July 16, 1950; both in General Correspondence, box 1, RG 6, MacArthur Papers.

59. Memo, undated, "This Is Background to Murrow 'Kill Order,'" file 343, Murrow Papers; Persico, *Murrow*, 244–46, 291–93. Paley soon reached the conclusion that formal censorship should be instituted in Korea. See Paley to Johnson, August 28, 1950, OPI files, Central Decimal File 000.73, box 17, RG 330.

60. "News Executives Prefer Voluntary Censorship Now," *Editor & Publisher*, August 19, 1950.

61. Parks to Early, August 7, 1950, Army CoS, Central Decimal File 091 (Korea), box 557, RG 319.

62. Alsop to Sommers, July 14, 1950; Sommers to Alsop, July 18, 1950; both in Special Correspondence: *Saturday Evening Post*, box 27, Alsop Papers, LC.

63. McGaw, "Commander's Public Relations Role," 25–31. For background on the Armed Forces Information School, see Binford, "Information Training for All Services," 3–10.

64. Collins to Kilbourne, August 4, 1950, Army CoS, Central Decimal File 000.74, box 548, RG 319.

65. Parks, "Commander and the Press," 17–34. Senior State Department officials also inclined toward censorship, on the grounds that "the communists are getting all the propaganda they need from news stories written by American correspondents." See Executive Secretariat, Summary of Daily Meeting, July 11, 1950, box 1, RG 59.

66. Parks to Early, July 17, 1950, Chief of I & E files, Unclassified Central Decimal File 000.73, box 5, RG 319.

67. "Lucas Urges Press, Radio Censor Selves"; "Censorship Plan Ready at Capital"; "Korean News Curb Urged"; all in *New York Times*, July 15 and 16, 1950. *Congressional Record, 1950*, 10175, 10357. Veterans of Foreign Wars also called for censorship; see Laporte to Johnson, July 12, 1950, OPI files, Central Decimal File 000.73, box 17, RG 330. Johnson's responses to numerous letters calling for censorship can also be found in this file.

68. Parks to Echols, July 22, 1950, Chief of I & E files, Unclassified Central Decimal File 000.73, box 5, RG 319.

69. "Beech Tells GI Blunders," *Chicago Daily News*, July 24, 1950.

70. Parks to Early, August 7, 1950, Chief of I & E files, Unclassified Central Decimal File 000.73, box 5, RG 319.

71. Parks to Early, August 7, 1950, Chief of I & E files, Unclassified Central Decimal File 000.73, box 5, RG 319.

72. Johnson to MacArthur, August 12, 1950, WARWX folder, box 113, RG 9, MacArthur Papers; Early to Bradley, August 7, 1950, OPI files, Central Decimal File 000.73, box 17, RG 330. On the battle, see Appleman, *South to the Naktong*, 270–74, 286–88.

73. "Press Asked Again to Guard Security," *New York Times*, August 12, 1950.

74. SCAP, press releases, July 11, July 12, July 13, July 20, 1950, PIO, subject file, box 27, RG 331.

75. FEC, PIO, "Amazingly Low Death Rate in Korea," October 23, 1950, box 362, RG 407; Higgins, "Newswoman Tells Harrowing Tale of Night Infiltration Raid on U.S. Command Post," *Washington Post*, August 4, 1950.

76. Fielder to Parks, July 21, 1950; Parks to Fielder, August 2, 1950; both in Chief of I & E files, Unclassified Central Decimal File 000.71, box 5, RG 319.

77. Roeder, *Censored War*, 7–25.

78. OPI, "Public Information Security Guidance No. 3: War Wounded," August 14, 1950, Policy, Planning, and Procedures for Release of Military Security Info, box 755, RG 330. When OPI did clear a picture of a wounded soldier for *Life*, it was careful to ensure "that the man's face was so obliterated that he would not be recognizable." See Levick to Mautner, August 17, 1950, OPI files, Central Decimal File 062, box 24, RG 330.

79. "Unproved Casualties Handed to Congress," *New York Times*, August 12, 1950.

80. "100 Seek War Beat Despite Privations"; "Communications Snag for War Reporters"; both in *Editor & Publisher*, August 12 and 26, 1950.

81. Blair to Bermingham, "Box Scores," July 28, 1950, folder 589, *Time* Dispatches, HU.

82. MacArthur to Department of Army, July 10, 1950, WARCXDA folder, box 26, RG 9, MacArthur Papers. OPI, "Press Branch Fact Sheets: Casualty Releases," August 10, 1950, Assistant Secretary of Defense for Public Affairs and Legislation, Press Releases Relating to Korean War Casualties, box 1, RG 330.

83. Memo for the Press, August 11, 1950, Assistant Secretary of Defense for Public Affairs and Legislation, Press Releases Relating to Korean War Casualties, box 1, RG 330. "U.S. Army Confirms 2,616 Casualties"; "Casualty Gap Denied"; both in *New York Times*, August 8 and 11, 1950.

84. Johnston, "GIs in Korea Handicapped by Unawareness of Mission," *New York Times*, August 13, 1950.

85. Andrews, "Korea Report Raises Spirits at Pentagon," *Washington Post*, August 10, 1950.

86. Bigart, "2 Generals Believe Reds Are Near End," *Washington Post*, August 25, 1950.

87. James, *Years of MacArthur*, 3:469–70; Schnabel and Watson, *Joint Chiefs of Staff and National Strategy*, vol. 3, 1:84–92.

88. Bolling to Ridgway, August 23, 1950; Bolling to Collins, September 7, 1950; both in Chief of I & E files, Central Decimal File, 000.73, box 194, RG 319.

89. MacArthur to Department of Army, September 28, 1950, WARZXDA folder, box 149, RG 9, MacArthur Papers.

90. Bigart, "The Marines' First Battle Action," *New York Herald Tribune*, August 8, 1950; "Why Are We Taking a Beating?" *Life*, July 24, 1950.

91. "Men under Fire: GIs versus Tanks"; "Where Did the Defense Billions Go?" both in *U.S. News & World Report*, July 14 and 28, 1950.

92. Smith to Johnson, July 7, 1950, Foreign Relations Committee: Korea, box 100, Smith Papers, PU. On the Alsops' campaign against Johnson, see Joseph Alsop, *"I've Seen the Best of It,"* 301–2; Hogan, *Cross of Iron*, 305–7.

93. Roosevelt to Truman, August 9, 1950, OF471B, box 1305, TP.

Chapter 3. Mobilizing for a Police Action

1. May, *American Cold War Strategy*, 11–15. Acheson, *Present at the Creation*, 374–75. Lawton, Memos for the Record, May 23 and 26, 1950, Meetings with Truman folder, box 6, Lawton Papers, HSTL.

2. The observation on Truman's speech was by Franks, January 7, 1950, FO371/81615, NA-UK. On Congress and defense spending, see Kolodziej, *Uncommon Defense and Congress*, 89–107, 119–23; Rearden, *History of the Office of the Secretary of Defense*, 1:75, 376–82.

3. *FRUS, 1950*, 1:185–87, 206–9, 225–26. Herter-Acheson, MemCon, March, 21 1950, Political files, bMS AM 1829 (c.890), Herter Papers, HU.

4. Schnabel and Watson, *Joint Chiefs of Staff and National Policy*, vol. 3, 1:73–79.

5. DA MC, July 14, 1950.

6. Booth to Bermingham, "Prex Week II," July 15, 1950, folder 593, *Time* Dispatches, HU. Ross relayed Truman's comment to this reporter.

7. Acheson, *Present at the Creation*, 413–14.

8. Truman, *Public Papers*, July 19, 1950; Ayers to Truman, July 20, 1950, PSF (Speech file): Public Reaction to Speeches, box 42, TP.

9. In fact, Truman did not come out in favor of NSC-68 until July 27, and even then it would take at least another month to finalize the programing and pricing. DA MC, July 27, 1950.

10. "Preparation of President's Message to Congress on Korea, July 19, 1950," subject file, Korea, box 71, Elsey Papers, HSTL. Hammond, "NSC-68," 352–53; *CQ, 1950*, 132; Condit, *History of the Office of the Secretary of Defense*, 2:226–27; Schnabel and Watson, *Joint Chiefs of Staff and National Policy*, vol. 3, 1:76–84.

11. "Preparation of President's Message," subject file, Korea, box 71, Elsey Papers. Hamby, *Beyond the New Deal*, 415; Pierpaoli, *Truman and Korea*, 33. On the previous political controversies surrounding controls, see Brinkley, *End of Reform*, 146–48; Hartmann, *Truman and the 80th Congress*, 4, 19–20. The Council of Economic Advisers also recommended curbing inflationary

pressures through fiscal and credit measures; see Council of Economic Advisers to Truman, August 9, 1950, box 9, Blough Papers, HSTL.

12. Steelman's comments were "not for attribution." Bookman, "Economic Mobilization," June 30, 1950, folder 589, *Time* Dispatches, HU.

13. U.S. Congress, Senate, *Hearings before Committee on Banking and Currency: Defense Production Act*, 26.

14. *FRUS, 1950*, 1:206–9, 225; *DSB* 22:673–75, 1038–39.

15. *FRUS, 1950*, 1:312–13, 323–24.

16. "Senator Demands U.S. Call Up Guard," *New York Times*, July 13, 1950; DOPS, July 13, 1950. According to one newspaper report, most mail to Indiana congressmen in the early days of the war "suggested the atomic bomb be used to end the fighting immediately." See Hall, "Crisis Cancels Many Campaign Plans," *Louisville Courier Journal*, July 23, 1950.

17. Marshall-Vorys, MemCon, July 15, 1950, CR Asst. SecState, subject file, box 1, RG 59. The day before, Vorys had commented privately that "we could be bled white by a series of incidents like Korea, while the other fellows are arming to the teeth. Some way or other, we have got to have a showdown before they are stronger than we are in atomic weapons, in addition to having superior strength in men and arms." At the same time, however, Vorys also opposed any public talk of using the A-bomb, especially in Korea, lest this encourage the Soviets to launch their own preventive strike. See Vorys to McClellan, July 14, 1950; Vorys to Giovanello, July 24, 1950; Vorys to Slick, August 2, 1950; General file, box 29, Vorys Papers, OHC.

18. U.S. Congress, Senate Foreign Relations Committee, *Reviews of the World Situation*, 321.

19. Hardy to Brown, August 9, 1950, PA Asst. SecState, subject file, box 10, RG 59; PA, "Info Objectives for the Rest of 1950," August 16, 1950, Info Memos, box 2, RG 59.

20. McWilliam to Dulles, July 20, 1950, correspondence file, Barrett folder, box 47, Dulles Papers, PU.

21. Elsey to Murphy, July 7, 1950, SMOF: Murphy, Korea folder, box 22, TP. Nitze to Webb and Acheson, July 6, 1950; Jessup to Mathews, Rusk, and Nitze, July 11, 1950; Acheson-Johnson-Harriman, MemCon, July 12, 1950; all in PPS files, State-Defense Relations, box 12, RG 59.

22. Notes on Cabinet Meetings, July 21, 1950, box 2, Connelly Papers, HSTL.

23. For a more positive view of Truman's cabinet appointments, see McCoy, *Presidency of Truman*, 147–49.

24. AFL, press release, July 11, 1950, Green files, NSRB folder, box 6, RG1–023, Meany Archives; Stieber, "Labor's Walkout from the Korean War Stabilization Board," 245.

25. Acheson, *Present at the Creation*, 368. In August, Acheson did meet secretly with Dewey to offer him the ambassadorship in London. But though an important post, this offer could also be viewed as an attempt to exile, rather than embrace, a senior Republican. And Dewey, keen to remain titular head of the GOP, turned it down. See Smith, *Dewey and His Times*, 562–63.

26. Truman, *Years of Trial and Hope*, 487; Princeton Seminar, March 14, 1954, Acheson Papers, HSTL; Kepley, *Collapse of the Middle Way*, 79–80.

27. Albright, "Truman Calls Senate Leaders to 4th 2-Party Meeting Today," *Washington Post*, July 11, 1950. See also " 'Citizen Cabinet' Urged as a Mobilization Guide," *New York Times*, July 24, 1950.

28. Schwerin Research Corporation, "Public Reaction to President Truman's Korea Speech, July 19, 1950," PSF (Speech): Public Reaction, box 42, TP.

29. Patterson to Russell, September 12, 1950, Foster files, box 20, RG 59.

30. U.S. Congress, Senate, *Hearings before Committee on Banking and Currency: Defense Production Act*, 97–99, 127, 135.

31. DOPS, July 17, 1950.

32. Gallup, "Stand-by Mobilization Bill Gets Increasing Public Support," August 6, 1950, newspaper clipping file, DNC Papers, HSTL.

33. Taft to Stapler, July 18, 1950, War (Korea) folder, box 924, Taft Papers, LC.

34. Patterson, *Mr. Republican*, 475–76; Hogan, *Cross of Iron*, 100–101, 329, 363–64.

35. Albright, "Taft and Martin Fight Idea of Controls by Compulsion," *Washington Post*, July 19, 1950. Taft, "The Economic Situation Produced by the Korean Crisis," July 24, 1950, Senate (Foreign Policy): MacArthur Hearings, box 628, Taft Papers.

36. U.S. Congress, Senate, *Hearings before Committee on Banking and Currency: Defense Production Act*, 135. On Capehart's role in the hearings, see Atwater to Bermingham, "Economic Mobilization II," July 28, 1950, folder 589, *Time* Dispatches, HU.

37. "House Upsurge Seen Favoring All-Out Wage, Price Controls"; Roberts, "15 Republicans Urge Standby Control Setup"; both in *Washington Post*, July 27 and 31, 1950. McNaughton and Deal to Bermingham, "Congress Week II," July 21, 1950; Atwater, "Controls," July 28, 1950; both in folder 589, *Time* Dispatches, HU.

38. Ayers Diary, August 1, 1950, box 20, Ayers Papers, HSTL; Elson, "Mobilization," August 2, 1950, folder 589, *Time* Dispatches, HU; Truman, *Public Papers*, August 1, 1950.

39. *CQ, 1950*, 626–30; McNaughton and Atwater to Elson, "Congress Week," August 11, 1950, folder 589, *Time* Dispatches, HU.

40. *CQ, 1950*, 631–34.

41. *CQ, 1950*, 634–35; McNaughton, "Congress Week," August 26 and September 1, 1950, folder 589, *Time* Dispatches, HU.

42. "Truman Is Accused of Playing Politics in Crisis," *New York Times*, August 14, 1950.

43. *Congressional Record, 1950*, A5497–98.

44. *Congressional Record, 1950*, 10839.

45. Griffith, *Politics of Fear*, 117.

46. Truman, *Public Papers*, August 8, 1950.

47. Tobey to Aiken, December 1, 1949, crate 34, box 1, GDA Campaign, Aiken Papers, University of Vermont; Tobey to Bickford, August 29, 1950,

Congressional Legislation file, box 54, Tobey Papers, Dartmouth College. For background, see Bell, *Liberal State on Trial*, 213–15.

48. *CQ, 1950*, 453–54; Reeves, *McCarthy*, 297, 308–11; Keith, *"For Hell and a Brown Mule,"* 69–73.

49. Griffith, *Politics of Fear*, 119–20.

50. Griffith, *Politics of Fear*, 120–21.

51. Booth to Bermingham, "Prex Week," August 26, 1950, folder 600, *Time* Dispatches, HU.

52. *Congressional Record, 1950*, 10959.

53. Griffith, *Politics of Fear*, 120–22.

54. "Political and Moral Reasons for a Presidential Veto of the Wood-McCarran Anti-subversive Bill," September 20, 1950, SMOF: Murphy, box 8, TP.

55. Truman, *Public Papers*, September 22, 1950.

56. Booth to Elson, "Prex Week II," September 23, 1950, folder 606, *Time* Dispatches, HU.

57. Griffith, *Politics of Fear*, 121–22; McNaughton to Elson, "Congress 1," September 23, 1950, folder 606, *Time* Dispatches, HU.

58. Smith Diary, July 2, 16, 18, 20, 28, August 3, 4, 5, 7, 8, 10, 1950, Smith Papers, PU. See also Smith, "Suggested Outline of a Republican Statement on Foreign Policy," July 24, 1950; Smith, Memos July 26 and August 8, 1950; all in Material re: Republican White Paper, box 100, Smith Papers. The Republican National Committee also engaged in an effort to forge a position on the war that all party members could endorse. See RNC Meeting, September 14, 1950, microfilm 10, frames 234, 369–71, 373–74, RNC Papers, LC.

59. "Text of GOP Senators' Statement," *New York Times*, August 14, 1950; Smith Diary, August 11 and 15, 1950; Meeting, August 9, 1950, Republican Conference Minority Policy Committee Minutes, box 3, RG 46; Kepley, *Collapse of the Middle Way*, 95–97.

60. Nitze to Webb, August 14, 1950, PPS files, Consultants, box 8, RG 59.

61. Tannenwald Diary, August 15, 1950, box 1, Tannenwald Papers, HSTL; McFall, "Material for Answer to Republicans," August 15, 1950, CR Asst. SecState, subject file, box 1, RG 59.

62. DA MC, August 14, 1940. On preventive-war sentiment at this time, see Trachtenberg, "A 'Wasting Asset,'" 20–21.

63. *Congressional Record, 1950*, 11431–32, 11511–12, 11616–17.

64. Press release, undated, PPS files, USSR, box 23, RG 59.

65. DOPS, August 16, 1950.

66. Krock, Memo, July 1950, Works and Memos Book 2, box 1, Krock Papers, PU.

67. Top Secret Memo, August 17, 1950, MemCon file, box 307, Harriman Papers, LC; MemCon, August 26, 1950, PPS files, State-Defense Relations, box 12, RG 59.

68. Matthews, "Aggressors for Peace Speech," August 25, 1950, Matthews Papers, HSTL; Alsop to Hibbs, August 31, 1950, Special Correspondence folder, box 27, Alsop Papers, LC.

69. DOPS, August 28, 1950. For the State Department's fears about the political consequences of public bickering, see Executive Secretariat, Summary of Daily Meeting, August 15, 1950, box 1, RG 59.

70. Shepley, "Rise and Fall of Louis Johnson II," September 16, 1950, folder 604, *Time* Dispatches, HU.

71. Leva to Johnson, September 9, 1950, Safe file, box 140, Johnson Papers, University of Virginia.

72. McNaughton, "Johnson-Acheson," September 1, 1950, folder 601, *Time* Dispatches, HU.

73. Jenner, "Can You Trust the Future to Those Who Betrayed the Past?" September 15, 1950, Presidential Powers folder, box 628, Taft Papers.

74. Ferrell, *Off the Record*, 191–93.

75. Waggoner, "U.S. Disowns Matthews' Talk of Waging War to Get Peace," *New York Times*, August 27, 1950; Matthews-Warner, TelCon, August 28, 1950, Matthews Papers, HSTL. Contrary to the claims of some historians, Matthews was not immediately sacked. He resigned in July 1951, and was appointed ambassador to Ireland. See Matthews to Truman, July 21, 1951, OF1285C, TP.

76. Norris, "Air College Head Suspended for 'Preventive War' Remarks," *Washington Post*, September 2, 1950. Within three months, Anderson had taken early retirement. See Henderson to Goodrich, April 20, 1951, folder 11, box 195-A, Marshall Papers.

77. On these two organizations, see Vaughn, *Holding Fast the Inner Lines*; Winkler, *Politics of Propaganda*.

78. Ross to Truman, undated, Truman: Misc., box 311, Harriman Papers, LC. Symington to Johnson, July 25, 1950, Security Classified Office files, Defense Department, box 14, RG 304. Warner, "Capital Studies a Possible New Domestic OWI," *New York Times*, August 2, 1950.

79. Elsey, Memo, undated; Davis to Symington, August 18, 1950; Elsey to Ross, August 28, 1950; all in Speech file: Speech Clearance, Elsey Papers, box 54. Ross to Truman, August 3, 1950, PSF (General), box 136, TP. Newlon to Stone, September 1, 1950, OPI files, Central Decimal File 350.05, box 35, RG 330.

80. Oechsner to Barrett, July 21, 1950, PA Asst. SecState, subject file, box 7, RG 59; Barrett to Elsey, September 22, 1950, PSF (General), box 119, TP; Sargeant to Elsey, October 4, 1950, box 54, Elsey Papers.

81. Truman, *Public Papers*, September 1 and 9, 1950.

82. "Sperry Union Sign 3-Year Peace Pact," *New York Times*, July 28, 1950; "New York, Center for Peace—or War?" *Newsweek*, September 18, 1950.

83. DOPS, July 12, 1950; Pace, Matthews, and Finletter to Johnson, July 13, 1950, Admin Sec files, Central Decimal File 092 (Korea: 38th Parallel), box 179, RG 330.

84. Merchant to Acheson, August 1, 1950; Webb to Matthews, August 10, 1950; both in Decimal File 795B.5, box 4306, RG 59. Schnabel and Watson, *Joint Chiefs of Staff and National Policy*, vol. 3, 1:61–72.

85. MacArthur to Joint Chiefs of Staff, July 15, 1950, Geographic file: Korea S.24, CCS 383.21, box 39, RG 218.

86. *Congressional Record, 1950,* 10996.

87. PA, "Current Public Opinion on Foreign Policy Matters," August 23, 1950, Office of PO Studies: Foster files, box 20, RG 59.

88. "Differences between World Federation Resolution, Culbertson Resolution, Atlantic Union Committee (Streit) Resolution," undated, World Government file, ML 3, box 63, Tobey Papers. For background, see Hays, *Politics Is My Parish,* 161–62; Woods, *Fulbright,* 139–40; Wooley, *Alternatives to Anarchy,* 85–120.

89. DA MC, August 14, 1940.

90. DOPS, June 2, 1950.

91. "Battle Report," SMOF: Jackson, box 18, TP; Bernhard, *U.S. Television News,* ch. 5.

92. Russell to Wood, September 21, 1950, PA Asst. SecState, subject file, box 8, RG 59.

93. Reston, "Soviet Union Seen Heading for New Diplomatic Error," *New York Times,* August 9, 1950.

94. Senate Foreign Relations Committee, Executive Session, August 22, 1950, Minutes and Hearings, box 11, RG 46; PA, "Public Opinion on the UN," July 17, 1950, Foster files, box 21, RG 59.

95. PA, "The UN Resists Aggression," September 8, 1950, Info Memos, box 2, RG 59.

96. Jebb to Miller, July 8, 1950, FO371/88446, NA-UK; Mazuzan, *Austin at the UN, 1946–53,* 152–58.

97. Hamilton, "Sees Zombie Rule," *New York Times,* August 11, 1950.

98. PA, "Public Opinion on the UN," August 16, 1950, Foster files, box 21, RG 59.

99. Wood to Barrett, September 21, 1950, PA Asst. SecState, subject file box 8, RG 59.

100. *DSB* 23: 523–29.

101. MSAO, September 1950.

102. Russell to Barrett, September 14, 1950, PA Asst. SecState, subject file, box 10, RG 59.

103. Wood to Barrett, September 21, 1950, PA Asst. SecState, subject file, box 8, RG 59.

104. Wood to Barrett, September 21, 1950, PA Asst. SecState, subject file, box 8, RG 59.

Chapter 4. On the Offensive

1. Higgins, *War in Korea,* 136; Martin, "Korea Commuter's War," *American War Correspondents Association Bulletin,* September–October 1950, box 27, Cochran Papers, DDEL; Erwin, "Korean Battle Story Unfinished," *Editor & Publisher,* October 7, 1950.

2. Shinn, *The Forgotten War Remembered, 120–28*; "Reporter in Korea Curbed after 'Beat,'" *New York Times,* September 16, 1950; Erwin, "Newsmen Hit 'Red Beach' in Bloody Inchon Invasion," *Editor & Publisher,* September 23, 1950.

3. MSAO, September 1950.

4. Sevareid, "New Analysis," September 26, 1950, I:D5, Sevareid Papers, LC.

5. *DSB* 23: 43–46.

6. MacDonald, *Korea*, 41; Stueck, *Korean War*, 92.

7. U.S. Congress, Senate Foreign Relations Committee, *Reviews of the World Situation*, 352–53.

8. *FRUS, 1950*, 7:272, 373, 386–87, 393–95, 506–8, 514.

9. Truman, *Public Papers*, August 31 and September 21, 1950; MemCon, September 2, 1950, PC file, box 82, Acheson Papers, HSTL.

10. "Austin Hints We Will Free Korea," *Washington Post*, August 18, 1950.

11. *DSB* 23:374–78; *FRUS, 1950*, 7:723; Truman, *Public Papers*, September 1, 1950. The service secretaries, who remained in the dark about State planning on the thirty-eighth parallel, believed that Austin's words on August 17 "imply all too clearly a military commitment on the part of the UN, and particularly the U.S., to use force to carry them out," and called for a firm policy decision to confirm this. Pace, Kimball, Finletter to Johnson, August 24, 1950, Admin Sec. files, Central Decimal File 092 (Korea: 38th Parallel), box 179, RG 330.

12. *FRUS, 1950*, 7:571–72; Stueck, *Rethinking*, 96.

13. *FRUS, 1950*, 7:686–87, 690–91; Stueck, *Road to Confrontation*, 219–20.

14. Stueck, *Korean War*, 91–94

15. For a synthesis of the recent literature, see Stueck, *Rethinking*, 102–11.

16. Stueck, *Road to Confrontation*, 227–36; Foot, *Wrong War*, 84–87.

17. Collins, *War in Peacetime*, 82–83; Foot, *Wrong War*, 74.

18. Smith, Memo of Meeting with Knowland, August 7,1950, Foreign Relations: Public Affairs Subcommittee, box 100, Smith Papers, PU; Marshall-Vorys, MemCon, July 15, 1950, CR Asst. SecState, subject file, box 2, RG 59.

19. Gallup, "Wide Public Backing for Crossing 38th Parallel Found in Opinion Survey," October 13, 1950, newspaper clipping file, DNC Papers, HSTL.

20. *FRUS, 1950*, 7:868–69. Stueck, *Road to Confrontation*, 230–31.

21. Blair, *Forgotten War*, 336; MacDonald, *Korea*, 210; Truman, *Public Papers*, October 10, 1950.

22. Casey, "Selling NSC-68," 662.

23. PA, "Popular Sentiment on the Handling of U.S. Foreign Policy," October 20, 1950; "Popular Attitudes toward Halting Further Communist Aggression," October 23, 1950; both in Foster files, box 20, RG 59.

24. Kuhn to Phillips and Micocci, October 3, 1950, box 5; Minutes of Meeting of PA Committee on National Security, Atomic Energy, and Politico-Military Affairs, October 11, 1950, box 6, RG 59; both in PA Asst. SecState, subject file, RG 59.

25. Marshall to Eisenhower, October 23, 1950, box 195, folder 53, Marshall Papers, Marshall Library; Poole, *Joint Chiefs of Staff and National Policy*, 4:35.

26. As early as October 9, Marshall detected this process at work, bemoaning the difficulties in calling up reserve officers. See MemCon, October 9, 1950, PPS files, Country and Area, Europe, box 28, RG 59.

27. Fordham, *Building the Cold War Consensus*, 175–78.

28. Pace, OH.

29. Fordham, *Building the Cold War Consensus*, 177–78.

30. Condit, *History of the Office of the Secretary of Defense*, 2:231–33, 235–37; Hogan, *Cross of Iron*, 308–10.

31. Norris, "U.S. Must Keep Up Its Forces Sent to Europe, Bradley Says"; Folliard, "Truman Hits Possible Cut in Arms Plan"; both in *Washington Post*, September 28 and 29, 1950.

32. Casey, "Selling NSC-68," 678–79.

33. National Advisory Board, Defense Bulletin, September 25, 1950, SMOF: Jackson, box 23, TP; Fritchey to Pace, December 29, 1950, OPI files, Central Decimal File 0001, box 19, RG 330. For background, see Griffith, "Selling of America," 389.

34. National Organizations Branch, Minutes of Meeting, October 17, 1950, Meetings Concerning Defense PR Programs, box 723, RG 330.

35. Field to Beach, August 22, 1950; Dillon to Saudek, October 30, 1950; both in OPI files, Central Decimal File 000.77, box 17, RG 330. *Time for Defense* was carried by 212 ABC stations at 10:00 on Thursday nights. For background see Dillon, Memo for Fritchey, January 29, 1951, OPI files, Central Decimal File 000.77, box 42, RG 330.

36. Bolte to CoS, October 13, 1950, Chief of Info files, Central Decimal File 062.2, box 194, RG 319. For its part, Hollywood volunteered "to cooperate fully in the government's film program, and to utilize all the industry's 'know-how' and the enthusiasm and experience of its creative talent and expert technicians in the process." "Motion Picture Industry Plan for Cooperation with Government in Production of Armed Services Information Films," undated, Motion Picture Industry Cooperation folder, SMOF: Halverstedt, box 3, TP.

37. Isaacson and Thomas, *Wise Men*, 337–38.

38. Vorhees, "CPD, 1950–53," April 1968, CPD Essay file, Vorhees Papers, Rutgers University. MSC to Marshall, October 31, 1950, folder 7, box 197, Marshall Papers.

39. Minutes of PA Staff Meeting, October 16, 1950, PA Asst. SecState, subject file, box 7, RG 59.

40. CPD to Marshall, October 24, 1950, CPD Office files, no.1, box 1, Voorhees Papers.

41. For background, see Coletta, "Matthews," 784–85.

42. Blair, "Secretary Matthews," September 22, 1950, folder 605, *Time* Dispatches, HU.

43. Symington to McKellar, September 14, 1950, Classified Office files, Cong. correspondence folder, box 13, RG 304. NSRB, *United States Civil Defense*.

44. Oakes, *Imaginary War*, 34–38.

45. Grossman, *Neither Dead nor Red*, 41–42; NSRB, *Civil Defense*, 7.

46. *CQ, 1950*, 430. Altshuler, "Unenthusiastic Congress Due to Shelve Agency Dispersal," *Washington Post*, September 2, 1950.

47. Gage to Stephens, October 9, 1950, FO 371/81733, NA-UK. "Civil Defense," *Newsweek*, October 16, 1950.

48. Hitchcock, *France Restored*, 133–42; Ireland, *Creating the Entangling Alliance*, 195–200; Condit, *History of the Office of the Secretary of Defense*, 2:320–23.

49. Cited in Beisner, *Acheson*, 367.

50. Parks, October 28, 1950, correspondence, box 6, Parks Papers, DDEL; "Pact Defense Chiefs Here," *Washington Post*, October 28, 1950; DOPS, October 20, 1950.

51. Blair, "NATO," November 3, 1950, folder 614, *Time* Dispatches, HU. The OPI also worked with newsreels, radio, and newspapers to ensure that the opening of the conference would be well publicized. Roberts to Marshall, October 16, 1950, OPI files, Central Decimal File 001, box 19, RG 330.

52. OPI, "Activity Reports," October 30 and 31, 1950, box 153, RG 330; Blair, "NATO," November 3, 1950, folder 614, *Time* Dispatches, HU.

53. Notes on Cabinet Meetings, September 29, 1950, box 2, Connelly Papers, HSTL; Foot, *Wrong War*, 70.

54. McConnell, "Candidates Watch Korea," *New York Herald Tribune*, August 27, 1950. "Tobey Trails in Hot Fight for Senate Nomination"; Folliard, "GOP Claims '50 Gains but Not Congress Control"; both in *Washington Post*, September 13 and October 8, 1950.

55. RNC, "Background to Korea," *Editorial Digest*, July 24, 1950, subject file, Korea as Political Issue, box 229, RNC Papers, LC.

56. White, "Truman Terms Contemptible wherry Attack on Acheson," *New York Times*, August 18, 1950.

57. Oshinsky, *A Conspiracy So Immense*, 174–76; Keith, *"For Hell and a Brown Mule,"* 93–94.

58. Minutes of RNC Meeting, September 14, 1950, microfilm 10, frames 234, 373–74, RNC Papers, LC.

59. This was what Bill Mylander, the GOP press chief, told a *Time* reporter. Booth, "Politics II," October 13, 1950, folder 609, *Time* Dispatches, HU. See also Knowles, "Republicans Stick to Korea as Issue," *New York Times*, September 16, 1950.

60. Republican Minority Policy Committee, "Observations on the Truman Administration's Relations with the People," October 1950, Speech Material, bMS AM 1829 (e.1360), Herter Papers, HU.

61. Minutes of RNC Meetings, July 31–August 1, 1950, and December 8, 1950, microfilm 10, frames 218 and 436–41, RNC Papers.

62. Smith to Aiken, November 2, 1950; Brewster to Aiken, November 9, 1950; both in GDA Campaign, crate 34, box 1, Aiken Papers, University of Vermont. "Visual Aid Presentations," undated, National Republican Congressional Committee: PR Director, box 9, Humphreys Papers, DDEL.

63. Savage, *Truman and the Democratic Party*, 74–79.

64. Heller, ed., *Truman White House*, 100.

65. Hechler, "Distribution of Presidential Policy Speeches," July 6, 1950, box 5; Hechler, "State Department Materials on Foreign Policy," August 31, 1950, box 1; Hechler to Armstrong, October 4, box 1; all in Hechler Papers, HSTL. For Democratic literature see also DNC, "Capitol Comment," October 28, 1950, Chronological file: Classified Subjects—DNC, box 584, Green Papers, LC.

66. Booth, "Tearing Off on Taft," September 22, 1950, folder 605, *Time* Dispatches, HU. On labor's efforts in Ohio, see LaPalombara, "Pressure, Propaganda, and Political Action," 319–21.

67. Harriman cited by Agronsky, ABC News Report, September 20, 1950, Special for Guylay, Radio Reports, 1950 Campaign file, box 276, Taft Papers, LC.

68. Truman, *Public Papers*, September 21, 1950.

69. Truman to Nolan, August 29, 1950, OF 471B, TP. Hamby, *Man of the People*, 549–51.

70. Murphy, OH; Ayers Diary, October 9–14, 1950, box 20, Ayers Papers, HSTL; DA MC, October 9, 1950.

71. James, *Years of MacArthur*, 3:500–512; Wilz, "Truman and MacArthur," 169–75; McCullough, *Truman*, 800–808.

72. Truman, *Public Papers*, October 15, 1950.

73. Booth to Bermingham, "Prex Week II," October 21, 1950, folder 612, *Time* Dispatches, HU.

74. Booth to Bermingham, "Prex Week II," October 21, 1950, folder 612, *Time* Dispatches, HU. Nixon, OH; Kent, OH; Morris, *Deadline Every Minute*, 324–25.

75. Truman, *Public Papers*, October 19, 1950.

76. PA, "Press and Radio Reaction to Truman's Meeting with MacArthur," October 24, 1950, Foster files, box 20, RG 59; Fitzgerald to Ross, PSF (Korean War file): Wake Island, General, box 244, TP.

77. PA, "Press and Radio Reaction to Truman's Meeting with MacArthur," October 24, 1950, Foster files, box 20, RG 59; Fitzgerald to Ross, PSF (Korean War file): Wake Island, General, box 244, TP.

78. Bell to Murphy, August 14, 1950, Speech file, UN Speech, box 47, Elsey Papers, HSTL.

79. DA MC, October 9, 1950.

80. Shulman to Jessup, October 12, 1950, SMOF: Murphy, box 8, TP.

81. *FRUS, 1950*, 7:1014, 1025–26, 1036.

82. Parrot, "Chinese Red Unit Helps Foe Drive Allies back in Korea," *New York Times*, October 31, 1950; DOPS, November 1, 1950.

83. Russell to Barrett, November 1, 1950, PA Asst. Sec State, subject file, box 2, RG 59.

84. Darby, "Prex Week I," November 17, 1950, folder 617, *Time* Dispatches, HU.

85. Bigart, "General Calls 'Alien' Reds a Grave Issue," *New York Herald Tribune*, November 6, 1951; DOPS, November 6 and 7, 1950.

86. Foot, *Wrong War*, 96; McNaughton, "The Election," November 10, 1950, folder 616, *Time* Dispatches, HU.

87. NPC008, November 6, 1950, folder 615, *Time* Dispatches, HU.

88. Hamby, *Man of the People*, 551.

89. Russell to Barrett, November 13, 1950, Barrett file, box 281, Harriman Papers, LC.

90. Griffith, *Politics of Fear*, 122–31; Keith, *"For Hell and a Brown Mule,"* 85–87; Hulsey, *Dirksen*, 26–29.

91. Acheson, *Present at the Creation*, 460–61.

92. McNaughton to Bermingham, "The New Congress," November 10, 1950, folder 615, *Time* Dispatches, HU. Democrats started the Eighty-First Congress with 262 seats, but had lost two by the end of the second session; see *CQ, 1950*, 20.

93. *FRUS, 1950*, 7:1102–3; Stueck, *Rethinking*, 114.

94. Foot, *Wrong War*, 90–91.

95. *FRUS, 1950*, 7:1148–49; James, *Years of MacArthur*, 3:527–29.

96. Foot, *Wrong War*, 92–95.

97. Executive Secretariat, Summary of Daily Meeting, November 10, 1950, box 1, RG 59; Truman, *Public Papers*, November 16, 1950.

98. Acheson, *Present at the Creation*, 466–67.

99. Schnabel and Watson, *Joint Chiefs of Staff and National Policy*, vol. 3, 1:141–45; Foot, *Wrong War*, 92–95, 99; Stueck, *Rethinking*, 114–15.

100. Casey, "Selling NSC-68," 682–83.

101. DA MC, November 27, 1950.

Chapter 5. An Entirely New War

1. "Temperature Skids 40 Degrees in Capital," *Washington Post*, November 26, 1950; "$400,000,000 Storm Loss Seen," *New York Times*, November 28, 1950.

2. "81st Congress Holds Brief Session in Social Mood," *Washington Post*, November 28, 1950.

3. *FRUS, 1950*, 7:1237.

4. McCullough, *Truman*, 816.

5. *FRUS, 1950*, 7:1242–49; Foot, *Wrong War*, 103–4. MIGs were small, fast jet fighters, named after their designers, Artem Mikoyan and Mikhail Gurevich.

6. *FRUS, 1950*, 7:1250.

7. *FRUS, 1950*, 7:1263, 1266–67.

8. "Truman Sees Security Council," *Washington Post*, November 29, 1950.

9. Elsey, Memo, December 15, 1950, subject file, National Emergency Proclamation, box 73, Elsey Papers, HSTL. On the mood in Washington, see "March of the News," *U.S. News & World Report*, December 8, 1950.

10. Darby, "Prex Week II," December 2, 1950, folder 602, *Time* Dispatches, HU.

11. Lanigan to Harriman, November 30, 1950, Congressional Liaison file, box 282, Harriman Papers, LC.

12. *DSB* 23: 962–67. Truman, *Public Papers*, December 1, 1950.

13. Elsey to Truman, December 4, 1950, PSF (General): Elsey, box 119, TP; Noble to Russell, December 6, 1950, PA Asst. SecState, subject file, box 5, RG 59; Hechler, Memo for Elsey, December 12, 1950, box 1, Hechler Papers, HSTL.

14. *DSB* 23: 962–67.

15. U.S. Congress, Senate Foreign Relations Committee, *Reviews of the World Situation*, 367–81. Truman, *Public Papers*, December 1, 1950.

16. "Points which the Secretary might wish to make in Presentation to Congressional Leaders," November 30, 1950, PPS files, Congressional folder, box 8, RG 59.

17. Truman, *Public Papers*, November 30, 1950.

18. Headline, *Washington Post*, December 1, 1950.

19. *FRUS, 1950*, 7:1266, 1326.

20. Darby, "Prex Week II," December 1, 1950, folder 620, *Time* Dispatches, HU.

21. *FRUS, 1950*, 7:1276; Beisner, *Acheson*, 418.

22. Harris, *Attlee*, 461–63; Folliard, "Attlee to See President on Tuesday," *Washington Post*, December 2, 1950.

23. Truman, *Public Papers*, November 30, 1950.

24. Darby, "Prex Week II," December 1, 1950, folder 620, *Time* Dispatches.

25. DOPS, December 1, 1950.

26. McNaughton, "Congress Week," December 1, 1950, folder 620, *Time* Dispatches, HU.

27. Appleman, *Disaster in Korea*, 262–336; Marshall, *River and the Gauntlet*, 251–348.

28. Brief, December 6, 1950, Admin. Sec. files, Central Decimal File 092 (Korea: folder 4), box 180, RG 330. Appleman, *Escaping the Trap*, 24.

29. *FRUS, 1950*, 7:1312–13.

30. *FRUS, 1950*, 7:1320–22.

31. *FRUS, 1950*, 7:1276–81, 1310–13; Foot, *The Wrong War*, 105.

32. *FRUS, 1950*, 7:1323–34, 1345–46; DA MC, December 4, 1950; Acheson, *Present at the Creation*, 476–77; Kennan, *Memoirs*, 2:32–33.

33. *FRUS, 1950*, 7:1382.

34. *FRUS, 1950*, 7:1367.

35. *FRUS, 1950*, 7:1366, 1369.

36. James, *Years of MacArthur*, 3:376.

37. "MacArthur's Own Story," *U.S. News & World Report*, December 8, 1950.

38. *FRUS, 1950*, 7:1337–38.

39. AP Report, December 2, 1950, copy in OF 584, box 1397, TP.

40. Bigart, "Ghastly Night Put in by Yanks," *Washington Post*, November 28, 1950.

41. *New York Herald Tribune* wire, "Many Chinese Closer to Seoul Than Yanks," *Washington Post*, December 2, 1950.

42. Sherrod, "Korean Situation," December 1, 1950, folder 620, *Time* Dispatches, HU.

43. Reston, "Washington Grim," *New York Times*, December 4, 1950.

44. Gonzalez, "Bipartisan Group Given Late Briefing," *Washington Post*, December 4, 1950.

45. Connally, PC, December 6, 1950, Senate Foreign Relations Committee, Minutes and Hearings, box 12, RG 46; OPI, "Activity Reports," December 5, 1950, entry 134, box 154, RG 330.

46. For Bradley's efforts to reassure legislators, see Smith, MemCon, December 12, 1950, Foreign Relations, PA Subcommittee, box 100, Smith Papers, PU.

47. Truman, December 3, 1950, PSF (longhand notes), box 333, TP.

48. Stone to Howard, December 1, 1950, City file (Washington): S-H Newspaper Alliance, box 251, Howard Papers, LC.

49. McCullough, *Truman*, 826.

50. Collins, Third Trip, December 1–8, 1950, Korea Trips file, box 23, Collins Papers, DDEL; *FRUS, 1950*, 7:1468–72.

51. Norris, "Korean Debacle Seen Avoided," *Washington Post*, December 9, 1950.

52. *FRUS, 1950*, 7:1469–72.

53. DOPS, December 6 and 14, 1950.

54. DOPS, December 1, 4, and 5, 1950; "Senators Want A-Bomb Use Left to MacArthur," *New York Herald Tribune*, December 4, 1950; Montgomery and Johnson, *One Step from the White House*, 97–98.

55. PA, "Main Trends of Opinion Regarding the Korean Crisis," December 5, 1950, PA Asst. SecState, subject file, box 5, RG 59.

56. DA MC, December 4, 1950

57. DOPS, December 4 and 7, 1950.

58. Albright, "Crisis in Korea Sidetracks Political Maneuvers on 'Hill,'" *Washington Post*, November 29, 1950. See also Berger to Harriman, December 6, 1950, Acheson file, box 281, Harriman Papers, LC.

59. *CQ, 1950*, 242.

60. White, "Taft Bids Truman Tell Public More," *New York Times*, December 6, 1950; DOPS, December 6, 1950.

61. Bermingham, "What Do We Fear?" December 16, 1960, folder 622, *Time* Dispatches; Berger to Harriman, December 6, 1950, Acheson file, box 281, Harriman Papers.

62. McNaughton, "Congress Week II," December 8, 1950, folder 621, *Time* Disptaches, HU.

63. DOPS, December 14, 1950; Russell to Truitt, December 19, 1950, Korea folder, series 16, box 21, Russell Papers, University of Georgia. See also Summary of Meeting, December 1, 1950, PA Asst. Sec State, PRWG file, box 1, RG 59.

64. Minutes of Meeting with Congressional Leaders, December 13, 1950, subject file, box 73, Elsey Papers.

65. Lanigan to Harriman, December 15, 1950, Congressional Liaison file, box 282, Harriman Papers. Barkley also reported: "there is a growing feeling

on the Hill that they are not being told enough as to what goes on." See Notes on Cabinet Meetings, December 8, 1950, box 2, Connelly Papers, HSTL.

66. McNaughton, "Congress Week II," December 8, 1950, folder 621, *Time* Dispatches, HU.

67. DA MC, December 2, 1950.

68. Darby, "Prex Week II," December 8, 1950, folder 621, *Time* Dispatches.

69. Elsey, Memo, December 15, 1950, subject file, National Emergency Proclamation, box 73, Elsey Papers. Darby, "Prex Week II," December 8, 1950, folder 621, *Time* Dispatches.

70. For stories on Truman's mental fitness, see "Truman's Snap Decisions Are Alarming Symptoms," editorial, *Chicago Daily News*, December 16, 1950; "Anvil of Office," *Time*, January 1, 1951. Back in September, Drew Pearson had got word that Truman's personal physician, Wallace Graham, "has been giving the chief executive a course in psychotherapy.... In these sessions, Truman pours out his innermost secrets to his doctor—such things as the worry he had over dropping the A-bomb, his worry over his dealings with Stalin, over his decision to send American boys to fight in Korea." This story now sparked a bout of speculation. See Meek, Memo, September 9, 1950, *St. Louis Post-Dispatch* files, box 25, Childs Papers, WHS.

71. DOPS, November 29, 1950.

72. Howard to Stone, December 18, 1950, City file (Washington): Scripps-Howard Newspaper Alliance, box 251, Howard Papers.

Chapter 6. Dealing with the "Disaster School of Journalism"

1. Bigart to Bigart, September 10, 1950, correspondence folder, box 1, Bigart Papers, WHS.

2. "War Writers Wander in Search of Front," *Editor & Publisher*, December 9, 1950; Thompson, *Cry Korea*, 243–57; Boyle, Dispatches, November 27 to December 11, 1950, Writings and Speeches folder, box 6, Boyle Papers, WHS.

3. Minutes of Meeting with Congressional Leaders, December 13, 1950, subject file, box 73, Elsey Papers, HSTL. Most stories on this particular incident were actually quite small and buried on an inside page. See, for instance, AP, "6,000 GIs Shut in Trap," *New York Herald Tribune*, December 10, 1950.

4. Appleman, *Escaping the Trap*, 11, 29.

5. FEC, PIO, SSR, December 1950.

6. FEC, PIO, SSR, December 1950. AP wire, "Note to Editors," December 14, 1950, copy in Chief of I & E files, Unclassified Central Decimal File 092 (Korea), box 17, RG 319.

7. FEC, PIO, SSR, December 1950.

8. "Army Tells How Casualty Reporting Is Speeded Up," *Editor & Publisher*, December 9, 1950.

9. Moran, "The Battle," December 6, 1950, folder 620, *Time* Dispatches, HU.

10. Sherrod, "Heavy Casualties" and "Add Heavy Casualties," December 9 and 11, 1950, folders 621 and 622, *Time* Dispatches, HU. AP, "Marines Halve Loss Figure in Death Trap," *Los Angeles Times*, December 13, 1950.

11. MacArthur to Boykin, December 13, 1950, White House Counsel file, box 1, Souers Papers, HSTL.

12. Willoughy, "The Truth about Korea," 37; Vorhees, *Korean Tales*, 82. See also Almond to Harrison, July 30, 1950, CoI, Central Decimal File 000.74, box 194, RG 319.

13. On MacArthur's efforts to put a more positive spin on events, see Thompson, *Cry Korea*, 263–65; James, *Years of MacArthur*, 3:540–41.

14. "Covering Korea," *Chicago Daily News* advertisement, *Editor & Publisher*, January 6, 1951. On the circulation of the *Chicago Daily News*, see Whited, *Knight*, 172–73. In February, the paper announced a net profit of $1.53 million, up more than $360,000 over the previous year. See "*Chicago News* Continues Gain," *Editor & Publisher*, February 10, 1951.

15. Sparks, "Nightmare Valley Ahead of 'Yanks'"; Beech, "Only 15 Minutes to Safety, but Marines Measure It in Blood"; both in *Chicago Daily News*, December 6, 1950.

16. Beech, "War-Battered Seoul Shrouded in Gloom," *Chicago Daily News*, December 13, 1950.

17. Higgins and Bigart, "On the Battlefront in Korea," *New York Herald Tribune*, December 6, 1950.

18. This assessment of Scripps-Howard coverage is based on what appeared in the *New York World-Telegram and Sun*. On Luce's cooperation, see Fritchey to AP, INS, and UP, December 28, 1950, Chief of I & E files, Unclassified Central Decimal File 000.7, box 5, RG 319. MacArthur, for his part, had long considered *Time*'s coverage of the war "a good example of objective reporting." See *Time*'s internal newspaper, *FYI*, July 14, 1950, copy in general correspondence, box 1, Rosengren Papers, WHS.

19. These paragraphs are based on an analysis of the stories in these six newspapers of November 28–December 15. I chose these papers so as to reflect a cross-section of regional and political organs; the arguments in Kern, Levering, and Levering, *Kennedy Crises*, heavily influenced my choice.

20. James, "Withdrawal a Rout"; Johnston, "Outnumbered GIs Lost Faith in Arms"; both in *New York Times*, December 5 and 9, 1950.

21. "Echols Says Rivalry Forced Strict Rules," *Editor & Publisher*, January 20, 1951.

22. See, for instance, Cannon, " 'They Blew Bugles,' " *Baltimore Sun*, December 2, 1950. On this battle, see Marshall, *River and the Gauntlet*, 251–348.

23. Higgins, "On the Battlefront in Korea," *New York Herald Tribune*, December 6, 1951, and "The Bloody Trail Back," *Saturday Evening Post*, January 27, 1951. "There Was Christmas," *Life*, December 25, 1950. On the marines' exploits, including flying in and constructing a treadway bridge, see Appleman, *Escaping the Trap*, esp. 296–98.

24. Parrott, "New Defenses Set," *New York Times*, December 1, 1950.

25. Thompson, *Cry Korea*, 20, 37–38.

26. AP Report, December 2, 1950, copy in OF 584, box 1397, TP.

27. Bigart, "GIs Pull Back Safely"; "MacArthur's Disaster," editorial; both in *New York Herald Tribune*, December 1 and 6, 1950. The next day,

another editorial was quick to claim that the Bigart and Higgins dispatches "both told better than a hundred communiqués what the Korean reversal means to those caught up in it." "Two Faces of the War," editorial, *New York Herald Tribune*, December 7, 1950.

28. MacArthur to All Units, December 10, 1950, War, Misc. Out folder, box 53, RG 9, MacArthur Papers, MacArthur Memorial Library.

29. FEC, PIO, SSR, December 1950; AP wire, "Note to Editors," December 14, 1950, copy in Chief of I & E files, Unclassified Central Decimal File 092 (Korea), box 17, RG 319; "Censor to 'Screen' Korean War News," *Washington Post*, December 21, 1951.

30. Lockhart to Howard, February 7, 1951, City file: NY: Lockhart, box 249, Howard Papers, LC.

31. Lockhart to Howard, February 1, 1951, City file: NY: Lockhart, box 249, Howard Papers. For the State Department's views on censorship see *FRUS, 1950*, 7:1330–34; Executive Secretariat, Summary of Daily Meeting, December 5, 1950, box 1, RG 59.

32. "Military Censorship Imposed by MacArthur," *Editor & Publisher*, December 23, 1950.

33. Lockhart to Young, December 20, 1950, City file: NY: Lockhart, box 249, Howard Papers; Parks, December 21, 1950, box 6, Parks Papers, DDEL.

34. "MacArthur Says Press Demanded Censorship," *Editor & Publisher*, January 20, 1951.

35. Eighth Army, PIO, Command Report, December 1950; "Military Censorship Imposed by MacArthur."

36. Appleman, *Escaping the Trap*, 319–44.

37. Universal Newsreel, December 18, 1950, 23/414, RG 200.UN; AP, "How 205,000 Escaped Reds," *Chicago Daily News*, December 23, 1950.

38. MacArthur, Communiqué, December 26, 1950, Korean War Communiqués, box 2, RG 319.

39. Appleman, *Disaster in Korea*, 354, 450.

40. Eighth Army, PIO, Command Report, December 1950.

41. Waugh, "3 of 4 Censors Have Been Reporters," *Editor & Publisher*, March 10, 1951.

42. Eighth Army, PIO, Command Report, December 1950 and January 1951.

43. Parks to Echols, December 21, 1950, Chief of I & E files, Unclassified Central Decimal File 092 (Korea), box 17, RG 319; Parks to Echols, December 23, 1950, Chief of I & E files, Unclassified Central Decimal File 000.74, box 5, RG 319.

44. Editorial, "News from Korea," *New York Times*, December 21, 1950.

45. Appleman, *Ridgway Duels for Korea*, especially 30–31, 41–58, 91–92; James, *Years of MacArthur*, 3:547–49.

46. Parks to Echols, January 23, 1951, Chief of I & E files, Unclassified Central Decimal File 091 (Korea), box 73, RG 319.

47. "'Momentous Blunder' in Korea Is Charged to MacArthur," *Washington Evening Star*, January 15, 1951. For Tokyo's reaction see SCAP, Govt. Section, Central files, box 2149, RG 331.

48. "Echols Says Rivalry Forced Strict Rules," *Editor & Publisher*, January 20, 1951. Later newspaper reports suggested that Beech's source was none other than MacArthur's closest adviser, General Whitney. See "Now It Comes Out"; "Now It Comes Out II"; both in *Washington Post*, April 13 and 14, 1951.

49. Whitney to Back, January 17, 1951, SCAP, Govt. Section, Central Files, box 2149, RG 331.

50. Eighth Army, PIO, Command Report, January 1951.

51. Fritchey to Wilson, December 28, 1950, Chief of I & E files, Unclassified Central Decimal File 000.73, box 60, RG 319.

52. OPI, Activity Report, January 10, 1951, box 155, RG 330.

53. Sherrod to Bermingham, "War News from Korea," January 5, 1951, folder 625, *Time* Dispatches, HU.

54. FEC, PIO, SSR, December 1950 and January 1951.

55. Eighth Army, PIO, Command Report, December 1950 and January 1951.

56. Eighth Army, PIO, Command Report, January 1951. See also UP, "Korean Censorship Tightened Again," *New York Times*, January 7, 1951.

57. "8th Army Censors Subject Press to Court Martial," *Editor & Publisher*, January 13, 1951.

58. "8th Army Censors Subject Press to Court Martial," *Editor & Publisher*, January 13, 1951.

59. Eighth Army, PIO, Command Report, January 1951; Info for War Correspondents, January 7, 1951, Censorship file, box 189, Senate Armed Services Committee, RG 46.

60. "Censorship," editorial, *Editor & Publisher*, January 13, 1951.

61. Eighth Army, PIO, Command Report, January and February 1951; AP, "8th Army Bars Word 'Retreat,' "; Johnston, "M'Arthur Limits Own War Reports" both in *New York Times*, January 10 and 11, 1951.

62. MacArthur to Brown, January 18, 1951, general correspondence, box 1, RG 6, MacArthur Papers.

63. The UP's Wilson now challenged the fact that this meeting had called for censorship at all, adding that he had certainly opposed it at the time but would now abide by the army's decision. "M'Arthur Asserts Press Asked Curb," *New York Times*, January 19, 1950.

64. Howard to Brown, City file (NY): *Editor & Publisher*, box 255, Howard Papers.

65. "8th Army Censors Subject Press to Court Martial," *Editor & Publisher*, January 13, 1951. "General Parks 'Disturbed,' " *New York Times*, January 11, 1951; Parks to Short, January 19, 1951, Chief of I & E files, Unclassified Central Decimal File 000.73, box 60, RG 319.

66. UP, "Echols Coming to U.S.," *New York Times*, January 14, 1951; Blair, "Colonel Echols," January 26, 1951, folder 629, *Time* Dispatches, HU.

67. "13th Reporter Loses Life in Korean War," *Editor & Publisher*, February 17, 1951; UP, "Marshall Says Press Helps Guard Liberty," *New York Times*, January 29, 1951.

68. Ridgway, *Korean War*, 79–83.

69. Appleman, *Ridgway Duels for Korea*, 162–348. James, *Refighting the Last War*, 58–60.

70. Eighth Army, PIO, Command Report, February 1951.

71. On Walker and the press, see Appleman, *South to the Naktong*, 417.

72. Eighth Army, PIO, Command Report, February 1951.

73. Appleman, *Ridgway Duels for Korea*, 1–24. See also "'I Aim to Stay,' Says Ridgway on Tour of Korean Front," *Chicago Daily News*, December 27, 1951; "Airborne Grenadier," *Time*, March 5, 1951.

74. Ridgway, *Korean War*, 111; Allen to Parks, July 23, 1951, Chief of I & E files, Unclassified Central Decimal File 000.74, box 60, RG 319.

75. Quirk biography, www.trumanlibrary.org/hstpaper/quirkja.htm#bio.

76. Ridgway to Quirk, February 5, 1951, Korean War folder 2, box 1, Quirk Papers, HSTL; Quirk Diary, February 1 and 21, 1951, Korean War folder 1, box 1, Quirk Papers. On the recruitment drive, see UP, "Publicity Personnel for Defense Up 60%," *New York Times*, June 30, 1951. Since the start of the war, the U.S. army had been aware of the need to educate GIs on the question, as it was called, "Why We Fight," and had set up a four-hour precombat orientation course for soldiers before they embarked for the front. See Collins to Greenbaum, September 22, 1950, Army CoS, Decimal File 091 (Korea), box 557, RG 319.

77. Eighth Army, PIO, Command Report, January and February 1951.

78. Euson and Hoffman, June 21, 1951, Korean folder 2, box 1, Quirk Papers. For another positive assessment of Quirk's performance see Dorn to Furuholmen, July 11, 1951, Chief of I & E files, Unclassified Central Decimal File 000.73, box 60, RG 319.

79. "Faris Assigns Young Staffers to Korean War," *Editor & Publisher*, March 24, 1951. See also Edwards, "On War Correspondents and Censorship," *American War Correspondents Association Bulletin*, March–April 1951, box 27, Cochran Papers, DDEL.

80. Eighth Army, PIO, Command Report, March 1951.

81. Hoberecht, "At 71, Gen. MacArthur Makes Jet-Age News," *Editor & Publisher*, January 27, 1951.

82. Eighth Army, PIO, Command Report, February 1951.

83. Quirk Diary, February 21 and 24, 1951. Ridgway, *Korean War*, 109–10.

84. Quirk Diary, February 24, 1951.

85. MacArthur, press statement, March 7, 1951, OF 584, box 1397, TP.

86. Quirk Diary, March 7 and 8, 1951.

87. Eighth Army, PIO, Command Report, March 1951.

88. Eighth Army, PIO, Command Report, March 1951.

89. Eighth Army, PIO, Command Report, March 1951. "Double Censorship in Korea," *American War Correspondents Association Bulletin*, March–April 1951, box 27, Cochran Papers, DDEL.

Chapter 7. Mobilizing with the Utmost Speed

1. Brinkley, *Washington Goes to War*, 73; Roberts, *Washington*, 146–47; McFarland and Roll, *Louis Johnson*, 154–55.

2. May, "The U.S. Government," 217–18.

3. Brackman, "Mr. Republican Visits the White House," December 14, folder 622, *Time* Dispatches, HU.

4. Minutes of Meeting with Congressional Leaders, December 13, 1950, subject file, box 73, Elsey Papers, HSTL.

5. PWT, Memo for Small, December 12, 1950; Corie, Memo for Garlock, December 13, 1950; both in Admin. Sec. files, Central Decimal File 350, box 194, RG 330. For details, see Leffler, *Preponderance*, 402.

6. Minutes of Meeting with Congressional Leaders, December 13, 1950, subject file, box 73, Elsey Papers. The possibility of declaring a national emergency, for psychological rather than legal reasons, had been under consideration from the very start of the new crisis. See DA MC, December 2 and 3, 1950.

7. "Theater TV Proves Box Office," *Variety*, December 20, 1950.

8. Cress, Memo for Joint Chiefs of Staff Chairman, December 13, 1950, Admin Section, Central Decimal File 350, box 194, RG 330. Some White House aides also worried about specific references to "Russia," "the Soviet Union," or "the Kremlin." See Houston to Steelman, Memo, December 12, 1950, Chronological file, box 36, Steelman Papers, HSTL.

9. Truman, *Public Papers*, December 16, 1950.

10. Leveiro, "Truman Sets Drive"; Egan, "Recent Auto Rises Canceled"; both in *New York Times*, December 17, 1950.

11. Economic Stabilization Agency, press release, December 18, 1950, Green files, Economic Stabilization Agency folder, box 5, RG1–023, Meany Archives.

12. Pierpaoli, *Truman and Korea*, 50–53.

13. Leveiro, "GE Chief Is Picked," *New York Times*, December 15, 1950. Officials also considered bringing Republicans into the cabinet, although this course was again rejected. See Hooker to Nitze, December 11, 1950, PPS files, Working Papers: Bipartisanship, box 73, RG 59.

14. Minutes of Meeting with Congressional Leaders, December 13, 1950, subject file, box 73, Elsey Papers.

15. Smith to Taft, Millikin, Wherry, Bridges, and Wiley, December 12, 1950, copy in Republican Party folder, box 310, Harriman Papers, LC.

16. Brackman, "Mr. Republican Visits the White House," December 14, folder 622, *Time* Dispatches, HU. Trussell, "Congress Chieftans Agree on Rapid Military Build-Up," *New York Times*. December 14, 1950.

17. *CQ, 1950*, 139–43, 669–77.

18. Eckel, "Strikers Return," *New York Times*, December 17, 1950.

19. "Sponsors Flocking to News Programs at Hyped Pace under War Crisis," *Variety*, January 10, 1951; Stanton to Marshall, December 18, 1950, OPI files, Central Decimal File 000.77, box 17, RG 330. The Pentagon also shifted its own radio shows "from a reliance on entertainment to a strong emphasis on news and information about the military establishment." And according to Nielsen ratings, there was now a large audience for such subject matter. Between December and February, the rating for *Time for Defense*, the Pentagon's flagship

program, went up from 2.5 to 5.1, making it one of ABC's top three shows. Fritchey to Marshall, April 4, 1951, OPI, 000.77, box 42, RG 330.

20. Hitchcock, *France Restored*, 146–47; Ireland, *Creating the Entangling Alliance*, 204–7; Schwartz, *America's Germany*, 151–54.

21. Leveiro, "Truman Will Send More Men to Europe as Soon as He Can," *New York Times*, December 20, 1950.

22. *CQ, 1950*, 242.

23. Bermingham, "What Do We Fear," December 16, 1950, folder 622, *Time* Dispatches, HU.

24. Truman, *Public Papers*, December 19, 1950.

25. Note, December 18, 1950, Republican file, ML 3, box 60, Tobey Papers, Dartmouth College.

26. Smith Diary, December 15 and 16, 1950, Smith Papers, PU; Leary, "Smith of New Jersey," 164–65.

27. Tobey to Smith, January 4, 1951, Senate Foreign Relations Committee file, ML 3, box 105, Tobey Papers.

28. "Text of Hoover's Speech," *New York Times*, December 21, 1950.

29. Brooks to McConnell, December 19, 1950, PA folder, Office files, PR (Brooks), box 131, NBC Records, WHS.

30. FRF to Symington, December 29, 1950, PSF (General): Hoover, box 122, TP; *DSB* 24: 83–84, 87–88.

31. Lisagor, "Dulles Gets Big Buildup in Reply to Hoover," *Chicago Daily News*, December 28, 1950.

32. *DSB* 24: 85–89; Dulles to Hoover, December 28, 1950, Taft folder, box 20, Dulles Papers, PU.

33. MSAO, December 1950 and January 1951.

34. Hoover to Knowland, January 16, 1951, Knowland folder, box 53, Dulles Papers, PU. Best, *Herbert Hoover*, 343–5.

35. Taft to Spieker, January 15, 1951, Subject: Foreign Policy, box 968, Taft Papers, LC.

36. *Congressional Record, 1951*, 56–58.

37. See, for instance, Millis, *Arms and the State*, 344–47; James, "Truman," 124–25; Pierpaoli, *Truman and Korea*, 57–58; Bell, *Liberal State on Trial*, 241. Beisner, *Acheson*, 452, also labels the GOP campaign "a weak attempt" and characterizes the administration's victory as "easy."

38. Egan, "Dewey Asks State War Footing," *New York Times*, January 4, 1951. On January 19, Biffle, the secretary of the Senate, told a reporter (off the record) that Morse, Lodge, Flanders, Knowland, Saltonstall, Bridges, and Tobey would all defect to the administration. McNaughton, "Presidency II," January 19, 1951, folder 628, *Time* Dispatches, HU.

39. Patterson, *Mr. Republican*, 475–76; Hogan, *Cross of Iron*, 100–101, 329, 363–64. On Taft the conviction politician, see Merry, "Taft," 179–80.

40. Taft to Curtis, December 22, 1950, Subject: Foreign Policy, box 968, Taft Papers.

41. Wainhouse-Lodge, MemCon, November 11, 1950, CR Asst. SecState, subject file, box 1, RG 59; Marshall to Nitze, November 15, 1950, PPS files,

Congressional, box 8, RG 59. See also "Poll Indicates Congress Views on Aid to Allies Sharply Divided," *New York Times*, January 7, 1951.

42. *Congressional Record, 1951*, 34, 94.

43. Lanigan to Harriman, January 8, 1951, Congressional Liaison folder, box 282, Harriman Papers.

44. Gellner, Clodfelter, and Shepard, "The 'Great Debate,'" 20.

45. Marshall to Nitze, January 16, 1951, PPS files, Congressional, box 8, RG 59.

46. "Taft Lacks 'Great Confidence' in U.S. Military," *Washington Post*, December 30, 1950.

47. *Congressional Record, 1951*, 54–60, 456.

48. Brinkley, "Draft 'Delinquents,'" January 26, 1951, folder 629, *Time* Dispatches, HU.

49. "Casualties Forcing Army to Add 50,000 Draftees"; Furman, "Educators Favor Draft Proposals"; both in *New York Times*, January 12 and 20, 1951.

50. DA MC, February 19, 1951.

51. Parks to Collins, February 26, 1951, Chief of I & E files, Unclassified Central Decimal File 000.7, box 54, RG319. According to one source, most of the president's mail now came from mothers who did not want their sons drafted. Darby, "Prex Week," February 16, 1951, folder 633, *Time* Dispatches, HU.

52. Truman, *Public Papers*, January 11, 1951; Leary, "Smith of New Jersey," 170–71.

53. Barrett to Webb, February 8, 1951, Barrett folder, box 281, Harriman Papers.

54. Murphy to Hechler, January 16, 1951; Benton to Hechler, January 26, 1951; both in Political file, Analysis of Taft's Votes, box 3, Hechler Papers, HSTL. Lend-Lease was Roosevelt's way of providing aid to those countries fighting Nazi Germany, at a time when isolationist opinion in the United States remained opposed to direct and formal American involvement in World War II.

55. Casey, "Selling NSC-68," 682–83.

56. Ferguson and Schwinn to Watts, January 5, 1951, PA, Policy Guidance and Coordination Staff, Records Relating to NSC, box 3, RG 59.

57. Vorhees, "CPD, 1950–53," April 1968, 24–28, CPD Essay file, Vorhees Papers, Rutgers University.

58. Lanigan to Harriman, December 21, 1950, CPD folder, box 299, Harriman Papers. Vorhees, Memo, January 17, 1951, CPD folder, box 92, Clayton Papers, HSTL. See also Russell to Barrett, January 30, 1951, PA Asst. SecState, Subject 1530, box 5, RG 59.

59. Darby, "Prex Speech: Color and Delivery"; Bermingham to Levison; January 8 and 20, 1951, folders 625 and 628, *Time* Dispatches, HU. Truman, *Public Papers*, January 8, 1951.

60. Webb to Truman, January 5, 1951, PSF (Subject): 82nd Congress, box 143, TP. DA MC, January 12, 1951.

61. Button to George, February 15, 1951, box 197, folder 6, Marshall Papers, Marshall Library.

62. U.S. Congress, Senate, *Hearings before the Committee on Armed Services, Preparedness Subcommittee: Universal Military Service and Training*, 42. Nelson, "Rosenberg," 133–61.

63. Vorhees, Memos, January 24 and 31, February 16, 1951, CPD Office files, no. 2, box 1, Vorhees Papers.

64. Truman, *Public Papers*, January 11, 1951.

65. Minutes of NSC Meeting, January 4, 1951, box 3, RG 273; Schwinn to John Ferguson, January 5, 1951, PA, Policy Guidance and Coordination Staff, Records Relating to NSC, box 3, RG 59. On the NSC-68 leaks, see Memo for Pulitzer, January 5, 1951, *St. Louis Post-Dispatch* files, box 25, Childs Papers, WHS.

66. Hunt, "Beijing and the Korean Crisis," 473–74; Foot, "Making Known the Unknown War," 428.

67. *DSB* 24: 363–64. The remark was by Jessup, in an extended speech warning of the perils of preventive war. No polling was done on preventive war between October 1950 and May 1951. The last poll, in October, found 79 percent opposed, but this was before the Chinese intervention. See Foster to Schwinn, May 28, 1951, Foster files, box 1, RG 59.

68. Joyce to Nitze, January 24, 1951, PPS files, Working Papers: War Aims, box 73, RG 59.

69. Joyce to Nitze, January 24, 1951, PPS files, Working Papers: War Aims, box 73, RG 59. *FRUS, 1951*, 1, 7–18.

70. Spaatz, "Preventive War?" and "The Prospects for Victory in Korea," both in *Newsweek*, September 4 and 11, 1950. In these articles, Spaatz was careful not to explicitly endorse a preventive war. For his part, Taft was always keen to stress that he was opposed to a preventive war. See Special for Guylay, September 5, 1950, Radio Reports, 1950 Campaign file, box 276, Taft Papers.

71. Alsop to Sommers, December 15, 1950, Special Correspondence, box 27, Alsop Papers, LC.

72. Marshall to Nitze, January 25, 1951; Joyce to Nitze, January 24, 1951; both in PPS files, Working Papers: War Aims, box 73, RG 59; Walsh, "Is It Immoral to Strike First If Attack Is Imminent?" *Washington Sunday Star*, December 24, 1950. Before the Chinese intervention, CPD leaders had maintained a strong opposition to preventive war; see Hershberg, *Conant*, 506, 531–33. In fact, when Conant had been consulted on NSC-68 back in March 1950, he had "put the value on avoiding war very high"; see *FRUS, 1950*, 1:182.

73. For the private debate on preventive war, see Trachtenberg, "A 'Wasting Asset,'" 21–27.

74. Walz, "U.S. Can Hit Back," *New York Times*, January 1, 1951; Minutes of Meeting with Milne, Martin, and Warner, January 18 1951, box 82, Acheson Papers, HSTL. As Acheson explained to one of his closest advisers a few weeks later, when discussing his forthcoming testimony on sending additional forces to Europe, the whole aim of the mobilization program, was not just to keep the United States out of a land war. "The whole idea of what

we are doing is to keep us out of any war." Battle, MemCon, February 12, 1951, CR Asst. SecState, subject file, box 1, RG 59.

75. *FRUS, 1951*, 7:68. Similar actions had been taken in November to dampen down preventive war sentiment. See Executive Secretariat, Summary of Daily Meeting, November 10, 1950, box 1, RG 59.

76. McFall to Webb, December 14, 1950, CR Asst. SecState, subject file, box 1, RG 59.

77. Schmeitzer, "Connally," 86–103; Connally, *My Name Is Tom Connally*, 166–75; Johnson, *Congress and the Cold War*, 15, 42–45.

78. Fite, *Russell*, 175–76, 199–200, 225, 238; Caro, *Master of the Senate*, 169–84.

79. Russell, press release, undated; Russell to Newton, December 24, 1951; both in Universal Military Training Correspondence folder, series 9, box 140, Russell Papers, University of Georgia. On UMST, Russell adopted his usual technique of letting others lead from the front, this time getting Lyndon Johnson's preparedness subcommittee to assume the public burden. See Legislative file, Dockets: S.1, Armed Services Committee, box 155, RG 46; Caro, *Master of the Senate*, 322–23 n.

80. "Commitment of Additional U.S. Troops to Western Europe," January 26, 1951, CR Asst. SecState, subject file, box 2, RG 59. Although he supported troops to Europe, Russell added the caveat that it needed to be "made clear to Congress that the European nations intend to do their part toward defending themselves."

81. Executive Secretariat, Summary of Daily Meeting, January 23, 1951, box 1, RG 59. Russell to Thomas, April 14, 1951, Troops to Europe Correspondence, series 9, box 140, Russell Papers.

82. *DSB* 24: 246–48, 285–86.

83. Smith Diary, February 2, 1951. Aiken to Beatty, January 26, 1951, Foreign Affairs file, crate 39, box 1, Aiken Papers, University of Vermont.

84. U.S. Congress, Senate, *Hearings before the Committees on Foreign Relations and Armed Services: Assignment of Ground Forces to Europe*, 40–41, 80–81, 481–83, 526–29.

85. *Congressional Record, 1951*, 55–56. U.S. Congress, Senate, *Hearings before the Committees on Foreign Relations and Armed Services: Assignment of Ground Forces to Europe*, 610–17.

86. U.S. Congress, Senate, *Hearings before the Committees on Foreign Relations and Armed Services: Assignment of Ground Forces to Europe*, 39, 80–81.

87. Chernow, *Alexander Hamilton*, 627.

88. U.S. Congress, Senate, *Hearings before the Committee on Armed Services, Preparedness Subcommittee: Universal Military Service and Training*, 25–26.

89. Taft to Gillilland, January 22, 1951, Subject: Foreign Policy, box 968, Taft Papers; White, "Curbs on Troops for Europe Fought," *New York Times*, March 20, 1951.

90. *CQ, 1951*, 275–82.

91. *CQ, 1951*, 223–24; *Congressional Record, 1951*, 3083, 3095–96, 3148, 3280–82; Carpenter, "United States' NATO Policy at the Crossroads," 412–13.

92. Reston, "U.S. Is Now Running a Marathon, Not a Sprint," *New York Times*, March 11, 1951.

93. Marshall, PC, March 27, 1951, box 206, folder 58, Marshall Papers. See also Harriman to Eisenhower, April 9, 1951, Harriman folder, box 55, Eisenhower, Pre-Presidential Papers, DDEL.

94. Stark, "Wilson Calls on Rail Men to Return," *New York Times*, February 6, 1951.

95. McClure, *Truman Administration and the Problems of Postwar Labor*, 35–37, 73–74, 213–18, 239–42; Marcus, *Truman and the Steel Seizure Case*, 17–19; Lichtensetin, *Labor's War at Home*, 238–39.

96. Stark, "Army Orders Rail Strikers to Return or Forfeit Jobs," *New York Times*, February 9, 1951.

97. Council of Economic Advisers to the President, March 9, 1951, box 9, Blough Papers, HSTL; Pierpaoli, *Truman and Korea*, 63; Rockoff, *Drastic Measures*, 178–79.

98. UP, "Hollywood's Wildest Ideas of Reporting Topped at Announcement of Freeze," *New York Times*, January 27, 1951. Senior officials wanted to act fast, on a Friday afternoon, in order "to utilize, for public education purposes, the full press coverage of Sunday, January 28, newspapers." See "Wage Stabilization Program History, 1950–53," 1:82, box 1, RG 293.

99. Zieger, *CIO*, 297–98; Lichtensetin, *Labor's War at Home*, 234–38.

100. AFL Research Staff, Report no. 10, December 11, 1950, Green files, Defense Production Admin. folder, box 5, RG 1–023.

101. Henle to Green, February 2, 1951, Green files, ULPC folder, box 6, RG 1–023.

102. Stieber, "Labor's Walkout from the Korean War Stabilization Board," 245–46; Houston to Steelman, November 7, 1950, Chronological file, box 36, Steelman Papers.

103. "Wage Stabilization Program History, 1950–53," 1:5, box 1, RG 293. On Clay's role in World War II, see Stein, "Labor's Role in Government Agencies during World War II," 399–401; Koistinen, "Mobilizing the World War II Economy," 459–60.

104. Green, Murray, Leighty, and Hayes to Wilson, February 9, 1951, ULPC press releases, Green files, box 6, RG1–023.

105. Loftus, "Labor Incensed by Defense 'Snub,'" *New York Times*, February 5, 1951. On the WSB meetings, see Ching, *Review and Reflection*, 95–96.

106. ULPC, press release, February 16, 1951, Green files, box 6, RG1–023.

107. Stark, "President Reassures Labor on Equity in Wage Controls"; Stark, "Truman Enters Pay Board Row"; Loftus, "Labor Quits All Mobilization Posts"; all in *New York Times*, February 20 and 24, and March 1, 1951.

108. *Business Week*, February 3, 1951; Pierpaoli, *Truman and Korea*, 79–81; Donovan, *Tumultuous Years*, 326–28, 331, 368–69.

109. Neustadt to Murphy, February 16, 1951, Lucas Committee Amendment folder, box 3, Enarson Papers, HSTL; Elsey to Murphy, February 16, 1951, box 89, Elsey Papers; Pierpaoli, *Truman and Korea*, 89–90.

110. Pierpaoli, *Truman and Korea*, 94–95.

111. Defense Mobilization Board, Minutes, March 14, 1951, Classified General files, box 2, RG 296.

112. Wilson, "Building America's Might," April 1, 1951, Security Classified files, ODM, box 14, RG 304.

113. Welch to Symington, April 2, 1951, Security Classified files, Economic Management Office, box 14, RG 304.

114. Reston, "Differing Views of Marshall and Wilson Puzzle Capital," *New York Times*, March 29, 1951.

115. Reston, "Differing Views of Marshall and Wilson Puzzle Capital," *New York Times*, March 29, 1951.

Chapter 8. Why Korea?

1. DOPS, January 10, 11, 19, and 29, 1951.

2. Patterson, *Mr. Republican*, 485–86. See also Taft to Chapple, January 10, 1951; Taft to McCamic, January 17, 1951; both in Subject: Foreign Policy, box 968, Taft Papers, LC.

3. Gallup, "Public Favors Withdrawing from Korea by Nearly 3 to 1," *Washington Post*, January 21, 1951.

4. Russell to Barrett and Webb, January 19, 1951, PA Asst. SecState, subject file, box 5, RG 59.

5. Summary of Meeting, January 23, 1951, PA Asst. SecState, PRWG file, box 1, RG 59; Barrett to McFall, Rusk, Fisher, January 23, 1951, PA Asst. SecState, subject file, box 2, RG 59.

6. Summary of Meeting, February 7, 1951, PA Asst. SecState, PRWG file, box 1, RG 59.

7. Elsey to Truman, February 2 and 9, 1951, PSF (General): Elsey, box 119, TP.

8. Notes on Cabinet Meetings, February 9, 1951, box 2, Connelly Papers, HSTL.

9. Kuhn, "President Flies to Capital," *Washington Post*, December 27, 1950. *FRUS, 1950*, 7:1570–73.

10. James, *Years of MacArthur*, 3:547–49. *FRUS, 1950*, 7:1630–33; *FRUS, 1951*, 7:55–56.

11. Truman, *Years of Trial and Hope*, 434; *MSFE*, 329, 1600

12. *FRUS, 1951*, 7:71–72, 77–78; Stueck, *Rethinking*, 123.

13. Kennedy, "Truman Cuts Short Holiday to See U.S. Chiefs in Capital," *New York Times*, December 26, 1950.

14. UP, "U.S. Planning to Remain and Fight in Korea," *Washington Post*, January 12, 1951.

15. Collins, Fourth Trip, January 12–18, 1951, Korea Trips file, box 23, Collins Papers, DDEL; Collins, *War in Peacetime*, 251–57.

16. *FRUS, 1951*, 7:93–94, 102–3; *MSFE*, 324.

17. Truman, *Years of Trial and Hope*, 461–63.

18. James, *Years of MacArthur*, 3:555.

19. However, in discussions with Collins and Vandenberg on January 15, MacArthur was keen to reassure them that Truman's message had clari-

fied Washington's policy for him. Collins and Vandenberg, Memo for the Joint Chiefs of Staff, January 19, 1951, Admin. Sec. files, Central Decimal File 092 (Korea), box 231, RG 330.

20. Erwin, "News Correspondents Move to New UN Home," *Editor & Publisher*, January 6, 1951.

21. DA MC, November 28, 1950.

22. *FRUS, 1951*, 7:8–9.

23. *FRUS, 1951*, 7:11, 18, 38.

24. *FRUS, 1951*, 7:23, 25–26, 38, 64, 76; Stueck, *Korean War*, 151–54.

25. DOPS, January 8, 1951. Editorials in this vein included "The UN Could Save Its Soul," *Cincinnati Times Star*, December 27, 1950; "The UN at the Crossroads," *New York Times*, January 4, 1951; "The Chinese Rejection," *New York Herald Tribune*, January 18, 1951.

26. *Congressional Record, 1951*, 457–61. For background see White, "House Bids UN Act at Once to Stamp Peiping Aggressor," *New York Times*, January 20, 1950; Levison, to Bermingham, January 20, 1951, folder 628, *Time* Dispatches, HU; "To the Point," *Time*, January 29, 1951.

27. *Congressional Record, 1951*, 344–46, 554–62; *CQ, 1951*, 238–39. Senator McClellan (D-AK) initially introduced this resolution on January 16, along with two others. One called for Beijing to be barred from the UN; the other requested economic sanctions against the Chinese. On January 23, the Senate voted ninety-one to zero for the first, but sent the second off to committee.

28. Acheson, *Present at the Creation*, 513.

29. *DSB* 24: 164–65; Austin-Hickerson, TelCon, January 17, 1951, UN: Korea, Ceasefire folder, box 49, Austin Papers, University of Vermont.

30. *FRUS, 1951*, 7:98–99, 123–24. Foot, *Wrong War*, 111–12.

31. *FRUS, 1951*, 7:136–37. Stueck, *Korean War*, 153–57; Foot, "Anglo-American Relations in the Korean Crisis," 53–56.

32. Acheson, *Present at the Creation*, 513. See, for instance, Caridi, *Korean War and American Politics*, 113–14.

33. DA MC, January 23, 1951.

34. *DSB* 24:60.

35. Noble to Russell, December 6, 1950, PA Asst. SecState, subject file, box 5, RG 59.

36. Barrett to Acheson, February 1, 1951, PA Asst. SecState, subject file, RG 59; Russell to Barrett and Webb, January 19, 1951, PA Asst. SecState, subject file, box 5, RG 59.

37. DA MC, January 18 and 23, 1951.

38. DA MC, January 16, 1951; McFall to Lodge, January 26, 1951, Asst. SecState for Cong. Rels, subject file, box 2, RG 59.

39. *DSB* 24:263, 297–98. Rusk's speech was also distributed to U.S. troops in Korea, as part of Ridgway's efforts to bolster morale; see Eighth Army, PIO, Command Report, March 1951.

40. MSAO, February 1951.

41. PA, "Popular Opinion on Handling of Foreign Affairs," undated, Foster files, box 20, RG 59.

42. Barrett to Acheson, February 1, 1951; Russell to Barrett, February 15, 1951; both in PA Asst. SecState, subject file, box 10, RG 59.

43. Tannenwald to Cooper, April 5, 1951, Political folder, box 5, Tannenwald Papers, HSTL.

44. Barrett to Webb, February 8, 1951, Barrett folder, box 281, Harriman Papers, LC.

45. Summary of Meeting, January 30, 1951, PA Asst. SecState, PRWG file, box 1, RG 59.

46. Russell to Lehrbas, March 30, 1951, PA Asst. SecState, subject file, box 8, RG 59.

47. Staats to Elsey, December 27, 1950; Elsey to Short, January 2, 1951; both in Speech file: Speech Clearance, box 54, Elsey Papers, HSTL. "Revived OWI Included in Emergency Planning," *Variety*, December 13, 1950, 2; "New Agency?" *Washington Post*, January 23, 1951.

48. *FRUS, 1950*, 7:1335–36.

49. Truman, press release, December 6, 1950, OF 584, box 1397, TP. James, *Years of MacArthur*, 3:540–41.

50. Stevens, "Censorship Is Put on Federal Data," *New York Times*, November 27, 1950; Elsey to Truman, December 4, 1950, Speech file: Speech Clearance, box 54, Elsey Papers; Truman to Senior Officials, December 5, 1950, PSF (General): Speech, Instructions for Public Statements, TP.

51. This naturally concerned some senior officials. See Harriman to Eisenhower, May 18, 1951, Harriman folder, Eisenhower, Pre-presidential Papers, DDEL.

52. PA, "Why We Are Staying in Korea," February 6, 1951, PA, Info Memos, box 2, RG 59.

53. Hechler to Elsey, January 9, 1950, box 1, Hechler Papers, HSTL.

54. Schatz, *Boom and Bust*, 307–13, 329–33;

55. Caute, *Great Fear*, 489–502.

56. "8 War Pix among '50 Top Grossers," *Variety*, January 3, 1951.

57. "COMPO Factions in Accord," *Hollywood Reporter*, January 15, 1951.

58. Mayer, "COMPO Formed to Combat Attacks on Filmdom," *New York Times*, October 29, 1950. "Top Execs Being 'Cast' for Last-Ditch Pitch to Preserve COMPO"; "COMPO Rides Again"; both in *Variety*, January 10 and 17, 1951.

59. Young, "Hard Sell," 9.

60. Spiro, "Korean War Fails to Affect Hollywood's Martial Affairs," *New York Times*, September 24, 1950; Coe, "First Korea Film a Patent Quickie," *Washington Post*, February 16, 1951. Hughes's film did not appear until July 1952. Entitled *One Minute to Zero* and now starring Robert Mitchum, it was one of the few Pentagon-sponsored movies the military refused to endorse. The Defense Department was annoyed by the final scene, in which Mitchum orders the artillery to fire on a line of refugees that also contains North Korean soldiers. Hughes only released the film after he received assurances from the Pentagon that it would not rescind his government contracts. See Suid and Haverstick, *Stars and Stripes on Screen*, 168–69.

61. Connolly, "Escapism the Trend among 68 Pix Going into Prod. in 1st 6 Weeks of '51," *Variety*, January 10, 1951.

62. Doherty, *Projections of War*, 276; Suid and Haverstick, *Stars and Stripes on Screen*, 4, 17, 20, 77, 93, 131, 168–69, 196, 221, 228, 251, 276.

63. *Yank in Korea*, a bigger release by Columbia, appeared in February.

64. Suid and Haverstick, *Stars and Stripes on Screen*, 224.

65. " 'Steel Helmet' Is Realistic Drama of Korean Conflict," *Hollywood Reporter*, December 28, 1950. For brief background, see Shindler, *Hollywood Goes to War*, 133.

66. Koppes and Black, *Hollywood Goes to War*, 54, 125–32; Myers, *Bureau of Motion Pictures*, 106, 157–58.

67. This film was *Retreat, Hell!*—a project about the marines' retreat from the Yalu that Warner Brothers pitched to the Pentagon on December 7, 1950, while the battle was still raging. See Suid, *Guts and Glory*, 138. Although various attempts were made in these years to centralize the Defense Department's liaison activities with Hollywood, in practice the services still retained control. see Suid, *Guts and Glory*, 136; and documents 71–73, in Suid, ed., *Film and Propaganda*, 4:196–204.

68. "White House Plugs Zanuck Production," *Hollywood Reporter*, January 3, 1951.

69. *Why Korea?* Director, Edmund Reek, 1951, LC.

70. Steelman to Wilby, January 13, 1951, OF 471B, box 1356, TP; UP, "White House Backs Korean Movie," *New York Times*, January 27, 1951.

71. On Marshall's sensitivity to congressional mail in World War II, see Reynolds, *Rich Relations*, 80–81.

72. Hines to Campbell, March 28, 1951, OPI, Decimal File 000.73, box 42, RG 330.

73. See, for instance, the correspondence in Decimal File 795.00, box 4271, RG 59; *Congressional Record, 1951*, 479; Case to Marshall, April 27, 1951, Admin. Sec. files, Central Decimal File 092 (Korea), box 233, RG 330.

74. Barrett to Acheson, February 1, 1951.

75. Moullette to Moullette, January 16, 1951; Moullette to Acheson, January 19, 1951; Acheson to Moullette, February 23, 1951; all in Acheson Correspondence folder, box 1, Moullette Papers, HSTL.

76. UP, "Marine Says He Is Convinced," *New York Times*, March 4, 1951.

77. Waggoner, "Acheson Tells Bitter Marine to Have Faith in U.S. Ideals," *New York Times*, March 4, 1951. AP, "There Is No East Past the Reds to Peace," *Washington Post*, March 4, 1951. Afterward, whenever the State Department drafted a similar letter, officials called it the "Corporal Moullette approach." Hadsel to Patterson, June 13, 1951, Decimal File 795.00, box 4273, RG 59.

78. Ruckh to Meley, March 12, 1951, Public Opinion Mail Concerning Moullette Letter, Acheson Papers, HSTL. Shulman to Barnes, Subsequent Acheson-Moullette Correspondence folder, box 1, Moullette Papers.

79. Review of *Why Korea?*; "Vagaries of Film Censorship"; " 'It's Too Long,' Sez Cincy Exhib: Duck 'Korea' Date"; all in *Variety*, December 24, 1950, January 3 and 31, 1951.

80. Wood to Steelman, January 22, 1951; Steelman to Zanuck, April 3, 1951; both in OF 471B, box 1356, TP.

81. Foot, *Substitute for Victory*, 15–16. See also Spanier, *Truman-MacArthur Controversy*, 2–7; Higgins, *Korea and the Fall of MacArthur*, viii; Rees, *Korea*, x–xvi.

82. Austin, "Is the World Ready for Collective Security?" February 12, 1951; handwritten note, February 15, 1951; both in Collective Security folder, box 37, Austin Papers.

83. *FRUS, 1951*, 7:196, 245.

84. *FRUS, 1951*, 7:189–93, 201–2. Minutes of State–Joint Chiefs of Staff Meetings, February 6, 13, 15, 1951, PPS files, box 77, RG 59. Schnabel and Watson, *Joint Chiefs of Staff and National Policy*, vol. 3, 1:206–12; Schnabel, *Policy and Direction*, 351–54.

85. Truman, *Public Papers*, February 15, 1951.

86. Eighth Army, PIO, Command Report, March 1951.

87. Eighth Army, PIO, Command Report, March 1951. Parrott, "5 UN Units 17 Miles South of Parallel," *New York Times*, March 20, 1951.

88. *FRUS, 1951*, 7:228–29.

89. Elsey, Memo, March 23, 1951, Speech file (Speech Clearance), box 54, Elsey Papers.

90. MSAO, March 1951.

91. James, *Years of MacArthur*, 3:582–83.

92. James, *Years of MacArthur*, 3:582–83.

93. James, *Years of MacArthur*, 3:582–83. Quirk Diary, March 8, 1951, Korean War folder 1, box 1, Quirk Papers, HSTL.

94. Schaller, *MacArthur*, 230–31. Schnabel and Watson, *Joint Chiefs of Staff and National Policy*, 3, 1:197.

95. Schaller, *MacArthur*, 231. James, *Years of MacArthur*, 3:587–88.

96. *FRUS, 1951*, 7:220.

97. *FRUS, 1951*, 7:246–47 251. Schnabel and Watson, *Joint Chiefs of Staff and National Policy*, vol. 3, 1:212–13.

98. MacArthur, press statement, March 24, 1951, OF 583, box 1397, TP. James, *Years of MacArthur*, 3:585–88.

99. *FRUS, 1951*, 7:266–67; Acheson, *Present at the Creation*, 518–19; Truman, *Years of Trial and Hope*, 442. On the reaction of the press corps, see "MacArthur Warning Given on Own Hook," *Washington Post*, March 25, 1951.

100. Stueck, *Rethinking*, 130–31.

101. Short to Truman, April 2, 1951, Truman, Misc., box 311, Harriman Papers; MemCon, March 30, 1951, Speech file (Speech Clearance), box 54, Elsey Papers.

Chapter 9. The MacArthur Controversy

1. Short, PC, April 11, 1951, SMOF: Short, box 1, TP; Donovan, *Tumultuous Years*, 335–36.

2. Ayers, "MacArthur," April 6, 7, 9, 1951, Korean War folder 3, box 9, Ayers Papers, HSTL.

3. Flesson, "Anything Can Take Place Now," *New York Post*, April 12, 1951.

4. Marshall to Nitze, April 11, 1951, Subject (Korea), Foreign Policy, MacArthur, box 74, Elsey Papers, HSTL; Drafts, April 11, 1951, PSF (Speech file), box 34, TP.

5. Truman, *Public Papers*, April 11, 1951.

6. On the atmosphere in the chamber, see W0409P, April 11, 1951, MacArthur file, box 87, DNC Papers, HSTL.

7. *Congressional Record, 1951*, 3640–49. On Kerr's speechmaking abilities, see Morgan, *Kerr*, 22, 110–11. The White House provided support for this attack; see Hechler to Carroll, April 17, 1951, Subject (Korea): Foreign Policy, MacArthur, box 74, Elsey Papers; Elsey Notes, "MacArthur," undated, Korean War folder 3, box 9, Ayers Papers.

8. Bell to Elsey, April 16, 1951, Speech file: Jefferson-Jackson Day, box 49, Elsey Papers; 7th Draft, PSF, Speech file, longhand notes, box 41, TP.

9. Truman, *Public Papers*, April 14, 1951.

10. Harris, "The MacArthur Dismissal"; Reeves, *McCarthy*, 370. GE1052A, April 13, 1951, MacArthur file, box 87, DNC Papers; White, "Taft Says Truman Hamper Integrity of U.S. Joint Chiefs," *New York Times*, April 27, 1951.

11. "Views of Nation's Newspapers on General MacArthur's Removal," *Baltimore Sun*, April 12, 1951; "U.S. Press Comment on Removal of MacArthur," *New York Times*, April 12, 1951.

12. "U.S. Press Comment on Removal of MacArthur," *New York Times*, April 12, 1951. "Widely Different Opinions Expressed in U.S. Newspapers," *Washington Evening Star*, April 12, 1951.

13. MSAO, April 1951.

14. Lippmann, "MacArthur in Person," *Washington Post*, April 19, 1951.

15. Short, PC, April 17, 1951, SMOF: Short, box 1, TP. White, "Congress to Hear MacArthur as Administration Yields"; "Truman Unlikely to Meet MacArthur"; both in *New York Times*, April 14 and 19, 1951.

16. Elsey, note for the file, April 19, 1951, Speech file: American Society of Newspaper Editors, box 49, Elsey Papers.

17. Korea had long been at the heart of broadcasters' efforts to sell television; see NBC, "TV to Watch," 1951, AD and Promotion, TV, folder, Office files, PR (Brooks), box 130, NBC Records, WHS.

18. Donovan, *Tumultuous Years*, 359–60; James, *Years of MacArthur*, 3:611–18.

19. Stokes, "GOP Faces a Great Decision," *Washington Star*, April 20, 1951.

20. Pearson, "GOP-MacArthur Friction Noted," *Washington Post*, April 18, 1951.

21. Lawrence, "Korean Policy in for Censure," *Washington Star*, April 12, 1951. On the telegrams to Congress, see G816P, April 11,1951, MacArthur file, box 87, DNC Papers.

22. *CQ 1951*, 243; Aiken to Howland, MacArthur Controversy file, crate 11, box 1, Aiken Papers, University of Vermont; "Sen. Duff Says Truman Had to Resolve Dispute," *New York Herald Tribune*, April 12, 1951.

23. Pearson, "GOP Held Wary of MacArthur," *Washington Post*, April 20, 1950. See also Sevareid, "News Analysis," April 16, 1951, box 1:D5, Sevareid Papers, LC; Lawrence, "MacArthur as Asset Stirs GOP Doubts," *New York Times*, April 18, 1951.

24. *Congressional Record, 1951*, 4462–64.

25. White, "Taft Says Truman Hamper Integrity of U.S. Joint Chiefs"; White, "Taft Demands U.S. End Fear of Russia, Go All-Out in Korea"; Loftus, "Taft Asks Cutback in Armament Goal"; all in *New York Times*, April 27 and 28, May 1, 1951.

26. Smith, Memo of Meetings with Hoover, April 14 and 26, 1951, MacArthur Dismissal file, box 106, Smith Papers, PU. Caridi, *Korean War and American Politics*, 150.

27. Lawrence, "Korean Policy in for Censure," *Washington Star*, April 12, 1951. Taft to Hick, April 20, 1951, MacArthur, 1951, files, box 995, Taft Papers, LC.

28. Meeting, April 16, 1951, Republican Minority Policy Committee Minutes, box 3, RG 46; White, "Republicans Call for Full Inquiry on Truman Policy," *New York Times*, April 17, 1951.

29. Truman, *Public Papers*, May 3, 1951.

30. PA, "Popular Attitudes on MacArthur Dismissal," May 8, 1951, Foster files, box 1, RG 59.

31. Elsey to Harriman et al., May 29, 1951, subject file: MacArthur Dismissal, box 75, Elsey Papers.

32. "4 Large Papers in NY Support General MacArthur," *Chicago Tribune*, April 13, 1951.

33. Harsch to Jandron, May 4, 1951, correspondence folder, box 38, Harsch Papers, WHS; Saville to Strout, May 2, 1951, Professional file, box 4, Strout Papers, LC.

34. DA MC, May 15, 1951. Even the *San Francisco Chronicle*'s initial support had been lukewarm, dismissing the idea of impeachment but calling for a clarification of the administration's Far East policy; see "But the Problem Remains," editorial, *San Francisco Chronicle*, April 13, 1951.

35. Hechler, Memo of Meeting at Barriere's, undated, MacArthur Hearings: Misc. Background file, box 304, Harriman Papers, LC.

36. Harris, "Kennedy Expresses Concern, Regrets MacArthur Removal," *Boston Globe*, April 11, 1951.

37. Editorial, "Republicans and MacArthur," *New York Herald Tribune*, April 18, 1951; "Venom in the Vacuum," editorial, *Washington Post*, May 1, 1951.

38. Elsey, Memo for the file, April 19, 1951, Speech file: Speech Clearance, box 54, Elsey Papers.

39. Murphy to Truman, April 16, 1951, PSF (General): Murphy, box 131, TP; Hechler, *Working with Truman*, 168–70.

40. Tannenwald to Carroll, April 16, MacArthur Hearings: Misc. Background, box 304, Harriman Papers.

41. Barriere, OH; Savage, *Truman and the Democratic Party*, 74–80.

42. Hechler to Tannenwald, April 25, 1951, MacArthur Hearings: Misc. Background file, box 304, Harriman Papers; Hechler, Memo of Meeting at Barriere's, undated, MacArthur Hearings: Misc. Background file, box 304, Harriman Papers.

43. Hechler, Memo of Meeting at Barriere's, undated, MacArthur Hearings: Misc. Background file, box 304, Harriman Papers. See also Vorhees, "CPD, 1950–53," April 1968, 49–50, CPD Essay file, Vorhees Papers, Rutgers University.

44. Hechler to Carroll, April 17, 1951, MacArthur Hearings: Misc. Background file, box 304, Harriman Papers.

45. Hechler to Murphy, May 7, 1951; Murphy to Pendleton, May 8, 1951; Tannenwald to Goodrich, May 14, 1951; Hechler to Tannenwald, May 15, 1951; all in MacArthur Hearings: Misc. file, box 304, Harriman Papers.

46. Elsey to Truman, March 28, 1951, PSF (General): Elsey, TP; Hechler to Carroll, April 17, 1951; Elsey to Tannenwald, April 30, 1951, SMOF: Lloyd (1), China Lobby folder, TP.

47. Elsey, Memo on China Lobby, June 8, 1951, China Lobby files, box 4, Tannenwald Papers, HSTL. The State Department did brief friendly journalists about the large bank accounts held by some nationalist leaders. See Childs to Behrle, April 25, 1951, correspondence folder, box 2, Childs Papers, WHS.

48. Leveiro, "Files Show That MacArthur Foresaw Quick Victory," *New York Times*, April 21, 1951. On the leak, Merz of the *New York Times* told Pulitzer of the *St. Louis Post-Dispatch* that Truman was personally responsible. See Pulitzer RPB, April 24, 1951, *St. Louis Post–Dispatch* files, box 25, Childs Papers. On Republican anger, see *MSFE*, 1686; To RH, Memo for the Record, May 14, 1951, folder 19, box 195A, Marshall Papers, Marshall Library; Walz, "Files on M'Arthur to be Fully Open, Pentagon Pledges," *New York Times*, April 23, 1951.

49. Lloyd to Tannenwald, May 10, 1951, MacArthur Hearings: Misc. Background file, box 304, Harriman Papers, LC. "Now It Comes Out"; "Now It Comes Out II"; both in *Washington Post*, April 13 and 14, 1951.

50. Summary of Meeting, May 4, 1951, PA Asst. SecState, PRWG file, box 1, RG 59.

51. Shulman to Acheson, May 15, 1951, PPS files, Subject: National Security, box 11A, RG 59.

52. Bell to Elsey, May 7, 1951, Civil Defense Dinner, box 49, Elsey Papers.

53. Shulman to Acheson, May 15, 1951, PPS files, Subject: National Security, box 11A, RG 59.

54. Lloyd to Murphy and Bell, April 25, 1951; Lloyd to Elsey, April 30, 1951; both in Speech file: Military Budget Message, box 49, Elsey Papers.

55. Truman, *Public Papers*, May 7, 1951. On the drafting of this speech, see Lloyd to Elsey, May 7, 1951, Civil Defense Dinner folder, box 49, Elsey Papers.

56. Kuter, *Wars of Watergate*, 351.

57. Caro, *Master of the Senate*, 311–31; Woods, *Fulbright*, 154–63; Wilson, "Kefauver Committee," 3439–43, 3460–63.

58. Doherty, *Cold War, Cool Medium*, 107–16.

59. Barriere, OH.

60. Memo to Harriman, undated, MacArthur files, Briefing Book 13, box 304, Harriman Papers.

61. Tannenwald to Carroll, April 16. Goodrich to Leva and Larkin, April 13, 1951, folder 11; Nash to Goodrich, May 5, 1951, folder 1; both in box 195A, Marshall Papers. On the administration's efforts to plant questions with friendly congressmen, see, Pearson, *Diaries*, 160–62.

62. Russell, Statement, April 13, 1951, Speeches and Statements folder, series 12, box 5, Russell Papers, University of Georgia.

63. Leveiro, "Joint Chiefs Will Answer M'Arthur and Will Analyze 'Basic Differences,'" *New York Times*, April 22, 1951; Russell to Marshall, April 25, 1951, folder 2, box 195A, Marshall Papers; Marshall to Russell, May 5, MacArthur Hearings: Misc. Background file, box 304, Harriman Papers.

64. White, "Republicans Call for Full Inquiry on Truman Policy"; Trussell, "Congress Spurred to Policy Inquiries"; White, "Taft Says Truman Hampers Integrity of U.S. Joint Chiefs"; all in *New York Times*, April 17, 20, and 27, 1951.

65. Russell to McGill, April 26, 1951, Special Correspondence folder, series 12, box 1, Russell Papers; "Senate GOP Asks M'Arthur Inquiry Be Held in Public," *New York Times*, April 26, 1951. MacArthur was perfectly happy to appear before the cameras. Gutzner, "M'Arthur Willing to Face Television," *New York Times*, April 26, 1951.

66. *Congressional Record, 1951*, 4772–76; *MSFE*, 93–96, 270, 293. White, "M'Arthur Hearings to Start in Secret"; White, "Democrats Filibuster to Bar Open MacArthur Hearing"; "GOP Loses Senate Fight For Open MacArthur Hearings"; all in *New York Times*, May 1, 3, and 5, 1951.

67. *Congressional Record, 1951*, 4180–86; White, "M'Arthur Hearing to be Opened May 3 by Senate Group," *New York Times*, April 25, 1951.

68. Memo to Harriman, undated, MacArthur files, Briefing Book 13, box 304, Harriman Papers. Smith Diary, May 2, 1951, Smith Papers, PU.

69. "Van Fleet Says Foe Lost First Phase"; Parrott, "Chinese Pull Back from Seoul Front"; Parrott, "UN Units Advance; Van Fleet Claims a 'Grand Victory'"; all in *New York Times*, April 30, May 2 and 3, 1951. On the battle itself, see Appleman, *Ridgway Duels for Korea*, 449–96.

70. Wilz, "MacArthur Inquiry," 3602–3.

71. *MSFE*, 68, 70, 133.

72. *MSFE*, 49, 66, 132.

73. *MSFE*, 39.

74. *MSFE*, 44, 65–66, 30.

75. Smith Diary, May 4 and 5, 1951.

76. *MSFE*, 308.

77. *MSFE*, 101, 142, 299–300. Higgins, *Korea and the Fall of MacArthur*, 149.

78. *MSFE*, 76–78, 140–42.

79. See Saltonstall to Barker, April 24, 1951, Correspondence 1951, box 14, Saltonstall Papers, MHS; Trussell, "Congress Spurred to Policy Inquiries," *New York Times*, April 20, 1950.

80. Bradley, Speech, April 17, 1951, Korean War folder 3, box 9, Ayers Papers.

81. *MSFE*, 324–25, 501, 736–37, 730–32.

82. *MSFE*, 1379, 1492–93, 1503. Wilz, "MacArthur Inquiry," 3615.

83. Cater, Memo for the Record, April 24, 1951, folder 1, box 195A, Marshall Papers.

84. *MSFE*, 1527–28

85. *MSFE*, 28–29.

86. McMaster, "Extra! All about Mac," *Editor & Publisher*, April 28, 1951. According to Drew Pearson, the American Society of Newspaper Editors "were not happy over the way MacArthur kept them waiting three hours yesterday while he took a nap." Pearson, *Diaries*, 157.

87. Meeting, May 16, 1951, Republican Conference Minority Policy Committee Minutes, box 3, RG 46.

88. *MSFE*, 610–11, 937, 950, 1278–79, 1286–88.

89. *MSFE*, 1286; Adams to Larkin, May 14, 1951, folder 4, box 195A, Marshall Papers.

90. *MSFE*, 1286–87.

91. "Poll of Newsmen Backs Truman, 6–1," *Washington Post*, June 9, 1951. Summary of Meeting, May 9, 1951, PA Asst. SecState, PRWG file, box 1, RG 59.

92. Memo Re Marshall Testimony, undated, Hearings Materials, series 12, box 7, Russell Papers.

93. Truman to Lowenthal, May 15, 1951, PSF (General): Lowenthal, TP.

94. "Most Who Follow Testimony Favor MacArthur's Policies," *Washington Post*, June 10, 1951.

95. Elsey to Harriman et al., May 29, 1951, subject file: MacArthur Dismissal, box 75, Elsey Papers.

96. *MSFE*, 646.

97. Pearson to Flanders, May 22, 1951, Presidential Appointments file, ML 3, box 71, Tobey Papers, Dartmouth College.

98. Summary of Meeting, May 31, 1951, PA Asst. Sec State, PRWG file, box 1, RG 59.

99. "Formosa Gets Equal Priority with Europe on Arms Help"; "News of the Week in Review"; both in *New York Times*, April 25 and May 13, 1951. Stueck, *Korean War*, 189–93.

100. *DSB* 24: 846–48.

101. Rusk, OH; Porter, "Rusk Hints U.S. Aid to Revolt in China"; Waggoner, "Acheson Disavows China Policy Shift"; both in *New York Times*, May 19 and 24, 1951.

102. Krock, "In the Nation," *New York Times*, May 24, 1951.

103. *FRUS, 1951*, 6: 34–37, 41–51.

104. Summary of Meeting, May 4 and 9, 1951, PA Asst. Sec State, PRWG file, box 1, RG 59.

105. On Acheson's office, see Chace, *Acheson*, 197–98. For rough notes on these meetings, see MacArthur Testimony file, Acheson Papers, HSTL. For his preparation, see also Beisner, *Acheson*, 433.

106. Russell to Barrett, May 29, 1951, PA Asst. SecState, subject files, box 5, RG 59.

107. *MSFE*, 1727–39, 1837–57. Wilz, "MacArthur Inquiry," 3617.

108. Smith Diary, June 4, 1951. Wiley also privately thought that "in all fairness he [Acheson] was deservent [*sic*] of a compliment for his ability in standing up under the tremendous pressure of very close questioning." Wiley to Dallman, June 15, 1951, Legislative: Foreign Relations folder, box 57, Wiley Papers, WHS.

109. *MSFE*, 1714–15.

110. *MSFE*, 1720.

111. James, *Years of MacArthur*, 3:624–25. Gallup, "U.S. Public Reveals Lack of Interest in Senate Inquiry on Policy Concerning Korea," June 9, 1951, Newspaper Clipping file, DNC Papers.

112. "Proposed Witnesses," undated, series 12, box 7, Russell Papers; Knowland to Russell, April 24, 1951, Correspondence, Knowland file, Senate Armed Service Committee Papers, box 201, RG 46.

113. McFarland and Roll, *Louis Johnson*, 112–16, 352–53.

114. *MSFE*, 2597–604. White, "Acheson, Not Joint Chiefs Urged War, Johnson Asserts," *New York Times*, June 15, 1951.

115. Hechler, *Working with Truman*, 183–84.

116. McCullough, *Truman*, 854–55; Hamby, *Man of the People*, 564–73.

117. Higgins, *Korea and the Fall of MacArthur*, 183; Caridi, *Korean War and American Politics*, 170–73, 204–5; Kaufman, *Korean War*, 151–52; Foot, *Substitute for Victory*, 8–10, 38.

118. University of Michigan Survey, "Public Reactions to American Foreign Policy," July 25, 1951, Subject (Korea): Foreign Policy, MacArthur, box 74, Elsey Papers. Gallup, "Eisenhower More Popular Than MacArthur as Choice for U.S. President"; "Disapproval of MacArthur Dismissal Found Declining"; May 13 and June 8, 1951, both in Newspaper Clipping file, DNC Papers.

119. Maverick to Truman, June 15, 1951, PSF (General): MacArthur, box 129, TP.

120. *MSFE*, 1398–1400.

121. Schwinn, Memo, June 5, 1951, PA, Policy Guidance and Coordination, National Security subject files, box 57, RG 59. During this period, the administration also worked with allies and made important advances in mobilization; see Stueck, *Rethinking*, 225–26.

122. Congress of Industrial Organizations, Political Action Committee, "Questions about Korea," May 1951, Presidential Campaign, 1952, Info file, DNC, Foreign Policy, Korea folder, box 348, Harriman Papers.

123. Wilson, "Building America's Might," April 1, 1951, Security Classified files, ODM, box 14, RG 304.

124. "Washington Outlook," *Business Week*, April 28, 1951.

125. Reeves, *McCarthy*, 371–72; DOPS, July 23, 1951.

126. Bell to Taft, undated; Taft to Cooper, April 16, 1951; Taft, press release, April 16, 1951; all in Senate (Foreign Policy): MacArthur Hearings file, box 628, Taft Papers. See also "Taft Says Truman Charge He Asks All-Out War on China Is Nonsense," *New York Times*, May 20, 1951.

127. *Congressional Record, 1951*, 5424. On the administration's response, see Merchant to Fisher, May 2, 1951, Decimal File 795.00, box 4273, RG 59. On discussions in the Republican Policy Committee, see Pearson, "GOP Held Wary of MacArthur," *Washington Post*, April 20, 1950.

128. See, for instance, DOPS, July 26, 1951.

129. Wilz, "MacArthur Inquiry," 3602, 3626; James, *Years of MacArthur*, 3:624–25, 639.

130. Schlesinger to Saltonstall, December 16, 1950, correspondence folder, box 14, Saltonstall Papers. For background, see Shaffer, *On and Off the Floor*, 52–53.

131. AP, "Morse Hits GOP Bias for M'Arthur," *Washington Post*, August 19, 1951; AP, "Chief Points Made by 8 Republican Senators," *New York Times*, August 20, 1950; DOPS, August 20 and 23, 1951.

132. *MSFE*, 1782–83

133. Summary of Meeting, July 3, 1951, PA Asst. Sec State, PRWG file, box 1, RG 59.

134. Lawrence, "But What Does Stalin Think?" *Washington Post*, July 4, 1951. See also Ward, "Republicans Troubled by Moves for Truce," *Baltimore Sun*, July 1, 1951; Krock, "Korea's Consequences Weighed in Washington," *New York Times*, July 8, 1951.

Chapter 10. Interminable Truce Talks

1. Rosenthal, "Soviet Calls for Truce Parley," *New York Times*, June 24, 1951.

2. Truman, *Public Papers*, June 25, 1951; *FRUS, 1951*, 7:558–59; Hermes, *Truce Tent*, 15–20.

3. Campbell and Jamieson, *Deeds Done in Words*; Smith and Smith, *White House Speaks*, 23.

4. Barrett to Matthews, February 4, 1952, PA Asst. SecState, Memos, box 2, RG 59.

5. Eighth Army, PIO, Command Report, July 1951.

6. Unnumbered press release, July 6, 1951, Korean War Communiqués, box 5, RG 319.

7. MacGregor, "Allied Delegates Kept from the Press," *New York Times*, July 16, 1951.

8. Pakenham, "Back at Peace Camp," *Newsweek*, July 23, 1951; O'Leary, press release, September 10, 1951, U.S. Marine Corps, Division of PI, Publicity Stories Relating to the First Marine Division in Korea, box 1, RG 127.

9. AP, "Story of the 1st Truce Meeting," *Chicago Daily News*, July 9, 1951.

10. Parrott, "UN Delegates Meet Reds," *New York Times*, July 8, 1951.

11. Sparks, "Sparks Busts Truce City Gap," *Chicago Daily News*; UP, "Reporters Call Kaesong a Red Camp, Cry 'Gag,'" *New York Herald Tribune*; both July 10, 1951.

12. *FRUS, 1951*, 7:639, 649–50.

13. Hermes, *Truce Tent*, 26–29.

14. Eighth Army, PIO, Command Report, July 1951; "Press Catches Blame for Stalling 'Peace,'" *Editor & Publisher*, July 14, 1951.

15. Allen to Parks, July 23, 1951, Chief of I & E files, Unclassified Central Decimal File 000.74, box 60, RG 319.

16. See, for instance, FEC, PIO, SSR, January and February 1952.

17. FEC, PIO, SSR, July 1951. Allen's World War II record, in contrast, did not spark confidence in the press corps, for he had been blamed for stopping all news stories on the Battle of the Bulge in December 1944. See "Correspondents at Bay," *Time*, July 23, 1951.

18. Stueck, *Rethinking*, 150–54.

19. FEC, PIO, SSR, January and February 1952. Barrett, "Truce Reporters Held Indiscreet," *New York Times*, February 8, 1952.

20. Knightley, *First Casualty*, 352–53; Aronson, *Press and the Cold War*, 114–16.

21. Pakenham, "Rendezvous in Kaesong," *Newsweek*, July 30, 1951.

22. Pakenham, "Appointment in Kaesong," *Newsweek*, July 16, 1951.

23. Parrott, "Truce Sessions Make 'Some Progress,'" *New York Times*, July 17, 1951.

24. Aronson, *Press and the Cold War*, 114–15.

25. McConnell, "Kaesong Resumes Deadlocked Talks," *New York Herald Tribune*, August 1, 1951.

26. Nuckols, U.S. Air Force Biography, www.af.mil.bios/bio. "Nuckols Proves Able in Role of Mediator between Army and Press on News of Truce," *New York Times*, August 1, 1951. For a far more critical view, see Burchett, *Again Korea*, 53–55.

27. Burchett, *Again Korea*, 33–35; Aronson, *Press and the Cold War*, 114–15.

28. Parrott, "Reds Suggest Breakdown," *New York Times*, August 2, 1951. Goodman, *Negotiating While Fighting*, 23.

29. *FRUS, 1951*, 7:758, 761.

30. Parrott, "Truce Parley Seeks Accord on Fixing Military Line," *New York Times*, July 28, 1951; McConnell, "Reds' Answer to Allies Due," *New York Herald Tribune*, July 31, 1951.

31. Foot, *Substitute for Victory*, 17.

32. Vorhees, *Korean Tales*, 15; *FRUS 1951*, 7:594.

33. "Press Restrained on 'Roaming' Around Kaesong," *Editor & Publisher*, July 21, 1951.

34. Allen to Parks, July 23, 1951, Chief of I & E files, Unclassified Central Decimal File 000.74, box 60, RG 319.

35. Parrott, "UN Delegates in Tokyo," *New York Times*, August 7, 1951.

36. AP, "Enemy Believed Ready to Accept Present Line as Truce Buffer Zone"; UP, "Statement to Japanese"; both in *New York Herald Tribune*, August 3 and 4, 1951.

37. Joy, PC, August 14, 1951, Korean War Communiqués, box 5, RG 319. "Still No Compromise at Parley"; Parrott, "Joy Asks Military Logic"; both in *New York Times*, August 14 and 15, 1951. AP, "Reds Spurn Conciliatory Bid by Allies," *New York Herald Tribune*, August 16, 1951.

38. Hayward, "UN Conferees Ask Line Deep in North Korea," *Christian Science Monitor*, August 4, 1951.

39. DOPS, July 16, 20, and 30, 1951.

40. Hermes, *Truce Tent*, 40–51.

41. O'Leary, press release, September 10, 1951.

42. FEC, PIO, SSR, October and December 1951. For the claim that Nuckols tried to mislead reporters but was caught out, see Burchett, *Again Korea*, 53–55; Aronson, *Press and the Cold War*, 115.

43. *FRUS, 1951*, 7:1080, 1088, 1101–2; Goodman, *Negotiating While Fighting*, 46, 68.

44. Goodman, *Negotiating While Fighting*, 68, 77.

45. FEC, PIO, SSR, July 1951 and November 1951.

46. *FRUS, 1951*, 7:1093.

47. Ridgway to Collins, September 26, 1951, Collins Papers, box 17, DDEL; *FRUS, 1951*, 7:1105, 1120–22; Foot, *Substitute for Victory*, 52–53, 66, 68.

48. Hermes, *Truce Tent*, 177.

49. FEC, PIO, SSR, November 1951; Eunson, "UN Censors Pass New Report of Disputed 'Ceasefire' Order," *Christian Science Monitor*, December 3, 1951.

50. Eighth Army, PIO, Command Report; FEC, PIO, SSR, November 1951; Eunson, "UN Censors Pass New Report."

51. *FRUS, 1951*, 7:1290–96.

52. AP, "4,500 GIs Called Prisoners in Korea," *New York Herald Tribune*, August 15, 1951.

53. Acheson to Marshall, August 27, 1951, Decimal File 693.0024, box 3003, RG 59. Fechteler, to Lovett, October 15, 1951; Ruffner to Acting Secretary, November 28, 1951; both in Admin. Sec. files, Central Decimal File 092 (Korea), box 233, RG 330. *FRUS, 1951*, 7, 1197–98. Foot, *Substitute for Victory*, 87–88.

54. Bridges, Cain, and Dirksen, press release, July 30, 1951, Senate Armed Services Committee Papers, Correspondence: Bridges file, box 187, RG 46; *Congressional Record, 1951*, 13086.

55. Schooley to Houser, January 8, 1952, Admin. Sec. files, Central Decimal File 092 (Korea), box 233, RG 330.

56. OPI, Activity Report, October 25, 1950, box 153, RG 330. See also Summary of Meeting, October 5, 1950, PA Asst. SecState, PRWG file, box 1, RG 59.

57. See, for instance, AP, "Americans Massacred by North Korean Captors," *New York Times*, October 23, 1950; Sharpe and Currie, "God Saved My Life in Korea," *Saturday Evening Post*, January 13, 1951.

58. Johnson to Lovett, October 8, 1951; Lovett to Joint Chiefs of Staff, October 17, 1951; Fechteler to Lovett, November 30, 1951; all in Admin. Sec. Central Decimal File 092 (Korea), box 233, RG 330.

59. FEC, PIO, SSR, November 1951; *FRUS, 1951*, 7:1137, 1143–44.

60. FEC, PIO, SSR, November 1951.

61. "Four-Star Blunder," *Time*, December 3, 1951. The letters and telegrams are in OF 325, HSTL.

62. "Terms for a Truce," editorial, *New York Times*, November 18, 1951.

63. Houser to Reber, November 30, 1951, Admin. Sec. files, Central Decimal File 092 (Korea), box 233, RG 330.

64. UP, "Congressmen Demand UN Use A-Bomb to Avenge Atrocities," *Washington Post*, November 15, 1951.

65. MemCon: Atrocity Reports, November 21, 1951, Decimal File 795.00, box 4276, RG 59.

66. FEC, PIO, SSR, December 1951; Parks for PIOs, December 18, 1951, Chief of I & E files, Unclassified Central Decimal File 000.7, box 54, RG 319. For details on the list, see Vatcher, *Panmunjom*, 126.

67. *FRUS, 1951*, 7:1421–22.

68. Foot, *Substitute for Victory*, 109–21; Manhard to Muccio, March 14, 1952, Decimal File 795.00, box 4278, RG 59; *FRUS, 1952–54*, 15:369–70.

69. Welch, Memo for the Chief of Legislative Liaison, June 19, 1952, Chief of I & E files, Unclassified Central Decimal File 000.73, box 60, RG 319.

70. Worden, "Our Lucky Red Prisoners," *Saturday Evening Post*, January 3, 1952.

71. Collins to Lovett, November 15, 1951, Admin. Sec. files, Central Decimal File 092 (Korea), box 233, RG 330; *FRUS, 1951*, 7, 1170–71.

72. Worden, "Our Lucky Red Prisoners," *Saturday Evening Post*, January 3, 1952; Robertson, "Chinese PWs Cling to Red Line," *Christian Science Monitor*, December 1, 1951; Beech, "UN Tries to Convert Prisoners," *Chicago Daily News*, December 3, 1951.

73. Webb, Meeting with President, October 29, 1951, PPS files, Subject: Korea, box 20, RG 59.

74. *FRUS, 1951*, 7:1232–33, 1278.

75. Goodman, ed., *Negotiating While Fighting*, 175–79, 181. On the communists' motivations, see Foot, *Substitute for Victory*, 219; Stueck, *Rethinking*, 163.

76. Truman, January 27, 1951, PSF (longhand notes), box 333, TP.

77. MSC to Foster, January 22, 1952, Admin. Sec. files, Central Decimal File 092 (Korea), box 319, RG 330. A few weeks earlier, at the start of the year, senior officials had been more optimistic; see Stueck, *Rethinking*, 164.

78. DOPS, January 23, 1952.

79. DOPS, January 24, 1952; Lippmann, "Blunder in Korea," *Washington Post*, January 24, 1951. See also Stelle to Nitze, January 28, 1951, PPS files, Subject: Korea, box 20, RG 59.

80. Barrett to Matthews, February 4, 1952, PA Asst. SecState, Memos, box 2, RG 59.

81. *FRUS, 1952–54*, 15:33–34, 41–42, 68–69; Bernstein, "Struggle over the Korean Armistice," 281–83; Stueck, *Rethinking*, 165–66.

82. *FRUS, 1952–54*, 15:100.

83. "Domestic Info Program on Korea," April 8, 1952, PA Asst. SecState, Memos, White House Meetings with Short, box 2, RG 59.

84. Marshall to Nitze, January 28, 1952, PPS files, Subject: Korea, box 20, RG 59.

85. Phillips to Bohlen, March 12, 1952, PA Asst. SecState, Memos, box 2; Phillips, "Some PR Questions on POW Issue," PA Asst. SecState, subject file, box 5, April 15, 1952; both in RG 59.

86. On Armstrong's views, see his letters to Rusk, May 25 and July 17, 1951, Decimal File 795.00, boxes 4273 and 4274, RG 59. On his final resolution, see *Congressional Record, 1952*, 3092.

87. Summary of Meeting, February 1, 1952, PA Asst. SecState, PRWG file, box 1, RG 59; DA MC, undated [filed in October 1952]. See also *FRUS, 1952–54*, 15:41, 100. Bernstein, "Struggle over the Korean Armistice," 281 n. 53.

88. FEC, PIO, SSR, January, 1952; Parrott, "Civilian Soldiers Repatriation Plan Is Proposed by UN," *New York Times*, January 2, 1952.

89. Phillips to Bohlen, March 12, 1952, PA Asst. SecState, Memos, box 2. PA, "Articulate and Popular Opinion on Issue of Involuntary Repatriations and POWs," April 16, 1952, PA Asst. SecState, subject file, box 5, RG 59.

90. *FRUS, 1952–54*, 15:103, 156; Phillips, "Psychological Aspects of Negotiations on Exchange of POWs in Korean Armistice," January 17, 1952, Decimal File 795.00, box 4277, RG 59.

91. *FRUS, 1952–54*, 15:82, 86–87, 89. Battle, MemCon, March 14, 1952, Decimal File 795.00, box 4278; Sargeant to Acheson, March 14, 1952, PA Asst. SecState, subject file, box 5; both in RG 59.

92. Parrott, "Foe Won't Discuss Soviet Truce Role"; "Foe Charges UN Violations of Truce Talk Secrecy Pact"; both in *New York Times*, March 26 and 29, 1951. Bernstein, "Struggle over the Korean Armistice," 272–74. Foot, *Substitute for Victory*, 97–98. *FRUS, 1952–54*, 15:108.

93. *Congressional Record, 1952*, 2323, 3985; Foot, *Substitute for Victory*, 99–100.

94. Goodman, *Negotiating While Fighting*, 355, 367–68, 384–86, 396–99; *FRUS, 1952–54*, 15:22, 58–59, 113, 148, 192–93; Bernstein, "Struggle over the Korean Armistice," 285–86; Foot, *Substitute for Victory*, 97–99.

95. "Acheson Declares Captives Key Issue"; Schumach, "UN Tells Full Story of Poll of Prisoners"; Parrott, "Red Reply Spurns Plan for Solving All Truce Issues"; all in *New York Times*, April 25 and 26, May 2, 1952.

96. Phillips to Tubby, April 25, 1952, White House Central File, Korean Emergency folder, box 22, TP; *DSB* 26:786–87.

97. Clark, *From the Danube to the Yalu*, 40–41; Official Press Release, May 12, 1952, FEC PIO Printed and Misc. Matter, box 6, Rosengren Papers, WHS.

98. Hermes, *Truce Tent*, 254–55.

99. Fritchey, Press Statement, May 13, 1952, FEC PIO Printed and Misc. Matter, box 6, Rosengren Papers; "Prisoner Snafu in Koje Camp," *Newsweek*, May 26, 1952.

100. *Congressional Record, 1952*, 5193–97; "Members of Congress Want Full Report on Koje Incident," *New York Times*, May 16, 1952. On the "coddle" accusation, see Morgan to Rosengren, May 22, 1952, FEC PIO Printed and Misc. Matter, box 6, Rosengren Papers.

101. DOPS, May 13 and 16, 1952

102. *FRUS, 1952–54*, 15:222–23, 259.

103. *FRUS*, 244–46; Dennison to Truman, May 19, 1952, PSF (Korean War): Armistice folder, box 243, TP.

104. *FRUS, 1952–54*, 15:73–74, 79, 210–12. On the actual charges, see Leitenberg, "New Russian Evidence," 185–96; Weathersby, "Deceiving the Deceivers," 176–80.

105. Sargeant to Acheson, March 14, 1952, PA Asst. SecState, subject file, box 5, RG 59. Even in July, after the administration had focused more attention on the issue, only 64 percent had heard of the germ warfare charges, which was a far lower level of public awareness than on other major issues. See Sargeant to PA, August 5, 1952, PA Asst SecState, Memos, box 1, RG 59.

106. "UN Tightens Ban on Germ Charges," *New York Times*, May 14, 1952.

107. *FRUS, 1952–54*, 15:223–24; Waggoner, "Acheson Calls Germ Charge Soviet 'Crime,'" *New York Times*, May 8, 1952.

108. "Prisoner Snafu in Koje Camp," *Newsweek*, May 26, 1952.

109. Eighth Army, PIO, Command Report, June 1952; Painton, UP dispatches, June 11 and 12, 1952, Korea Reports folder, box 6, Rosengren Papers.

110. Rosengren to Rosengren, May 17, 1952, Korean Letters folder, box 2, Rosengren Papers. See also Clark, *From the Danube to the Yalu*, 50–54.

111. Rosengren, Memo, undated, FEC PIO Printed and Misc. Matter, box 6, Rosengren Papers. Parks thought the Koje-do incident would make a good case study to teach PI students. See Parks to Rosenberg, General Correspondence, box 1, Rosengren Papers.

112. Stueck, *Rethinking*, 169, 196–99.

113. Hamby, *Man of the People*, 593–97; Marcus, *Truman and the Steel Seizure Case*, 83–101, 249–60.

114. Gallup, "Truman Popularity at New Low," *Washington Post*, December 30, 1951.

115. Gallup, "Vote Agrees Korean War Is 'Useless,'" *Washington Post*, November 4, 1951.

116. Gallup, "Popularity of Truman Rises from Low Point Last Winter," *Washington Post*, June 20, 1952.

117. Russell, "Comparison of American Popular Opinion on Foreign Policy a Year Ago and Today," January 2, 1952, Foster files, box 20, RG 59.

118. MSAO, July 1951, February and June 1952.

119. PA, "Articulate and Popular Opinion on Issue of Involuntary Repatriations and POWs," April 16, 1952.

120. MSAO, July 1952; Summary of Meeting, July 24, 1952, PA Asst. Sec State, PRWG file, box 1, RG 59; on the petitions, see Phillips to Tubby, July 3, 1952; Sargeant to Boughton, July 9, 1952; PA Asst. SecState, Memos, box 2, RG 59.

Chapter 11. Steady Improvements

1. Eighth Army, PIO, Command Report, December 1951.
2. Foot, *Substitute for Victory*, 208.
3. Knightley, *First Casualty*, 353.
4. James, *Refighting the Last War*, 66–67; Braim, *Will to Win*, 239.
5. Eighth Army, PIO, Command Report, March 1952.
6. Braim, *Will to Win*, 240, 297–98.
7. AP, "Ridgway Appoints Allen New Information Chief"; AP, "Buffalo Editor on Way to Tokyo"; both in *New York Times*, July 4, 1951, and January 3, 1952.
8. Eighth Army, PIO, Command Report, December 1952.
9. Eighth Army, PIO, Command Report, December 1952. FEC, PIO, SSR, November 1951.
10. Vorhees, *Korean Tales*, 80–96. FEC, PIO, SSR, January and February 1952.
11. James, *Refighting the Last War*, 66–68, 72; Braim, *Will to Win*, 239.
12. Eighth Army, PIO, Command Report, November 1952.
13. Ridgway to Parks, March 21, 1951, Chief of I & E files, Unclassified Central Decimal File 000.73, box 60, RG 319.
14. FEC, PIO, SSR, May and June 1951; FEC, PIO, Press Release, June 5, 1951, UN Command, Liaison Section: subject file, box 15, RG 333.
15. Eighth Army, PIO, Command Report, June 1951; FEC, PIO, SSR, May, June, and October 1951.
16. Allison, "Black Sheep Squadron," 472–77; "Truman Likens 'Propaganda' of Marines to Stalin Set-Up," *New York Times*, September 6, 1950.
17. Denig, OH.
18. Interview with Stahey, January 28, 1952, MCHC. For a sample of these stories, see U.S. Marine Corps, Division of PI, Publicity Stories Relating to the First Marine Division in Korea, boxes 1–4, RG 127.
19. First Marine Division, press releases, September 10, 1951 and undated, Publicity Stories Relating to the First Marine Division in Korea, box 1, RG 127.
20. Headline, *San Francisco Chronicle*, May 1, 1951.
21. Interview with Stahey; Geer to McQueen, April 16, 1951; both in U.S. Marine Corps, Division of PI, General files, KP-9, box 5, RG 127. *Marine Corps Gazette*, July 1950, 20–21, and September 1952, 32–34.
22. Parks to Deputy Chief, March 15, 1951; see also Parks to Quirk, May 2, 1951; and for an assessment of the reasons behind the marines' success, see Hickey to Parks, February 10, 1951; all in Chief of I & E files, Unclassified Central Decimal File 000.7, box 54, RG 319.

23. Parks to Collins, March 7, 1951, Chief of I & E files, Unclassified Central Decimal File 000.7, box 54, RG 319. The marines' statement stressed that this rotation would only be "small scale." Press Release, February 24, 1951, Division of Information, Special Action folders (Policy), box 24, RG 127.

24. Parks to Van Fleet, October 27, 1952, Chief of I & E files, Unclassified Central Decimal File 000.7, box 54, RG 319.

25. Parks to Quirk, March 1, 1951; Parks to Ridgway, March 8, 1951; Collins to Ridgway, May 8, 1951; all in Chief of I & E files, Unclassified Central Decimal File 000.7, box 54, RG 319. Van Fleet was hesitant to institute this reform, fearing that it might give the enemy important intelligence. See Van Fleet to Parks, June 14, 1951, Chief of I & E files, Unclassified Central Decimal File 000.73, box 60, RG 319. On the press coverage of the Second Division, see Marshall, *River and the Gauntlet*, 49.

26. Eighth Army, PIO, Command Report, September, November, and December 1951.

27. "Rotation for Korean Veterans," April 9, 1951, Korean War Communiqués, box 4, RG 319.

28. Rosenberg to Russell, January 18, 1952, Senate Armed Services Committee Records, Correspondence: Def. Sec. file, box 193, RG 46; "Risky Promise," *Time*, October 29, 1951.

29. Notestein to Fowler, September 4, 1951, Unclassified Central Decimal File 000.75, box 61; Fowler to DeWitt, May 12, 1952, Unclassified Central Decimal File 000.7, box 54; both in Chief of I & E files, RG 319.

30. FEC, PIO, SSR, July 1951.

31. Eighth Army, PIO, Command Report, May and August 1951, and November 1952.

32. Lane, "Officer PI Course," March 20, 1951; Binford to Parks, January 17, 1951; both in U.S. Marine Corps, Division of Info, General files, P11–6ER, box 6, RG 127.

33. Eighth Army, PIO, February and September 1952.

34. Parks to Wiggins, August 25, 1952, Chief of I & E files, Unclassified Central Decimal File 000.73, box 60, RG 319.

35. Parks to Lochner, June 4, 1952; Merrick to Notestein, October 13, 1952; both in Chief of I & E files, Unclassified Central Decimal File 000.73, box 60, RG 319.

36. FEC, PIO, SSR, December 1952; Berding to Williams, December 16, 1952, OPI, 000.73, box 70, RG 330; Joint Field Press Censorship, January 6, 1953, UN Command, Liaison Section: subject file, box 15, RG 333.

37. Eighth Army, PIO, Command Report, June 1951. AP, "Korea Censorship Branded Erratic"; Baldwin, "Too Few Facts on Korea"; both in *New York Times*, September 29 and October 2, 1951.

38. "Simmons Has No Censorship Gripe in Korea"; "Tokyo Correspondents Battle Inflation"; both in *Editor & Publisher*, September 6 and November 1, 1952.

39. Schakne, "Reporters Fight War of Tedium in Korea," *Editor & Publisher*, January 24, 1953.

40. AP, "Korean Guerrillas Fire on Train," *New York Times*, August 19, 1952; "CBS Reporter Hit by Shrapnel in Korea," *Editor & Publisher*, October 25, 1952.

41. This is based on a sample of reporting in three papers noted for their coverage in 1950: the *Chicago Daily News*, *Christian Science Monitor*, and *New York Herald Tribune*.

42. Schakne, "Reporters Fight War of Tedium in Korea," *Editor & Publisher*, January 24, 1953. Rosenberg to Parks, June 27, 1952, General Correspondence, box 1, Rosengren Papers, WHS.

43. Collings, "Communications Setup in Korea 'Fabulous,'" *Editor & Publisher*, June 23, 1951.

44. FEC, PIO, SSR, January 1952.

45. Schakne, "Reporters Fight War of Tedium in Korea," *Editor & Publisher*, January 24, 1953.

46. Foot, *Substitute for Victory*, 63; Hermes, *Truce Tent*, 80–103.

47. For a vivid description see Blair, *Forgotten War*, 947–50.

48. Hermes, *Truce Tent*, 80–97. Unnumbered Press Release, September 5, 1951, Korean War Communiqués, box 5, RG 319.

49. UP, "18-Day Fight Won!" *Chicago Daily News*, September 5, 1951. See also "U.S. Troops Battle for Weeks," *Washington Post*, September 5, 1951; AP, "U.S. Forces Win Korea Ridge in 17-Day Battle," *New York Herald Tribune*, September 6, 1951.

50. Bernhardt, "White Horse Mountain Covered by Army PIO," *Editor & Publisher*, November 1, 1952.

51. Bernhardt, "White Horse Mountain Covered by Army PIO," *Editor & Publisher*, November 1, 1952; AP, "Bayonets Drive Reds from Peak," *Chicago Daily News*, October 8, 1952.

52. FEC, PIO, SSR, December 1952.

53. FEC, PIO, SSR, December 1951.

54. Dorn to Marshall, November 20, 1951, Chief I & E files, Unclassified Central Decimal File 000.73, box 60, RG 319; Barrett, "Non-U.S. Reporters Protest Navy Ban," *New York Times*, October 16, 1952. During 1952 there were roughly 220 correspondents accredited to FEC, of whom about a third were non-U.S. In March, a fairly normal month, 20 were Japanese, 18 British, 11 South Korean, 10 Chinese nationalist, 3 Philippine, and one each from a range of other countries.

55. For an excellent discussion, see Connelly, *Diplomatic Revolution*, 56.

56. PA, "Television and Popular Attitudes toward Foreign Policy," January 22, 1952, Foster files, box 20, RG 59.

57. Dillon, Memo for Director, December 28, 1951, OPI 000.77, box 42, RG 330; Bernhard, *U.S. Television News*, 49; Doherty, *Cold War, Cool Medium*, 83.

58. Prochnau, *Once upon a Distant War*, 29–30.

59. Dillon, Memo for Director, December 28, 1951.

60. Doherty, *Cold War, Cool Medium*, 168.

61. Eighth Army, PIO, Command Report, October 1952.

62. Persico, *Murrow*, 303–5.

63. On Dulles as "bipartisan accommodator," see Cumings, *Origins*, 2:14.

64. Truman-Dulles, MemCon, October 3, 1951, Japanese Peace Treaty, box 53, Dulles Papers, PU; Pruessen, *Dulles*, 499–500.

65. *Congressional Record, 1951*, 10824–25. Truman to McCarran, September 24, 1951, OF 207, TP. Barrett to Short, October 24, 1951, box 5; Crosby to Russell, December 27, 1951, box 2; both in PA Asst. SecState, subject file, RG 59.

66. Bernhard, *U.S. Television News*, 92.

67. Sargeant, Memo, February 5, 1952, Asst. SecState Correspondence folder, box 4, Sargeant Papers, HSTL.

68. Lovett, press briefing, January 31, 1951, OPI 000.78, box 70, RG 330.

69. MSC to Lovett, September 13, 1951, Central Decimal File 350.01, box 265, RG 330.

70. PA, "Television and Popular Attitudes toward Foreign Policy," January 22, 1952, Foster files, box 20, RG 59.

71. DOPS, September 12, 1951; "Victory at San Francisco," *Time*, September 17, 1951; Sullivan, "Politics and San Francisco," *Washington Post*, September 16, 1951. Beisner, *Acheson*, 477.

72. White to Acheson, January 29, 1952, PA Asst. SecState, Memos, box 2, RG 59.

73. Marshall to Truman, July 5, 1951, PSF (Korean War): Marshall folder, box 243, TP.

74. *CQ, 1951*, 455; Enarson to Carroll, June 25, 1951, Lucas Committee Amendment folder, box 3, Enarson Papers, HSTL.

75. Knowles, "Peace Issue in Controls Fight," *New York Times*, July 9, 1951.

76. *DSB* 25: 47–49, 206.

77. *CQ, 1951*, 460–61; "Wilson Fears for Defense Plans," *New York Times*, July 10, 1951.

78. "Week in Review," *New York Times*, July 15, 1951; Roberts, "House Unit Again Cuts Controls Bill," *Washington Post*, June 21, 1951.

79. *CQ, 1951*, 451.

80. "Riddled Controls"; "Blunted Attack"; both in *Newsweek*, July 23 and 30, 1951.

81. Hamby, *Man of the People*, 579–80.

82. Flynn, *Hershey*, 180–87; Flynn, *Draft*, 114–25. Compared to World War II, however, a number of draft boards noticed more griping and less enthusiasm. See Rose, *Cold War Comes to Main Street*, 262–63.

83. Niegarth, Memo, July 18, 1952, Defense folder, box 3, Lambie Records, DDEL.

84. Kane to Chapin, September 27, 1951; Pace to Publicity Asst. SecDef, January 19, 1952; Dorn to Chief of Chaplains, July 28, 1952; all in Chief of I & E files, Unclassified Central Decimal File 000.7, box 54, RG 319.

85. MacGregor, *Integration of the Armed Forces*, 433–35, 457.

86. Fousek, *To Lead the Free World*, 179–82.

87. McAuliffe, Summary Sheet, December 29, 1951, Racial Integration folder, box 22, Collins Papers, DDEL; MacGregor, *Integration of the Armed Forces*, 437–39; Bowers, Hammond, and MacGarringle, *Black Soldier, White Army*, 263–70; Blair, *Forgotten War*, 147–52, 683–84.

88. MacGregor, *Integration of the Armed Forces*, 433–35, 457.

89. Hargus to Thomas, August 1, 1950, OPI Central Decimal File 000.7, box 17, RG 330.

90. Dillon to Kaufman, May 8, 1951, OPI 000.77, box 42, RG 330. MacGregor, *Integration of the Armed Forces*, 447.

91. Marshall, Statement, September 10, 1951; Lovett, Statement, September 20, 1951; OPI, Military Production News, September 10, 1951; PR Progress Report, October 1 to November 1, 1951; all in SMOF: Jackson, box 21, TP.

92. OPI, "Blood Donor Program Again Exceeds Quota," December 14, 1951; Healy to Advertising Managers, December 7, 1951; Ad Council to Miller, June 9, 1951; all in SMOF: Jackson, box 21, TP.

93. Poster, undated, SMOF: Jackson, box 21, TP.

94. Ridgway Statement, November 11, 1951, SMOF: Jackson, box 21, TP.

Chapter 12. The Advent of Eisenhower

1. Lodge, "Campaign to Win the Republican Nomination for Eisenhower," undated, AWF, Administration series, Lodge folder, box 23, Eisenhower Papers, DDEL.

2. Parmet, *Eisenhower and the American Crusades*, 4–5; Greene, *Crusade*, 94–95; Eisenhower, *Mandate for Change*, 33.

3. Eisenhower, PC, June 4, 1952, AWF, Campaign series, Eisenhower on Korea folder, box 8, Eisenhower Papers.

4. DOPS, June 3, 1952. For an assessment of the Democratic candidates, see Greene, *Crusade*, 33–47.

5. "Some Notes on Republican Campaign Statements Regarding Korea," undated, White House files, Eisenhower Korean Troops, box 10, Lloyd Papers, HSTL.

6. Taft, Speech, March 30, 1952; Taft, NBC Radio Broadcast, June 1, 1952; Speech Material folder, box 463, Taft Papers, LC. See also "Taft on the Korean War," undated, Taft Campaign folder, box 9, Benedict Papers, DDEL; Divine, *Foreign Policy and U.S. Presidential Elections, 1952–1960*, 10.

7. Memo, October 17, 1951, PSF (Political): Taft folder, box 50, TP.

8. Ayers, Note, March 29, 1952, Politics folder, box 11, Ayers Papers, HSTL.

9. Truman, *Years of Trial and Hope*, 561–62.

10. Johnson, *Papers of Stevenson*, 4:91; Broadwater, *Stevenson and American Politics*, 76.

11. Johnson, *Papers of Stevenson*, 4:viii, 18, 28.

12. On the prospects for Taft's campaign, see Greene, *Crusade*, 86 96; Patterson, *Mr. Republican*, 505. On the moderates' reaction, see Lodge,

"Campaign to Win the Republican Nomination," undated, AWF, Administration series, Lodge folder, box 23, Eisenhower Papers. Stassen did enter the primaries, largely to block Taft but also in the hope that, if the convention deadlocked, the party would turn to him. See Shanley Diaries, "The Delaying Action," box 1, Shanley Diaries, DDEL.

13. Pickett, *Eisenhower Decides to Run*, 87–88, 97.

14. Ambrose, *Eisenhower*, 1:498–99.

15. Clay to Eisenhower, April 2, 1952, Clay folder, box 24, DDE PP.

16. DOPS, July 18, 1952. For Wiley's private views of how the campaign should be conducted, see Wiley to Summerfield, July 23, 1952, Legislative: Foreign Relations, box 57, Wiley Papers, WHS.

17. DOPS, July 11 and 14, 1952.

18. Johnson, *Papers of Stevenson*, 4:67.

19. Greene, *Crusade*, 174–75, 204–7.

20. Divine, *Foreign Policy and Presidential Elections*, 43–44. "Document X," undated, Campaign and Election folder, box 10, Humphreys Papers, DDEL.

21. Divine, *Foreign Policy and Presidential Elections*, 50–54; Bowie and Immerman, *Waging Peace*, 75.

22. Eisenhower Speeches, September 15, 16, 18 and 22, 1952, 1952 Campaign, Speeches and Statements folder, boxes 1–3, Benedict Papers.

23. Eisenhower Speeches, September 4 and 22, 1952; Notes on Speech Writing Session, August 29, 1952; both in 1952 Campaign: Speeches and Statements folder, box 1, Benedict Papers. Divine, *Foreign Policy and Presidential Elections*, 45–46.

24. Larmon to Robinson, October 16, 1952, Larmon folder, box 9, Robinson Papers, DDEL.

25. Robinson to Cake, October 10, 1952, Eisenhower folder, box 2, Robinson Papers; Eisenhower to Stassen, October 5, 1952, AWF, Administration series, Stassen folder, box 34, Eisenhower Papers.

26. Russell to Lunsford, October 14 1952, series 6, box 152, Russell Papers, University of Georgia; Leuchtenberg, *White House Looks South*, 220–21. Greene, *Crusade*, 159–69, 210–12.

27. Broadwater, *Stevenson and American Politics*, 121, 130; Muller, *Stevenson*, 95.

28. Johnson, *Papers of Stevenson*, 4:133–34, 82–84, 118.

29. Johnson, *Papers of Stevenson*, 80, 96.

30. Johnson, *Papers of Stevenson*, 115–17, 127.

31. *FRUS, 1952–54*, 15:512–14, 522–25, 533, 537, 545–48, 554–57, 563; Foot, *Substitute for Victory*, 142–50.

32. DOPS, September 16 and 19, October 10 and 17, 1952.

33. Foot, *Substitute for Victory*, 136–37.

34. DOPS, July 1, 1952. On the bombing campaign see Hermes, *Truce Tent*, 320–24.

35. Hermes, *Truce Tent*, 303–18; Blair, *Forgotten War*, 970.

36. DOPS, October 8 and 13, 1952.

37. MSAO, January, October, and November 1952. See also Greene, *Crusade*, 215. For anecdotal evidence to support this see Lubell, *Revolt of the Moderates*, 39.

38. Eisenhower Speech, October 24, 1952, Korea Speech folder, box 1, Hughes Papers, PU.

39. DOPS, October 27 and 30, 1952. For analysis, see Medhurst, "Text and Context in the 1952 Presidential Campaign," 464–82.

40. DOPS, November 4, 1952.

41. Even Nixon, who was the GOP's central attack dog, was careful to distance himself from those who thought Truman had been wrong to intervene in the first place. See DOPS, August 26, 1952.

42. Hughes, *Ordeal of Power*, 33. See also Divine, *Foreign Policy and Presidential Elections*, 76.

43. Greene, *Crusade*, 224–25; Ambrose, *Eisenhower*, 1:571; Kaufman, *Jackson*, 69–70.

44. Hagerty to Hagerty, November 29 and 30, December 6, 1952, Korean Trip file, box 11, Hagerty Papers, DDEL.

45. Hagerty to Hagerty, November 29, 1952, Korean Trip file, box 11, Hagerty Papers.

46. Eighth Army, PIO, Command Report, November and December 1952.

47. Hagerty to Hagerty, December 6, 1952, Korean Trip file, box 11, Hagerty Papers.

48. Hagerty to Hagerty, December 7 and 8, 1952, Korean Trip file, box 11, Hagerty Papers. Rosengren to Rosengren, December 7, 1952, Eisenhower Story folder, box 6, Rosengren Papers, WHS.

49. Rosengren to Rosengren, December 7, 1952, Eisenhower Story folder, box 6, Rosengren Papers. Eighth Army, PIO, Command Report, December 1952.

50. Eighth Army, PIO, Command Report, December 1952.

51. DOPS, December 8, 1952; MSAO, December 1952.

52. Hamby, *Man of the People*, 615–6; Hagerty to Adams, undated, Transition folder, box 10, Hagerty Papers.

53. Bowie and Immerman, *Waging Peace*, 79, 84–92.

54. For details, see Reichard, *Reaffirmation of Republicanism*, 48–50.

55. Minutes of Cabinet Meeting, January 12, 1953, AWF, Cabinet series, box 1, Eisenhower Papers.

56. On Persons, see Hughes, *Ordeal of Power*, 66. On bipartisanship, see Minutes of Meeting with Congressional Leaders, January 26, 1953, AWF, Legislative Meetings series, box 1, Eisenhower Papers. Eisenhower to Cabinet Officers, March 6, 1953, AWF, Eisenhower Diary series, box 3, Eisenhower Papers.

57. Merry, "Taft," 189–90. Eisenhower's new secretary of defense should not to be confused with the *other* Charles E. Wilson, former president of General Electric, whom Truman had appointed to head the ODM.

58. Hoopes, *Devil and John Foster Dulles*, 146–47, 152–53.

59. Ambrose, *Eisenhower*, 2:42–43; Parmet, *Eisenhower and the American Crusades*, 156; Eisenhower, *Public Papers*, January 20, 1953.

60. Ferrell, *Eisenhower Diaries*, 226.

61. Bowie and Immerman, *Waging Peace*, 9–108.

62. *FRUS, 1952–54*, 15:743–45, 769–70; Keefer, "Eisenhower and the End of the Korean War," 268, 270–74.

63. Eisenhower, *Public Papers*, January 20, February 2 and 17, 1953. On the drafting of the State of the Union address, see Hughes Diary, January 23 and 28, 1953, Hughes Papers.

64. *DSB* 28: 382–83, 413–14; Stueck, *Korean War*, 306.

65. DOPS, January 15 and 22, February 17, 1953.

66. DOPS, January 26, February 10, and March 9, 1953. See also Hughes Diary, February 6, 1953.

67. Rosengren to Rosengren, January 30 and February 6, 1953, General Correspondence folder, box 1, Rosengren Papers.

68. Norris, "Van Fleet Says UN Can Win Korean War," *Washington Post*, March 5, 1953; Hinton, "Ammunition Short, Van Fleet Asserts," *New York Times*, March 6, 1953; DOPS, March 17, 1953.

69. Lawrence, "Eisenhower Calls Chief Aides to Hear Van Fleet on Korea," *New York Times*, March 1, 1953; Eisenhower, *Public Papers*, March 3, 1953.

70. DOPS, February 10, 1953; Eisenhower, *Public Papers*, February 17, 1953.

71. DOPS, February 13, 1953.

72. Hughes Diary, February 24, 1953.

73. Stueck, *Korean War*, 308–9.

74. Eighth Army, Press Release, April 5, 1953, Command Reports, box 1472, RG 319; FEC, PIO, SSR, March and April 1953.

75. FEC, PIO, SSR, April 1953.

76. FEC, PIO, SSR, April 1953.

77. FEC, PIO, SSR, April 1953.

78. DOPS, April 23 and 28, 1953.

79. AP, "Ike Sad but Cautious on POW 'Atrocities,'" *San Francisco Chronicle*, April 24, 1953; AP, "Senators Shelve Probe of PW Atrocity Reports," *Christian Science Monitor*, April 23, 1953. For the administration's statements on Indochina, see Anderson, *Trapped by Success*, 22.

80. TelCon Re: *New York Times* Story, April 9, 1953, Subject, Telephone Memos, box 1, Dulles Papers, DDEL; Taft to Bill [Knowland?] April 9, 1953, Subject, Korea folder, box 1234, Taft Papers.

81. Eisenhower, *Public Papers*, April 16, 1953; *DSB* 28: 605. For background, see Bowie and Immerman, *Waging Peace*, 109–22; Osgood, *Total Cold War*, 57–67.

82. DOPS, April 9, 10, and 13, 1953.

83. *FRUS, 1952–54*, 15:805–6, 893–94; Hughes Diary, March 15 and 20, 1953; Bowie and Immerman, *Waging Peace*, 124.

84. Notes on Legislative Leadership Meeting, April 30, 1953; Legislative Leadership Meeting, Supplementary Notes, May 12, 1953; both in AWF, Eisenhower Diary series, Staff Notes folder, box 4, Eisenhower Papers.

85. *FRUS, 1952–54,* 15:826, 854–56. In public, the Joint Chiefs' response to Van Fleet's allegations about ammunition shortages also made it clear that while there had always been a sufficient stockpile to fulfill the current mission, a more grandiose enterprise would be far costlier. See Sawyer, "What Is U.S. Goal in Korea?" *Christian Science Monitor,* April 21, 1951; Eisenhower, *Public Papers,* March 26, 1953.

86. *FRUS, 1952–52,* 15:893–94, 1015–16.

87. Stueck, *Korean War,* 318–19.

88. Stueck, *Korean War,* 320–21; Dulles, MemCon, May 9, 1953, Subject, Korean Armistice folder, box 10, Dulles Papers, DDEL.

89. Stueck, *Korean War,* 322–23.

90. *FRUS, 1952–54,* 15:1068–69; Keefer, "Eisenhower and the End of the Korean War," 280.

91. Dulles, TelCons with Wiley and George, June 4, 1953, Subject, Korean Armistice folder, box 10, Dulles Papers, DDEL.

92. Legislative Leadership Meeting, Supplementary Notes, May 19, 1953, AWF, Eisenhower Diary series, Staff Notes folder, box 4, Eisenhower Papers.

93. Notes on Legislative Leadership Meeting, April 30, 1953, AWF, Eisenhower Diary series, Staff Notes folder, box 4, Eisenhower Papers. Foot, *Substitute for Victory,* 173.

94. On Knowland's position, see Dulles, MemCon, May 9, 1953, Subject, Korean Armistice folder, box 10, Dulles Papers, DDEL; DOPS, June 2, 1953. On his statement, see Dulles-Knowland, TelCon, June 8, 1953; Knowland, Statement, June 8, 1953; both in Subject, Korean Armistice Matter folder, box 10, Dulles Papers, DDEL.

95. Merrill, *Korea,* 168–72; Cumings, *Origins,* 2:697–702.

96. See, for instance, Beech, "1200 Red Agents Put to Death in South Korea," *St. Louis Post-Dispatch,* July 12, 1950; Grutzner, "27 Executed in Seoul Cemetery for Collaboration with Red Foe," *New York Times,* November 3, 1950. For similar reports, see Cumings, *Origins,* 2:700–701.

97. Johnston, "Seoul to Mitigate Prisoners' Terms," *New York Times,* December 22, 1950.

98. See, for instance, Jaffe, "Uncle Sam's Bitter Nephew," *Nation,* December 29, 1951. On the military's attitude toward South Korea, see Cumings, *Origins,* 2:692–93.

99. "Rhee's Fight with Assembly Threatens Democracy in Korea," *Newsweek,* June 9, 1952; DOPS, June 6, 1952. On the 1952 political crisis, see Stueck, *Rethinking,* 196–99; Keefer, "Truman Administration and the South Korean Political Crisis of 1952," 145–68.

100. Rosengren to Parks, September 16, 1952, General Correspondence, box 1, Rosengren Papers. On the decision to expand the South Korean army, see Hermes, *Truce Tent,* 340–45.

101. *FRUS, 1950,* 7:630–31.

102. Cumings, *Origins,* 2:701.

103. On the guerrilla problem, see Merrill, *Korea,* 146–57, 160–65; Cumings, *Origins,* 2:250–60, 268–90; Birtle, *U.S. Army Counterinsurgency Doctrine,* 85–98.

104. Eighth Army, PIO, Command Report, December 1951 and January 1952. For details of the operation see Hermes, *Truce Tent*, 182–83.

105. See, for instance, McGregor, "Guerrilla Region Invested in Korean War," *New York Times*, December 3, 1951; UP, "ROK Troops Out to Destroy 10,000 Bandits," *New York Herald Tribune*, December 3, 1951.

106. Brown to Pettitt, November 8, 1952, Cables and Dispatches folder, box 2, Brown Papers, WHS.

107. "The Forgotten People," *Time*, July 16, 1951.

108. See, for instance, "Tough Stuff"; "Eleventh-Hour Reprieve"; both in *Time*, June 9 and 16, 1952.

109. MacGregor, "Koreans' Regard for U.S. Lessens," *New York Times*, June 21, 1953.

110. *Congressional Record, 1952,* 6816–17, 7985–87; DOPS, June 6, 1952.

111. DOPS, June 1 and 11, 1953.

112. *FRUS, 1952–54,* 15:1200–1201. Stueck, *Korean War,* 337.

113. DOPS, June 25, 1953.

114. Dulles-Eisenhower, TelCon, June 24, 1953, Subject, Korean Armistice Matter folder, box 10, Dulles Papers, DDEL.

115. DOPS, June 19, 22, and 23, 1953.

116. White, "Korea Puts New Strain on Bipartisan Policies," *New York Times*, June 21, 1951.

117. *FRUS, 1952–54,* 15:1217, 1219.

118. DOPS, July 9, 1953. See also "Rhee Called Great Patriot by Knowland"; "Wiley Says Rhee Perils World Peace"; both in *Washington Post*, June 28 and July 8, 1953.

119. Dulles-Eisenhower, TelCon, June 20, 1953, Subject, Korean Armistice Matter folder, box 10, Dulles Papers, DDEL.

120. Hermes, *Truce Tent*, 474–76; Stueck, *Korean War*, 335–36.

121. "Knowland Flubs the Job," editorial, *Washington Post*, June 25, 1953. White, "Korea Puts New Strain on Bipartisan Policies," *New York Times*, June 21, 1951. For background on Ike's relationship with congressional Democrats, see Reichard, "Divisions and Dissent," 53–54.

122. Dulles to Robertson and Briggs, June 26, 1953, Subject, Korean Armistice Matter folder, box 10, Dulles Papers, DDEL; *FRUS, 1952–54,* 15:1291–92.

123. Stueck, *Korean War,* 337; *FRUS, 1952–54,* 15:1413.

124. Alden, "Rhee's Secret Concessions to U.S. Called Sweeping," *New York Times*, July 13, 1953; *DSB* 28:101–2.

125. DOPS, July 14 and 16, 1953.

126. Memo on Recent Polls, June 2, 1953, Korea folder, box 4, Jackson Records, DDEL; MSAO, July 1953.

127. MSAO, July 1953. The breakdown of U.S. casualties was 33,629 dead, 103,284 wounded, 5,178 missing or captured. See Hermes, *Truce Tent*, 500–501.

Conclusion

1. Alden, "Panmunjom Is Set for Truce Signing"; Reston, "Korea Almost Too Skeptical to Believe She Has a Truce"; both in *New York Times*,

July 26 and 27, 1953. Clark, *From the Danube to the Yalu*, 275–78. Eisenhower, *Public Papers*, July 27, 1953.

2. FEC, PIO, SSR, June and July 1953.

3. Hammond, "NSC-68," 370; Bernstein, "Week We Went to War," 9; Jervis, "Impact of the Korean War on the Cold War," 563; Gaddis, *Strategies*, 109; Fousek, *To Lead the Free World*, 165–69. Some historians have even speculated that Acheson invited the North Korean attack in order to rally support for NSC-68, or at least encouraged Truman to intervene for this reason. See Cumings, *Origins*, 2:431–35; Fordham, *Building the Cold War Consensus*, 68–69, 115–16.

4. Osgood, *Limited War*, 13; Spanier, *Truman-MacArthur Controversy*, 2–7; Higgins, *Korea and the Fall of MacArthur*, viii; Rees, *Korea*, x–xvi.

5. Albright, "Truman Calls Senate Leaders to 4th 2-Party Meeting Today," *Washington Post*, July 11, 1950.

6. The exception is the work on the rise of McCarthy, where historians have demonstrated how the administration's ineffectual response allowed him to flourish. But little attention has been paid to how this symbiosis affected issues like the initial Korean crisis or mobilization. Here, the extant literature tends to depict the administration simply being in the vanguard of the public debate.

7. Taft to LeVander, August 11, 1950; Taft to Conners, July 20, 1950; both in War (Korean) folder, box 924, Taft Papers, LC.

8. McCullough, *Truman*, 854–55; Hamby, *Man of the People*, 564–73; Higgins, *Korea and the Fall of MacArthur*, 183; Caridi, *Korean War and American Politics*, 170–73, 204–5.

9. Hermes, *Truce Tent*, 500–501.

10. Short to Flack, June 5, 1951, OF471B, box 1305, TP; PA, "Glossary on Far Eastern Situation," Special Guidance no. 51, July 27, 1951, Admin Sec, Central Decimal File 092 (Korea, 1951), box 233, RG 330.

11. Bell to Elsey, May 7, 1951, Civil Defense Dinner, box 49, Elsey Papers, HSTL.

12. Edwards, *On Deaf Ears*, 241.

13. Reeves, *McCarthy*, 371–72; DOPS, July 23, 1951.

14. White, "Congress Cautious in Korean Comment," *New York Times*, July 28, 1953; Gallup, "Survey Shows Public Feels Korean War Will Not Resume," *Washington Post*, January 2, 1954.

15. Kaufman, *Korean War*, 211.

16. Khong, *Analogies at War*, 59, 62, 110–16; Jones, *Death of a Generation*, 45.

BIBLIOGRAPHY

Archives and Manuscripts

Columbia University, Butler Library, New York

Koo, Wellington. Papers.

Cornell University, Ithaca, N.Y.

Ives, Irving M. Papers.
Taber, John. Papers.

Dartmouth College, Rauner Special Collections Library, Hanover, N.H.

Tobey, Charles W. Papers.

Eisenhower Library, Abilene, Kans. (DDEL)

Benedict, Stephen. Papers.
Brownell, Herbert. Papers.
Cochran, Jacqueline. Papers.
Collins, J. Lawton. Papers.
Dulles, John Foster. Papers (1952–53).
Eisenhower, Dwight D.
    Pre-Presidential Papers.
    Presidential Papers.
        Ann Whitman File (AWF).
        White House Central File (WHCF).
Hagerty, James C. Papers.
Humphreys, Robert. Papers.
Jackson, C. D. Papers and Records.
Lambie, James M. Papers and Records.

McCann, Kevin. Collection of Press Releases.
McCardle, Carl W. Papers.
Parks, Floyd L. Papers.
Pyle, Howard. Records.
Robinson, William E. Papers.
Shanley, Bernard. Diaries.

Harvard University, Houghton Library, Cambridge, Mass. (HU)

Herter, Christian A. Papers.
Time Inc. Dispatches from *Time* Magazine Correspondents.

Library of Congress, Manuscripts Division, Washington, D.C. (LC).

Alsop, Joseph and Stewart. Papers.
Bush, Vannevar. Papers.
Connally, Thomas T. Papers.
Green, Theodore Francis. Papers.
Harriman, W. Averell. Papers.
Howard, Roy W. Papers.
Jessup, Philip C. Papers.
McMahon, Brien. Papers.
Meyer, Eugene. Papers.
Murrow, Edward R. Papers.
Nitze, Paul H. Papers.
Reid Family. Papers.
Republican Party, National Committee (RNC). Papers .
Sevareid, A. Eric. Papers.
Strout, Richard L. Papers.
Taft, Robert A. Papers.
Vandenberg, Hoyt S. Papers.

MacArthur Memorial Library, Norfolk, Va.

MacArthur, Douglas. Papers.

Marine Corps Historical Center, Navy Yard, Washington, D.C. (MCHC)

Korean War Files.

Marshall Library, Lexington, Va.

Marshall, George C. Papers.

Massachusetts Historical Society, Boston (MHS)

Lodge, Henry Cabot, Jr. Papers.
Saltonstall, Leverett. Papers.

Meany Memorial Archives, Silver Spring, Md.

American Federation of Labor (AFL). Legislative Department Files.
Green, William. President's Files.

National Archives II, College Park, Md. (NARA)

Record Group (RG) 59. Department of State.
Record Group (RG) 127. U.S. Marine Corps.
Record Group (RG) 200.LW. Longines Chronoscope.
Record Group (RG) 200.MT. *March of Time* Newsreels.
Record Group (RG) 200.UN. Universal Newsreels.
Record Group (RG) 218. Joint Chiefs of Staff.
Record Group (RG) 273. National Security Council (NSC).
Record Group (RG) 293. Economic Stabilization Agency (ESA), Records of Wage and Salary Stabilization Boards.
Record Group (RG) 296. Economic Stabilization Agency (ESA), General Records.
Record Group (RG) 304. Office of Civil and Defense Mobilization.
Record Group (RG) 319. Army Staff.
Record Group (RG) 330. Office of Secretary of Defense.
Record Group (RG) 331. Allied Operational and Occupation Headquarters, World War II.
Record Group (RG) 333. United Nations Command (UNC).
Record Group (RG) 338. Eighth Army.
Record Group (RG) 407. Army Department, Adjutant General's Office.
   UN, Far East Command (FEC), General Headquarters.
   Eighth Army (EUSAK).
Record Group (RG) 554. United Nations Command (UNC).

National Archives: Center for Legislative Archives, Washington, D.C. (CLA)

Record Group (RG) 46. U.S. Senate.
Record Group (RG) 233. U.S. House of Representatives.
Republican Party, Minority Policy Committee. Papers.

National Archives, UK, Kew Gardens, London, England (NA-UK)

Foreign Office (FO).

Ohio Historical Center, Columbus (OHC)

Vorys, John M. Papers.

Princeton University, Seeley G. Mudd Manuscript Library, Princeton, N.J. (PU)

Baruch, Bernard M. Papers.

Dulles, John Foster. Papers (1950–52).
Hughes, Emmet. Papers.
Krock, Arthur. Papers.
Lawrence, David. Papers.
Smith, H. Alexander. Papers.

Russell Library, University of Georgia, Athens, Ga.

Russell, Richard B., Jr. Papers.

Rutgers University, Alexander Library, New Brunswick, N.J.

Vorhees, Tracy S. Papers.

Truman Library, Independence, Mo. (HSTL)

Acheson, Dean G. Papers.
Ayers, Eban A. Papers.
Blough, Roy. Papers.
Clayton, William L. Papers.
Connelly, Mathew J. Papers.
Democratic Party, National Committee (DNC). Papers.
Elsey, George M. Papers.
Enarson, Harold L. Papers.
Hechler, Kenneth W. Papers.
Lawton, Frederick J. Papers.
Lloyd, David D. Papers.
Matthews, Francis P. Papers.
Moullette, John B. Papers.
Quirk, James T. Papers.
Ross, Charles G. Papers.
Sargeant, Howland H. Papers.
Souers, Sidney W. Papers.
Spingarn, Stephen J. Papers.
Steelman, John R. Papers.
Tannenwald, Theodore. Papers.
Truman, Harry S. Papers (TP).
    President's Secretary's Files (PSF).
    Staff Member and Office Files (SMOF).
        Connelly, Mathew J. Files.
        Halverstedt, Dallas C. Files.
        Jackson, Charles W. Files.
        Lloyd, David D. Files.
        Murphy, Charles S. Files.
        Short, Joseph H. Files.
        White House Central Files (WHCF).
        Confidential File.

Official File (OF).
Webb, James E. Papers.

University of Vermont, Bailey/Howe Library, Burlington

Aiken, George D. Papers.
Austin, Warren R. Papers.

University of Virginia, Small Special Collections Library,
Charlottesville, Va.

Johnson, Louis A. Papers.

Wisconsin Historical Society, Madison (WHS)

Bigart, Homer. Papers.
Boyle, Harold V. Papers.
Brown, Cecil. Papers.
Childs, Marquis W. Papers.
Harsch, Joseph C. Papers.
Jaffe, Sam A. Papers.
National Broadcasting Company (NBC). Records.
Pierpoint, Robert C. Papers.
Rosengren, Roswell P. Papers.
Rovere, Richard. Papers.
Wiley, Alexander. Papers.

Oral History Transcripts (OH)

Acheson, Dean. HSTL.
Anderson, Vernice. HSTL.
Barrett, Edward W. HSTL.
Barriere, John E. HSTL.
Battle, Lucius D. HSTL.
Denig, Robert L. Marines Corps Historical Center.
Elsey, George M. HSTL.
Finletter, Thomas. HSTL.
Folliard, Edward T. HSTL.
Kent, Carleton. HSTL.
Nixon, Robert. HSTL.
Pace, Frank. HSTL.
Perlmeter, Irving. HSTL.
Rusk, Dean. Russell Library.
Russell, Francis. HSTL.
Stowe, David H. HSTL.
Symington, Stuart. HSTL.
Walsh, Robert K. HSTL.

Published Documents

Bigart, Homer. *Forward Positions: The War Correspondence of Homer Bigart*. Fayetteville: University of Arkansas Press, 1992.

Eisenhower, Dwight D. *Public Papers of the Presidents, 1953*. www.presidency.ucsb.edu/index.php.

Ferrell, Robert H., ed. *Off the Record: The Private Papers of Harry S. Truman*. Columbia: University of Missouri Press, 1980.

——. *The Eisenhower Diaries*. New York: Norton, 1981.

Goodman, Allan E., ed. *Negotiating While Fighting: The Diary of Admiral C. Turner Joy at the Korean Armistice Conference*. Stanford, Calif.: Hoover Institution Press, 1978.

Johnson, Walter, ed. *The Papers of Adlai E. Stevenson*. Vol. 4. *"Let's Talk Sense to the American People," 1952–1955*. Boston: Little Brown, 1974.

McMillan, James E., ed. *The Ernest W. McFarland Papers: The United States Senate Years, 1940–1952*. Prescott, Ariz.: Sharlot Hall Museum Press, 1995.

Pearson, Drew. *Diaries, 1949–1959*. Tyler Abell, ed. New York: Holt, Rinehart, and Winston, 1974.

Suid, Lawrence H., ed. *Film and Propaganda in America: A Documentary History*. Vol. 4. *1945 and After*. New York: Greenwood Press, 1991.

Truman, Harry S. *Public Papers of the Presidents, 1950–1953*. www.presidency.ucsb.edu/index.php.

U.S. Congress. *Congressional Quarterly Almanac*. Washington, D.C.: CQ News Features, 1949–53.

——. *Congressional Record*. Washington, D.C.: GPO, 1950–53.

——. *Official Congressional Directory*. Washington, D.C.: GPO, 1950–53.

U.S. Congress. House. *Hearings before the Committee on Appropriations, Military Subcommittee*. Washington, D.C.: GPO, 1950.

U.S. Congress. Senate. *Hearings before the Committee on Armed Services*. Washington, D.C.: GPO, 1950–51.

——. *Hearings before the Committee on Armed Services, Preparedness Subcommittee: Universal Military Training*. Washington, D.C.: GPO, 1951.

——. *Hearings before the Committee on Armed Services and the Committee on Foreign Relations: Assignment of Ground Forces to Europe*. Washington, D.C.: GPO, 1951.

——. *Hearings before the Committee on Armed Services and the Committee on Foreign Relations: Military Situation in the Far East (MSFE)*. Washington, D.C.: GPO, 1951.

——. *Hearings before the Committee on Banking and Currency: The Defense Production Act*. Washington, D.C.: GPO, 1950–51.

——. *Hearings before the Committee on Foreign Relations*. Washington, D.C.: GPO, 1950–51.

——. *Reviews of the World Situation: 1949–1950. Hearings Held in Executive Session before the Committee on Foreign Relations, U.S. Senate*. Washington, D.C.: GPO, 1974.

U.S. Department of State. *Department of State Bulletin*. Volumes 23–28, Washington, D.C.: GPO, 1950–53.

——. *The Conflict in Korea*. Washington, D.C.: GPO, 1951.

——. *Foreign Relations of the United States, 1950–1954*. Washington, D.C.: GPO, 1976–84.

U.S. National Security Resources Board, *United States Civil Defense*. Washington, D.C.: GPO, 1950.

Newspapers and Magazines

Baltimore Sun
Boston Globe
Business Week
Chicago Daily News
Chicago Daily Tribune
Christian Science Monitor
Collier's
Editor & Publisher
Fortune
Hollywood Reporter
Leatherneck
Life
Los Angeles Times
Louisville Courier Journal
Marine Corps Gazette
New York Herald Tribune
New York Times
New York World-Telegram and Sun
Newsweek
St. Louis Post-Dispatch
San Francisco Chronicle
Saturday Evening Post
Time
U.S. News & World Report
Variety
Vital Speeches of the Day
Washington Evening Star
Washington Post

Memoirs

Acheson, Dean. *Present at the Creation: My Years in the State Department*. New York: Norton, 1969.

Allison, John M. *Ambassador from the Prairie, Or Allison Wonderland*. Boston: Houghton Mifflin, 1973.

Alsop, Joseph W. *"I've Seen the Best of It": Memoirs*. New York: Norton, 1992.

Baillie, Hugh. *High Tension*. Freeport, N.Y.: Libraries Press, 1959.

Barrett, Edward R. *Truth Is Our Weapon*. New York: Funk and Wagnalls, 1953.

Beech, Keyes. *Tokyo and Points East*. New York: Doubleday, 1954.

Burchett, Wilfred G. *Again Korea*. New York: International, 1968.

Ching, Cyrus S. *Review and Reflection: A Half-Century of Labor Relations*. New York: B. C. Forbes, 1953.

Clark, Mark. *From the Danube to the Yalu*. London: Harrap, 1954.

Collins, J. Lawton. *War in Peacetime: The History and Lessons of Korea*. Boston: Houghton Mifflin, 1969.

Connally, Tom. *My Name is Tom Connally*. New York: Crowell, 1954.

Eisenhower, Dwight D. *Mandate for Change, 1953–1956*. London: Heinemann, 1963.

Elsey, George M. *An Unplanned Life: A Memoir*. Columbia: Univeristy of Missouri Press, 2005.

Hays, Brooks. *Politics Is My Parish*. Baton Rouge: Louisiana State University Press, 1981.

Hechler, Kenneth W. *Working with Truman: A Personal Memoir of the White House Years*. New York: Putnam, 1982.

Higgins, Marguerite. *War in Korea: The Report of a Woman Combat Correspondent*. Garden City, N.Y.: Doubleday, 1951.

Hoberecht, Earnest. *Asia Is My Beat*. Rutland, Vt.: Tuttle, 1961.

Hughes, Emmet J. *The Ordeal of Power: A Political Memoir of the Eisenhower Years*. New York: Atheneum, 1963.

Johnson, Walter. *How We Drafted Adlai Stevenson*. New York: Knopf, 1955.

Kennan, George F. *Memoirs, 1950–1963*. London: Hutchinson, 1973.

MacArthur, Douglas. *Reminiscences*. New York: McGraw-Hill, 1964.

Martin, Joe. *My First Fifty Years in Politics*. New York: McGraw-Hill, 1960.

Reston, James. *Deadline: A Memoir*. New York: Random House, 1991.

Ridgway, Matthew B. *The Korean War*. New York: Doubleday, 1967.

Roberts, Chalmers M. *First Rough Draft: A Journalist's Journal of Our Times*. New York: Praeger, 1973.

Shaffer, Samuel. *On and Off the Floor: Thirty Years as a Correspondent on Capitol Hill*. New York: Newsweek Books, 1980.

Shinn, Bill. *The Forgotten War Remembered, Korea: 1950–1953. A War Correspondent's Notebook and Today's Danger in Korea*. Elizabeth, N.J.: Hollym International, 1995.

Smith, Merriman. *Thank You, Mr. President: A White House Notebook*. New York: Harper, 1946.

Thompson, Reginald. *Cry Korea*. London: MacDonald, 1951.

Trohan, Walter. *Political Animals: Memoirs of a Sentimental Cynic*. Garden City, N.Y.: Doubleday, 1975.

Truman, Harry S. *Memoirs: Years of Trial and Hope, 1946–1952*. New York: Signet, 1965. (First published 1956)

Vorhees, Melvin B. *Korean Tales*. New York: Simon and Schuster, 1952.

Secondary Sources: Books

Accinelli, Robert. *Crisis and Commitment: United States Policy toward Taiwan, 1950–1955*. Chapel Hill: University of North Carolina Press, 1996.

Allen, Craig. *Eisenhower and the Mass Media: Peace, Prosperity, and Prime-Time TV*. Chapel Hill: University of North Carolina Press, 1993.

Almond, Gabriel A. *The American People and Foreign Policy*. 2nd ed. Westport, Conn.: Greenwood Press, 1960.

Ambrose, Stephen E. *Eisenhower*. 2 vols. London: Allen and Unwin, 1983–84.

Anderson, David L. *Trapped by Success: The Eisenhower Administration and Vietnam, 1953–1961*. New York: Columbia University Press, 1991.

Appleman, Roy E. *South to the Naktong, North to the Yalu, June-November 1950. The United States Army in the Korean War*. Washington, D.C.: Office of the Chief of Military History, Department of the Army, 1961.

———. *Disaster in Korea: The Chinese Confront MacArthur*. College Station: Texas A&M University Press, 1989.

———. *Escaping the Trap: The U.S. Army X Corps in Northeast Korea, 1950*. College Station: Texas A&M University Press, 1990.

———. *Ridgway Duels for Korea*. College Station: Texas A&M University Press, 1990.

Aronson, James. *The Press and the Cold War*. Indianapolis: Bobbs-Merrill, 1970.

Barnouw, Erik. *Tube of Plenty: The Evolution of American Television*. Rev. ed. New York: Oxford University Press, 1978.

Baughman, James L. *Henry R. Luce and the Rise of the American News Media*. Baltimore: Johns Hopkins University Press. 2001.

Bayley, Edwin R. *Joe McCarthy and the Press*. Madison: University of Wisconsin Press, 1981.

Beisner, Robert L. *Dean Acheson: A Life in the Cold War*. New York: Oxford University Press, 2006.

Bell, Jonathan. *The Liberal State on Trial: The Cold War and American Politics in the Truman Years*. New York: Columbia University Press, 2004.

Berebitsky, William. *A Very Long Weekend: The Army National Guard in Korea, 1950–1953*. Shippensburg, Pa.: White Mane, 1996.

Bernhard, Nancy E. *U.S. Television News and Cold War Propaganda, 1947–1960*. Cambridge: Cambridge University Press, 1999.

Best, Gary Dean. *Herbert Hoover: The Post-presidential Years. Vol. 2.1946–1964*. Stanford, Calif.: Hoover Institution Press, 1983.

Birtle, Andrew J. *U.S. Army Counterinsurgency and Contingency Operations Doctrine, 1942–1976*. Washington, D.C.: Center of Military History, 2006.

Blair, Clay. *The Forgotten War: America in Korea, 1950–1953*. Annapolis: Naval Institute Press, 2003. (First published 1987)

Bowers, William T., William M. Hammond, and George L. MacGringle. *Black Soldier, White Army: The 24th Regiment in Korea*. Washington, D.C.: Center of Military History, U.S. Army, 1996.

Bowie, Robert R., and Richard H. Immerman. *Waging Peace: How Eisenhower Shaped an Enduring Cold War Strategy*. New York: Oxford University Press, 1998.

Braestrup, Peter. *Battle Lines: Report of the Twentieth Century Fund Task Force on the Military and the Media*. New York: Priority Press, 1985.

Braim, Paul F. *The Will to Win: The Life of General James A. Van Fleet*. Annapolis: Naval Institute Press, 2001.

Brinkley, Alan. *The End of Reform: New Deal Liberalism in Recession and War.* New York: Knopf, 1995.

Brinkley, David. *Washington Goes to War.* New York: Ballantine, 1988.

Broadwater, Jeff. *Adlai Stevenson and American Politics: The Odyssey of a Cold War Liberal.* New York: Twayne, 1994.

Campbell, Karlyn K., and Kathleen Hall Jamieson. *Deeds Done in Words: Presidential Rhetoric and the Genres of Governance.* Chicago: University of Chicago Press, 1990.

Caridi, Ronald J. *The Korean War and American Politics.* Philadelphia: University of Pennsylvania Press, 1968.

Caro, Robert A. *The Years of Lyndon Johnson: Master of the Senate.* New York: Knopf, 2002.

Carruthers, Susan L. *The Media at War.* Basingstoke, England: Palgrave, 2000.

Casey, Steven. *Cautious Crusade: Franklin D. Roosevelt, American Public Opinion, and the War against Nazi Germany.* New York: Oxford University Press, 2001.

Cater, Douglass. *The Fourth Branch of Government.* Boston: Houghton Mifflin, 1959.

Caute, David. *The Great Fear: The Anticommunist Purge under Truman and Eisenhower.* New York: Simon and Schuster, 1978.

Chace, James. *Acheson: The Secretary of State Who Created the American World.* Cambridge, Mass.: Harvard University Press, 1998.

Chen, Jian. *China's Road to the Korean War: The Making of Sino-American Confrontation.* New York: Columbia University Press, 1994.

Chernow, Ron. *Alexander Hamilton.* New York: Penguin, 2004.

Christensen, Thomas J. *Useful Adversaries: Grand Strategy, Domestic Mobilization, and Sino-American Conflict, 1947–1958.* Princeton, N.J.: Princeton University Press, 1996.

Cohen, Bernard C. *The Press and Foreign Policy.* Princeton, N.J.: Princeton University Press, 1963.

——. *The Public's Impact on Foreign Policy.* Lanham, Md.: University of America Press, 1983.

Cohen, Warren I. *Dean Rusk.* Totowa, N.J.: Cooper Square, 1980.

Condit, Doris M. *History of the Office of the Secretary of Defense.* Vol. 2. *The Test of War, 1950–1953.* Washington, D.C.: GPO, 1988.

Connelly, Matthew. *A Diplomatic Revolution: Algeria's Fight for Independence and the Origins of the Post–Cold War Era.* New York: Oxford University Press, 2002.

Coughlin, William J. *Conquered Press: The MacArthur Era in Japanese Journalism.* Palo Alto, Calif.: Pacific Books, 1952.

Cumings, Bruce. *The Origins of the Korean War.* Vol. 2. *The Roaring of the Cataract, 1947–1950.* Princeton, N.J.: Princeton University Press, 1991.

——, ed. *Child of Conflict: The Korean-American Relationship, 1943–1953.* Seattle: University of Washington Press, 1983.

Detzer, David. *Thunder of the Captains: The Short Summer of 1950.* New York: Crowell, 1977.

Divine, Robert. *Foreign Policy and U.S. Presidential Elections, 1952–1960.*
New York: New Viewpoints, 1974.

Doherty, Thomas. *Projections of War: Hollywood, Culture, and World War II.*
New York: Columbia University Press, 1993.

———. *Cold War, Cool Medium: Television, McCarthyism, and American Culture.*
New York: Columbia University Press, 2003.

Donovan, Robert J. *Conflict and Crisis: The Presidency of Harry S. Truman,
1945–1948.* Columbia: University of Missouri Press, 1977.

———. *Tumultuous Years: The Presidency of Harry S. Truman, 1949–1953.*
Columbia: University of Missouri Press, 1982.

Dubofsky, Melvyn, and Warren Van Tine. *John L. Lewis: A Biography.* Urbana:
University of Illinois Press, 1986.

Edwards, George C. III. *The Public Presidency.* New York: St. Martin's Press,
1983.

———. *On Deaf Ears: The Limits of the Bully Pulpit.* New Haven, Conn.: Yale
University Press, 2003.

Eisinger, Robert M. *The Evolution of Presidential Polling.* Cambridge: Cambridge
University Press, 2003.

Elder, Robert Ellsworth. *The Policy Machine: The Department of State and
American Foreign Policy.* Syracuse, N.Y.: Syracuse University Press, 1960.

Farrar, Ronald T. *Reluctant Servant: The Story of Charles G. Ross.* Columbia:
University of Missouri Press, 1969.

Farrar-Hockley, Anthony. *The British Part in the Korean War.* 2 vols. London:
HMSO, 1990–95.

Fite, Gilbert C. *Richard B. Russell, Jr., Senator from Georgia.* Chapel Hill: University of North Carolina Press, 1991.

Flynn, George Q. *Lewis B. Hershey: Mr. Selective Service.* Chapel Hill: University
of North Carolina Press, 1985.

———. *The Draft, 1940–1973.* Lawrence: University Press of Kansas, 1993.

Foot, Rosemary. *The Wrong War: American Policy and the Dimensions of the
Korean Conflict, 1950–1953.* Ithaca, N.Y.: Cornell University Press, 1985.

———. *A Substitute for Victory: The Politics of Peacemaking at the Korean Armistice Talks.* Ithaca, N.Y.: Cornell University Press, 1990.

Fordham, Benjamin O. *Building the Cold War Consensus: The Political Economy
of U.S. National Security Policy, 1949–1951.* Ann Arbor: University of
Michigan Press, 1998.

Fousek, John. *To Lead the Free World: American Nationalism and the Cultural
Roots of the Cold War.* 2000.

Foyle, Douglas C. *Counting the Public In: Presidents, Public Opinion, and Foreign
Policy.* New York: Columbia University Press, 1999.

Freeland, Richard M. *The Truman Doctrine and the Origins of McCarthyism.*
New York: New York University Press, 1985.

Gaddis, John Lewis. *The United States and the Origins of the Cold War,
1941–1947.* New York: Columbia University Press, 1972.

———. *Strategies of Containment: A Critical Appraisal of Postwar American
National Security Policy.* Oxford: Oxford University Press, 1982.

Gaddis, John Lewis. *The Long Peace: Inquiries into the History of the Cold War*. New York: Oxford University Press, 1987.

———. *We Now Know: Rethinking Cold War History*. Oxford: Clarendon Press, 1997.

Gallup, George H. *The Gallup Poll: Public Opinion, 1935–1971*. 3 vols. New York: Random House, 1972.

George, Alexander L. *Presidential Decisionmaking: The Effective Use of Information and Advice*. Boulder, Colo.: Westview Press, 1980.

Ginneken, Jaap van. *Understanding Global News: A Critical Introduction*. London: Sage, 1998.

Greene, John Robert. *The Crusade: The Presidential Election of 1952*. New York: Lanham, 1985.

Greenstein, Fred I. *The Hidden-Hand Presidency: Eisenhower as Leader*. New York: Basic Books, 1982.

Griffith, Robert. *The Politics of Fear: Joseph R. McCarthy and the Senate*. 2nd ed. Amherst: University of Massachusetts Press, 1987.

Grossman, Andrew D. *Neither Dead nor Red: Civilian Defense and American Political Development during the Early Cold War*. New York: Routledge, 2001.

Hallin, Daniel C. *The "Uncensored War": The Media and Vietnam*. Berkeley: University of California Press, 1986.

Hamby, Alonzo L. *Beyond the New Deal: Harry S. Truman and American Liberalism*. New York: Columbia University Press, 1973.

———. *Man of the People: A Life of Harry S. Truman*. New York: Oxford University Press, 1995.

Hammond, William M. *Reporting Vietnam: Media and Military at War*. Lawrence: University Press of Kansas, 1998.

Harris, Kenneth. *Attlee*. London: Weidenfeld and Nicolson, 1982.

Hart, Roderick P. *The Sound of Leadership: Presidential Communication in the Modern Age*. Chicago: University of Chicago Press, 1987.

Hartmann, Susan M. *Truman and the 80th Congress*. Columbia: University of Missouri Press, 1971.

Heller, Francis H., ed. *The Korean War: A 25-Year Perspective*. Lawrence: Regents Press of Kansas, 1977.

———. *The Truman White House: The Administration of the Presidency, 1945–1953*. Lawrence: Regents Press of Kansas. 1980.

Hermes, Walter G. *Truce Tent and Fighting Front. The United States Army in the Korean War*. Washington, D.C.: Center of Military History, U.S. Army, 1992.

Herring, George C. *LBJ and Vietnam: A Different Kind of War*. Austin: University of Texas Press, 1994.

Hershberg, James G. *James B. Conant: Harvard to Hiroshima and the Making of the Nuclear Age*. Stanford: Stanford University Press, 1995.

Hess, Stephen. *The Ultimate Insiders: U.S. Senators and the National Media*. Washington, D.C.: Brookings, 1986.

Hickey, Michael. *The Korean War: The West Confronts Communism, 1950–1953*. London: John Murray, 1999.

Higgins, Trumbull. *Korea and the Fall of MacArthur: A Précis in Limited War*. New York: Oxford University Press, 1960.

Hildebrand, Robert C. *Power and the People: Executive Management of Public Opinion in Foreign Affairs, 1897–1921*. Chapel Hill: University of North Carolina Press, 1984.

Hitchcock, William I. *France Restored: Cold War Diplomacy and the Quest for Leadership in Europe, 1944–1954*. Chapel Hill: University of North Carolina Press, 1998.

Hixson, Walter L. *Parting the Curtain: Propaganda, Culture, and the Cold War, 1945–1961*. Basingstoke, England: Macmillan, 1997.

Hogan, Michael J. *A Cross of Iron: Harry S. Truman and the Origins of the National Security State, 1945–1954*. Cambridge: Cambridge University Press, 1998.

Holsti, Ole R. *Public Opinion and American Foreign Policy*. Ann Arbor: University of Michigan Press, 1996.

Hoopes, Townsend. *The Devil and John Foster Dulles*. London: Andre Deutsch, 1974.

Hulsey, Byron C. *Everett Dirksen and His Presidents: How a Giant Shaped American Politics*. Lawrence: University Press of Kansas, 2000.

Ireland, Timothy P. *Creating the Entangling Alliance: The Origins of the North Atlantic Treaty Organization*. London: Aldwych Press, 1981.

Isaacson, Walter, and Evan Thomas. *The Wise Men: Six Friends and the World They Made*. New York: Simon and Schuster, 1986.

James, Clayton D. *The Years of MacArthur*. 3 vols. Boston: Houghton Mifflin, 1970–85.

———. *Refighting the Last War: Command and Crisis in Korea, 1950–1953*. New York: Free Press, 1993.

Johnson, Robert David. *Congress and the Cold War*. Cambridge: Cambridge University Press, 2006.

Jones, Howard. *Death of a Generation: How the Assassinations of Diem and JFK Prolonged the Vietnam War*. New York: Oxford University Press, 2003.

Kaufman, Burton I. *The Korean War: Challenges in Crisis, Credibility, and Command*. 2nd ed. New York: McGraw-Hill, 1997.

Kaufman, Robert G. *Henry M. Jackson: A Life in Politics*. Seattle: University of Washington Press, 2000.

Keith, Caroline H. *"For Hell and a Brown Mule": The Biography of Senator Millard E. Tydings*. Lanham, Md.: Madison Books, 1991.

Kepley, David R. *The Collapse of the Middle Way: Senate Republicans and the Bipartisan Foreign Policy, 1948–1952*. New York: Greenwood Press, 1988.

Kern, Montague, Patricia W. Levering, and Ralph B. Levering. *The Kennedy Crises: The Press, the Presidency, and Foreign Policy*. Chapel Hill: University of North Carolina Press, 1983.

Kernell, Samuel. *Going Public: New Strategies of Presidential Leadership*. 3rd ed. Washington, D.C.: Congressional Quarterly, 1997.

Khong, Yuen Foong. *Analogies at War: Korea, Munich, Dien Bien Phu and the Vietnam Decisions of 1965*. Princeton, N.J.: Princeton University Press, 1992.

Kiepper, James J. *Styles Bridges: Yankee Senator*. Sugar Hill, N.H.: Phoenix, 2001.

Knightley, Phillip. *The First Casualty. From the Crimea to the Falklands: The War Correspondent as Hero, Propagandist and Myth Maker*. Rev. ed. London: Pan Books, 1989.

Koen, Ross Y. *The China Lobby in American Politics*. New York: Harper and Row, 1974.

Kofsky, Frank. *Harry S. Truman and the War Scare of 1948: A Successful Campaign to Deceive the Nation*. New York: St. Martin's Press, 1993.

Kolodziej, Edward A. *The Uncommon Defense and Congress, 1945–1963*. Columbus: Ohio State University Press, 1966.

Koppes, Clayton R., and Gregory D. Black. *Hollywood Goes to War: How Politics, Profits, and Propaganda Shaped World War II Movies*. New York: Free Press, 1987.

Krugler, David F. *The Voice of America and the Domestic Propaganda Battles, 1945–1953*. Columbia: University of Missouri Press, 2000.

Kuter, Stanley I. *The Wars of Watergate: The Last Crisis of Richard Nixon*. New York: Knopf, 1990.

Lacey, Michael J., ed. *The Truman Presidency*. Cambridge: Cambridge University Press, 1989.

Lapomarda, Vincent A. *The Boston Mayor Who Became Truman's Secretary of Labor: Maurice J. Tobin and the Democratic Party*. New York: Peter Lang, 1995.

Leffler, Melvyn P. *A Preponderance of Power: National Security, the Truman Administration, and the Cold War*. Stanford, Calif.: Stanford University Press, 1992.

Leigh, Michael. *Mobilizing Consent: Public Opinion and American Foreign Policy, 1937–1947*. Westport, Conn.: Greenwood Press, 1976.

Leuchtenberg, William E. *The White House Looks South: Franklin D. Roosevelt, Harry S. Truman, and Lyndon B. Johnson*. Baton Rouge: Louisiana State University Press, 2005.

Lichtenstein, Nelson. *Labor's War at Home: The CIO in World War II*. 2nd ed. Philadelphia: Temple University Press, 2003.

Lincoln, George A. *Economics of National Security: Managing America's Resources for Defense*. 2nd ed. New York: Prentice-Hall, 1954.

Lubell, Samuel. *Revolt of the Moderates*. New York: Harper, 1956.

Lucas, Scott. *Freedom's War: The U.S. Crusade against the Soviet Union, 1945–56*. Manchester: Manchester University Press, 1999.

MacDonald, Callum A. *Korea: The War before Vietnam*. New York: Free Press, 1986.

———. *Britain and the Korean War*. Oxford: Blackwell, 1990.

MacGregor, Morris J. *Integration of the Armed Forces, 1940–1965*. Washington, D.C.: Center of Military History, U.S. Army, 1981.

Marcus, Maeva. *Truman and the Steel Seizure Case: The Limits of Presidential Power*. New York: Columbia University Press, 1977.

Markel, Lester, ed. *Public Opinion and Foreign Policy*. New York: Harper, 1949.

Marshall, S. L. A. *The River and the Gauntlet: Defeat of the Eighth Army by the Chinese Communist Forces, November 1950*. New York: Time, 1962.

May, Ernest R., ed. *American Cold War Strategy: Interpreting NSC-68*. Boston: St. Martin's Press, 1993.

Mazuzan, George T. *Warren R. Austin at the UN, 1946–1953*. Kent, Ohio: Kent State University Press, 1977.

McClure, Arthur F. *The Truman Administration and the Problems of Postwar Labor, 1945–1948*. Cranbury, N.J.: Associated University Presses, 1969.

McCoy, Donald R. *The Presidency of Harry S. Truman*. Lawrence: University Press of Kansas, 1984.

McCullough, David. *Truman*. New York: Simon and Schuster, 1992.

McFarland, Keith D. and David L. Roll. *Louis Johnson and the Arming of America*. Bloomington: Indiana University Press, 2005.

McGlothlen, Ronald. *Controlling the Waves: Dean Acheson and U.S. Foreign Policy in Asia*. New York: Norton, 1993.

Merrill, John. *Korea: The Peninsular Origins of the War*. Newark: University of Delaware Press, 1989.

Milliken, Jennifer. *The Social Construction of the Korean War: Conflict and Its Possibilities*. Manchester: University of Manchester Press, 2001.

Millis, Walter, with Harvey C. Mansfield and Harold Stein. *Arms and the State: Civil Military Elements in National Policy*. New York: Twentieth Century Fund, 1958.

Miraldi, Robert. *Muckraking and Objectivity: Journalism's Colliding Traditions*. New York: Greenwood Press, 1990.

Mitchell, Franklin D. *Truman and the News Media: Contentious Relations, Belated Respect*. Columbia: University of Missouri Press, 1998.

Montgomery, Gayle B., and James W. Johnson. *One Step from the White House: The Rise and Fall of Senator William F. Knowland*. Berkeley: University of California Press, 1998.

Morgan, Anne Hodges. *Robert S. Kerr: The Senate Years*. Norman: University of Oklahoma Press, 1977.

Morris, Joe Alex. *Deadline Every Minute: The Story of the United Press*. New York: Doubleday, 1957.

Mueller, John E. *Wars, Presidents and Public Opinion*. New York: Wiley, 1973.

Muller, Herbert J. *Adlai Stevenson: A Study in Values*. London: Hamish Hamilton, 1968.

Myers, James M. *The Bureau of Motion Pictures and Its Influence on Film Content during World War II*. Lewiston, N.Y.: Edwin Mellen Press, 1998.

Nagai, Yonosuke, and Akira Iriye, eds. *The Origins of the Cold War in Asia*. Tokyo: University of Tokyo Press, 1977.

Neustadt, Richard E. *Presidential Power and the Modern Presidents: The Politics of Leadership from Roosevelt to Reagan*. New York: Free Press, 1990.

Oakes, Guy. *The Imaginary War: Civil Defense and American Cold War Culture*. New York: Oxford University Press, 1994.

Offner, Arnold A. *Another Such Victory: President Truman and the Cold War, 1945–1953*. Stanford, Calif.: Stanford University Press, 2002.

Osgood, Kenneth. *Total Cold War: Eisenhower's Secret Propaganda Battle at Home and Abroad*. Lawrence: University Press of Kansas, 2006.

Osgood, Robert Endicott. *Limited War: The Challenge to American Strategy*. Chicago: University of Chicago Press, 1957.

Oshinsky, David M. *A Conspiracy So Immense: The World of Joe McCarthy*. New York: Free Press, 1983.

Paige, Glenn D. *The Korean Decision, June 24–30, 1950*. New York: Free Press, 1968.

Parmet, Herbert S. *Eisenhower and the American Crusades*. New York: Macmillan, 1972.

Patterson, James T. *Mr. Republican: A Biography of Robert A. Taft*. Boston: Houghton Mifflin, 1972.

Pedelty, Mark. *War Stories: The Culture of Foreign Correspondents*. New York: Routledge, 1995.

Persico, Joseph E. *Edward Murrow: An American Original*. New York: Da Capo Press, 1988.

Pickett, William B. *Eisenhower Decides to Run: Presidential Politics and Cold War Strategy*. Chicago: Ivan Dee, 2000.

Pierpaoli, Paul G., Jr. *Truman and Korea: The Political Culture of the Early Cold War*. Columbia: University of Missouri Press, 1999.

Pleasants, Julian P., and Augustus M. Burns III. *Frank Porter Graham and the 1950 Senate Race in North Carolina*. Chapel Hill: University of North Carolina Press, 1990.

Pomeroy, Charles. *Foreign Correspondents in Japan: Reporting a Half Century of Upheavals: From 1945 to the Present*. Rutland, Vt.: Tuttle, 1998.

Poole, Walter S. *The Joint Chiefs of Staff and National Policy*. Vol. 4. *The Joint Chiefs of Stafff and National Security Policy*. Washington, D.C.: Office of Joint History, Office of the Chairman of the Joint Chiefs of Staff, 1998.

Prochnau, William. *Once Upon a Distant War: David Halberstam, Neil Sheehan, Peter Arnett—Young War Correspondents and Their Early Vietnam Battles*. New York: Vintage, 1995.

Pruessen, Ronald W. *John Foster Dulles: The Road to Power*. New York: Free Press, 1982.

Rearden, Steven L. *History of the Office of the Secretary of Defense*. Vol. 1. *The Formative Years, 1947–1950*. Washington, D.C.: GPO, 1984.

Rees, David. *Korea: The Limited War*. London: Macmillan, 1964.

Reeves, Thomas C. *The Life and Times of Joe McCarthy*. New York: Stein and Day, 1982.

Reichard, Gary W. *Reaffirmation of Republicanism: Eisenhower and the 83rd Congress*. Knoxville: University of Tennessee Press, 1975.

Reynolds, David. *Rich Relations: The American Occupation of Britain*. London: HarperCollins, 1995.

Ritchie, Donald A. *A History of the U.S. Senate Republican Policy Committee, 1947–1997*. Washington, D.C.: GPO, 1997.

———. *Reporting from Washington: The History of the Washington Press Corps*. New York: Oxford University Press, 2005.

Roberts, Chalmers M. *Washington, Past and Present*. Washington, D.C.: Public Affairs, 1950.

Rockoff, Hugh. *Drastic Measures: A History of Wage and Price Controls in the United States*. Cambridge: Cambridge University Press, 1984.

Roeder, George H. *The Censored War: American Visual Experience during World War II*. New Haven, Conn.: Yale University Press, 1993.

Rose, Lisle A. *The Cold War Comes to Main Street: America in 1950*. Lawrence: University Press of Kansas, 1999.

Rovere, Richard H., and Arthur Schlesinger, Jr. *The MacArthur Controversy and American Foreign Policy*. New York: Noonday Press, 1965.

Sandler, Stanley. *The Korean War: No Victors, No Vanquished*. Lexington: University Press of Kentucky, 1999.

Savage, Sean J. *Truman and the Democratic Party*. Lexington: University Press of Kentucky, 1997.

Schaller, Michael. *Douglas MacArthur: The Far Eastern General*. New York: Oxford University Press, 1989.

Schatz, Thomas. *Boom and Bust: The American Cinema in the 1940s*. New York: Scribner's, 1997.

Schlesinger, Arthur M., Jr., and Roger Bruns, eds. *Congress Investigates: A Documented History, 1792–1974*. New York: Chelsea House, 1975.

Schnabel, James F. *Policy and Direction: The First Year. The United States Army in the Korean War*. Washington, D.C.: Center of Military History, U.S. Army, 1992.

Schnabel, James F., and Robert J. Watson. *The Joint Chiefs of Staff and National Policy*. Vol. 3. *The Korean War*. 2 pts. Washington, D.C.: Office of Joint History, Office of the Chairman of the Joint Chiefs of Staff, 1998.

Schwarz, Benjamin C. *Casualties, Public Opinion, and U.S. Military Intervention*. Santa Monica, Calif.: Rand, 1994.

Schwartz, Thomas Alan. *America's Germany: John J. McCloy and the Federal Republic of Germany*. Cambridge, Mass.: Harvard University Press, 1991.

Shindler, Colin. *Hollywood Goes to War: Films and American Society, 1939–1952*. London: Routledge, 1979.

Shlaim, Avi. *The United States and the Berlin Blockade, 1948–1949: A Study in Crisis Decision-Making*. Berkeley: University of California Press, 1983.

Sigal, Leon V. *Reporters and Officials: The Organization and Politics of Newsmaking*. Lexington, Mass.: Heath, 1973.

Small, Melvin. *Johnson, Nixon and the Doves*. New Brunswick, N.J.: Rutgers University Press, 1988.

——. *Democracy and Diplomacy: The Impact of Domestic Politics on U.S. Foreign Policy, 1789–1994*. Baltimore: Johns Hopkins University Press, 1996.

Smith, Craig Allen, and Kathy B. Smith. *The White House Speaks: Presidential Leadership as Presidential Persuasion*. Westport, Conn.: Praeger, 1994.

Smith, Jean Edward. *Lucius D. Clay: An American Life*. New York: Holt, 1990.

Smith, Richard Norton. *Thomas E. Dewey and His Times*. New York: Simon and Schuster, 1982.

Spanier, John W. *The Truman-MacArthur Controversy and the Korean War.* Cambridge, Mass.: Harvard University Press, 1959.

Stacks, John F. *Scotty: James B. Reston and the Rise and Fall of American Journalism.* Boston: Little, Brown, 2003.

Steel, Ronald. *Walter Lippmann and the American Century.* New York: Vintage Books, 1981.

Stromer, Marvin. *The Making of a Political Leader: Kenneth S. Wherry and the U.S. Senate.* Lincoln: University of Nebraska Press, 1969.

Stueck, William W. *The Road to Confrontation: American Policy Toward China and Korea, 1947–1950.* Chapel Hill: University of North Carolina Press, 1981.

——. *The Korean War: An International History.* Princeton, N.J.: Princeton University Press, 1995.

——. *Rethinking the Korean War: A New Diplomatic and Strategic History.* Princeton, N.J.: Princeton University Press, 2002.

Suid, Lawrence H. *Guts and Glory: The Making of the American Military Image in Film.* Rev. ed. Lexington: University Press of Kentucky, 2002.

Suid, Lawrence H., and Dolores A. Haverstick, *Stars and Stripes on Screen: A Comprehensive Guide to the Portrayal of American Military on Film.* Lanham, Md.: Scarecrow Press, 2005.

Sweeney, Michael S. *Secrets of Victory: The Office of Censorship and the American Press and Radio in World War II.* Chapel Hill: University of North Carolina Press, 2001.

Talese, Gay. *The Kingdom and the Power.* New York: World, 1969.

Taylor, Philip M. *Munitions of the Mind: A History of Propaganda from the Ancient World to the Present Day.* 2nd ed. Manchester: Manchester University Press, 1995.

Theoharis, Athan G. *The Yalta Myths: An Issue in American Politics, 1945–1955.* Columbia: University of Missouri Press, 1970.

Towle, Michael J. *Out of Touch: The Presidency and Public Opinion.* College Station: Texas A&M University Press, 2004.

Trimble, Vance H. *The Scripps-Howard Handbook.* 3rd ed. Cincinnati: E. W. Scripps, 1981.

Truman, David B. *The Congressional Party: A Case Study.* New York: Wiley, 1959.

Tucker, Nancy Bernkopf. *Patterns in the Dust: Chinese-American Relations and the Recognition Controversy, 1949–1950.* New York: Columbia University Press, 1983.

Turner, Kathleen J. *Lyndon Johnson's Dual War: Vietnam and the Press.* Chicago: University of Chicago Press, 1985.

Vatcher, William H. *Panmunjom: The Story of the Korean Military Armistice Negotiations.* New York: Praeger, 1958.

Vaughn, Stephen. *Holding Fast the Inner Lines: Democracy, Nationalism, and the Committee on Public Information.* Chapel Hill: University of North Carolina Press, 1980.

Wainstock, Dennis D. *Truman, MacArthur, and the Korean War.* Westport, Conn.: Greenwood Press, 1999.

Weintraub, Stanley. *MacArthur's War: Korea and the Undoing of an American Hero.* New York: Free Press, 2000.

Westerfield, H. Bradford. *Foreign Policy and Party Politics, Pearl Harbor to Korea.* New Haven: Yale University Press, 1955.

Whited, Charles. *Knight: A Publisher in the Tumultuous Century.* New York: Dutton, 1988.

Whitfield, Stephen J. *The Culture of the Cold War.* 2nd ed. Baltimore: Johns Hopkins University Press, 1996.

Williams, Herbert Lee. *The Newspaperman's President: Harry S. Truman.* Chicago: Nelson Hall, 1984.

Winfield, Betty Houchin. *FDR and the News Media.* New York: Columbia University Press, 1994.

Winkler, Allan M. *The Politics of Propaganda: The Office of War Information.* New Haven, Conn.: Yale University Press, 1978.

Woods, Randall Bennett. *Fulbright: A Biography.* Cambridge: Cambridge University Press, 1995.

Wooley, Wesley T. *Alternatives to Anarchy: American Supranationalism since World War II.* Bloomington: Indiana University Press, 1988.

Zelizer, Julian E. *On Capitol Hill: The Struggle to Reform Congress and Its Consequences, 1948–2000.* Cambridge: Cambridge University Press, 2004.

Zieger, Robert H. *The CIO, 1935–1955.* Chapel Hill: University of North Carolina Press, 1995.

Secondary Sources: Articles

Bacchus, Wilfred A. "The Relationship between Combat and Peace Negotiations: Fighting while Talking in Korea, 1951–1953." *Orbis* 17 (1973): 545–74.

Belmonte, Laura. "Anglo-American Relations and the Dismissal of MacArthur." *Diplomatic History* 19 (1995): 641–67.

Berger, Henry W. "Bipartisanship, Senator Taft, and the Truman Administration," *Political Science Quarterly* 90 (1975): 221–37.

Bernhard, Nancy E. "Clearer Than Truth: Public Affairs Television and the State Department's Domestic Information Campaigns, 1947–1952." *Diplomatic History* 21 (1997): 545–67.

Bernstein, Barton J. "The Week We Went to War: American Intervention in the Korean Civil War." Pt. 1. *Foreign Service Journal* 54 (January 1977): 6–9, 33–35.

——. "The Week We Went to War: American Intervention in the Korean Civil War." Pt. 2. *Foreign Service Journal* 54 (February 1977): 8–11, 33–34.

——. "The Policy of Risk: Crossing the 38th Parallel and Marching to the Yalu." *Foreign Service Journal* 54 (March 1977): 6–22, 29.

——. "The Origins of America's Commitments in Korea." *Foreign Service Journal* 55 (March 1978) 10–13, 34.

——. "The Struggle over the Korean Armistice: Prisoners or Repatriation?" In Cumings, *Child of Conflict,* 261–307.

Binford, Thomas H. "Information Training for All Services." *Army Information Digest* 6 (May 1951): 3–10.

Burke, Lee H., and Dana J. Johnson. "The Department of State's Congressional Relations Office." *Foreign Service Journal* 57 (February 1980): 29–34, 44–45.

Carlin, Diana B. "Harry S. Truman: From Whistle-Stops to the Halls of Congress." In Kurt Ritter and Martin J. Medhurst, eds., *Presidential Speechwriting: From the New Deal to the Reagan Revolution and Beyond.* College Station: Texas A&M University Press, 2003, 40–67.

Carpenter, Ted Galen. "United States' NATO Policy at the Crossroads: 'The Great Debate' of 1950–1951." *International History Review* 8 (1986): 389–414.

Casey, Steven. "Selling NSC-68: The Truman Administration, Public Opinion, and the Politics of Mobilization, 1950–51." *Diplomatic History* 29 (2005): 655–90.

——. "White House Publicity Operations during the Korean War, June 1950–June 1951," *Presidential Studies Quarterly* 35 (2005): 691–717.

Coletta, Paolo E. "Francis P. Matthews." In Coletta, ed., *American Secretaries of the Navy.* Annapolis: Naval Institute Press, 1980, 2:783–822.

Cumings, Bruce. "Introduction: The Course of Korean-American Relations, 1943–1953." In Cumings, *Child of Conflict*, 3–55.

Dingman, Roger. "Atomic Diplomacy during the Korean War." *International Security* 13 (1988–89): 50–91.

Dorn, Frank. "Briefing the Press." *Army Information Digest* 6 (May 1951): 36–41.

Echols, Marion P. "Information in the Combat Zone." *Army Information Digest* 6 (April 1951): 61–64.

Flynn, George Q. "The Draft and College Deferments during the Korean War." *Historian* 50 (1988): 369–85.

Foot, Rosemary. "Anglo-American Relations in the Korean Crisis: The British Effort to Avert an Expanded War, December 1950–January 1951." *Diplomatic History* 10 (1986): 43–57.

——. "Making Known the Unknown War: Policy Analysis of the Korean Conflict in the Last Decade." *Diplomatic History* 15 (1991): 411–31.

Ford, John W. "The McCarthy Years inside the Department of State." *Foreign Service Journal* 57 (November 1980): 11–13.

Gaddis, John Lewis. "Korea in American Politics, Strategy and Diplomacy, 1945–1950." In Nagai and Iriye, *Origins of the Cold War in Asia*, 277–98.

Griffith, Robert. "The Selling of America: The Advertising Council and American Politics, 1942–1960. *Business History Review* 57 (1983): 388–412.

Hamby, Alonzo. "Comments on Wilz, 'The Korean War and American Society.'" In Heller, *The Korean War*, 168–73.

——. "Public Opinion: Korea and Vietnam." *Wilson Quarterly* 2 (1978): 137–41.

Hammond, Paul Y. "NSC-68: Prologue to Rearmament." In Warner R. Schilling, Paul Y. Hammond, and Glenn H. Snyder, eds., *Strategy, Politics, and Defense Budgets.* New York: Columbia University Press, 1962, 271–378.

Hart, Roderick P. "Why Do They Talk That Way? A Research Agenda for the Presidency." *Presidential Studies Quarterly* 32 (2002): 693–709.

Howard, Michael. "The Historical Development of the UN's Role in International Security." In Adam Roberts and Benedict Kingsbury, eds., *United Nations, Divided World.* 2nd ed. Oxford: Clarendon Press, 1993, 63–80.

Hunt, Michael. "Beijing and the Korean Crisis, June 1950–June 1951." *Political Science Quarterly* 107 (1992): 453–78.

Hurwitz, John. "Presidential Leadership and Public Followership." In Michael Margolis and Gary A. Mauser, eds., *Manipulating Public Opinion: Essays on Public Opinion as a Dependent Variable.* Pacific Grove, Calif.: Brooks Cole, 1989, 222–49.

James, D. Clayton. "Harry S. Truman: The Two War Chief." In Joseph G. Dawson, ed., *Commanders in Chief: Presidential Leadership in Modern Wars.* Lawrence: University Press of Kansas, 1993, 107–26.

Jervis, Robert. "The Impact of the Korean War on the Cold War." *Journal of Conflict Resolution* 24 (1980): 555–72.

Keefer, Edward C. "President Dwight D. Eisenhower and the End of the Korean War." *Diplomatic History* 10 (1986): 267–89.

———. "The Truman Administration and the South Korean Political Crisis of 1952: Democracy's Failure?" *Pacific Historical Review* 60 (1990): 145–68.

Koistinen, Paul A.C. "Mobilizing the World War II Economy: Labor and the Industrial-Military Alliance." *Pacific Historical Review* 42 (1973): 443–78.

Kotch, John. "The Origins of the American Security Commitment to Korea." In Cumings, *Child of Conflict,* 239–59.

LaFeber, Walter. "Crossing the 38th: The Cold War in Microcosm." In Lynn H. Miller and Ronald W. Preussen, eds., *Reflections on the Cold War: A Quarter Century of American Foreign Policy.* Philadelphia: Temple University Press, 1974, 71–90.

———. "American Policymakers, Public Opinion, and the Outbreak of the Cold War, 1945–50." In Nagai and Iriye, *Origins of the Cold War in Asia,* 43–65.

LaPalombara, Joseph G. "Pressure, Propaganda, and Political Action in the Elections of 1950." *Journal of Politics* 14 (1952): 300–325.

Leitenberg, Milton. "New Russian Evidence on the Korean War Biological Warfare Allegations: Background and Analysis. *Cold War International History Project Bulletin* 11 (1998): 185–96.

McGaw, E. J. "A Commander's Public Relations Role." *Army Information Digest* 6 (March 1951): 25–31.

Martin, Robert P. "The MacArthur Censorship." *Nieman Reports* 2 (1948): 3–4.

Matray, David. "Truman's Plan for Victory: National Self-Determination and the Thirty-Eighth Parallel Decision in Korea." *Journal of American History* 66 (1979): 314–33.

———. "Korea: Test Case of Containment in Asia." In Cumings, *Child of Conflict,* 169–93.

May, Ernest R. "The U.S. Government, A Legacy of the Cold War." In Michael J. Hogan, ed., *The End of the Cold War: Its Meaning and Implications.* Cambridge: Cambridge University Press, 1992, 217–43.

Medhurst, Martin. "Text and Context in the 1952 Presidential Campaign: Eisenhower's 'I Shall Go to Korea' Speech." *Presidential Studies Quarterly* 30 (2000): 464–84.

Merry, Robert W. "Robert A. Taft: A Study in the Accumulation of Legislative Power. In Richard A. Baker and Roger H. Davidson, eds., *First among Equals: Outstanding Senate Leaders of the Twentieth Century.* Washington, D.C.: Congressional Quarterly, 1991, 163–97.

Nelson, Anna Kasten. "Anna M. Rosenberg, an 'Honorary Man.'" *Journal of Military History* 68 (2004): 133–61.

Neustadt, Richard E. "The White House Staff: Later Period." In Heller, *Truman White House,* 93–117.

Oldfield, Barney. "USAF Press Relations in the Far East." *Army Information Digest* 5 (November 1950): 40–45.

Parks, Floyd L. "The Commander and the Press." *Army Information Digest* 6 (May 1951): 17–34.

Paterson, Thomas G. "Presidential Foreign Policy, Public Opinion, and Congress: The Truman Years." *Diplomatic History* 3 (1979): 1–18.

Pelz, Stephen. "U.S. Decisions on Korean Policy, 1943–1950: Some Hypotheses." In Cumings, *Child of Conflict,* 93–132.

Powlick, Philip J. "The Sources of Public Opinion for American Foreign Policy Officials." *International Studies Quarterly* 39 (1995): 427–51.

Reichard, Gary W. "Divisions and Dissent: Democrats and Foreign Policy, 1952–1956." *Political Science Quarterly* 93 (1978): 51–72.

Rottinghaus, Brandon. "Reassessing Public Opinion Polling in the Truman Administration." *Presidential Studies Quarterly* 33 (2003): 325–32.

Russett, Bruce M., and Thomas W. Graham. "Public Opinion and National Security Policy: Relationships and Impacts." In Manus I. Midlarsky, ed., *Handbook of War Studies.* London: Unwin Hyman, 1989, 239–57.

Schaller, Michael. "MacArthur's Japan: The View from Washington." *Diplomatic History* 10 (1986): 1–23.

Schmeitzer, Janet. "Tom Connally." In Kenneth E. Hendrickson, Jr., Michael L. Collins, and Patrick Cox, eds., *Profiles in Power: Twentieth-Century Texans in Washington.* Austin: University of Texas Press, 2004, 86–103.

Schonberger, Howard. "The Japanese Lobby in American Diplomacy, 1947–1952." *Pacific Historical Review* 46 (1972): 327–59.

Sparrow, Bartholomew H. "Limited Wars and the Attenuation of the State: Soldiers, Money, and Political Communication in World War II, Korea, and Vietnam." In Ira Katznelson and Martin Shefter, eds., *Shaped by War and Trade: International Influences on American Political Development.* Princeton, N.J.: Princeton University Press, 2002, 267–300.

Stein, Bruno. "Labor's Role in Government Agencies during World War II." *Journal of Economic History* 17 (1957): 389–408.

Stieber, Jack. "Labor's Walkout from the Korean War Stabilization Board." *Labor History* 21 (1980): 239–60.

Stueck, William. "The March to the Yalu: The Perspective from Washington." In Cumings, *Child of Conflict*, 195–237.

Trachtenberg, Marc. "A 'Wasting Asset': American Strategy and the Shifting Nuclear Balance, 1949–54." *International Security* 13 (1988–89): 5–49.

Tuchman, Gaye. "Objectivity as Strategic Ritual: An Examination of Newsmen's Notions of Objectivity." *American Journal of Sociology* 77 (1972): 660–79.

Wala, Michael. "Selling the Marshall Plan at Home: The Committee for the Marshall Plan to Aid European Recovery." *Diplomatic History* 10 (1986): 247–65.

Weathersby, Kathryn. "Korea, 1949–1950: To Attack, or Not to Attack? Stalin, Kim Il Sun, and the Prelude to War." *Cold War International History Project Bulletin* 5 (1995): 1–9.

———. "Deceiving the Deceivers: Moscow, Beijing, Pyongyang, and the Allegations of Bacteriological Weapons Use in Korea." *Cold War International History Project Bulletin* 11 (1998): 176–80.

Wells, Samuel F. "Sounding the Tocsin: NSC 68 and the Soviet Threat." *International Security* 4 (1979): 116–58.

Willoughby, Charles A. "The Truth about Korea." *Cosmopolitan*, December 1951, 35–37, 133–39.

Wilson, Theodore. "The Kefauver Committee, 1950." In Schlesinger and Bruns, *Congress Investigates*, 5:3439–66.

Wilz, John Edward. "The MacArthur Inquiry, 1951." In Schlesinger and Bruns, *Congress Investigates*, 5:3593–635.

———. "The MacArthur Hearings of 1951: The Secret Testimony." *Military Affairs* 39 (1975): 167–73.

———. "The Korean War and American Society." In Heller, *Korean War,* 112–58.

———. "Truman and MacArthur: The Wake Island Meeting." *Military Affairs* 42 (1978): 169–75.

Zaller, John. "Elite Leadership of Mass Opinion: New Evidence from the Gulf War." In W. Lance Bennett and David L. Paletz, eds., *Taken By Storm: The Media, Public Opinion, and U.S. Foreign Policy in the Gulf War*. Chicago: University of Chicago Press, 1994, 186–209.

Unpublished Works

Allison, Fred H. "The Black Sheep Squadron: A Case Study in Marine Corps Innovations in Close Air Support." Ph.D. diss., Texas Tech University, 2003.

Gellner, Charles R., Ellen Clodfelter and Mary Shepard. "The 'Great Debate' on U.S. Foreign Policy: Hearings and Discussion on the Wherry Resolution." Washington, D.C.: Library of Congress Legislative Reference Service, 12 March 1951. (Copy in Legislation File: Foreign Resolutions, 82nd Congress box 295, Connally Papers, LC.)

Harris, Merne Arthur. "The MacArthur Dismissal: A Study in Political Mail."
Ph.D. diss., University of Iowa, 1966.

Leary, William M. "Smith of New Jersey: A Biography of Alexander Smith, U.S.
Senator from New Jersey, 1944–59." Ph.D. diss., Princeton University,
1966.

Young, Marilyn B. "Hard Sell: The Korean War." In Kenneth Osgood, ed.,
Selling War (forthcoming).

INDEX

appeasement
  in administration rhetoric, 176, 215,
    222–23, 224
  in MacArthur's rhetoric, 100, 250
  in 1930s, 20, 215
  in Republican rhetoric, 38, 111, 117, 118,
    258, 262
Armed Forces Information School, 58–59,
  305
Armstrong, Orland Kay, 287
Arnell, Ellis, 220
Associated Press (AP), 42, 48, 55
  and armistice talks, 269, 278
  and censorship, 155–56
  and Chinese intervention, 146
  and communications, 54
  and competition, 52
  coverage of stalemate war, 307, 311
  and June (1950) crisis, 36
  and MacArthur's threats, 57
  and McCarthy, 15
  and Quirk, 168
  sends correspondents to Korea, 45
  and Taft, 260
  See also wire services
Atlanta Constitution, 139
Atlantic Charter, 245, 256
Atlantic Union, 90–91
Attlee, Clement, 133, 135, 138, 235
Austin, Warren, 8, 133
  and ceasefire resolution, 212
  speeches and statements, 92–93, 98,
    222, 226

Bailey, Thomas A., 101
Baltimore Sun
  and aggressor resolution, 211
  and armistice talks, 276
  and Chinese intervention, 152
  and MacArthur's recall, 235
Barkley, Alben, 73, 129, 206
Barrett, Edward R.
  experience, 7
  and Korea, 27, 214
  and low-key rhetoric, 72
  and NSC-68, 67
  and POWs, 268, 286
  and Republican attacks, 216
  resignation, 314
Barriere, John, 242–43
Baruch, Bernard, 75
Battle Report, Washington, 91, 312
Battleground, 219
Beatty, Morgan, 353
Beech, Keyes, 58, 307, 311
  and casualties, 63–64
  and censorship, 161
  and Chinese intervention, 149–50, 152
  impact of reporting, 60

and June (1950) crisis, 42–43
and MacArthur, 150, 159, 208
and POWs, 283
Bell, David, 332
Bell, Ulric, 222
Bennett, Wallace F., 120
Bentsen, Lloyd, 71
Biffle, Leslie, 92, 120
Bigart, Homer
  and army's lack of equipment, 66
  and Chinese intervention, 136, 146,
    150, 152
  and conditions in Korea, 145
  impact of reporting, 58
  and Korean battles, 53, 65
  leaves Korea, 150, 307
  and MacArthur, 150, 154, 159
  relations with Higgins, 52, 150
Bloody Ridge battle, 267, 309–10
Boatner, Haydon L., 291
Bob Hope Show, 101
Bohlen, Charles, 341
Boston Globe, 235
Boston Herald, 235, 345–46
Boyle, Harold, 45, 146
Bradley, Omar N., 206
  and blood campaign, 322
  and Chinese intervention, 127, 134
  "Dunkirk" statement, 137, 154
  and MacArthur hearings, 251
  and mobilization, 77, 103
  in World War II, 166
Brewster, Owen
  and A-bomb, 71, 133–34
  and Acheson, 180
  attacks administration, 24
  and election (1950), 111
  and Johnson (Louis), 7
Bricker amendment, 354
Bridges, Styles, 174, 341
  and casualties, 63
  and communist brutality, 345–46
  and June (1950) crisis, 38
  and MacArthur's recall, 238
  and mobilization, 177
Brines, Russell, 48
Brinkley, David, 22
Britain
  See United Kingdom
Buckhart, E.C., 155
Buffalo Courier-Express, 298
Burma, 213
Bush, Vannevar, 191
business
  and price freezes, 178
  and Wilson, 202
  in World War II, 72
Business Advisory Council, 103
Business Week, 259, 322

Butler, John Marshall, 120
Byrnes, James F., 86

Cain, Harry P.
  and A-bomb, 139
  and election (1952), 336
  and MacArthur's recall, 253, 261
Canada, 212, 311, 348
Cannon, Clarence, 178
Cannon, James S., 152
Capehart, Homer
  and election (1950), 112, 120
  and MacArthur's recall, 234, 235
  and mobilization, 76
  and UN, 90
Carlson, Frank, 120
Carroll, John A., 242, 243, 252
Case, Francis, 120, 234, 235
Catholic Church
  and MacArthur, 241, 242
  and Matthews, 105
  and POWs, 287
casualties
  and blood campaign, 323
  in MacArthur's communiqués, 50, 250
  in political debate, 62–64, 148, 185, 250,
    252–53
  political scientists and, 4
  total U.S., 296, 356, 361, 423n127
CBS, 307
  and Acheson, 217
  and Inchon, 96, 97
  loyalty oaths, 12
  and mobilization, 178–79
  self-censorship, 56–57
  and Truman's A-bomb statement, 133
  war coverage, 312–13
censorship
  at armistice talks, 270, 273, 277
  "double censorship," 170–72, 299
  established, 158
  implementation of, 9, 158–63, 167–68
  improvements in, 299–300, 305–
    307, 362
  lingering problems, 311
  self-censorship, 15, 56, 352
  and thirty-eighth parallel, 228
  voluntary code, 45–46
Central Intelligence Agency (CIA), 19,
  117, 120
Chavez, Dennis, 184, 198
Chiang Kai-shek, 14, 24, 35, 205, 208, 237,
  239, 283, 342
Chicago Daily News, 42, 60, 208
  and Chinese intervention, 149–50, 152
  circulation of, 149, 396n14
  coverage of stalemate war, 311
Chicago Sun-Times, 46
  self-censorship, 56

and South Korea, 353
Chicago Tribune, 52
  and censorship, 306
  and Chinese intervention, 151
  and June (1950) crisis, 36, 41
  and MacArthur, 163, 233, 235
  and Truman, 14
China (People's Republic of), 24, 35, 97
  and armistice talks, 267
  and ceasefire resolution, 212
  Easter offensive, 249, 252, 263
  First Phase Offensive, 117
  and POWs, 285, 288
  Second Phase Offensive, 127–29, 131,
    134, 136, 145–53
  and stalemate war, 310–11, 334, 354
  Third Phase Offensive, 157, 159–62,
    164, 207
China lobby, 24, 243, 341, 349
Chipyong-ni battle, 164
Chonan battle, 49, 50, 53
Christian Science Monitor
  and armistice talks, 276, 347
  and Chinese intervention, 151
  and Eisenhower's trip to Korea, 339
  favors negotiated peace, 139
  and MacArthur, 46, 235, 240–41
  and South Korea, 353
  and UN, 90
Christmas in Korea, 312
Church, John H., 42–43
Cincinnati Times Star, 14, 211
civil defense, 106–7, 245–46
civil rights,
  integration of armed forces, 319–22
  Truman and, 10, 332
  Russell and, 194
Clark, Mark C., 289–91, 342, 345, 357
Clay, Lucius, 201, 328
Clayton, William, 104, 105
Cleveland Plain Dealer, 38, 235
Cohen, Bernard, 9
Collier's, 322
Collins, J. Lawton, 296
  Korean trips, 135, 138, 208–209
  and media relations, 59
  and POWs, 284
  public statements, 136, 163, 253
Colson, Charles F. 289–91
Committee on the Present Danger
  activities of, 187, 189
  and administration, 187, 242–43
  formation of, 105
  and MacArthur's recall, 243
  and preventive war, 105, 191, 403n72
Committee on Public Information, 6, 87, 88
Committee to Sell the Marshall Plan, 11, 187
Compton, Wilson, 314
Conant, James B., 104, 105

PIO and PI personnel, 9, 46, 167, 298–99, 338–39
reasons for defeats, 49, 164
relations with UNC, 160, 169–72, 298–300
retreats, 49–50, 53, 157
sent to Korea, 45
and stalemate war, 295–96, 309–11
and television coverage, 312
and UP, 159–60
War Crimes Section, 280
See also Press Security Division; specific units; U.S. army
Eisenhower, Dwight D., 35, 187, 250, 253
and armistice, 355–56, 357
and cabinet, 340–41
and Congress, 340–41
and Democrats, 340, 354
and election (1952), 325–26, 328–32, 335–36, 364–65
and great debate, 195, 196–97, 216
and Korean policy, 342, 347–49, 353–54
Korean trip, 336–39, 355
and McCarthy, 330
media briefings and releases, 325–26, 339, 343, 346
and mobilization, 104
and NSC, 340
and nationalist Republicans, 330, 354
and NATO, 108, 179
speeches, 325, 330–31, 334–35, 341, 342, 346, 357
and Taft, 328–29, 330
and Truman, 339–40
and UMST, 105
and Van Fleet, 343
election (1944), 329
election (1946), 70, 86
election (1948), 10, 24, 330, 332
election (1950)
administration and, 109, 112–13, 116–17
Democrats and, 111–12
and Korea, 109, 117–19
Republicans and, 109–11
result, 119–20
Wake and, 113, 115–16
election (1952)
campaign, 325–36
and Korea, 325–29, 331–36, 364–65
MacArthur and, 258
result, 326
See also Eisenhower; Stevenson
Elsey, George
and MacArthur hearings, 254
presidential speech suggestions, 206, 229
and State Department, 39
See also White House aides

Faris, Barry, 156, 168
Ferguson, Homer, 81, 248

First Marine Division, 45, 301
See also U.S. Marines
Fisher, Adrian, 71
Flanders, Ralph E., 23
and A-bomb, 133
and Chinese intervention, 118
Ford, Gerald R., 78
Formosa (Taiwan), 14, 24, 35, 100, 205, 255, 267, 346, 371n22
Foster, William C., 289
Four Freedoms, 245, 256
France, 107–8, 179, 348
Frear, Allen, 184, 198
Fritchey, Clayton, 156, 160
Fulbright, J. William
and committee hearings, 246
and MacArthur hearings, 247, 250, 254
and mobilization, 77

Gabrielson, Guy, 109, 111
"gagging orders," 141, 189–90, 217–18, 242
Galbraith, Kenneth, 332
Gallup poll
on A-bomb, 139
on election (1948), 31
on June (1950) crisis, 35
on MacArthur hearings, 257
on mobilization, 75, 102, 318
on thirty-eighth parallel, 100, 229
on withdrawing from Korea, 205, 292
Gaynor, Paul, 322
Geneva Convention, 280, 283
German rearmament, 107–8, 179
Gibney, Frank, 42
Godwin, Earl, 346
Gough, Lewis, 343
Gould, Alan J., 155–56
Grant, Cary, 221
Greece, 30
Green, William, 75
Gross, Ernest A., 213
Gurney, Chan, 180

Hagerty, James C., 338–39
Hale, Robert, 84
Hall, Leonard, 111
Halls of Montezuma, 225
Handleman, Howard, 306
Hanley, James N., 280–82
Harding, Victor, 118
Harper's, 322
Harriman, Averell, 61, 72, 85, 192
and economic controls, 70
and election (1950), 112
and Truman's A-bomb statement, 133
Hayward, Henry S., 276
Hearst newspapers, 14, 334
Heartbreak Ridge battle, 268, 309–10
Heatter, Gabriel, 75

Lippert, 221
Lippmann, Walter
  and Acheson, 140
  and armistice talks, 334
  and media speculation, 344
  and POWs, 285
  and withdrawal from Korea, 205
Lodge, Henry Cabot, 26
  and Eisenhower, 328
  and GOP white paper, 82
  and MacArthur's recall, 238
  and UN, 92
  as UN ambassador, 341, 342
Loews theaters, 222
Los Angles Times
  and aggressor resolution, 211
  and Chinese intervention, 151
  and escalation, 334
  and MacArthur's recall, 235
  and Truman, 14
Lovett, Robert A.
  appointed defense secretary, 280, 314
  congressional testimony, 139
  and establishment, 104–5
  and MacArthur, 121, 231
  and media relations, 314–15
  and POWs, 280, 281, 284
Lucas, Scott W.
  and Acheson, 140
  and censorship, 59–60
  and congressional authorization for war, 34
  and election (1950), 113, 119, 120
  and Kem resolution, 180
  and McCarran Act, 81
  and McCarthy, 80
Luce, Henry, 328
Luce magazines, 14, 206
  and China, 14
  and Chinese intervention, 151
  See also Time; Life.

MacArthur, Douglas, 22, 29
  appointed UNC, 44–45
  and casualty reporting, 148, 250
  and censorship, 8, 45–49, 66, 154–55,
    156–57, 158, 162, 172
  and Chinese intervention, 117, 118,
    120–21, 127, 154, 157
  communiqués, 8, 41, 43, 47–48, 50, 55,
    118, 136
  and Formosa, 100, 208
  and Inchon, 47, 65
  and June (1950) crisis, 28
  and Korean policy, 49, 65, 100, 120–21,
    207–208, 230, 236–37, 251, 342
  and MacArthur hearings, 249–50,
    252–53, 260
  and media's Korean coverage, 53, 149,
    150, 155, 207, 360

  media relations, 46–49, 230
  and medical teams, 62
  meets wire service bosses, 55
  offensives, 101, 121
  and "palace guard," 48, 169
  personality, 46–47, 229–30
  pessimism of, 134, 135, 154, 207–208
  recall and return, 233, 236–39, 296
  and Ridgway, 164, 230
  trips to Korea, 28, 168–69, 170–71
  unauthorized comments, 8, 100, 136,
    142, 157, 169, 170, 171, 217–18,
    230–31
  and UN, 90
  and Wake Island conference,
    113–15
  and war correspondents, 53, 148–149,
    150, 155, 207, 360
  See also United Nations Command
MacGregor, Greg, 352
Malenkov, Georgiy, 344
Malik, Jacob, 91–92, 94, 267
Mansfield, Mike, 185
Mao Zedong, 99
Markel, Lester, 214
Marshall, Charles, 286
Marshall, George C., 35, 206
  advisers, 104
  appointed Defense Secretary, 86
  and censorship, 163
  and Chinese intervention, 121, 134, 207
  congressional testimony and briefings,
    188, 195–97, 216
  and Korean policy, 209, 227
  low-key rhetoric and actions, 192
  and MacArthur, 121, 208, 231
  and MacArthur hearings, 251
  media briefings and releases, 199, 322
  and mobilization, 103, 174, 202
  and NATO, 108
  and UMST, 199
  and volatility of public opinion, 102–3,
    156, 199
  and war correspondents, 147
Marshall, Thurgood, 321
Martin, Joseph W.
  and aggressor resolution, 211–12
  and mobilization, 76
Martin, Robert, 96
Matthews, Burrows, 298
Matthews, Francis P.
  declares end to the war, 105–6
  and MacArthur's recall, 242
  preventive war speech, 85–86, 87
Maverick, Maury, 233
Maybank, Burnet R., 133
McCardle, Carl W., 56
McCarran, Pat, 80, 198, 248
McCarran Act, 78–82

McCarthy, Joseph
  allegations, 15, 23–24, 79, 83, 189,
    260, 363
  and election (1950), 109, 110
  and election (1952), 330, 336
  and MacArthur's recall, 235, 260
  and media, 14, 15
  and Tydings, 79–80, 110, 120, 250
McCarthyism
  before Korea, 16
  and election (1950), 110, 120
  and MacArthur, 241
  and media, 12
McClellan, John
  and aggressor resolution, 211–12
  and presidential power, 184
McCormack, John
  and aggressor resolution, 212
  and election (1950), 120
  and mobilization, 77
McCormick newspapers, 334
McFarland, Ernest, 199–200
McKellar, Kenneth D., 177
McLeod, Scott, 341
McMahon, Brien, 113
  and MacArthur hearings, 247, 248,
    250–51
McNamara, James C., 298
media and the press
  African American newspapers, 321
  and armistice, 285, 355, 357
  and casualties, 148
  and censorship, 55, 59, 153, 155–56, 158,
    161–63, 167–68, 172, 306
  and Chinese intervention, 117, 118,
    150–54
  and communist brutality, 280, 345–46
  and Defense Department, 22, 62
  and Dulles, 346–47
  and Eisenhower's Korean trip, 338–39
  and escalation, 334
  and germ warfare allegations, 291,
    422n105
  and GOP white paper, 83
  and June (1950) crisis, 22–23, 36–39
  and Koje-do, 283–84, 290–91
  and MacArthur, 153–54, 172
  and MacArthur's recall, 235–36,
    240–41, 252, 253, 257
  and MacArthur's threats, 57–58
  and marines, 301
  and McCarthy, 14
  and McCarthyism, 12
  non-U.S. media, 311–12
  pack reporting, 12, 14
  partisanship, 14
  and POWs, 281, 282–84, 347
  and rumors, 22, 36–37, 343–44
  self-censorship, 15, 56–57, 143, 352

  and South Korea, 350–53
  and stalemate war, 310–11, 331–32, 362
  and thirty-eighth parallel, 97, 100,
    228–29, 263, 276, 347
  and Truman's A-bomb
    statement, 132, 133
  and UN, 211, 212
  and Wake Island conference, 113,
    115–16
  and withdrawal from Korea, 205
  See also objective journalism; *specific
    publications*; television; war
    correspondents; wire services.
Merrick, Richard H., 305–306
Millikin, Eugene
  and A-bomb, 133
  attacks administration, 25
  and election (1950), 109, 120
  and MacArthur's recall, 239–40
  and mobilization, 177
Millis, Walter, 334
Minneapolis Star and Tribune, 96
Morse, Wayne
  and censorship, 161
  and MacArthur's recall, 262
  and McCarthy, 79
Moullette letter, 224–25
movies
  administration's plans to use, 104,
    389n36
  and Korean War, 219–23
  and Truman's speeches, 176
  and World War II, 219
  See also newsreels
Mowrer, Edgar, 290
Muccio, John J., 23
  and Rhee, 226
  and war correspondents, 43
Mundt, Karl E., 78
Mundt bill
  See McCarran Act
Murphy, Charles S., 6
Murrow, Edward
  dispatches censored, 57
  television shows, 312–13
  and Truman's A-bomb statement, 133
Myers, Francis J.
  and Acheson, 140
  and election (1950), 113, 119, 120
  and McCarthy, 80

National Association for the Advancement
  of Colored People (NAACP), 321
National Association of Broadcasters, 156
National Business Publications, 104
National Guard, 68, 186
National Opinion Research Center poll
  on European security, 182
  on withdrawing from Korea, 215

personnel, 314
and POWs, 286–87
Public Studies Division, 32
speech suggestions, 32, 41, 122, 187,
206, 214, 215, 218–19, 286
and television, 91, 94
and volatility of public opinion, 101–2
See also U.S. State Department
Office of Public Information (OPI)
and blood campaign, 322–23
and integration, 321–22
organization of, 7
See also U.S. Defense Department
Office of War Information, 87, 88, 217, 222
"Operation Common Knowledge," 95–96
Operation Killer, 164, 166, 169
Operation Little Switch, 344–46, 348
Operation Ratkiller, 351
Operation Ripper, 164
Operation Thunderbolt, 164
opinion polls
on armistice, 355, 365
on election (1952), 332
on escalation, 240
on European security, 182, 258
on germ warfare allegations, 422n105
on Korea as mistake, 206, 215, 292,
334–35
on Korea as campaign issue, 334–35
on likelihood of world war, 32
on MacArthur's recall, 240, 253–54, 258
on mobilization, 75, 102, 258
on thirty-eighth parallel, 263, 292
Truman and, 6, 31
Truman's approval ratings, 215
on Truman's speeches, 75
on UN, 92
on voluntary repatriation, 292–93
See also Denver Post; Gallup poll; National
Opinion Research Center poll
Osan battle, 34, 49

Pace, Frank, 102, 322
Paley, William S., 57
Panikkar, K.M., 99–100
Panmunjom, 268, 277, 288, 333, 344–45,
348–49, 357
Parks, Floyd L.
and armistice talks, 275
and censorship, 59–61, 155, 156, 158, 163
and lack of PR personnel, 47
and marines, 301–302
and media relations, 59
and PR campaigns, 302–303, 319
Patten, Harold A., 334
Patterson, Robert P., 104, 105
Patton, George S., 166
Pearson, Drew
and casualties, 63

and June (1950) crisis, 38
and MacArthur's recall, 238
and preventive war, 87
self-censorship, 56
and Truman, 16
Pentagon
construction of, 173
See also U.S. Defense Department
Pentagon-Washington, 312
Persons, Wilton B., 340
Philadelphia Evening Bulletin, 56
Philadelphia Inquirer, 166
and aggressor resolution, 211
and communist brutality, 345
and McCarthy, 14
and Wake Island conference, 115
Policy Planning Staff
and June (1950) crisis, 31
and preventive war sentiment, 191
speech suggestions, 234
and volatility of public opinion, 102
and voluntary repatriation, 286
See also U.S. State Department
political scientists
and casualties, 4
and public opinion, 101
and rally effect, 12
Poynter, Nelson, 161
press
See media and the press
Press Advisory Division (PAD)
established, 155, 158
and implementation of censorship, 171,
300, 306–307
See also United Nations Command
Press Security Division (PSD)
established, 158
and implementation of censorship, 162,
163, 170–72
importance of military success, 164–66
and war correspondents, 168
See also Eighth Army
Preston, Walter J., 270
preventive war sentiment, 32–33, 71–72,
84–85, 190–91, 383n16, 403n67
prisoners of war (POWs)
communist POWs, 268, 282–84
exchange of sick and wounded, 344–46
negotiations over in 1953, 348–49
screening of, 288–89, 290
UN POWs, 279–82
voluntary repatriation, 284–89
propaganda
agency, 6, 87–88, 217, 362
communist, 275–77, 290–91
definition of, 5
foreign, 5, 224, 284, 290–91
World War I, 6
World War II, 6

propaganda (*continued*)
    See also Committee on Public
        Information; Office of War
        Information
Providence Journal, 228–29
public opinion
    and armistice, 228–29, 275, 285,
        356, 365
    and Chinese intervention, 139
    and defense spending, 68
    and escalation, 236, 261
    and European security, 181
    and Inchon, 97
    and MacArthur's recall, 236, 253–54, 258
    and POWs, 280, 282, 284, 293–93
    and thirty-eighth parallel, 100,
        228–29, 263
    and UN, 90–92, 94, 211–214
    and withdrawing from Korea, 139,
        205–206, 214
    volatility of, 32–33, 71, 101–3, 215,
        316, 359
    See also opinion polls
Pusan
    conditions in, 52
    perimeter, 61, 64
Pyongyang, 101, 114, 275

Quirk, James T.
    appointed Ridgway's adviser, 166–67, 298
    experience, 166
    and MacArthur, 169–70
    media briefings and releases, 167, 170
    media's view of, 168
    relations with PI officers, 167

radio, 97, 104, 133, 205
    and Acheson, 216–17
    and armistice talks, 285, 334
    and MacArthur's recall, 239, 248
    and mobilization, 178–79, 400n19
    and Truman's speeches, 27, 176
    See also ABC; CBS; NBC; individual
        broadcasters
Rayburn, Sam
    and election (1950), 120
    and Johnson (Louis), 86
    and June (1950) crisis, 27
    and mobilization, 77
Red Cross, 322, 352
Republican Party (GOP)
    and Acheson, 119–20, 180–81, 216
    and casualties, 63, 252–53, 322
    and censorship, 60
    and China, 261
    difficulty of opposing war, 10, 74
    divisions in, 10, 183, 196, 261–62,
        328–29, 330, 340, 354, 363–64
    and election (1948), 10, 24, 330, 332

and election (1950), 78, 82–83, 109–11,
    119–20
and election (1952), 329, 336
and Hollywood, 219
and Johnson (Louis), 66
and June (1950) crisis, 23–25, 38
and Korean policy, 139, 342–43, 360–61
and MacArthur's recall, 237–40, 244,
    247–48, 257, 262, 364
and McCarthyism, 23–24, 78–80
Minority Policy Committee, 24, 26, 83, 239
and mobilization, 74–78, 177–78, 316–18
and POWs, 280, 348–49
and South Korea, 353–54
and UN, 90, 211, 338
white paper, 82–83
See also internationalist Republicans;
    nationalist Republicans
Reston, James
    and Acheson, 11, 254
    and Chinese intervention, 137
    and GOP white paper, 83
    and lack of government coordination,
        203
    and letdown, 198–99
    and Malik, 91
Reuters, 162
Rhee, Syngman, 39
    brutality of regime, 97, 349–50, 352
    declares martial law, 292, 350, 352
    and Eisenhower's trip, 337
    and POWs, 353
    and Robertson trip, 354–55
    and thirty-eighth parallel, 226
    U.S. sympathy for, 352
Ribicoff, Abraham, 185
Richmond Post-Dispatch, 205
Ridgway, Matthew, 61, 208
    appointed Eighth Army
        commander, 163, 164
    appointed UNC, 233, 263, 296
    and armistice talks, 271, 277–78, 288–90
    and censorship, 166, 299–300, 311
    hands over UNC, 289
    and MacArthur, 169–70, 229
    media briefings and releases, 166, 170,
        229, 249, 281, 289, 322–23
    and media relations, 166–67, 270–71,
        296–98
    offensives, 164, 195, 198
    and POWs, 281, 288–89
    strategy and tactics, 164, 299
    and Van Fleet, 299
RKO, 221
Robertson, Walter, 341, 353–55
Roeder, George H., 62
Roosevelt, Eleanor, 66
Roosevelt, Franklin D., 237
    appointments, 73, 74

South Korean Second (II) Corps, 117
South Korean Third Division, 101
Soviet Union
  A-bomb test, 10–11, 32, 67
  and June (1950) crisis, 19, 30–31
  MIG fighters, 128, 392n5
  and North Korea, 19, 21
  TASS agency, 48
Spaatz, Carl, 191
Sparkman, John J., 247
Sparks, Fred, 311
  and armistice talks, 270
  and Chinese intervention, 149
  leaves Korea, 305
Sperry Gyroscope, 89
Spofford, Charles, 179
Stahey, Carl E., 301
Stalin, Josef, 30–31, 97, 99, 344
Stassen, Harold
  and great debate, 196
  and mobilization, 104
  as presidential candidate, 85, 328,
    427–28n12
  and Soviet Union, 85
Steel Helmet, 221–22
Steelman, John
  and emergency powers, 70
  and Hollywood, 223
Stevens, William P., 96
Stevenson, Adlai
  and Eisenhower, 329–30, 333
  and Korea, 327–28, 330, 333, 335
  political style, 327, 332–33
  and Truman, 327, 333
Stimson, Henry, 73
Sullivan, Mark, 16
Swing, Raymond Gramm, 205
Symington, Stuart
  and civil defense, 106
  and economic controls, 70, 71
  and labor, 72, 201
  and need for tougher Cold War stance, 191

Taber, John, 178
Taejon battle, 49
Taft, Robert A., 174, 206
  and Acheson, 180–81, 315
  and allies, 185
  attacks administration rhetoric, 86,
    185, 260
  and China, 24, 205
  and Chinese intervention, 185
  and congressional authorization for
    war, 34, 185
  and congressional committees, 193
  and consultation, 26, 140
  and Eisenhower, 330, 340–41
  and election (1950), 109, 112, 120, 183
  and election (1952), 326–28, 330

and GOP white paper, 83
and great debate, 182–86, 196–97
and June (1950) crisis, 38
and Korean policy, 205, 260, 363, 365
and MacArthur's recall, 238–39, 250
and Marshall, 86
and McCarran Act, 82
and McCarthy, 23
and media bias, 187, 197, 260
and mobilization, 75–76, 177–78,
    182–83, 238, 347
and preventive war, 191
and public opinion, 182, 183
Tauriello, Anthony F., 86
Taylor, Maxwell B., 343
television, 138, 215, 219, 260
  and Acheson, 94
  and administration, 12
  and congressional committees, 246
  and Japanese peace treaty, 315
  and MacArthur's recall, 236, 238, 248
  and Truman's speeches, 176
  and UN, 91–92, 94
  war coverage, 312–13
Tenth (X) Corps
  and Chinese intervention, 134, 136, 138
  evacuation from Hungnam, 147,
    149–50, 152–53, 157
Third Infantry Division, 45
thirty-eighth parallel, 72, 95
  and armistice negotiations, 272, 274–76
  debate in 1951, 225–29, 263
  decision to cross, 97–100, 121–22
Thomas, Elbert D., 23, 26
Thomis, Wayne, 52
Thompson, R.L., 56
Thurmond, Strom, 194
Time, 42
  and Acheson, 315
  background briefings, 70
  and casualties, 64, 148
  and China, 14
  and Korean policy, 139, 342, 347
  praised by MacArthur, 396n18
  and South Korea, 352
Time for Defense, 104, 322, 400n19
Tobey, Charles W., 23
  and Acheson, 180–1
  and McCarthy, 79
Tobin, Maurice J., 201
Tokyo Press Club, 48, 96
Truman, Harry S
  and A-bomb, 132
  approval ratings, 215, 258, 292, 365
  and armistice talks, 267, 279
  assassination attempt on, 118
  and Attlee, 135, 138
  and bipartisanship, 26, 74
  and cabinet, 69, 72–74, 206–207

and Chinese intervention, 118–19, 128, 135
and civil defense, 106–7
and civil rights, 10, 320, 332
and Congress, 10, 26, 28, 32, 77
and congressional authorization for war, 34
congressional briefings, 26–27, 29, 174–75, 177
decision-making style, 190
and Defense Department, 35
and Democratic Party, 10, 188
and economic controls, 69, 70, 76–77, 318
and Eisenhower, 339–40
and election (1950), 112–13, 118–19
and election (1952), 326–27, 333
and emergency declaration, 175
fear of World War III, 30–31
and Formosa, 24
"gagging orders," 141, 189–90, 217–18
and the great debate, 186, 188–90, 192
and H-bomb, 15, 32, 37
and Johnson (Louis), 35, 86
and June (1950) crisis, 19–20, 21, 25–26, 28–29
Korean War decisions, 21, 25–26, 28–29, 44, 99–100, 135, 209–10
and labor, 199, 201–202
as lame duck, 258, 292, 361
and leaks, 21, 189–90, 243–44
low-key rhetoric and actions, 19–20, 34, 72, 74, 84, 97, 129–30, 192, 362–63
loyalty of, 141, 180
and MacArthur, 44, 100, 141, 208, 209–10
and MacArthur's recall, 231–32, 233–36, 240, 253
and marines, 300
and Marshall, 86
and McCarthyism, 79
and media, 13, 138
media statements and releases, 22, 26–27, 37, 77, 79, 101, 121, 130, 131, 208, 215–16, 227–28, 279, 289
mental state, 138, 285, 395n70
and NSC-68, 67, 69–70, 122–23, 189–90
and opinion polls, 6, 31
and overheated rhetoric, 4
press conferences, 28, 103, 132, 138, 180
and POWs, 284–86, 289, 363
and propaganda agency, 88, 217
PR decisions, 142, 203, 206, 231–32
and Republicans, 74, 110, 128, 180, 234–35
speeches, 6, 21, 27, 69, 88–89, 98, 116–17, 141, 175–76, 188, 209, 222, 234–35, 245–46, 267, 363
and steel seizure, 292
and Symington, 191

and thirty-eighth parallel, 98, 227–28
on vacation, 198, 215, 279
veto, 81–82
and Wake Island conference, 113–16
and Wilson, 201–202, 258
Truman Doctrine, 30, 375n39
Tubby, Roger, 206
Tucker, Richard K., 152–53
Turkey, 30
Twentieth Century-Fox, 220–23
Twenty-Fourth Infantry Division, 321
Tydings, Millard E.
    and Acheson, 140
    and election (1950), 119, 120
    and McCarran Act, 81
    and McCarthy, 79–80, 110, 250, 364

unions
    See labor
United Kingdom
    and aggressor resolution, 210–12
    and armistice talks, 348
    and bombing, 334
    and demilitarized zone, 121
    reassures China, 99
    sends troops to Korea, 90
    and Truman's A-bomb statement, 133
    war correspondents, 311–12
United Labor Policy Committee, 200, 317
United Nations (UN), 3, 29
    in administration rhetoric, 8, 27, 30, 89–90, 116–17, 226, 256
    and armistice, 333
    criticisms of, 89–90
    and June (1950) crisis, 21–22
    mandate for intervention, 27, 30, 97
    offices, 89, 210
    reform of, 90–92, 93–94
    resolutions, 21, 44, 99, 210–14, 348
United Nations Command (UNC)
    and armistice coverage, 269, 270–71, 273–79, 282, 348–49, 357–58
    and armistice talks, 267, 269–70, 272–78
    attacks Bigart, 159
    and casualties, 50, 64, 148
    and censorship, 157, 170–72, 228, 299–300
    and communications, 54, 148, 269–71, 308
    and Eisenhower's trip to Korea, 339
    established, 44, 372n24
    media briefings and releases, 48, 147, 154–55, 160, 170, 249, 269, 273, 276, 280, 281, 304
    and POWs, 281, 282, 288–89
    PIO and personnel, 47, 167, 271, 298, 311
    relations with Eighth Army, 160, 169–72, 298–300

Printed in Great Britain
by Amazon.co.uk, Ltd.,
Marston Gate.